THE LIGHTS OF GUIDANCE

FROM THE KNOWLEDGE OCEANS OF THE DIVINE SIDE

THE LIGHTS OF GUIDANCE

FROM THE KNOWLEDGE OCEANS OF THE DIVINE SIDE

The Early Lebanon Suhbas of

Shaykh Muhammad Nazim al-Haqqani

I

Preface by

Shaykh Muhammad Hisham Kabbani

Translated with notes, glossary & indexes by

Gibril Fouad Haddad

Translation from the Arabic of *Anwār al-hidāya min buḥūr al-ʿulūm al-ladunniyya: al-Juz' al-awwal* by Shaykh Muhammad Nazim al-Haqqani. Ed. Muhammad Ghazi ʿAbd al-Rahman Ghannoum. 2nd ed. Tripoli and Beirut: al-Mu'assasat al-Ḥadītha lil-Kitāb, 2015.

Volume I first English edition 2024 at
Institute for Spiritual & Cultural Advancement, Fenton, MI (USA)

Published in the US by Institute for Spiritual & Cultural Advancement
17195 Silver Parkway #401, Fenton, MI 48430 USA
Tel: (810) 593-1222 Fax:(810) 815-0518
Email: info@sufilive.com Purchase online at: http://www.isn1.net

Front cover image: *thuluth jalīy* calligraphy of the Quranic verse *and We have certainly honored the children of Ādam* (17:70) by the Trabzon, Turkey master Mehmed Özçay (b. 1961). Courtesy of *Kurrāsat al-khaṭṭ al-ʿArabī*. Back cover image: Shaykh Nazim in Shaykh Hisham's house, Tripoli, Lebanon in the early 80s. Photo courtesy of Shaykh Hisham Kabbani Family Archive.

ISBN: 978-1-938058-82-0

Cataloging-in-Publication Data

al-Haqqani, Shaykh Muhammad Nazim Adel, 1922-2014; Ghannoum, Muhammad Ghazi ʿAbd al-Rahman, 1950- ; Haddad, Gibril Fouad, 1960-

The Lights of Guidance from the Knowledge Oceans of the Divine Side: The Early Lebanon Suhbas of Shaykh Muhammad Nazim al-Haqqani. Volume I. Preface by Shaykh Muhammad Hisham Kabbani. Translated with notes, glossary and indexes by Gibril Fouad Haddad.

500 pp. 23 cm. Bibliography.

1. Naqshbandiyya. 2. Sufism. 3. Spiritual life. 4. Muḥammad, Prophet -- advice. 3. ʿAbd Allāh Fā'iz al-Dāghistānī -- teachings. I. Author. II. Title. III. Title: *Anwār al-hidāya min buḥūr al-ʿulūm al-ladunniyya.*

There exist types of secrets and realities that cannot be expressed with the tongue. As for the heart, it gathers up the realities and the secrets. To Allah belong momentous matters regarding His servants. *Every day He is in a great affair* (al-Raḥmān 55:29).

Suhba I.34

Translation of a note written by Mawlana Shaykh Nazim

01 *Ḥaḍrat al-Ustādh* (Mawlana Shaykh ʿAbd Allah Faʾiz al-Daghistani) said in al-Madīnat al-Munawwara on 24 Dhū al-Ḥijja 1386 (5 April 1967):

02 In the Name of Allah the All-Beneficent the Most Merciful.

03 The spirit of the Tariqa is tied to love and followership.

04 We begin the *awrād* (devotions) of the distinguished Tariqa and its duties in conformity in accordance with the level of the affiliate and his spiritual energy,

05 on the basis of the fact that Allah Most High has made the Umma three tiers. The people of the first tier of the Umma,

06 they are a party that are named *ahl al-ʿazāʾim* (the people of high resolves), and they are the *fardāniyyūn*, and the station of the *fardānī* is the most advanced

07 of stations and the nearest in the presence of Allah Most High in preferment. From the exaltation of their energies, they leave no level except

08 they are gaining it. And they shall never come out of their worldly life until they have attained the covenants taken

09 in the presence of Allah Almighty and Exalted on the Day of the promise and the solemn covenant, the Day of *am I not your nurturing Lord* etc.

10 – Be careful and let never any of you write without *basmala* for verily the devil would put his filth there –

11 The first of the three, the *ahl al-ʿazāʾim* in the distinguished Tariqa must

12 The *ahl al-ʿazāʾim*—and they are the first of the three—must

13 The first party in the distinguished Tariqa—and they are the *ahl al-ʿazāʾim*—must renew their *īmān* (belief) and their *islām* (submission)

14 with three [times] the *shahādatayn* (two testimonies of faith) in every twenty-four hours once.

15 The Pride of existing beings–upon him the best blessing and peace–has firmly renewed this matter so that there would be

16 a universalization of the bounty to all three of the abovementioned three tiers of the Umma.

17 Then let one ask forgiveness of Allah 70 times. This is a protocol taught to us by the Messenger of Allah which is required before everything,

18 and the Messenger of Allah–upon him the blessings and peace of Allah–has certainly said, "My nurturing Lord has raised me," etc.

19 And there is also an important remark, which is that Allah Most High has chosen *adab* for His Beloved, the Pride of existing beings

20 one and all, and He has raised him with the most perfect manner, **and Shariʿa consists in rulings while Tariqa consists in high manners.**

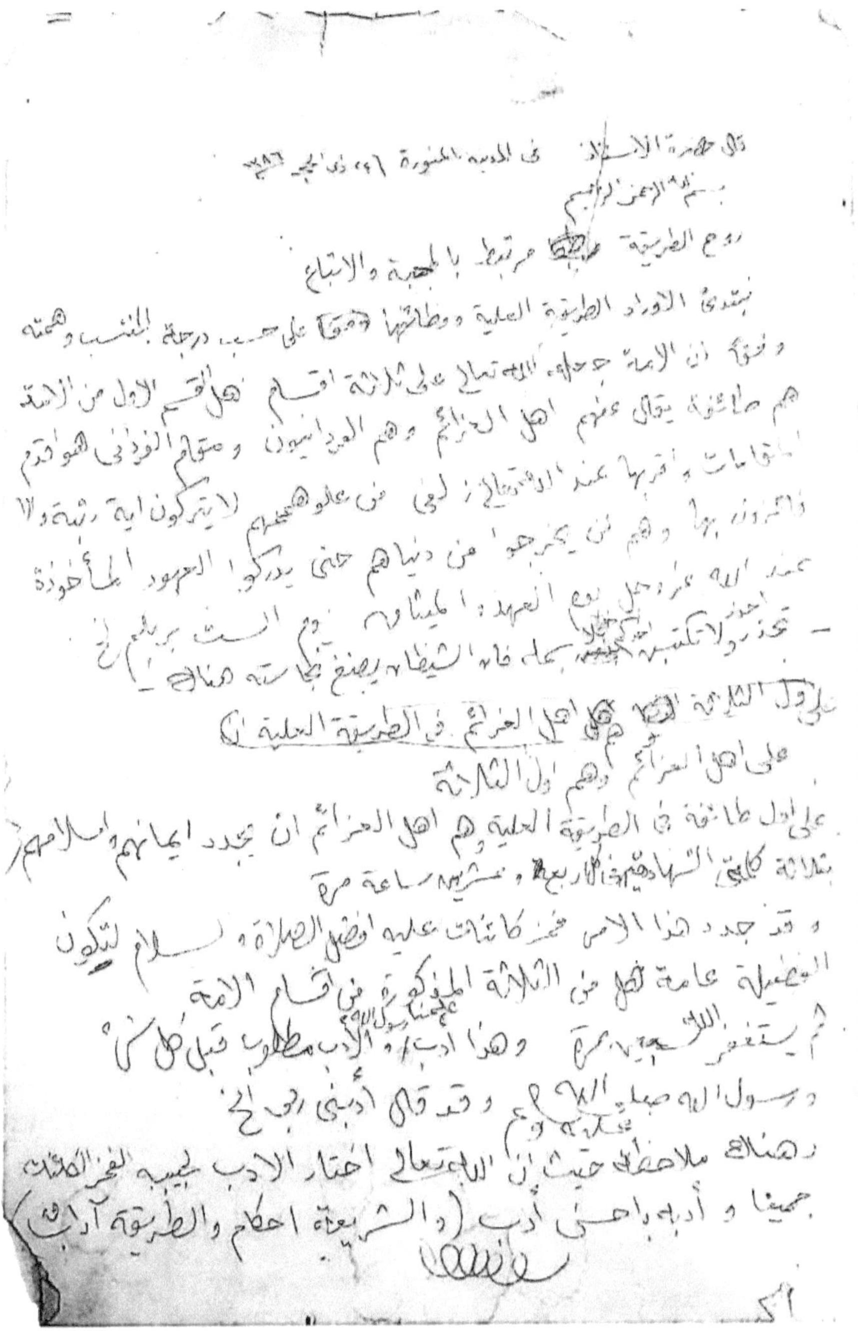
قال حضرة الأستاذ في المدينة المنورة ٢٤ ذي الحجة ١٣٨٦

بسم الله الرحمن الرحيم

روح الطريقة مرتبط بالمحبة والاتباع

على أول طائفة في الطريقة العلية هم أهل العزائم أن تجدد إيمانهم وإسلامهم

الفضيلة عامة لكل من الثلاثة المذكورة من أقسام الأمة

جميعا وأدبه فأحسن أدب (والشريعة أحكام والطريقة آداب)

Mawlana Shaykh Nazim's handwritten note
Medina 24 Dhū al-Ḥijja 1386 / 5 April 1967

Contents

Epigraph 7

Frontispiece: Translation of a handwritten note by Mawlana Shaykh Nazim 8
Original - Medina 24 Dhū al-Ḥijja 1386 / 5 April 1967 9

Mawlana Shaykh Hisham Kabbani's Preface 19

Transcriber's Foreword 21

Translator's Introduction 23

Glossary of Mawlana Shaykh Nazim's Arabic Terms 35

The Lights of Guidance from the Knowledge Oceans of the Divine Side[1] 39

1. The blessing of the supplication of forefathers for the people of Tripoli, Lebanon - The perfect spiritual guide - The one to whom intercession does not apply 41
2. Concern for the cleanness of the heart - The divisions of the ego for men and women - [The earth of love - Acquiring the character of Allah] - The intuitions coming on the part of the Messenger - "If my Umma keeps straight then it has one day" 45
3. The divine good pleasure in voluntary deeds - Imam Ghazālī's heavenly ascent - The reason Allah granted our liege Lord 'Umar mercy 51
4. The signs of real belief - [To hear creation's glorification increases nearness to Allah - No end to knowledge of Allah - *Barzakh* meetings] 55
5. The cycles in which the Umma passes - Duty for religious authorities to humble themselves 59
6. The wisdom of Allah's testing of His servants - [The reward for *ṣabr* (steadfast endurance) is without count] 61
7. The loveliest of deeds to Allah is the dawn prayer of the Awliya - [Keep Sharī'a - Praying in the *Bayt al-ma'mūr* with the Prophet and Abū Bakr - Level of Naqshbandi Masters - Vanquishing the ego with *fajr* and *'ishā*] 63
8. One's state is more important than his statement - [Our intentions are better than our deeds] - Modality of jihad to quit reprehensible traits 67
9. Excellence of belief in the unseen - [Believe like Abū Bakr al-Ṣiddīq] 71

[1] The numbers and titles assigned by the transcriber to each of the suhbas in the Arabic edition have been kept in full. Additions by the translator are in square brackets.

10. [The faith-system is all faithful advice] - Searching out flaws in people 73

11. [Three types of people – Whoever makes the world his goal becomes nothing in the sight of Allah] – What is meant by *a heart most pure* – [Living for the meeting with the Beloved – The purpose of life] 75

12. Difference between outward and inward knowledge – To arrive at the world of invisible sovereignty you need a guide from there 79

13. Distinction between knowledge of something and arriving there 83

14. The *himma* (spiritual energy) of true men 85

15. Pure repentance – [Two dangerous faculties in human beings] – The stomach is a receptacle – [The world is not a place of pleasure but work] 89

16. People are either wrongdoers or victims of wrongdoing; [be the latter and not the former] 93

17. The reality of *kufr* (unbelief) for the people of reality [is the *takfīr* of other human beings – The secret of Allah is in every human being] 95

18. The reality of humanhood – The levels of belief – [Definition of the unbeliever – Self-sacrifice and its divine compensation] 99

19. The harm caused by the ego's attributes – [Enduring harm is the way of self-purification] 101

20. [The spiritual powers of the Prophets] – The greatest *muʿjiza* (staggering miracle) of the Messenger –upon him blessings and peace 103

21. [12,000 *miʿrāj*s – *Ṣiddīqīn*'s heart-knowledge raises you to the Throne – Grandshaykh is the Seal of the *Ṣiddīqs* in the Tariqa] - Reality of the heavenly Ascent to honor human beings – [The Prophet's intermediacy] 105

22. Predetermination of animals – [Reason and wisdom in the creation of everything – Connecting makes you vicegerent of Allah on earth – *Quṭb al-mutaṣarrif*'s power] 109

23. The spiritual powers of the Awliya – ["The Ulema carry their knowledge whereas knowledge carries the Awliya"] 111

24. Reality of familiarity with people – [Prophetic inheritors – Knowledge of spiritual realities – 12,000 night ascents and 124,000 Ādams that passed] – Number of the beautiful Names of Allah – [Overriding mercy] 113

25. [The five stations of the heart – The station of ego-incapacity] 121

26. [Have concern for the spiritual life – The Day of Promises is continuous – *Adab*] – Modality of murid's obedience to Shaykh's order and to Allah – Shaykh Nazim's seclusion in Jaylānī's *maqām* – Story of ʿAzrā'īl and Jaylānī – Awliya's service to murids – Shah Naqshband's service 123

27. Allah does not change what is in a people until they change what is in themselves – As you are, so shall your governors be – [Politics] 129

28. Meaning of being a human being – *He subjected to you what is in the skies* – [Women and men show divine beauty and majesty] – Each reality has a basis – [Secret of *mukallaf*] – Your acts are your workers – [Power of intention] – Signs of WW3 131

29. [The mark of servanthood is prostration – The coming punishment] 139

30. Meaning of *we belong to Allah and to Him do we return* – Meaning of *We exalted for you your name* – [Allah has honored our realities] – Spiritual powers are something absolute – [Prophet received Qur'ān directly] – Attribute *Mālik al-mulk* – Oneness is knowable – [Divine power over subatomic particles] 141

31. [12,000 heavenly Ascents] – Requital of whoever reviles Allah's servants – [Infinite] number of the beautiful Names of Allah – Tidings of the gardens to the Umma of end time – [Seeking Allah alone] 149

32. The hadith "Die before you die" – [Ego, whim, world and devil] – Prophets direct humankind to Allah – The faith-system is all transaction – A spiritual state is taken from its possessor – "My Companions are like the stars" – [Impotence of the ulema of our time] – Mahdi shall stop war 157

33. Meaning of *sulṭān al-dhikr* (arch-authority of Allah's remembrance) 165

34. Unbelief is of inessential nature – [Men of the unseen – *Sufi* means pure – Station of absoluteness – Human souls are uncompassable – 124k Ādams] – *Mālik yawm al-dīn* – Prophet's test of Jibril – *The piercing star* – Prophet has the absolute Message – [Perpetual creation] – Rifa'i's unveiling 167

35. [The reality of the human being – The Prophet's instruction to welcome foreign converts] – The greatest jihad – [Leaving what is of no benefit] 175

36. [Everyone receives spiritual intuitions from the Prophet but their power to hear and see is out of order] – Reality of the station of human beings – Various types of shaykhs 179

37. How to arrive at the reality of belief – [Strength of presence with Allah and His Messenger – Two kinds of life of a human being – True life] 183

38. [All that is created is for the Prophet's honor – Age of *lā ilāha illā-l-Lāh Muḥammadun Rasūlu-l-Lāh* and the Prophetic mission – Station of Jibril and the Muhammadan reality] – The Messenger is the teacher of all the Prophets – [A guide must be from the *malakūt*, not earth] 185

39. Who practices what he knows – [Allah does not accept deeds done by coercion – Eating manners in honor of the Prophet – Q&A at the British Library] – Knowledge is a power that points to the All-True's magnificence [and keeps increasing] 191

40. [Saṭīḥ the pre-Islamic soothsayer] – Meaning of *and when the wild beasts are assembled* 195

41. [Our way is companionship and immense good is in keeping good company] – Abū Yazīd and the *Quṭb* of the time – The meaning of *He does not acquaint of His unseen anyone* – [Awliya partake of the Prophet's *jawāmi' al-kalim* – The *kashf* of newborns and of Shaykh 'Abd Allah Daghistani – Shaykh 'Azīz Maḥmūd Hudā'ī] 197

42. [Reason for material losses] – The knowledge of the tongue and the knowledge of the heart 205

43. The obligation to keep an Islamic appearance 209

44. Absence of supporters of truth in the era of tyrants – [Categorical obligation of an Islamic caliphate] 211

45. The duty to rid oneself of egotism – [Egotism and anger in this life will burn one in the hereafter – Whoever says "I" and "me" is as if fighting Allah – Repeating *astaghfiru-l-Lāh* is best to leave anger] 215

46. Duty to wage war against egos so as to behold the magnificence of the All-True – [True knowledge] 221

47. The fire of unlawful appetite shall be put out by the Mahdī's sword 223

48. Question on why Iblīs exists – Ja'farī fiqh – *The All-Merciful has taught the Qur'ān* – Balqīs's throne – Usury – The orphan's maintainer 225

49. Duty of jihad to obtain purity of heart – What is the *dunyā*? – [Allah's 24,000 manifestations to the heart – Your heart is the house of Allah] 233

50. [Magnifying the Holy Prophet ﷺ – The Companions repelled Iblīs from their gatherings] – The happiest of people is the one well-pleased with his Lord – Love for the righteous – 24 hours in a day – Harmony with the servants of Allah 237

51. Do not argue even if you are in the right 243

52. Duty to consult with the Shaykh [on three matters] and to give thanks to Allah for His blessings 247

53. Matters are pledged to their own times 249

54. Doubt with regard to *rizq* – [Shaykh 'Abd al-Khāliq al-Ghujduwānī's two lessons and the murid's attainment of perfection] 251

55. Importance of *Khatm al-khwājagān* 255

56. Foundations of asking for help towards reform 257

57. He has put the servants wherever He wants – [Keep busy with your own faults] 259

58. Spending will be a reason for meeting the Mahdi 261

59. [Prophets and Awliya prefer seclusion but are commanded to show themselves – Seeing Allah –The ego's arrogance] – The Israelites' repentance – [Die before you die] – Allah purifies whom He wishes – [The worst enemy – *Mawlā* not *dunyā*] 263

60. We must work to put out the fire of wrongdoing 271

61. [Two words from the Prophet – Seek your time's mercies] – Allah's hand is on the group – Reality of tasking – [Definition of muridship – Subjection of heaven and earth to the murid] 273

62. Problems of nations caused by holding on to what vanishes 279

63. [Mawlana Shaykh Nazim's heritage of knowledge] – With wisdom the servant draws near to Allah – Hārūt, Mārūt and magic 281

64. [Entrusting our testimony of faith to the Prophet – Strength in contrition] – Patient endurance in affliction is the key to deliverance 283

65. The need for a divine pull 285

66. [Reward of attending gatherings of faithful advice – Hankering after this world] - Contentment is an inexhaustible treasure - [Ḥabīb al-ʿAjamī's *yaqīn* vs. externalities – *A seating-place of truthfulness*] – The Day of promise and covenant – Certainty is transmitted from its possessors 287

67. [Tariqa principles] – Bearing with contrarieties and reverses will make you reach the reality of life 293

68. [The Umma's inheritance of the *Miʿrāj* – Everything is in the Qur'ān] – Murid's surrender to the spiritual guide – [The veil of egotism – Confirmation of belief – Spiritual illness causes remoteness from Allah] 299

69. The *rūḥ* (spirit) is the vicegerent of Allah 303

70. Duties and benefits of reflecting about death – [*Sulṭan al-khawf* and *ʿazīmat al-sharīʿa*] 305

71. Ḥasan Baṣrī's advice on non-obligatory orders – [Bane of smoking] 309

72. *Whoever believes in Allah He shall guide his heart* and he will be at peace 311

73. The soul of deeds is humbleness 313

74. Everything that began must have a first mover – [Those who view the cosmos as random chaos] – Real friendship – [Era of *Ṣāḥib al-zamān*] 315

75. [Sin results in a repulsive savage human nature – This world is finishing] – The glad tidings of the Night journey and the Heavenly ascent 319

76. [Purifying humbleness is the prayer of *miʿrāj*] – The Attribute of Allah is Power and Might [while ours is absolute incapacity – Folding of time and space at the time of the last breaths of life] 325

77. Who recited the marriage sermon for our liege lord Ādam–upon him peace? 329

78. The spirit of the Tariqa is love and followership – [Difference between love in Allah and love in the ego – The Prophet has a deputy who meets him every 24 hours and conveys from him] 331

79. Attribute of the greatest mujahid – The Prophet's renewal of the matter of Tariqa – [The possessor of *himma* obtains all the spiritual ranks before death – Pledge of dhikr from all human beings, not just Tariqa people – Mercies descend daily to the number of human beings but only rememberers get them, not violators of the solemn Covenant] 335

80. Grandshaykh's service in the Dardanelles [and Palestine (1915-1917)] – The breath of holiness – The Ikhwān al-Muslimīn have incurred condemnation – [Prophet's] knowledge of the Tablet and the Pen 341

81. The world is under control 349

82. Some virtues of the blessings on the Prophet – Praying at the times of greatest merit – [Tariqa high resolve forbids speaking of people's defects – Keep steadfast endurance and do not get angry] 351

83. The excellence of the *basmala* – The Praiseworthy Station – The nib of the Pen 357

84. "Fitna is dormant, Allah curses whoever awakens it" – *Whoever pardons and conciliates, his wage rests upon the One God* – Rank of readiness in Tariqa – Pharaoh's judgment against himself – [Can women be soldiers?] – *Fiṭra* in slaughtering 359

85. One's safety is in keeping custody of the tongue – [Allah curses whoever awakens fitna] 365

86. [The wali is nothing without the divine gift] – Who is the sincere one? – [The Umma's three types: Prophet-like, interceded for, honored] 369

87. Attributes of the [five] stations of the heart – How the servants will see their deeds on the Day of Resurrection – [The greatest Name of Allah in the human being] 375

88. Questions and answers on creed and Quranic commentary 383

89. "Tie down knowledge with writing" – [Purpose of knowledge – Faith in Awliya increases you in faith in Allah and His Prophet – Real love of the Shaykh – Coming to the houses through their doors] 385

90. No harm ensues for Allah from the unbelief of the servants – [Breath of holiness – Prophethood and sainthood are bestowed not acquired – The pursuit of spiritual knowledge – Divine mercy far exceeds the mercy of Prophets and Awliya] 391

91. [Rebelling against authority] – Who sows the wind reaps the whirlwind – Reason has limited power – Solving the world crisis 397

92. Slander causes diminishment in the faith of the slandered – Allah is the wisest of judges – Awliya are sources of the holiest outpouring 401

93. Divine help through the servant's acknowledgment of his incapacity – The least level of the people of Paradise – [*The nurturing Lord of the worlds*] 405

94. Individual and public right – Rights of Allah and rights of servants 409

95. [God-given knowledge is partial: no partnership for anyone with Allah in knowledge] – Station of judgeship is for the Messenger – [Prostration is indispensable in worship] – Actions are according to conclusions 411

96. Meaning of fear of Allah – Real servanthood is to follow the divine will free of *shirk khafīy* – Abū Bakr and 'Alī's high station – [Secret of the Qur'ān] 417

97. [Ka'b al-Aḥbar – 'Umar and 'Uthmān – Prophets and Awliya] 423

98. Have faith in the shaykh's knowledge of this world and of the *dīn* equally – Miraculous gifts of Shaykh 'Abd al-Khāliq al-Ghujduwānī – [All human beings have goodness in them] 427

99. [Be patient and do not pass judgment on others] – A murid's following of his shaykh's order – Reality of "Whoever depends on Allah it is enough for him" – [Why does a person not reach unveiling?] 431

100. The hearts of kings are in the Hand of the All-Merciful – Was al-Ḥajjāj an evildoer or a just man? 437

101. Who is the companion of *Ṣāḥib al-zamān*? –Miraculous gifts of the Muhammadan inheritor 443

102. [*Adab* with Allah and His apportionment] – A person's worth is the worth of his manners – He has put the servant where He wanted – [Do not question the position of others and their doings] 447

103. [Spiritual intuitions are from divine *fayḍ* in the Shaykh's heart] – Bearing with reverses is [the one sign of belief and] the means to spiritual sciences

and openings – [The servants' sins cannot overcome the mercy of their Lord] – Deeds of human beings between the spirit and the body 451

104. [*Dastūr* and *madad* signify breaking of the ego] – Story of Ahmad al-Badawi with the *Quṭb* – Tariqa is for piercing through the veils – Be with the truthful – [The lights of Naqshbandis prevail] 457

105. *Fiṭra* matters more than Islam, belief [and deeds] – Did the Messenger rely on his work? – [*Fiṭra* takes you to your station] – Story of our liege lord ʿAlī with the Jewish doctors of the Law 465

106. Be a searcher for the truth – The submission of our liege lord ʿUmar – Deeds have no inherent result in the divine presence – Meaning of "The best of deeds are the most arduous" 471

Bibliography 475

Index of Quranic Verses 483

Index of Hadiths 487

General Index 495

Mawlana Shaykh Hisham Kabbani's Preface

بسم الله الرحمن الرحيم

This advice is enough for this whole universe. It comes from the heart of Mawlana Sheikh Nazim, from the heart of Mahdi[1] and from the heart of the Prophet–upon him the blessings and peace of Allah. These jewels are not thrown into the hands of the ignorant. These jewels have been brought and put between the hands of those that deserve them; and you deserve them. Such lectures do not come every time. Sometimes only, for special people. These are very deep secrets of sufi teachings and you can never find these things in books. When Mawlana Sheikh Nazim opens something, if that is to be found in books then it is not important. He only opens something that has never been written. Every second there is creation of knowledge.

They write things in books and then they place references to Sayyidina Jalaluddin Rumi, Sayyidina Muhyiddin Ibn ʿArabi, Sayyidina Hasan al-Basri, Sayyidina al-Hallaj, Sayyidina ʿAbd al-Qadir Gilani, Sayyidina Abu Yazid al-Bistami, all these saints. This is not their time anymore. Their knowledge has become as nothing in the ocean of knowledge of the saints of this present-day Nation. Every second, there is creation of new knowledge. Previous knowledge is over and done with. It is now limited to its own time and place. Next to the knowledge that is in the heart of Mahdi–upon him peace–their knowledge is as a drop in an ocean.

When Mahdi appears or gives the order to open this knowledge, people are going to dance with joy, because they did not and will not hear of such knowledge such as the knowledge that will open up in his time. He will come on the Day of Reckoning at the end of time, when the role of this particular Umma will be ended, which will bring the end of all knowledge as far as this particular world is concerned. All the oceans of knowledge that had been heretofore forbidden to previous saints and hidden within the hearts of later saints will be opened in the time of *Ṣāḥib al-zamān*,[2] to the point that the knowledge of all people and all saints, with the sole exception of Mahdi, will become like the knowledge of children.[3]

[1] See Suhba I.76.

[2] See on this point Suhbas I.48, tenth note; I.47, 58, 74, 76, 98-99.

[3] Shaykh Muhammad Hisham Kabbani, "The ocean of knowledge in Mahdi's heart" in *Pearls and Coral: Secrets of the Sufi Way*, 2 vols. (Fenton: ISCA, 2004-2005).

Transcriber's Foreword

Praise belongs to Allah the nurturing Lord of the worlds. I ask for blessings and salutations on our liege lord Muhammad and on his Family and Companions and all the Prophets and Messengers, and upon their Families and Companions one and all.

I have seen a group of the lovers of our Shaykh and Master, possessors of high energies, gathering much of the admonishments and suhbas, publishing volumes of the talks and teachings of our teacher and refuge, and composing many books on that, each book singling itself out with unique benefits not found in the other. I had been writing and compiling what my shaykh and refuge was teaching in his gatherings for a period of more than 30 years. I had always wanted to publish it so that whoever sought shelter in my shaykh, followed him and loved him might benefit from it if Allah wills. On one of my visits to Mawlana al-Shaykh–may Allah sanctify his secret–in Cyprus in the summer of 2004, my shaykh and master authorized me to bring out those suhbas and teachings and to publish them.

I devoted myself to the revision of these suhbas and made them ready—*bi-taṣarruf* (adapting them)—in the hope their readers might find everything they are looking for from the choicest, most precious and beneficial suhbas. I aimed to write them in simplified classical Arabic that is easy to understand by the general public and the specialized one. I gathered in this book many of the abundant nuggets of wisdom that Mawlana al-Shaykh was recounting in the years 1978-1979, arranged as individual suhbas just as Mawlana was narrating to us in his sittings and his teachings. I pray for the facilitation of the attainment of my goal.

This book is but the first volume of a series. I hope and pray that Allah will help me bring it out in full so that the seekers might turn to it whenever they are in need of it, finding every meaning in its specific chapter if Allah wills. Allah is He Whom we beseech for the fulfillment of the quest. May He inspire whoever looks into it to cover up whatever they might detect in it of gaps and faults. Verily He has power to do what He wishes and is prompt to answer. He alone makes what is difficult easy. May He grant mercy to whoever shows me lenience in my incapacity to fulfill what I attempted to do. Allah is enough for us *and what a wonderful Trustee! What a wonderful protecting friend and what a wonderful helper!*

Translator's Introduction

Glory, praise and thanks belong to the One God. Blessings and peace on our liege lord the Prophet Muḥammad and upon his Family and Companions one and all, and upon all the Prophets and Messengers, the Friends of Allah, the angels and those brought near. I seek refuge in Allah from the accursed devil. In the Name of Allah the All-Beneficent the Most Merciful do I begin and strive to follow guidance. There is no power nor strength but with Allah the Exalted, the Magnificent. Your permission, my master and guardian, support! "Our Tariqa is companionship, and goodness is in collectedness."

This is the first English translation of the first volume—covering the years 1978-1979—of Mawlana Shaykh Nazim al-Haqqani's (1922-2014) 1,700-page hexalogy entitled *Anwār al-hidāya min buḥūr al-ʿulūm al-ladunniyya* (The lights of spiritual guidance from the knowledge oceans of the divine side), which is the Arabic transcription by Shaykh Muhammad Ghazi ʿAbd al-Rahman Ghannoum of Tripoli, Lebanon, the meticulous reporter of these suhbas in Mawlana Shaykh Nazim's original Arabic—colloquialisms, Turkish turns and all. He took these suhbas live and directly from Mawlana over the years and he completed their final draft from his own notes and transcripts after Mawlana gave him permission to do so in Lefke in the summer of 2004. As of writing these lines the first four volumes have been published while the fifth and sixth are still in digital format. The timeline of their original delivery can be summarized as follows:

> Volume I: 1978-1979 – Volume II: *al-Baḥr al-masjūr* (The Plenished Sea), 1979-1980 – Volume III: *al-Luʾluʾ al-wardī* (The Rose-Red Pearl), 1979-1980 – Volume IV: 1980-1981 – Volume V: 1982 – Volume VI: 1983-1984.

He informed me towards the end of Shaʿbān 1445/February 2024 that he had told Mawlana he had in his possession enough material for not just five or six but fifteen books of suhbas. May he and his family be rewarded on behalf of the Umma and may Allah bring it all to the best completion!

Giving thanks and rightful acknowledgment where thanks are due

May Allah sanctify the pure souls of our blessed masters in the Golden Chain of the most distinguished Naqshbandi Sufi path, particularly my beloved teachers and spiritual parents, our guides and refuges Mawlana Shaykh Nazim al-Haqqani and Mawlana Shaykh Hisham Kabbani, and our teachers' teacher Mawlana Shaykh ʿAbd Allah Faʾiz al-Daghistani. The blessings of Allah that have come to the writer of these lines at the hands of these masters are beyond encompassment and can never be truly thanked.

Our greatest gratitude goes to the one that has prepared us for this moment with the patience and magnanimity of mountains and seas and "everything in the universe moving," Mawlana Shaykh ʿAbd Allah al-Daghistani's successor after Mawlana Shaykh Nazim and the latter's son-in-law, the *Quṭb al-mutaṣarrif*, our master and teacher Mawlana Shaykh Muhammad Hisham Kabbani, the Prophetic descendant, caliph and inheritor of the Khwajagan and Naqshbandi Golden Chain, the teacher of *ḥusn al-ẓann* in Allah, without whom there would not have been the first inkling of a motion for putting pen to paper.

Mawlana Shaykh Hisham has brought us forth, and countless multitudes, from delivery, then toddlerhood in faith, into the race to *islām, īmān, iḥsān, maḥabba* and *ḥikma*, east and west. Thanks also to our spiritual mother—his wife and Mawlana Shaykh Nazim's daughter—Hajjah Naziha; their family of light, especially Dr. Nour Mohamad Kabbani who was the first to bring these suhbas to the attention of the English-speaking world in a series of suhbas on the shoulders of his father and grandfather's *fayḍ*; his brother Shaykh Omar Kabbani who asked me to translate them; and all murids, lovers and helpers who have striven to be, in the words of Mawlana Shaykh Nazim in the Mercy Oceans series and the Lefke suhbas, "if not a sun or a moon, then at least a ray from the shining lights of your Shaykh."

These then are some of the heavenly suhbas–"friendly spiritual discourses"–spoken during shaykh-murid associations in the historic Sunni cities of Beirut and Tripoli among other venues in Lebanon in the late 1970s and early 1980s by the possessor of holy breaths, spiritual attraction and angelic manners, the master who freed us from slavery and the compass of our love, Mawlana Shaykh Muhammad Nazim al-Haqqani of Cyprus and Damascus.

The miraculous gift contained in experiencing these suhbas

This is a manual about the knowledge and practice of the Prophets and the Awliya (Friends of the One God) as communicated in the spoken teachings, the life directives and the spiritual states of the foremost living Sufi master of this age. These suhbas are from the spiritual world. They wake up the reader from the sleep of this world. They remind human beings of the wisdom of their particular destiny. "If the human being does not think about himself and about the wisdom for which he was brought into existence, he will be lower than the level of animals. Likewise, Allah gives power to whoever connects himsef of human beings, such that he becomes able to have control over all creatures on the face of the earth. And with this power he becomes the vicegerent of Allah on earth."[1]

[1] Suhba I.22, "The predetermination of animals."

The English-speaking reader will not see anything like these talks gathered under one roof with respect to content of Divine and Prophetic inspiration, holy advice, precious reminders, invaluable directives to goodness and truth in the language of our time. They are a fountain of life flowing from beyond this world to everyone's doorstep, a unique source of healing for minds and hearts. Mawlana Shaykh Nazim's suhba is often experienced as no less than what Ibn 'Abd al-Salām said of Ibn 'Aṭā' Allāh Sakandarī's discourse, "it is as if descending fresh from the heavens" and going straight into the hearts. The long advice on the Tariqa principle derived from the hadith of "Pray your prayer as if it were your last" turns our eyes into our souls and cleaves the heart in two.[1] The linking of the commentary on the verse of divine *istiwā'* (establishment) on the Throne to the principle that the servant's heart is the Throne of Allah is found in the rarest Sufi *tafsīr*s (such as Ruzbehan Baqli's *'Arā'is al-bayān*) but only Mawlana connects it to the fifth and highest station of the heart in Mawlana Shaykh 'Abd Allah al-Daghistani's teachings, *maqām al-khafā'* (the station of hiddenness) which no one but Allah sees.[2]

Many or most of these suhbas are about the spiritual world and the hereafter. They uplift and bring one to that new world and time. Before you is the threshold of end time events. Here you are, as part of the last band of the believers in Allah and the Messenger, standing by the side of our liege Lord 'Īsā (Jesus), then flying in the company of the angels, singing to the Creator a praise of indescribable beauty. The glad tidings of such events includes the reassurance of safety as proclaimed in the Qur'ān—*say: "Nothing shall happen to us except what the One God has decreed for us; He is Our protecting friend; and in the One God let the believers trust"* (Tawba 9:51)—with an unbreakable link to Sultan al-Awliya Mawlana Shaykh 'Abd Allah in this world and the next without difference. "He was given the power of *al-taṣarruf fil-qulūb* (discretionary power in the hearts)."[3]

The grounding of Mawlana's teachings in the knowledge of divine mercy

Mawlana Shaykh Nazim's emphasis on the linguistic intensive forms of the Attributes of Divine forgiveness in *Raḥmān, Rahīm, Ghafūr, Ghaffār, Karīm, Arḥam al-rāḥimīn, Akram al-akramīn* etc.[4] is an elucidation of the Divine Hadith "I am exactly as My servant thinks of Me" and an apt example of why Shaykh Nazim named Mawlana Shaykh 'Abd Allah *Sultan al-awliya* (the supreme authority of the Friends of Allah) and the *Murabbī al-'ārifīn* (the

[1] Suhba I.70.

[2] Suhba I.87. On the five stations of the heart see also Suhba I.25.

[3] Suhba II.2 on the time of Mahdi.

[4] Suhba II.3.

educator of the spiritual knowers of Allah) and why Shaykh Nazim himself has been described as *Shaykh al-awliya* (teacher of the Friends of Allah).[1] Likewise, Grandshaykh and Mawlana have lavished on Shaykh Hisham the most numerous and sumptuous names that any Master in living memory has yet received.[2]

It is noteworthy that none of those three masters ever claimed leadership for themselves. "Mawlana Shaykh Nazim never once claimed leadership. Love of leadership is the sickness of the murid. The secret of *irshād* (spiritual guideship) is humbleness. It opens the door to the *imdādāt* (reinforcements) of the Awliya."[3] One of the late contemporary masters of Damascus, Shaykh Shukri Luhufi, a scholar of the Qur'ān who had written a manual on the Ten Quranic Readings, spent his whole life out of the limelight. He was content ordering the shoes of murids at the door of his Shaykh's zawiya. He was then ordered to stop ordering the shoes and to start serving everyone water at the gatherings of dhikr. He did so for decades. After the third successor to his Shaykh died he was finally appointed to succeed. When this happened he made the rounds of all the younger shaykhs and murids, asking their forgiveness, kissing their hands and asking for their blessing and permission, although he was everyone's senior by far. More than that, he was considered one of the *Abdāl* (Substitutes) of Syro-Palestine.

"The soul of deeds is humbleness."[4] In light of all of the above it is no wonder even for a beginner to discover that the overwhelming traits in the teachings of Mawlana Shaykh 'Abd Allah al-Daghistani and his successors are unlimited forbearance, tolerance, sufferance, good cheer, good pleasure, good humor, exalted aims, humbleness, forgiveness and keeping family ties, all so as to practice and teach one of the magnificent Sunnas of guidance and creed: *ḥusn al-ẓann bi-l-Lāh*, keeping the highest good opinion in Allah. A suhba's titles reflect Mawlana's emphasis of the connection between the high level of

[1] By Shaykh Rajab Dib (1931-2016) of Damascus.

[2] (1) Madadul-Haqq (the Support from Allah); (2) Hujjatullah al-Mukhlis (the Sincere Proof from Allah); (3) Thamirul-Haqq (The Abundant Fruit-Bearer from Allah); (4) Zaynul-'Abidin (the Adornment of Worshippers); (5) Muradullah al-Dhakir (the Divinely-Intended Rememberer); (6) Qutbul-Mutasarrif (the Pole of Complete Discretion); (7) Lisanul-Awliya (the Spokesman of the Friends of Allah); (8) Khalifatul-Mahdi (al-Mahdi's Caliph); (9) Mahbub (Well-Beloved); (10) Mahbub al-Kull (Well-Beloved by All), meaning by the Prophets, Awliya, and *Ahl Dīwan al-Nabī* (People of the Prophet's Assembly)—upon him and them blessings and peace—and the Righteous. "The multitude of names spells the honor of the one named" (al-Nawawī).

[3] Suhba by Mawlana Shaykh Hisham.

[4] Suhba I.73.

a servant's *riḍā* (full contentment) and the Divine Attributes.[1]

The war against the ego and its dominant characteristics; real repentance

Mawlana's suhbas are a Shaykhly sword drawn against the idol of Ego, an anatomy of that creature conducted in his clinic for our benefit. Throughout he cites Grandshaykh's directives and the latter's diagnosis that we as murids are in kindergarten, a continuation of the *ghayr mukallaf* (unaccountable) station mentioned in many suhbas, where we are stuck until we pick up the fight against our egos once and for all. "The one that simply waits for natural death, this one has gone and has not benefited from his life. But as for the one that uses a sword in struggling with his own ego and kills it or subdues it and causes it to die, then he severs himself from his wicked natural characteristics, because the ego is *maghḍūb ʿalayh* (incurring divine anger); and what is mentioned in the Qur'ān is that very ego; for the one that comes [to Allah] with his ego has incurred divine anger."[2] Until it is cleaned our *tablīgh* (conveyance) remains an imitation of real conveyance.[3]

What are the dominant characteristics of the ego? "The origin of emotions in a human being will be from one of two paths: the path of the appetitive lustful faculty or the path of the faculty of anger. The servant must master these two faculties so that he will get to the station of human perfection. The human being that does not keep watch over these two faculties will be a follower of his whim. People are two kinds. One kind is under subjection and one kind is ruling. The one that is truly ruling is the one that is ruling over those two faculties. As for the one that is under the rule of his lust and his anger, he is truly under subjection whether he is a *ʿallāma* (erudite scholar), a *ʿābid* (worshipper), or a king or anything else. For the people of spiritual reality the whole world is in this order.... The foundations of all sins go back to those two origins. For this reason pure and sincere repentance is not ascertained until he is able to rule over his anger and over his lust."[4]

The spiritual guide supports the murid that declares war upon his ego and the latter becomes affiliated to one who is affiliated with the world of *malakūt* (invisible spiritual sovereignty).[5] In terms reminiscent of Imam Ghazali in his

[1] Suhba II.3, "When Allah is well-pleased with the servant – Difference between full contentment and patient endurance – The palace of full contentment in Paradise – The Attributes of Allah Almighty."

[2] Suhba II.4.

[3] Suḥba I.78.

[4] Suhba I.15.

[5] Suhba I.12. "The human being's own *malakūt* is his own *rūḥ* (soul)" (Shaykh ʿAbd Allāh Sirāj al-Dīn al-Ḥalabī, suhba on *isrāʾ* and *miʿrāj*).

proclamation of the knowledge of *mukāshafāt* (spiritual unveilings) as dominating all the other types of knowledge in the first of the forty books of *Iḥyā' 'ulūm al-Dīn* (the Book of knowledge), Mawlana describes the three signs of real belief that appear in a human being. The first is the servant's audition of the glorifications of all creatures. The second is the opening of the door of wisdom to hear and understand each single glorification. The third is the free meeting with the Holy Prophet–upon him blessings and peace–and the people of *barzakh*. "And all of this is to draw nearer to Allah."[1]

The knowledge and practice of spiritual intuitions

The principal method of the transmission of knowledge that Mawlana speaks about is what the Sufis called *'ilm al-wāridāt*, the science of spiritual intuitions. "My coming to your country [Lebanon] is not for the sake of this world. This world is under our feet. However, it is to give you glad tidings that the event is taking place soon, and so that you may get ready to be among the men of that age, and some spiritual intuitions are coming to us for the purification of your hearts from the illnesses that block one from being present together with the Owner of the time.[2] Make your intention and Allah shall support you in accordance with your intentions. Likewise, in every sitting, something is cast into our hearing of the intuitions that reach me from the side of the Messenger, upon him the blessings and peace of Allah, and from the great spiritual masters. So take heed and think well on this discourse, and do not say, 'This one is talking on his own.'"[3]

Thus Mawlana explicitly reassured us that such intuitive teachings are not a function of our qualifications or preparedness but of our intentions, and "our intentions are definitely better than our deeds."[4] The important thing is to form the intention and put our best foot forward. "When the servant resolves on seeking the good pleasure of Allah he has become a true seeker. It is guaranteed that Allah and His Messenger and His Awliya will teach him through the sending of spiritual intuitions to his heart as long as he recognizes that the purpose of life is to obtain the love of Allah and His Messenger and His Awliya."[5] "Some people, their hearts are like an international airport: from every side the spiritual intuitions and the secrets of the Qur'ān land on them. And some people, their hearts are constricted."[6]

[1] Suhba I.4.

[2] *Ṣāḥibu al-zamān*, also known as *Ṣāḥibu al-'aṣr*, i.e. the Mahdī.

[3] Suhba I.2.

[4] See Suhbas I.8 and I.61, twelfth note.

[5] Suhba I.11.

[6] Suhba II.2.

Some of Mawlana's main themes in the Tariqa navigation of endtimes

There are too many light-filled themes in Mawlana's suhbas for any single reader to attempt to summarize them. The following themes are a summarized selection. Each reads like a different life of the soul that opens up as the pages containing their blessed words turn. They all speak to excellent opinion of Allah and the immense honor He has lavished on human beings.

I. Infiniteness of spiritual knowledge

The place of the special divine gifts of this Umma at the hands of its Prophet–upon him the blessings and peace of Allah–in the definition of human *khilāfa* (vicegerency) on earth is such that "if the angels were given pens and were ordered to write the glad tidings that Allah has prepared for the children of Ādam until the Day of Resurrection they would be unable."[1]

II. Divine mercy overrides all following the Judgment

At the very end of the Armageddons and Apocalypses of here and hereafter the separation of servants into Paradise and Hell, the ultimate primacy and last word shall belong to all-encompassing, overriding divine mercy, and all bad deeds will be replaced by good ones.[2]

III. Pre-existence of the address of divine generosity to creatures

Indescribable infinite divine generosity is the underpinning of creation from its very first moment, and we – all humankind – were there.[3]

IV. Naqshbandi inheritorship of the 12,000 Prophetic heavenly ascents

"The secret of the existence of 12,000 heavenly ascents, that the *ṣuḥba* of our nurturing Lord granted to the Messenger–upon him the blessings and peace of Allah–in the heavenly ascents was not only to magnify the person of the Messenger but also consisted in glad tidings about the honoring of the children of Ādam in the presence of Allah."[4] "Mawlana [Shaykh ʿAbd Allah al-Daghistani] has explained this noble verse for 40 years: *and We have certainly honored the children of Ādam* (Banū Isrā'īl/Isrā' 17:70)."[5]

V. Inessentiality of unbelief and primordiality of belief

Unbelief is inessential and passing, while belief is the original state of humankind, and the loftiness of the human station in the divine presence at a time

[1] Suhba I.21.

[2] Suhbas I.24; I.31, 11th paragraph; I.87; I.103; II.4.

[3] Suhba I.28.

[4] Suhba I.21.

[5] Suhba I.84. See also I.17, 21, 25, 28, 30, 34, 48, 75, 82, 84.

before time is inexpressible beyond the Divine speech (*Am I not your Lord? They said yes*) and the Prophetic disclosures themselves ("Every human being is born with true submission"), naturally leading to the conclusion that "What is originally the creed of the people of Scripture? Belief. What is originally the creed of all humankind? Belief also. Unbelief is *'āriḍī ṭāri'* (inessential, passing). It is baseless!"[1]

VI. The possessors of spirit vs. those still controlled by their egos

The possessors of the spirit are those who have conquered their egos and to whom the trust of the secret of the Qur'ān has been granted. "They are a party named *ahl al-'azā'im* (the people of high resolves), the *fardāniyyūn* (exalted solitary ones). The station of the *fardānī* is the most advanced of stations and the nearest in the presence of Allah in preferment. From the exaltation of their energies they leave no level but they are gaining it. They shall never come out of their worldly life until they have attained the covenants taken in the presence of Allah Almighty and Exalted on the Day of the promise and the solemn covenant, the Day of *am I not your nurturing Lord*."[2] They are fewer than few even among the Companions.[3] Those who are still controlled by the ego are everyone else at the station of *the lowest of the low* (Tīn 95:5).[4] "As long as a human being remains at the *maqām* (station) of ego and his blameworthy traits are controlling him, his journeying will be *then they believe, then they disbelieve* (Nisā' 4:137)."[5]

VII. This knowledge is not found in books

"I am not speaking these words from books. Rather it is from the heart to the heart, and the sight of the eyes from my Master who has caused my tongue to speak."[6] "Mawlana [Shaykh 'Abd Allah al-Daghistani] says that if you were to look for this knowledge in the books from the beginning of this world until the end of this world, it would be extremely difficult for you to obtain the like of these sciences. For they are not derived from book-reading but rather they are a manifestation of *and whom We had taught, from Our side, a certain knowledge* (al-Kahf 18:65)."[7]

[1] Suhba I.34.

[2] See Mawlana's note to that effect at the frontispiece of this volume, lines 6-9.

[3] Suhbas I.96-97.

[4] Suhba I.11, 67, 96.

[5] Suhba I.37. See also I.15, 66, 80, 86.

[6] Suhba I.75.

[7] Suhba I.98. See also I.31, 76.

VIII. Sultans mirror divine will despite the failure of human governance

Exactly as you are, so shall your governors be. Your acts are your workers. The Prophet–upon him the blessings and peace of Allah–has predicted all the successive types of historic governance, so Allah is in charge of history and world order, not us. "We are not walking with uprightness but according to our likes and our whim. After that we say we want all people and governors to be the way we want!" *Allah does not change what is in a people until they change what is in themselves* (Ra'd 13:11) and Prophets were not revolutionaries. So our way in Tariqa is against revolutionary acts and revilement of authority. Reform yourself first.[1]

~

The above are but glimpses of some of the *fuyūḍāt* (spiritual outpourings) brimming in this treasury of suhbas. They illustrate their nature as a map to be long perused and studied for the safe spiritual crossing of the endtimes of our lives. They form a reminder of the Sunni creed for our times enfolding a fresh contemplation of the Qur'ān and the Sunna, from the laser-like interventions of the shorter suhbas[2] to the roaring seas of the major ones.[3] They are a proof for the Khwajagan Masters' parable that *Shari'a is the oceans, Tariqa is the ship serving to navigate them, and Ḥaqīqa is the deep-sea pearl*:

> Each Quranic verse represents the knowledges of the All-True and likewise the Prophet's hadiths–upon him the blessings and peace of Allah–are like the signs of Allah Almighty. The Awliya swim in those oceans to the extent of their ability in knowledge and in accordance with *and above every possessor of knowledge there is one with vaster knowledge* (Yūsuf 12:76). In this fashion each wali plunges into those oceans and takes of the pearls and jewels to the extent of his ability.[4]

It takes nothing short of the Saint of the Age to plumb their depths and resurface with treasures for our greatest benefit here and hereafter. We might then say, with the certainty with which Aḥmad b. Ḥanbal said after hearing al-Ḥārith al-Muḥāsibī speak, "I have never heard such *ḥaqā'iq* (spiritual realities) before."

~

[1] See Suhbas I.5, 27, 28, 40, 75, 80, 91, 100.

[2] See, e.g., Suhbas I.13, 29, 33, 55, 58, 60, 62, 69, 77.

[3] See, e.g., Suhbas I.4, 24, 26, 28, 30-31, 41, 59, 61, 66, 67, 75, 79, 87, 99, 104.

[4] Suhba I.92.

Our *Quṭb* on contemplation of Mawlana's suhbas

Of the crucial advice Mawlana al-Shaykh Hisham has also given the writer of these lines—in addition to what he mentioned in the preface—is that Mawlana al-Shaykh Nazim's suhbas are not monolithic style-wise, content-wise or audience-wise: "Be attentive to what is meant for *you*. It might come in the middle of the suhba or at the end, or it might be mentioned among other things which are meant for others."

Authenticity and authority of this work

This translation is controlled by the blessing of the written and signed *ijāza*; the verbal authorization; and the strict instruction to the translator by our grandmasters Mawlana al-Shaykh Hisham Kabbani and Mawlana al-Shaykh Nazim al-Haqqani–may Allah sanctify their souls and raise their stations. They ordered for Tariqa teachings to be conveyed only by their representatives and deputies. They never gave permission for their teachings to be misrepresented by someone whose affiliation is partnered with self-promotion. Any subsequent translation of the same Arabic work or any translation of this translation must therefore abide by the same standards of faithfulness to Mawlana's discourse, accuracy and precision in wording, clarity in style and the required grasp of *Ahl al-Sunna wal-Jamā'a* orthodoxy he reflected as defined by the established practice of the predecessors and their consensus. Whatever contravenes the latter is from our own shortcomings and misunderstandings as narrators, translators and/or transcribers from Mawlana.

We wrote in *The Joy of Cyprus in the Association of Rajab* (1422/2002):

> One of the murids asked Mawlana, "*Yā Sayyidī*, do you authorize and entitle us to narrate from you all your answers?" He replied: "Honey is not taken from the mouth of the bee. We wait until it digests it." The bee is the murid and the digestion is divinely-granted spiritual maturity. May this transcription approximate the latter! And "Many a transmitter of knowledge does not himself understand it, and many may transmit knowledge to others who are more versed in it than they are."[1]

May this translation, also, approximate Mawlana's spiritual honey and its special benefit here and hereafter.

Editorship and footnote documentation

Artefacts such as suhba titles, bold type for emphasis, paragraphing and the glossary are added in support of the basic work of translation as embellishments serving to enhance the reader's experience of Mawlana's suhbas.

[1] *Mutawātir* (mass-transmitted) Prophetic hadith narrated from 19 Companions.

The footnote documentation illustrates Mawlana's vast purview of the Prophetic Hadith and of the terminology of the Sufi authorities, both of which complement his constant recourse to the Qur'ān. May it facilitate a better grasp of Mawlana's inspired speech, demonstrate the extent to which the latter represents a summa of classical *taṣawwuf* in our time, and provide reliable sourcing for the treasure-trove of its proof-texts. It is also intended as a double preventive. On the one hand it mutes Mawlana's detractors and their materialistic understanding of Shari'a and Tariqa, let alone of the dimension of *ḥaqīqa* which they have abjured—like Satan refusing to bow to Ādam—on the formal grounds of strict monotheism. On the other hand it fends off do-it-yourself novices-turned-guides looking to market their brand as would-be representatives of Sufism whose common traits are emphasis on this world and the fact that they were never authorized to give *irshād*—if they were authorized at all.

May our Masters be well-pleased with this work and sign it by the Holy Prophet's hand with his acceptance. May Allah forgive its mistakes and reward all those that use it for His sake with unending success and provision.

Blessings and peace on the Prophet, his Family, his Companions, his Awliya, most especially our teacher and our teachers' teacher and their teachers, and us and all their followers with them, and all his Umma.

Brunei Darussalam
21 Ramadan 1445 / 1 April 2024

Glossary of Mawlana Shaykh Nazim's Arabic terms

abad: eternity, everlastingness
ʿabd: servant of Allah
adab: (high) manners; discipline; spiritual practice
al-aḍdād: reverses
ahl al-ḥaqīqa: the people of spiritual reality
al-ʿaql; the intellect
ashhadu an lā ilāha illā-l-Lāh wa-ashhadu anna Muḥammadan rasūlu-l-Lāh: I bear witness that there is no god but the One God and that Muhammad is the Messenger of the One God
Awliya: Friends of Allah
ʿayn al-yaqīn: the sight of certainty
azal: pre-existence; beginninglessness
ʿAẓamūt: (world of) divine magnificence
ʿazīma: high resolve, strictness
ʿazīmat al-sharīʿa: the high resolve of the sacred Law
baqāʾ fi-l-Lāh: abiding in Allah
barzakh: interlife
barzakhīy: living here and hereafter
basmala: the theonymic phrase *bismi-l-Lāhi-r-Raḥmāni-r-Raḥīm* (in the Name of the One God the All-Beneficent the Most Merciful)
al-bātin: the inward
dastūr: permission
dhikr: remembrance (of Allah)
al-dīn: the faith-system
dunyā: this life, this world
fardānī: exalted solitary one
fayḍ: spiritual outpouring, pl. *fuyūḍāt*
fitna: sedition, strife, temptation, trial
fiṭra: primordial state / disposition / nature
ḥaqīqa: spiritual reality
ḥaqīqat al-jadhba: the reality of attraction
ḥaqīqat al-tawajjuh: the reality of focusing the heart
ḥaqq al-yaqīn: the reality of certainty
hawā: whim; proclivity
ḥaẓīrat al-quds: the sanctuary of holiness
ḥikma: wisdom

himma ʿāliya: high spiritual energy. See also *ʿulūw al-himma*
iḥsān: doing what is best; excellence; kind generosity
ʿilm al-bātin: inward knowledge
ʿilm ladunnī: knowledge from the divine side
ʿilm maʿnawī: a type of knowledge related to spiritual meanings
ʿilm al-nafs: self-knowledge; psychology
ʿilm al-yaqīn: knowledge of certainty; certain knowledge
ʿilm al-ẓāhir: outward knowledge
īmān: belief
islām: submission
isrāʾ: night journey
istighfār: contrition; asking forgiveness
Jabarūt: (world of) divine omnipotence
jihad: struggle, striving
karāma: miraculous gift of a wali
kashf: spiritual unveiling
khalīfat Allāh: successor / vicegerent appointed by Allah
khilāfa: divinely-appointed vicegerency / lieutenancy
al-Mahdi: the well-guided one. See also *ṣāḥib al-zamān*
Lāhūt: (world of) Godhead
mā siwā-l-Lāh: something/everything other than the One God
madad: spiritual supply, support and help
maʾdhūn: deputy
majāl al-iṭlāq: the realm of absoluteness (beyond time and place)
Malakūt: (world of) invisible sovereignty
maqām: spiritual station; gravesite
maqām al-nafs: the station of ego
maqām al-ṣiddīqiyya: the station of veraciousness
maʿrifa: spiritual knowledge
miʿrāj: heavenly ascent
mujahid: practitioner of jihad
muʿjiza: staggering miracle of a Prophet
mulk: visible world of creation
murshid: spiritual guide
al-nafas al-qudsiyya: the breath of holiness
nafs: ego
nafs al-ṭifl al-madhmūma: the child's blameworthy ego
naṣīḥa: transparent, faithful, pure counsel

Nāsūt, nāsūtiyya: (world of) human nature
al-qadar: the foreordained Decree
Quṭb: spiritual pole, axis, pivot
Quṭb al-mutaṣarrif: spiritual Pole with discretionary power
quṭbāniyya: spiritual poleship
rābiṭa: firm connection
al-rūḥ: the spirit
rūḥaniyya: spiritual presence; spiritual extension; spiritual world
rukhṣa: dispensation, allowance
Ṣāḥib al-waqt, Ṣāḥib al-zamān: the spiritual leader of endtimes
Sharīʿa: sacred Law
shayṭān: the devil
ṣiddīq: most veracious believer; as a proper noun it refers to Abū Bakr
ṣiddīqī: Ṣiddīq-affiliated; title used to refer to a Naqshbandi master
ṣiddīqiyya: veraciousness; used as a name for the Naqshbandi Sufi way
ṣuḥba: spiritual companionship; spiritual discourse
sulṭan al-khawf: dominant fear
sulṭan al-dhikr: dominant remembrance
sulūk: spiritual wayfaring; following tariqa discipline
taḥammul al-aḍdād: bearing with reverses
tajallī, pl. *tajalliyāt*: spiritual manifestations
takbīr: magnification; the exclamation *Allāhu akbar!* (God is greatest)
takfīr: declaring others to be unbelievers
takhliya: self-clearance, self-purification (from spiritual ills)
tamkīn: firmness and strength
taqwā: guarding oneself from divine displeasure
ṭarīqa: spiritual path
taṣdīq: giving credence
ṭifl al-nafs al-madhmūma: the childish blameworthy ego
ʿubūdiyya: servanthood, worshipfulness
ʿulūm maʿnawiyya: plural of *ʿilm maʿnawī*
ʿulūw al-himma: high spiritual energy
walī: friend of Allah; rightful ally; guardian; near friend
wārid, pl. *wāridāt*: spiritual intuitions
wasīla: intermediary
wilāya: friendship (with Allah); sainthood
al-yaqīn: certainty
yawm al-maḥshar: the Day of the Regathering

yawm al-qiyāma: the Day of Resurrection
zāhid: person of simple living, ascetic
al-ẓāhir: the outward
zuhd: simple living

THE LIGHTS OF GUIDANCE

FROM THE KNOWLEDGE OCEANS
OF THE DIVINE SIDE

The Early Lebanon Suhbas of

Shaykh Muhammad Nazim al-Haqqani

I

1
The blessing of the forefathers' supplication for the people of Tripoli, Lebanon – The perfect spiritual guide – One to whom intercession does not apply

I seek refuge in Allah from the accursed devil
In the Name of Allah the All-Beneficent the Most Merciful
There is no power nor strength but with Allah the High, the Magnificent
Permission, O my Master, support!
Our way is companionship, and goodness is in the congregation

This blessing has reached all of you as a result of the supplication of your righteous forefathers. You will get, in every age, an increase of those excellent virtues. Here, in this country (Tripoli), a spiritual manifestation such as that of Sham (Greater Syria), where it is forbidden for its hypocrites to prevail over its believers, including in this very country of Tarabulus al-Sham (Tripoli of Greater Syria) which is famous among Allah's Friends.

So the people of falsehood cannot prevail over the people of the truth in this country. This is glad tidings and a protection as well. At the same time it is a protection for the people of the region. Then there will appear things that are of the miraculous gifts which Allah has given exclusively to this Umma from among the people of this country, so that its status among the Islamic countries will be like that of a star in the sky. It will give light by the blessing of the presence of the truthful, the righteous, the lovers, and the supporters of the truth that hail from this country. Those that raced with one another as soon as the sign of truth appeared so that they will obtain something from it and take their share of it. Praise be to Allah Who has gathered us around love of the truth! O Allah! inspire us our right way and be our refuge away from our own bad deeds.

It is a must for the human being to be more concerned about the traps of the *nafs* (ego) and of the devil. For it is not possible for the human being to resist his ego. Rather he needs a helper such as a truthful brother or such as a perfect *murshid* (spiritual guide). The *murshid* is the foundation of all quests. And when the servant of Allah finds the perfect *murshid*, he has won every success and has reached salvation for all his hopes in this world and the next. But when he is without the perfect *murshid*, then he must look for a truthful brother who will help him in his affair in this life and the next, and that is the important thing. If you cannot find a truthful brother, then you will never ever find a perfect spiritual guide.

When craftsmen need something that is necessary for their crafts, for example, they search every country until they find it, because they need it. And this is for a worldly matter. Likewise when there is in our country a truthful brother or a perfect *murshid*, then it is an obligation for us to search for him until we find him, because the presence of the perfect *murshid* pertains to eternal life. And when we find that perfect *murshid* or truthful brother, that will be an illustration of the Quranic verse, *We shall strengthen your arm with your brother* (Qaṣaṣ 28:35).

The truthful brother is a brother in the faith. It is not necessary for him to be a son of your mother and father. So when you find a truthful brother, through him the quest for the perfect *murshid* will become easier. For without the perfect *murshid* it will be impossible for your endeavor to succeed.

Why has the practice of the faith declined? Because there is no interest in searching for a perfect *murshid*. The perfect *murshid* nurtures the human being in his faith-system and teaches him to truly hold fast to his belief, Likewise, the human being's certainty becomes stronger by sitting with the perfect *murshid*. When people started to deny the Sufi paths and their masters, they plummeted to earth, whereas before they were flying in the sky and reaching to the world of the angels. They became characterized by *is he then that goes groveling on his face better-guided?* (Mulk 67:22).

And whoever has no Shaykh and no Imam showing him the way, Iblis shall be his instructor and his guide. The first of those on whom Iblis inflicts his authority are the people of knowledge. He fills them with egotism until they admit no one as being above them. He says to them, "You are the learned scholar, you are the unique one of your time, and the rest of the eminent scholars are all beneath you!" The ulema of this type are sick, and whoever listens to them, self-admiration will contaminate him also, and they will become proud of their deeds, their prayers and their own presence in the congregations. Pride is the heritage of Iblis. Whoever has an ant's weight of pride will be affiliated with Iblis and it will be forbidden for him to enter Paradise. That is because:

- if a proud person enters Paradise then Iblis must also enter Paradise;
- if an obdurate person enters Paradise then Iblis must also enter Paradise;
- if an envious person enters Paradise then Iblis must also enter Paradise;
- if an angry person enters Paradise then Iblis must also enter Paradise.

That to which intercession does not apply consists in four human traits: **anger, envy, pride and obduracy. Whoever has any single one of these traits is**

an inheritor of Iblis and there is no possibility of intercession for him on the Day of Resurrection, because Iblis is not included in the Messenger's intercession and his affair is resigned to Allah. Likewise, whoever possesses these traits cannot enter Paradise, because these traits are a moral impurity. And whoever does not condescend to listen to one of the Shaykhs and follow him is overproud. If you were to question him he will absolve himself, although absolving oneself is forbidden: our liege Lord Yūsuf –upon him peace– said, *and I do not absolve myself* (Yūsuf 12:53).

He absolves himself and says, "Where can a perfect *murshid* be found nowadays?" Many of the ignorant ones even say, "The Messenger of Allah –upon him the blessings and peace of Allah– is my Shaykh!" But the Messenger –upon him the blessings and peace of Allah– himself was following our liege Lord Jibril and took him as a guide, and he would not make one step until Jibril first came down to him and signaled him. This would be enough for them if there was a trace of light in their hearts or any intelligence in them and if they understood at all the meaning of following the Sunna of the Messenger of Allah –upon him the blessings and peace of Allah. The fact that the Messenger followed Jibril is as if he were saying to us, "O my nation! You as well must take one whose path you follow;" and Allah says *and follow the path of him who has abundantly repented to Me* (Luqmān 31:15), i.e. him who has left everything other than Allah.

Where and how can you find one of them? They are the red Sulphur.[1] When you firmly believe that "their existence is necessary and my life is that short time," you will leave everything and you will look for them the way that our liege Lord Mūsā –upon him peace– did. He had a great need to see "one of the slaves of Allah" (cf. Kahf 18:65) who was more knowledgeable than him. Hence he searched until he found him. And this is a teaching for us, that *man ṭalabanā wajadanā* (whoever searches for us finds us). However, **due to arrogance in the ego, due to mindlessness, and due to the absence of light in the heart, many are claiming to know something of the faith-system when in reality they know nothing. That is why it is a must to find a truthful brother or a perfect *murshid*.** An example for that is when they bring a patient to the emergency room in a hospital. The nurses that are present there administer the first aid until the doctor comes. Likewise the truthful brother provides service and assists us in our need. Likewise, **if three individuals gather together, singlehearted, then truly their voice will be heard from east to west.**[2] And this is an important matter.

[1] I.e. the pure gold.

[2] Cf. the Prophetic hadith, "The hand of Allah is with the *jamāʿa* (congregation),"

The basic foundation is for the human being either to have a truthful brother or a perfect *murshid*. The Messenger –upon him the blessings and peace of Allah– all of his life never walked one step except with the command of Allah which he would receive from Jibril –upon him peace– and he would wait, in all his movements and all his pauses, for the command to come to him from Allah. This is the Sunna of the Messenger of Allah –upon him the blessings and peace of Allah– and we are followers of his Sunna. But as for one who claims that he is a follower of the Sunna of the Messenger of Allah –upon him the blessings and peace of Allah– but does not take a trusted authority for him in all his movements and pauses to consult him and to be under his command, then he is a liar. This is why our liege Lord Abū Yazīd al-Bisṭāmī says:

"Whoever has no Shaykh, his Shaykh is the devil."

"Whoever has no Imam, his Imam is the devil."

"Whoever has no guide, his guide is the devil."

"Whoever has no teacher, his teacher is the devil."

And this is how the first *khamīra* (leaven) for Islam will be: a group gathering together for the cause of the truth, in support of the truth. From them, the truth will spread like ember lighting up stacks of coal. These attributes were dressed upon our brothers that live in Tripoli of Greater Syria, and from them, the truth will spread, whereby all of them are part of this circle of truth. They will become supporters of the truth and they will be given help to victory with the truth on the part of Allah. And they will be drawn swords in support of the truth in the way of Allah.

These glad tidings have come for their sake. This is what my liege Lord and Master has told me.

O nurturing Lord! You are the All-True. O nurturing Lord! make us of the people of truth. O nurturing Lord! keep us away from falsehood and protect us with the truth. By the sanctity of the Beloved, by the sanctity of the Fatiha.

narrated from Ibn ʿAbbās by al-Tirmidhī and Bayhaqī in *al-Asmā' wal-ṣifāt* (Ḥāshidī ed. 2:136 §702, *isnād ṣaḥīḥ*), a mass-transmitted report in meaning according to al-Jaṣṣāṣ in *al-Fuṣūl*, al-Ghazālī in *al-Muṣtaṣfā*, Ibn Rushd the Grandson and others such as Ibn Qudāma in *Rawḍat al-nāẓir*.

2

The concern for the cleanness of the heart – The divisions of the ego for men and women – [The earth of love – Acquiring the character of Allah] – Intuitions coming on the part of the Messenger – "If my Umma keeps straight then it has one day"

I seek refuge in Allah from the accursed devil
In the Name of Allah the All-Beneficent the Most Merciful
There is no power nor strength but with Allah the High, the Magnificent
Permission, O my Master, support!
Our way is companionship, and goodness is in the congregation

And the One God summons to the Abode of Wholeness (Yūnus 10:25). We are summoned to be with our almighty nurturing Lord.

When a summoning has come to us from the President of the Republic or from any important direction, we start preparing ourselves for that invitation and we do not go without putting our external appearance in order. Now we are being invited into the presence of our nurturing Lord. This is why we must take much more care for that attendance for *yawm al-ʿarḍ* (the Day of display) before Allah, where all creatures will be standing on their feet, present and waiting for the Day of display.[1] **We did not come to this world to play the way the minions of this world do. Rather we came to this world to prepare ourselves for the display before the All-True.**

At the time of the big display in the various countries and in celebratory parades, those who possess distinctions and grades do not leave out anything except they hand it on their chests so that they will come out before people wearing them. *And verily the hereafter is vaster in levels and vaster in preferential treatment!* (Isrāʾ 17:21). This world is nothing; the real levels and preferential treatment is in the hereafter. This is why we must prepare ourselves day after day for the display before Allah, because we do not know when we will be summoned to go back to His presence.

Imam Ghazālī mentioned this issue as part of the types of spiritual disclosures. He says: "When the funeral bier is carried to the grave, on the way, Allah asks the deceased 40 questions 'and there is no translator between Him and

[1] *On that Day you shall be displayed, not one secret of yours remaining hidden* (al-Ḥāqqa 69:18).

His servant,'[1] and the first thing Allah shall ask him is, 'O My servant, you used to put so much care in your external appearance because the gaze of people was trained on your outward look and so that you would obtain their respect. O My servant, have you taken care, even once, of your heart, bearing in mind that "My nurturing Lord is looking at my heart, so I must make my heart a house for Him?"'"

For Allah says, "All the limbs are yours but as for the heart it belongs to me.[2] Have you purified My house, O My servant?" Allah Most High says, *and purify My House* (al-Ḥajj 22:26), and the meaning is not that our liege Lord Ibrāhīm should only purify the House of Allah outwardly. Rather the goal is for every servant to purify his heart, because it is the house of Allah and the locus of His gaze. Our liege Lord al-Ghazālī has said this was the first question, and there is no need to discuss the rest of the questions, since the first question contains everything. And this impels the servants to take much more care of their hearts.

Among women there are nine parts of ego and one part of reason, whereby Allah has divided the ego into ten parts and has placed nine in women and a single one in men, and He has divided reason into ten parts of which He put nine among men and a single one in women. If man cannot keep a single part of ego under his control, the whole retribution will be against him. For the burden of women is heavy, and *men are caretakers over women* (al-Nisā' 4:34). Women, whatever they do, their egos will overcome them; as for men, with nine parts of reason and yet one cannot keep a single part of ego under his control – then he will be exposed to retribution.

This is why we have to think about the matter of our hearts, since we do not know when our lives will be taken back and our nurturing Lord will ask us about the matter of our hearts. Hence the Prophet's –upon him the blessings and peace of Allah– great concern for the hearts of the Umma, because when the servant's heart is fit then his entire situation becomes right, but if the heart is spoiled then all his affairs become spoiled. But **concern for the hearts does not become easy except by sitting with Prophets or Friends of Allah, and likewise there is no Prophet after the Prophet of the end of times –upon him the blessings and peace of Allah. However, his inheritors endure until the Day of Resurrection.**

This is why the Prophet –upon him the blessings and peace of Allah– said, "There will never cease to be a group from my Umma who prevail, standing

[1] Hadith from 'Adī b. Ḥātim in the *Musnad*, the two *Ṣaḥīḥ*s and the *Sunan*.

[2] Cf. Report from Wahb b. Munabbih in Aḥmad, *al-Zuhd* (chapter on Yūsuf).

firm on truth, until the Hour rises."[1] These ones, the world will never be devoid of them, but we must only look for them. And whoever looks for these ones truthfully, Allah shall give him a way to reach them. All he needs is a truthful quest, and a truthful quest is only for the sincere ones. The sincere one is the one who does not become tired in his wayfaring to Allah Almighty. Every time he reaches a new high station he does not suffice himself with it. No, he climbs up to the next one. And thus he does not grow tired of climbing higher and progressing in stations, and he does not become lazy in obedience of Allah. That is the sincere one.

We are in need of truthfulness. Whoever is truthful with his nurturing Lord will be truthful with all. **We want for love of Allah and of His Messenger–upon him the blessings and peace of Allah–and love of Awliya and of one's teacher and of Mahdi (the rightly-guided one) and of brethren to settle in our hearts. For once we firmly plant love in our hearts, that is where faith and submission will grow, and in the earth of love all of the excellent traits of character will come to fruition**, but when the earth of love is nowhere to be found, it is like seeds that are impossible to plant.

So this is love. As part of the last will of Shaykh Sharaf al-Dīn Dāghistānī before he left this world he called Shaykh 'Abd Allāh and said to him, "**My last will for the brothers is that they must love and respect whoever is affiliated to us and has become, in relation to us, like their love for me, and that they prize him the same as their prizing of me.**" This is why, to the extent that we can, we must love one another and disregard the shortcomings found in some of us. For when we cover up one another's blemishes Allah covers us. **We must also adorn ourselves with the manners of Allah,**[2] and of His manners is that He is *Sattār al-'uyūb* (All-Covering of blemishes). **Mention the excellencies of creatures and do not mention their evil traits because, at the mention of excellent traits mercy descends; whereas at the mention of evil traits darkness and curses descend, and you will be far from the mercy of Allah.** When a person just looks at the excellencies of others, Allah shall give him a type of wisdom and knowledges that were not consigned in books. Your nurturing Lord shall lift the veil for you, and this is from the foundation of *taqwā* (God-fearingness).

[1] Mass-transmitted from sixteen Companions per Kattanī, *Naẓm al-mutanāthir.*

[2] "We must acquire as our own traits the entirety of the Attributes of the divine Essence to the extent that we can. Most of the human appropriation of divine traits is divided into (i) individual categorical obligation, (ii) sunna, (iii) and collective categorical obligation. So look at His beautiful Names and acquire as your trait, from every Name among them, its *muqtaḍā* ⟨requisite⟩ as much as possible." Ibn 'Abd al-Salām, *Shajarat al-ma'ārif wal-aḥwāl.* See also Suhbas I.31, third note; I.50, last note; I.59.

We must medicate ourselves against those illnesses, against looking at the evils of others, from the perspective that ahead of us lies a new era in which nothing will remain except what is pure. But whoever has sickness in him, then he will be cast into the quarantine, i.e. the *barzakh* (interlife). And we are aiming to reach the age of al-Mahdi about whom the truthful one, our liege Lord the Messenger of Allah –upon him the blessings and peace of Allah– told us, whereby he has given us the glad tidings that before the Day of Resurrection there shall be the age of al-Mahdi and the age of ʿĪsā (Jesus) –upon them peace, when there shall emerge the age of absolute glory for Islam and the believers. The earth itself is awaiting those days and is tolerating for impurities, unbelievers and injustice to fester on top of it, otherwise it would have swallowed them up. But it keeps still, only so that it will reach the time of al-Mahdi. Likewise there remained none of the Companions of the Prophet–upon him the blessings and peace of Allah– when he told them of the age of al-Mahdi, but they all asked to be reaching that age. When they realized that it was not possible for them to reach that age, they supplicated Allah to make some of their offspring reach it, so that they themselves would reach those lights through them. And we are now standing at the doors of that age, and whoever lives a natural life should reach that age.

My coming to your country is not for the sake of this world. This world is under our feet. However, it is to give you glad tidings that the event is taking place soon, and so that you may get ready to be among the men of that age, and some spiritual intuitions are coming to us for the purification of your hearts from the illnesses that block one from being present together with the owner of the time. Make your intention and Allah shall support you in accordance with your intentions. Likewise, in every sitting, something is cast into our hearing of the intuitions that reach me from the side of the Messenger, upon him the blessings and peace of Allah, and from the great spiritual masters. So take heed and think well on this discourse, and do not say, "This one is talking on his own."

If we brought a radio – which is a wooden box – and it said, "This is London," you would believe it, yet when I say, "I am speaking to you on the part of the Messenger –upon him the blessings and peace of Allah–and on the part of the great spiritual masters," you do not concern yourselves! The meaning of this is there is absence of certainty.

The more a human being increases in certainty, he increases in faith, just as our generation shall reach the Mahdi, per the evidence that the Messenger of Allah –upon him blessings and peace of Allah– has said that "Every hundred years there shall come someone who will renew the matter of this faith-system."[1] And we are about to reach the beginning of the Hijri year 1400 (21 November 1979).

It has also been narrated in the hadith of the Messenger –upon him the blessings and peace of Allah: "If my Umma has followed uprightness then they have one day, and if they have not followed uprightness then they have half a day, *and verily one day in the presence of your nurturing Lord is as a thousand years of what you count* (Ḥajj 22:47)."[2] I.e. the meaning of one day is a thousand years, and if it has not followed uprightness then it will have half a day, i.e. 500 years. This is a sign that the age of the Umma is 1,500 years, and we are now reaching the Hijri year 1,400. We are awaiting deliverance – we are commanded to wait, and the Prophet, upon him blessings and peace, said, "Awaiting deliverance is worship."[3] By virtue of our awaiting we will be recompensed and it is as if we are in the midst of worship.

Our request is only that Allah will bring into being His promise to us, since He says, *the One God has promised those of you who believe and do righteous deeds that He shall indeed grant them succession in the land just as He granted those who were before them succession; and that He shall indeed empower for them their faith-system with which He is well-pleased for them; and that He shall indeed give them in exchange, after their fear, safety, as they worship Me without associating anything with Me* (Nūr 24:55). The granting of succession that our nurturing Lord has mentioned: first He gave the rule to our forefathers over the earth; and He shall repeat this matter as an honor lavished upon the people of belief and the people of righteous deeds. And He shall empower us to establish our faith-system, then He shall substitute our fear with safety, for the Muslims now are afraid and there is no power to establish their faith-system but Allah has given His promise and glad tidings.

[1] Narrated from Abū Hurayra by Abū Dāwūd, Ḥākim, Bayhaqī and others, a sound hadith per Ibn Ḥajar, *Tawālī al-ta'nīs*; Sakhāwī, *al-Maqāṣid al-ḥasana*; 'Ajlūnī, *Kashf al-khafā*; and al-Suyūṭī, *Mirqāt al-ṣu'ūd ilā Sunan Abī Dāwūd.*

[2] The wording "Truly I swear that I hope my Community will not be denied by their Lord a respite of half a day" is narrated from Abū Tha'laba al-Khushanī and Sa'd b. Abī Waqqāṣ by Aḥmad, Abū Dāwūd, Ḥākim and Abū Nu'aym, a fair report per the editor of Ibn al-Mulaqqin's *Mukhtaṣar istidrāk al-Dhahabī 'alā Mustadrak al-Ḥākim*, with Ibn Abī Waqqāṣ's additional comment, "and half a day is five hundred years." Suhaylī said there is nothing in this hadith that precludes additional time per Ibn Ḥajar, *Fatḥ*.

[3] Narrated from (i) Ibn Mas'ūd by al-Tirmidhī; al-Ṭabarānī; (ii) 'Alī b. Abī Ṭālib by Ibn Abī al-Dunyā; (iii) Anas by al-Bazzār, al-Bayhaqī and al-Khaṭīb; (iv) Jābir by al-Ḥakīm al-Tirmidhī; (v) Ibn 'Abbās by Ibn 'Adī, Ibn al-Muqri' and al-Quḍā'ī; and (vi) Ibn 'Umar by Ibn Ḥibbān, Ibn Jumay', al-Mālīnī, al-Quḍā'ī and al-Silafī.

Our hope is that we shall reach the age of al-Mahdi and strive against the unbelievers, from the perspective that in his age firearms will no longer function, and Allah shall support Islam with magnification and bring their power to nought. The matter will revert to sword-fighting. This is our hope, that our nurturing Lord will give the young men of Islam this sword until they will be of the strivers with al-Mahdi. The matter is in the hand of Allah and it is not in our hands. We are servants who possess for ourselves neither harm nor benefit, neither life nor death nor resurrection. When al-Mahdi appears there shall descend, in support of him, heavenly hosts whom the earthly hosts will join. If Allah wills we shall attain those days.

By the sanctity of the Beloved, by the sanctity of the Fatiha.

3
The divine good pleasure in voluntary deeds – Imam Ghazālī's heavenly ascent – The reason for which Allah granted our liege Lord 'Umar mercy

I seek refuge in Allah from the accursed devil
In the Name of Allah the All-Beneficent the Most Merciful
There is no power nor strength but with Allah the High, the Magnificent
Permission, O my Master, support!
Our way is companionship, and goodness is in the congregation

Every day a human being goes through motions and pauses. From the time of puberty to the time of death our acts are counted against us. Either they are in agreement with the command of Allah and His Messenger –upon him the blessings and peace of Allah– or they are in agreement with the cravings of the ego, of one's whim, of the devil and of this lower world.

Imam al-Ḥasan al-Baṣrī says, "Every day one chances upon one of two things: either something of the commands the Prophet–upon him the blessings and peace of Allah–has brought, or something of the prohibitions." Imam al-Ḥasan al-Baṣrī instructed the following: "When you chance upon one of the 500 commands the Prophet –upon him the blessings and peace of Allah– has brought, do not neglect it by saying, 'This is neither a categorical obligation nor a requirement' or 'This is merely desirable.' Rather hold fast to it and seize the opportunity!" Hold fast to it and do not consider it insignificant, as small as it might be. Here is the Messenger's statement –upon him the blessings and peace of Allah: "Never dismiss any *ma'rūf* (goodness) as insignificant!"[1] It is a teaching and a directive for all humankind.

The human being must stand apart from the animal. For the animal does not recognize goodness. Anyone that does not practice goodness is not a human being other than in appearance. That is why the *awliyā* have striven to honor the human being, to the point that Imam al-Ḥasan al-Baṣrī would address people with the phrase "O my children." Most of the love and compassion of the human being is directed at his children, and the believers are all, in his [=al-Ḥasan al-Baṣrī's] eyes, like his children. This is the attribute of the

[1] Narrated from (i) Jābir b. Sulaym al-Hujaymī by Ibn al-Mubārak, Ibn Wahb, al-Ṭayālisī, Ibn Sa'd, Aḥmad, al-Bukhārī in *al-Adab al-mufrad* and others; and (ii) Abū Dharr by Aḥmad, Muslim, al-Bazzār, Ibn Ḥibbān, al-Bayhaqī and others.

great spiritual guides. Just as the Messenger of Allah–upon him blessings and peace of Allah–was described by his nurturing Lord as *anxious over you, towards the believers tenderest, most compassionate* (Tawba 9:128), likewise, the inheritors of the Messenger are anxious over the Umma of the Messenger and are striving for their salvation, their ultimate triumph and their eternal happiness. For it might be that a servant is doing some work that consumes a lot of his time and requires endurance – and that is because he expects great goodness from it – but it is probable that the greater divine good pleasure will be in a little, partial work that the human being is neglecting. That is why **it is imperative to pay attention to everything that the Prophet–upon him blessings and peace of Allah–has brought, even if it is small.**

In the same way the ego, whims, the devil and the lower world pounce on the human being to embellish for him the neglect of that work as some paltry matter, and yet Allah's good pleasure might be in it. This is a secret Allah has placed in deeds.

Mawlana Sultan al-Awliya Shaykh 'Abd Allah Fa'iz al-Daghistani said of this matter that when the Proof of Islam Imam al-Ghazālī died, the *awliyā* were looking at his spiritual presence as it was ascending in the sky from the same station the Messenger–upon him the blessings and peace of Allah– had ascended from, and they were asking themselves: "Perhaps Imam al-Ghazālī reached this rank because of his prayer, or his night vigil prayer, or his fasting, or the books he wrote, or his spiritual directives, or his simple living," etc. But confirmation from Allah Almighty did not come to any of them, until the divine call came that , "My servant Imam Ghazālī obtained this rank because of a simple, partial deed, namely that he was writing an epistle in a hurry on the night of the noble Mawlid (birth of the Prophet–upon him blessings and peace of Allah), when a fly alighted on the edge of the paper and started to drink from the ink so Imam Ghazālī stopped writing and did not kill it or shoo it away, as a mark of respect for the Prophet–upon him the blessings and peace of Allah–and his birth, noting to himself that this fly had been created for his sake. And by reason of this simple deed I have given him this station so that he would climb up to the station of the *fardāniyyīn* (solitary ones)."[1]

Similarly, our liege Lord 'Umar b. al-Khaṭṭāb was seen in a dream after he moved from this world and he was asked: "What has Allah done with you, O

[1] See al-Ḥakīm al-Tirmidhī, *Khatm al-awliyā'* (section 7, *khiṣāl al-wilāyat al-'ashr*; section 13, *khātam al-awliyā'*; section 20, *al-walī wal-khaṭī'a*). Shaykh 'Abd al-Qādir mentions *dār al-fardāniyya* (the abode of exalted solitary rank) among the levels reached by the Sufi in the "Book of the manners of the murids" in his *Ghunya*. In Akbarī terminology the *fard* is the one who lies beyond the gaze of the *quṭb*.

'Umar?" He said, "He forgave me." He was asked, "By what special deed?" He said, "One day I saw in one of the alleys of Medina the Illuminated some children tormenting a bird so I compensated them and set the bird free.[1] Because of this deed, my nurturing Lord has forgiven me." Everyone considers that our liege Lord 'Umar–Allah be well-pleased with him–[soared] because of his immense services in the time of the Messenger of Allah–upon him the blessings and peace of Allah–or his caliphate after his time and his Companionship to the Messenger, but he did not mention any of that; and Allah said, "I granted you mercy because of the bird." This is a sufficient teaching for the intelligent one that he should not leave out anything of the *ma'rūf* (good deeds) if he is able to do it.

There is also another example there to clarify that the *ma'rūf*, even something minimal, directs the servant—even if he is an unbeliever—to faith, and from wretchedness to bliss. It is related that there was in Baghdad a Zoroastrian who worshipped fire. In one of the days of Ramadan he saw one of his small children eating a piece of bread so he disciplined him, saying, "Are you not ashamed to eat during the day of Ramadan while the Muslims are fasting?" This is what he happened to do. After the man died, he was seen in Paradise and he was asked, "How did you enter Paradise when you used to be a Zoroastrian?" He said, "Allah honored me with faith because I prevented my child from eating on one of the days of Ramadan and I even disciplined him although he was not legally tasked, and I did that out of respect for Islam, and that was accepted in the presence of my nurturing Lord, so He guided me to Islam."

Yet another example that shows how Allah will forgive everything from a person's past life because of a small deed is the story of the prostitute from Mūsā's people. She was travelling from one country to another and had reached a water well. She saw a dog there that was licking the sand in extreme thirst. She took pity on it, went down into the well, drank from it, then filled her shoe with water and tied it up with her scarf. Then she gave the dog water to drink. Later, when she reached the town of one of the Prophets of the Israelites, Allah revealed to that Prophet, "Give glad tidings to So and so that I have forgiven her all her sins because of the mercy she showed to that dog."[2]

By the sanctity of the Beloved, by the sanctity of the Fatiha.

[1] Something similar is narrated about Ibn 'Umar by Aḥmad, Bukhārī and Muslim.

[2] Prophetic report narrated in substance from Abū Hurayra by Bukhārī and Muslim.

4

Signs of real belief – [To hear creation's glorifying increases nearness to Allah – There is no end to knowledge of Allah – *Barzakh* meetings]

I seek refuge in Allah from the accursed devil
In the Name of Allah the All-Beneficent the Most Merciful
There is no power nor strength but with Allah the High, the Magnificent
Permission, O my Master, support!
Our way is companionship, and goodness is in the congregation

Up to this point we have been in the age of imitative faith, and the age of real faith shall begin with the beginning of the 15th century [November 21, 1979] i.e. the age of Muḥammad al-Mahdī–upon him peace.[1] Our belief as of now is imitative belief. Such a belief is accepted in the presence of Allah but we are tasked with rising up from imitative belief to real belief. If we abandon this matter we shall be sinful in the presence of Allah–exalted is He. **Real belief has signs. When they appear in a human being, one has reached the station of real belief.** We shall mention three of these signs:

1. The first is the servant's audition of the glorifications of all creatures.

Allah Most High said in His glorious Book, *and there is not one thing in existence but extols His praise* (Banū Isrā'il/Isrā' 17:44). So whoever is counted among the things must make glorification. This is important: every part of the human being's body actually makes glorification while he is heedless of it.[2] But

[1] A reference to the final age predicted in the authentic Prophetic hadith, "There shall be Prophethood among you for as long as Allah wishes. He shall lift it up when He wishes. Then there shall be caliphate after the pattern of Prophethood for as long as Allah wishes. He shall lift it up when He wishes. Then there shall be a difficult kingship for as long as Allah wishes. He shall lift it up when He wishes. Then there shall be a tyrannical kingship for as long as Allah wishes. He shall lift it up when He wishes. Then there shall be caliphate after the pattern of Prophethood." Narrated from (i) Ḥudhayfa b. al-Yamān, (ii) Abū 'Ubayda b. al-Jarrāḥ and (iii) Mu'ādh b. Jabal by Ṭayālisī, Aḥmad, Abū Ya'lā, Ṭabarānī (*Awsaṭ*; *Kabīr*), Ibn 'Abd al-Barr (*Tamhīd*), al-Bayhaqī (*Sunan*; *Shu'ab*). Ba'lī in *al-Arba'ūn min riyāḍ al-janna* cites it (§20) and declares it sound, cf. Haythamī, *Majma' al-zawā'id* (5:188-189); Ibn Rajab, *Jāmi' al-'ulūm wal-ḥikam* (§28).

[2] "In the morning every joint of yours must pay a *ṣadaqa*. Every *tasbīḥ* is a *ṣadaqa*, every *taḥmīd* is a *ṣadaqa*, every *tahlīl* is a *ṣadaqa*, every *takbīr* is a *ṣadaqa*, every commanding good is a *ṣadaqa* and every forbidding evil is a *ṣadaqa*, and all this is accomplished through two *rak'as* one can pray in *ḍuḥā*." A Prophetic hadith narrated from

the glorifications of created things differ from one another, and each thing has its special glorification with a special wording.

Mawlana Shaykh ʿAbd Allah Fa'iz al-Daghistani says that the audition of the glorifications of created things appear in the real believer in three stages. (i) In the first stage, one hears the glorifications of created things in their entirety as a single sound, like the buzzing of bees. (ii) In the second stage one draws near to that station and becomes strengthened with those powers, distinguishing the sounds of the glorifications of created things the way the sounds of things are distinguished from one another. One distinguishes between them: water, trees, inanimate things. (iii) In the third stage what takes place is the perfection of the sign of the audition of the glorification of created things: one recognizes in what wording each of those things glorifies Allah, just as the glorification of colors differs.

The hearing of this glorification will be part of the perfection of the first of the signs of true belief. The giving of this light for the audition of the glorifications may be gradual, and it may take place in one day, or over several months or a year. That is all according to the person's readiness. And all things say *subḥān Allah* (glory to Allah), each with a better wording than the next. There is nothing in the world like the glorification of water. *And We made, from water, everything that lives* (al-Anbiyā' 21:30). Then, when one hears the glorification of things, one hears the glorification of all of them without limits. I.e. one hears the glorifications of the angels of the heavens and the earth and the angels of the Footstool and the Throne. **The power of real belief gives whoever has it the power to hear the glorifications of each thing on a par, and the audition of any given one of them never prevents him from hearing the glorifications of the millions in the seas and the skies and the glorifications of the angels.**

People deem that belief in Allah is something simple; but **how will the human being be a *khalīfat Allāh* (successor/vicegerent appointed by Allah) and how can he be a representative of the All-True but not hear the glorifications**? However, what is the benefit of hearing the glorifications? With the audition of the glorifications the human being increases in every moment in knowledge of Allah–exalted is He–and without this power there will not be a drawing near to Allah. [The Prophet–upon him the blessings and peace of

Abū Dharr by Muslim. "There are 360 joints in a human being and he must pay a *ṣadaqa* for each one of them." They said, "Who can do such a thing, Messenger of Allah?" He replied, "Bury the sputum you see in the masjid, remove a dangerous object from the road, [etc.]; and, if you are unable, then the two *rakʿas* of *ḍuḥā* accomplish it for you." Aḥmad, Abū Dāwūd, Ṭaḥāwī, Ibn Ḥibbān from Abū Burayda.

Allah–held pebbles in his hand and let the Companions hear their glorification.[1]]

2. [The second is the opening of the door of wisdom.]

The second sign of the entering of the light of real belief into the servant's heart is that Allah opens up for you the door of wisdom, from the perspective that one will hear the glorification of something and recognize the wisdom of its existence in the created universe. To the extent of one's acquired knowledge through wisdom one will increase in nearness to and knowledge of Allah. Likewise creation never stops. Rather, *and He creates that which you do not know* (Naḥl 16:8)[2] i.e. creation is constantly appearing at all times from inexistence to existence, carrying one of the beautiful Names of Allah, glorifying its nurturing Lord – exalted is He – with a glorification befitting that Name. Hence the door of the knowledge of wisdom is increasing at all times and we shall never find an end to the knowledge of Allah.

Creation is perpetual. He has always been and continues to be al-Khallāq (The All-Creating) since before time;[3] and whensoever our nurturing Lord creates, creations appear; and each creature will be under the upbringing of one of His beautiful Names. This is why the servant increases in knowledge in every second through the appearance of the Names from [created] things and, with his knowledge of those things, His knowledge of Allah increases. Hence knowledge of Allah is an ocean without shore and without bottom![4]

[1] Narrated from Abū Dharr by al-Bukhārī, *al-Tārīkh al-kabīr* (8:442) and others. The bracketed clause is mistakenly moved to the title of the next suhba in the Arabic text.

[2] Cf. *glory to Him Who created the species—all of them—from what the earth grows, and from themselves, and from what they do not know* (Yā Sīn 36:36); *and raising you up into that which you know not* (al-Wāqiʿa 56:61).

[3] Cf. Ibn Khafīf, *al-ʿAqīda al-ṣaḥīḥa* (Mss. Fātih. 5381, 5391 and Hagia Sophia 4792, f° 746b-748a, ed. Ibrāhīm Dusūqī Shaṭṭā, *Sīrat al-shaykh al-kabīr Muḥammad Ibn Khafīf al-Shīrāzī* (Cairo: al-Hay'at al-ʿĀmma li-Shu'ūn al-Maṭābiʿ al-Amīriyya, 1977) pp. 340-365 §19: *lam yazal Khāliqun wa-lā makhlūq* "He was ever Creator even when there was nothing created;" Ṭaḥāwī, *ʿAqīda* (§15), "to Him belonged the meaning of Lordship even when there was nothing lorded over." This is a point of similarity between the Ashʿarī and Māturīdī creeds. Later Ashʿarīs further specified that the Attributes of act have two types of *taʿalluq* (linkage) to the act, *ṣalūḥī qadīm* (beginninglessly potential) and *tanjīzī ḥādith* (newly actualizing): Būṭī, *Kubrā al-yaqīniyyāt al-kawniyya* (p. 121); Sakūnī, *Arbaʿūna mas'ala fī uṣūl al-dīn* (§19, "the linkage of the pre-eternal divine Attributes").

[4] *Behold the Throne over its water // as a ship coursing with His Names,*
And wonder at the vessel, revolving, // in whose entrails He placed creatures!
It is glorifying in a shoreless ocean, // in the unseen's deep night and its darkness,
*Its waves the states of His lovers, // its wind the breaths of His children.**

Abū Bakr Muḥyī al-Dīn Muḥammad b. ʿAlī b. Muḥammad al-Ṭā'ī al-Ḥātimī al-Mursī,

3. [The third is the meeting with the people of the *barzakh*.]

With the appearance of the third sign for the possessor of true belief, it becomes easy for him to encounter and assemble with all of the people of the *barzakh* (interlife), whereby he meets with the *rūḥāniyya* (spiritual presence)[1] of the Messenger–upon him the blessings and peace of Allah. At the occurrence of this meeting he becomes able to meet with any human being in the interlife because he has become *barzakhī* (living both here and hereafter).[2] Yet there is no way to express the modality of the spiritual meeting. However, the door of *kashf* (spiritual unveiling) is opened there for the servant, whereupon he is now at the station of real belief, where belief is through witnessing. That in which he had believed without seeing has now become witnessed to him. At that point he is able to meet with the spiritual presence of any Prophet or any Companion or any Shaykh without impediment.

These are the signs and the levels of the possessor of real belief. What is demanded from us is to obtain this belief. This is the fruit of a life. We did not come here to obtain the rubble of this world. We came here to obtain this reality.

By the sanctity of the Beloved, by the sanctity of the Fatiha.

Dīwān Ibn 'Arabī, ed. 'Alī Afandī Jawdah and Muḥammad b. Ismā'īl Shihāb al-Dīn (Bulāq: Dār al-Ṭibā'at al-'Āmira, 1271/1855, rept. Baghdad: Maktabat al-Muthannā, [1963]) pp. 10-11 = *Dīwān Ibn 'Arabī*, ed. Aḥmad Ḥasan Basaj (Beirut: Dār al-Kutub al-'Ilmiyya, 1416/1996) p. 15 (*min bāb al-kawri wal-dawr*).

* *His true sons* أبنائه i.e. *khulafā'ih*, can also be read أنبائه translatable as *His great news*.

[1] On the *rūḥāniyya* see the answer to the 58th question of al-Ḥakīm al-Tirmidhī's *Khatm al-awliyā'* (p. 225) given by Ibn 'Arabī, *al-Futūḥāt al-Makkiyya* (Osman Yahya ed. 12:348 §282, conclusion of Chapter 73).

[2] See for example al-Ḥasan al-Baṣrī's words in his letter to the Caliph 'Umar b. 'Abd al-'Azīz, كأنك في الدنيا لم تكن وفي الآخرة لم تزل "you are as if you had never been in this world, and you have never ceased to be in the hereafter." Narrated by Ibn 'Abd al-Ḥakam, *Sīrat 'Umar b. 'Abd al-'Azīz 'alā Mā Rawāh al-Imām Mālik b. Anas wa-Aṣḥābuh*, ed. Aḥmad 'Ubayd, 6th ed. (Beirut: 'Ālam al-Kutub, 1404/1984) p. 94; Aḥmad, *al-Zuhd* (p. 197); al-Fasawī, *Ma'rifa* (1:594, 3:344); Balādhūrī, *Ansāb* (8:138); Ibn Abī al-Dunyā, *Dhamm al-dunyā* (p. 104 §213); *Qiṣar al-amal* (p. 146 §226); *al-Zuhd* (p. 127 §263); Abū Nu'aym, *Ḥilya* (5:305). This description applies to Mawlana al-Shaykh Nazim and Mawlana Shaykh Hisham–may Allah raise their ranks.

5
The cycles in which the Umma passes – Duty for religious authorities to humble themselves

I seek refuge in Allah from the accursed devil
In the Name of Allah the All-Beneficent the Most Merciful
There is no power nor strength but with Allah the High, the Magnificent
Permission, O my Master, support!
Our way is companionship, and goodness is in the congregation

Allah the exalted said, *and when it is said to them, "Do not spread corruption in the land," they say, "We are but redressers!"* (al-Baqara 2:11). But people are in fact corrupters although they claim the contrary. This is why we need a heavenly governance, because human judgments have corrupted things. Allah Most High said, *corruption has appeared in the land and the sea with what the hands of the people have earned* (Rūm 30:41), and the Messenger–upon him the blessings and peace of Allah–is saying of this time that it is the time of strifes, whereby the one sitting is safer than the one standing, the one standing is safer than the one walking, and the one walking towards it has definitely fallen into strife.[1] This is pointing to the fact that whoever has no work to do must stay at home. For we are in the cycles about which the Messenger has related, "There shall be after me caliphs [who will practice what they know], and after the caliphs emirs [who will not practice what they know]."[2]

We are now in the cycle of the tyrants and that of al-Mahdī.[3] Our time is the time of the tyrants in the world, those that rule according to their whim and do not comply with a single one of the commands of Allah. That is why,

[1] "Verily there shall be strifes in which the one lying down is better than the one sitting, the one sitting down better than the one standing up, the one standing up better than the one walking, and the one walking better than the one running to them. Behold! Once they befall, whoever has camels let him retire to them; whoever has sheep let him retire to them; whoever has a plot of land let him retire to it; whoever has none of that, let him take his sword and strike its sharp edge against a rock. Then let him find salvation wherever he can. O Allah! Have I conveyed? O Allah! Have I conveyed? O Allah! Have I conveyed?" Narrated from Abū Bakrat al-Thaqafī by Muslim (*al-Fitan wa-ashrāṭ al-sāʿa, nuzūl al-fitan ka-mawāqiʿ al-qaṭr*); Abū Dāwūd (*al-Fitan wal-malāḥim, fil-nahy ʿan al-saʿy fil-fitna*, with *fitna* in the sing.); Aḥmad (34:130 §20490, 34:54 §20412, both wordings); Ibn Ḥibbān (13:303 §5965); Ṭabarānī.

[2] See its full wording and documentation in Suhba I.44, second note.

[3] See the first footnote for Suhba 4 in this volume.

without ruling by the Law of Allah, the rule will be arbitrary and the result will be injustice. It will not satisfy the old or the young or the learned or the unlearned. No one can attain his right in this time. It is the duty of the religious authorities to humble themselves more than those that humble themselves before them. The one that wishes to be respected, let him have more respect for the common public than their respect for him.

By the sanctity of the Beloved, by the sanctity of the Fatiha.

6
The wisdom of Allah's testing of His servants – [The reward for *ṣabr* (steadfast endurance) is without count]

I seek refuge in Allah from the accursed devil
In the Name of Allah the All-Beneficent the Most Merciful
There is no power nor strength but with Allah the High, the Magnificent
Permission, O my Master, support!
Our way is companionship, and goodness is in the congregation

The servant must know that in all his movements and his pauses there is a test. The test will be either on the part of Allah - exalted is He - for His servant, or on the part of the Messenger–upon him the blessings and peace of Allah–for his Umma, or on the part of the Shaykhs for their sons and daughters. At the time of the test, a human being becomes honored or dishonored.

Mawlana al-Shaykh is saying, verily Allah knows the state of His servant without test. So why this test? He is answering, the wisdom of the test on the part of Allah for His servant or on the part of the Messenger –upon him the blessings and peace of Allah–for his Umma or on the part of the Shaykhs for their followers is "for *taraqqī* (rising in levels) and manifesting the truth." For testing weighs heavily on the egos and requires endurance, and the Messenger of Allah–upon him the blessings and peace of Allah–said, *man ṣabara ẓafira* (whoever endures succeeds).[1] Hence it is a must for the servant's principle in life to be patience.

Whoever has *ṣabr* will always be granted success. For the motions and the pauses of a human being are all subsumed either under what the Prophet–upon him the blessings and peace of Allah–has brought or under what he has prohibited. In order to establish a command out of what the Prophet–upon him the blessings and peace of Allah–has brought, a human being needs utmost endurance against his own ego, his whim, his world and his devil[2] because they are all standing against him and pushing him very hard towards

[1] A saying of the *mukhaḍram* tricentenarian Hijazi sage Aktham b. Ṣayfī b. 'Abd al-'Uzzā (a paternal uncle of the Companion Ḥanẓala b. al-Rabī' al-Tamīmī) cited by al-Qālī, *Amālī*; Māwardī, *Adab al-dunyā wal-dīn* and others, a proverbial statement per to Ibn 'Abd al-Barr in *Bahjat al-majālis*. Cf. Aktham's entry in Ibn Ḥajar, *Iṣāba*.

[2] *Nafs, hawā, dunyā, shayṭān.*

what is forbidden. Then the All-True will test His servant with goodness and evil as a strife. He will grant him goodness and test him over that goodness: will he spend it on the purpose for which he was created or spend it on his ego's whim? This is the testing. Or He will test him through evil: will he endure steadfastly? Or something else? Harm will smite one in one's body, one's family, one's situation. If he endures patiently over problems he will be given reward without count. This is wisdom. And the one who has no endurance, He will also give him some bounties out of His munificence – exalted is He – from 10 to 700 levels of bounties even if he did not succeed. But to those that succeed, then without count!

By the sanctity of the Beloved, by the sanctity of the Fatiha.

7
The loveliest of deeds to Allah is the dawn prayer of the Awliya – [Keeping Sharīʿa – Praying in the *Bayt al-maʿmūr* with the Prophet and Abū Bakr - Level of the Naqshbandi Masters – Vanquishing the ego with *fajr* and *ʿishā*]

I seek refuge in Allah from the accursed devil
In the Name of Allah the All-Beneficent the Most Merciful
There is no power nor strength but with Allah the High, the Magnificent
Permission, O my Master, support!
Our way is companionship, and goodness is in the congregation

What is the duty of someone who says, "I am a believer in Allah and His Messenger and the last Day"? The duty of the believer is to find out what the loveliest of all deeds to Allah is and to put it into practice. Mawlana al-Shaykh ʿAbd Allah Fa'iz al-Daghistani said that Allah has sworn by His glory and might and has informed us that there are some deeds that will be accepted by Him and that are better and more beautiful than others.

Mawlana al-Shaykh is saying that the best of the deeds which the people of certainty have agreed upon – those that have acquired the knowledge of certainty, the vision of certainty and the reality of certainty, namely the possessors of the tongue of truthfulness, namely our Naqshbandi Masters – they said that the dawn prayer is the loveliest of deeds and the best of them in the presence of Allah. The evidence to this matter is that the Prophets and the Awliya, when they leave this world, all legal responsibilities cease for them except the dawn prayer. For all the Awliya are a manifestation of the verse, *rather they are alive with their nurturing Lord, receiving provision* (Āl ʿImrān 3:169).[1]

Whoever is dressed with this attribute among the Awliya has to pray the dawn prayer with the Messenger of Allah–upon him the blessings and peace of Allah–in the *Bayt al-maʿmūr* (the frequented House). Likewise our liege lord Bilāl raises the call to prayer in the *Bayt al-maʿmūr*, and the Friends of

[1] See also the next note and the divine Hadith "My servant approaches me with nothing lovelier to Me than what I have made obligatory upon him" (Bukhārī); the hadith "the best of deeds is prayer" (Aḥmad); the hadith "the best prayer is to stand long" (Aḥmad, Nasā'ī); the hadith of the Prophet Mūsā seen praying in his grave during the *Isrā'*; etc.

Allah still alive [in the world] that hear Bilāl's call to prayer are tasked with and permitted to attend in in the *Bayt al-maʿmūr* to pray their current dawn prayer with the Messenger–upon him the blessings and peace of Allah. Mawlana [Shaykh ʿAbd Allah al-Daghistani] is saying that the Awliya that are still alive also pray with us in observance of the sacred Law. That takes place by means of their corporeal image remaining with us while their reality is praying their current dawn prayer with the Messenger–upon him the blessings and peace of Allah.

Mawlana is adding that **the Awliya are very insistent on the observance of the sacred Law in its manifest forms as a proclamation to us that they never reached that station except by keeping strictly all the outward forms of the sacred Law, because it is the servant's means to reach the *malakūt* (world of invisible sovereignty).[1] Hence the smallest defect on the servant's part concerning the external forms of the Sharīʿa will block him from reaching that station. Likewise, whoever leaves one of the sunnas of the Prophet–upon him the blessings and peace of Allah–will not reach that station.**

As for the generality of the Muslims, whoever of them attends the dawn prayer with the congregation, Allah shall appoint on his behalf one of the angels who will pray that prayer with the Prophet–upon him the blessings and peace of Allah–and it shall be recorded in the servant's record of deeds, unless there is one of the three valid excuses preventing him from going out to the dawn prayer with the congregation, namely sickness, fear and travel. If he has is any of these excuses, that angel will be deputized on his behalf.

But why was the prayer dawn given such preference? Because the start of daily life is from the dawn prayer, and if the servant's affair is upright from the start of the day, it will be upright all day long. This is why Allah gave special importance to the dawn prayer[2] and He made it *al-ṣalāt al-wusṭā*[3] because it

[1] "The human being's own *malakūt* is his own *rūḥ* (soul)" (Shaykh ʿAbd Allāh Sirāj al-Dīn al-Ḥalabī).

[2] Per the verse *verily the Qur'ān of the dawn is ever witnessed* (Banū Isrā'īl/al-Isrā' 17:78), "because it is heavily attended by the angels of the day and the angels of the night" per (i) the Prophetic hadith to that effect narrated from Abū al-Dardā' by al-Ṭabarī and Ibn Abī Ḥātim under the latter verse; and the glosses of (ii) Qatāda (d. 118/736) in Ṭabarī and (iii) the Syrian muezzin al-Qāsim b. Mukhaymira al-Hamdānī al-Kūfī (d. 107/725) in Abū Shuʿayb al-Ḥarrānī's *Fawā'id*.

[3] *Guard prayers jealously and the* ṣalāt al-wusṭā, *and stand before the One God in complete devotion* (Baqara 2:238). "The *ṣalāt al-wusṭā* is 'the middle one among them' or 'the choicest one among them especially'" per al-Bayḍāwī in his *Tafsīr*. Its gloss as the dawn prayer is the position reported from (i-iii) Ibn ʿAbbās, ʿAlī b. Abī Ṭālib and Ubay b. Kaʿb by Ṭabarī and (iv) al-Shāfiʿī by al-Thaʿlabī. For this and other glosses see also

is the hardest prayer for the human being. Among the five prayers there is no harder prayer than the dawn prayer, so if a servant is able to make himself pray it then even more must the rest of the prayers be fulfilled; and when he orders himself to perform the dawn prayer he is able to control himself the rest of his day. When the human being controls himself at the beginning of his day, this shall be a cause for his protection from the banes of the ego all his day long. Likewise, the dawn prayer will protect him from banes and hardships and calamities that might befall him on that day. Thus is ascertained the meaning of the verse *verily the prayer forbids indecency and wrongdoing* ('Ankabūt 29:45), just as it protects him here and hereafter from hardships and shameful acts.

Abū Bakr al-Ṣiddīq asked the Messenger of Allah–upon him the blessings and peace of Allah, "Messenger of Allah, what is the status of the servant who is thus described?"[1] He replied, "Even if he says *Allāhu akbar* and starts praying the dawn prayer then gets lost, as if he prayed absent-minded, then, upon giving salam, he remembers that he got lost away from the prayer, then he makes two prostrations of inadvertence, that is enough for him."[2]

Mawlana Shaykh added that just as the dawn prayer is the most important of prayers, likewise the prayer of *'ishā'* (the night) is difficult on the ego. Whoever attends it with the congregation, Allah creates angels from the light of the Essence in his particular image, not resembling any other and whom no one can bear except the Naqshbandi Masters. They pray with Abū Bakr in the *Bayt al-ma'mūr*, and the immense merit of that prayer is recorded for that one. No one has any knowledge or awareness of these angels among the rest of the Imams of the Sufi paths – including our liege lord 'Abd al-Qādir al-Jaylānī. None knows them except the Naqshbandi Masters.

Just as our liege Lord Jibril never moved past his station – and had he moved past it he would have been burnt[3] – when our liege lord the Messenger of Allah

'Abd al-Mu'min b. Khalaf al-Dimyāṭī, *Kashf al-mughaṭṭā fī tabyīn al-ṣalāt al-wusṭā*, ed. Majdī al-Sayyid (Ṭanṭā: Dār al-Ṣaḥāba, 1410/ 1989).

[1] I.e. as an indecent wrongdoer who starts to pray.

[2] Per the Prophetic Hadith, "the two prostrations of inadvertence compensate every addition and deficiency" narrated from 'Ā'isha by Abū Ya'lā, al-Bazzār, al-Ṭabarānī, al-Bayhaqī and al-Khaṭīb. This was done even when no perceptible mistake was committed, as in the prostrations narrated from al-Ḥasan b. 'Alī and Ibrāhīm al-Nakha'ī by Ibn Abī Shayba, *Muṣannaf* (*man kāna yasjudu lil-sahwi wa-lam yas-hu*).

[3] Cited from Junayd by Qushayrī, *Mi'rāj* (p. 115), cf. *Laṭā'if al-ishārāt* (Baqara 2:124), "i.e. from the light" in Muḥ. b. 'Umar Nawawī al-Bantanī, *al-Durar al-bahiyya fī sharḥ al-Khaṣā'iṣ al-Nabawiyya fī akhbār al-laylat al-isrā'iyyati wal-mi'rājiyya* (Cairo: al-Maṭba'at al-Sharafiyya, 1298/1881) p. 40. Narrated without mention of the burning as *fa-ta'akhkhara Jibrīl* (Jibril stayed back) from Anas by Ibn Abī Ḥātim in Ibn Ḥajar, *Fatḥ*

–upon him the blessings and peace of Allah–completed his ascent, likewise, if the forty Imams of the forty Sufi paths had moved to look upon the reality of these angels they would have been burnt, because these angels are created from the light of the Essence, upon which none can bear to gaze except the Naqshbandi Shaykhs.[1]

Mawlana added: such is the extent that the benefits of the prayers of *subḥ* and *'ishā* reach. This is why Iblīs and his soldiers assail people to make them leave those two prayers. Just as between the two poles [of a magnet] it is impossible for a metal to let go, likewise the ego has to be [held] between two extremities. **So whoever wants to be delivered from the domination of his ego which is his most relentless enemy, his greatest jihad will be in this manner, between the prayer of the dawn and the prayer of the night**. For these two prayers assist the servant to conduct the greatest jihad and bring him into the compass of protection, and with them the servant will vanquish his ego. Otherwise it is impossible to control the ego and to rid oneself of its evil.

By the sanctity of the Beloved, by the sanctity of the Fatiha.

(7:217, *qawluhu bāb al-mi'rāj*); *fa-rafaḍanī Jibrīl* (Jibril did not accompany me) in Ibn Kathīr (Banū Isrā'īl/Isrā' 17:1), cf. Qurṭubī citing Muqātil under Ṣāffāt 37:165-166; Muḥ. b. 'Alawī al-Mālikī, *Wa-Huwa bil-ufuqi al-a'lā* (Cairo: Maṭba'at al-Fārūq, 1419/1998) p. 279; *al-Anwār al-bahiyya min isrā' wa-mi'rāj khayr al-bariyya* (1419/1998) p. 75. "The *sidrat al-muntahā* (lote-tree of the farthest boundary) is where the angels' knowledge ends" per Ka'b al-Aḥbār as narrated from Ibn 'Abbās by Ibn Abī Shayba, *Muṣannaf* (last report of *Kitāb al-janna*); al-Ṭabarī and Wāḥidī, *Basīṭ* (Najm 53:14-16). "The *sidrat al-muntahā* (lote-tree of the farthest boundary) is where the angels end up without going further: none has gone past it except Muḥammad" in Qushayrī, *Mi'rāj* (p. 54). Cf. the Prophet's question to Jibril, "Do you see your nurturing Lord?" to which he replied, "Between me and the Throne are seventy veils of light; were I to approach any of them I would burn." Narrated from (i) Zurāra b. Awfā by Ibn Abī Shayba, *al-'Arsh*; Dīnawarī, *Mujālasa*; Abū al-Shaykh, *'Aẓama*; (ii) Anas by Abū Nu'aym, *Ḥilya*, cf. Bayhaqī, *Asmā'* (*mā jā'a fil-'arshi wal-kursī*).

[1] A reference to the light of the Muhammadan essence in the Prophet's assembly upon which only whoever he allows has permission to look as related from 'Abd al-'Azīz al-Dabbāgh by Ibn Mubārak in *Kitāb al-Ibrīz*.

8

One's state is more important than his statement – [Our intentions are better than our deeds] – Modality of jihad to quit reprehensible traits

I seek refuge in Allah from the accursed devil
In the Name of Allah the All-Beneficent the Most Merciful
There is no power nor strength but with Allah the High, the Magnificent
Permission, O my Master, support!
Our way is companionship, and goodness is in the congregation

One's state matters more than one's statement, because what is required is a high state.[1] This discourse which we are reading is all from the states of the Shaykh which typified his character and attributes. This is why he would bring this speech and quote it to the listeners as a state. And the state of the Shaykh must appear in his followers sooner or later. These states must appear in the lives of the murids, and so must their meanings on the Day of Resurrection.

Our liege lord the Shaykh ['Abd Allah Fa'iz al-Daghistani] says about the foundations of *mujāhada* (jihad against the ego), in commentary on the statement of Allah Almighty, *but the ones that strove in Us, We will indeed show them Our ways* (al-ʿAnkabūt 29:69), that the nature of the ego is loaded with vicious traits of character. These vicious traits has foundations. From the foundations, thousands of vicious traits branch out also.

The servant is legally tasked with purification in the life of this world, until he is brought before the All-True – exalted is He – with complete and perfect purity. Therefore *mujāhada* is obligatory for all of us, each according to his capacity. For the human being ought to be ashamed of being brought before Allah while he is soiled with the dirt of reprehensible traits. Because of this, Allah has ordered us to practice prayer, from the perspective that *verily the prayer forbids indecency and wrongdoing* (al-ʿAnkabūt 29:45). The basis of the wisdom for being legally tasked to perform the obligations is so that one will acquire complete and perfect purity. These are means to an end, which is *the Day no wealth benefits and no sons, except whoever comes to the One God with a heart most pure!* (al-Shuʿarā' 26:88-89).

[1] Cf. "Sit with the one whose limbs speak to you, not the one whose tongue speaks to you," spoken by Tustarī and narrated from him by Abū Nuʿaym in *Ḥilyat al-awliyā'*.

Part of the foundations of *mujāhada*, Mawlana al-Shaykh says, is that there are twelve months in the year, so that if a human being strives, each month, to leave one of the blameworthy traits, he will be able in the course of one year to rid himself of twelve bad traits of character. This is the easiest way for *mujāhada*. When a human being intends to quit the characteristic of anger in himself for example, because of this intention, he can keep watch over himself in all of his motions. If he is able to control his nerves and not get angry, this will be a great gain for him, whereby he will be watching over himself – and keeping watch over one's ego is one of the most important matters of the faith. For it has been transmitted in the divine Hadith, "Whoever strives to come nearer to Me one hand-span, I come near him one cubit. If he comes near Me one cubit I come near him an arm's length. If he comes to Me walking, I come to him running."[1] When the servant makes the intention – with all his weakness – to leave that vicious trait of character which is buried deep in the nature of the ego, he will be taking a step in the direction of Allah. At that time Allah shall help him and support him to make him reach his goal, and the divine lordly assistance will reach him.

In allusion to this [divine support] the Prophet's Hadith states, "Every serious matter that is not begun *bismi-l-Lāhi-r-Raḥmāni-r-Raḥīm* (in the Name of the All-Beneficent, the Most Merciful), it will be stunted."[2] The meaning of this hadith is that the servant, by saying *bismillāh*, has in effect resolved upon a certain intention, acknowledged his helplessness and relied upon his nurturing Lord. Let it not be thought that this work will remain fruitless! But the one that did not invoke the Name, his deed is without fruit.

And when the divine lordly help attains the servant, nothing remains to prevent him from reaching his objective and his goal. This is why it is very clear that "the mere intention is better than the deed,"[3] and our nurturing Lord is waiting for us to correct our intention. Mawlana adds to this that in this

[1] Narrated from Abū Hurayra and Anas by al-Bukhārī, Muslim, Tirmidhī, Ibn Mājah and Aḥmad, all with the beginning, "I am exactly as My servant thinks of Me and I sit with him when he remembers Me. If he mentions Me in himself I mention him in Myself. If he mentions Me in a gathering I mention him in a better gathering. If he comes near Me one hand-span," etc. Bayhaqī said in *al-Asmā' wal-ṣifāt*, "by 'coming near' is meant the swiftness of Allah's response and forgiveness as we narrated from Qatāda." Nawawī said in *Sharḥ Ṣaḥīḥ Muslim*, "The message is that His reward is many times over proportional to one's coming near."

[2] Narrated from Abū Hurayra by al-Khaṭīb al-Baghdādī, *Jāmi'* (2:87 §1232), rated fair by al-Nawawī in *al-Adhkār*. The sound version has the wording "every serious matter that is not begun with *al-ḥamdu li-l-Lāh*" per Ibn Ḥajar, *Fatḥ al-Bārī* (*Tafsīr*, Āl 'Imrān 3:64), which illustrates the same point.

[3] See Suhba I.61, twelfth note.

manner, **when the servant makes the intention of striving yet he has not ridden himself from any blameworthy trait, still Allah shall record him as one of the ascetics in this world because of his intention. To the extent of his effort in this world, Allah shall make him reach, in the end, the highest levels of the greatest jihad**. The evidence to this matter is the transmitted noble hadiths to the effect that if someone were to intend the pursuit of knowledge, then begins to learn the alphabet, then dies, Allah will appoint for him an angel that teaches him forever until that person will be resurrected with the assembly of the ulema.[1]

Mujāhada has foundations, namely to let it be for a single day. It is part of the foundations of *mujāhada* to set a limited time for the ego, because the shorter the time is, the more a human being will ready himself to complete the *mujāhada*, but when the goal takes a long time, for many there does not remain for them any energy to complete it. *Mujāhada* is for you to tell yourself, "Today there is jihad and tomorrow death in which there is no jihad." And so forth. Cut off the hope of the ego for the next day and you will be successful. You will be able to take full control of it.

By the sanctity of the Beloved, by the sanctity of the Fatiha.

[1] Related hadiths state, (i) "Verily the angels indeed lower their wings in approval of the student of knowledge," narrated from Abū al-Dardā' by Abū Dāwūd, al-Tirmidhī and Ibn Mājah; (ii) "Whoever pursues knowledge and dies in that state dies as a shahid," narrated from Abū Hurayra and Abū Dharr by Ya'qūb b. Sufyān in *al-Ma'rifa wal-tārīkh*; Bazzār; Ibn 'Abd al-Barr; al-Khaṭīb al-Baghdādī and others; (iii) "Whoever pursues knowledge then he is in the way of Allah until he returns," narrated from Anas by Abū Nu'aym in *Ḥilyat al-awliyā'*.

9
The excellence of belief in the unseen – [Giving credence like Abū Bakr al-Ṣiddīq]

I seek refuge in Allah from the accursed devil
In the Name of Allah the All-Beneficent the Most Merciful
There is no power nor strength but with Allah the High, the Magnificent
Permission, O my Master, support!
Our way is companionship, and goodness is in the congregation

Mawlana Shaykh ʿAbd Allah Faʾiz al-Daghistani says that it is an obligation for human beings to believe in the unseen. Without it, it will be impossible for the servant to obtain any merit in the life of this world or in the hereafter. Belief in the Prophets–upon them peace–in their reports about Allah and about the matter of the hereafter raises the servant to the very stations in which he has declared his belief. Whoever falls short of belief in something will not obtain it.

The affairs of the hereafter are something unseen for us. Our belief in the speech of the Prophets and our giving credence to them make us reach those levels in the hereafter and in the knowledge of Allah. Just as this is through firm belief in the Prophets–upon them peace–likewise the thing takes place concerning the inheritors of the Prophets.[1] The noble Companions would fully believe the Messenger–upon him the blessings and peace of Allah–in his reports, and just by virtue of their credence that they gave him, they would reach the highest levels and the highest stations.

The Messenger–upon him the blessings and peace of Allah–related the news of the heavenly ascent, which is something unseen, and the Companions believed him. However, their confirmation fid not reach the level of the confirmation given by Abū Bakr al-Ṣiddīq–may Allah be well-pleased with him. This is why the Ṣiddīq obtained from the reality of the heavenly ascent that which no other Companion obtained. When they heard the news of the heavenly ascent some went to Abū Bakr and asked him, "What has your companion said tonight?" Abū Bakr said, "Has faith not yet taken place in you that all created things Allah has created for his sake? And when He invites him to this [ascent] that is too much for you?" Then our liege lord Abū Bakr said, "I

[1] I.e. those that have knowledge of Allah.

believe the Messenger–upon him the blessings and peace of Allah–in what is beyond that also."[1]

And there are also reports about the heavenly ascent for the generality of people, and according to their confirmation of them as true they obtain those levels. This is why, in the company of Shaykhs, those that are in attendance rise to spiritual stations in proportion with their giving credence. Whoever uses their cerebral powers when attending the presence of the noble Shaykhs remains on earth. As for the one that uses his spirituality, he will fly with the Shaykh in his stations.

By the sanctity of the Beloved, by the sanctity of the Fatiha.

[1] Narrated (only with Abū Bakr's second reply and with the mention of the *isrā'* but not the *mi'rāj*) from (i-ii) al-Zuhrī from Ibn al-Musayyib and Abū Salama by 'Abd al-Razzāq, al-Ṭabarī (Banū Isrā'īl/Isrā' 17:1) and al-Bayhaqī, *Dalā'il* (2:360-361); (iii) 'Ā'isha by 'Abd al-Razzāq, *Muṣannaf* (5:321-328 §9719); al-Ḥākim (3:65 §4407, *ṣaḥīḥ al-isnād*; 3:81 §4458, *ṣaḥīḥ*); al-Wāḥidī, (Banū Isrā'īl/Isrā' 17:1); (iv) al-Ḥasan by Ibn Hishām, *Sīra* (1:398-399); (v) 'Abd al-Raḥmān b. Zayd by Ṭabarī (Banū Isrā'īl/Isrā' 17:60); (vi) 'Urwa by al-Ājurrī, *al-Sharī'a* (3:1538-1540 §1030, 4:1799-1800 §1259); (vii) Ibn 'Abbās and 'Ā'isha by al-Tha'labī and al-Baghawī (Banū Isrā'īl/Isrā' 17:1).

10
[The faith-system is all faithful advice] – Searching out flaws in people

I seek refuge in Allah from the accursed devil
In the Name of Allah the All-Beneficent the Most Merciful
There is no power nor strength but with Allah the High, the Magnificent
Permission, O my Master, support!
Our way is companionship, and goodness is in the congregation

He said–upon him the blessings and peace of Allah–"The *dīn* (belief system) is all *naṣīḥa* (absolute good faith, sincere advice)."[1] But to merely hear the *naṣīḥa* is not enough, because matters is the application on the ego. Likewise, one is required to learn from the cradle to the grave in every age, since the Messenger of Allah–upon him the blessings and peace of Allah–said, "He whose two days are identical has been defrauded;"[2] "There is no blessing for me in a morning wherein I have not gained more knowledge."[3]

Now there is an categorically obligatory knowledge which must be learnt, and there are also, of the types of knowledge, the adornment or the perfections. There must be in the Umma those that learn the latter type in order to preserve the manifest form of the Sharī'a from every side. Also of the

[1] The continuation states: "They asked, 'To whom, Messenger of Allah?' He replied, 'To Allah; to His Book; and to His Messenger, the leaders of the Muslims and their multitude.'" Narrated from (i) Tamīm al-Dārī by Muslim, Abū Dāwūd and al-Nasā'ī; (ii) Abū Hurayra by al-Tirmidhī (*ḥasan ṣaḥīḥ*), Aḥmad and al-Nasā'ī; (iii) Ibn 'Umar by al-Bazzār; and (iv) Thawbān by al-Bukhārī in *al-Tārīkh al-Kabīr*.

[2] Narrated as I. a saying of (i) the ascetic Medinan Companion Abū Ḥāzim al-A'raj Salama b. Dīnār Mawlā Banī Layth al-Ashja' the admonisher by Ibn 'Asākir, *Tārīkh* (22:59); (ii) 'Alī by al-Daylamī, *al-Firdaws* with a weak chain per Suyūṭī, *Durar* and Sakhāwī, *Maqāṣid*; II. a dream vision of the Prophet by (iii) an unnamed "shaykh from the Banū Sulaym" by Ibn Abī al-Dunyā, *Manāmāt* (p. 116 §243); cf. Ibn Rajab, *Laṭā'if* (conclusion of the month of Dhūl-Ḥijja); (iv) Ibn Abī Rawwād by al-Bayhaqī in *al-Zuhd* (p. 367 §986); (v) another unnamed man by al-Khaṭīb in *Iqtiḍā' al-'ilm al-'amal* (p. 112 §196); and (vi) al-Ḥasan al-Baṣrī by Abū Nu'aym, *Ḥilya* (8:35) through Ibrāhīm b. Ad-ham. Al-Qārī in *al-Asrār al-marfū'a* cites it and declares its meaning confirmed by the Sura of al-'Aṣr (103).

[3] Narrated from 'Ā'isha by Isḥāq b. Rāhūyah, *Musnad* (2:553 §1128); al-Ḥakīm al-Tirmidhī, *Nawādir* without chain in the wording "more knowledge that brings me near to Allah;" al-Ṭabarānī, *Awsaṭ* (6:367 §6636); Abū Nu'aym, *Ḥilya* (8:188) in the same wording as al-Ḥakīm al-Tirmidhī; Ibn 'Abd al-Barr, *Jāmi' bayān al-'ilm* (1:259 §318); al-Khaṭīb, *Tārīkh Baghdād* (Ibrāhīm b. Shammās Abū Isḥāq al-Samarqandī).

necessary type of knowledge that we need to learn is for the servant to know what it is that Allah and His Messenger love and what it is that Allah and His Messenger hate. The latter type is extremely precise. Mawlana [Shaykh ʿAbd Allāh al-Dāghistānī] is asking, what is the deed that Allah and His Messenger hate? And to whom does this world belong? Mawlana is answering: this world is the servants of Allah, and both the believers and the unbelievers are the servants of Allah. Also, both are part of the Umma of the Messenger of Allah–upon him the blessings and peace of Allah–and the nurturing Lord of the worlds says, "I am the Mover and the All-Doer of what I want."[1]

The responsibility for the Umma falls on the shoulders of the Messenger–upon him the blessings and peace of Allah–because he is the Prophet of end-times and the carrier of the entire Umma. Because of this, the Messenger–upon him the blessings and peace of Allah–hates it for someone to interfere between the servant and his nurturing Lord, and to search out flaws in people, and this is the most hated thing in the presence of Allah and in the presence of His Messenger. Anyone whose characteristic is to search out flaws in people is categorized, in the presence of Allah and in the presence of the Messenger and in the presence of the people of truth, as a type of fly that only sets on filth, and just as killing flies is required, likewise whoever possesses their characteristics exposes himself to the vengeance of Allah Almighty. The first duty of a servant is to cleanse oneself of that attribute.

Purity of the body is important but the most important is inward purity, so that you will not stand before Allah Almighty with that impure characteristic which Allah and His Messenger hate. Therefore, Mawlana al-Shaykh's instruction is for you not to look anywhere in the street except at yourself, and not look with the gaze of an inspector of the flaws of Allah's servants and the Umma of our liege lord Muhammad–upon him the blessings and peace of Allah. And when you arrive at your house, do not carry with you filth from the outside and retell it to your spouse, nor let her also convey to you the news so that both would delight in the flaws of people. This is why he said–upon him the blessings and peace of Allah–"Blessings to him whose flaws keep him busy and away from [searching out] the flaws of people."[2]

By the sanctity of the Beloved, by the sanctity of the Fatiha.

[1] Cf. *the One God has created you and all that you do* (al-Ṣāffāt 37:96); *verily your nurturing Lord is All-Effecter of what He wishes* (Hūd 11:107); and Yūnus 10:31.

[2] Narrated from (i) Anas by Bazzār (12:348 §6237), cf. Haythamī, *Majmaʿ al-zawāʾid* (10:229); al-Bayhaqī, *Shuʿab* (Branch 71: *al-zuhd*); Ibn ʿAsākir, *Tārīkh* (54:240) and *Muʿjam al-shuyūkh* (2:1052 §1358); (ii) ʿĀʾisha by Dīnawarī, *Mujālasa* (4:108 §1288); (iii) al-Ḥusayn b. ʿAlī by Abū Nuʿaym, *Ḥilya* (3:202-203); (iv) Sufyān b. Usayd al-Ḥaḍramī by al-Quḍāʿī, *Musnad al-Shihāb* (Ḥamdī ed. 1:357-358 §613).

11

[Three types of people – Whoever makes the world his goal becomes nothing in Allah's sight] – Meaning of *a heart most pure* – [Living for the meeting with the Beloved – The purpose of life]

I seek refuge in Allah from the accursed devil
In the Name of Allah the All-Beneficent the Most Merciful
There is no power nor strength but with Allah the High, the Magnificent
Permission, O my Master, support!
Our way is companionship, and goodness is in the congregation

Sultan al-Awliyā' Mawlana Shaykh ʿAbd Allāh al-Dāghistānī says there are three types of people. The first is the one that does not understand anything of the speech of the All-True, and they are counted among the heedless. The second is the one that does not listen to anything of the speech of the All-True, and they are counted among the obdurate. The third is the one that understands and follows the speech of the All-True, and they are called *yaqẓān* (awake). They have wakefulness. Whoever possesses the latter discernment from understanding and followership will be a student also, and it is required for human beings to be students.[1]

Someone came to our liege lord Jalaluddin Rumi weeping and begging him to return to him his lost son. He said, "My son is seven years old and I do not know where he is. All the doors are closed except your door until you return him back to me. I do not know whether he has died or whether he is still alive." The Shaykh said to him, "Glory to Allah! And why are you looking for the child?" He said, "He is my child and I would ransom him for the whole world." Hearing this the Shaykh said, "People have all lost Allah yet no one is asking about Him or looking for Him! Has Allah become cheaper than this child? O man, go in quest of your nurturing Lord and you will find Him, then your child will be returned to you just as Yūsuf was returned to Yaʿqūb–upon them the blessings and peace of Allah."

You see people running in quest of something but they do not know the object of their quest. If we said that they want influence or wealth, we would

[1] See the first paragraph of the preceding suhba.

find that when they reach just that they relax; but instead we see them persist in their search even then, and they say, "our goal is still unfulfilled."

Even if a human being is able to fulfill his goal and what he is in search for is the whole world, nevertheless the whole world, in the sight of Allah, is not worth the wing of a gnat. So that searcher's own worth is that low. The one that makes the enjoyment of the world his objective has himself become nothing in the sight of Allah. This is why it is very rare for the common person to understand this matter, from the perspective that the speech of the All-True orients the servant from what is lowest to what is highest; from nothing to everything; from the extinct to the ever-abiding.

If the servant fails to understand this speech he will be of the heedless. It is the same with the speech of the All-True with the Prophets–upon them peace–and with the Awliya–upon them good pleasure–because they summon people from the extinct to the ever-abiding. Blessing be upon whoever orients himself from the *dunyā* (life of this world) to the *Mawlā* (protecting Friend). If a man were to live a hundred years and more, his life filled with ease and food and drink, and he never turned his face from the *dunyā* to the *Mawlā*, what would be the upshot of his life? Nothing. His type will be like that of a dumb beast. The one in whose heart the fire of live for Allah and His Messengers and His Awliya was never kindled, and he never wore those lights, the upshot of his life will be like that of dumb beasts. Nothing.

This is why the fruit of real life has become burning love for Allah and for His love, love of the Messenger–upon him the blessings and peace of Allah–and of His Awliya–upon them His good pleasure.[1] Yet people make their purpose in life *wealth and sons,*[2] although neither will benefit in the presence of Allah, since He says–may He be exalted–*the Day no wealth benefits and no sons, except whoever comes to the One God with a heart most pure!* (al-Shuʿarāʾ 26:88-89).

What is meant by *a heart most pure*? What is meant is for the human being to work hard to acquire the love of Allah and His Messenger and His Awliya; and the love of Allah burns away the love of this world so that his heart will be clear of it, thereby becoming *most pure.* As for whoever has as his sole

[1] Per the Prophetic supplication, "I ask Your love, the love of those who love You and the love of acts that bring one closer to Your Love," and he added, "It is the truth, so study it and learn it." Narrated from Muʿādh b. Jabal by al-Tirmidhī (*ḥasan ṣaḥīḥ*), Aḥmad and others.

[2] *Wealth and sons are the ornament of the life of this world, but the ever-abiding righteous deeds are better in the presence of your nurturing Lord for reward, and better for hope* (al-Kahf (18:46).

purpose the love of this world and its acquisition, then he will reap nothing but anxieties and sorrows due to the loss of possessions and the end of happiness. And you might find the nearest of people to you—namely your children and your wife—tied to you with a thread of cotton. You cannot protect them. When they grow up they run away. As for him in whose heart there is love of Allah and His Messenger and His Awliya then his happiness increases and his anxieties die down, because the more the days pass, the nearer he gets to meet his nurturing Lord and with his beloved the Messenger–upon him the blessings and peace of Allah–and with the Friends of Allah. **Whoever lives for the sake of the meeting with the Beloved, does any sadness remain with him? Rather, if the happiness that exists in the hearts of the lovers of Allah and of His Messenger -upon him the blessings and peace of Allah–and of His Awliya were distributed to the people of the earth, there would not remain in the hearts of all the servants any trace of sadness or anxiety**.

The Prophets came to banish all kinds of sadness from the hearts of servants and they filled them with love of Allah. But people do not believe the speech of the All-True. This is why they have become heedless. What is transmitted (from the Qur'ān and the Hadith) and what is inferred from mere reason both agree with this speech. It cannot be reasonably denied. When the servant refuses to accept it, he will join the ranks of the obdurate. But whoever follows the Prophet's discourse obtains happiness and peace of mind here and hereafter.

In summary let our purpose be the All-True and the divine good pleasure. It is necessary for us to direct ourselves to search for that. Whoever only wants the enjoyment of this life as his sole purpose has put himself into the well of woes and has imprisoned himself *into the lowest of the low* (al-Tīn 95:5). The Prophets want to deliver the servant from such prisons. So **when the servant resolves on seeking the good pleasure of Allah he has become a true seeker. It is guaranteed that Allah and His Messenger and His Awliya will teach him through the sending of spiritual intuitions to his heart as long as he recognizes that the purpose of life is to obtain the love of Allah and His Messenger and His Awliya**. This discourse is the edification of the Prophets one and all. No one rejects it but an obdurate one, and the obdurate are with Abū Jahl.

By the sanctity of the Beloved, by the sanctity of the Fatiha.

12

Difference between outward and inward knowledge – To arrive at the world of invisible sovereignty you need a guide from there

I seek refuge in Allah from the accursed devil
In the Name of Allah the All-Beneficent the Most Merciful
There is no power nor strength but with Allah the High, the Magnificent
Permission, O my Master, support!
Our way is companionship, and goodness is in the congregation

Mawlana Shaykh ʿAbd Allah al-Daghistani says that there are two types of knowledge: the *ẓāhir* (outward) and the *bāṭin* (inward), i.e. the *ʿilm maʿnawī* (knowledge of spiritual meanings). There is none with more knowledge of the outward knowledge than Iblīs, since he knows the Gospel, the Psalms, the Torah and the Qur'ān by heart.

Outward knowledge refers to the letters and will be on the tongue. As for inner knowledge its place is the heart. What settles in the heart is called *ʿilm al-yaqīn* (knowledge of certainty). For example, a believing person knows that if he said *bismi-l-Lāhi al-Raḥmāni al-Raḥīm* (in the Name of the One God, the All-Beneficent, the Most Merciful) he could walk on water, or that when he drank poison it would not harm him if he first said *bismi-l-Lāhi al-ladhī lā yaḍurru maʿa smihi shay'un fil-arḍi wa-lā fil-samā'i wa-Huwa al-Samīʿu al-ʿAlīm* (in the Name of the One God with Whose Name nothing can harm on earth or in the sky and He is the All-Hearing, the All-Knowing). Yet, despite this [knowledge], he cannot walk on water nor drink poison. Why? Because there is no confirmation in his heart for the truth of what he states. This is why Iblīs was and still is memorizing the letter of the four Scriptures, but he has no acquaintance with the *ʿulūm maʿnawiyya* (types of knowledge related to spiritual meanings) found inside these Scriptures.

Likewise, outward knowledge nurtures egotism in the human being the more his knowledge increases. As for the types of knowledge related to spiritual meanings, their upshot removes egotism to the point it leaves no trace of it in the servant. The representative of the types of knowledge related to spiritual meanings – the knowledge of *ḥaqīqa* (spiritual reality) – is the Messenger–upon him the blessings and peace of Allah–while the representative of outward knowledge is Iblīs. The latter has remained confined in the limits of outward knowledge, and upon reaching the apex of these types of knowledge he has reached the apex of egotism. Because of the intensity of his egotism he will not accept that anyone should be a guide for him, and by rejecting the guide he has rejected the door of Allah. That is the reason for the absence of anything related to the knowledge of spiritual reality with him.

The greatest Imam—Abū Ḥanīfa—said, "Were it not for two years, al-Nuʿmān[1] would have perished," because he had stayed with his spiritual guide for two years before the latter passed from this world and he considered himself to be among those who were bound for destruction if he had not spent time with his guide. For the science of Abū Ḥanīfa benefits at the station of the uneducated masses; but at the level of the people of *ḥaqīqa* (spiritual reality), his sciences are of no use to the Awliya because they are outward sciences.[2] As for the *ʿulūm maʿnawiyya* (types of knowledge of spiritual meanings) they cannot be acquired except by way of a guide who must himself be affiliated to the *malakūt* (invisible sovereignty). But he did not get to meet his guide except two years before the latter died. For this reason he would regret what he had missed of sciences and stations.

The four Imams were all, each of them, followers of one of the Shaykhs, just as the Prophets themselves, before Jibril would descend to them, did not have any Prophetship and any arrival to the world of invisible sovereignty, but when he descended to them they acquired Prophetship and connection to invisible sovereignty. By the above it can be recognized that whoever wants to reach the *malakūt*, it is necessary for them to have a guide from the *malakūt*. The four mujtahid Imams recognized this secret and each followed a guide[3] from the *malakūt* until they obtained something from the sciences of spiritual reality—

[1] Abū Ḥanīfa's name was al-Nuʿmān b. Thābit b. Kawūs b. Hurmuz b. Marzubān.

[2] "Because the jurist does not go beyond the confines of this world to the hereafter... and he does not consider, in relation to *islām*, other than the tongue. As for the heart, it is beyond the compass of the jurist's jurisdiction. For the Messenger of Allah–upon him the blessings and peace of Allah–kept away from it the possessors of swords and authority by saying, 'And did you cut open his heart?' to the one who had killed a speaker of the testimony of faith and excused himself on the grounds he had spoken it only for fear of the sword [narrated from Usāma b. Zayd by Aḥmad, Muslim, Abū Dāwūd, Ibn Mājah].... Sufyān al-Thawrī would say—and he was an Imam in outward knowledge—'This is not from the provision of the hereafter.' And how can it be imagined that the latter consists in knowledge of *ẓihār* (divorce), *liʿān* (mutual imprecation), *salam* (advance sale), *ijāra* (hire) and *ṣarf* (morphology)? And whoever learns these matters for the sake of drawing near to Allah—then he is a madman." Ghazālī, *Iḥyāʾ ʿulūm al-Dīn*, Book I (*Kitāb al-ʿilm*).

[3] Abū Ḥanīfa (d. 150/767): Jaʿfar al-Ṣādiq (d. 148/765); Mālik b. Anas (d. 179/795): Ibn Hurmuz (d. 148/765); al-Shāfiʿī (d. 204/819): Shaybān al-Rāʿī (d. circa 170/786); Aḥmad b. Ḥanbal (d. 241/855): Maʿrūf al-Karkhī (d. 200/816).

but they did not show them. Also, it is impossible for anyone to obtain those sciences until they complete the Sharīʿa and they take a guide. Thereafter, the guide gives them those sciences.

Having said this [we ask], why did Allah Almighty order the angels and Iblīs also to prostrate to our liege lord Ādam? If Iblīs had prostrated to our liege lord Ādam, he would have been accepting for our liege lord Ādam to be his guide, because our liege lord Ādam was carrying in himself the seed of the Messenger of Allah–upon him the blessings and peace of Allah. Thereupon the Messenger–upon him the blessings and peace of Allah–would have been a guide to Iblīs unto stations unimaginable to the latter. But when he refused through his egotism, he was banished even from that station in which he already was, and he was deprived of the knowledges of spiritual meanings. Mawlana al-Shaykh would say "If Iblīs had one speck of the knowledges of spiritual meanings, he would not tire himself with any of the human beings, but because of his ignorance of these sciences he tries to induce them into unbelief and sins.

By the sanctity of the Beloved, by the sanctity of the Fatiha.

13
The distinction between knowledge of something and arriving at something

I seek refuge in Allah from the accursed devil
In the Name of Allah the All-Beneficent the Most Merciful
There is no power nor strength but with Allah the High, the Magnificent
Permission, O my Master, support!
Our way is companionship, and goodness is in the congregation

Does our knowledge of something well-known[1] mean arrival at the object of knowledge? For example, there is a beauty queen whose picture everyone has seen and they have learnt her name. But does this knowledge of theirs mean that they have reached her? Therefore, knowledge of something is one thing, and arrival at the object of knowledge is something else.

Our knowledge of the Shaykh is something. But our arrival at his station is something else. Knowledge of the Messenger–upon him the blessings and peace of Allah–is something, from the perspective that people have recognized him by his name and his physical aspects. But for them to be with him and in his presence—is it the same thing?

We say, "we believe in Allah, and we know, about Allah, that He is All-Hearing, All-Generous, Strong, Able, Living." Does this knowledge of ours mean that we have reached Him? And has the one that knows these things about Allah reached?

What is more difficult? To obtain the knowledge, or to obtain the arrival? This is why this question is important. This is the laying of the foundation for the arrival to Allah. This means that the acquisition of knowledge of something that is well-known is something easy. By simply searching, the servant acquires knowledge of something well-known. But the arrival to what is well-known needs a *himma ʿāliya* (high spiritual energy).

May Allah provide us and you.

[1] *Al-maʿlūm*. Mawlana would exclaim *maʿlūm!* to signify "of course! no question!"

14
The *himma* (spiritual energy) of true men

I seek refuge in Allah from the accursed devil
In the Name of Allah the All-Beneficent the Most Merciful
There is no power nor strength but with Allah the High, the Magnificent
Permission, O my Master, support!
Our way is companionship, and goodness is in the congregation

There is a difference and a distinction between knowledge of something well-known and arrival at something well-known. Knowledge of the existence of the Kaʿba is one thing. Arrival to it is something else. There are many who know of the Kaʿba with *ʿilm al-yaqīn* (certain knowledge) and they have seen its pictures. But this does not mean they have reached it.

Acquiring knowledge of something is an easy matter but arriving to it is difficult, it needs high spiritual energy and strong resolve. For example, the car when it goes to the mountain: does it go at the same power that it goes when it is driven on the coast? Likewise you may see the plane pushing with all its power at the time it takes off and rises.

Likewise, the one with small energy remains on earth while those with high spiritual energies reach to the *malakūt* (world of invisible sovereignty). Mawlana told a story about this. A long time Ka'ba ago a young man entered the masjid to pray. He heard the shaykh teaching there saying, "the high energy of true men uproots mountains,[1] and high energy is part of belief." And he explained this subject. Then he said, "truly whoever has high spiritual energy, even if he decided to marry the king's daughter it would take place for him, and the possessor of high spiritual energy is not deprived of anything in the world." The young man said to himself, "This is enough for me." He got up from the gathering and headed for his village, where he sold everything he owned and then headed to the king's palace.

When he tried to enter the palace, the guards blocked him. He kept trying to enter and the guards kept blocking him for four years. One day, as he was peering inside the palace, he notice the king taking a walk in his garden as the

[1] It is supported by the Prophetic hadith, "If a man with full certainty were to recite *qad aflaḥa al-mu'minūn* to the conclusion of ten verses (Mu'minūn 23:1-11) on a mountain, it would cease to be." Narrated from Ibn Masʿūd by Ibn Abī Ḥātim under this verse and al-Bayhaqī, *al-Daʿawāt al-kabīr* (1:155-156 §209) with a sound chain as indicated by Ibn Ḥajar, *Natā'ij al-afkār fī takhrīj aḥādīth al-afkār* (4:155).

guards were looking at the king. He seized the opportunity and ran towards him but the guards caught him. He started shouting, "Let go of me! I am the king's son-in-law!" The king was curious about his statement so he asked him about his purpose. The young man said, "I want to marry your daughter." The king agreed, on condition that the dowry must be seven camel-loads of jewels engraved with the image of the angel Jibril!—the cost of each of these jewels being equal to the entire treasury of seven countries. The young man said, "I accept; but tell me, where can I find them?" The king said, from the greatest ocean, where the fish that go hunting will have such jewels in their bellies.

The young man took his leave from the king. He went and bought a pail, then he sat on the shore of the greatest ocean with the intention of emptying it of all its water so that he would acquire those jewels. He started filling up the pail and emptying it time after time behind him on the shore. He kept at it for seven years. For a wisdom Allah knew of, the king happened to pass by near that beach as he was strolling in the countryside. His gaze fell on the young man who was busy emptying the ocean. He sent his vizier to enquire about that man. When the vizier went to him to ask him, the young man expelled him, saying, "do not delay me from my work!" The vizier was perplexed and informed the king.

When the king came in person to ask the man about his story, he replied to him that he wanted to put together a dowry for the king's daughter. At that time the king remembered him and took him with him, saying, "my daughter's dowry has certainly reached me. Whoever is like you, the greatest king's daughter would be fit for him." After that the king abdicated his throne in favor of him. That is due to his high spiritual energy and his perseverance in his work. How much hardship did this man endure in order to marry the king's daughter!

Likewise knowledge about Allah is an easy matter and every person reads the *ʿilm al-ḥāl* (presently-needed knowledge)[1]—that "Allah is absolutely One, eternally besought, Creator" [etc.],[2] just as the children learn this, and they can memorize the divine Attributes. However, is it in this way that they will arrive at Allah Almighty? Or that the young men will arrive at the beauty

[1] An allusion to opening of Burhān al-Islām al-Zarnūjī's (d. circa 640/1243) oft-read educational manual *Taʿlīmu al-mutaʿallimi ṭarīqa al-taʿallum* (Teaching the student the proper way to learn), *afḍalu al-ʿilmi ʿilmu al-ḥal wa-afḍalu al-ʿamali ḥifẓu al-ḥāl*, "the best knowledge is the knowledge of what is urgently needed and the best deed is the guarding of one's state."

[2] Because everyone urgently needs knowledge of the foundations of faith at all times.

queen,[1] or to the king's daughter? How much hall would it cost them of hardships? What do you think then, O servants of Allah, about the arrival to Allah—is it an easy matter when you are neck-deep in the world? Reaching Allah demands effort, and standing firm, and constant endeavor. And here, our intention will be better than our actions. Therefore, whoever keeps knocking at the door, it must be opened for him in the end.

May Allah grant us and you to stand firm. By the sanctity of the Beloved, by the sanctity of the Fatiha.

[1] A reference to the previous suhba, which may form one and the same with this.

15

Pure repentance – [Two dangerous faculties in human beings] – The stomach is a receptacle – [The world is not a place of pleasure but of work]

I seek refuge in Allah from the accursed devil
In the Name of Allah the All-Beneficent the Most Merciful
There is no power nor strength but with Allah the High, the Magnificent
Permission, O my Master, support!
Our way is companionship, and goodness is in the congregation

What makes repentance pure, which is an obligation for every legally-tasked person? **Pure repentance is to leave behind the ego's will. As long as the servant is still at the station of the ego then every time they repent they will do away with their repentance.**

Allah Most High said, *have you seen him who has taken up as his god his own whim?* (al-Jāthiya 45:23). For when the servant follows his ego, he has certainly taken up his whim as his god. This is why, at the station of the ego, the servant cannot stand long on the straight path. His journeying will be *then they believe, then they disbelieve* (al-Nisā' 4:137).

It is a mistake for a person to follow his emotions, because emotions will always be in conformity with the whim of the ego. The origin of emotions in a human being will be from one of two paths: the path of the appetitive lustful faculty or the path of the faculty of anger.[1] With the severing of these two

[1] *Quwwat al-shahwa... quwwat al-ghaḍab.* In his commentary on *depart to a shadow with three branches* (Mursalāt 77:30) al-Bayḍāwī said, "the particularity of the three is either because the veil of the self from the lights of holiness is sensory perception, imagination and estimation, or because what led to this punishment is the *quwwat al-wāhima* (estimative faculty) residing in the brain, the *ghaḍabiyya* (irascible faculty) in the right side of the heart, and the *shahwiyya* (lustful faculty) in its left." The gates of Gehenna are seven (Ḥijr 15:44) "perhaps thus specified to reflect the confinement of all destructive sins to slavishness to the [five] senses and the constant pursuit of the lustful and wrathful faculties." Lust is assimilated to the golden Calf: "whoever wants to know his worst enemy—which strives in every way to inflict true death upon him —the way for him is to slaughter the cow in his own self, namely the lustful faculty" per al-Bayḍāwī at the end of the commentary on Baqara 2:73. See also his commentary on Allah's statements, *verily he was ever most unjust, most ignorant* in the verse *verily We have presented the trust before the heavens and the earth and the mountains but they*

faculties life stops, since the faculty of appetitive lust is the pursuit of existence to maintain a human being's life while the faculty of anger is a pressure given to the body which, once it falls to zero, no life remains. Our motion pours out from this direction.

The explanation of anger is that it is a propulsive power from the human being towards work. As for the lustful faculty it is to draw up that propulsive power to action. When it passes the limit it becomes blameworthy anger. "Do not be angry"[1] means, "do not rush impetuously lest your rushing becomes blameworthy and lest you can no longer control yourself due to the intensity of your rushing." For this reason the servant must master these two faculties so that he will get to the station of human perfection. The human being that does not keep watch over these two faculties will be a follower of his whim.

People are two kinds. One kind is under subjection and one kind is ruling. The one that is truly ruling is the one that is ruling over those two faculties. As for the one who is under the rule of his lust and his anger, he is truly under subjection, whether he is a *ʿallāma* (erudite scholar) or a *ʿābid* (worshipper) or a king or anything else. For the people of spiritual reality the whole world is in this order.

One of those that mastered his ego visited a king and spoke with him. The king felt wonder at his words and said to him, "Ask of me whatever you wish." The master answered, "How can I ask anything of you when you are a slave to my slaves? For you are ruled by your lustful appetite and your anger. As for me, verily anger and lustful appetite are slaves in my presence. Yet they are ruling over you."

This is a yardstick for the human being. He has to know: is he ruling over his ego at the time of anger and lust? Does he endure patiently at the time the causes for anger appear? At that time he can distinguish whether he is ruling or ruled. But as long as the servant is still at the station of ego, everything will

refused to assume it and they shrank in dread of it, and the human being assumed it (al-Aḥzāb 33:72); *do not follow whim* (Ṣād 38:26).

[1] Narrated from Jāriya b. Qudāma al-Saʿdī, Abū Hurayra, Abū Saʿīd al-Khudrī and Sulaymān b. Ṣurad by Ibn Wahb, Ibn Saʿd, Ibn Abī Shayba, Aḥmad, Bukhārī, al-Tirmidhī and others. The questioner was Jāriya per Ibn Abī Shayba (13:61 §25889), al-Ḥākim (3:713 §6578) with a chain of trustworthy narrators (cf. Nūr al-Khayriyya bint Khālid al-Mālīziyya and Fāḍila Yāmā al-Faṭāniyya, *al-Aḥādīth al-latī sakata ʿanhā al-Ḥākim wal-Dhahabī maʿan fil-Mustadrak wa-Talkhīṣih*, Kuala Lumpur: IIUM, 2007, pp. 360-361 §6578/277) and Ibn ʿAbd al-Barr, *al-Tamhīd* (7:246-248), "and the same question [and answer] took place with Abū al-Dardāʾ, ʿAbd Allāh b. ʿUmar, and Sufyān b. ʿAbd Allah al-Thaqafī" per Ibn Ḥajar, *Hadyu al-sārī* (7: *bayān al-asmāʾ al-muhmala al-latī yakthur ishtirākuhā, kitāb al-adab, ḥadīth Abī Hurayra, lā taghḍab*).

be ascribed to his ego. When he rises above the level of his ego—at that time things shall change.

There are 800 prohibited things which Allah neither loves nor accepts. Their origin is either from anger or from lust. When one of them dominates a human being his mind stops functioning. The foundations of all sins go back to those two origins. For this reason pure and sincere repentance is not ascertained with the servant until he is able to rule over his anger and over his lust.

The Naqshbandi path call for the relinquishment of anger and watchfulness over lust. Who can claim that he is ruling his lust while he is looking at women right and left in the streets? And you can find in the eyes of young men, at the very least, 12,000 darknesses of *zinā* (fornication).

Our liege lord the Shaykh has said of the pure and sincere repentance that proclivity, the devil, the world and the ego are allies in the destruction of the servant by means of pleasure. The servant must know that because of the pleasure of the ego, proclivity, the devil and the world, all the sins and acts of disobedience come. Whoever leaves no avenue for experiencing pleasure this way has become truly and sincerely repentant.

There is an example from Prophetic medicine that the stomach is a container[1] that must be given three parts: one third for food, one third for drink and one third for air.[2] And the believing servant eats so that he will have energy in life. He will not eat more than what sates him purely for hedonistic pleasure, because Allah has set the limits of the licit and the illicit for human beings. Wherever the limits of the licit end, the limits of the illicit begin. Whatever is enough for the servant to perpetuate his life and his lineage and his species Allah has made permitted. As for its surplus, it will be for hedonistic pleasure.

When you leave what your ego loves and what your whim and your devil and your world love, you will have truly repented and returned to your nurturing Lord. For this world is not an abode of taking pleasure but an abode of work whose recompense is in the hereafter. This is what the believers must know.

May Allah grant us sincerity in deeds. By the sanctity of the Beloved, by the sanctity of the Fatiha.

[1] *Wiʿāʾ*, as in the hadith, "No human being fills a worse vessel than a belly." Narrated from al-Miqdām b. Maʿdīkarib al-Kindī by Ibn Saʿd, Aḥmad, Tirmidhī (*ḥasan ṣaḥīḥ*), Ibn Mājah, Ibn Abī al-Dunyā, al-Nasāʾī and others.

[2] Continuation of the abovementioned hadith in al-Tirmidhī and Ibn Mājah.

16

People are either wrongdoers or victims of wrongdoing; [be the latter and not the former]

I seek refuge in Allah from the accursed devil
In the Name of Allah the All-Beneficent the Most Merciful
There is no power nor strength but with Allah the High, the Magnificent
Permission, O my Master, support!
Our way is companionship, and goodness is in the congregation

The Messenger of Allah–upon him the blessings and peace of Allah–said, "People are either a *ẓālim* or a *maẓlūm* (an oppressor or a victim of oppression)."[1] Mawlāna al-Shaykh explains this hadith to mean that a lion possesses honor, so it devours a single prey, eats from it and does not return to it. The wolf, however, if it were to find before itself a hundred sheep, its greed will not be satisfied until it chokes them all. The wolf is the worst of wild predators and has extraordinary eagerness to inflict harm. Sheep, on the other hand, are the archetype of that from which no harm comes nor even a sound even when it is struck or harmed,[2] although goats yell. And this is the meaning of the Messenger's hadith "Be a victim of oppression and do not be an oppressor."[3] But how many people will you find nowadays that have the characteristics of wolves from east to west! All of them are known by their names and their places, and the arrows of divine revenge will target them, and none of them will be saved. For the shepherd protects his sheep. So woe to the sheep for the wolves, and woe to the wolves for the final outcome! This is what the characters of people have become now.

May Allah protect us and you from the evils of our souls and the wrongs of our deeds. By the sanctity of the Beloved, by the sanctity of the Fatiha.

[1] Narrated as a statement of the Companion (i) al-Zubayr b. al-ʿAwwām at the Battle of the Camel (36/656) by Ibn Saʿd, *Ṭabaqāt al-kubrā* (*al-Badriyyīn min al-muhājirīn, waṣiyyat al-Zubayr*); Ibn Abī Shayba; al-Bukhārī (*Farḍ al-khumus, barakat al-ghāzī fī mālihi ḥayyan wa-mayyitan*); al-Ḥākim; Bayhaqī; and (ii) ʿAmr b. al-ʿĀṣ at the Battle of Ṣiffīn (37/657) by Abū Ḥanīfa Aḥmad b. Dāwūd al-Dīnawarī, *al-Akhbār al-ṭiwāl*, ed. ʿAbd al-Munʿim ʿĀmir (Cairo: ʿĪsā al-Bābī al-Ḥalabī, 1960) p. 181.

[2] Pain in sheep is assessed through observation of changes in their normal behavior and even their facial expressions.

[3] Narrated to this effect in the wording, "Let one be like the better one of the two sons of Ādam" from Abū Mūsā al-Ashʿarī by Ibn Abī Shayba, Aḥmad, Abū Dāwūd, al-Tirmidhī (*ḥasan ṣaḥīḥ*) and Ibn Mājah, spoken in the context of end time strifes.

17
The reality of *kufr* (unbelief) for the people of reality [is the *takfīr* of other human beings – The secret of Allah is in every human being]

I seek refuge in Allah from the accursed devil
In the Name of Allah the All-Beneficent the Most Merciful
There is no power nor strength but with Allah the High, the Magnificent
Permission, O my Master, support!
Our way is companionship, and goodness is in the congregation

Allah Most High said *and We have certainly honored the children of Ādam* (Banū Isrā'īl/Isrā' 17:70). Mawlana al-Shaykh ['Abd Allah Fa'iz Daghistani] explains this by asking, what is unbelief for the people of spiritual reality? All of the children of Ādam are honored in the presence of their nurturing Lord, and this is an ennoblement and a magnification on the part of Allah. It is particularly obligatory to believe this with respect to the believers. And if it is obligatory for us to believe that the children of Ādam are honored in the presence of Allah, it is also a must for us to implement this matter in practical terms and to respect all, and this is a very high manner.

Mawlana asks, through what did Allah honor human beings? He adds that Allah Almighty has honored human beings by making them His vicegerents. From this perspective **every single creature of the human beings is prized in the sight of his nurturing Lord, and it is not permissible to deprecate the essence of any individual human being**. And the meaning of unbelief for the people of truth is the deprecation of that which Allah has magnified. For this reason **the deprecation of human beings is the foundation of unbelief and its origin,**[1] **just as unbelief is the origin of every evil; and the truth is that were it not for the servants' revilement of one another there would be no evil on the face of the earth**. If every human being respected the other, could you find any strife on the face of the earth? This is why Mawlana says, the dwellers of the lowest depth of Hellfire are those that revile the servants of Allah and look upon them with contempt.

Whatever appears of sins, transgressions and ugly deeds from human beings, your duty is to treat them as an expert physician that does not despise his patients no matter how grave their disease gets. You must look at the

[1] I.e. their deprecation by Iblīs through his refusal to bow to Ādam.

servants with a look of mercy, asking from Allah to cure them or to deliver them from those wrongs until their essences show with all their lights, and no trace of ills remains on that original essence. You must, when you find a servant drowning in transgressions and sins, consider him a jewel that fell among impurities. And when you find a jewel among impurities, do you leave it or do you take it out and clean it so you can recover the jewel? And does not the essence which Allah has stored in human beings at least amount to one of the jewels of this world? Therefore consider the servant—even if he is mired in sins and polytheism—as a jewel, because sins and polytheism are accidents and not part of the original essence.

Part of the formal custom of our honorable masters is that Mawlana Shaykh Sharaf al-Din al-Daghistani, even if a child of four years of age came to the gathering, would get up from his place, take him by the hand, sit him by his side and ask him about his family and how they were. One day our liege lord Shaykh Jalal al-Din al-Rumi, the Imam of the Mevlevi Tariqa and one of the major spiritual authorities, was passing through the souk when he encountered a priest. The priest lowered his head out of respect for our liege lord the Shaykh, as the latter had imposing stature. But Mawlana lowered his head even more on the spot, as if bowing. They asked him, "Our master, this is a priest and you have given him so much respect!" He replied, "This is good manners with Allah and thus has the Messenger of Allah trained us to do."[1]

The Messenger–upon him the blessings and peace of Allah–would stand up when a funeral bier passed, even that of an unbeliever.[2] For what reason? He would say about it that the angel of death is accompanying the bier.[3]

[1] See the important suhba detailing the three levels of explanation for this account (Shariʿa, Tariqa and *Ḥaqīqa*) by Dr Nour Mohamad Kabbani entitled "Realities are understood by examples" (https://www.youtube.com/watch?v=c5z0rBFHS3M) given in Fenton, MI on 16 September 2023).

[2] Narrated from (i) Jābir by al-Bukhārī, Muslim, Abū Dāwūd, al-Nasāʾī; Aḥmad; (ii-iv) Abū Hurayra, al-Sharīd b. Suwayd and Abū Mūsā al-Ashʿārī by Aḥmad; (v) Anas by al-Nasāʾī; al-Bukhārī, *al-Tārīkh al-kabīr*. (vi-vii) The Companions Sahl b. Ḥunayf and Qays b. Saʿd were sitting in al-Qādisiyya (Iraq) when a funeral bier happened to pass by them so they stood up. They were told that it belonged to one of the dhimmis so they said, "The Prophet–upon him the blessings and peace of Allah–stood up for a funeral bier that was passing him and he was told it was that of a Jew, whereupon he replied, 'Is it not a human soul?'" Narrated from ʿAbd al-Raḥmān b. Abī Laylā by al-Bukhārī and Muslim, Ibn al-Jaʿd, Ibn Abī Shayba and others. (viii) Ibn ʿUmar stood for the funeral bier of a Jew and ordered his student Mujāhid b. Jabr to get up as well. Narrated from Mujāhid by al-Ṭaḥāwī, *Sharḥ maʿānī al-āthār*.

[3] Per Anas's narration: "You are only standing up for your brothers the angels." Per Abū Mūsā al-Ashʿarī's: "You are only standing up for the angels accompanying it." Also

That servant is carrying the secret of Allah; out of magnification for the secret of Allah there shall be respect. For **there is none that is self-sustaining except Allah, and everything in existence stands through Allah Almighty**. Why is the Name of Allah *al-Qayyūm* (The Ever-Sustainer)? Because absolutely everything is standing by means of Him.[1] And the perspective of the people of spiritual truth is that the secret is with each and everyone, and that if people held fast to this high manner, the manner of the Master of Messengers–upon him the blessings and peace of Allah–the whole world would certainly become an abode of peace, security and purity at once. This is why our nurturing Lord says, *and keep reminding, for verily the reminder benefits the believers* (al-Dhāriyāt 51:55). We must always remind ourselves that if we respect one another, we will never find among the servants any trace of enmity, or hatred, or envy.

O Allah, grant us *adab*! By the sanctity of the Beloved, by the sanctity of the Fatiha.

narrated from Abū Mūsā by al-Rūyānī in his *Musnad* and al-Ṭaḥāwī, *Maʿānī*.

[1] Per the verse *Is He Who is overseeing every soul with what it earns—?* (al-Raʿd 13:33) as stated by Dr Nour Kabbani (see three notes up).

18
The reality of humanhood – The levels of belief – [Definition of the unbeliever – Self-sacrifice and its divine compensation]

I seek refuge in Allah from the accursed devil
In the Name of Allah the All-Beneficent the Most Merciful
There is no power nor strength but with Allah the High, the Magnificent
Permission, O my Master, support!
Our way is companionship, and goodness is in the congregation

The more the servant rises in the stations of nearness to Allah, the more his ego's arrogant pride leaves him. No importance or trace of it remains. Human perfection appears in him. In this station the servant readies himself to sacrifice himself for all the servants of Allah or for the Umma of our liege lord Muhammad–upon him blessings and peace. That consists in his sacrificing himself on behalf of any human being at all whatever his school of thought, because his perspective is that this human being is, first of all, one of the servants of Allah, and then from the Umma of the Beloved–upon him the blessings of Allah. He sacrifices himself and his wealth for the sake of any individual human being or any individual from the Umma of our liege lord Muhammad–upon him the blessings and peace of Allah.

This is why the first station of the stations of nearness to Allah begins when the servant enters into the realm of belief. For the servant is far from Allah until he believes. Belief has levels. The more the servant's strength of belief increases, the nearer to Allah Almighty he gets. Mawlana Shaykh ['Abd Allah al-Daghistani] explains this by asking, what is it that distinguishes the servant from the rest of people at the station of belief? The unbeliever is unconcerned by other than his own ego—and we do not mean, by "unbeliever," the people of the Book or whoever believes in Allah or in any of the Prophets or in any of the Books or in the Last Day or in the angels. So **the unbeliever, for the people of spiritual reality, is the denier of the existence of Allah and the denier of His Books or His Messengers or His Prophets or the Last Day or Paradise and Hell.**

The materialists—they are the unbelievers who do not acknowledge the existence of Allah Almighty. This is why eating their slaughtered meat is categorically forbidden as is marrying their daughters. As for the people of the Book, Allah gave dispensation for them to live together with the people of

Islam, and more than that, He has made it halal for Muslims to eat their food and marry their women. But for the unbeliever, his own ego is the absolute judge, so he does not recognize any immense favors other than the godhood of his own self. If he found the opportunity he would certainly make all people his servants. This is why you see atheists adopting the ruthlessness of tyrants, so that they will always make people subservient to them.

Materialists do not acknowledge anything of spiritual meanings ever. They do not acknowledge other than materiality. They want to turn people into automatons and they want them to confine all their thoughts to their bellies and underbellies so that they will never think of exalted things or virtues. This is the attribute of the unbeliever that is ruled by his ego's will.

When the servant comes out of the prison of his ego, he will set his foot in belief and come out of his egotism. The first of the travel-stations of belief is for the servant to view all people in their due rights as equal with himself in the way he preserves his own rights. This is the first of the outward travel-stations of belief. This creed makes sure there is equality in the world. From the recognition of the rights of people the servant continues to journey to the stations of nearness to Allah. The more he climbs up from one station to another, the more he keeps back his own ego from claiming its rights, putting the rights of others first. For example, in the first station it will be one morsel for him and one morsel for other than him. Thereafter, the more he climbs up from that principle to the second station—the station of giving preference to others—he will increase in [the meaning of] *and they give preference over themselves even if there is penury in them* (al-Ḥashr 59:9).

Thus, even if they found a morsel they would not eat it but would give it to someone in the same need as they are. They have now become, with this station, a sacrifice on behalf of the servants of Allah and the Umma of the Beloved of Allah and His Messenger–upon him the blessings and peace of Allah. The meaning is that no importance remains for the ego in their sight. Their life has become in the way of Allah. Once they have made their lives in the way of Allah, Allah has compensated them with the best of what they have devoted to His way. As for the one that does not devote himself or his wealth to the way of Allah and to the way of the Umma of the Beloved–upon him the blessings and peace of Allah–such a one will remain at the first of the stations of belief, which is the nearest to the station of unbelief. This is a weighing scale by which the human being may know himself as to which of the stations of nearness he occupies. And this is the way by which to arrive at the reality of humanhood.

May Allah grant it to us and you. By the sanctity of the Beloved, by the sanctity of the Fatiha.

19
The harm caused by the ego's attributes – [Enduring harm is the way of self-purification]

I seek refuge in Allah from the accursed devil
In the Name of Allah the All-Beneficent the Most Merciful
There is no power nor strength but with Allah the High, the Magnificent
Permission, O my Master, support!
Our way is companionship, and goodness is in the congregation

Our liege lord the Shaykh [ʿAbd Allah al-Daghistani] told us about a bird living in the region of Yemen called *milḥān*.[1] It is a big bird that lives 200 years. For the first 100 it sires and provides food for its offspring, then it sheds its feathers, sits in its nest and grows old while its offspring feed it. The wisdom of this bird's longevity is that when it flies it does not flap its wings for fear of hurting any creature in the air. It flies with its wings outstretched. It means that it is anxious to avoid harming anything.

There are also other animals that live long lives such as the elephant for example. It also does not harm others and its food is foliage. As for ferocious animals such as the lion and the tiger, their lives are short. This is the meaning of the noble hadith, "Injustice does not last, and if it lasts, it destroys."[2] Likewise whoever represents injustice does not last either, whether a human being or an animal.

Harming is from injustice and it is not part of the character of humanhood, so how can it be found in the Muslim? Whoever calls himself a human being ought never to commit injustice; how much more so when it comes to those whom Allah has honored by making them able to say, "I am a believer"! How can he possibly harm others? Harming is part of the characteristics of the ego. A servant's belief does not become perfect until people are safe from his harm.[3] The mark of perfect belief in the servant is to keep his harm far from

[1] "Hoar-frost," a name for extreme cold applied to the second of the two months of *kānūn* (December and January) per Abū Manṣūr al-Azharī, *Tahdhīb al-lugha* (*m-l-ḥ*).

[2] Attributed to Kisrā Anūsharwān "as I have seen it cited in one of the ancient books" per Tāj al-Dīn al-Fākihānī in *Riyāḍ al-afhām fī sharḥ ʿUmdat al-aḥkām* and cited as a wise dictum by later scholars such as Jamāl al-Dīn al-Fattanī in *Majmaʿ biḥār al-anwār*, Zayn al-Dīn al-Munāwī in his two commentaries on Suyūṭī's *Jāmiʿ al-ṣaghīr*, al-Ṭāhir Ibn ʿĀshūr in his *Tafsīr* and others.

[3] Per the Prophetic hadith, "The Muslim is he from [the harm of] whose tongue and

people and to put up with their harm. Whoever is thus described will be on a footing with the Prophets–upon them peace–because all the Prophets were harmed and they never requited harm with harm.

To refrain from harming people is a command in all the heavenly laws. The jihad against one's ego begins with it. From there does excellent character begin. The envier harms people the most, likewise people of falsehood and obduracy. Any blameworthy trait of character that appears in the human being, we will see that he will harm people because of it. This is why we have said that the first of all the praiseworthy traits of character is for us to never harm people.

As for putting up with the harm of people, it will be the station of *tamkīn* (firmness and strength)[1] in belief. Anyone that bears with harm climbs up the stations of belief. The people of spiritual reality have said that harm is the avenue of purification. I.e. because of enduring harm, purity ensues in the hearts. This is why it was directed at the Prophets then at the Awliya, and the Prophet–upon him the blessings and peace of Allah–said, "None has been harmed as much as I have been harmed for the sake of Allah."[2] That is just like gold when it is placed in the fire, how it glows! And without fire—the harm of people—the heart will not become pure.

May Allah grant us and you to follow Him and to support Him. By the sanctity of the Beloved, by the sanctity of the Fatiha.

whose hand people are safe." Narrated from ʿAbd Allāh b. ʿAmr, Abū Hurayra, Muʿādh b. Anas al-Juhanī and Faḍāla b. ʿUbayd al-Anṣārī by Aḥmad and al-Nasāʾī. It is also related from Anas b. Mālik, Abū Dharr, Wāthila b. al-Asqaʿ and Ibn ʿUmar.

[1] As opposed to *talwīn*, cf. chapter on *tamkīn* and *talwīn* in *al-Risāla al-Qushayriyya.*

[2] Narrated from (i) Anas by Ibn Abī Shayba, Aḥmad, al-Tirmidhī in the *Sunan* and *Shamāʾil*, Ibn Mājah, Ibn Ḥibbān, Abū Nuʿaym, al-Bayhaqī in the *Shuʿab*, and others; (ii) Jābir by Ibn ʿAdī and Ibn ʿAsākir; (iii) Burayda by Daylamī, *Musnad al-firdaws*. Its basis in al-Bukhārī according to al-Sakhāwī, *al-Maqāṣid al-ḥasana*. Suyūṭī declared it *ḥasan ṣaḥīḥ* in *al-Jāmiʿ al-ṣaghīr* (Bulāq 1286/1869 ed. 2:298).

20
[The spiritual powers of the Prophets] – The greatest *muʿjiza* (staggering miracle) of the Messenger –upon him blessings and peace

I seek refuge in Allah from the accursed devil
In the Name of Allah the All-Beneficent the Most Merciful
There is no power nor strength but with Allah the High, the Magnificent
Permission, O my Master, support!
Our way is companionship, and goodness is in the congregation

All the Prophets–upon them peace–brought powerful, overwhelming staggering miracles. Were it not for the *muʿjizāt*, they would be ordinary men and no one would pay attention to them. The staggering miracles are the sign that there are custom-breaching powers in them.

There are two powers in human beings: outward, and spiritual. The spiritual powers show in all their perfection in the Prophets–upon them peace– and they dominate the outward powers. **A single possessor of the spiritual powers is able to repel the outward powers of the nations in their entirety**. At the same time, spiritual powers do not appear in the servant until the ego-related powers are extinguished once and for all in him.

The spiritual powers that appear in the servant are originally a power from their nurturing Lord. Our liege lord the Shaykh [ʿAbd Allah Fa'iz al-Daghistani] has mentioned, as the greatest staggering miracle of the Messenger–upon him the blessings and peace of Allah–that he emerged in a society that was in the greatest time of ignorance and among people whose unbelief was the staunchest unbelief, and there was no outward helper with him on whom he could rely. Yet, despite that, he stood and proclaimed *There is no god but the One God, and Muhammad is the Messenger of the One God* when there was no army with him, no men, and no wealth. But there were spiritual powers with him, so that he went against all of them, and he began alone, and he vanquished all of them.

Can any human being call to something and stand his ground against people without men or wealth? The Messenger–upon him the blessings and peace of Allah–was supported from above, and the spiritual powers that were with him are evidence that his affair is from the *malakūt* (world of invisible sovereignty). And this is enough for the possessors of hearts to affirm the Prophethood of our Prophet–upon him blessings and peace.

Our liege lord ʿĪsā–upon him peace–came to a people that had with them a sacred Law from Allah that Mūsā–upon him peace–had brought, and they knew Prophets and Scriptures. He came among the Israelite people and conditions were ripe for accepting him. His people did not oppose him the way the Quraysh did with our liege lord Muhammad–upon him the blessings and peace of Allah–because the Quraysh were not familiar with any Prophet or any Scripture at the time the Beloved of Allah called them. Also, Allah supported our liege lord Mūsā–upon him peace–with outward powers such as his staff. His heart depended on his staff which, when he cast it, became a huge snake swallowing up everything, although he was a Prophet from among the Prophets of great resolve, and he had said, *it is my staff, I lean on it and I strip off the tree leaves with it over my sheep, and I use it for other needs* (Ṭa Ha 20:18).

In light of the above, the staggering miracle of our Prophet has become the greatest of all staggering miracles, from the perspective that the Messenger of Allah–upon him the blessings and peace of Allah–has alone founded the faith-system of the truth and called to it, saying that this faith-system shall remain until the Day of Resurrection. And were are now 1400 years after the time of the Messenger, and we may well see: has his call endured and does it perpetuate or not? Christians and foreigners are entering Islam. On the night of the Mawlid we find more than 100 million Muslims magnifying the Messenger of Allah, invoking blessings on him and celebrating in his honor; and this is the greatest demonstration and proof to the soundness of the Messenger's Prophethood–upon him the blessings and peace of Allah.

Mawlana al-Shaykh is giving glad tidings and is saying that at the end of time, when the Umma becomes weak, *ṣāḥib al-zamān* (the spiritual guide of endtimes) will emerge following that very way, and he will also come bringing custom-breaching spiritual powers. It is because of this that we said that if a single man possessed the spiritual powers, he could resist the world and everything in it. When the spiritual guide of the times appears he shall indeed resist the world and raise the cry of magnification, *Allāhu akbar!* (The One God is greatest) three times, and with these magnifications every falsehood will perish and the truth shall appear. The Mahdi–upon him peace–shall also make use of extraordinary miracles.

May Allah grant us to follow him and to support him. By the sanctity of the Beloved, by the sanctity of the Fatiha.

21

[12,000 *miʿrājs*[1] – *Ṣiddīqīn*'s heart-knowledge raises you to the Throne – Grandshaykh is the Seal of the *Ṣiddīqs* in Tariqa] - Reality of the heavenly Ascent to honor human beings – [Prophet's intermediacy]

I seek refuge in Allah from the accursed devil
In the Name of Allah the All-Beneficent the Most Merciful
There is no power nor strength but with Allah the High, the Magnificent
Permission, O my Master, support!
Our way is companionship, and goodness is in the congregation

Our liege lord Shaykh ʿAbd Allah al-Daghistani says that Allah Almighty did not invite the Messenger one time to the heavenly Ascent but rather He invited him 12,000 times,[2] and that the one the Messenger–upon him the blessings and peace of Allah–spoke about was one of those heavenly ascents. As for the rest, they remained in the heart of Abū Bakr al-Ṣiddīq–may Allah be well-pleased with him. Hence the Prophet–upon him blessings and peace–said, "Whatever Allah has poured into my chest I have certainly poured it into Abū Bakr's chest."[3]

[1] See also Suhba I.24 on the status of this knowledge in the Naqshbandi Tariqa.

[2] "The Prophet–upon him blessings and peace of Allah–had many *miʿrājs*" per Abū Saʿīd al-Kharkūshī (d. 406/1015), *Sharaf al-Muṣṭafā* (2:140); cf. Ibn Ḥajar, *Fatḥ* (7:197, *qawuluhu ḥadīth al-isrāʾ wa-qawlu-l-Lāhi subḥān al-ladhī asrā*); Muḥammad b. Jaʿfar al-Kattānī, *Miʿrāj al-Nabī*, 4th ed. (Damascus: Dār al-Qurʾān, 1392/1072) pp. 4-5.

[3] Cited chainless in latter-day non-Arab Sufi exegeses e.g. Rashīd al-Dīn Maybodī's (d. 530/1136) commentary on al-Harawī al-Anṣārī's *Tafsīr*; Rāzī; Najm al-Dīn Kubrā; Niẓām al-Dīn Naysābūrī; Ismāʿīl Ḥaqqī and the generality of the Naqshbandi masters in their works as the corollary of the Quranic verse, *the second of two as they were both in the cave, as he was saying to his companion, "Grieve not! Verily the One God is with us"* (Barāʾa/Tawba 9:40). "True in meaning although unestablished in transmission and I have always heard the general public attribute it to the Messenger of Allah–upon him blessings and peace" per Ibn al-Jawzī, *Mawḍūʿāt*. That meaning is allusively supported by one of the the very last Prophetic *khuṭbas*, "Truly there is a servant to whom Allah gave the choice between this world and the hereafter so he chose the hereafter," by which Abū Bakr sensed the Prophet meant himself so he wept and the Prophet–upon him blessings and peace–said to him, "slow down." Then he said, "wall up these doors leading into the Mosque except the door of Abū Bakr–Allah have mercy on him–for verily I know not any man among all the Companions who has helped me more than Abū Bakr!" Narrated from (i) Ayyūb b. Bashīr al-Anṣārī in *mursal* mode by ʿAbd al-

Yet our liege lord Abū Bakr did not narrate, of the Prophet's hadiths–upon him the blessings and peace of Allah–except some twenty-odd hadiths approximately. Is this everything that he had heard from the Messenger–upon him the blessings and peace of Allah–whereas he was the first of the believers,[1] his Companion and minister for 23 years of the Prophethood? So where did those sciences that he learnt from the Messenger go? Where is the center of the sciences for the servant? The place where knowledge descends is the servant's heart, just as the place where revelation descends is the Muhammadan heart. As for the realities and the secrets and the sciences found in the heart of the Ṣiddīq, where are they? Did he kept them concealed? It is known, of course, that it is impermissible for anyone to conceal a knowledge he has learnt when he knows that the servants of Allah will benefit from it. What then when the matter pertains to the most veracious believer? Is it rationally conceivable that he would conceal knowledge that he had received from the magnified Messenger?

The Messenger–upon him the blessings and peace of Allah–has taught two types of knowledge: the knowledge of the Shari'a with the tongue, and the knowledge of the *Ḥaqīqa* (spiritual reality) with the heart, and it moved to the heart of Abū Bakr the Most Veracious. As for the one that did not acquire the

Razzāq, *Muṣannaf* (5:431); Ibn Hishām, *Sīra* (2:649); Bayhaqī, *Dalā'il* (7:177-178); (ii) Abū Sa'īd al-Khudrī by Ibn Sa'd, *Ṭabaqāt* (*Tatimmat al-Sīra, dhikr sadd al-abwāb ghayr bāb Abī Bakr*); Ibn Abī Shayba; Aḥmad; al-Bukhārī (*Ṣalāt, al-khawkha wal-mamarr fil-masjid* and *Aṣḥāb al-Nabī, qawl al-Nabī suddu al-abwāb illā bāb Abī Bakr*) with the addition, "Truly the one I owe the greatest favor among people in his companionship and wealth is Abū Bakr, and if I were taking a beloved intimate out of my Umma it would be Abū Bakr" and "indeed let no door ever remain in the Mosque except it has been closed up but the door of Abū Bakr;" Muslim (*Faḍā'il al-Ṣaḥāba, min faḍā'il Abī Bakr*); (iii) Abū al-Ḥuwayrith by Ibn Sa'd (ditto); (iv) Ibn 'Abbās by Aḥmad (4:252 §2432); Bukhārī (*Ṣalāt, al-khawkha wal-mamarr fil-masjid*); (v) 'Ā'isha by Dārimī; Bukhārī, *al-Tārīkh al-kabīr* (1:407-408 §1304, 2:67-68 §1710); al-Tirmidhī; (vi) 'Utba b. Ghazwān by Ibn Abī 'Āṣim, *al-Sunna* (*Faḍā'il Abī Bakr*); (vii) Anas by Bazzār (13:150 §6557, *isnāduhu ḥasan* per al-Haythamī, *Majma' al-zawā'id* 9:43); al-Ṭaḥāwī, *Mushkil* (9:181 §3550); and others; (viii) Ka'b b. Mālik by Ṭaḥāwī, *Mushkil* (9:180 §3547) and others; (ix-x) Jābir b. 'Abd Allāh and Ḥakīm b. 'Umar al-'Absī by Ibn 'Asākir (30:249, 30:256-257). The walling-up hadith points to Abū Bakr's caliphate per Ibn Baṭṭāl, as is the school of Imam Aḥmad and as concluded by Ibn Ḥajar in his analysis in *Fatḥ al-Bārī* (7:12-16). The above mass transmission is not contradicted by the report that the Prophet also ordered for 'Alī b. Abī Ṭālib's door to be kept open in a separate narration from Zayd b. Arqam, Jābir b. Samura and Ibn 'Umar as shown by al-Ṭaḥāwī, *Mushkil* (8:181-189); Ibn Ḥajar, *al-Qawl al-musaddad* (2nd-3rd hadiths); Kattānī, *Naẓm al-mutanāthir* (pp. 191-194 §229, §231).

[1] See the documentation to that effect in the chapter on Abū Bakr al-Ṣiddīq in Gibril Fouad Haddad, *The Rightly-Guided Caliphs* (Fenton: ISCA, 2023) p. 73 §21.

rank of most-veraciousness, the knowledge of spiritual reality is impermissible for such a one. With all the knowledges that the human being memorizes and relates with the tongue, however, he cannot rise from the earth. For knowledge-driven [spiritual] power will be through the heart. **The knowledges whose headquarters are the heart shall carry you from the earth to the Throne**. This is why the Messenger–upon him the blessings and peace of Allah–retold one of the accounts of the heavenly Ascents while he directed the rest to the heart of the Ṣiddīq, whereby the Ṣiddīq's heart is like the sea: it is wide enough to contain those sciences and to confirm them as true. Likewise, **whoever inherits from the Ṣiddīq, his heart will also be like the sea, so that the sciences of spiritual reality will be poured into it**. The sciences of the 40 Imams of Tariqa do not exceed the like of a demitasse from the sea of the *ṣiddīqīn* of the *Ṭarīqa 'aliyya*. So do not be surprised when you hear that the number of the heavenly ascents of the Messenger are 12,000 ascents but believe! For a person keeps believing until he is written in the presence of Allah as a most veracious one. The *maqām al-ṣiddīqiyya* (station of veraciousness) cannot be obtained except with *taṣdīq* (giving credence). And the servant's heart will not become vast enough to give credence until the light of belief enters it. Otherwise he will keep objecting, belying and dissembling.

Our noble liege masters sometimes speak of certain matters which murids have never heard of, or never read about in any book. This is a teaching for us and to recognize whether the light of belief has entered into the hearts of the addressees. Do they give credence or are they still trying to use their minds to estimate and assess? For the mind cannot comprehend all realities. It might comprehend the obligations of ablution, ritual shower and prayer. These are very external matters which are easy to comprehend and give credence to. However, what lies beyond that of realities cannot be comprehended by the human mind. It would be like addressing non-Muslims about the benefits of *ṣalāt*. They will not believe what is related to its merits in the hereafter and they will admit that it is a beneficial exercise only. They do not believe that the human being will be rewarded for it in the hereafter. In order for a human being to believe the light of belief must enter his heart.

When our liege lord 'Umar came to our liege lord Abū Bakr to enquire about the report of the heavenly Ascent the latter replied to him, "This is little with regard to the Prophet–upon him the blessings and peace of Allah. If I said what I knew you yourself would run away O 'Umar!" This is why, the more a servant gives credence the more he rises, and the reverse takes place when he asks, "Why is it so?" He does not rise. For the question means narrowness of the servant's chest with respect to giving credence.

Mawlana [Shaykh 'Abd Allah Daghistani] says—from the perspective that **he is the seal of the Ṣiddīqs in the most distinguished Tariqa**—concerning the secret of the existence of 12,000 heavenly ascents, that the *ṣuḥba* of our nurturing Lord granted to the Messenger–upon him the blessings and peace of Allah–in the heavenly ascents was not only to magnify the person of the Messenger but also consisted in glad tidings about the honoring of the children of Ādam in the presence of Allah. He says–exalted is He–*and We have certainly honored the children of Ādam* (Banū Isrā'īl/Isrā' 17:70). Allah was informing the Messenger with what He had honored His servants, exalted them and magnified them. As part of His honoring of His servants, **if the angels were given pens and were ordered to write the glad tidings that Allah has prepared for the children of Ādam until the Day of Resurrection they would be unable to do so**, because *never was the giving of your nurturing Lord restricted* (17:20). *And they never reckoned the One God with the reckoning that is truly His* (An'ām 6:91, Zumar 39:67). Therefore:

blessing and happiness for us, assembly of humankind,[1] *truly we have,*
of immense divine care, a Pillar indestructible!

Just as our nurturing Lord would give the Messenger good news regarding his nation in particular and human beings in general, He would also give him some spiritual powers for the protection of human beings, from the perspective that **the Messenger–upon him the blessings and peace of Allah–has been put in charge of the servants of Allah from the Day of *"am I not your nurturing Lord?" They said yes*** (al-A'rāf 7:172), and so that Iblīs will not be able to steal any of the human beings. Allah has dressed His Messenger with powers from His side to protect them from the first to the last of them, and the existence of injustice or bad things or the denial of the servants does not matter to Him, not even the unbelief of unbelievers. For our Messenger is none other than the all-trustworthy Muhammad–upon him the blessings and peace of Allah. Would a shepherd be trustworthy if he lost one of his sheep? Even more so when it comes to the Messenger of Allah.

The lesson from this discourse is that we must always be wide awake in giving value to human beings, for in our time human beings have lost all value. Our nurturing Lord loves for His servants to be given value. Likewise, giving value to human beings makes love grow for human beings in the hearts of the servants. This is the secret. However, deprecating the servants causes enmity, hatred and aversion from others in the hearts. And all the blameworthy traits of character fester behind the contempt of the servant. By the sanctity of the Beloved, by the sanctity of the Fatiha.

[1] *Ma'shara al-insāni* in the Arabic edition, either Mawlana's intended rewording of the original (see e.g. Suhbas I.26, I.31) or a slip of the pen on the transcriber's part.

22
The predetermination of animals – [Reason and wisdom in the creation of everything – The human being that connects himself becomes vicegerent of Allah on earth – The *Quṭb al-mutaṣarrif*'s power]

I seek refuge in Allah from the accursed devil
In the Name of Allah the All-Beneficent the Most Merciful
There is no power nor strength but with Allah the High, the Magnificent
Permission, O my Master, support!
Our way is companionship, and goodness is in the congregation

Do bees have intelligence? If they had minds they would have been legally liable. For this reason the mind of all keep them busy, because they are under injunction. Just as one whose mind is deficient or an orphan is placed under an effective injunction or under a trustee until they reach maturity, likewise everything outside the human beings is under the injunction of the All-True–Almighty is He. For example, whenever a piece of bread falls on the ground you will see ants after a little while coming and taking it. Who then is putting these ants to work? Animals have no mind. Bees do not make honey through their knowledge or their reason. So then reason was given to human beings as an honor. Whoever thinks about this matter must acknowledge the existence of the Creator Who moves everything and directs it to a specific goal.

Allah Most High says, *and to each one his orientation that he turns to*[1] (al-Baqara 2:148). What is considered to be subsumed under *each*, whether it is an inanimate object or a plant or an animal or a human being, must necessarily have an orientation and a goal to which Allah turns them.[2] You cannot find any part of the universe without orientation. Otherwise there would not appear out of the elements different combinations oriented towards their purposes. If there were a single atom in creation without orientation its existence would be for nothing but play. It was said in the noble verse, *our nurturing Lord! You did not create this in vain* (Āl 'Imrān 3:191). What He pointed out by saying *this* is that even the least thing is subsumed under that status and

[1] Also parsable and translatable as *that He turns him to* (Bayḍāwī).

[2] The verse can be glossed two ways: "that he turns his face to," or "that Allah Most High is orienting him to" (Bayḍāwī).

has a reason and a wisdom for which Allah brought it into existence. How much more true it is of the human being that is adorned with a mind!

So if the human being does not think about himself and about the wisdom for which he was brought into existence, he will be lower than the level of animals. Likewise, Allah gives power to whoever connects himsef of human beings, such that he becomes able to have control over all creatures on the face of the earth. And with this power he becomes the vicegerent of Allah on earth. Allah Most High said, *and He made subservient to you what is in the skies and what is on earth entirely from Him* (al-Jāthiya 45:13). But the human being will not be given that power until he has complete mastery over his ego and frees himself of its will. Then he will connect himself with the *malakūt* (invisible sovereignty). The *Quṭb al-mutaṣarrif* (spiritual Pole with discretionary power) was given governance for the determination of animals towards what Allah created them for and he alone has power to govern all creatures, and there is no limit to what he possesses of spiritual powers from the world of invisible sovereignty.

May Allah grant it to us and you. By the sanctity of the Beloved, by the sanctity of the Fatiha.

23

Spiritual powers of the Awliya – ["The Ulema carry their knowledge whereas knowledge carries the Awliya"]

I seek refuge in Allah from the accursed devil
In the Name of Allah the All-Beneficent the Most Merciful
There is no power nor strength but with Allah the High, the Magnificent
Permission, O my Master, support!
Our way is companionship, and goodness is in the congregation

Students strive to receive the disciplines and you may see them struggling to memorize and fix them in their minds. Whoever uses his intellectual powers, acquiring knowledge and memorizing it will be difficult and you will find that the mind slowly forgets it after a while. As for him that uses his spiritual powers then nothing is difficult for him to acquire and he does not struggle to memorize it. You see its example in the Prophets and the Awliya.

I have kept company with Mawlana Shaykh 'Abd Allah al-Daghistani a long time—40 years—and when he moved to the world of invisible sovereignty he was 115 years old. Any time that he spoke of his childhood and his boyhood he would not forget anything. How many times we heard him repeat it, and I would notice that nothing was missing from his discourse. On the contrary he would add more details. As for us, if we tell any story then we retell it after a month or more, we miss something from it because we forget. *Sulṭān al-ʿārifīn* Abū Yazīd al-Bisṭāmī would say that "the ulema carry their knowledge"—in the sense that if they had not read and memorized they would not have knowledge—"but as for us"—the Awliya—"knowledge carries us." And in any sitting or for any cause we may speak and say what is required for those who are present, without need to look it up or to study the sciences.[1]

[1] This is the upshot of al-Ghazālī's differentiation between the foremost knowledge—knowledge of Allah—and other types of knowledge in the first book of *Iḥyā' ʿulūm al-dīn* and the gist of another famous statement of Abū Yazīd to the ulema, "You take your knowledge from the dead" (i.e. the letter) "whereas we take it from the Living Who does not die." It is also what Mawlana Shaykh Nazim means by focusing on the *wāridāt*—spiritual intuitions—over and above bookish knowledge. Contrary to the bibliophobic misinterpretations of some, never did he forbid study or the reading of books. On the contrary he practiced them all his life, first in Istanbul, then in Homs, then in Damascus, then in Cyprus as illustrated by his extensive handwritten annotations and bookmarks in the several libraries that he owned and as demonstrated by his

Mawlana al-Shaykh is saying that the human being has a physical power and a spiritual power. However, the physical power is in constant diminishment until death. As for the Prophets and the Awliya, they are the representatives of the spiritual power, and we cannot find with them any weakness or diminishment in their powers—even the physical ones. Even if the age of one of them reaches 100 we will find he still have complete virile power. Likewise when they move to the highest world of invisible sovereignty, the earth does not consume their bodies.

By the sanctity of the Beloved, by the sanctity of the Fatiha.

constant references to Islamic sources and scholarly terminology.

24

The reality of close familiarity with people – [Prophetic inheritors – Heart knowledge of spiritual realities – The 12,000 night ascents – The 124,000 Ādams that have passed] – Number of the beautiful Names of Allah – [Overriding mercy]

I seek refuge in Allah from the accursed devil
In the Name of Allah the All-Beneficent the Most Merciful
There is no power nor strength but with Allah the High, the Magnificent
Permission, O my Master, support!
Our way is companionship, and goodness is in the congregation

Souls are stamped with the instinct of wildness while social conversation creates close familiarity among people. **The more a human being develops close familiarity with other people, the more his close familiarity with Allah increases, and the more estranged and distant from people he gets, the more he deprives himself from close familiarity with Allah Almighty**. This is why, when we see a person get along with the rich and the poor, the old and the young, we recognize in him close familiarity with Allah Almighty. However, if we were to leave the ego to its nature, then it would not get along with anyone and it would wish to remain alone.

The Prophets have come to found social closeness between the servants. This does not occur except through belief in Allah Almighty, and belief in the Messengers is the door to belief in Allah Almighty. Close familiarity with the Prophets yields close familiarity with Allah. Prophethood has now been sealed with the Seal of Prophets since there is no Prophet after him–upon him the blessings and peace of Allah. However, one can find inheritors to the august Messenger who are always in existence, and so until the Day of Resurrection. The earth shall never be devoid of them.[1] When the Messenger moved on, the

[1] Per the Prophetic hadiths, "The Substitutes in this Nation are thirty like Ibrāhīm the Friend of the Merciful. Every time one of them dies, Allah substitutes another one in his place." Narrated by Aḥmad through trustworthy narrators per Haythamī, *Majmaʿa al-zawāʾid* (10:62) and Suyūṭī rated it *ṣaḥīḥ* in *al-Jāmiʿ al-ṣaghīr*. Ibn Kathīr cited it in his *Tafsīr* under the verse *and if Allāh had not repelled some men by others the earth would have been corrupted* (al-Baqara 2:251). Another version states, "The earth will never lack forty men similar to the Friend of the Merciful. Through them people receive rain and are given help. None of them dies except Allah substitutes another in his

earth wept and said, "O my nurturing Lord, none remains walking on my shoulders of the Prophets!" Whereupon Allah Most High addressed it and said, "In honor of My Beloved Muḥammad, there are over there 124,000 of his Umma on a footing with 124,000 Prophets, relaying the Prophets without cease until the Day of Resurrection."[1]

These inheritors exist. However, in our time, it is not allowed for their suns to appear because our time is the time of darkness and of "fitnas that are like chunks of dark night."[2] If the lights of those Awliya were to appear there would not remain any darkness at all on the face of the earth, but the Messenger–upon him the blessings and peace of Allah–is a truthful reported and it is necessary for what he predicted of strife to emerge. But keeping company with the Awliya yields close familiarity and revives the hearts and, since the darkness of strifes has certainly reached a maximum, it is also necessary for the time of deliverance to be near, just as the Messenger–upon him the blessings and peace of Allah–gave glad tidings of it.

Part of what our liege lord *Sulṭān al-awliyā'* (The supreme authority of the Friends of Allah) Shaykh 'Abd Allah al-Daghistani said, is that the knowledge of reality will not be by the tongue. Rather, its headquarter is the heart. It is defined as the knowledge that makes the servant reach from *mulk* (the visible world of creation) to *malakūt* (the invisible world of sovereignty), and it is what Allah asks and loves.

We know that there are some priests and some of the people of Scripture and Orientalists who have more acquaintance with the Qur'ān and the noble

place." Narrated from Anas by Ṭabarānī, *Awsaṭ* with a fair chain per Haythamī (10:63). Qatāda said, "We do not doubt al-Ḥasan [al-Baṣrī] is one of them."

[1] واعلم أن من رحمة الله بخلقه أن جعل على قدم كل نبي ولياً وارثاً له فما زاد. فلا بد أن يكون في كل عصر مائة ألف ولي وأربعة وعشرون ألف ولي؛ على عدد الأنبياء؛ ويزيدون ولا ينقصون. فإن زادوا قسم الله علم ذلك النبي على من ورثه. فإن العلوم المنزلة على قلوب الأنبياء لا ترتفع من الدنيا وليس لها إلا قلوب الرجال فتقسم عليهم بحسب عددهم. فلا بد من أن يكون في الأمة من الأولياء على عدد الأنبياء وأكثر من ذلك in Ibn 'Arabī, *Futūḥāt* (Būlāq ed. 3:208, ch. 349). "Le nombre total des saints, toutes catégories confondues, est en permanence au moins égal à celui des prophètes… soit cent vingt-quatre mille. S'il est supérieur à ce chiffre, c'est que l'héritage de tel ou tel des ces prophètes a été fractionné entre plusieurs *awliyâ*" in Michel Chodkiewicz, *Le Sceau des saints* (Paris: Gallimard, 1986) pp. 73, 107.

[2] From a Prophetic hadith narrated from (i-ix) Ḥudhayfa b. al-Yamān, Abū Hurayra, Ibn Mas'ūd, Anas b. Mālik, Abū Mūsā al-Ash'arī, Sa'īd b. Zayd b. 'Amr b. Nufayl, Abū Umāma al-Bāhilī, al-Ḍaḥḥāk b. Qays, Jundub b. Sufyān and, in *mursal* mode, (x-xi) Ka'b al-Aḥbar and Mujāhid by Ma'mar b. Rāshid, *Jāmi'*; Nu'aym b. Ḥammād, *Fitan*; Ibn Sa'd; Ibn Abī Shayba; Aḥmad; Muslim; Ibn Mājah; al-Tirmidhī; al-Dānī, *al-Sunan fil-fitan*; Abū Dāwūd; al-Ṭabarānī; al-Ḥākim, *Mustadrak*; and others.

hadiths than Muslims, but those knowledges remained on their tongues and never entered their hearts, whereby they have not shown their belief. So there is no benefit from knowledge that remains on the tongue. As for the knowledge of reality that settles in the heart, it revives the hearts. This is why the Awliya do not die but they disappear from the life of this world and become present in the *malakūt*. When they are in the world they are also present in the *malakūt*, and none of them would be a wali otherwise. And the believer is the *wali* (rightful ally, guardian, friend) of the truth. This is why we must acquire the light of *wilāya* (friendship with Allah) in our lifetime. It is for this reason that we came to this world, and Allah Almighty says, *then search for a light!* (al-Ḥadīd 57:13); and of the ways of searching for the light is to keep company with the Awliya - may Allah be well-pleased with them.

Mawlana al-Shaykh ʿAbd Allah would explain that the Messenger–upon him the blessings and peace of Allah–went on 12,000 heavenly ascents,[1] although only one of them has become famous in the Umma—and yet what the Messenger related from the ocean of that latter *miʿrāj* is as a drop in the sea and to the extent of the understanding of the generality of the Umma. For the *miʿrāj* is a breach of natural custom and none believes it but a believer. Whoever asks himself whether the *miʿrāj* was in body or in spirit, has a half-belief. Allah says *subḥān al-ladhī asrā—Glory to the One Who took His servant on a journey by night* (Banū Isrāʾīl/al-Isrāʾ 17:1), and *subḥān* means, "Do not try to weigh this matter with your mind, for it lies beyond its capacity and necessitates belief only.

The Night journey and Heavenly ascent (12YP/1BH/621CE)[2] took place with the complete person and reality of our liege lord Muhammad–upon him the blessings and peace of Allah–all the way to the highest Assembly and to that which is above the Throne, where none has reached.[3] The Messenger then abridged the narratives of the heavenly Ascent within the parameters of the understanding of people, to the point our liege lord ʿUmar asked our liege lord Abū Bakr about what the Messenger–upon him the blessings and peace of Allah–was saying of the narrative of the heavenly Ascent, and the Ṣiddīq would reply that he believes him with regard to what is more that that yet.

[1] Expansion of the discourse begun in Suhba I.21.

[2] In the 12th of the 23 historical years of Prophetship, one year before the Hijra, 621 of the Common Era.

[3] The hadiths to that effect are mass-transmitted from no less than 45 Companions as documented in al-Kattānī, *Naẓm al-mutanāthir* (pp. 207-209 §258).

So the Ṣiddīq became "a Most veracious one" because he is the first to believe[1] that Muhammad was the Messenger of Allah–upon him the blessings and peace of Allah–and the Messenger is the first who believed that *there is no god but the One God.*[2] This is why the servant's belief is invalid if he does not also say *Muhammad is the Messenger of the One God* together with *there is no god but the One God.* Thus the report of the Night ascent entered the heart of our liege lord 'Umar thanks to the Ṣiddīq's communication, and the rank of the Ṣiddīq none knows but Allah and His Messenger.

Whoever obtains the rank of *Ṣiddīqiyya* (station of veraciousness)[3] among the Awliya also becomes an inheritor of the reality of those heavenly ascents that reach 12,000 in number, and the Messenger had five heavenly ascents daily. The Messenger of Allah–upon him the blessings and peace of Allah–said, "The believer's prayer is his *mi'rāj*."[4] This is what is well-known among the Naqshbandi masters. And beyond this matter upon which none has looked other than Allah and His Messenger and the first one that gave credence to them among the first and the last, namely Abū Bakr al-Ṣiddīq,[5] from whom issues the Naqshbandi chain of transmission.

Mawlana says that those knowledges and realities are inherited from the Muhammadan heart to the heart of Abū Bakr, then to the hearts of the Ṣiddīqīn and down to our present day. This inheritance has never stopped existing in the Umma. And it is from those knowledges that Allah has invited the Messenger–upon him the blessings and peace of Allah–to the night Ascent 12,000 times for the sake of the magnification, the honor and the lavish gifting of his Umma, and that our Prophet Muhammad is the Messenger of the two dense species of the humans and the jinns, he is the Imam of the Messengers and the absolute Envoy, and his Prophethood and Messengership is not

[1] See Suhba I.21, fourth note.

[2] See Suhba I.30 also.

[3] See Suhba I.21 and glossary.

[4] Thus cited by al-Rāzī in his *Tafsīr* (1:226, al-Fātiḥa). "I heard my master Abū 'Alī al-Daqqāq–Allah be well-pleased with him–say, 'Truly our Prophet–upon him blessings and peace–has brought the Umma an ascent to heaven *'alā al-taḥqīq* (in the truest sense), for prayer for us is tantamount to the *mi'rāj*.'" Qushayrī, *al-Mi'rāj*, ed. 'Alī 'Abd al-Qādir (Cairo: Dār al-Kutub al-Ḥadītha, 1384/1964) p. 80. Abū al-Qāsim al-Qushayrī was one of Khwājā Abū 'Alī al-Farmadī's direct teachers. A Prophetic hadith states, "Whenever you see the dying person's gaze stretched and raised to the sky it is for no other reason than his state of wonder at the *mi'rāj* (heavenly ladder) on which the souls of human beings climb." Narrated from Abū Sa'īd al-Khudrī by Kharkūshī, *Sharaf al-Muṣṭafā* (2:169 §365) and Bayhaqī, *Dalā'il al-Nubuwwa* (2:391).

[5] See Suhba I.21, fourth note.

restricted to a time or a place, since his Prophethood and Messengership are from the time of *lā ilāha illā-l-Lāh* in front of which there is *Muḥammadun Rasūlu-l-Lāh.*

And is there anyone that knows from what time it was written *lā ilāha illā-l-Lāh Muḥammadun Rasūlu-l-Lāh*?[1] No one knows this but Allah. This is the meaning of *and We exalted for you your name!* (Sharḥ 94:4);[2] and the Prophet–upon him the blessings and peace of Allah–says, "I was a Prophet when Ādam was still between water and clay."[3] And this means that the Prophethood of the Messenger is from before there was a beginning until everlastingness. This wording, therefore, signifies that the nations one and all are subsumed under the flag of the Messenger, as indicated by his statement–upon him the blessings and peace of Allah, "Ādam and everyone after him are under my flag on the Day of Resurrection."[4] This also alludes to the all-inclusivity of his Prophethood.

How many are the human beings? How many are the servants of Allah whom He has honored? They are not the ones that once lived and now have gone from the time of our liege lord Ādam—and you already know that our liege lord Ādam is the last Ādam of the past ones that came before him and whose number is 124,000 Ādams whose nations came and went, and their resurrections came, and they ended up in Paradise or Hellfire, and lastly in the

[1] "Written in light on the leg of the Throne" as narrated from (i) Wahb b. Munabbih by Ibn Hishām, *Tījān* (p. 14); (ii-iii) Abū al-Dardā' and 'Alī Zayn al-'Ābidīn by Abū al-Qāsim Isḥāq b. Ibrāhīm al-Khatlī, *al-Dībāj*, ed. Ibrāhīm Ṣāliḥ (Damascus: Dār al-Bashā'ir, 1994) pp. 21-23; Abū Muḥ. al-Ḥasan b. Muḥ. b. Ḥasan al-Khallāl, *al-Majālis al-'asharat al-amālī*, ed. Majdī Fatḥī al-Sayyid (Ṭanṭā: Dār al-Ṣaḥāba, 1411/ 1990) p. 63 §65); (iv) Ibn 'Abbās by Abū Bakr Aḥmad b. Muḥammad b. Hārūn al-Khallāl, *al-Sunna*, ed. 'Aṭiyyat al-Zahrānī, 7 vols. (Riyadh: Dār al-Rāya, 1410/1989) 1:261 §316); Ḥākim, *Mustadrak* (2:671 §4227); (v) 'Umar b. al-Khaṭṭāb by Ṭabarānī, *Awsaṭ* (6:313 §6502) and *Ṣaghīr* (2:182 §992); al-Ḥākim, *Mustadrak* (2:672 §4228); Bayhaqī, *Dalā'il* (5:488-489); (vi) Abū al-Ḥamrā' by by al-Ṭabarānī, *Kabīr* (22:200 §526); (vii-viii) 'Alī and Jābir by al-Tha'labī, *Tafsīr* (al-Baqara 2:37, al-Qamar 54:55). See also Suhba I.38.

[2] "I have expanded your breast for you and relieved you of your burden and exalted your name, for I am not mentioned except you are mentioned with Me." A Prophetic *ḥadīth qudsī* (divine saying) narrated from Abū Hurayra by al-Ṭabarī (Banū Isrā'īl/ Isrā' 17:1). "He paired his name with His Name in the two testimonial phrases" per al-Bayḍāwī (*A-lam nashraḥ* 94:3).

[3] "I am the servant of Allah in the Motherbook and verily I was already the Seal of Prophets when Ādam was still kneaded in his clay." Narrated from 'Irbāḍ b. Sāriya and Abū Umāma al-Bāhilī by Aḥmad, Ibn Ḥibbān and al-Ḥākim through trustworthy narrators per al-Haythamī, *Majma' al-zawā'id* (8:221).

[4] Narrated from Abū Sa'īd al-Khudrī by al-Tirmidhī, *Sunan* (*Tafsīr, Sūrat Banī Isrā'īl, ḥasan ṣaḥīḥ*); Ibn 'Abbās by Aḥmad, *Musnad* (4:330 §2546, 4:427 §2692).

mercy of Allah, and that the Message of our Prophet–upon him the blessings and peace of Allah–is absolute for all 124,000 Ādams that have come and their respective progenies.[1]

Likewise, when our resurrection comes so that we would settle in Paradise or Hellfire, and finally in the mercy of Allah,[2] will our nurturing Lord be sitting and has creation finished, whereas He is al-Khallāq (The All-Creator)? He has said–exalted is He– *and He creates that which you do not know* (al-Naḥl 16:8).[3] The latter address is for everyone, the general public, the special public, the Prophets and the angels. Our nurturing Lord creates new universes like

[1] Cf. Muṭahhar b. Ṭāhir al-Maqdisī (d. circa 355/966), *al-Bad' wal-tārīkh*, ed. Clément Huart, 6 vols. (Paris: Ernest Leroux, 1899-1919) 2:69 (1,200 Ādams); "it was related in the books of the Shī'a from Muḥammad b. 'Alī al-Bāqir–upon him peace–that he said, 'There has passed before the Ādam that is our father *alfu alfi* (one million) Ādams or more'" per Rāzī (19:37 under al-Ḥijr 15:26) and others, in reference to Abū Ja'far Muḥammad b. 'Alī b. al-Ḥusayn b. Bābawayh al-Qummī, known as al-Shaykh al-Ṣadūq (d. 381/991), *al-Khiṣāl*, ed. Aḥmad al-Māḥūzī, 3 vols (Tehran: Nashr Ṣādiq, 2018) 3:212 (12,000 worlds), 3:215-216 (124,000 Prophets), 3:240-241 (one million worlds and one million Ādams); ditto in Ibn Bābawayh's *al-Tawḥīd*, ed. Ḥāshim al-Ḥusaynī al-Ṭahrānī (Qum: Mu'assasat al-Nashr, 1430/2009) pp. 270-271 as noted by al-Ālūsī (al-Nisā' 4:1-4); 100,000 Ādams in Ibn 'Arabī, *Futūḥāt* (Būlāq ed. 3:348, 549, ch. 390): قال لي أنا من أجدادك قلت له كم لك منذ مت فقال لي بضع وأربعون ألف سنة فقلت له فما لآدم هذا القدر من السنين فقال لي عن أي آدم تقول عن هذا الأقرب إليك أو عن غيره فتذكرت حديثاً عن رسول الله ﷺ إن الله خلق مائة ألف آدم cf. Chodkiewicz, *Sceau des saints* (p. 108 n. 2); Claude Addas, *Ibn 'Arabī ou La quête du Soufre Rouge* (Paris: Gallimard, 1989) p. 258. See also Suhba I.34.

[2] Per A'rāf 7:156, whence Ibn 'Arabī's doctrine that universal mercy follows the closure of the Judgment after heaven and hell, *Futūḥāt* (1:656, 2:408, 4:120, 137, 248); *Fuṣūṣ al-ḥikam*, ed. Abū al-'Alā 'Afīfī (Beirut: Dār al-Kitāb al-'Arabī, 1365/1946) p. 94 (quatrain at the end of the *ḥikma ismā'īliyya*), 169. "La colère divine s'éteindra au Jour du Jugement et le dernier mot appartiendra à la Miséricorde universelle (*al-raḥmat al-'āmma*). Cette universalité de la Miséricorde, qui exclut donc l'éternité des châtiments infernaux, est un des traits fondamentaux de la doctrine akbarienne." Chodkiewicz, *Sceau des saints* (p. 195). "Interprétant de manière strictement littérale les versets du Coran (par exemple 6:128, 9:68, 16:29 etc.) qui affirment l'éternité du *séjour* en Enfer mains non l'éternité du *châtiment*, Ibn 'Arabi estime que l'immensité de la Miséricorde divine–qui selon un verset coranique 'embrasse toute chose'–interdit la perpétuité des peines infernales. Les êtres voués à demeurer éternellement en Enfer y resteront effectivement. Mais, pour eux, le feu deviendra félicité." Addas, *Ibn 'Arabī* (pp. 188-189). See also Su'ād al-Ḥakīm, *al-Mu'jam al-Ṣūfī* (pp. 786-788 §442, *al-'adhāb*; 1060-1062 §612, *al-na'īm*; 1088-1091 §644, *al-nār*. Aḥmad b. Taymiyya held the vaguely similar position that the Fire of Hell goes out, for which he was pilloried. See 'Ā'isha bint Yūsuf Mannā'ī, *'Aqīdat fanā' al-nār bayn Ibni 'Arabī wa-Ibni Taymiyya* (Qatar: Jāmi'at Qaṭar, 2002). See also Suhbas I.34, ninth note; I.83; II.4.

[3] See above, Suhba I.4.

this world for all of which our liege Lord Muḥammad–upon him the blessings and peace of Allah–is the exclusive Messenger. For his Message will be inclusive of them because his Message and his Prophethood are absolutely without beginning and without end.

Just as there is no limit to Allah or to His Essence or His Attributes or His Names—together with the fact that they are 99 Names[1]—and from the perspective that there are beautiful Names for Allah to the number of atoms,[2] over each of which appears something of the creation of Allah, *and they never reckoned the One God with the reckoning that is truly His* (Anʿām 6:91, Zumar 39:67); likewise, our Messenger is the gatherer of the Names and Attributes. Among those Names are *the First and the Last and the Outward and the Inward* (al-Ḥadīd 57:3), and the Messenger is himself the Ẓāhir[3] whereas Allah is a *huwiyya* (an absolute Essence) that is impossible to fathom. So the Messenger is the gatherer of the Names and the Attributes, and whatever appears of the Attributes and the Names is from creatures, i.e. it appears from the Messenger–upon him the blessings and peace of Allah.

Our nurturing Lord invited the Messenger to the Heavenly ascent as a proclamation of the honoring of the children of Ādam, and He would also teach him of the beautiful Names of Allah to the number of every atom; and when the matter of the teaching of the beautiful Names was completed with 12,000 heavenly ascents the Messenger moved on from the life of the world for his work was finished. This is the wisdom of his moving on. Externally, it was that revelation had stopped coming to him; but among the people of spiritual reality the teaching of the beautiful Names to the Messenger had been completed through 12,000 heavenly ascents. And with every Name he learnt, a new high honor would descend upon his Umma first, and thereafter upon all the nations.

May Allah grant us and you of those lights and before moving on. This is the real honor. By the sanctity of the Beloved, by the sanctity of the Fatiha.

[1] "Per the Legislator–upon him the blessings and peace of Allah–or the narrator [of the hadith of the 99 Names]" per al-Bayḍāwī, *Muntahā al-munā* (p. 41).

[2] Cf. al-Rāzī, *Tafsīr* (al-Fātiḥa, §8: *fī baqiyyat al-mabāḥith fī asmā'i-l-Lāh, bayān anna asmā' Allāh lā tuḥṣā*). "The sound position is that the Names of Allah and the Names of His Prophet are uncountable because their respective perfections are without limit" per al-Suyūṭī, *Muʿtarak al-aqrān fī iʿjāz al-Qur'ān* (2:300).

[3] In two different senses: "outward," i.e. eminently visible to all in history, and "prevailing" over his opponents.

25
[The five stations of the heart – The station of ego-incapacity]

I seek refuge in Allah from the accursed devil
In the Name of Allah the All-Beneficent the Most Merciful
There is no power nor strength but with Allah the High, the Magnificent
Permission, O my Master, support!
Our way is companionship, and goodness is in the congregation

There are five stations in the servant's heart: *qalb* (heart); *sirr* (secret); *sirr al-sirr* (secret of the secret); *akhfā* (more hidden); *khafā'* (hiddenness). Allah has consigned in every station treasures that nothing in the universes can match. However, a *mahr* (dowry) is due on them since the Day of *"am I not your nurturing Lord?" They said yes* (al-Aʿrāf 7:172).

These treasures were given by Allah without anything in exchange. But so that His servants would not feel ashamed before their nurturing Lord He has tasked them with worshipfulness. This way the servant would say, "I did a righteous deed and this is in exchange for it," the way a generous man would order a person that was once mighty but has been brought low, telling him, "Sit and count the people, and here is your hire which I am paying you."

This is from the Attribute of generosity. For is our nurturing Lord awaiting this deed from us? Truly human beings are highly honored in the presence of their nurturing Lord without beginning: *and We have certainly honored the children of Ādam* (Banū Isrā'īl/Isrā' 17:70). And has Allah given this munificence in order to return it back to Himself? Far from it. Part of this munificence also is His statement–exalted is He–*verily those who believe and do good deeds, gardens of Paradise are ever theirs as hospitality* (al-Kahf 18:107). He did not say *sa-takūnu* (there shall be) but *kānat* (were ever). The servant will say, "I did a righteous deed and I have acquired Paradise."

However, **in the understanding of the Awliya, the people of spiritual reality are ashamed to say "we have prayed and we have fasted." Rather, out of His bounty and munificence has He bestowed these treasures. And when the right guidance of the servant has become firm and he has left the station of the ego, he will be given these treasures**. otherwise they will be kept in reserve. And when the servant attains the station of incapacity from[1] Allah

[1] *Maqām al-ʿajzi min Allah.* I.e. "before Allah and in His presence," or "against Him" in

Almighty and surrenders his state, the power of the All-True shall take its course in him and he shall be dressed with one of the Attributes of the All-True. The station of incapacity is a recognition that there is no longer any trace of the ego-faculty in the servant.

Mawlana [Shaykh ʿAbd Allah] explains the station of incapacity saying that it is like every truth that needs to be established with a conclusive argument and a demonstrative proof. The realization of this station instructs the human being to "test yourself and try with everyone else." At that time you will know when the servant is given his trust. For example, if you happen to be sitting in the room of a luxurious hotel and a beautiful girl enters showing you all her charms and sits next to you. If you keep sitting with your hands, your feet, your eyes and your heart motionless like the dead, you will be at that time at the station of incapacity. That is what proves the discourse true. It is like the dead person or the one who is in agony: if one girl lies down next to him and another on the other side, and yet he does not move, he will be at the station of incapacity and at that time he will be trusted with his treasure, because the ego has died.

And this discourse concerns the first station of belief which we ourselves have covenanted with Allah on the Day of *"am I not your nurturing Lord?" They said yes* (al-Aʿrāf 7:172). Without it there is no station of belief. This is the station of whoever says, "I believe in Allah," and without it, one's belief cannot be established. So whoever says, "I believe in Allah," and then a woman enters to be with him, who is the third present with them? Allah. But as for him who is oblivious of Allah, at that time the devil is the third one who is present with them, and his belief is belief in the devil.

The station of incapacity is for one to be incapable of implementing anything forbidden. Whoever claims incapacity and yet implements something forbidden, the care and concern of Allah move away from him and he is left to his own ego. This is why arrival is a difficult matter. It is not a matter of narration. Rather, one must be dressed with this state and this is what matters. Otherwise is no benefit comes from reading many books or memorizing them, because the examination will be with a practical test. At that time the matter will be correct and valid.

By the sanctity of the Beloved, by the sanctity of the Fatiha.

the sense of "apart from Him and His decree."

26
[Have concern for the spiritual life – The Day of Promises is continuous – *Adab*] – Modality of murid's obedience to Shaykh's order and to Allah – Shaykh Nazim's seclusion in Jaylānī's *maqām* – Story of ʿAzrāʾīl and Jaylānī – Awliya's service to murids – Shah Naqshband's service

I seek refuge in Allah from the accursed devil
In the Name of Allah the All-Beneficent the Most Merciful
There is no power nor strength but with Allah the High, the Magnificent
Permission, O my Master, support!
Our way is companionship, and goodness is in the congregation

As much as we concern ourselves with the body, still this is temporary. As for the true obligation then it is to be concerned with the life of the spirit because it remains and never dies. **The least that a believer who truly believes that there is a hereafter should do, is to take great care of the matter of his spiritual life just as he takes care of his corporeal life. Otherwise he cannot be described as truly believing in the hereafter**.

At the beginning of creation, before the children of Ādam showed up in the world, before Allah ordered for the spirits to be joined with the bodies, our nurturing Lord gathered all the spirits on a Day that is called the Day of the Promise and the solemn Covenant. And every single individual of the children of Ādam was present at that great place of witnessing with his spiritual reality, when their nurturing Lord asked them, ***"am I not your nurturing Lord?"*** whereupon all acknowledged His absolute Lordship and ***they said yes*** (al-Aʿrāf 7:172).

When the sultan of the spiritual knowers Abū Yazīd al-Bisṭāmī was buried the angels came for the questioning. When they asked him, "Who is your nurturing Lord?" He replied, "Ask Him if Abū Yazīd is His slave or not." Then he said, "It does not matter whether I say that my nurturing Lord is Allah, for He is my nurturing Lord whether I like it or not. But what matters is, is He pleased with me as a slave or not?" They said, "This is a strange thing!" He said, "Were you two present when Allah took the Covenant from His slaves and they all acknowledged His absolute Lordship?" They said no —for this is exclusive to human beings alone. He said, "Then do not interfere between me and my nurturing Lord, because He has taken my answer since that Covenant!" This answer none can give except the one from whom the veils have been lifted. **For they hear at every moment the address of the All-True, *"am I not your nurturing Lord?"* And this is the attribute of the wali. Also, the address of the All-True is without beginning and without end, it is never absent, and He waits for us to say** ***yes!***, especially in the context of what we have been ordered to do, when we obey His command and refrain from prohibitions.

Mawlana [Shaykh ʿAbd Allah al-Daghistani] would ask **where do we stand on Awliya? If we have not studied with them there is no hope of salvation for us. For Allah is saying, *and follow the path of him who has abundantly repented to Me*** (Luqmān 31:15). **And the awliya—they alone are the ones that have abundantly repented to Allah in every moment.**

The faith-system was brought on the foundation of *adab* (high manners), and if there is no *dīn* there is no *adab* for human beings. The Messenger–upon him the blessings and peace of Allah–has come as a teaching of manners for human beings: "My nurturing Lord has raised me and He has perfected my manners."[1]

Our liege lord Mūsā–upon him peace–asked, "O my nurturing Lord! What human being is accepted in Your presence?" The divine Majesty answered him, "Whoever watches everything about Me the way the tiger watches its prey. The loveliest servant is the one that obeys My command with eagerness and quickly, and with high energy." For Allah does not love laziness whether in the work of this world or the next. But you will find people skillful in the work of this life. As for the work of the hereafter, they are lazy. Yet Allah is Most Forgiving, Most Merciful. He shall set up the tent of His immense mercy on the Day of Resurrection, and you will not cease feeling ashamed in front of your nurturing Lord—why did you not obey His commands? In that spot at that time the human being will reprimand himself and will wish for a thousand deaths out of shame before the Lord of Might. This is the realm of *adab*.

[1] Narrated from (i) Ibn Masʿūd by Abū Saʿd al-Samʿānī, *Adab al-Imlā' wal-Istimlā'* per al-Suyūṭī who rated it *ṣaḥīḥ* in *al-Jāmiʿ al-Ṣaghīr* (1:32); (ii) ʿAlī b. Abī Ṭālib by al-ʿAskarī, *Amthāl* per al-Sakhāwī, *Maqāṣid* and Ibn Ṭūlūn, *al-Shadhara* (1:44-45 §42); al-Rifāʿī in *Ḥāl Ahl al-Ḥaqīqati maʿa Allāh* (Cairo 1315 ed. p. 74 §18)—which is his commentary on his own forty hadiths—per Aḥmad al-Ghumārī, *Mudāwī* (1:249-250 §310); (iii) ʿAbd al-Raḥmān al-Zuhrī by Ibn ʿAsākir per al-Suyūṭī in *Ziyādat al-Jāmiʿ al-Ṣaghīr*; (iv) Ibn ʿUmar by Abū Nuʿaym in *Tārīkh Aṣbahān*. The hadith scholars considered that its meaning is sound and true by consensus.

The murid must fly like an arrow to fulfill the order of his Shaykh so that he will learn the modality of rising to the task of serving his nurturing Lord with such speed. Allah Most High is saying [in the abovementioned verse and reports] that the one who rises to serve Him with this speed, and resorts to the holy, righteous ones the way the child resorts to his parents—that one is the loveliest of servants in His presence. So the one who is a true son and daughter or the one who is a true follower in the eyes of the righteous will be accepted in the presence of Allah,[1] and through their blessing we succeed in our life and our hereafter.

Sayyidi ʿAbd al-Qadir al-Jaylani, when he buried his murids in the grave, would be present with them when the two angels would come to question them—even if, in his outward gathering, he did not leave his seat. He would say to the angels, "Do not interrogate him. I am the one who is responsible by law. Ask me instead of him." This is a miraculous gift, and another miraculous gift given to Shaykh ʿAbd al-Qadir is that whoever pronounces his name will be part of his assembly on the Day of Resurrection. For at that time they will be the sultans, and we are considered to be their followers, so we are not qualified for the Reckoning! And by their blessing we shall enter Paradise *in shāʾ Allāh*.

Mawlana Shaykh ʿAbd Allah ordered me to enter seclusion in the *maqām* of our liege lord ʿAbd al-Qadir al-Jaylani for 40 days. I met with Sayyidi Shaykh ʿAbd al-Qadir spiritually and he spoke to me a suhba that has been engraved in my heart. In the first night that I attended in his Maqam a tall man came to me—he was the attendant of the Maqam—and said to me, "Are you Shaykh Nazim?" I said yes. He said, "Sayyidi al-Shaykh has ordered me to serve you for as long as you are in seclusion, and he showed you to me." Then he kept serving me for 40 days.

On the Day of the Promise and the Covenant, our nurturing Lord presented to our liege lord Muḥammad–upon him the blessings and peace of Allah–all human beings. He is the one that received them all before they came to this world, for he is Muḥammad the Trustworthy in the presence of his Lord! Was his trustworthiness only in this world or rather he is the Trustworthy one since before the beginning? And our nurturing Lord said to him, "Just as I have handed them over to you pure, you must return them back to me pure." And the Messenger–upon him the blessings and peace of Allah–accepted that. Then Allah disclosed to him what was going to descend on all the Umma from the beginning to the end of darknesses, what the servants would commit of crimes and unbelief. When the Messenger saw that, he asked for helpers to

[1] "The good pleasure of Allah is in the good pleasure of the parents" (Hadith).

shoulder him, so Allah showed him the souls of all the Awliya. Then He divided the Umma in batches, every wali becoming responsible for a batch, and He equipped the awliya with the lights of Prophethood found in the Muhammadan heart and made them shepherds for all the servants.

The gaze of the Awliya on their followers dates from *ʿālam al-dharr* (the world of atoms) so that they will not be harmed by the aggression of Iblīs and enemies against them. And through how many worlds they will be passing until they finally appear in this world thoroughly protected! Each wali is protecting his followers.

Mawlana spoke to us of the great virtues of Sayyidi ʿAbd al-Qadir al-Jaylani, that he was always watching his followers between the easts and the wests. Between the first look and the second look ʿAzrāʾīl seized the soul of one of his murids. He looked at the murid and found out that he had died, although his covenant was that he would obtain seven of the levels of faith. Right away, the Shaykh reached ʿAzrāʾīl in the nearest sky and asked him for the soul of his murid. He refused, saying, "Allah has ordered me to seize his soul, so how can *you* ask me to leave it?" At that time al-Jaylani took the soul of his murid by force and took from him the souls of 37 more people he had seized—for he is *mutaṣarrif* (having discretionary power) over all the universes—and he set the souls free. So one would get up while he was on his funeral bier, another would get up at the time they placed him in his grave, and so forth. ʿAzrāʾīl stopped where he stood, neither rising up the sky nor descending to the earth, until Allah addressed him, "Why are you standing still?" He replied, "By Your binding command I seized the souls of 37 men and this shaykh came and took them. His nurturing Lord said to him, "Do you not know that I entrusted him *taṣarruf* in all the universes? I have given the 37 souls he released an additional life of 37 years, after which you may seize them."

Such is the work of the Awliya. If the murid or the servant is lazy and does not have energy for worship and before he parts with life by seven breaths the Awliya pounce on him, since Iblīs comes to make him of his foot soldiers, but he runs away at the sight of the light of divine Friendship. And in the last seven breaths, wherein Allah is able to cause a long time to intervene —even seven centuries' time!—He causes it [=worship] to enter inside the seven breaths, and our nurturing Lord puts that time under the control of the wali so that he will perfect him in the space of seven breaths. Then the Shaykh calls to the Messenger–upon him the blessings and peace of Allah–that the murid has become perfect and is presently ready to receive. At that time the spiritual presence of the Messenger comes and dictates belief, saying to him: "I bear witness that there is no god but the One God and that I am Muhammad the Messenger of the One God," and the Messenger witnesses his witnessing. Once his dictation to his Umma finishes, his nurturing Lord addresses him, "Leave My servant." For at that time no one interferes between the servant and his nurturing Lord, and what happens between them is known only to Allah.

There, the servant shall see. This is why **every servant without exception sweats at the time the soul is departing, in shame before Allah when He discloses to them something of the reality of the honor which He has lavished on human beings**. This is why no one knows what ultimate end a servant experiences in the world. This is a secret and Allah knows best about it. Therefore the Shariʿa has forbidden it to pass judgment about any servant that he has died as an unbeliever, even if at times we see the sign of unbelief on the human being. However, in the space of seven breaths, the wali sees but within limits. Likewise the light of Prophethood sees even farther. As for what Allah will do with His servant then this is a secret, and it is part of the unseen that Allah knows exclusively as *no one knows the unseen but Allah* (cf. Naml 27:65).

The miraculous gifts of the Awliya are real, and **Allah does not give miraculous gifts to the awliya so that we may see them flying in the air or walking on water. He gave them miraculous gifts for the sake of the Umma. And the meaning of the *karāma* is that he has a word that will not be turned down in the presence of Allah. The Awliya use this word in order to deliver the Umma in this world and the hereafter**. Blessings, therefore, to whoever got to know a wali and has come under his canopy! Then, on the Day of the Regathering, each wali will look at his followers with *ḥaqīqat al-jadhba* (the reality of attraction), with which he will gather up his followers next to him. On that day things will be "each footstep is seventy footsteps."

Shah Naqshband was corpulent in his appearance and he had eyes like those of a horse, they were constantly rolling. There was with his gaze *ḥaqīqat al-naẓar* (the reality of sight) and he was saving the light that was in his eyes for the Day of the Regathering. Whoever entered into the realm of lights would come under his canopy. These are the Friends of Allah—so:

blessing and happiness for us, assembly of Submission, truly we have,
of immense divine care, a Pillar indestructible![1]

And whoever has no shaykh then there is still the *quṭb al-ghawth* (the spiritual Pole of help), *quṭb al-aqṭāb* (the spiritual Pole of poles), *quṭb al-irshād* (the spiritual Pole of direction), *quṭb al-mutaṣarrif* (the spiritual Pole of

[1] *Ṭūbā lanā maʿshara al-islāmi fa-inna lanā // min al-ʿināyati ruknan ghayra munhadimi*, one of Mawlana's favorite verses from the Algerian Berber poet Abū ʿAbd Allāh Muḥ. b. Saʿīd b. Ḥammād al-Ṣanhājī al-Būṣīrī's (608-696/1212-1297) *al-Kawākib al-durriyya fī madḥi khayr al-bariyya* (The pearl-like stars in the praise of the Best of creation), known as *Qaṣīdat al-Burda* (Poem of the mantle).

discretionary power), and *quṭb* [*al-bilād*] (the spiritual Pole of all regions) for the general public.[1] All of these are responsible for the generality of people and their protection.

We have now reached a time in which Resurrection is near. Allah Most High says, *the Hour has drawn near* (Qamar 54:1). So momentous events are going to take place which will boggle the minds. There will be years of difficulty for deterrence and to discipline the world. Whoever goes through such a phase will reach a time that has no precedent. The world is now on the cusp of a deep, dark tunnel. All of the Awliya are awaiting the opening of the door promised by Allah and His Messenger–upon him blessings and peace of Allah–whereby the reality of *verily We have conquered for you—a signal conquest!*—(Fatḥ 48:1) will emerge, beginning with the 15th/ 21st century, whereupon the station of *kashf* (spiritual unveiling) will take place for every servant that reaches the time of the spiritual leader of endtimes.

Therefore human beings must pay attention to the matter of their spiritual state and enter into the realm of *adab* with Allah. Let each remember he is a servant of Allah and not a servant of ego or of the devil or of whim or of the world. For there is not going to remain, until the time that the spiritual leader of endtimes appears, except those with a pure heart— *except whoever comes to the One God with a heart most pure!* (al-Shuʿarā' 26:89).

By the sanctity of the Beloved, by the sanctity of the Fatiha.

[1] On the *quṭbs* see Ibn ʿArabī, *Futūḥāt*, chapters 462-464 and the excerpt from ʿAlā' al-Dawla Simnānī's book *al-ʿUrwa* in Osman Yahya's edition of Ḥakīm al-Tirmidhī, *Khatm al-awliyā'* (p. 489).

27
Allah does not change what is in a people until they change what is in themselves – As you are, so shall your governors be – [Politics]

I seek refuge in Allah from the accursed devil
In the Name of Allah the All-Beneficent the Most Merciful
There is no power nor strength but with Allah the High, the Magnificent
Permission, O my Master, support!
Our way is companionship, and goodness is in the congregation

When the people of ʿĀd went against their Prophet Hūd–upon him peace–they went through a terrible drought. Then a big black cloud showed up on the horizon, whereupon the people started moving towards it, saying, *here is a dark cloud that will rain on us!* (al-Aḥqāf 46:24). Thus they thought that it was outwardly a raincloud of mercy, but after they gathered under it, a fire came down, burning them.

People now, because of their very bad circumstances, every time they see a dark cloud near, they say, *here is a dark cloud that will rain on us!* but it brings something uglier than what they were experiencing. Allah has mentioned in the noble Qur'ān what happened with the people of ʿĀd, al-Ayka, al-Mu'tafikāt and *Yawm al-ẓilla.*[1] People in our time, when they see a cloud or anything, they estimate that there is mercy in it. Why should there not be mercy? Because those people are persisting in their unbelief, going against their Prophets, and they never changed, and their never replaced [evildoing with uprightness]. For *verily the One God does not change what is in a people until they change what is in themselves* (Raʿd 13:11).

[1] *The people of Nūḥ lied before them, as did ʿĀd and Firʿawn of the Stakes, and Thamūd, and the people of Lūṭ, and the dwellers of al-Ayka* ʿthe thick tanglewoodʾ*! Those are the factions. Each did nothing but belie the Messengers, and so My punishment came true* (Ṣād 38:12-14); *and verily the people of al-Ayka were indeed wrongdoers, so We took revenge from them, and they are both on a high road plain to see* (Ḥijr 15:78-79); *has there not come to them the news of those before them—the people of Nūḥ, ʿĀd, Thamūd, the people of Ibrāhīm, the dwellers of Madyan and the Mu'tafikāt* ʿoverturned townsʾ*? Their Messengers came to them with the manifest signs; for never was the One God to wrong them but they themselves were wronging themselves* (Barā'a /Tawba 9:70); *so they* [=*the people of al-Ayka*=Madyan] *belied him* [=Shuʿayb] *and the punishment of Yawm al-ẓilla* ʿthe Day of the overshadowingʾ *seized them. Verily it was the punishment of a terrible day!* (al-Shuʿarā' 26:189)

Did the Persians change anything of their state?[1] Rather, they changed from bad to worse, and this is not from the effect of mercy. So the state in which they have now become is not because of a cloud raining on them but because of a fire that descends upon them. And this is just the beginning. When people do not accept to change their state and they want the changing of the *tajallī al-Ḥaqq* (divine manifestation) from *qahr* (subjugation) to *luṭf* (kindness), yet they continue to reside in the area of divine avengement, what is going to rain down on them? That dark cloud rains down subjugation on them. This is not an easy matter. What they have done is the revolution of egos, and the first revolutionary is Iblīs. He made a revolution against his nurturing Lord, and he fell into affliction and curses forever. Praise be to Allah that it is never said, "Muḥammad's revolution." Far be it from the Prophets to be "revolutionaries"!

Every human being is enslaved under his ego. However, when he becomes a servant to his nurturing Lord, Allah will put his like in authority over him: "As you are, so shall your governors be."[2] [But] it is impossible for our leaders now to be like the rightly-guided caliphs. **Our directive to people asking "when they should rise?" We say to them: whoever tries to get something before its time shall be sanctioned by being deprived of it. Until the knowledge of the Messenger appears,[3] all the matters shall run just as our nurturing Lord has arranged and there is no need of some leader or of fighting**. For everyone that goes out is definitely exposed to danger, but who can take responsibility for a single drop of blood that people might shed? This is why we must wait until deliverance comes from Allah.[4]

By the sanctity of the Beloved, by the sanctity of the Fatiha.

[1] I.e. with the 1979 Iranian revolution.

[2] A Prophetic hadith narrated from (i) Abū Bakrah by al-Quḍā'ī, *Musnad al-shihāb* (1:336) and Ḥākim in *Tārīkh Naysābūr* per Suyūṭī, *al-Durr al-manthūr*; (ii) Abū Bakr al-Ṣiddīq by Ibn Jumay' al-Ṣaydāwī, *Mu'jam al-shuyūkh* (p. 149 §104) and Daylamī in *al-Firdaws*; (iii) the *Tābi'ī* Abū Isḥāq al-Sabī'ī by al-Bayhaqī, *Shu'ab al-īmān*. Al-Ṭabarānī narrated to that effect, "Every epoch has a king whom Allah sends in the semblance of the hearts of its people." He also narrated that al-Ḥasan al-Baṣrī heard a man supplicating against al-Ḥajjāj whereupon he said to him: "Do not do that! Truly you are all the same and were treated accordingly. The only thing we fear, if al-Ḥajjāj were to be put away or die, is that apes and pigs will be made rulers over you! It has been narrated: *a'mālukum 'ummālukum* (your deeds are your workers) and as you are, so will your leaders be."

[3] I.e. until his Prophecy of the well-guided Mahdi comes true.

[4] A reference to the hadith "Waiting for deliverance is worship," narrated from Ibn Mas'ūd and 'Alī, Anas, Jābir, Ibn 'Umar and others by Tirmidhī, Ibn Abī al-Dunyā, al-Bazzār, al-Ṭabarī, al-Ḥakīm al-Tirmidhī, Ibn Ḥibbān, al-Ṭabarānī and others.

28

Meaning of being a human being – *He subjected to you what is in the skies* – [Women and men show divine beauty and majesty] – Each reality has a basis – [Secret of *mukallaf*] – Your acts are your workers – [Power of intention] – Signs of WW3

I seek refuge in Allah from the accursed devil
In the Name of Allah the All-Beneficent the Most Merciful
There is no power nor strength but with Allah the High, the Magnificent
Permission, O my Master, support!
Our way is companionship, and goodness is in the congregation

When Allah inspires a servant to be well-directed then he has certainly followed guidance. The Messenger–upon him blessings and peace–said, "The *dīn* is *naṣīḥa*."[1] I.e. the upholding of the faith-system is through transparent sincere advice, and a human being needs *naṣīḥa* because it is the cause for the emerging of inspiration to the heart, without which the servant will not follow guidance. For example in winter, cars will not start and they need someone to push them. Likewise a human being needs faithful advice so that it will push him to work. And when the human being's heart works, that will be enough for him. This is why the Messenger said, "*Dīn* is *naṣīḥa*." And we are asking for the latter.

Furthermore, listening is preferable to speaking for the human being. Allah Most High said, *and when the Qur'ān is recited, then listen to it and be silent—perhaps you will be granted mercy* (al-A'rāf 7:204). To listen to the Qur'ān is better and nobler and more beneficial. But *sam'* (hearing) is one thing and *istimā'* is another. You may *hear* the sound of cars and planes without paying any attention, but as for *listening*, then you summon your heart's presence for understanding and acceptance. This is why it is obligatory for us to **listen to the Qur'ān so that strength and spiritual power will ensue for the hearts.**

For the human being is not human only through his body; rather he has a body and a soul, too. Glory to Him Who has paired the souls with the bodies! And this is the perfection of the human being—with the marrying of the bodies with the souls. For this reason the children of Ādam have become legally tasked. When Allah married the souls with the bodies, He

[1] See Suhba I.10.

honored them by making them successors/vicegerents on the earth. More than that, the human being is the caliph of Allah Almighty in the universes, whereby our nurturing Lord is saying, *and He subjected to you what is in the heavens* (Jāthiya 45:13). Therefore, all of the upper and lower visible universes, the earths and the heavens, have been subjected.

So there exists a subjection, but do you yourself see it? This *taskhīr* (subjection) exists in its entirety for the human being, but it will not come into sight until the human being has become complete and perfected. Otherwise he remains in the image of a human being but the meanings of humanness have not yet come to light in him. For the meaning of the human being with his spiritual dimension contains and encompasses the universes, although his physical mass is insignificant next to the immensity of the universes.[1] Likewise the human being's body does not amount to anything, not even the extent of a small ant,[2] but with his spiritual power he has immense worth and status.

The human being is a human being through his meaning, not his image. In his first 40 days of gestation he is given form and his image emerges in his mother's womb. This image is easy and a small matter for Allah. However, for the human being to obtain the full meaning of humanness—this is a very difficult matter, and not easily achieved. And our nurturing Lord Almighty has subjected to the perfect human being what is in the heavens and what is in the earth, all of it![3]

Mawlana is asking, "In what thing does the human being's perfection consist?" and he answers us, **the perfection of the human being emerges once he has mastered the control of his ego. As for the one that is ruled by his ego, he will never be a complete human being or a master. People are either controlled by their egos or in control. The one that controls himself will be trustworthy in the divine presence and trusted.**

[1] "Each human being is a world in the sense of comprising the equivalents of the substances and accidents the macrocosm contains by which the Maker can be known just as He can be known through what He fashioned in the macrocosm. Hence He made studying each the same as studying the other and said *and in yourselves; can you then not see?* (Dhāriyāt 51:21). There is nothing in the world but its equivalent is found in human beings." Bayḍāwī (Fātiḥa 1:2, Baqara 2:34, Dhāriyāt 51:21). See also Ghazālī, *al-Intiṣār li-mā fīl-Iḥyā' min al-Asrār* and Rukn al-Islām Ibrāhīm b. Ismā'īl al-Ṣaffār (d. 534/1139) in *Talkhīṣ al-Adilla li-Qawā'id al-Tawḥīd*, ed. Angelika Brodersen (Beirut: Orient-Institut, 2011) p. 193. See also Suhba I.34, seventh note; I. 69, first note.

[2] Ants are astronomically stronger than human beings despite their small size.

[3] *And He made subservient to you what is in the skies and what is on earth entirely from Him* (al-Jāthiya 45:13).

Allah Most High said, *verily the soul indeed incites to evil* (Yūsuf 12:53): it commands you to do evil. It is not of the attributes of the ego to command goodness, nor was this ever conveyed whether in the Book or in the Sunna. Even if times have changed! The human being says, "We are now in the age of progress." But has your ego become ever-inciting to goodness or has it remained ever-inciting to evil? If it is still in control of you the case is closed, even if you lived to the 40th century! This is the attribute of the ego, it is always commanding evil. Do not hope for any goodness from it. **As for the one who says, "I can trust my ego," his nurturing Lord will test him with something**. This is why the Prophet–upon him the blessings and peace of Allah–raised this supplication: "O Allah, do not leave me to my ego for the blink of an eye."[1] Then what can we say about us? If he is supplicating one time, we ourselves must supplicate a thousand times.

Your ego is a perfidious traitor, cunning, unbelieving, tyrannical. All the bad attributes apply to it. Do not be on your ego's side. When you pamper it, it rules you and increases in toughness, and when you revile it, it submits to you. This is from psychology and the servants must have this knowledge about themselves. It is like the physician. If he has not recognized the illness of the patient, how can he treat him? We must know our own illnesses so that we may treat them. Otherwise, why did the Prophets come? They came to guide people.

And why this interest in people? It is because the human being is the cream of creatures, the quintessence of creatures. Among all creatures there is nothing with a more beautiful stature than the human being and a more excellent honorable status, neither in our image nor from the aspect of our spiritual reality. Even the angels are not like us. If a man had wings, would he become handsome? Even outwardly, our nurturing Lord fashioned us in such a form that it is inconceivable to any thinker to think of a more beautiful one. If we had four eyes, would that be better? People run a lot. If they had four legs, would it be better? Because in the time of progress, he has to reach his work with four legs—what do you think? In a traffic jam, if we have wings to fly off, would this be better? You cannot find better.

[1] Narrated from (i) Abū Bakrat al-Thaqafī by al-Ṭayālisī; Ibn Abī Shayba; Aḥmad; Bukhārī, *Adab al-mufrad*; Abū Dāwūd; Nasā'ī; Ṭabarānī (ii) Anas by Bazzār; Nasā'ī; Ibn Abī al-Dunyā; Ibn al-Sunnī; Ma'marī; Ḥākim; Kharā'iṭī; Ṭabarānī; Bayhaqī; (iii) Abū Hurayra by Abū Bakr al-Shāfi'ī (*Ghaylāniyyāt*); (iv) Jābir by al-Ṭabarānī; (v) Ibn 'Umar by Bazzār; Khaṭīb; Dāraquṭnī (*'Ilal*), who corrected it to (vi) 'Ubayd b. 'Umayr in *mursal* mode; and (vii) Qatāda in *mursal* mode by Ṭabarī; Wāḥidī, *Basīṭ*. The hadith was rated fair by al-Ḍiyā' in *al-Aḥādīth al-mukhtāra* and Ibn Ḥajar in *Natā'ij al-afkār*, his documentation on the hadiths of al-Nawawī's *Adkhār*.

Allah Most High said, *We have certainly created the human being in the best of proportions* (al-Tīn 95:4). This is the human species. Many people look at themselves in the mirror and do not like their form. They go to plastic surgeons. Give praise to your nurturing Lord and say, "Praise be to Allah who has made beautiful my outward form and my character, and has made me *in the form of a perfect human being* (Maryam 19:17)! Especially ladies. They are not pleased with their forms, whereas they are the outward manifestation of the beauty of the All-True. He sprinkled upon them from the ocean of beauty, while the men are the outward manifestation of the majesty of the All-True.[1] From the aspect of moral perfection, the All-True says, swearing by His Majesty and Might, *and We have certainly honored the children of Ādam* (Banū Isrā'īl/Isrā' 17:70).

From what time has your nurturing Lord honored you? Have you yourself written a petition stating, "Honor me, O my nurturing Lord"? If He had made you one of the animals that crawl, what would you have said? Is there any complaint to be found on the part of the animals that crawl? The human being is never pleased with his state—poor, rich, sick, healthy, young, old, tall, short—except he complains. You can never find someone who will reply to you, "Praise be to Allah." There is always some complaint. Look at the creatures of Allah. He has honored you by making you be, among them, of the human beings. This is ancient munificence and it is a free gift for nothing in exchange. You never asked, "O my nurturing Lord, make me one of them!" Rather, out of His bounty and generosity He has made us of the human beings.

Honored in His presence since when? You do not know, or rather we forgot. He is worshipped in truth since before the beginning and forever. And the One Who is worshipped, how is He worshipped if there is no worshipper worshipping Him? Was He an imaginary object of worship and a deity and lord in form without the existence of a worshipper? How would he be worshipped? Who was worshipping Him before the beginning? So then **the history of the human species is not 5,000 or 7,000 years in this world. No. We were a foundation.**

For everything there is a reality and for every reality there is an origin. We have a reality and we have an origin. From it we are appearing, we, the human beings that exist and are alive century after century. **This is an offshoot from the origin that is never ever distanced in the presence of Allah. Allah Almighty has always been ever worshipped without beginning and He had worshippers worshipping Him, and we are worshippers of our nurturing Lord since *al-azal* (before the beginning of time). We have covenanted with**

[1] See the words of Shaykh 'Abd al-Qādir al-Jaylāni on this in Suhba I.34 note 5.

Allah to servantship since before the beginning of time, and this is a bestowal of honor. And He has *certainly honored the children of Ādam* (Banū Isrā'īl/Isrā' 17:70) by making them, in His august presence, worshippers of His–exalted is He. This is *takrīm*, the foundation of the bestowing of honor! **And this bestowal of honor is an ocean whose depth cannot be fathomed. Even the Prophets cannot encompass, of the reality of the bestowal of honor of human beings, other than a portion.** It is all in the presence of our nurturing Lord.

This is why we have become *mukallaf* (legally tasked): because of the honoring there is legal liability. I.e. to the extent of the honor bestowed there comes legal tasking, and with that tasking comes responsibility. The President of the Republic at this time has the position of honor, so is his responsibility the same as our responsibility? We sleep until morning, there is no telephone ringing and asking for us and there are no soldiers at the door confining us, "Do not go out, do not come in." Allah Almighty has placed the servants wherever He wanted. This is why He does not entrust anyone to govern us other than our like.

Have we now understood that we are legally tasked, with what we are legally tasked? Allah has ordered us to be on the side of the truth always and forever, and our mistake is that we lean away from the side of the truth to the side of falsehood. We must be forever with the truth. Every human being is responsible for himself. Let him ask his conscience. "O my ego, are you following right guidance or whim?" Every human being knows, and if he has a conscience he must admit it. Nevertheless our nurturing Lord is Most Merciful, Most Forgiving. He is full of pardon and He loves pardoning, *and He pardons much* (al-Shūrā 42:30). Were it not the case we would have perished. What little remains? The little does not matter.

Allah Most High has made the tongue of His Prophet–upon him blessings and peace of Allah–proclaim, "Your deeds are your workers."[1] The correcting of the deeds will be the cause for the correcting of the workers. Moreover Allah Almighty has promised us, *the One God has promised those that believe and do good deeds: theirs is immense forgiveness and recompense* (Mā'ida 5:9). This is a promise most true as a great honor for the truthful believers even if they are very few. For their sake Allah shall change our state. This promise is in honor of them, *He shall indeed grant them succession in the land* (Nūr

[1] Narrated from al-Ḥasan al-Baṣrī in anonymized mode by Ṭabarānī. See Suhba I.27, third note. Cf. Baghawī, *Sharḥ al-Sunna* (14:59 §3845); Sakhāwī, *Maqāṣid* (*ka-mā takūnūn yuwallā ʿalaykum*); ʿAjlūnī, *Kashf al-khafā* (*aʿmālukum ʿummālukum*).

24:55).[1] Our forefathers and ancestors have now gone but He has promised that the grant of succession would be with us. He will change everything. And Allah is saying, *a victory from the One God and a conquest at hand. And give the glad tidings to the believers*, O Muḥammad! (Ṣaff 61:13). **When the servant repents, Allah relents towards him. If the servant changes his intention and inclines away from falsehood to the truth it is enough. If he thinks upon the matter of the truth it is sufficiency for him.**

As for the one who gives no thought—not to mention deeds—then his heart has become dead. And these ones die. This is why the days ahead of us are going to bring a divine *ghirbāl* (sieve) that is going to sift the people of our time: either an instrument of goodness or an instrument of evil. Whoever is an instrument of goodness will remain and whoever is an instrument of evil is sifted away to the afterlife. For ahead of us is coming a big massacre which the Messenger–upon him the blessings and peace of Allah–has described by saying, "The Hour [of Judgment] shall not rise until two very large factions fight one another and there will be between them *malḥamatun ʿaẓīma* (a massive slaughter). Their respective claims are one and the same."[2]

There has happened in human history fighting and wars, but what the Messenger–upon him the blessings and peace of Allah–described has not happened until now. World War I took place but the world was not two sides,[3] and in World War II they were three sides[4] that destroyed one another. Now there are two powers in the field. "The Hour shall not rise," i.e. when the Hour is near the world will be two sides, east and west facing one another, each having power over the other, preparing himself to eradicate the opposite side, and this, in relation to the proximity of the Hour, shall take place without the shadow of a doubt. "There will be between them a massive slaughter" that cannot be described.

[1] *The One God has promised those of you who believe and do righteous deeds that He shall indeed grant them succession in the land just as He granted those who were before them succession; and that He shall indeed empower for them their faith-system with which He is well-pleased for them; and that He shall indeed give them in exchange, after their fear, safety, as they worship Me without associating anything with Me. But whoever disbelieves after that, then those ones—they are the depraved* (al-Nūr 24:55).

[2] Narrated from (i) Abū Hurayra by Aḥmad (13:485 §8136); al-Bukhārī (*Manāqib, ʿAlāmāt al-Nubuwwa; Fitan, khurūj al-nār*); Muslim (*Fitan, idhā tawājaha al-Muslimān bi-sayfayhimā*); al-Baghawī, *Sharḥ al-Sunna* (15:38 §4244); (ii) Abū Saʿīd al-Khudrī by ʿAbd al-Razzāq, *Muṣannaf* (10:151 §18658); al-Ḥumaydī, *Musnad* (2;15 §766); Aḥmad (18:401 §11906); al-Baghawī, *Sharḥ al-Sunna* (10:229 §2555).

[3] Perhaps in reference to China's neutrality.

[4] The Axis, the Allies and the Soviet Union.

The people of spiritual reality say in description of that disaster that out of every seven people only one will be saved and six will die. Fourteen hundred years ago the bewilderment of that war was expressed to us as "a huge massacre."[1] Mawlana al-Shaykh ['Abd Allah al-Daghistani] says there is no precedent for it. For every seven only one will remain. That operation has to happen, because we have reached a time in which the sciences and the arts have reached the top and yet, despite that, the atheism of people has also reached the top, and with all their sciences and arts they are ignorant of the greatest of all realities, which is the existence of the One God.

They say *lā ilāha* (there is no god) but they do not say *illā-l-Lāh* (except the One God). This is what their knowledge has reached. So whoever says "there is no god" will be a person of progress and whoever says "except the One God" will be a person of backwardness. This is why Allah's punishment will not be like the one He took from the people of Nūḥ (Noah) whom He caused to die by water. The punishment against this world will be by fire.

They would fear a Day whose direness is universal (al-Insān 76:7). This is the fear of who is going to begin—American or Russia? At what time? In the morning? The daytime? At night? It is not known. Fear grips the world, a black cloud overcovers the hearts. Allah has cast terror over the servants one and all. This is the requital of whoever says "there is no god." This statement attracts Allah's punishment. Therefore there is no way out other than for the world to say "except the One God."

At the time the punishment befalls it is not known whether a president called Ahmad, or Hasan, or Ali will say *lā ilāha illā-l-Lāh* first. Will he be on the side of the truth or not? Many of the people, their heads are snakes. Thus do the people of spiritual reality see them. A black cloud is coming from the far ends of the world from four sides. It is coming and it is not far. *And the One God is warning you of Himself* (Āl 'Imrān 3:28, 30). And the first safety is to clear oneself of atheism and for one to say, "O Allah, You are my nurturing Lord, there is no god but You, You created me and I am Your slave."[2]

By the sanctity of the Beloved, by the sanctity of the Fatiha.

[1] Per the Prophetic hadith from Muʿādh b. Jabal in Aḥmad, Tirmidhī and others.

[2] A Prophetic Hadith narrated from (i) Burayda al-Aslamī by Ibn Fuḍayl al-Ḍabbī, *al-Duʿāʾ*; Aḥmad; Ibn Mājah (*Duʿāʾ, mā yadʿū bihi al-rajul idhā aṣbaḥa*); Abū Dāwūd (*Adab, mā yaqūl idhā aṣbaḥa*); al-Tirmidhī (*Daʿawāt, bāb minh*) and others; (ii) Shaddād b. Aws by Ibn Abī Shayba; Aḥmad; al-Bukhārī (*Daʿawāt, afḍal al-istighfār*); *Adab al-mufrad*; Nasāʾī (*Istiʿādha min sharri mā ṣanaʿ*) and others; (iii) Jābir by ʿAbd b. Ḥumayd; Nasāʾī, *Kubrā*; and others; (iv-vii) Abū Hurayra, Ibn ʿUmar, Ibn Masʿūd and Ibn Abzā per al-Tirmidhī.

29
[The mark of servanthood is prostration – The coming punishment]

I seek refuge in Allah from the accursed devil
In the Name of Allah the All-Beneficent the Most Merciful
There is no power nor strength but with Allah the High, the Magnificent
Permission, O my Master, support!
Our way is companionship, and goodness is in the congregation

Whoever is too stingy to prostrate to his nurturing Lord is not a true servant of his nurturing Lord. The mark of servanthood is prostration. Even if you know everything that is good and yet you do not prostrate to the One God then you are not a servant.

We have not come to this world to play. No, there is service to be done here. There is a wisdom here for whoever wants his safety. Ahead of us lie mind-boggling events, the like of Resurrection. Young men will become white-haired from them and mothers will cast off what their wombs carry, except whomever Allah protects, except whomever Allah grants mercy! This is the requital of the atheism of the world according to the reports of the All-True and the reports of the Prophet–upon him the blessings and peace of Allah.

O You besides Whom there is no refuge other than to Him! We are taking refuge in you, O my nurturing Lord! *So take flight unto the One God!* (al-Dhāriyāt 51:50). "*Lā ilāha illā-l-Lāh* is My fortress, and whoever enters My fortress is certainly safe from My punishment."[1]

By the sanctity of the Beloved, by the sanctity of the Fatiha.

[1] A divine Hadith narrated from ʿAlī b. Abī Ṭālib, from the Prophet–upon him peace –by al-Quḍāʿī, *Musnad al-shihāb* (2:323 §1451); al-Shajarī, *Amālī* (1:54-55 §185); Ibn ʿAsākir, *Tārīkh* (5:462, 7:115, 48:367) and *Muʿjam* (2:680 §845); Abū Ṭāhir al-Silafī, *Muʿjam al-safar* (pp. 141-142 §433). Cf. al-Suyūṭī, *Jāmiʿ al-ṣaghīr* (1:268, no rating).

30

Meaning of *we belong to Allah and to Him do we return* – *We exalted for you your name* – [Allah has honored our realities] – Spiritual powers are something absolute – [Prophet received Qur'ān directly] – Attribute *Mālik al-mulk* – Oneness is knowable – [Divine power over subatomic particles]

I seek refuge in Allah from the accursed devil
In the Name of Allah the All-Beneficent the Most Merciful
There is no power nor strength but with Allah the High, the Magnificent
Permission, O my Master, support!
Our way is companionship, and goodness is in the congregation

Allah alone is al-Mudabbir (the Knower and Disposer of conclusions).[1] Yet people have immense anguish in their hearts.

From every letter in the Qur'ān are manifested, through the light of *wilāya*, 24,000 meanings at the lowest level and more. And every single one of the letters is an ocean. What is with our Prophet–upon him the blessings and peace of Allah–of the meaning of the *alif*, for example, none knows, not even our liege lord Jibril–upon him peace–who is the angel of revelation. When the noble verse *kāf; hā; yā; ʿayn; ṣād* (Maryam 19:1) came down, Jibril said, *kāf*. The Messenger said, "I know." And so forth until the last of the letters. Our

[1] Narrated from Abū Hurayra through ʿAbd al-ʿAzīz b. Ḥuṣayn among the 99 Names by Abū Sulaymān Ḥamd b. Muḥ. al-Khaṭṭābī, *Sha'n al-duʿā'*, ed. Aḥmad Yūsuf al-Daqqāq, 3rd ed. (Damascus: Dār al-Thaqāfat al-ʿArabiyya, 1412/1992) pp. 98-99 §36; Ḥākim, *Mustadrak* (1:63 §42); Abū Nuʿaym, *Ṭuruq ḥadīth inna lil-Lāhi tisʿatan wa-tisʿīna ismān*, ed. Mashhūr Salmān (Medina: Maktabat al-Ghurabā', 1413/1993) p. 128 §52; al-Bayhaqī, *Asmā'* (1:32 §10) and *al-Iʿtiqād wal-hidāya ilā sabīl al-rashād ʿalā madhhab al-salaf wa-aṣḥāb al-Ḥadīth*, ed. Aḥmad Abū al-ʿAynayn (Riyadh: Dār al-Faḍīla, 1420/1999) p. 46; Ibn Ḥajar, *Takhrīj ḥadīth al-Asmā' al-ḥusnā*, ed. Mashhūr Salmān (Medina: Maktabat al-Ghurabā', 1413/1993) pp. 56-67 §40. "Name 38 [of the Names of Knowledge]: al-Mudabbir. The Qur'ān has adduced this name verbally, not nominally, and it came up in Abū Hurayra's hadith gloss through ʿAbd al-ʿAzīz b. Ḥuṣayn" per Abū Bakr Muḥammad b. ʿAbd Allāh b. Muḥ. Ibn al-ʿArabī al-Maʿāfirī al-Ishbīlī al-Mālikī, *al-Amad al-aqṣā fī sharḥ Asmā'i-l-Lāhi al-ḥusnā wa-Ṣifātihi al-ʿulā*, ed. ʿAbd Allāh al-Tawrātī and Aḥmad ʿArrūbī, 2 vols. (Tangiers and Beirut: Dār al-Ḥadīth al-Kattāniyya, 1436/ 2015) 2:260.

liege lord Jibril said, "O Muhammad! This is the first time I bring these verses. How did you know them when I myself did not know that?"[1] This is evidence that there is a connection between the Messenger–upon him the blessings and peace of Allah–and Allah Almighty which Jibril never looked upon, nor did any other Messenger. For Allah Almighty says *and verily you are indeed made to receive the Qur'ān from the side of an All-Wise, All-Knowing One* (al-Naml 27:6) directly—but in observance of high manners, through the intermediary of Jibril.

The Messenger of Allah–upon him the blessings and peace of Allah–is receiving because he is a Prophet of realities. And our bodies—are they our reality, of which Allah says, *and We have certainly honored the children of Ādam* (Banū Isrā'īl/Isrā' 17:70)?[2] And is the grant of honor [only] befalling this body? But when the body disappears, where does the honoring go? **Rather the address of the All-True befalls the reality of the children of Ādam. And far be it that the reality should disappear. However, our images take form in this world while our reality has always been and continues to be in the presence of the All-True–exalted is He**. And He says, without beginning, *We have certainly honored the children of Ādam*. The Messenger–upon him the blessings and peace of Allah–points to this [fact] with his statement, *kuntu nabiyyan wa-Ādamu bayna al-mā'i wal-ṭīn*: "I was already a Prophet when Ādam was still between water and clay."[3] *Kāna* (he was) is a verb in the past tense, i.e. before Ādam's physical frame existed.

The Messenger–upon him the blessings and peace of Allah–was a Prophet since his name was written and raised in the presence of Allah: *and We exalted for you your name* (Sharḥ 94:4). So since what time has the name of the Messenger been exalted, in light of the fact that the divine speech is *qadīm*

[1] See below, Suhba I.38.

[2] "With beautiful form, the most balanced temperament, symmetry of stature, mental discernment, power to make oneself understood through speech, signing and writing, being guided to the avenues of livelihood and the great Return, empowerment over what is on earth, mastery of industries, the channeling of celestial and terrestrial causes and results towards outcomes that benefit them, and other than that which is beyond count. Part of that is what Ibn 'Abbās mentioned, namely, that every animal takes hold of its food with its mouth except the human being, for he takes hold of it with his hand and raises it to his mouth" per Bayḍāwī under this verse. "The objection that this is also done by apes is answered by the fact that their walking on all fours gives their hands the same status as their feet" per Shihāb al-Dīn al-Khafājī, *Ḥāshiyat al-Shihāb 'alā Tafsīr al-Bayḍāwī*. Mawlana is dialoguing with such outward interpretations of this verse in a literal fashion to show there us more than what the commentaries limited themselves to.

[3] See Suhba I.24, 14th note.

(without beginning)? It means that in pre-existence his name was exalted already, and wherever it was written *lā ilāha illā-l-Lāh* (there is no god but the One God) there was in front of it *Muḥammadun Rasūlu-l-Lāh* (Muhammad is the Messenger of the One God), inseparably. The name of the Messenger–upon him the blessings and peace of Allah–was written with the Name of Allah Almighty. Likewise, since when was *lā ilāha illā-l-Lāh* written? Does anyone know? And who is the first to have confirmed as true the magnificent reality without beginning that *lā ilāha illā-l-Lāh* and witnessed to its truth? Muḥammad, the Messenger of Allah–upon him blessings and peace. And who is the first to believe that Muḥammad is the Messenger of Allah without beginning? It is Abū Bakr al-Ṣiddīq–may Allah be well-pleased with him.[1] This is why "If the faith of Abū Bakr was weighed against that of the Umma, the faith of Abū Bakr would be heavier."[2]

Was *lā ilāha illā-l-Lāh* ever something or some name without reality and without a referent? Or do the images require a reality? Just as *lā ilāha illā-l-Lāh* is the truth, *Muḥammadun Rasūlu-l-Lāh* is the truth also. And if both [statements] were present, then to whom was His Message directed on *al-yawm al-azalī* (the Day without beginning)? Over whom was He a Messenger? Over nothing? Did Allah construct the Message for His Messenger without the existence of any recipients of the Message? Is the Message a mere symbol? An image without a reality? Allah says, *verily I alone, I am the One God* (Ṭa Ha 20:14): to whom was this address in pre-existence? Was He a Lord to Himself and an object of worship for Himself? But if He is the One worshipped in truth without any worshipper, how is He worshipped? And was He a nurturing Lord in pre-existence without anything lorded over?[3]

Just as Allah on the Day without beginning caused His beloved–upon him the blessings and peace of Allah–to appear, i.e. since the time there was, in pre-existence, *lā ilāha illā-l-Lāh*, Muḥammad was the Messenger of Allah in pre-existence, likewise there was, in pre-existence, the reality of the children of Ādam and not the image. The image is for the world of possibles, and we are now in the world of possibility for which remaining and extinction are both possible. However, there is something that extinction

[1] See Suhba I.21, fourth note.

[2] A Prophetic Hadith narrated from ʿUmar, Ibn ʿUmar and Abū Bakrat al-Thaqafī as documented by al-Sakhāwī, *Maqāṣid* (*law wuzina īmānu Abī Bakr*).

[3] In the Ashʿarī school the answer is yes, "He was al-Razzāq even when there was no one to sustain, etc." (Ibn Khafīf's *Correct Islamic Doctrine*), but Mawlana points out that such Attributes, like the second phrase of the *kalima*, presuppose the existence of their referents in order for their sense to be complete.

cannot reach. This is why the divine address and the Message were made according to the realities of human beings. And just as *lā ilāha illā-l-Lāh* has always existed without beginning, likewise *Muḥammadun Rasūlu-l-Lāh* has always existed without beginning, and likewise the realities of human beings have always existed without beginning since that time, in that lordly presence, and this is never disappearing. [This is true] no matter how long you might be in this worldly life. This [worldly life] counts as nothing. For Allah has caused us to appear from the ocean of *waḥdāniyya* (oneness), and this is a manifestation tantamount to a flash of lightning. For us it will be like the length of years but in the presence of our nurturing Lord it is like a flash of lightning that has appeared and disappeared.

The matter of this universe and its like begins and ends in a moment which is beyond the comprehension of human beings, because it is the matter of *al-azal wal-abad* (beginninglessness and everlastingness). And this is one manifestation. From it these universes have appeared with human beings, with the life of this world. Likewise, on the spot, we are returning to the ocean of *waḥdāniyya* (oneness), so this means "we belong to Allah and unto Him we are returning." This happened from the ocean of power to the ocean of power; from the ocean of oneness to the ocean of oneness.

If we ask, "what is the benefit? We have existence," [the benefit is that] this knowledge has taken place. Otherwise, in the ocean of oneness we are not perceiving, whereas here, and in this manner, we have realized, because "Whoever recognizes himself has certainly recognized his nurturing Lord."[1] And this is the secret. This is the style of the beginningless Speech of Allah.

[1] A Sufi wisdom narrated from (i) Sahl al-Tustarī per Abū Nu'aym, *Ḥilya* (10:208) and (ii) Yaḥyā b. Mu'ādh al-Rāzī per Abū al-Muẓaffar Manṣūr b. Muḥammad b. 'Abd al-Jabbār al-Sam'ānī (426-489/1035-1096) in his *Qawāṭi' al-Adilla fī Uṣūl al-Fiqh*, ed. 'Abd Allāḥ Ḥāfiẓ al-Ḥakamī, 5 vols. (Riyadh: Maktabat al-Tawba 1419/1998) 3:439, both as their own statement; and (iii) cited forty times as a chainless Prophetic statement by Ibn 'Arabī (558-638/1163-1241), *Futūḥāt* incl. chapter 364 where he assimilates it to the verse *We shall make them see Our signs in the horizons and in themselves until it becomes manifest to them that it* [the Qur'ān or pure monotheism]*/he* [the Messenger]*/He* [Allah] *is the truth* (Fuṣṣilat 41:53), following Rāghib al-Aṣfahānī (d. 502/1109, see below); Sharīf al-Murtaḍā 'Alī b. al-Ḥusayn al-Mūsawī (355-436/966-1045) who cites it without chain in *Amālī al-Murtaḍā* (*Ghurar al-fawā'id wa-durar al-qalā'id*), ed. Muḥ. Abū al-Faḍl Ibrāhīm (Cairo: 'Īsā al-Bābī al-Ḥalabī, 1373/1954) p. 274; and Māwardī (364-450/974-1058), *Adab al-dunyā wal-dīn* (pp. 131, 374) in the report from 'Ā'isha, "Messenger of Allah, when does one know his nurturing Lord?" He replied, "When one knows oneself." In *al-Risāla al-Niẓāmiyya* ("What is impossible to attribute to Allah Almighty") Imam al-Ḥaramayn (419-478/1028-1085) states, "no attribute of which *jawāz* (possibility) is part can describe the exalted Godhead, for *qidam* (beginninglessness) and contingency are complete opposites. Createdness is

Al-qiwā al-rūḥaniyya* (spiritual powers) are something unlimited, whereby the spirit in *ʿālam al-iṭlāq* (the world of absoluteness) was in the *malakūt*; but Allah confined us here in the dimension of the body. This is why it became limited from all sides. Its vision, its hearing, its smelling, its taste, its touch, its knowledge, its capability all became subject to limitations. However, originally and in its own world there is no limit to the spirit's vision, because it is *of Our spirit (Anbiyā' 21:91, Taḥrīm 66:12). **For Allah has breathed of His spirit into the children of Ādam** (al-Sajda 32:9). This is why the spirit is ascribed to Allah (Banū Isrā'īl/Isrā' 17:85). And the spirit is not restricted by anything, nor is it restricted by the senses. yet we have remained confined to this existence, so everything is limited. But when the servant breaks his prison and connects with his station in the *malakūt* (world of invisible sovereignty), all his powers become limitless. There, the servant becomes capable of entering into the oceans of the Qur'ān and receive the sciences and the wisdoms.

Why did Allah make those sciences and those wisdoms and for what benefit? That is the rarest and most precious of all the kinds of knowledge. The wayfarer to Allah is in need of those sciences. It is for the sake of this that **Allah from the start put in the Qur'ān an unlimited munition or fuel that is necessary for the servant in his wayfaring to Allah**. This is why, every time the wali looks at the ocean of the Qur'ān, he draws help from it for his wayfaring to Allah. Likewise, **for each human being there is the share from the Qur'ān that he or she needs so that they might increase with it in knowledge and wisdom and light and certainty. Each according to his or her level, even the humblest level of human being has a share from the Qur'ān.**

Allah says to His Messenger–upon him the blessings and peace of Allah–*verily you are indeed made to receive the Qur'ān from the side of an All-Wise, All-Knowing One* (Naml 27:6). This receiving of the Qur'ān, does it benefit our nurturing Lord? And is this limited in time? Far from it. Therefore the Messenger has never stopped receiving, because his Message is unlimited, and also because creation is continuous and does not consist exclusively in the one that we ourselves know in this world. Likewise, there are no limits to the sovereignty of Allah as He says, *say: "O the One God, the Owner of Sovereignty!*

typified by contingency so we declare Allah transcendent above it. This is the meaning of the saying of the liege lord of humankind, upon him the blessings and peace of Allah, 'Whoever knows himself knows his nurturing Lord.' I.e. whoever knows himself to be utterly dependent, knows his Lord's utter exemption of his own [human] attributes." The very first chapter of Rāghib al-Aṣfahānī's *Tafṣīl al-nash'atayn wa-taḥṣīl al-saʿādatayn* is devoted to the congruity expressed by this wisdom.

(Āl 'Imrān 3:26). Does His sovereignty consist in this world only? Such a sovereignty would then be limited and very small, whereas it is imperative for His sovereignty to be without limit and unencompassed. When we put limits to the sovereignty of Allah His Attribute becomes the attribute of the servant. However, no one knows the limits of the sovereignty of *the Owner of Sovereignty* because it has no limits.

Our liege lord 'Abd al-Wahhāb al-Sha'rānī (d. 973/1566) mentioned that one of the people of spiritual reality would see all of this universe from top to bottom, despite its immensity, as a drop in the ocean of divine power. It did not appear to them other than as a drop. This [perception] is what makes way for the reality of pure monotheism, because people consider these worlds extremely vast. As a result it dawns on their minds to ask, "Where is Allah?" The creed of *ḥulūl* (immanence). But when these worlds appear to the wali as no more than a drop in the ocean of divine power, where would Allah be so as to be immanent in it?

And these worlds are as a drop in an ocean without shore and without bottom. In other words they are nothing. The upshot is that everything is in the ocean of divine power, and Allah Most High gathers them and causes them to appear out of the ocean of divine power. This is why there is no acquaintance of the sovereignty of Allah for any unauthorized Prophet—because not every Prophet is authorized. Allah Almighty said of our liege lord Muhammad the Messenger of Allah–upon him the blessings and peace of Allah–*indeed he saw of the signs of his nurturing Lord the greatest* (Najm 53:18). This is why *they have not reckoned the One God by His true reckoning* (al-Ḥajj 22:74). For He cannot be comprehended, because there is no way to understand the reality of His creatures in relation to His power–exalted is He! All that appears in the worlds is the trace of His power.

Science has now reached the conclusion that all the worlds go back to power or energy, i.e. a *kutla* (lump) that goes back to energy. So this origin has solved the issue. From the sea of power, Allah causes the different kinds of worlds to show. When He wants something He says, "Be!" and it appears, and He says "Be!" and it disappears. For example the icebergs in the North or the South Poles. Anytime they approach the warm sea they melt and no trace of them remains, although they possessed existence at the Pole. Likewise all the worlds fade away before divine power, but through His handiwork they appear. This is *the handiwork of the One God* (al-Naml 27:88).

So all the worlds are appearing because of one of the Attributes of Allah that cannot be limited nor can they counted. For it is impossible for His Attributes to be limited. These Attributes that we know point to the foundations, but out of each of them further Attributes branch out, pointing to the Essence. And

His Essence–exalted is He–is an absolute Essence. That is why His Attributes are absolute, and what is indicative of the Attributes of Allah is His Names. Yet His Names also cannot be given a limit, as an indication of His existing Attributes. We are only explaining a single Attribute which is the Attribute of power. We have not spoken about the rest of the Attributes. From a single Attribute, the Attribute of power, all the universes have appeared.

If we asked, "Where is Allah?" He is an absolute Essence that all ignore. None knows it, not even a Prophet. *Say, "It/He is the One God.*[1] *One*" (Ikhlāṣ 112:1)—an absolute Essence, were it not for His appearance through His Attributes. In *say, "It/He," it/He* is a substitute for *Allah*. "One" [means] in contradistinction to a multitude: one. Oneness is known, but as for *aḥadiyya* (unicity), it cannot be known. Glory to Him and exalted is He!

I was in London and there was a university professor, an atomic physicist. I asked him, "You say that every atom has a nucleus at the edge of which there a electrons revolving. And you say that between the electrons and the center there is a distance equal to that of the earth from the sun in a smaller proportion. I ask you, is this distance empty or full?" He said "I have not thought of that question before. I will think about it." I said, "Even if you think until the end of the world you will not reach a solution, because it is established that nothing can enter between the nucleus and the electrons, as it will be expelled. On top of that there are positive and negative elements around the center which are mutually attractive, but the positive ones repel one another. The nucleus stands alone and the protons carry the positive charges, but there are some rare ones that do not repel one another. What is the secret of this? For there is no exception, yet this is against the rule. And what is it that forces them to stay together? Therefore this distance that lies between them is filled with the power of Allah. This power ties them together whether they like it or not." At that time he said, *ashhadu an lā ilāha illā-l-Lāh wa-ashhadu anna Muḥammadan rasūlu-l-Lāh*, because if there is one that has power to effect such action on one of those atoms, it means he controls all atoms. And this is Allah.

By the sanctity of the Beloved, by the sanctity of the Fatiha.

[1] "The [third-person] pronoun is referring I. to the matter at hand, as when you say, *huwa Zaydun munṭaliqun* 'the fact is that Zayd is departing'; or II. to what he was asked about, i.e. 'the One regarding Whom you have asked me about, *He is the One God*.' For it was narrated the Quraysh had said, 'O Muḥammad! Describe for us your Lord unto Whom you are calling us,' whereupon it was revealed" (Bayḍāwī).

31

[12,000 heavenly Ascents] – Requital of whoever reviles Allah's servants – [Infinite] number of the beautiful Names of Allah – Tidings of the gardens to the Umma of end time – [Seeking Allah alone]

I seek refuge in Allah from the accursed devil
In the Name of Allah the All-Beneficent the Most Merciful
There is no power nor strength but with Allah the High, the Magnificent
Permission, O my Master, support!
Our way is companionship, and goodness is in the congregation

Isma'ū wa-'ū (hear and grasp) *wa-idhā wa'aytum fa-'ntafi'ū* (and once you have grasped, then benefit),[1] and hear with a hearing of acceptance so that you will benefit from what you hear, because hearing without acceptance carries no benefit!

Mawlana [Shaykh 'Abd Allah al-Daghistani] is saying that the gate of wise knowledge is opened when you realize that you are a slave of Allah and not a

[1] Alliterative proverbial, sapiential and oratorical phrases. The first is narrated from (i) Ibn Isḥāq by Ibn Hishām, *al-Tījān fī mulūk Ḥimyar*, ed. Sayyid Zayn al-'Ābidīn Mūsawī (Hyderabad: Dā'irat al-Ma'ārif al-'Uthmāniyya, 1347/1928) p. 115; (ii) Sa'd b. Abī Waqqāṣ by Abū Bakr Muḥ. b. Dāwūd b. 'Alī b. Khalaf al-Ẓāhirī, *al-Zahra*, ed. Ibrāhīm Sāmurā'ī, 2nd ed., 2 vols. (Zarqa: Maktabat al-Manār, 1406/1985) 2:504; (iii) Ibn 'Abbās by Abū 'Umar Shihāb al-Dīn Aḥmad b. Muḥammad Ibn 'Abd Rabbih al-Qurṭubī, *al-'Iqd al-Farīd*, ed. Mufīd Muḥ. Qumayḥa and 'Abd al-Majīd Tarḥīnī, 9 vols. (Beirut: Dār al-Kutub al-'Ilmiyya, 1404/1984) 4:215; al-Ṭabarānī, *al-Aḥādīth al-ṭiwāl*; Ibn 'Adī, *Kāmil* (Muḥ. b. Ḥajjāj al-Lakhmī); (iv) Ibn Mas'ūd by 'Askarī, *Awā'il* (p. 67), all four (Ibn Isḥāq, Sa'd, Ibn 'Abbās and Ibn Masūd) from the Prophet–upon him blessings and peace of Allah–from the pre-Islamic sage and poet Qiss b. Sā'ida b. Ḥudhāfa al-Iyādī (d. circa 22BH/ 600) "whom I remember seeing perched on a red camel addressing people at the market of 'Ukāẓ." Both phrases are narrated in this sequence from Ibn 'Abbās from (i) the Prophet, from Qiss b. Sā'ida as a continuation of Ibn 'Abbās' above-cited report by Abū Sa'īd Muḥ. b. 'Alī b. 'Umar al-Naqqāsh, *Funūn al-'ajā'ib fī akhbār al-māḍīn min Banī Isrā'īl wa-ghayrihim min al-'ubbād wal-zāhidīn*, ed. Ṭāriq al-Ṭanṭāwī (Cairo: Maktabat al-Furqān, [1410/1990]) p. 43 §28; al-Bayhaqī, *Dalā'il* (2:108-109); and (ii) Abū Bakr al-Ṣiddīq, from Qiss b. Sā'ida by Ibn 'Asākir, *Tārīkh* (3:428-431) as cited by Shurayshī in *Sharḥ Maqāmāt al-Ḥarīrī* (40: *al-maqāmat al-tibrīziyya, Qiss b. Sā'ida al-Iyādī*). See discussion in Ibn Ḥajar, *Iṣāba* (Qiss b. Sā'ida); Suyūṭī, *al-La'ālī' al-maṣnū'a* (*al-Anbiyā' wal-qudamā'*). Cf. Mufaḍḍal b. Muḥammad b. Ya'lā al-Ḍabbī (d. 168/785), *Amthāl al-'Arab*, ed. Iḥsān 'Abbās, 2nd ed. (Beirut: Dār al-Rā'id al-'Arabī, 1403/1983) p. 113.

slave of yourself. At that time you have certainly become a faqih possessing spiritual knowledge. And when the servant confesses that he is a servant of Allah, he has equipped himself for the task of his servanthood. Otherwise he is a slave of himself. In proportion to our confirmation [of that truth] there is for us, in the presence of Allah, reward, merit, high rank and high level. Therefore great blessings to the confirmers, and woe to the beliers!

It is not possible for the human being to know everything since knowledge is an ocean without bottom, and it is obligatory for us to believe that there is always someone who is more knowledgeable than us. Allah says, *and above every possessor of knowledge there is one with vaster knowledge* (Yūsuf 12:76). When the servant admits this matter, it becomes easy for him to confirm every truth as true. As for the one that claims that he knows everything, then that is pure ignorance for the servant does not encompass anything of knowledge other than what Allah wishes (Baqara 2:255). So we might very well hear of things which we had never heard of before and we never read about; therefore we cannot say that is rejected. Such would be the soul of foolishness, for there are so many lordly wisdoms, secrets and spiritual realities that Allah has reserved for his elect sincere servants of the Prophets and Awliya! When we hear of them we must always leave room for confirmation and say, "it might be Allah has honored His servants with these sciences and He did not give them to others, and these sciences are of the type *and whom We had taught, from Our side, a certain knowledge* (al-Kahf 18:65)."

***ʿIlm ladunnī* (knowledge from the divine side) is not acquired through reading but as a gift from Allah.**[1] When the servant is ready, Allah teaches him. We recollect with one another from the discourse of Sultan al-Awliya Shaykh ʿAbd Allah al-Daghistani, who did not read or write,[2] but who had some knowledge from the divine side. Part of what he spoke about was the sciences and secrets and spiritual realities that had taken place for the Messenger of Allah–upon him the blessings and peace of Allah–among the glad tidings of the night of the Heavenly ascent—and the subject of the Heavenly ascent is a very deep ocean. Mawlana would say that "Allah invited His Messenger–upon him the blessings and peace of Allah–to the *Miʿrāj* 12,000 times and not only one time, and we do not speak about them all, because a single report of the *Miʿrāj* was too great for the Umma, then what to say of all of them?"

Yet, despite that, there can be found those that can carry and mutually inherit from those spiritual realities from the Muhammadan heart. And that

[1] See also Suhba I.79 on the acquirability of all the stations below Prophethood.

[2] *Kāna ummiyyan.*

which the Messenger–upon him the blessings and peace of Allah–let show of the report of the *Miʿrāj* is like a drop in the sea, while the rest remained in his noble chest, and from there it moved to the chest of Abū Bakr al-Ṣiddīq. Those sciences are not cheap. Rather they are of the dearest of substances. The Messenger preserved them in his noble chest so that they would be given to those that are qualified for them, and he has fulfilled the trust. Among those to whom those sciences moved from heart to heart is our liege lord Shaykh ʿAbd Allah al-Daghistani. He says, from those spiritual intuitions, that Allah Almighty has praised His Messenger and has invited him to His exalted presence to teach him Himself, in all the ascents, about the immense honor lavished on human beings.

Here it can be seen how precious the value of human beings is in the divine presence. As for their value among people then human beings are cheap —and whoever makes the value of human beings cheap is an enemy of Allah, and Allah shall exact punishment from him in this world or on the Day of Resurrection. And whoever despises the servants of Allah will become despicable and under the feet of all on the Day of Resurrection, so that he will taste the requital of having reviled human beings.

The more Allah taught His Messenger about the great honor of human beings, the more he would give him strength and power to protect them all in the world and in the hereafter, so that none of them would be lost or fall into Iblīs' hand. For **each individual of the human beings is precious in the presence of his nurturing Lord; and the attribute of the Messenger of Allah–upon him the blessings and peace of Allah–who is the representative of the All-True is likewise, since he is the one that is high-mannered with the high manners of Allah.[1] To him also the Umma is precious.**

[1] Per the Hadith from ʿĀʾisha, "Truly his character was the Qurʾān" in Muslim (*Ṣalāt al-musāfirīn, jāmiʿ ṣalāt al-layl*); Nasāʾī (*Qiyām al-layl wa-taṭawwuʿ al-nahār; qiyām al-layl*); Aḥmad (41:314-7 §24269, 42:183 §25302, 43:15 §25813); Abū Dāwūd (*Ṭahāra, ṣalāt al-layl; Ṣalāt, abwāb qiyām al-layl*) and others. The Shāfiʿī master and Shaykh al-Islam Shihāb al-Dīn ʿUmar al-Suhrawardī (539-632/1145-1235) said in commentary of this hadith in *ʿAwārif al-maʿārif (29: fī akhlāq al-ṣūfiyya wa-sharḥ al-khuluq)*: "Know that in the statement of ʿĀʾisha, 'his character was the Qurʾān,' there is a hidden sign and subtle hint pointing to the *akhlāq al-rabbāniyya* (divine manners). She was too shy before Allah to say 'His character was the character of Allah' so she expressed the same meaning by saying 'his character was the Qurʾān' out of modesty before the glories of divine Majesty and as a cover for the actual state of affairs through fine language. This is from her superior intelligence and accomplished manners. There is also, between the sayings of Allah *We have given you Seven of the Oft-repeated and the great Qurʾān* (Ḥijr 15:87) *and truly you are of a magnificent character* (Qalam 68:4) a congruence that proclaims the saying of ʿĀʾisha, 'his character was the Qurʾān.'" See also Suhbas I.2, fifth note; I.50, last note; and I.59.

Here is an example of that. If a person has 40 children and is able to save them from the enemy, would he leave behind one of them? Likewise the Messenger: is he not able to free his Umma from the grip of Iblīs? Or is Iblīs stronger than the Messenger? When Allah is saying, *truly the guile of the devil is ever weak* (al-Nisā' 4:76)? Whereas the Messenger of Allah–upon him the blessings and peace of Allah–is supported by Allah, and he is the manifestation of the address of the All-True, "O My Beloved, ask and you shall be given!"[1] And he is the manifestation of the divine address, *and indeed soon shall your nurturing Lord give you, then you shall be pleased* (Ḍuḥā 93:5). So would he leave his Umma to Iblīs and enter Paradise, while we are at the Resurrection waiting to see where our place will be—in Paradise or Hellfire? How would he rest easy in the gardens of Paradise? This is the Messenger of Allah, and every time that his nurturing Lord invited him to the Heavenly ascent He would give him and He would say to him, "Ask, O My Beloved, and you shall be given." And this is the meaning of:

blessing and happiness for us, assembly of Submission, truly we have,
of immense divine care, a Pillar indestructible![2]

And Allah would say to His Beloved–upon him the blessings and peace of Allah–"My storehouses are for you and for your Umma, My mercy is for you and for your Umma and for My servants." And these are glad tidings.

Then Mawlana al-Shaykh explains the statement of Allah, *and to the One God belong the most beautiful Names* (A'rāf 7:180). What is the count of the Names of Allah? Mawlana says that it is to the number of atoms. To Allah belong the most beautiful Names. And what is the atom? **If the measure of one bead of atoms was taken out of the prayer-beads and the people of the whole world sat to count them until the hereafter, they would be unable to count them! What to say of these worlds and universes—how many atoms are there in them? To that number there are Names for Allah**. But human beings are unable to write down or read out the number of the atoms that are present in a single prayer-bead, so what do you think of the whole world, the heavens, the Throne and the Footstool? And the Names of Allah are to their number!

Our nurturing Lord was teaching His Messenger His most beautiful Names. When the teaching of them to the Messenger ended, the Messenger–upon him the blessings and peace of Allah–was taken back and he was 63 years of age. He became present in the *malakūt* (world of invisible sovereignty), and in the

[1] "Ask and you shall be given" is part of the hadith of the great intercession narrated from at least 17 Companions in all the main Hadith compilations.

[2] See Suhba I.26.

jabarūt (world of divine omnipotence), and in the *lāhūt* (world of Godhead), and in the *'aẓamūt* (world of divine magnificence) also.[1] Just as he was present in the world, likewise was he present in the *malakūt*. He completed his learning and he remained there. And every time the Messenger of Allah–upon him the blessings and peace of Allah–was in the *Mi'rāj* his nurturing Lord was giving him glad tidings. Among the glad tidings of the All-True to His Messenger He was telling him, **"O My Beloved! I have given you an Umma that is never sated with sinning; and I am their nurturing Lord, I am never sated of forgiving them. And just as they never tire of committing sins, likewise I never tire of substituting their sins with good deeds. *The One God shall replace their evil deeds with excellent deeds* (Furqān 25:70). This is the attribute of your Umma and this is the attribute of your nurturing Lord."**

And He would, in every *Mi'rāj*, support him with a power without any precedent. Thus has our nurturing Lord requested from His Messenger–upon him the blessings and peace of Allah–that he should supplicate and ask on behalf of his Umma. **The servant's request will always be according to the servant's knowledge of the generosity of the All-True and His munificence, and there is none in existence that has more knowledge of the All-True than our Prophet–upon him the blessings and peace of Allah–for he is the most knowledgeable of creatures.** This is why, when Allah Almighty told him, "Ask and you shall be given," the Messenger did ask, whereupon his nurturing Lord said to him, "I have given you, but is this all that you want to ask?" At that time the Messenger was shy. The All-True is saying to His Messenger, "As a special bestowal to you, in magnification of you and in honor of you, O My Beloved, I have given you ten of your Companions that already have the glad tidings of Paradise[2] (and this a magnification of the Messenger of Allah–upon him the blessings and peace of Allah), and likewise I have given you an Umma from the end of times that shall live in the time of the Mahdi–upon him peace–about whom the gardens of Paradise received the glad tidings that they will enter it."[3] The gardens of Paradise have received the glad tidings that they shall be granted the honor to host the lights of the Umma of the Beloved who will come at the end of time.

[1] "O *Ghawth al-a'ẓam*!... Every state between *nāsūt* and *jabarūt* is a Shari'a; and every state between *malakūt* and *jabarūt* is a Tariqa; and every state between *jabarūt* and *lāhūt* is a *Ḥaqīqa*." 'Alī b. 'Abd al-Malik al-Muttaqī al-Hindī, *Khamsata 'ashara maktūban lil-Shaykh 'Abd al-Qādir al-Jaylānī*, incipit, Ann Arbor, University of Michigan, Special Collections Research Center, Isl. Ms. 257.

[2] Per the Prophetic hadith, "Abū Bakr is in Paradise, 'Umar is in Paradise," etc.

[3] Narrated from Ibn 'Umar by al-Bazzār and al-Rūyānī among other Companions; also see the hadith of the victorious Group from Mu'āwiya in the two *Ṣaḥīḥs*.

This glad news for the gardens of Paradise has emerged because of those men at the end of times. When our liege lord Sharaf al-Din al-Daghistani enumerated their names he counted the first name as that of Mawlana Shaykh 'Abd Allah al-Daghistani. Mawlana explained, about the description of the gardens of Paradise, that if one of the houris extended her hand from Paradise to the nearest sky, this world would become drunk from her beauty and her lights, people would forget eating and drinking and they would become enraptured until they died. This is if she were to extend her hand to the sky. Thus there are indescribable and infinite blessings there.

Our master the Shaykh recounted that the lands of Russia are cold and olives do not thrive there. One time, he said, a man came carrying [uncured] olives for sale and a woman bought them because of Allah's praise of them in the Qur'ān. When she put one in her mouth [and chewed it], her palate smarted from the bitterness and she said, "O my nurturing Lord, is this the olive that You have praised?" She thought it was just like a fruit. Mawlana is saying, if a person were to eat a single olive from the olives of the gardens of Paradise, following which he ate of the most sumptuous food of the earth for 40 days, it would all be as if he was eating sand. What do you think of the rest of the blessings? Likewise the voices of the people of Paradise: if any human being heard them and then heard the most beautiful voices in the world he would feel sick to his stomach from the ugliness of the latter voices in comparison to the former.

If we wanted to describe the blessings of Paradise from now until the Day of Resurrection we would be unable to describe them except as "a drop in the sea." For the blessings of Paradise increase every day, and **the least level of the sovereignty of someone who enters Paradise will be to the extent of 10 times that of the whole world.**[1] *And We have more* (Qāf 50:35). Thus the bestowal from Allah is constantly increasing, and this extent itself is always increasing the more the believer's longing and love for Allah increase. It is like a tree whose yield increases the more you take from it.

Mawlana [Shaykh 'Abd Allah] is saying that the blessings of Paradise are for the general public, i.e. those that used to work as seekers of recompense and reward.[2] As for those that were worshipping Allah for His own sake without request or ulterior motive, and they do not want anything in exchange whether in this world or in the hereafter, but rather their objective is, "My

[1] Prophetic hadith of the very last of the *jahannamiyyūn* (the people of Hell that are brought into Paradise) narrated from Ibn Mas'ūd by Ibn Abī Shayba, Aḥmad, Muslim, Ibn Mājah, al-Tirmidhī and others.

[2] See Suhba I.104, fifth note.

God, You are my goal and Your good pleasure is my quest."[1] There are some among them concerning whom Allah orders His angels, "Take My servant and bring him into Paradise," but that servant will not accept. Even if they shackled him with chains and put him in Paradise, he would return to the place of the regathering. Then Allah orders for him to be taken to Paradise again. Then the servant returns again, and so forth until Allah asks him, "What do you want?" Whereupon the servant will tell Him, "O my nurturing Lord! Give Paradise to whoever was seeking it, but I did not seek it, I only sought You." Whereupon a cloud of lights will descend on him and take him, and no trace of him will remain.[2]

This is why the servant must always ask for the highest. If the servant has the chance of choosing between a tent and a palace, will he choose the tent? We are fools because we are choosing the tent and we are neglecting the palace. And these eight Paradises with their blessings which are beyond description, next to the request of that man who disappeared in the lights, are less than a tent.[3] This is why whoever has faith asks for what is most precious. And Mawlana is saying, if Allah were to open the extent of a pinhole of these stations over the eight Paradises even for a moment, the eight Paradises and their dwellers would burn away. This is why Allah has hidden them within His power and does not show them. He said–exalted is He– *verily the Godfearing are in gardens and river water, in a seating-place of truthfulness with an All-Sovereign absolutely All-Powerful* (al-Qamar 54:54-55).

By the sanctity of the Beloved, by the sanctity of the Fatiha.

[1] This is the dhikr of the murid in practice of Shaykh 'Abd al-Khāliq al-Ghujduwānī's principle of باز گشت (baz gasht) which is explained as "the rememberer's recursiveness in negation and affirmation after releasing himself to intimate conversation with this noble phrase, إلهي أنتَ مقْصُودي وَرِضَاكَ مَطْلوبي (my God, You are my goal and Your good pleasure is my quest), observing which emphasizes negation and affirmation and causes to result, in the rememberer's heart, the secret of true pure monotheism until he banishes from his view the existence of all creation" per Muḥammad Amīn al-Kurdī al-Irbilī's 1322/ 1904 book *Tanwīr al-qulūb fī mu'āmalat 'Allām al-ghuyūb*, 9th ed. (Cairo: Maṭba'at al-Sa'āda, 1372/1953) p. 507.

[2] See the Prophetic hadith of the man in the light of the Throne narrated in *mursal* mode from Abū al-Mukhāriq by Ibn Abī al-Dunyā, *al-Awliyā'*.

[3] This is established by analogy with the four schools' consensus that even the place on earth where the Prophet–upon him the blessings and peace of Allah–presently is, is "better than the Ka'ba, better than the Throne, better than the carriers of the Throne and better than Paradise" as stated by Ibn 'Aqīl al-Ḥanbalī (431-513/1040-1119) in *al-Funūn* and Ibn Qayyim al-Jawziyya in *Badā'i' al-fawā'id*. Cf. Qadi 'Iyāḍ in *al-Shifā*, al-Nawawī in *al-Majmū'* and others.

32

The hadith "Die before you die" – [Ego, whim, world and devil] – Prophets direct humankind to Allah – The faith-system is all transaction – A spiritual state is taken from its possessor – "My Companions are like the stars" – Impotence of the ulema of our time – The Mahdi shall stop war

I seek refuge in Allah from the accursed devil
In the Name of Allah the All-Beneficent the Most Merciful
There is no power nor strength but with Allah the High, the Magnificent
Permission, O my Master, support!
Our way is companionship, and goodness is in the congregation

One does not say about the Prophet–upon him the blessings and peace of Allah–that "he was a *'ābid* (worshipper)," but rather "he was His *'abd* (servant)." And it is possible for every human being to be a *'ābid*, but for one to be at the station of *'ubūdiyya* (servanthood), then such is not facilitated other than for a few. **It is possible for the worshipper to still be with his ego. But at the station of servanthood there is no ego. If one does not cause one's own ego to die then one will not be a servant to Allah. So whoever wants servanthood must agree to execute himself.**

Mawlana al-Shaykh would talk about this secret, that in the time of our liege lord 'Abd al-Qadir al-Jaylani—he was contemporary to Harun al-Rashid[1] – whoever was affiliated to our liege lord al-Jaylani was exempt from serving in the military. Everyone started to affiliate themselves to al-Jaylani. It so happened that an attack from the unbelievers took place and the Muslim army was not present because all were affiliated to our liege lord 'Abd al-Qadir. At that time Harun al-Rashid wrote to al-Jaylani[2] asking him what he should do as he was in need of the army, but he could not revoke the agreement made with al-Jaylani. Our liege lord al-Jaylani answered, "I will send you an army of unlimited size." Then our liege lord al-Jaylani ordered the public crier to call for the people to gather up, especially all those that were affiliated to him, in a

[1] Jaylāni (470-561/1077-1166) was a contemporary of the Caliph al-Mustarshid and his successor al-Rāshid bil-Lāh, while Hārūn al-Rashīd died in 193/809.

[2] See previous note.

certain large public place in Baghdad, in the center of which there was a sandhill. Our liege lord al-Jaylani set up a tent on the sandhill and when the people gathered he came out of the tent carrying a sword and said, "O my brothers! I was commanded to slaughter everyone that is affiliated to me." And he asked them to surrender themselves to be slaughtered. Whereupon a man went up and our liege lord al-Jaylani made him lie down and said to him, "Act as if you had been slaughtered." Then he slaughtered a ram next to his head and the man started to agitate his arms and legs as if he had been slaughtered. Then he called out again, "Who is next?" Seeing that, half the people fled. Then a woman climbed up. She was the wife of the one who had been "slaughtered." He slaughtered another ram next to her head. At that time all the people fled. Al-Jaylani wrote to the caliph, "O Commander of the believers! I have one murid and a half, and the rest are all soldiers for you."

This is why it is very difficult for a human being to agree to kill himself of his own will. Yet **Allah is calling out, *kill yourselves* (Baqara 2:54), and this ruling remains with respect to us, not in its same form as with the Israelites, for they were judged outwardly, but the ruling for us remains to kill the ego,**[1] since the Messenger of Allah–upon him the blessings and peace of Allah–said, "Die before you die."[2] And this is the voluntary death. Hence those who have arrived are few and the claimants are many. This is what the Sulṭān al-ʿĀrifīn Abū Yazīd al-Bisṭāmī would say: "All people are afraid of the horror

[1] As per the story of the yellow cow: "whoever wants to know his worst enemy—which strives in every way to inflict true death upon him—the way for him is to slaughter the cow of his own self" per al-Bayḍāwī, commentary on al-Baqara 2:73. see also al-Sulamī's *Ḥaqā'iq al-tafsīr* on the same verse.

[2] Cited thus by al-Qārī (*Asrār, Mirqāt, Sharḥ al-Shifā*) as a Sufi saying in the sense of dying to sins and the pleasures of the ego and narrated as a Prophetic hadith (i) from Abū Hurayra by al-Ḥākim (4:481 §8338, *ṣaḥīḥ al-isnād*; 4:486 §8357, *ṣaḥīḥ ʿalā sharṭ Muslim*) in the wordings, "You shall indeed be hand-picked the way the date is hand-picked out of the bowl, then the best of you shall indeed go away and the most evil of you shall indeed remain, until none remains but those about whom Allah does not care one whit, so die if you can" and "Woe to the Arabs from an evil that has certainly drawn near! Die if you can;" i.e. very dark times are coming; and (ii) by al-Ḥākim (4:595 §8656) from Kurayb the Mawlā of Ibn ʿAbbās who was with Ibn ʿAbbās in Ibn al-Zubayr's company in a group when Abū Hurayra joined them and said, "Die!" Ibn al-Zubayr said to him, "O Abū Hurayra! The faith-system is standing, jihad is standing, prayer, zakat, the Hajj and the fast of Ramadan are standing!" Abū Hurayra said, "[It is better] if you die before you reach [a time] when the doer of good is unable to increase in doing good and the evildoer is unable to desist from his evildoing!" Other established Prophetic narrations to that effect are, (iii-v) "Whoever of you is able to die in Medina, let him do so;" "Whoever of you is able to die debt-free, let him do so;" and "Whoever of you is able to die a pilgrim or on a raid or while transporting raiders, let him do so, and let him never die as a merchant or a tax-collector."

of the Regathering but I am eagerly waiting for my nurturing Lord to call me 'O My servant! Rise for your reckoning.' And this address intoxicates me to the end of time. I do not want anything else. Even if He put me in Hellfire I would not feel it due to the pleasure of this address. It would be enough that my nurturing Lord had made me, despite my insignificance and my weakness, His addressee!"

Allah has created the human being, from the time of Ādam to the Day of Resurrection, as possessing a spirit and possessing an ego. **As much as the centuries progress, still the nature of the ego remains the same with all its emotions, its lusts and its wants. And from the time of Ādam to this time of ours, what has directed the human being is his ego, his whim, his worldliness and his devil. In our time, has anything changed of these four directors? Never!** When the servant remains in the hand of the four directors the result shall remain the same. Then why have the Prophets come, and also why has our nurturing Lord made the first human being the first Prophet? Because the Prophets are the true director of humankind to Allah. As for the four partners—*nafs, hawā, dunyā, shayṭān*—they only direct the human being away from Allah and to one's own egocentrism. **The conflict from the time the human being has existed to our present time has been going on with these four enemies.**

Likewise the representative of the *malakūt* (world of invisible sovereignty) in the human being is his spiritual reality. This conflict is standing and permanent. And the Prophets direct the servant to Allah and to *malakūt*, because the servant's origin is from *malakūt* and his presence on earth is temporary. Allah kept renewing the vigor of humankind with the Prophets until the matter has reached to the Seal of Prophets–upon him the blessings and peace of Allah. For the Messenger has come directing all to Allah, and the world was, before his mission, in the most intense need for a peerless director without any precedent. This is why the wisdom of the All-True dictated the sending of the Seal of Prophets–upon him the blessings and peace of Allah.

Every Prophet has used three integral pillars to direct humankind, without which it is impossible to direct creatures to the Creator. **The first is the pillar of *aqīda* (the creed)**, upon which are built the other two pillars. For without creed this directing never starts. The foundation of the creed is belief, i.e. the fact that a human being believes in something will give him strength to start, regardless whether it is a belief in falsehood or a belief in the truth. Do you not see the people of falsehood in our time, how they believe in their falsehood even more than the believers believe in the truth? Communists believe in that notorious Jew[1]—and what believer believes in the Book of Allah the way Communists believe in Marx? From that principle they start with strength in order to rule the world, although they deny eternal life. Despite that, they sacrifice their lives for the sake of their creed. We believe in Allah and in the last Day, yet there is not found among us this kind of self-sacrifice for Allah and His Messenger–upon him blessings and peace of Allah–and His Book. This is why the first thing that must be done is to instill the creed into young Muslims, for without creed there is no deed, since "the faith-system is all transaction."[2] **Then *ʿamal* (practice) comes after the creed, then *akhlāq* (high manners) that direct people to Allah.**

The Prophets came to teach people how they should interact with one another and how their manners should be so that, by virtue of these manners, they would direct themselves to Allah. This cannot be realized until the human being becomes firmly grounded in the creed. However, **we need for those who call to Allah to be from those whose faith and creed are at the level of *yaqīn* (certainty), because what matters in creed is the strength of certainty, not just verbal narrative. Many are those who declare verbally, but confirmation has not yet taken place in their hearts!** And this affects the second pillar. The creed that necessitates certainty does not happen for a person through reading, but rather one needs to receive it from the people of certainty. For **certainty is a state among other states, and a state does not move through hearsay. A state moves from the possessor of that state to the other person.** It is like an empty battery when you connect it with a wire to a full battery. Electricity runs through it and it fills up without a sound. Likewise the state does not move other than from the possessor of that state to the heart of the seeker.

[1] Leon Trotsky or Karl Marx.

[2] Ghazālī, *Iḥyā' 'ulūm al-dīn*, Book of *murāqaba* and *muḥāsaba*: "We mean by the *dīn* (faith-system) the *muʿāmala* (transacting) that takes place between the servant and his nurturing Lord." See e.g. Ibn 'Āshūr, *Taḥrīr* ('Ankabūt 29:65; Zumar 39:2; Ghāfir 40:65). As for the faith-system consisting in the transacting that takes place between the servant and other creatures it is supported by various Quranic verses such as *and speak excellence to people* (Baqara 2:83); *the One God commands you to deliver trusts to their rightful owners, and, when you judge between people, to judge with justice* (Nisā' 4:58); and hadiths such as "I was only sent to complete the highest of manners" (narrated from (i) Abū Hurayra by al-Bazzār, al-Quḍā'ī, al-Bayhaqī; (ii) Jābir by al-Baghawī, *Sharḥ al-Sunna*); "The most perfect of believers is the most excellent of them in character" (narrated from (i) Abū Sa'īd al-Khudrī by Ibn Wahb; (ii-iii) Abū Hurayra and 'Ā'isha by Ibn Abī Shayba and Aḥmad; (iv) Jābir by Ibn Abī Shayba; (v) Anas from al-Bukhārī, *al-Tārīkh al-kabīr*).

If the Book of Allah was sufficient without [the need for] a Prophet to be sent Allah would have sent down a Book like scrolls and He would have ordered people, "Take the scrolls and read them and practice what is in them." He would not have sent the Prophets. So for what reason did He send the Prophets together with the Scriptures? In the Book there are letters that move to the tongue whereas when it comes to the state, then it moves from the heart to the heart. That is why the Messenger–upon him the blessings and peace of Allah–was the speaking Qur'ān while the Companions were taking from the states of the Prophet and from the company of the Prophet. They became oceans of knowledge outwardly and inwardly, in action and in speech, having inherited from the Messenger.

The Messenger–upon him the blessings and peace of Allah–was always in a state of witnessing and there was no veil between him and his nurturing Lord, or between him and the *malakūt* and *jabarūt*. Rather he was constantly connected. That is why his state would move to the Companions, and they became a part of the ocean of the Prophet. Each one of them would represent the perfection of the Messenger. This is why they are an assembly whom the Messenger–upon him the blessings and peace of Allah–highly praised by saying, "My Companions are as the stars; whomever you take from, you shall be well-guided."[1] The Umma needs, in every age, men of truth who are constantly in a state of presence with the All-True and a state of presence with the Messenger–upon him the blessings and peace of Allah–and whom this world does not distract.

Whoever has a heart distracted with the world, his state and his sickness are going to contaminate those that are listening to him. This is why he has no power to direct. His tongue speaks but his heart directs him in the direction opposite to what he says. As for him whose heart is wholly directed towards Allah and towards His Messenger, his state will be transmitted to

[1] Narrated from (i) Jābir by al-Dāraquṭnī in *Faḍā'il al-Ṣaḥāba* and *al-Mu'talif wal-mukhtalif* (4:1778), also (ii-vi) Abū Hurayra, 'Umar, Ibn 'Umar, Ibn 'Abbās, Anas; and (vii) Jawwāb b. 'Ubayd Allāh in *mursal* mode. Laknawī declared it *ṣaḥīḥ* (sound) in *Tuḥfat al-akhyār*. Ṣāghānī rated it *ḥasan* (fair) per Sharaf al-Dīn al-Ṭībī and others in their commentaries on the *Mishkāt*, followed by 'Abd al-Fattāḥ Abū Ghudda. Al-Bayhaqī in *al-I'tiqād* and Ibn Ḥajar in *Talkhīṣ al-ḥabīr* said it is supported by the sound hadith narrated from Abū Mūsā al-Ash'arī by Muslim and Aḥmad, "**The stars are trustees for the sky** and when the stars wane, the sky is brought what was promised [*i.e.* of the corruption of the world and the coming of the Day of Judgment]; and I am a trustee for my Companions, so when I go, my Companions will be brought what was promised them [*i.e.* of *fitna* and division]; **and my Companions are trustees for my nation**, so when they go my nation will be brought what was promised to you [*i.e.* following *hawā* and vying for *dunyā*]."

those that listen to him while he himself is journeying to Allah. This type is all but lost in our time until Allah delivers the Umma from its predicament. For our Prophet is the Prophet of the end of times and the Hour shall come in the time of his Umma.

The Messenger is a truthful reporter and he has informed us about the signs of the Hour. The appearance of the signs of the Hour requires that the lights of sainthood be extinguished so that people will remain in complete darkness and the preconditions of the Hour will spread, then the Resurrection will come. We now live in the time of strifes and darkness. This is why the Umma needs special care from its nurturing Lord, and that has been promised by our Prophet–upon him the blessings and peace of Allah–namely that at the end of times, "even if there remains only one day, Allah shall cause the renewer of the faith to appear in one night"[1] so that submission will prevail over the world and *over faithful obedience in its entirety* (al-Tawba 9:33, al-Fatḥ 48:28, al-Ṣaff 61:9). And we are waiting. And this corruption is part of the signs of the Hour. It cannot be removed. Even if all the ulema gather up to repel this trend, what they do will be like someone attempting to block the flood of a huge river with straw.

The aptest way to describe the ulema of this time is incapacity. They cannot do anything at all. Only He that opened that door can close it, and everything will be finished. Otherwise the matter is completely out of the hands of human beings, and it is out of the hands of the ulema, the presidents and the kings. It is completely impossible for any king or president to enforce his will as he wants, for **they are predetermined and they do not have any choice**. This is the true description of how the world is going. As long as this trend is going, there is an overriding wisdom that is part of His judgment–exalted is He–so that every human being's foulness that is hidden in his heart must appear. Then Allah will remove it from them in honor of the Prophet by means of events, wars and strifes. Allah has appointed an expiation for this Umma in this world before the hereafter, from the perspective that evil will devour itself until goodness comes.

Allah Most High has said, *the Hour has drawn near* (al-Qamar 54:1). This verse came down 1,400 years ago. That long ago, it had already drawn near! So in this present time what has happened? How much closer have we come? Also of the signs of the Hour is the adornment of this world, *until, when the*

[1] The two clauses are from two separate hadiths narrated from I. Muḥammad b. al-Ḥanafiyya, Ibn 'Abbās, 'Alī b. Abī Ṭālib and Ibn Mas'ūd by al-Dānī, *al-Sunan al-wārida fil-fitan*; and II. 'Alī b. Abī Ṭālib by Nu'aym b. Ḥammad, *al-Fitan* and al-Dānī, *al-Sunan al-wārida fil-fitan*. See Ibn Kathīr, *al-Nihāya fil-fitan wal-malāḥim*.

land has put on its adornment and has decked itself (Yūnus 10:24).[1] This is why we are the Umma of the end of time. Also of the signs of the Hour is the appearance of our liege lord the Mahdi (well-guided one)–upon him peace–and the coming out of the Dajjal (arch-liar), then ʿĪsā (Jesus), then Yaʾjūj and Maʾjūj (Gog and Magog). Once the first of these signs shows up the rest will follow in succession like the string of prayer-beads. Between us and the Mahdi there is a world war. When the world war befalls—as the Prophet–upon him the blessings and peace of Allah–said, "A huge slaughter shall take place"[2] in which billions will die and not just millions like previously, and out of every seven only one will remain.

Nations are now ready to enter the war. Now, when small countries fight one another, major powers intervene and stop them; but when the major powers go to war against one another who will stop them? At that time we will need a special care from our nurturing Lord, whereby the Mahdi shall raise the *takbīr* after three months of war. At the very first *takbīr* all the nuclear weapons the people of unbelief rely upon will be neutralized—because the next war is coming for the destruction of unbelief and atheism. When the killing reaches a certain fixed count our liege lord the Mahdi will raise the *takbīr*, then the war shall stop, just as our liege lord Mūsā (Moses) did when he prostrated with our liege lord Hārūn (Aaron) and asked for the fighting to stop. Their nurturing Lord answered their prayer. The number of those that had been determined to be killed had been reached. In the third world war, when the number of those that had been determined to be killed will be reached, Allah shall command the Mahdi to raise the *takbīr* and stop the war that took place in requital of the people that are saying "there is no god," which will be six in every seven people. This is why Allah has empowered them over one another: as a requital for what they are saying. This is the forthcoming result.

May Allah protect us and you. By the sanctity of the Beloved, by the sanctity of the Fatiha.

[1] The continuation states, *and its dwellers think they are controlling it, Our command visits it by night or by day, then We leave it rooted out, as if it was never there the day before. Thus do We detail the signs for a people that reflect.*

[2] See Suhba I.28, eighth note.

33
The meaning of *sulṭān al-dhikr* (the arch-authority of the remembrance of Allah)

I seek refuge in Allah from the accursed devil
In the Name of Allah the All-Beneficent the Most Merciful
There is no power nor strength but with Allah the High, the Magnificent
Permission, O my Master, support!
Our way is companionship, and goodness is in the congregation

Of our honorable liege lords are those that remember Allah with *sulṭān al-dhikr. Sulṭān al-dhikr* takes place when one says *lā ilāha* (there is no god) until one reaches *illā-l-Lāh* (but the One God), and how much there is of *mā siwā-l-Lāh* (something other than the One God), and as many as there are in them of atoms, one gathers them up and encompasses them with the wisdom of existence, i.e. that wisdom by which Allah has brought them into existence: *there is no god* that brought these universes into existence with these wisdoms *other than the One God* Who has brought them into existence. With the wisdom itself his gaze takes control and at that very moment [of saying] *lā ilāha* he gathers all, *illā-l-Lāh* he encompasses the wisdom of their existence.

Our liege lord Khālid al-Baghdādī Dhū al-Janāḥayn (the two-winged)[1] has practiced remembrance with *sultān al-dhikr* six times. As for our liege lord Jamāl al-Dīn al-Ghumūqī al-Ḥusaynī—nine times. Our liege lord Shah Naqshband would make dhikr with *sultān al-dhikr* in every step he walked. As for our liege lord Sharaf al-Dīn al-Dāghistānī, he would make a *khatm* (complete reading) of the Qur'ān in every breath of his, and conclude with *sulṭān al-dhikr* and receive from every letter of the noble Qur'ān three meanings that did not resemble [those of] the next letter. **As for Mawlana Shaykh ʿAbd Allah al-Daghistani then no one knows his station. His teacher our liege lord Sharaf al-Din al-Daghistani would say of him, "Starting with myself, how many awliya can be found that do not even approach the station that Shaykh ʿAbd Allah al-Daghistani has reached!"**

May Allah benefit us with the blessing of their holy breaths. Āmīn! By the sanctity of the Fatiha.

[1] I.e. of the outer knowledge and the inward knowledge as stated by Mawlānā Khālid al-Baghdādī's student Muḥammad Amīn Ibn ʿĀbidīn in his catalogue of teachers entitled *ʿAqd al-la'ālī fil-asānīd al-ʿawālī.*

34

Unbelief is of an inessential nature – [Men of the unseen – *Sufi* means pure – Station of absoluteness – Human souls are uncompassable – 124k Ādams] – *Mālik yawm al-dīn* – Prophet's test of Jibril – *The piercing star* – Prophet has the absolute Message – [Perpetual creation] – Rifaʿi's spiritual unveiling

I seek refuge in Allah from the accursed devil
In the Name of Allah the All-Beneficent the Most Merciful
There is no power nor strength but with Allah the High, the Magnificent
Permission, O my Master, support!
Our way is companionship, and goodness is in the congregation

What is originally the creed of the people of Scripture? Belief. What is originally the creed of humankind? Belief also. **Unbelief is *ʿāriḍī ṭāriʾ*** (inessential, passing).[1] **It is baseless! For there was no servant but all were believers in their nurturing Lord from the Day of *"am I not your nurturing Lord?" They said yes* (Aʿrāf 7:172). And each is born with this faith**![2] This

[1] This doctrinal *qāʿida* (foundational rule) of *Ahl al-Sunna wal-Jamāʿa* is stated time and again by Imam al-Bayḍāwī in his *Tafsīr*. e.g. *in Your hand is all goodness; verily You are All-Powerful over all things* (Āl ʿImrān 3:26): "He mentioned goodness by itself (i) because it is decreed *bil-dhāt* (essentially) while evil is decreed *bil-ʿaraḍ* (unessentially), as no particular evil exists except it must imply some universal good;" *verily your nurturing Lord is swift in punishment and verily He is indeed Most Forgiving, Most Merciful* (al-Anʿām 6:165): "He described punishment without ascribing the latter to Himself whereas He described Himself as forgiving and added to that His being described as merciful, superadding the syntax of intensity and the emphatic *lām* [in *la-ghafūr* (indeed Most Forgiving)] as a notification that He is *ghafūrun bil-dhāt muʿāqib bil-ʿaraḍ* (essentially forgiving, occasionally punishing), abundant in mercy and forceful in it, abundant in punishment but sparing in it." See also under Aʿrāf 7:131; Yūnus 10:4, 10:107; Qaṣaṣ 28:37; ʿAnkabūt 29:44; Rūm 30:45; Fatḥ 48:14.

[2] Per the Prophetic hadith "Every newborn is born in conformity with the *fiṭra* (primordial state / disposition / nature) of *islām* (submission) then, when they reach the age of reason, their parents make Jews or Christians or Zoroastrians of them." Narrated from (i) al-Aswad b. Sarīʿ by Ibn Ḥibbān, *Ṣaḥīḥ* (1:341-342 §132); al-Ṭabarānī, *Kabīr* (1:283 §827); (ii) al-Zuhrī as his own statement by Bukhārī (*Janāʾiz, idhā aslama al-ṣabiyyu fa-māt*). Its basis is in Mālik's *Muwaṭṭaʾ*, Aḥmad's *Musnad*, the two *Ṣaḥīḥ*s and

is why whatever child of the people of Scripture dies before reaching puberty will be in Paradise while part of those who die after puberty are dressed with the vestment of unbelief—and this is justice from Allah—or dressed with the vestment of faith—and this is bounty from Him.[1]

The servant is between the bounty of Allah and His justice. This is why the dreams of the people of Scripture might be true and might be mercy-bearing, and because of them they might ultimately be guided to the truth, and many of them conceal true belief in their consciences and preserve it, but they find no opportunity to show it and they die with this belief concealed in themselves. The question is asked with what *sāʾiq* (conveying angel)[2] will this person be adduced?[3] The answer is, with the conveying angel of [the carriers of] faith, because belief is a foundation, and belief is averse to unbelief, and in the hearts of the people of Scripture, because the foundation therein is belief, they will lean towards belief even if there is outwardly unbelief in them. This is an important matter.

A person might come to us and identify himself as So and so, but he might be someone you do not recognize. More than that, he might be one of the men of the unseen who has come for some important matter. For it is possible for the men of the unseen to appear in any form, and to have a sanction to meet at this very time and in this very form, without permission to meet other than in this place to say what he wants, so the manifestation that he needs takes place for him in order to fulfill his mission. Our liege lord ʿAbd al-Qadir al-Jaylānī asked to meet with one of them but he was unable to. It is also possible for the men of the unseen to appear in a form to which no one pays any attention. You [think you] recognize it as being So and so but in fact he is not the one that you know.

A man of the unseen might appear in different forms, for example there was once a qadi in a certain country where there dwelled a Sufi who was *ṣāfī* (pure). "Sufi" is an allusion to one's inward purity and a servant will never be a Sufi until he is first *ṣāfī*. Now the qadi did not like that Sufi. He would say that he was mad and he would say, "when I see him I shall give him a lesson so that he will know his limit." One day the Qadi was walking on a long alleyway. He looked up and saw the Sufi walking in his direction in the distance. He said to himself, "now I will give him a lesson." Then he looked again and

others as narrated from (iii) Abū Hurayra.

[1] See to that effect the chapter on children in al-Bayhaqī's *al-Iʿtiqād.*

[2] *And each soul has come, and with it a conveyor and a witness* (Qāf 50:21).

[3] I.e. the "part of those [of the people of Scripture] who die after puberty" that are then "dressed with the vestment of faith."

saw him in the form of a ploughman. There was no one but the two of them in the alley. Then he looked again and now he saw him in the form of a soldier! He wondered and thought, "where did the other two go?" He continued to walk until he reached his side and now he found him in the form of a merchant. At that time the Sufi addressed him and said, "according to what form will you pass judgment, O qadi?" The qadi was dumbstruck and asked the other man's forgiveness. This story signifies that the men of the unseen are able to re-form themselves in different forms and in different places wherever they are ordered, because they have become part of *majāl al-iṭlāq* (the realm of absoluteness), i.e. outside of time and place.

This is why, when the servants show pure sincerity to their nurturing Lord–may He be exalted–He dresses them with something of His Attributes —the attribute of absoluteness. That is because their origin in the realm of being is at the station of absoluteness, unrestricted by any time or place, and they are able to appear in the shapes and the places they want. Most of the time they are found in the visible world of creation or the world of invisible sovereignty. **It is their miraculous gift for them to be present in the *malakūt* because they cut themselves off their own egos and present them to Allah as a self-sacrifice. They are well-pleased with Allah in respect of His rulings over them and no will of theirs remains with them. They made themselves die so that no trace remains of what was left of their existence. At that time some of the lights of the All-True conquer them and give them a stable, firm existence that neither changes nor wanes, and that is their miraculous gift.**

Allah caused them to be joined to their spiritual reality. He did not leave them in their forms but He returned them to their realities since before time. For **human beings possess realities that are immutable, and the realities of human beings are highly honored in the presence of their nurturing Lord since before time and everlastingly forever**. Furthermore, no one can be excluded from the compass of that divine address, *and We have certainly honored the children of Ādam* (Banū Isrā'īl/Isrā' 17:70). And just as there is no *ḥaṣr* (encompassment) for Allah–exalted is He–likewise, the spirits of human beings cannot be encompassed, and **every individual among human beings is an appearance for one of the beautiful Names of Allah and under the upbringing of that Name**. When the servant reaches the knowledge of that Name and mentions it he becomes *rabbānī* (lordly). He says to a thing, "Be" and it will be.[1] Likewise that human being enters into the ocean of the mercy

[1] Cited from ancient Scripture by Shaykh 'Abd al-Qādir al-Jaylānī, *Futūḥ al-ghayb* (Discourse 13 before the end; Discourse 16 at the end; Discourse 46 at the end), i.e. as the believer is given to do in Paradise per the Prophetic hadiths to that effect.

of that Name and the garden of Paradise that was made specific to that Name of the All-True–exalted is He.[1] There exist types of secrets and realities that cannot be expressed with the tongue. As for the heart, it gathers up the realities and the secrets. To Allah belong momentous matters with His servants. *Every day He is in a great affair* (al-Raḥmān 55:29).

Mawlana [Shaykh ʿAbd Allah al-Daghistani] says that **this century comes in sequel to our liege lord Ādam and his progeny whose turn is nearly coming to an end. Inspiration is coming to us to speak out of those spiritual intuitions as a consolation because souls have ended up in darkness in our time. They find no rest unless they can enter into the oceans of such spiritual realities. For spirits relax and hearts find peace at the news of heavens.** And the role of our liege lord Ādam–upon him peace–and his children has almost finished. For the people of spiritual truth Ādam is but one of the Ādams whose number reaches up to 124,000 Ādams.[2] Each one of them was brought into existence by the All-True, then He produced a progeny from him, and He appointed for him and his progeny a fixed time in one of the worlds just like this world of ours. Messengers have come to them and their resurrection took place, and they were regathered and the Owner of the Day of Reckoning passed judgment on them, then He put one section of them in Paradise, and one section He doomed to Hellfire. Then they both ended up thus in the mercy of Allah.[3] Then came the turn of the next Ādam, then Allah appointed for him his progeny and a time and a resurrection and so forth.

I have asked one of the ulema about Allah Almighty describing Himself as *the Owner of the Day of Reckoning* (Fātiḥa 1:4): is Allah "going to be" the Owner of the Day of Reckoning or was He so before? Will this attribute by which He is described take place in the future, or has He been so from pre-eternity? Has no Day of Reckoning yet passed for Him? So He became the Owner of the Day of Reckoning without any Day of Reckoning coming to pass, and it has not yet been realized for Him as He is waiting for the Day of Resurrection so that He "will be" the Owner of the Day of Reckoning? Or was

[1] Cf. "the human being is <the copy of the Motherbook, and> the mirror of the All-True–in majesty and beauty, and the totality of the universe—and he is named 'a complete universe' and 'a macrocosm'—because Allah created him 'with His hands' (Ṣād 38:75) i.e. with the Attributes of dominance and kindness... so that he will be the manifestation of the comprehensive Name contrary to the rest of things, for they were created 'with a single hand,' i.e. with a single Attribute" per Muḥyī al-Dīn Abū Muḥ. 'Abd al-Qādir al-Jaylānī, *Sirr al-asrār wa-maẓhar al-anwār* (Cairo: al-Maṭbaʿat al-Bahiyya, 1374/1955) pp. 52-53. (Bracketed phrase missing from the latter ed.). See also Suhba I.28, second note; I. 69, first note.

[2] See Suhba I.24.

[3] See Suhba I.24, 17th note.

He so before? And the attribute of the Owner of the Day of Reckoning, is it a symbol or a certainty? And if He was not in pre-eternity the Owner of the Day of Reckoning then it is a symbol. Furthermore, after the Day of Resurrection, will Allah "cast off this Attribute" and will it no longer be the case that He will be the Owner of the Day of Reckoning? According to the ulema of outward knowledge He casts off this Attribute!

The reality is that in every moment there rises the Resurrection of a people, and a people are regathered. This is why there is no end and no limit to human beings. And as for us our turn has come for Resurrection, and we are one part of the children of Ādam whom Allah has highly honored, but no one know the first of them or the last of them.

Mawlana Shaykh is saying that our liege lord the Messenger of Allah–upon him the blessings and peace of Allah–was standing in front of his Umma on the night of the heavenly Ascent with Jibril by his side. His nurturing Lord had made him stand to show him a magnificent sight. In front of the most noble Messenger were passing mounted riders with their weapons at the ready, each row of them extending beyond the reach of eyesight, and they were passing with the speed of lightning for the Messenger's review. The Messenger–upon him the blessings and peace of Allah–asked, "Who are these, O Jibril?" as a test to see whether Jibril's knowledge had reached this or not. He said, "You know best, Messenger of Allah, but I have been seeing them marching in this way ever since the time that I was created, and I have never seen the first of them or the last of them. There the verse came down, *and none knows the legions of your nurturing Lord but He* (Muddaththir 74:31). Then a star appeared. The Messenger asked Jibril what this star was. Jibril said, "Messenger of Allah, this star appears once every 70,000 years, and since Allah created me I have seen it 70,000 times, and I do not know how many times it had already appeared before the time that I was created." At that time the Messenger–upon him the blessings and peace of Allah–said, "This star is your companion O Jibril,"[1] and he was alluding to the *ḥaqīqa Muḥammadiyya* (Muhammadan Reality)—for if the Muhammadan Reality appeared, would this universe remain [seen apart] from its lights? It is also indicating the age of our liege lord Jibril[2] and the numerousness of the marching soldiers that are unending. Allah is the One that is worshipped in truth, and He is our nurturing Lord, and we are His slaves!

Mawlana is saying that our Messenger Muḥammad–upon him the blessings and peace of Allah–is the owner of the absolute Message, from the perspective

[1] See Suhba I.88, penultimate note.

[2] $70{,}000^2 + 1400 = 4{,}900{,}001{,}400$ years or more.

that the original Message of all of the Prophets comes from the Message of *Muḥammadun Rasūlu-l-Lāh*–upon him the blessings and peace of Allah. Likewise, how many will Allah created –and forever—of worlds and Ādams that are also subsumed under the mercy of Allah, either Paradise or Hellfire, and the upshot is that **the people of Hellfire are also subsumed under the mercy of Allah, and "there shall come a day when Gehenna itself will see its open doors agitated by the winds,"[1] because even the Fire is surrounded with mercy**. Allah shall put whoever is in the abyss of Gehenna in worlds wherein they are senseless, and the punishment of Hellfire will change if they are to remain therein, since Allah says "My mercy has primacy over My wrath;"[2] *and My mercy encompasses everything* (al-Aʿrāf 7:156). The Fire is one of the things. Were it not for its encompassment by Allah's mercy, it would have burnt up the heavens and the earths! And creation is perpetual: *and He creates that which you do not know* (al-Naḥl 16:8).

Allah shall gather up the first and the last that are specific to a single Ādam. Our liege lord Ahmad al-Rifaʿi says that there is in the fourth sky an ocean whose beginning cannot be distinguished from its end, and at each of its grains of sand there is a universe such as our world, each one of which has a resurrection, a regathering, a Paradise and a Hell. That is a spiritual unveiling for our liege lord al-Rifaʿi concerning the skies.

Thus whoever appears of the children of Ādam shall eventually settle in the mercy of Allah in Paradise and in the good pleasure of Allah forever, and they shall be in perpetual elevation, for Allah says, *you* [pl.] *shall indeed ride layer upon layer* (Inshiqāq 84:19), i.e. in perpetual rising through the stations of nearness [to Allah] forever. And things over there are not like the things of the life of this world. Rather, over there, everything is in an utmost state of

[1] Its continuation is "with no one inside." Narrated as a Prophetic hadith from (i) Abū Umāma by al-Ṭabarānī, *Kabīr* (8:247 §7969); al-Khaṭīb, *Tārīkh Baghdād* (Sahl b. ʿUbayd Allāh b. Dāwūd Abū Naṣr al-Bukhārī); (ii) Anas by Ibn ʿAdī, *al-Kāmil fīl-ḍuʿafāʾ* (al-ʿAlāʾ b. Zaydal); and as their own statement from (iii) ʿAbd Allāh b. ʿAmr b. al-ʿĀṣ by Yaʿqūb b. Sufyān, *al-Maʿrifa wal-tārīkh* (2:103, Bundār); Ḥarb b. Ismāʿīl al-Kirmānī (190-280/806-893), *Masāʾil Ḥarb*, ed. Fāyiz b. Aḥmad Ḥābis, unpubl. doct. diss., 3 vols. (Mecca: Jāmiʿat Umm al-Qurā, 1422/2001) 3:1158-1159 §1869 through trustworthy narrators; Bazzār, *Musnad* (6:442 §2478) through trustworthy narrators per Ibn Ḥajar, *al-Kāfī al-shāf fī aḥādīth al-Kashshāf* (p. 148 §528) with the addition "meaning of the pure monotheists" which Ibn Ḥajar questions as spurious; (iv) Ibn ʿAbbās by Ṭabarī (Hūd 11:107); (v) Ibn Masʿūd by Thaʿlabī and Makkī in their *Tafsīrs* (ditto). Cf. Ibn al-Muẓaffar al-Rāzī, *Mabāḥith fīl-tafsīr*, ed. Ḥātim ʿĀbid al-Qurashī (Riyadh: Dār Kunūz Ishbīliā, 1430/2009) pp. 168-177 §88-101 and two notes up.

[2] Narrated from Abū Hurayra by Aḥmad, al-Bukhārī and Muslim.

perfection and beauty, and it is perpetually in ascension from perfection to perfection, for it will be *this is Our grant... without account* (Ṣād 38:39).

This knowledge is from the heart to the heart, and *this is from the bounty of my nurturing Lord* (al-Naml 27:40). And this is nothing, for there exists, of things, that which is greater. And we hope and ask Allah to make us reach the time of al-Mahdi–upon him peace–so that you will see the great wonders, whereby if we sit with him or in his suhba, he will put us in the station that he speaking about.

May Allah grant it to us and you by the sanctity of the Fatiha.

35

[The reality of the human being – The Prophet's instruction to welcome foreign converts] – The greatest jihad – [Leaving what is of no benefit]

I seek refuge in Allah from the accursed devil
In the Name of Allah the All-Beneficent the Most Merciful
There is no power nor strength but with Allah the High, the Magnificent
Permission, O my Master, support!
Our way is companionship, and goodness is in the congregation

This suhba is for those whose covenant is to show belief in this time of ours, and these words will be a means for them to show their belief and to follow the truth of faith-systems. Allah Almighty has sent the Prophets–upon them peace–and has informed them of the case of human beings. For **it is impossible for the creature to recognize his own reality until his Creator teaches him**. And the sign of faith in the human being is that, just as he has become a believer, he wants all of creation to submit as well.

It is mentioned in the noble Hadith that people shall be requited on the Day of Resurrection in proportion to their respective intentions and not their acts. Hence whoever comes out in the way of Allah calling to the faith-system of Allah shall be regathered on the Day of Resurrection together with the Prophets, and he will acquire the merit of whoever has called the world to submission and they became Muslim at his hand. There are those among the young men from the west who have left everything and came to learn the reality of submission, after which they call [others] to it. They will be part of the thousands about whom the Messenger of Allah–upon him the blessings and peace of Allah–gave glad tidings at the end of times, "There shall come up to you from the different regions of the world students of knowledge, so tell them 'welcome!'"[1] And the foreigners who followed guidance are the very ones

[1] Narrated from Abū Sa'īd al-Khudrī by Ma'mar b. Rāshid, *Jāmi'* (11:252 §20466); al-Ṭayālisī, *Musnad* (3:644 §2305); Ibn Mājah (*Iftitāh, 'ilm, al-waṣāt bi-ṭalabat al-'ilm*); al-Tirmidhī (*'Ilm, mā jā' fīl-istīṣā' bi-man yaṭlub al-'ilm*); al-Ṭabarānī, *Musnad al-Shāmiyyīn* (1:226 §405); Ḥākim, *Mustadrak* (1:164 §298); Ibn al-Muqri', *Arba'ūn* (§4) and others. Baghawī included it among the fair narrations in *Maṣābīḥ al-Sunna*. This rating is in light of a stronger chain narrated from Ibn Ma'īn by Abū Isḥāq Ibrāhīm b. 'Abd Allāh b. al-Junayd al-Khutalī, *Su'ālāt Ibn al-Junayd li-Ibn Ma'īn*, ed. Aḥmad Muḥammad Nūr Yūsuf (Medina: Maktabat al-Dār, 1408/1988) pp. 275-276 §17. See

about whom the Messenger–upon him the blessings and peace of Allah–gave glad tidings, just as they are in pursuit of the reality of Islam and not its image.

Allah Almighty has sent forth the Messengers and has informed them about the reality of the human being, namely that our nurturing Lord has mounted an ego on every child of Ādam and, at the same time, he has made them His vicegerents on earth. Thus Allah has gathered together darkness and light inside the person of every human being, whereby the representative of the light on earth is the spirit and the representative of the darkness is the ego. **When the human being's spiritual power rules over him the servant will bask in light and when his egotism rules him he will forever remain in darkness. This is why the conflict stands between the ego and the spirit, and this conflict is dubbed *al-jihād al-akbar* (the greatest jihad). The Messenger himself named it "a greater jihad,"[1] because the ego is the most relentless enemy of a human being.[2] When the servant realizes that his salvation is through the salvation of his spirit, it becomes obligatory for him to use every available means to vanquish his ego in this jihad.**

This said, who are the victors and the conquerors in the greatest jihad? They are the Prophets–upon them peace–after whom come their inheritors, the Awliya of Allah.

Likewise it is obligatory for each person to raise the flag of pure monotheism in his heart so that his ego will not hold sway over him. Whoever acquires this knowledge must know the basic rules in the greatest jihad. Our liege lord the Shaykh ['Abd Allah al-Daghistani] has spoken about that. He said that among the weapons that are used in the greatest jihad are al-Ḥasan al-Baṣrī's instructions whereby whatever deed the servant does there needs to be a wisdom to it, and he must not do any deed that will serve against him. Allah has said, *verily your nurturing Lord indeed lies in ambush* (al-Fajr 89:14). Also among the instructions of al-Ḥasan al-Baṣrī, every human being must apply whatever he heard of advices to his physical frame, otherwise involvement in

also Suyūṭī, *al-Jāmiʿ al-ṣaghīr* (1:215) and Ghumārī, *Mudāwī* (2:426 §990).

[1] In his statement, "We have returned from the minor jihad to the greater jihad." Narrated from (i) Jābir by Bayhaqī in *al-Zuhd al-Kabīr* and Khaṭīb, *Tārīkh Baghdād*; and as a saying of (ii) Ibrāhīm b. ʿAbla by Nasāʾī per al-Mizzī, *Tahdhīb* (2:144); (iii) Ibrāhīm b. Ad-ham and (iv) Abū Ḥātim al-Aṣamm by Bayhaqī in *al-Zuhd*; and (v) ʿAbd Allāh b. ʿAmr b. al-ʿĀṣ by Ibn Rajab in *Sharḥ Ḥadīth Labbayk*.

[2] Narrated from (i) Abū Mālik al-Ashʿarī from the Prophet–upon him the blessings and peace of Allah–by al-Kharāʾiṭī in *Iʿtilāl al-qulūb*; Ibn Bashrān, *Amālī*; (ii) Ibn ʿAbbās by al-Bayhaqī, *al-Zuhd al-kabīr*; (iii) Anas and others per Ibn Ḥajar as cited by Murtaḍā al-Zabīdī, *Itḥāf al-sādat al-muttaqīn bi-sharḥ Iḥyāʾ ʿulūm al-dīn* (7:206).

what is of no benefit to him will follow. For the care shown by the servant will preserve him against falling into disliked matters, and therefore from falling into prohibited matters; and the care he shows in not falling into prohibited matters will preserve him against falling into unbelief. Falling into unbelief will lead to falling under the power of the ego.

Our liege lord al-Baṣrī would say, "O my children, whoever busies himself with what is of no concern to him has fallen under the meaning of the hadith, 'Whoever targets us is not part of us.'"[1] I.e. he falls under the punishment incurred per that hadith. Furthermore the Prophet–upon him the blessings and peace of Allah–did not say "part of me" but "part of us," i.e. the assembly of the Prophets. And in all of the faith-systems those that work against their Prophets are recorded as acting against their faith-community. Working with what is of no concern to one is forbidden in the revealed laws of all the Prophets, and no Prophet has ever busied himself with what is of no concern to him. For it is impermissible for any follower of a faith-system to busy himself with what is of no concern to him. What to say of its authority figures?

Yet you see in our time many of those that claim that they are men of faith—including Muslims, Christians and Jews—busying themselves with what is of no concern to them. Then how can one hope for the betterment of the world when the betterer is the one corrupting it? And when the authority figures cannot stop the general public from working with what is of no concern to them, the meaning of that is that they have no moral power to stop them from foul deeds. This is why the first thing the Sufis focused on was to leave what was of no concern to them, for the Prophet–upon him the blessings and peace of Allah–says, "Part of the excellence of one's submission is to leave what is of no concern/benefit to him."[2] And they would teach that faith and the prohibited do not coincide. The focus of the great Shaykhs was to teach people to leave what was of no concern to them. For it goes against transmitted teachings for the believer to commit what is prohibited. For then he is leaving the compass of belief, and the darkness of unbelief descends into his heart until he involves himself in what is illicit.

By the sanctity of the Beloved, by the sanctity of the Fatiha.

[1] Narrated as "Whoever shoots at us at night is not one of us" from (i) Abū Hurayra by Aḥmad; Bukhārī, *al-Adab al-mufrad*; Ṭaḥāwī, *Sharḥ mushkil al-āthār*; and others (ii) Burayda by al-Bazzār; (iv) Ibn ʿAbbās by Ṭaḥāwī, *Sharḥ mushkil al-āthār*; al-Ṭabarānī, *al-Kabīr*; and (v) ʿAbd Allāh b. Jaʿfar b. Abī Ṭālib in *al-Kabīr* also.

[2] *Mā lā yaʿnīh*. Narrated from Abū Hurayra by Ibn Mājah; al-Tirmidhī (*gharīb*); Ibn Ḥibbān and others. Al-Nawawī rated it fair in *al-Adhkār* and *Riyāḍ al-ṣāliḥīn*. Imam Aḥmad said its sound chain is from ʿAlī b. Ḥusayn b. ʿAlī b. Abī Ṭālib in *mursal* mode as related by Ibn Rajab, *Jāmiʿ al-ʿulūm wal-ḥikam*.

36

[Everyone receives intuitions from the Prophet but their hearing and seeing is out of order] – Reality of the human station – Various types of shaykhs

I seek refuge in Allah from the accursed devil
In the Name of Allah the All-Beneficent the Most Merciful
There is no power nor strength but with Allah the High, the Magnificent
Permission, O my Master, support!
Our way is companionship, and goodness is in the congregation

The faith-system is not just with externalities. Rather it addresses the deepest fibers of a human being. Mawlana Shaykh [ʿAbd Allah Daghistani] would say there are two types of shaykh: a shaykh of externalities and a shaykh of inner meanings. The shaykh of externalities is the one that knows about the façade of the Shariʿa and its boundaries. As for the shaykh of inner meanings then he is the one that knows about the secrets of the Shariʿa. One might find many shaykhs of externalities. As for finding a shaykh of inner meanings that knows about the reality of the Shariʿa—that is extremely rare.

Mawlana Shaykh ʿAbd Allah al-Daghistani was certainly one of those that knew the secret of the Shariʿa. He used to say that **in every prayer of the five prayers the Messenger–upon him the blessings and peace of Allah–is directing the Umma with his spiritual reality, and that every single one of the legally-tasked individuals of the Umma is receiving *wāridāt* (spiritual intuitions) on the part of the Messenger. Whoever is not deaf and dumb of heart will hear and whoever is not blind of heart will see.** Every single human being is being addressed by the Messenger of Allah–upon him the blessings and peace of Allah–for he is the Messenger to the Two Heavy Ones (human beings and jinns), and Allah Most High has said, *and know that in your midst is the Messenger of the One God* (Ḥujurāt 49:8) to the Day of Resurrection. **Spiritual intuitions from the Messenger will be like a broadcasting center that reaches all. With each individual of the Umma that exists there is power to catch and receive, but it is dysfunctional.**

This is why Mawlana says that whoever is not deaf shall hear the speech of the Messenger; and whoever is not blind shall see the spiritual presence of the Messenger addressing him. For **his spiritual presence fills the world.**[1] **And**

[1] See the epistle by the Shāfiʿī exegete and Hadith master Shams al-Dīn Muḥ. ʿAlī b. Muḥ. ʿAllān b. Ibrāhīm al-Makkī al-Bakrī al-Ṣiddīqī (996-1057/1588-1647), *Itḥāf ahl*

part of the reality of the Prophethood of the Messenger is that he directs his Umma with a spiritual direction to the One they worship according to their covenant with Him on the Day of the promise and the covenant. He lets every individual of his Umma see Whom he worships, and this is the reality of the station of *iḥsān* (excellence)—"that you worship Allah as if you see Him."[1] For whomever the human being turns to with his worship, that is his object of worship; or for whatever reason or purpose he worships Allah—that purpose is your lord.[2] Allah states, *and of people is he who worships the One God from afar, so if some good happens to him he feels at peace with it, but if a trial befalls him he recedes to his former way* (Ḥajj 22:11), and many worship Allah for a worldly motive or a next-worldly one, whereas your worship must be for your nurturing Lord without any ulterior motive. *Behold! To the One God belongs the absolute faith* (Zumar 39:3).

Some people work to become rich; or as a protection against hardships; or for the sake of the ranks of the gardens of Paradise. But this worship contradicts the speech of the All-True, *Behold! To the One God belongs the absolute faith.* I.e. **the servant ought never to intend, by his worship, anything other than the face of Allah. This is why, for the people spiritual reality, as long as the servant is till under the control of his ego, the ego will definitely lead him astray and away from pure worship of Allah. It will drag him away to its own goals. As has been made clear already, the servant whose station is**

al-īmān fī anna al-Nabīyya lā yakhlū ʿanhu zamānun aw makān (The gift to the people of belief that there is no time or place devoid of the Prophet) of which a fine ms. copy is in Damascus, Maktabat al-Asad ms. 9276, folios 157v-164v which I read to f° 161r. See Riyāḍ al-Māliḥ, *Fahras makhṭūṭāt Dār al-kutub al-Ẓāhiriyya: al-taṣawwuf*, 3 vols. (Damascus: Majmaʿ al-Lugha al-ʿArabiyya, 1398/1978) 1:4 §4. Nabhānī reproduced it in *Jawāhir al-biḥār fī faḍā'il al-Nabīy al-mukhtār* (The jewels of the seas on the elect Prophet's virtues), 4 vols. (Cairo: Muṣṭafā Bābī al-Ḥalabī, 1379/1960) 2:111-125 as *Taʿrīf ahl al-islām wal-īmān* etc. It was also published as a 70-page book entitled *Risāla fī ithbāt wujūd al-Nabīy fī kulli makān* (Cairo: Dār Jawāmiʿ al-Kalim, 1992) misattributed to "Ḥusayn b. Muḥ. al-Shāfiʿī," probably the copyist. On Ibn ʿAllān see Muḥ. Amīn al-Muḥibbī, *Khulāṣat al-athar fī Aʿyān al-qarn al-ḥādī ʿashar*, 4 vols. (Cairo: al-Maṭbaʿat al-Wahbiyya, 1284/1868; rept. Beirut: Dār Ṣādir, n.d.) 4:184-189.

[1] Per the Prophet hadith "*Iḥsān* (excellence) is for you to worship Him as if you are seeing Him." Narrated from ʿUmar in the Six Books and the *Musnad*. Al-Nawawī in the commentary on his own 40-Hadith compilation entitled *Sharḥ Matn al-Arbaʿīn al-Nawawiyya fil-Aḥādīth al-Ṣaḥīḥa al-Nabawiyya*, 2nd ed. (Cairo: Muṣṭafā al-Bābī al-Ḥalabī, 1385/1966) p. 22 equates *maqām al-iḥsān* ʿstation of practicing excellenceʾ with *maqām al-mushāhada* ʿreciprocal vision of Allahʾ and *maqām al-ṣiddīqīn* ʿstation of the most-veracious onesʾ in commentary of this clause. See Suhba I.59 and Ibn Ḥajar's detailed analysis of the whole hadith in *Fatḥ al-Bārī* and his discussion of Ibn ʿArabī's take on this passage translated in full in Haddad, *Sunna Notes III*.

[2] لأنَّ من يقصده الإنسان بعبادته، فذاك معبوده أو لأي شأن أو قصد عبد الله، فذاك المقصود هو ربّك

the station of the ego, his worship will be for his ego. This is why, to destroy the rule of the ego, the sword of pure monotheism—*lā ilāha illā-l-Lāh* (there is no god but the One God)—is empowered over it. This is why all the roads lead to the reality of pure monotheism, and their aim is to bring out the servant's servanthood from an ego-driven servanthood to the station of servanthood for Allah Almighty. The quest of common people is deliverance from Hellfire and the gaining of the gardens of Paradise while the special ones are those that delivered themselves from the station of ego and whose quest is the good pleasure of Allah.

Mawlana says that at the station of ego the servant will be controlled by the ego's blameworthy traits of character. Even if there remained a single blameworthy trait in the servant, that trait would make his deeds ugly and would push him back from the road of uprightness. An example of that is that if there is a single mistake on the part of the car's driver, this mistake will push it back from the right way. In the calculations of rockets if there is a single millimeter's error at the time of takeoff, it will become thousands of kilometers in the end. Likewise a single blameworthy trait opens the chance for it to repel him from his goal. This is why you should never say, with regard to obligations, "this is [just] Sunna" or "this is [just] disliked." For whoever cancels one of the Sunnas, he will replace it with a *bid'ā* (blameworthy innovation), and the meaning of *bid'a* is the following of the ego. As for the Sunna it is the following of the Messenger–upon him blessings and peace of Allah. To leave it is something easy for us but with Allah it is enormous.

Mawlana always said that this is why the reality of arrival is a difficult matter that needs detailed inspection of the state of the servant in order for him to ascend to the *malakūt*. It is like a rocket that is not allowed to take off before a careful detailed inspection. Likewise, when the Messenger signs off on the cleanness of the servant, the servant will be allowed to ascend. Otherwise we remain like animals on the ground. For the servant to come out of the station of ego, the murid is first given the word of *lā ilāha illā-l-Lāh* to repeat it, since the Prophet–upon him the blessings and peace of Allah–says, "I was commanded to fight people until they say *lā ilāha illā-l-Lāh*."[1]

And from Allah comes success by the sanctity of the Fatiha.

[1] "I was ordered to fight people until they say 'There is no god but the One God' believing in me and what I brought. When they do they have made their lives and properties untouchable by me except for the right due over them; and their reckoning is with Allah," a *mutawātir* (mass-transmitted) Prophetic hadith narrated from 19 Companions by al-Bukhārī, Muslim and others as detailed by al-Kattānī in *Naẓm al-mutanāthir*.

37

How to arrive at the reality of belief – [Strength of presence with Allah and with His Messenger – The two kinds of life of a human being – The true life]

I seek refuge in Allah from the accursed devil
In the Name of Allah the All-Beneficent the Most Merciful
There is no power nor strength but with Allah the High, the Magnificent
Permission, O my Master, support!
Our way is companionship, and goodness is in the congregation

Mawlana Shaykh 'Abd Allah Daghistani said—and he is a Muhammadan inheritor—that **there is no possibility for any person to know whether he is following the truth or falsehood before he first rids himself of his blameworthy traits of character; and we are ordered and legally tasked to follow the truth. So as long as a human being remains at the *maqām* (station) of ego and his blameworthy traits are controlling him, his journeying will be *then they believe, then they disbelieve* (al-Nisā' 4:137). At times he will be a believer and at times an apostate.** It is like a bird tied to a child's hand. Every time it tries to fly away the child pulls it back. Likewise our blameworthy traits that are affiliated with our egos: every time we direct ourselves to Allah Almighty they drag us downwards. **This is why, in all our movements and our moments of stillness, we must renew our belief. The renewal of our belief corrects our orientation.**

This is knowledge that is never wrong, and no human being is exempt from its universality. Just as our expressing the word of *shahāda* (witnessing) at every movement of ours—such as our standing for prayer, or in dhikr, or before eating or sleep—straightens up that matter and turns the servant's orientation to Allah, likewise the frequent repetition of the *shahāda* gives the human being *yaqaẓa* (wakefulness) that constantly reminds him that he is in *īmān* (belief) and *islām* (submission), and that he bears witness to Allah and to His Messenger–upon him the blessings and peace of Allah. For this truly gives him *quwwatun ḥuḍūriyya* (strength of presence) so that he will be present at all times in the presence of the Almighty All-True and in the presence of the Messenger–upon him the blessings and peace of Allah–and he will be watchful over all his acts.

Mawlana al-Shaykh says that it is impossible for a human being to obtain the reality of belief until he rids himself of his blameworthy traits of

character wholly. Likewise, whoever has not reached the reality of belief has not reached *ḥaqq al-ḥayāt* (the true life).

Mawlana says a human being has two kinds of life: a natural life which is the life of the animal, and a spiritual life, which is the real life. The natural life courses through the human being by means of what is eaten and what is drunk, and by their means he propels himself towards life. With this external power his life is standing. After the completion of this life it begins to diminish like a battery-powered mechanical man that reaches its peak then collapses. But **as for the one that has reached the level of true life, then a ray from the life of Allah Almighty has reached his heart, and his life is standing by the life of Allah. There is no death for him. When he has reached the true life, his powers are at the intensity of perfection and they remain so all his life long. In his grave he will be the manifestation of *rather they are alive with their nurturing Lord, receiving provision*** (Āl ʿImrān 3:169). And this station does not take place for the servant until he rids himself of his blameworthy characteristics and his ego dies. Connection with the reality of life with his heart does not become possible for him except after he divests himself of the blameworthy traits of character. This is why you will see the Prophets and the Awliya alive in their graves. After hundreds and thousands of years, if their graves are opened, you will find them as on the day that they were placed in there.

May Allah grant is to us and you by the sanctity of the Fatiha.

38

[All that is created is for the Prophet's honor – Age of *lā ilāha illā-l-Lāh Muḥammadun Rasūlu-l-Lāh* and of the Prophetic mission – The station of Jibril and the Muhammadan reality] – The Messenger is the teacher of the Prophets one and all – [The guide must be from the *malakūt*, not earth]

I seek refuge in Allah from the accursed devil
In the Name of Allah the All-Beneficent the Most Merciful
There is no power nor strength but with Allah the High, the Magnificent
Permission, O my Master, support!
Our way is companionship, and goodness is in the congregation

The foundations of obligatory belief for the believers are the firm belief that Allah Almighty has created the universes for the sake of the honor of our liege lord Muhammad–upon him the blessings and peace of Allah–who is the mercy for the worlds, and that everything that is created, is created as an increase for the honor of the Prophet, just as Allah Almighty Himself has honored His Prophet. For the Messenger of Allah was created from the light of Allah Almighty, and all the universes were created from the light of the Prophet–upon him the blessings and peace of Allah.[1]

The Messenger of Allah is the representative of the All-True in all the universes, and he is the greatest *wasīla* (intermediary) for creatures one and all to their nurturing Lord Almighty. Without him it is impossible for anyone to reach to Allah Almighty. For the Messenger of Allah–upon him the blessings and peace of Allah–is the first to confirm that *lā ilāha illā-l-Lāh* (there is no god but the One God), and the name of the Messenger was certainly written together with the Name of Allah Almighty: *lā ilāha illā-l-Lāh Muḥammadun Rasūlu-l-Lāh* (there is no god but the One God, Muhammad is the Messenger of the One God).[2] Since what time has *lā ilāha illā-l-Lāh* been written? No one

[1] Per the glosses of the verses *There has come to you from Allah a Light and a manifest Book* (al-Mā'ida 5:15) and *Allah is the Light of the heavens and the earth* (al-Nūr 24:35) among other proofs. See their review and discussion by the authorities in chapters 4-6 of Haddad, *The Muhammadan Light* (ISCA, 2012) pp. 103-224.

[2] See Suhba I.14, 12th note.

knows that but Allah. Since that time, *Muḥammadun Rasūlu-l-Lāh* has been written together with it. When *lā ilāha illā-l-Lāh* existed, *Muḥammadun Rasūlu-l-Lāh* existed. And this is a deep ocean, whoever enters it seldom comes out.

More than that—when did Allah Almighty send him *as a mercy to the worlds* (Anbiyā' 21:107)? Since there was *lā ilāha illā-l-Lāh Muḥammadun Rasūlu-l-Lāh*, and the first creation is the Messenger of Allah.[1] All existents and creatures use him as their intermediary to Allah Almighty. Likewise the Messenger of Allah is perpetually in His presence and receiving the Qur'ān *from the side of an All-Wise, All-Knowing One* (Naml 27:6). And this means that the reality of *Muḥammadun Rasūlu-l-Lāh* never moved away from its station in the presence of the All-True since before time. Then what do you think about him who is mentioned in the name *Muḥammadun Rasūlu-l-Lāh*: is he a name without referent? *Lā ilāha illā-l-Lāh Muḥammadun Rasūlu-l-Lāh*: where is the place of Muhammad–upon him the blessings and peace of Allah? Is it not in His presence–may He be exalted? This is being present from before time until forever:[2] *lā ilāha illā-l-Lāh*, in Whose presence is *Muḥammadun Rasūlu-l-Lāh*.

And has the Messenger of Allah–upon him the blessings and peace of Allah–come to the world and then died? Never. That was a single ray from the sun which his Almighty nurturing Lord had dressed him with, with the garment of *nāsūtiyya* (human nature), and He sent him to our side. What has appeared in the world of the sun of the Muhammadan reality is a single ray, not more. When our nurturing Lord had sent him to the world, Jibril came to him one day and the Messenger of Allah asked him, "How do you receive the Quranic verses, O Jibril?" He said, "I receive them from behind a curtain. A bright hand stretches out and gives me the verses and I bring them and recite

[1] Per the Prophetic hadith, "When Allah Almighty created Ādam He showed Ādam the excellence of his offspring. Ādam beheld their respective ranks and precedence. Then he saw me, a dazzling light beneath all of them. He said, 'O my Lord, who is this?' Allah replied, 'This is your son Aḥmad; he is the First and the Last and he is the first intercessor.'" Narrated from Abū Hurayra with a fair chain by Abū al-'Abbās Muḥammad b. Isḥāq b. Ibrāhīm al-Sarrāj al-Thaqafī (d. 313/925), *Ḥadīth al-Sarrāj*, ed. Ḥusayn 'Ukāsha Ramaḍān, 4 vols. (Cairo: al-Fārūq al-Ḥadītha, 1425/2004) 3:236 §2628; and through him by al-Bayhaqī, *Dalā'il* (5:483). See also two notes up.

[2] From before time: see Suhba I.24, 12th note; until forever: it is written as the third line below *bismi-l-Lāh al-raḥmān al-raḥīm* and *al-ḥamdu li-l-Lāhi rabbi-l-'ālamīn* on the standard of the Prophet on the Day of Resurrection as narrated from Abū Zayd Maḥdūj b. Zayd al-Bāhilī by Aḥmad in *Faḍā'il al-Ṣaḥāba* (2:663 §1131) and Abū al-Ḥasan 'Alī b. Muḥammad Ibn al-Maghāzilī al-Wāsiṭī, *Manāqib Amī al-Mu'minīn 'Alī b. Abī Ṭālib*, ed. Turkī al-Wādi'ī (Sanaa: Dār al-Āthār, 1424/2003) p. 94 §65.

them to you." The Messenger–upon him the blessings and peace of Allah–said to him, "You must find out who is behind the curtain and then tell me." When our liege lord Jibril was next ordered to receive revelation he lifted the curtain to see to whom belonged the bright hand that was handing him the verses and he saw the Messenger of Allah there. Then he sped to the Messenger of Allah, who asked him, "Did you see whose hand it was?" Jibril replied, "From you and back to you, O Muhammad!"[1]

Our liege lord Jibril also represents *al-'aql* (the intellect). When he stopped from advancing with the Messenger of Allah–upon him the blessings and peace of Allah–during the heavenly Ascent,[2] it signifies that there is where the limits of the intellect stop. Whatever lies beyond Jibril–upon him peace–is what lies beyond the intellect. The intellect cannot function without the five senses. Likewise, the station of our liege lord Jibril has senses the intellect comprehends, but its does not comprehend what lies beyond the station of Jibril. And from [the end of] the station of Jibril upwards, the one that receives over there is the Muhammadan Reality which our liege lord Jibril saw. That Reality is always in the divine presence. *And verily you are indeed made to receive the Qur'ān from the side of an All-Wise, All-Knowing One* (Naml 27:6).

Higher than the station of Jibril, therefore, there is the station of *lāhūt* (Godhead) and below his station there is the world of *nāsūt* (human nature). I.e. from *lāhūt* to *nāsūt* the transmitter is Jibril–upon him peace. From this it can be known that Jibril, as many as he brought down of revelation to the

[1] "For every Umma there is a special divine gate whose gatekeeper is their lawgiver, through which they enter to Allah Most High; and Muḥammad–upon him the blessings and peace of Allah–is the gatekeeper of gatekeepers due to the universality of his Message, unlike the rest of the Prophets–upon them peace–who are the gatekeepers to him–upon him the blessings and peace of Allah… in light of his statement, 'Ādam and all those after him are under my flag.' So they were his deputies in the world of creation while he was a pure spirit fully cognizant of that, before the emergence of his body." Ibn 'Arabī, *Futūḥāt* (1:259 at the bottom, ch. 42). Its Quranic proof is the verse *and when the One God took the binding pact of the Prophets, "that, indeed, whatever I give you of Scripture and wisdom, then a Messenger comes to you confirming what you already have, you shall be bound to believe in him and you shall be bound to support him!" He said, "Do you avouch it and bind yourselves to that with My bond?" They said, "We avouch it." He said, "Then bear witness, and I am with you, one of the witnesses"* (Āl 'Imrān 3:81). Its Sunna proof is the Prophetic hadith, "If Mūsā were alive he would have no alternative but to follow me," narrated from (i) Jābir by Aḥmad; al-Dārimī; Ibn Abī 'Āṣim, *al-Sunna*; Ibn 'Abd al-Barr, *Jāmi' bayān al-'ilm* (2:805-806 §1497); al-Bayhaqī, *Shu'ab al-īmān*; (ii) 'Abd Allah ibn Thābit by 'Abd al-Razzāq, *Muṣannaf* (6:113); Aḥmad; Ṭabarānī; al-Bayhaqī in *Shu'ab al-īmān*.

[2] Suhba I.7, penultimate note.

Prophets—Leaves, Gospel, Psalms, Torah—it was from that station that he would bring down every Scripture. And who was *made to receive the Qur'ān from the side of an All-Wise, All-Knowing One*? The Muhammadan Reality.

From this perspective our Prophet Muhammad–upon him the blessings and peace of Allah–is the teacher of all the Prophets. Then who taught the Names to our liege lord Ādam–upon him peace? The Messenger of Allah himself–upon him the blessings and peace of Allah–taught him, because our liege lord Ādam could not carry the direct teaching of Allah. And he carried only *the Names* (al-Baqara 2:31), but as for the meanings and their wisdom then it is with the Messenger of Allah, and through Jibril's intermediary every Prophet is taking from the Messenger. Allah says, *there was ever for you, in the Messenger of the One God, a fine model* (al-Aḥzāb 33:21). **The Messenger of Allah–upon him the blessings and peace of Allah–accepted for Jibril to be his guide, although in reality he is the guide for Jibril.**

One day Jibril brought the verse *kāf, hā, yā, ʿayn ṣād* (Maryam 19:1). Jibril said, *kāf*. The Messenger of Allah–upon him the blessings and peace of Allah–said, "I know." Jibril said, *hā*. The Messenger of Allah–upon him the blessings and peace of Allah–said, "I know." Jibril said, *yā*. The Messenger of Allah–upon him the blessings and peace of Allah–said, "I know." Jibril said, *ʿayn*. The Messenger of Allah–upon him the blessings and peace of Allah–said, "I know." Jibril said, *ṣād*. The Messenger of Allah–upon him the blessings and peace of Allah–said, "I know." Jibril wondered and said, "This is the first time I bring these verses. How did you know them when I myself did not know them?"[1] This means that there is a connection between Allah and His Messenger–upon him the blessings and peace of Allah–about which Jibril has not been told.

However, for the preservation of principles with the Prophets one and all, our liege lord Jibril would bring down the [Scriptural] signs from Allah Almighty and likewise to our liege lord the Messenger of Allah–upon him the blessings and peace of Allah–and that was as a teaching for his Umma that it is impossible for anyone to reach the *malakūt* (world of invisible sovereignty) without the intermediary of a guide. **The teaching of the Messenger consisting in his acceptance for Jibril to be a guide for him outwardly is to teach that whoever wants a connection between the *mulk* (visible world of creation) and the *malakūt* is in need of a guide**, although the Messenger's connection with Allah Almighty is continuous and he is also continually present in His presence. Despite that, the Messenger–upon him the blessings and peace of Allah–would not proceed with any movement or action without first

[1] Cited unsourced in Ismāʿīl Ḥaqqī Burusawī, *Rūḥ al-bayān* (al-Baqara 2:1, Maryam 19:1, Yā Sīn 36:1).

waiting for the descent of Jibril and receiving from him, then he would proceed. This means that his restricting himself to a guide is as a teaching for the Umma that whoever wants to reach the *malakūt* must take a guide to walk with him. **And it is not allowed for the guide to be earthly; he has to be from the *malakūt*.**

The Prophets are affiliated to the *malakūt*. They have taken a guide from the *malakūt* and they have reached. They have taken Jibril who is from the *malakūt* and he has made them reach the *malakūt*. And **just as the Prophets are connected to the *malakūt* through the intermediary of Jibril, the person who is unconnected with the *malakūt* would be unsuitable as someone to follow. Whoever follows such a one will remain on the surface of the earth and will not reach the *malakūt*. This is the quality of the guide: he must be *malakūt*-affiliated. *Malakūt*-affiliated men exist, and their number reaches 99 men in every age.**

By the sanctity of the Beloved, by the sanctity of the Fatiha.

39

Who practices what he knows – [Allah does not accept deeds done by coercion – Eating manners in honor of the Prophet – Q&A at the British Library] – Knowledge is a power that points to the All-True's magnificence [and keeps increasing]

I seek refuge in Allah from the accursed devil
In the Name of Allah the All-Beneficent the Most Merciful
There is no power nor strength but with Allah the High, the Magnificent
Permission, O my Master, support!
Our way is companionship, and goodness is in the congregation

The Messenger of Allah–upon him the blessings and peace of Allah–said, "Whoever practices what he knows, Allah shall make him inherit the knowledge of what he does not know."[1] Therefore **the more a human being gives attention to knowledge, the more Allah gives him of it. Knowledge is with the people of spiritual reality and all we have to do is search for it then put it into practice.** Mawlana al-Shaykh ['Abd Allah al-Daghistani] explains this verse, *there is no compulsion in the faith-system* (Baqara 2:256) by saying that **Allah does not accept from the servant any deed that he did while coerced to do it. For this reason, if you hate to do it then do not pray and do not fast, because Allah does not love acts that are done out of coercion. However, He accepts the deed that is offered with yearning and longing and love. This is why the foundation of the faith-system is love. To the extent that there is love, energy for deeds will increase.**

Mawlana Shaykh also says there is no benefit from medication or food that a human being is forced to take. It is originally part of high manners, when you sit at a dining table, to know that that table is the Messenger's table, and

[1] Narrated from (i) Ibn 'Abbās by Abū al-Shaykh per Suyūṭī in *al-Durar al-muntathira fīl-aḥādīth al-mushtahara*, ed. Muḥ. 'Abd al-Raḥīm (Beirut: Dār al-Fikr, 1415/1995) pp. 259-260 §423; *al-Jāmi' al-ṣaghīr* (2:107); cf. Ghumārī, *Mudāwī* (4:524-525 §5711); and, as their own saying, (ii) Awzā'ī by Abū al-Layth al-Samarqandī in *Tanbīh al-ghāfilīn*; Ibn 'Asākir, *Tārīkh*; (iii) Abū al-Dardā' in the wording "Whoever practices one tenth of what he knows, Allah shall teach him what he does not know" by al-Khaṭīb, *Jāmi'*; (iv) Sufyān al-Thawrī by Abū Ya'qūb Isḥāq b. Abī Isrā'īl al-Baghdādī al-Manjanīqī al-Warrāq in *Riwāyat al-kibār 'an al-ṣighār* per Suyūṭī, *Durr*; (v-ix) 'Īsā b. Maryam, Anas, 'Umar b. 'Abd al-'Azīz, Fuḍayl b. 'Iyāḍ and 'Abd al-Wāḥid b. Zayd.

that he has gathered the Umma around it. Then, to the extent of your body's need, take from it what is enough for you. For there is no shyness over food. And **you must intend, when you eat this food, for the honor of the Prophet–upon him the blessings and peace of Allah–to increase. For Allah has created all the dining tables and all the blessings as an increase in the honor of the Prophet**. Likewise the foundation of servanthood is the licit morsel, and the licit morsel cannot be ascertained until the servant recognizes that it is because of the Messenger–upon him the blessings and peace of Allah–and in honor of him and as benevolence to him that Allah gave it to us. This high manner causes a light to shine for the human being, an expansion in his heart, strength in his body, and honor here and hereafter. I have heard from my master and patron that whoever deprives himself of his right to eat out of shyness, will be fighting himself on the Day of Resurrection harder than the kind of fighting that kills 40 people. Give yourself the right due in food. Moreover do not eat just to please someone or another, for such would be a waste of blessings and cause the body harm.

Likewise there is no benefit in sleep that is by force. When a person is unable to sleep let him get up, make ablutions and pray. At that time Iblīs will come and try to make him fall asleep. So he does not need a sleeping pill. It is the same with speech. Whoever speaks by force and without inspiration being sent to the heart will be a follower of whim. But when inspiration for speech comes then speak. There will be a secret and a light in your speech, and love will be generated from it. You can see the students in our time having no appetite for study so do not force them to do that. Shut down schools for a month with wisdom and you will find them fed up with their free time and asking for schools to be reopened. This is the biggest principle of all, that you should not do some work without love for it or by coercion.

I went to the most famous library in the world, the British Library in London, wherein are found seven million volumes on the most precious and highest of the sciences.[1] There, I asked the director of the library, "To what do these volumes point?" He replied, "This question never crossed my mind. I do not know the answer." In that spot my liege lord inspired me the answer. I said, "All of the sciences in all of those volumes are pointing to the existence of the Almighty Creator. They open avenues for acquiring knowledge of the magnificence of the All-True. And everyone of the different sciences indicates and opens more avenues for the understanding of the magnificence of Allah." Hearing this he said, "I am going to record these words and put them up. I never heard such a reply but my heart finds peace in it."

[1] As of 2024 the British Library is one of the largest world libraries with over 170 million items including electronic and printed books, periodicals and manuscripts.

The more a servant increases in knowledge, the more the All-True becomes manifest to him with His magnificence. This is why no one can duly estimate the magnificence of the All-True like our Prophet can, because the magnificence of the All-True manifests itself to the extent of the servant's knowledge of his nurturing Lord. The more the magnificence of the All-True manifests itself to His servant, the more he increases in magnifying Allah. This is why two prayer cycles from the Messenger of Allah–upon him the blessings and peace of Allah–are more precious than all the worship of human beings and jinns. If it were placed in the pan of the balance it would weigh heavier than all of the sins put together and would make them *scattered motes* (al-Furqān 25:23). This is the Messenger of Allah; and where is our proper estimation of him?

Knowledge is a power that points to the magnificence of the Exalted All-True. Since there is no end to the magnificence of Allah, there is no end to knowledge. And knowledge increases in accordance with the manifestation of the magnificence of the All-True. There is no limit to the magnificence of Allah. This is why Allah orders His Prophet, *and say, "My nurturing Lord, increase me in knowledge!"* (Ṭa Ha 20:114)—knowledge of Allah. **And the more the servant's knowledge of Allah increases, the more the magnificence of the All-True manifests itself to him. And the more the magnificence of the All-True manifests itself to him, the more his own existence diminishes until no trace of him remains. For our existence is delusive while the existence of Allah is absolutely certain. And when the servant's existence disappears in the ocean of Allah's unicity, he will find complete joy and happiness. There is where real honor for the servant is, when he gets to the station of *baqā' fi-l-Lāh* (abiding in Allah).**

Knowledge appears and is given to the extent that people turn to it and the more the intellects of humankind develop and attain it. The Messenger–upon him the blessings and peace of Allah–knew the reality of matters and things with a complete and thorough knowledge. For were it not for the complete and thorough knowledge of the Messenger for things, it would be impossible to attain the knowledge of the Creator of things. This is why, before knowledge of Allah, the Knower of Allah must first get to know the creation of Allah, and then know the Creator. For which of the two is the vastest knowledge? Creation or the Creator? There is no doubt that the knowledge of the Creator is vaster. Next to the knowledge of the Creator, knowledge of creation is like a drop in the sea. He will drink it then he will turn himself to the knowledge of Allah.

May Allah grant it to us and you. By the sanctity of the Beloved, by the sanctity of the Fatiha.

40
[Saṭīḥ the pre-Islamic soothsayer] – Meaning of *and when the wild beasts are assembled*

I seek refuge in Allah from the accursed devil
In the Name of Allah the All-Beneficent the Most Merciful
There is no power nor strength but with Allah the High, the Magnificent
Permission, O my Master, support!
Our way is companionship, and goodness is in the congregation

Before the sending of the Prophet–upon him the blessings and peace of Allah–a group came to a soothsayer named Saṭīḥ.[1] This man had lived 600 years[2] and his form was strange. They would wrap him up in cloth and carry him from country to country. He had no neck. His face was on his chest and his body was devoid of bones and the jinn would inform him of future events by means of eavesdropping (cf. al-Ḥijr 15:18).[3] His jinns had eavesdropped at the time that Allah had spoken with Mūsā–upon him peace –on the Ṭūr (Mount).[4]

The aim of the group that had come to him was to ask him about what was going to happen in the future. They brought him a gift which happened to be a sword. When they entered and greeted him they did not tell him about the gift. He said to them, "Where is the sword first of all?" They said, "Oh! We forgot!" and they gave it to him. Then he asked them, "From what tribe do you hail?" They named a tribe but lied to him. He said, "No. Rather, from such and such a tribe," and named the correct one. After they had tested him with these things they began to rely on what he said and they asked him, "What lies ahead of us?" He said, "O assembly! You have become like wild beasts dispersed in the world. Soon there shall come the Prophet of endtimes to discipline the world. Such and such will take place in his time," until he named this time.

[1] Saṭīḥ Rabīʿ b. Rabīʿa b. Masʿūd b. Māzin b. Dhiʾb al-Ghassānī in Ibn Hishām (1:15). He was nicknamed *kāhin al-kuhhān* (the soothsayers of all soothsayers) per Masʿūdī in *Akhbār al-zamān* (Beirut: Dār al-Andalus, 1416/1996) p. 118.

[2] Per Abū Ḥātim Sahl b. Muḥammad b. ʿUthmān al-Jushamī al-Sijistānī (d. 248/862) in *al-Muʿammarūn* (*thalāthīna qarnan*) and Ibn al-Jawzī in *Aʿmār al-aʿyān*.

[3] As mentioned in *Murūj al-dhahab*, *al-Rawḍ al-unuf*, *al-Miṣbāḥ al-madīy*, *Subul al-hudā wal-rashād* and *Tārīkh al-khamīs* among other books of Prophetic *Sīra*.

[4] Per al-Suhaylī, *al-Rawḍ al-unuf* and al-Kilāʿī, *al-Iktifāʾ*.

The noble verse states, *and when the wild beasts are assembled* (al-Takwīr 81:5). This is it, the time of the second Jahiliyya, the time of the people that are like wild beasts dispersed all over the world. Wild beasts are animals. When you encounter them you can protect yourself from them as much as you can. But as for the wild beasts that exist now, you cannot protect yourself from them whether inside your house or outside it. This is from the signs of the final Hour. Vicious harmful souls have filled the world, so that the status of belief no longer has any effect on people unlike its effect before. Beastly souls now have taken over government. You see people as human outwardly, whereas their way of life is savage. That is also what you see on the news and in the newspapers daily—the savagery of the world with lies, hypocrisy, atheism and wars. You will never hear in the news a single report about one of the righteous ever. All the reports are about the wicked and their acts.

And when the records are rolled open (al-Takwīr 81:10), *and when the wild beasts are assembled* (81:5), this will be just before the Hour. This indicates, *when the records are rolled open*, i.e. when evil spreads and moves from one country to another, and the savage souls learn more corruption from the *ṣuḥuf* (newspapers). As for the *ṣuḥuf* (records) that are rolled open on the Day of Resurrection, that is something else.

Allah does not like for evil to spread among people. This is why He said–exalted is He–*verily those who love for an indecency to circulate far and wide among those who believe—theirs is a painful punishment in this life and the hereafter* (al-Nūr 24:19) and He also said, *the One God does not love the publicizing of evil-doing, except by whoever has been wronged* (al-Nisāʾ 4:148). And now evildoing has reached its apex. My master and patron has compared the upshot of this matter for me to a scorpion when it despairs of its own life: it stings itself on its own head. And the upshot of this evil shall be like that of the scorpion.

It is the same with the evil of the ego. You cannot prevent it except by taking refuge in Allah Almighty.

May Allah protect us and you from the evils of our egos. May Allah grant it to us and you by the sanctity of the Fatiha.

41

[Our way is companionship and immense good is in keeping good company] – Abū Yazīd and the *Quṭb* of the time – The meaning of *He does not acquaint of His unseen anyone* – [The Awliya partake of the Prophet's *jawāmiʿ al-kalim* – The *kashf* of newborns and of Shaykh ʿAbd Allah Daghistani – Shaykh ʿAzīz Maḥmūd Hudāʾī]

I seek refuge in Allah from the accursed devil
In the Name of Allah the All-Beneficent the Most Merciful
There is no power nor strength but with Allah the High, the Magnificent
Permission, O my Master, support!
Our way is companionship, and goodness is in the congregation

We creatures are all slaves and Allah does with us whatever He wishes. *Allāhu al-muqaddir wal-ʿālam shuʾūn* (Allah is the Apportioner while the world is full of tumults).[1] We are asking of Allah to pour over us from the blessings of the Messenger of Allah–upon him the blessings and peace of Allah–and the blessings of our noble liege lords so that our hearts shall become full of light, our longing shall increase, our *himma* (spiritual energy) shall rise, our certainty shall increase, our belief shall strengthen; so that we shall approach the majestic presence of the All-True–Almighty is He. This is why the Messenger of Allah–upon him the blessings and peace of Allah–said, "The *dīn* (faith-system) is all transparent, faithful counsel,"[2] and our liege lord Shah Naqshband would say, "Our way is companionship, and immense goodness is in keeping good company." For **the servant keeps drawing nearer to Allah in every association, and the one that is unable to draw nearer to Allah through his deeds can do so through keeping company with the righteous**

[1] From a famous Sufi poem by the Cairo-born Libyan Shaykh Abū ʿAbd Allāh Muḥ. b. Aḥmad b. Muḥammad ʿUlaysh al-Mālikī (1802-1882) who was thrown in jail bedridden from terminal illness at the time of the minister of war Aḥmad ʿArābī's failed 1881 revolt against the Khedive of Egypt.

[2] See Suhba I.10, first note.

ones, being present with them and hearing their speech, for in their speech there is life for one's spiritual side.

Our liege lord Abū Yazīd al-Bisṭāmī would say that the station of *Quṭb* in his time belonged to a certain blacksmith, although there were many in his time that possessed *wilāya*, spiritual unveiling and miraculous gifts. Yet that blacksmith had not reached the station of *kashf*. He did not know himself but the Awliya knew him as the *Quṭb*. Our liege lord Abū Yazīd said, "I wondered at him, how this blacksmith was given the station of *Quṭb* in the presence of thousands of Awliya. I decided to visit him to see his quality and how he had reached this level. When I entered his workshop he dropped everything and wanted to kiss my hand. I said to him, 'It is I that must kiss your hand.' He replied, 'My master, if, by your kissing my hand, the fire that is in my heart were extinguished, I would let you kiss it.'" Our liege lord Abū Yazīd asked him, "What fire do you mean?" He said to him, "My master, at the time of the Regathering, when people are down on their knees, how will the conditions of this Umma be? Will Allah manifest Himself with overwhelming power? My liege lord, I am constantly thinking of the Muhammadan Umma, and how they will fare on that tremendous Day in light of their rebellious sins. This is what is burning my heart and my thought."

At that time the All-True addressed our liege lord Abū Yazīd with the *hātif Rabbānī* (lordly call), saying, "O Abū Yazīd, this is his quality among those that say, *ummatī Ummat* (my nation, my nation!) and not *nafsī nafsī* (myself, myself!)." "At that time," Abū Yazīd said, "I realized why his nurturing Lord had dressed him with the station of the *Quṭb*, for his heart was on a footing with the Muhammadan heart. This is why his nurturing Lord elected him although he was a mere blacksmith and devoid of *kashf*, but his material was the material of Prophethood. I sat with him for a long while, and that was the avenue by which stations opened up for me which I had been unable to attain for forty years. During that while I would teach him some of the short Suras so that he might complete his prayer."

In our gathering we look at one another as if we know one another. However, it might be there are in our gathering some men of the unseen in our image whom we do not know. This is why high manners are required with everyone. It is which his high manners that our liege lord Abū Yazīd obtained some of these lordly outpourings. Glory to Him that placed His secret in the weakest of His creation! "There might be someone whose famous name has filled the east and the west, but he has no value in the presence of his nurturing Lord, not even that of the wing of a gnat, and there might be some disheveled one covered in dust, if he were to swear by Allah, Allah would fulfill his oath, although among people he was shoved out of doors."[1] The meaning of this is that the high energy of men uproots mountains.

Question: what is the meaning of *the Knower of the unseen! So He does not acquaint of His unseen anyone* (al-Jinn 72:26)?

Answer: Allah alone is *the Knower of the unseen and the seen* (Anʿām 6:73; Tawba 9:94, 9:105; Raʿd 13:9; Mu'minūn 23:92; Sajda 32:6; etc.), and He has created the human being weak (al-Nisā' 4:28). When He created him weak, Allah lightened his load by tasking him with what is in him. Hence the believer is *ibn waqtih* (living in his moment). He is tasked with the time that he is in. He is not charged with a future task because the servant is weak. This is why Allah made the matter of the future hidden and He did not show what would come about for people individually. For whoever knows what will befall him after an hour or a day or a month or a year, his high energy wanes and he might be overwhelmed by the thought of what is going to happen to him.

This is why Allah kept those matters hidden to him so that free choice would be sure to take place for the servants and so that one might be able to use the *irādat al-juz'iyya* (partial will) that is with him.[2] If what was going to take place were unveiled to him the servant would become pre-determined and would not be tasked. This is why Allah kept this matter hidden. And the meaning of *so He does not acquaint of His unseen anyone* is the absolute unseen that is with Allah. There is no acquaintance of it for anyone—not Prophets, not Awliya, and not angels. His absolute *huwiyya* (quiddity) and the divine types of knowledge are ascribed to Him and are unobservable.

However there is, of those types of knowledge, something that Allah pours out for the sake of the servants. And what Allah unveils for a Prophet from his time until the Day of Resurrection, or from his time until that of the next Prophet, are like road signs pointing you to the country ahead.

[1] Narrated from (i) Anas by Aḥmad (19:459 §12476); Tirmidhī (*Manāqib, manāqib al-Barā' b. ʿĀzib, ḥasan*); (ii) Abū Hurayra by Muslim (*al-Birr wal-ṣila wal-ādāb, faḍl al-ḍuʿafā' wal-khāmilīn; al-Janna wa-ṣifat naʿīmihā, al-nār yadkhuluhā al-jabbārūn*); (iii) Muʿādh b. Jabal by Ibn Mājah (*Zuhd, man lā yu'bahu lah*).

[2] See Mawlana Khālid al-Baghdādī's (1193-1242/1779-1827) *Risāla fī taḥqīq mas'alat al-irādat al-juz'iyya fīl-farq bayna kasbay al-Māturīdī wal-Ashʿarī* (Treatise on the verification of the question of partial will concerning the difference between the Māturīdī understanding of earning and the Ashʿarī); ʿAbd al-Ghanī al-Nābulusī's *al-Kawkab al-sārī fī ḥaqīqat al-juz' al-ikhtiyārī* (The moving star on the reality of the decisional particular); and Muḥammad Zāhid al-Kawtharī's *al-Istibṣār fīl-taḥadduth ʿani al-jabr wal-ikhtiyār* (Insights on the discussion of determinism and free choice).

Since our Prophet is the Prophet of the end of times and the end of his Umma reaches to the Resurrection, and since he is *al-Ḥāshir* (the Gatherer)[1] and people shall be regathered at the end of his time, Allah has made things clear to him from his time until the Day of Resurrection from the perspective that he is a *nabī* (Prophet), and the station of *nubuwwa* (Prophethood) consists in *inbā'* (informing) about the future. If the Prophet were not informing about the future of the world, how could he be a Prophet? In that case he would be like an ordinary human being. But at the station of Prophethood, the future is opened up for him so that he may teach his Umma to recognize all the phases that it is going to go enter until the Resurrection comes.

The Messenger–upon him the blessings and peace of Allah–also says, "I was given *jawāmi' al-kalim* (the pithiest of all discourses),"[2] i.e. the briefest word from the Messenger contains volumes of sciences in proportion with the light of belief and the light of spiritual knowledge. The Awliya are subsumed under that hadith.[3] So if the Messenger–upon him the blessings and peace of Allah–says something, every wali goes hunting out of that ocean that the Messenger has spoken, each according to the light of his *wilāya*. This is why, when a wali speaks, his speech is from the ocean of the Prophet–upon him the blessings and peace of Allah.

An example of that is in the statement of Allah Almighty, *its preconditions have certainly come already* (Muḥammad 47:18). Who is to explain the preconditions that Allah has spoken of? Common people? Rather the Messenger of Allah explains them to humankind. He is the one that explains the discourse of Allah and clarifies its meaning and elucidates it. Teaching is from him–upon him the blessings and peace of Allah. Hence when a wali speaks, his reliance is on the speech and explanation of the Messenger. And there are thousands of Prophetic hadiths, which are impossible for a single person to have exhaustive knowledge of, which is too difficult.

In addition some might have some critique on certain hadiths, however, the people of the truth have signs of the veracity of the hadith. For when any of

[1] A Prophetic Hadith narrated from (i) Jubayr b. Muṭ'im by Aḥmad, al-Dārimī, al-Bukhārī, Muslim and al-Tirmidhī; (ii) Ibn Ghanm by al-Dārimī; (iii) Abū Mūsā al-Ash'arī by Aḥmad and Muslim; (iv-v) Ḥudhayfa b. al-Yamān and 'Awf b. Mālik al-Ashja'ī by Aḥmad; and (vi) Muḥammad b. Jubayr b. Muṭ'im by Mālik.

[2] Narrated from (i) Abū Hurayra by Aḥmad; al-Bukhārī; Muslim; al-Tirmidhī, al-Nasā'ī; and (ii) Abū Mūsā al-Ash'arī by Muslim.

[3] I.e. they have been given a share of the knowledge of *jawāmi' al-kalim*. Hence the objection by one of the critics of Ibn 'Arabī that "the speech of Awliya is not open to interpretation; only the Qur'ān and the Sunna are," is inaccurate.

the hadiths of the Messenger is read, it comes with a light which the Awliya see, whereupon they give credence to the hadith even if the ulema concur on its weakness. Furthermore the people of *kashf* infer some of the secrets of that hadith through *kashf*. **Whoever has reached the station of *kashf*, the Muhammadan light is shown to him and the veils are lifted from him so that he might see the spiritual presence of the Messenger–upon him the blessings and peace of Allah. The people of *kashf* all convene with the Messenger in wakefulness and with their spiritual reality**. They say, "If the Messenger were veiled away from us a single moment we would no longer count ourselves among the believers."[1] These are the possessors of *kashf*.

Likewise the Messenger–upon him the blessings and peace of Allah–is alive, hearing, seeing and speaking in his grave. Nor has revelation been cut off from him, nor have the lordly outpourings. The evidence to that effect is the statement of Allah Most High, ***you*** [sing.][2] ***shall indeed ride layer upon layer*** (Inshiqāq 84:19) **is an address to the Messenger with the juratory *la*** (indeed) **of oath and the geminated *nūn*** [in *la-tarkabanna*], **which imparts the sense, "from pre-existence to everlastingness We shall indeed raise you one level after another, to that which has no end." And this comprises the friends of Allah, because they are the inheritors of the Messenger**.

These realities will never be reached through the mind. If the magnificence of the created universe were to appear the mind would come to a stop. The Awliya are the true inheritors of the Messenger–upon him the blessings and peace of Allah–and those that inherit from the perfection of the Messenger. The one that shows a *muʿjiza* (staggering miracle) in the Messenger, it shows in his inheritance as a *karāma* (miraculous gift). The Messenger tells about the unseen as a *muʿjiza* while his inheritors tell about it as a *karāma*. The *karāma* of a wali is a *muʿjiza* of the Prophet–upon him the blessings and peace of Allah. Moreover, have *karāmāt* appeared in any of the people of Scripture? Have any appeared from other than *Ahl al-Sunna*? Never.[3] Because *karāmāt* are not given to other than the people of uprightness.

Whoever walks in the steps of the Messenger–upon him the blessings and peace of Allah–*and be upright as you are commanded* (al-Shūrā 42:15), shall be dressed with the manifestation of the noble verse, *and they comprehend nothing of His knowledge except what He wishes* (al-Baqara 2:255). At that time,

[1] A statement famousy related from Abū al-ʿAbbās al-Mursī by Ibn ʿAṭāʾ Allāh in his *Laṭāʾif al-minan*.

[2] Per the reading of Ḥamza, al-Kisāʾī, Ibn Kathīr and Khalaf.

[3] As stated by al-Nabhānī in *Ḥujjat Allāh ʿalā al-ʿālamīn* and *Shawāhid al-Ḥaqq*.

when Allah shows His servant His knowledge, is there any to be found objecting? And after the Messenger, his inheritors are found until the Day of Resurrection.

Mawlana Shaykh ʿAbd Allah al-Daghistani is one of those inheritors. He was born already in a state of *kashf* just as **every newborn is born in a state of *kashf*.** At birth Allah sends two angels to show it its exit into the world. One of them holds it by one end to bring him out, so the child refuses and directs himself to the other corner whereby the second holds it so it refuses again and directs itself to another corner. The hardship of delivery for the woman is for that reason. The reason is that **the soul possesses perfection and it knows that the world is an abode of trial and strifes. This is why it does not want to come out into it.** When the angels become powerless to bring out the child, Allah manifests Himself and orders the angels to leave the child alone. **When Allah manifests Himself the child goes into prostration and comes out in a state of prostration. The child remains in a state of *kashf* for seven or eight days. Out of the darkness of the blameworthy manners of the father and mother the child is gradually veiled until it no longer sees. Were it not for that the human being would remember his birth. The near-totality of people become veiled in seven or eight days. Among them rare individuals are not veiled, such as our liege lord Shaykh ʿAbd Allah al-Daghistani. He did not reach a state of *kashf* through discipline or seclusions but from the day of his birth.** This is why he was remembering the worlds from where he had come.

The person who is in a state of *kashf* recognizes every human being he sees, at what level of belief he is, and whether he will be wretched or blissful, and when he passes near a cemetery, he sees the punishment or the bliss of the dwellers of the graves.

An example of the power of Awliya is Shaykh ʿAzīz Maḥmūd Hudāʾī, the Shaykh of Sultan Ahmad who built the Blue Mosque in Istanbul. This Sultan never failed to stand up whenever the name of the Messenger–upon him the blessings and peace of Allah–was mentioned in his gathering, and he would wear on top of his head the image of the Messenger's foot that is found among the sacred relics, the one where the Messenger is placing his foot on top of a rock as if it were treading dough. He brought them [=the relics] from Egypt. There is a specialized wali in Turkish lands that is connected with the Messenger–upon him the blessings and peace of Allah–and is found in Istanbul who keeps the relics together with a group of jinns. One of the tyrants tried to enter the place of the relics but he was struck in the face. The Shaykhs had to recite over him until he was cured.

The Companions would not leave a single hair of the Messenger fall on the ground or the water. The sign that it is the hair of the Messenger–upon him the blessings and peace of Allah–is that it has no shadow, only light. When the Messenger walks he has no shadow. And the sacredness of the part is as the sacredness of the whole. This is why in every place where there is a part [of the Messenger–upon him the blessings and peace of Allah] it is required to greet the Messenger as if you were seeing him.

Our liege lord Khālid b. al-Walīd would place on his head some of the Messenger's hair. This is why he never headed for any place except he would always be victorious. The Messenger's crown—his turban—is found among the sacred relics since they received it from Egypt from the last Abbasid Caliph. In every 24 hours there sat 24 memorizers of the noble Qur'ān reciting the discourse of Allah. This had lasted from the year 423/1032 until Mustafa Kemal took over. He banished the Caliph and the reciters and he shut down the place of the sacred relics. This is why their honor plummeted.

When the Mahdi–upon him peace–comes, as his first service he will head for Istanbul together with 12,000 soldiers and Awliya from the descendants of our liege lord 'Alī–may Allah ennoble his countenance–in his bearing and carrying his knowledge, in the hand of each of whom there will be a Dhūl-Fiqār [sword]. Their horses will place their hooves wherever their gazes reach. They will be possessors of *khuṭwa* (distance-folding steps). When they pass, you see them as if flying.

Shaykh 'Azīz passed by one of the most famous cemeteries in Anatolia together with Sultan Ahmad. The Shaykh was riding a horse while the Sultan was walking by the side of the Shaykh. The Sultan's heart moved, longing to see the *karāma* of his Shaykh, whereupon the Shaykh shouted at the top of his lungs to the dead, "Rise by permission of Allah!" Not one grave remained but its dweller appeared, in their shrouds, as if they were on the Day of the Regathering. The Sultan saw this sight. His Shaykh unveiled it for him. After a little while he said to them, "Return." They returned. This is a manifestation of the power that is found with the Awliya.

By the sanctity of the Beloved, by the sanctity of the Fatiha.

42
[Reason for material losses] – The knowledge of the tongue and the knowledge of the heart

I seek refuge in Allah from the accursed devil
In the Name of Allah the All-Beneficent the Most Merciful
There is no power nor strength but with Allah the High, the Magnificent
Permission, O my Master, support!
Our way is companionship, and goodness is in the congregation

My Master the Shaykh recounted that a man made the intention to sow his land on condition that he would give half its yield in the way of Allah. The harvest came to term. At the threshing floor, when the man saw how abundant his crop was, he said, "My nurturing Lord! You are not in need of the half but I am in need of it." When he formed his intention and decided to take home the whole crop a black cloud came and rain began to fall hard. A flood rose and took exactly half the yield. This indicates that **whatever a person loses of money or other than it will be for the reason of the rights owed to others and which one has not fulfilled.**

"Knowledge is two types: one is by the tongue and the other by the heart."[1] As for the knowledge of the tongue, all people learn it. Even in these parts there are found priests and lay Christians that are proficient in the fiqh of

[1] Part of a longer Prophetic hadith rated *ḥasan* by Suyūṭī, *al-Jāmiʿ al-ṣaghīr* (2:108) in the wording "Knowledge is two types: one is by the heart—and that is the beneficial knowledge—and the other is by the tongue, and the latter is the final proof of Allah over His servants." Narrated from (i) Anas by Abū al-ʿAbbās al-Aṣamm, *Majmūʿ* (p. 302 §559); Abū al-Shaykh, *Ṭabaqāt* (4:101); Abū ʿAbd al-Raḥmān Muḥ. b. al-Ḥusayn b. Muḥ. al-Sulamī al-Naysābūrī, *Arbaʿūn fil-taṣawwuf*, ed. Muḥ. Sūrī in Sulamī, *Collected Works on Early Sufism*, ed. Narsollah Pourjavady and Mohammed Soori, 3 vols. (Tehran: Iranian Institute of Philosophy and Institute of Islamic Studies, Free University of Berlin, 2009) 3:296 §7; Abū Nuʿaym al-Aṣbahānī, *al-Arbaʿīn ʿalā madhhab al-mutaḥaqqiqīn min al-ṣūfiyya*, ed Badr ʿAbd Allāh al-Badr (Beirut: Dār Ibn Ḥazm, 1414/1993) p. 85 §43; Qawwām al-Sunna, *al-Targhīb* (3:94 §2139); al-Shajarī, *Amālī* (1:80 §300) and others; (ii) Jābir by al-Khaṭīb, *Tārīkh Baghdād* (Aḥmad b. al-Faḍl b. Sahl) with a good chain per al-Mundhirī, *Targhīb* and al-ʿIrāqī, *al-Mughnī*; (iii) al-Ḥasan in *mursal* mode by Ibn al-Mubārak, *al-Zuhd* (p. 407 §1161); Ibn Abī Shayba, *Muṣannaf* (19:88 §35502); Dārimī (*Muqaddima, al-tawbīkh li-man yaṭlub al-ʿilm li-ghayri-l-Lāh*); al-Ḥakīm al-Tirmidhī, *Nawādir* (*Aṣl* 190, 3:255 §979) and others, with a sound chain per al-Mundhirī, *Targhīb* and al-ʿIrāqī, *al-Mughnī*; (iv) al-Ḥasan as his own statement by al-Dārimī (*Muqaddima, al-balāgh ʿan Rasūli-l-Lāh*); (v) al-Fuḍayl b. ʿIyāḍ as his own statement by al-Bayhaqī, *Shuʿab* (18: *Nashr al-ʿilm*).

Islam, the commentary of the Qur'ān, the Hadith of the Prophet–upon him the blessings and peace of Allah–and the legal rulings. Despite that, these sciences are only on their tongues. Despite their sciences they do not say *lā ilāha illā-l-Lāh Muḥammadun Rasūlu-l-Lāh*. They do give any thought to Whom these sciences came from, who represents them, and what the attribute of our liege lord Muhammad is—their translator. Can some ordinary man from common individuals have brought those oceans of knowledge that have no shore? If his attribute is not that he is sent as a Messenger from Allah and that his sciences are a bestowal from Allah, let them show us any man—we do not say unlettered, but even superlatively learned and schooled —and let that man produce such sciences. But they are devoid of reflection.

More than that, the sciences of the Awliya of this Umma boggle the minds. Among them are the sciences of our liege lord Muḥyī al-Dīn Ibn 'Arabī for example. Do they also not give any thought to where the Awliya took their sciences from? As an example of that, one learned scholar of the Muslims met with one of the learned scholars of the people of Scripture and asked him, "What do you say about our liege lord Muhammad–upon him the blessings and peace of Allah?" He replied, "A man of reason and wisdom rarely found." The Muslim scholar asked him, "Your testimony about our Prophet is that he is a man of reason and wisdom. So what do you say? Will a man of reason and wisdom be an arch-liar? And is lying congruent with wisdom?" The scholar from the people of Scripture said to him, "It is impossible that he is lying." The Muslim scholar said, "Verily our Prophet says that there is no doubt at all in the Qur'ān and that it comes from the nurturing Lord of the worlds." Thereupon the priest got up and left the meeting without replying.

This story shows that among them there are those that recognize the truthfulness of the Messenger of Allah–upon him the blessings and peace of Allah–but the arrogance that nests in their transgressive souls prevents them from confessing the truth. This is why their knowledge is only by the tongue. Moreover, when they are not admitting the truth they will be ignorants and not scholars of knowledge. As for the inward knowledge then it is in the heart, and the Messenger–upon him the blessings and peace of Allah–says of it, "That is the beneficial knowledge."[1] So whoever possesses knowledge yet does not acknowledge the truth, his type is *as the likeness of the ass carrying tomes* (al-Jumu'a 62:5), or as the donkey that is carrying jewels without benefiting from them even after the passing of many years.

[1] See previous note.

More than that, *Allah does not task any soul except to its capacity* (Baqara 2:286). Allah knows the capability of each person. There are some priests found to confess the One God but they are not able to openly declare it for fear of strife. Our Shari'a gives them leeway for that. I myself know many priests that recite the Qur'ān and pray wearing a turban and a *jubba* (robe) by themselves, then they come out to do their duties as priests. My liege lord and master has informed me that forty priests have entered Islam at his hands in Syro-Palestine, and he ordered them to keep their belief hidden.

By the sanctity of the Beloved, by the sanctity of the Fatiha.

43
The obligation to keep an Islamic appearance

I seek refuge in Allah from the accursed devil
In the Name of Allah the All-Beneficent the Most Merciful
There is no power nor strength but with Allah the High, the Magnificent
Permission, O my Master, support!
Our way is companionship, and goodness is in the congregation

The Messenger of Allah–upon him the blessings and peace of Allah–said, "Turbans are the crowns of the Arabs."[1] He specified the Arabs as having turbans as their sole crowns, i.e. so that they would hold fast to the outward aspects of their national identity and faith-system and not change their garb, for the outward preserves the inward. Take fruit for example. If they were without skins, how would their types be known and their pulps preserved? Can it be without wisdom that the Messenger–upon him the blessings and peace of Allah–said, "Do not imitate the Jews and the polytheists"?[2] Yet people today want Islam to remain confined to one's conscience. This is from the Communists' and the atheists' war against us, and the latter goes back to the Jews. We have become agents for them, yet we claim to be fighting them! If you indeed want to fight them then wear the turban of the Messenger–upon him the blessings and peace of Allah–and then fight. At that time if you walked with a stick they would be afraid of you. But now, they are not even afraid of warplanes.

An example for the above. There was a Prophet named Shamshūn (Samson) whose power was connected to his hair. The Israelites tried to punish him in every way they could but they were unsuccessful until they found out the secret of his strength from his wife and they induced her into cutting his hair. At that time they were given power over him.[3] This is a lesson for us that Islam

[1] Narrated from (i) 'Alī by al-Quḍā'ī, *Musnad al-shihāb* (1:75 §68); and, as their own saying, (ii) 'Alī by Ibn Hishām, *Sīra* (1:633); (iii) al-Zuhrī by al-Bayhaqī, *Shu'ab* (40: *al-Malābis, faṣl fīl-'amā'im*); (iv) al-Awzā'ī by al-Dhahabī, *Tadhkirat al-ḥuffāẓ* (1:137).

[2] Narrated from (i-ii) Abū Hurayra and Jubayr b. Muṭ'im by Ibn Sa'd (1:439); (iii-iv) al-Zubayr and Abū Hurayra by Aḥmad (3:31-32 §1415, 12:507 §7545); (v) Jābir by al-Ṭabarānī, *Awsaṭ* (5:227 §5160). It is also narrated by Ibn Sa'd and Ibn Abī Shayba among others as a statement of 'Ā'isha, Ibn 'Abbās and 'Umar b. al-Khaṭṭāb.

[3] See al-Ṭabarī and al-Tha'labī's *Tafsīrs* under the verse *the Night of worth is better than a thousand months* (al-Qadr 97:3). Cf. Judges 13:1-16:31 and Andrew Rippin, "The Muslim Samson: medieval, modern and scholarly interpretations" in *Bulletin of SOAS,*

cannot be vanquished except from inside it, and that there is no external power that can vanquish it.

Those that rose in Turkey and forbade the faith and all of its outward manifestations, as well as religious garb for religious people, men and women, are all from our own kith and kin. They did not spare the mosques except because they were historical buildings. Otherwise they would have laid them to ruin—as they did with many of them, which they turned into stables for animals. This indicates that the Jews of the Umma are worse than the Jews of the children of Israel. The Messenger–upon him the blessings and peace of Allah–said of them, "Do not greet the Jews of my Umma with salam."[1] For it is "from them that strife issues and to them that it returns."[2]

By the sanctity of the Beloved, by the sanctity of the Fatiha.

Vol. 71 no. 2 (2008), 239-253.

[1] Cited among the forgeries by Raḍīy al-Dīn al-Ḥasan b. Muḥammad b. al-Ḥasan al-Ṣaghānī al-Qurashī, *al-Mawḍūʿāt*, ed. Najm ʿAbd al-Raḥmān Khalaf (Damascus: Dār al-Ma'mūn, 1405/1985) p. 41 §45 while al-Suyūṭī in *al-Ḥāwī* said he could not find it, but its gist is supported by the report cited next. Another narration states, "The Jews of my Umma are the Murji'a," rated a forgery by consensus. An authentic wording states, "Do not initiate salam to the Jews and the Christians," narrated from Abū Hurayra by Maʿmar b. Rāshid, *Jāmiʿ*; Aḥmad (13:56 §7617); al-Tirmidhī (*Siyar, mā jā' fil-taslīm ʿalā ahl al-Kitāb, ḥasan ṣaḥīḥ*); al-Bayhaqī, *Shuʿab* (61: *Muqārabat ahl al-Dīn, al-salām ʿala ahl al-dhimma*); and others.

[2] Part of the hadith, "There shall come a time when nothing shall remain of Islam but its name and nothing shall remain of the Qur'ān but its writing. Their hearts will have left guidance while their mosques will be prosperous. Their scholars shall be the worst of all that is under the sky at that time. Out of them dissension came forth and back to them shall it return." Narrated from (i) ʿAlī b. Abī Ṭālib as his own statement by Ibn Abī al-Dunyā, *ʿUqūbāt*; al-Dīnāwarī, *al-Mujālasa wa-jawāhir al-ʿilm*; Ibn ʿAdī, *al-Kāmil*; Abū al-Layth al-Samarqandī, *Tanbīh al-ghāfilīn*; Ibn Baṭṭa, *Ibṭāl al-ḥiyal*; al-Dānī, *al-Sunan al-wārida fil-fitan*; al-Bayhaqī, *Shuʿab* (18: *Nashr al-ʿilm* towards the end); and, in part, by al-Bukhārī, *Khalq afʿāl al-ʿIbād*; (ii) Muʿādh b. Jabal by Daylamī; (iii) Ibn ʿUmar by al-Ḥākim in *Tārīkh Naysābūr*. ʿAlawī b. Aḥmad al-Ḥaddād (1216/1801) said in the introduction to *Miṣbāḥ al-anām fī radd shubuhāt al-Najdī al-bidʿī al-ladhī aḍalla bihā al-ʿawāmm* (The light of mankind on the refutation of the dubious matters raised by the Najdi innovator by which he led astray the common public), "the words 'out of them dissension came forth' refer to Musaylima the Arch-Liar while the words, 'and back to them shall it return' refer to Muḥammad b. ʿAbd al-Wahhāb and his followers."

44
Absence of supporters of truth in the era of tyrants – [Categorical obligation of an Islamic caliphate]

I seek refuge in Allah from the accursed devil
In the Name of Allah the All-Beneficent the Most Merciful
There is no power nor strength but with Allah the High, the Magnificent
Permission, O my Master, support!
Our way is companionship, and goodness is in the congregation

We are living in a time in which no supporters of the truth are found whereas supporters of falsehood are many. This is why, when the Messenger of Allah–upon him the blessings and peace of Allah–commended the Umma of the end of times, whereby a single person would be given the reward of fifty, the Companions asked him, "Fifty of us or fifty of them?" The Messenger–upon him the blessings and peace of Allah–said to them, "Nay, fifty of you! For you have helpers in support of the truth whereas they will not find anyone to help them defend the truth."[1] And in their time, whoever stands for the truth they pounce on him to eradicate him.

There remains no more defenders of the truth. We are now in the time of the tyrants, whereby our Prophet–upon him blessings and peace–has told us of the stages through which the Muhammadan Umma shall pass so that we would know in what stage we find ourselves. He said, "There shall be after me caliphs, and after the caliphs emirs, and after the emirs kings, and after the kings *jabābira* (tyrants). After that there shall come out a man from the people of my House that will fill the earth with justice and right just as it had been filled with injustice and transgression."[2] I.e. "there will be the rightly-guided

[1] Narrated from (i) Abū Tha'labat al-Khushanī by Abū Dāwūd (*Malāḥim, al-amr wal-nahy*); Ibn Abī al-Dunyā, *al-Amr bil-ma'rūf*; *al-Ṣabr wal-thawāb 'alayh*; *al-'Uqūbāt*; Ibn Ḥibbān, *Ṣaḥīḥ* (2:108-109 §385); Bayhaqī, *Ādāb*, *Shu'ab*, *al-Sunan al-kubrā* and others; (ii) Ibn 'Umar by Ibn Waḍḍāḥ, *al-Bida'*; (iii) 'Utba b. Ghazwān by Marwazī, *al-Sunna*; Ṭabarānī, *Awsaṭ* (3:272 §3121), *Kabīr* and *Musnad al-Shāmiyyīn*. Cf. the hadith, "My Umma is like the rain: it is unknown whether its beginning is better or its end." Narrated from (i) Anas by Aḥmad; Tirmidhī (*ḥasan*); (ii-v) 'Ammār b. Yāsir, 'Abd Allāh b. 'Amr, Ibn 'Umar and 'Alī by Abū Ya'lā and others. It is the last hadith in al-Baghawī's *Maṣābīḥ al-Sunna* and Nabhānī's *Arba'īn fī amthāl afṣaḥi al-'ālamīn*.

[2] Narrated from (i) Jābir al-Ṣadafī or his father Mājid by Ibn Abī Ḥātim, *al-Jarḥ wal-ta'dīl*, 9 vols. (Hyderabad: Dā'irat al-Ma'ārif al-'Uthmāniyya, 1373/1953, rept. Beirut: Dār Iḥyā' al-Turāth al-'Arabī, n.d.) 2:494 §2029; Ṭabarānī, *Kabīr* (22:374 §937); Abū Nu'aym, *Ma'rifat al-Ṣaḥāba* (2:553-554 §1538, 5:2857 §6737); Ibn 'Asākir, *Tārīkh*

caliphs after me, then the Umayyad emirs in Syro-Palestine, then the Abbasid emirs in Baghdad," then Sultan Selim received the sacred relics from the last Abbasid caliph, whereupon began the era of the kings, which then ended in the time of Sultan 'Abd al-Ḥamīd, after which began the time of the tyrants. It is in the latter era that the flag of the Messenger–upon him the blessings and peace of Allah–has disappeared. Thus you will not find defenders of the truth in the time of the tyrants.

In Turkey, after the abolition of the Caliphate, they put to death 40,000 major ulema. They abolished all madrasas and all show of religion, and they forbade the recitation of the Qur'ān and its teaching. Then that [behavior] spread to the countries of Islam. You will not find, in the time of the tyrants, anyone gathering under the leadership of a single leader to lift up the flag of the Messenger–upon him the blessings and peace of Allah–which will not be surrendered to a tyrant's hand but rather it has its qualified carrier who will lift it up. This is why you see in this time many Islamic flags lifted up, but which of them contains Islam and subsumes the Umma? You cannot find anything other than the Messenger's flag to contain them. Moreover, all the Crusaders and the Jews are in agreement over the division of the Muhammadan Umma and the prevention of its gathering under a single flag so that they can more easily swallow them up. This has been an ongoing conspiracy since Islam first appeared until we reached what we have reached today.

Before the deposition of Sultan 'Abd al-Ḥamīd (1909) Islam possessed *hayba* (awe), as all feared the Prophet's flag which, if it were unfurled, made jihad an obligation on all. Now we stand in need of someone that will unfurl the flag of the Messenger–upon him the blessings and peace of Allah. Such an Imam must be followed, not be a follower, and his ruling is enforced, and the presidents and common Muslims submit to him east and west. The existence of such an Imam is a *farḍ* (categorical obligation) for the Umma. This is why they are all sinful. Thus you will see there are no defenders of truth now. For the conditions of everyday life have become the principal concern of people. The lower-middle class work for their bellies while the upper-middle class run after the world in mutual pride and the pursuit of pleasure. They are not thinking about the issue of caliphate or the Imam or whoever will carry up the flag of the Messenger–upon him the blessings and peace of Allah. That is why the people of the truth have become complete strangers. Most certainly "The

(14:282-283, 61:195) cf. Ibn Kathīr, *al-Bidāya wal-nihāya* (*Fitan, dhikr al-Mahdī*) and *Jāmi' al-masānīd wal-sunan* (2:66-67, 9:220-221); Ibn Ḥajar, *al-Iṣāba* (1:551 §1041, Jābir b. Mājid al-Ṣadafī); (ii) Abū Hurayra in a similar wording by Ibn Ḥibbān (15:41 §6658); Bayhaqī, *Dalā'il* (6:521).

faith-system began as a stranger and it shall end up again as it began, so blessings to the strangers!"[1]

Deliverance has certainly drawn near, and our Prophet–upon him blessings and peace of Allah–says, "To await deliverance is worship,"[2] and *the promise of the One God is truth* (Yūnus 10:55, Kahf 18:21, Qaṣaṣ 28:13 etc.), as He has said, *the One God has promised those of you who believe and do righteous deeds that He shall indeed grant them succession in the land just as He granted those who were before them succession* (Nūr 24:55). And this is glad tidings from Allah that the second succession in the land is near, and there will be *a victory from the One God and a conquest at hand* (Ṣaff 61:13).

By the sanctity of the Beloved, by the sanctity of the Fatiha.

[1] A Prophetic hadith narrated as "Islam began as a stranger, etc." from (i-xiv) Ibn Mas'ūd, Anas, Sa'd b. Abī Waqqāṣ, 'Abd al-Raḥmān b. Sanna, 'Abd Allāh b. 'Umar, Abū Hurayra, 'Amr b. 'Awf, Sahl b. Sa'd al-Sā'idī, Jābir b. 'Abd Allāh, Abū al-Dardā', Abū Umāma, Wāthila b. al-Asqa', Ibn 'Abbās and Abū Sa'īd al-Khudrī by Ibn Abī Shayba, Aḥmad, al-Dārimī, Muslim, Ibn Mājah, al-Tirmidhī, al-Bazzār, Abū Ya'lā, al-Dūlābī, al-Ṭaḥāwī, Ājurrī, Ṭabarānī and others. Kattānī in *Naẓm al-mutanāthir* cites four more Companions narrating it.

[2] See Suhba I.2, eighth note.

45

The duty to rid oneself of egotism – [Egotism and anger in this life will burn one in the hereafter – Whoever says "I" and "me" is as if fighting Allah – Repeating *astaghfiru-l-Lāh* is best to leave anger]

I seek refuge in Allah from the accursed devil
In the Name of Allah the All-Beneficent the Most Merciful
There is no power nor strength but with Allah the High, the Magnificent
Permission, O my Master, support!
Our way is companionship, and goodness is in the congregation

We are humble students. And we are hoping that Allah Almighty is giving, and His Messenger–upon him blessings and peace of Allah–is giving, and the Muhammadan inheritor and the inheritors of all the Prophets are all giving to the student. Mawlana used to say that the full jug, you cannot put anything in it. This is why whoever comes to the Messenger as a humble student must for sure take his share; but whoever comes to him obdurate will be left disappointed.

We are imitating students. We want them to extend their help to us. Whoever exposes himself to the help of the possessor of help must for sure obtain it. Whoever acts self-sufficient is left to himself. And whoever is left to himself will be like Iblīs. This is why we are humble students and we do not claim to have knowledge. Rather we benefit from what they have bestowed on us through their blessing, and we benefit from the speech of our liege lord the Shaykh ['Abd Allah al-Daghistani]. For his *kalām* (discourse) points to his *kamāl* (perfection). And whoever wants perfection must keep close company with the possessors of perfection. An example for us is the noble Companions, how they were before and how they became by keeping company with the Messenger–upon him the blessings and peace of Allah.

A person's speech points to their perfection or lack thereof. Since all the speech of Mawlana Sultan al-Awliya is pointing to his perfection, he is explaining the magnificent verse *nor have I created the jinns and human beings but so that they would worship Me* (al-Dhāriyāt 51:56), i.e. **the servants were not created to busy themselves with the matters of this world but for worship**, and Allah has tasked with it the jinns and human beings. Mawlana is saying that Allah wants us to worship Him with a pure worship exclusively for

Him, since Allah says, *behold! To the One God belongs the absolute faith* (Zumar 39:3); *and they were never commanded but to worship the One God, dedicating to Him alone the faith* (Bayyina 98:5). And this is telling us that we should not offer to our nurturing Lord a fake worship, when the Messenger–upon him the blessings and peace of Allah–is telling us, "Whoever deceives us then he is not of us."[1]

When will worshipfulness be purely for Allah? When there is no share of ego in it. There are 500 types of worshipfulness that the Prophet–upon him the blessings and peace of Allah–brought and the human being's ego wants to have a share in them. I.e. it will not do any deed unless it receives some compensation for it. It does not accept for the deed to be purely for the sake of Allah. Mawlana would say, "Allah does not want any prayer or fasting; rather He wants purely sincere deeds for His sake only–exalted is He. O my God, You alone are my goal." For if you prayed or fasted for other than the sake of Allah, you will have associated a partner with your nurturing Lord in your worship of Him. That is why we are legally tasked with implementing purely dedicated worship for the sake of Allah.

This [task] demands effort against your ego until it submits to you. Every human being knows best what deficiency there is in him, for Allah Almighty says, *rather the human being is against himself an all-seeing eye* (al-Qiyāma 75:14). The above is all showing the human being that he must reform himself so that his works will be purely and exclusively for the sake of Allah. It is possible for the human being to become motivated for self-reform if only with his intention. Even if his spiritual wayfaring was not completed, Allah will complete it for him. He will not leave His servant that formed the intention and walked in His way. The Qur'ān bears witness that whoever comes out of his house to go to Allah and His Messenger, then death overtakes him, then for certain his recompense has fallen upon Allah.[2]

[1] Narrated from (i) Abū Hurayra by al-Ḥumaydī; Ibn Abī Shayba; Aḥmad; Muslim; Ibn Mājah; Abū Dāwūd and others; (ii) Abū al-Ḥamrā' by Ibn Abī Shayba; Ibn Mājah; al-Dūlābī and others; (iii) Abū Burda b. Niyār by Ibn Abī Shayba; Aḥmad; al-Bazzār; al-Ḥākim and others; (iv) Ibn 'Umar by Aḥmad; al-Dārimī; al-Bazzār and others; (v) al-Barā' b. 'Āzib by al-Bukhārī, *al-Tārīkh al-kabīr*; al-Ṭabarānī, *Awsaṭ*; (vi) Qays b. Abī Gharaza by Ibn Abī 'Āṣim, *al-Āḥād wal-mathānī*; (vii) Ibn Mas'ūd by Ibn Ḥibbān; al-Ṭabarānī, *Ṣaghīr*; (viii-ix) Ḥudhayfa and Abū Mūsā al-Ash'arī by al-Ṭabarānī, *Awsaṭ*; (x-xi) Ḍumayra and Ibn 'Abbās by Ṭabarānī, *Kabīr*; (xii) Abū Sa'īd al-Khudrī by Tammām al-Rāzī. Kattānī cites five more Companions in the *Naẓm*.

[2] *And whoever should leave his home as an emigrant to the One God and His Messenger, whereupon death should come to him, then, assuredly, his wage has fallen upon the One God* (al-Nisā' 4:100).

What is asked of us is to migrate from our egos to Allah Most High. This emigration is perpetual and until the Day of Resurrection. The Messenger–upon him the blessings and peace of Allah–migrated from Mecca to Medina the Illuminated, and we have, in the Messenger of Allah, an excellent model. Let us migrate of our own wills to Allah Most High. In all of the faith-systems it is required to migrate from the ego to Allah. Allah Most High said, *and the One God summons to the Abode of Wholeness* (Yūnus 10:25). The entirety of the Abode of Wholeness is with Him.

Allah Most High is saying, *and We have more* (Qāf 50:35). Yet people are running away *as if they were startled onagers fleeing from a mighty lion* (al-Muddaththir 74:50-51). But they must realize that tomorrow is the Day of *ʿarḍ* (Exposition) and today is the Day of *tadāruk* (Amendment). This is why Mawlana [Shaykh ʿAbd Allah al-Daghistani] is saying that **the beginning of the way is love, and whoever you tie your heart to with love, you shall be with them on the Day of Resurrection.**

Mawlana also says there are 80,000 bad characteristics in the human being, and the meaning is that there are 80,000 veils between the human being and the Messenger–upon him the blessings and peace of Allah. When the human being cuts them, he will see the spiritual reality of the Messenger and he will be in his presence. Allah Almighty said, *and know that in your midst is the Messenger of the One God* (Ḥujurāt 49:8), i.e. from pre-existence to everlastingness. For the origin of existence and the foundation of creation is from the light of the Beloved–upon him the blessings and peace of Allah. It is from this light that all the universes have emerged, and he is in us. However, we are veiled from him with the veils of the ego.

The greatest of these veils is the anger of the ego because, at the time of anger, the light of belief is extinguished and the fire of anger flares up. The origin of anger is the ego's selfishness that claims that it is Allah. Its beginning is anger and its end is woe and regret. For at the time of anger, Iblīs blows arrogance into the human being to the point he sees nothing and no one as greater than himself or as lord other than himself. The meaning of this is as Allah said, *self-importance spurs him on to sin* (al-Baqara 2:206).

Anger prevents the servant's arrival at the presence of the All-True. With the fire of anger the fire of Gehenna increases to burn his egotism so that he can enter Paradise. From here the fire of anger is kindled out of our egotism, and over there our nurturing Lord stores it up. This is why the *ḍirs* (molar tooth) of the people of hellfire is as big as Mount Uḥud,[1] because of their

[1] Narrated from (i-iii) Ibn ʿUmar, Abū Saʿīd al-Khudrī and Abū Hurayra by Aḥmad;

egotism in this life. **This is knowledge from the sciences of the secrets of the Qur'ān. Whoever has egotism and anger in this life shall carry them with him so that they will burn him in the hereafter.** Thus do you see people and nations burning up with the fire of anger in this life, whose origin is from the selfishness of egos. For every human being is claiming that he is Allah and no one concedes to the other. This is why the Prophets came to deliver people from their egotism so that they will worship Allah alone. Whoever acknowledges servanthood, no trace of egotism remains with him. For whoever says, "I am a servant," how will he claim that he is a god? But when servanthood is not purely and exclusively for Allah, the egotism of many people is fostered therein. And whoever becomes an ego-driven person his egotism shall burn him.

Mawlana is saying that **whoever says "I" is as if fighting Allah. This is why it is our duty to strive with all our strength to leave egotism. Every time the servant bows and prostrates he must rid himself of his egotism and not increase it. Until the ego's anger goes away from the servant his deed is not accepted because it is counterfeit.** And the evidence of the effect of egotism in the human ego is that what he loves makes him happy but what he does not love he loathes. Mawlana is saying that without leaving the ego's selfishness and the ego's anger, every time the servant mentions "Allah, Allah," the angels rebut him by saying, "Liar, liar! For you are not intending Allah with your dhikr nor do you know Allah for you to mention Him, so we will never believe you until you leave your ego's selfishness." And the Awliya of Allah hear this angelic speech.

This is why Mawlana al-Shaykh is instructing that **when the murid's anger shows, instead of saying, "Allah," he must say *astaghfiru-l-Lāh* (I ask Allah forgiveness) to the number of the word "Allah" so that it will be an aide for him to leave egotism. More than that, asking forgiveness at that station itself requires asking renewed forgiveness. That is why we repeat *istighfār*. This is the way of the Folk, the way and the *adab* of Allah's pure and sincere servants, and we are legally tasked to be pure and sincere servants of our Almighty nurturing Lord. Servants must make every effort towards this matter because it might carry the meaning of the whole life of a human being.** This is why when the desert Arab asked of the Messenger–upon him the blessings and peace of Allah–to instruct him he only said to him, "Do not be angry," and he did not add anything to it.[1]

and Abū Hurayra by Muslim and al-Tirmidhī.

[1] See Suhba I.15, second note.

What is the secret of this hadith? It is that **the presence of anger is evidence of the presence of egotism, and whoever has egotism in him then he is claiming that he is Allah**. So what will the result of his deeds be? *Have you seen him who has taken up as his god his own whim?* (al-Jāthiya 45:23). But getting read of egotism is not easily achieved. *Innamā al-ʿilmu bil-taʿallum* (knowledge can only be through learning) *wal-ḥilmu bil-taḥallum* (and patient wisdom can only be through patient wisening).[1] **When this discourse finds a place of eminence in the heart of the servant in the time of need, it[2] will point out to him, "Leave your egotism."** At that time he shall hear the speech of the Prophet–upon him the blessings and peace of Allah–in his heart. Otherwise that fire will burn him, for it is impossible for the servant to enter Paradise together with egotism. He must first burn away the egotism, out of which all the impurities are generated.

From Allah is all success. By the sanctity of the Beloved, by the sanctity of the Fatiha.

[1] A Prophetic hadith narrated from (i) Abū Hurayra by Ibn Abī al-Dunyā, *al-Ḥilm*; al-Dāraquṭnī, *ʿIlal*; (ii) Abū al-Dardāʾ by Ṭabarānī, *al-Awsaṭ*; *Musnad al-Shāmiyyīn*; Ibn Shāhīn, *al-Targhīb*; Dāraquṭnī, *ʿIlal*; Abū Nuʿaym, *Ḥilya*; and as a saying of Abū al-Dardāʾ by Hannād b. al-Sarīy, *al-Zuhd*; Ibn Ḥibbān, *Rawḍat al-ʿuqalāʾ*; al-Bayhaqī, *al-Madkhal ilā al-Sunan* and *Shuʿab al-īmān*; Ibn ʿAbd al-Barr, *Jāmiʿ bayān al-ʿilm*.

[2] I.e. the presence of the *murshid* in the heart of the murid. See Bayḍawī's *Tafsīr* and the commentaries on *burhān Rabbih* (the demonstration of his nurturing Lord) in Yūsuf 12:24 in the manuals of the Naqshbandi masters.

46

Duty to wage war against egos so as to behold the magnificence of the All-True – [True knowledge]

I seek refuge in Allah from the accursed devil
In the Name of Allah the All-Beneficent the Most Merciful
There is no power nor strength but with Allah the High, the Magnificent
Permission, O my Master, support!
Our way is companionship, and goodness is in the congregation

Our gathering is by order of the Messenger–upon him blessings and peace–and by order of Sultan al-Awliya and our noble masters. I do not come to Tripoli except by his permission. Nor do I come in pursuit of this world. For "the world is a carcass and its seekers are dogs."[1] I have come for the purpose of war against transgressive, rebellious sinful egos and my call is to myself, not anyone else, and to egos that are thus described. Our war is against transgressive, tyrannical, rebellious, unbelieving egos.

Every human being must be an enemy of his ego because it is the worst enemy, and he must help us over this matter.[2]

[1] Narrated from 'Alī b. Abī Ṭālib as his own saying by Abū Isḥāq Ibrāhīm b. Muḥ. b. Yaḥyā b. Sakhtawayh al-Naysābūrī al-Muzakkī (d. 362/973), *al-Muzakkiyāt wa-hiya al-fawā'id al-muntakhaba al-gharā'ib al-'awālī min ḥadīth Abī Isḥāq al-Muzakkī intiqā' al-Dāraquṭnī*, ed. Aḥmad Fāris al-Sallūm (Beirut: Dār al-Bashā'ir al-Islāmiyya, 1425/2004) p. 250 §152; Abū Ṭālib Muḥ. b. 'Alī b. 'Aṭiyya al-Ḥārithī al-Makkī (d. 386 /996), *Qūt al-qulūb* (32: *Sharḥ maqāmāt al-yaqīn, maqām al-zuhd*); Abū Nu'aym, *Ḥilya* (8:238); Shajarī, *Amālī* (2:267); Nawawī, *Tahdhīb al-asmā' wal-lughāt* (1:346).

[2] Per the Prophetic reports I. "Your enemy is not the one who, when he kills you, causes you to enter Paradise and, when you kill him, it accrues light for you; your worst enemy is your own ego that is between your flanks," narrated in *mursal* mode through the narrators of the *Ṣaḥīḥayn* from (i) Abū Mālik al-Ash'arī by Abū Bakr Muḥ. b. Ja'far b. Muḥ. al-Kharā'iṭī, *I'tilāl al-qulūb*, ed. Ḥamdī al-Dimardāsh, 2nd ed., 2 vols. (Mecca: Nizār Muṣṭafā al-Bāz, 1421/2000) 1:26 §32; Ibn Bishrān, *Amālī*; al-Daylamī, *Firdaws* (3:408 §5248); (ii) Anas per Ibn Ḥajar in Zabīdī, *Itḥāf* (7:206); Ibn Rajab, *Nūr al-iqtibās fī mishkāt waṣiyyat al-Nabī ṣallā Allāhu 'alayhi wa-sallam li-Ibni 'Abbās* in *Majmū' rasā'il Ibni Rajab*, ed. Ṭal'at al-Ḥulwānī, 2nd ed. 4 vols. (Cairo: al-Fārūq al-Ḥadītha, 1424/2003) 3:157 and in his *Sharḥ hadīth "Labbayk."* The latter also cited Abū Bakr as saying to 'Umar upon appointing him as his successor, "the first thing I warn you against is your own ego between your flanks;" (iii) Ibn 'Abbās by al-Bayhaqī, *Zuhd* (p. 156 §343) but the latter is probably a forged chain; II. "O Allah, protect me from the evil of my own ego," from 'Imrān b. Ḥuṣayn and Abū Hurayra by Aḥmad, al-Dārimī, al-Bukhārī in *Khalq af'āl al-'ibād*, Abū Dāwūd, Tirmidhī and others; III. "The mujahid

We want to erase ourselves until we are nothing. I am not giving you ranks. On the contrary, what is required of you is self-extinction. Whoever accepts is welcome. Our egos make us low and despised. We must sacrifice this ego so that our worship will be for Allah Almighty. I never want for any of you to pride himself over the other as being richer, or more knowledgeable in fiqh, or more intelligent. For this is how people are now, but this is unrightful proudness. For pride belongs to Allah alone–Almighty is He. Knowledge teaches us that we are nothing and ensures that we have power to look at the magnificence of Allah. The more we increase in knowledge the more we must belittle ourselves until we disappear and no trace remains of our egos. This alone is knowledge.

When you look at the magnificence of Allah you lose sight of yourself until nothing remains of yourself. This is why I do not like for people of egos to be present in my gathering, because my enmity is for egos. I do not give leeway to anyone—not to Muslims and not to other than them. Whoever raises his head in this time I shall cut it down. This is my function.

Let none of you pride himself over the other. Focus only on the magnificence of Allah and you will see that you are nothing. This is spiritual knowledge. And I want you to erase the word *za'l* (displeasure) from your vocabulary, because our way is the way of the truth and not the way of playing games. Rather it is the way of high manners. As the Messenger is saying, "My nurturing Lord has raised me and He has perfected my manners."[1]

From Allah is all success. By the sanctity of the Beloved, by the sanctity of the Fatiha.

is he who makes jihad against his ego for the sake of obeying Allah" narrated from Faḍāla b. 'Ubayd by Aḥmad, al-Tirmidhī, Ibn Ḥibbān and Ḥākim; IV. "The strong man is not he who wrestles down others but he who controls his ego when he is angry," narrated from Abū Hurayra by Mālik, Aḥmad, Bukhārī and Muslim; V. "Help me against your own *nafs*," narrated from Rabī'a b. Ka'b al-Aslamī by Aḥmad, al-Dārimī, Muslim, Nasā'ī, Abū Dāwūd; and other hadiths. "Putting one's lust to death by warning the ego of the punishment of Allah and fear of His threat so that one will subdued it or repel it from the impulse of its whim and what stirs up in it to straighten it so that it will keep to the divine command that Allah ordered it to follow: **this alone is the greatest jihad, greater than which there is no jihad,** and Ḥasan [al-Baṣrī] used to say, 'Your enemy is not the one you have killed and of whom you are now relieved; but rather your enemy is your own ego that is between your flanks,' to control **which receives, without doubt, greater reward in the presence of Allah than the jihad against the polytheists"** per Ṭabarī, *Tahdhīb al-āthār wa-tafṣīl al-thābit 'an Rasūl Allāh min al-akhbār*, ed. Maḥm. Muḥ. Shākir, 6 vols. (Cairo: Maṭba'at al-Madanī, 1402/1982) 5:812-813 (*Musnad 'Umar b. al-Khaṭṭāb*). Cf. also Tustarī, *Tafsīr* (Baqara 2:30, Aḥqāf 46:6).

[1] See Suhba I.26, first note.

47

The fire of unlawful appetite shall be put out by the Mahdī's sword

I seek refuge in Allah from the accursed devil
In the Name of Allah the All-Beneficent the Most Merciful
There is no power nor strength but with Allah the High, the Magnificent
Permission, O my Master, support!
Our way is companionship, and goodness is in the congregation

Fire cannot be put out except by water but the fire of illicit appetite is now blazing in the whole world. This is why water will not extinguish it, but only the sword of *Ṣāḥib al-zamān* (the spiritual leader of endtimes). Now, it is difficult for a person to master the matter of his faith-system, because with a single look the heart becomes poisoned and the light of faith goes out. For whoever looks at a woman that is not closely related to him for example, will be as if touching her with his gaze, and if he were able to get her he would not delay it. For whoever looks at the matters of fornication does not delay committing fornication. But the Messenger–upon him the blessings and peace of Allah–said, "The fornicator does not fornicate while he is a believer."[1] This is why we are taking shelter in the kind forgiveness of our nurturing Lord. But as for the sake of reaching the station of the sincere elect, then that is in need of earnest effort because it is prized.

From Allah is all success. By the sanctity of the Beloved, by the sanctity of the Fatiha.

[1] Narrated from (i) Abū Hurayra by Aḥmad; Dārimī; Bukhārī; Muslim; Ibn Mājah; Abū Dāwūd; al-Tirmidhī; Nasā'ī; (ii) Jābir b. 'Abd Allāh by Aḥmad; (iii) Ibn 'Abbās by al-Bukhārī; al-Nasā'ī.

48

Question on why Iblīs exists – Jaʿfarī fiqh – *The All-Merciful has taught the Qur'ān* – Balqīs's throne – Usury in Islam – The orphan's maintainer

I seek refuge in Allah from the accursed devil
In the Name of Allah the All-Beneficent the Most Merciful
There is no power nor strength but with Allah the High, the Magnificent
Permission, O my Master, support!
Our way is companionship, and goodness is in the congregation

The question puts the questioner under legal liability. For when he asks the question and gets to know, he becomes bound to act accordingly. Also, questions must be motivated by belief or worshipfulness or excellent high manners. If they are none of those three categories they are part of *mā lā yaʿnī* (what is of no benefit),[1] which is rejected in Islam.

Answers to questions put by some teachers
to Shaykh Muhammad Nazim al-Rabbani

Question 1: "In a certain book there is a thorough description for Iblīs's tragedy. In the author's view 'Iblīs disobeyed at the very time that he was obeying.' He obeyed the divine will in the absence of prostration to Ādam so he was counted as rebelliously disobeying the divine command, but had he obeyed the command he would have rebelliously disobeyed the divine will. So he has no way out whether in obedience or disobedience."

Answer: According to the people of truth Iblīs is a servant under order and he is bound under the will of the Almighty All-True. The *murīd* (willer) is Allah. And He has a far-reaching wisdom in every matter without exception, from the perspective that our nurturing Lord never created anything in vain. He says in the Qur'ān, *our nurturing Lord! You did not create this in vain* (Āl ʿImrān 3:191). Iblīs is something among other things and he was not created in vain. This is why, before the question, the questioner must first realize the wisdom of the existence of Iblīs so that he may base his question on this fact. For our nurturing Lord never created anything in vain—and because, if He had created something in vain, it would inseparably follow that there is, because of that vain thing, a deficiency in the world. But when our nurturing Lord has

[1] See Suhba I.35, note 5.

created everything with wisdom and with truth, then there is an objective and an aim, so that He will raise the servants to the presence of the Almighty All-True. And for the people of truth, Iblīs is a stepladder to reach high stations and Allah Almighty has certainly created Iblīs and given him a chance for servanthood, and he did worship his nurturing Lord.

When Allah wanted to bring out the children of Ādam from absolute inexistence into existence, the wisdom of our nurturing Lord dictated for Iblīs—whose name was ʿAzāzīl—to be an intermediary for making human beings reach their levels in the presence of Allah. So He commanded him and all the angels to prostrate. Our nurturing Lord had proclaimed that he would be ordering the angels to prostrate through a certain command, and that one of them would disobey. When He proclaimed that, all the angels wept, each fearing that he himself might be that servant and that the garland of malediction would be placed on his neck.

Of wisdoms there is a type that is spoken and there is a type that is left unspoken. And of the secret wisdoms that were not proclaimed is the fact that [ʿAzāzīl] knew of this matter, and the angels asked him to supplicate for them so that they would be safe of that rebellious sin. Since [ʿAzāzīl] was one whose supplication was answered, he supplicated for them. In the sacred Law when the servant supplicates for his brother and he does not mention himself the angels will say, *wa-laka mithluh* (and to you the same).[1] What about when ʿAzāzīl supplicated, "O my nurturing Lord, keep safe Your servants the angels from falling into rebellious sin?"

Allah did answer his supplication, and in the manifest locution of the Law he says *ansānīhi-l-Lāh* (Allah caused me to forget it). I.e. he supplicated for everyone and forgot himself. Since he became overproud, the divine curse descended on him because of that violation; or maybe he had forwarded himself under that curse, as a deliverance for the rest of the angels and a safety for them. This is a secret that is not known. And when our nurturing Lord ordered the angels to prostrate he was standing to see that servant who had not prostrated to Allah, whereas all the angels were prostrating. At that moment, as he was standing, and without his realizing, the divine curse descended on him, since the divine will dictated this matter.

Thereupon a state of intoxication descended on Iblīs. He lost his mind and became heedless of reality by the wisdom of the divine will that had dictated

[1] Narrated thus as a Prophetic hadith from Abū al-Dardā' by Abū al-Shaykh, *Aḥādīth Abī al-Zubayr ʿan ghayr Jābir*, ed. Badr b. ʿAbd Allāh al-Badr (Riyadh: Maktabat al-Rushd, 1417/1996) p. 132 §77; in the wording *wa-laka bi-mithlih* by Ibn Abī Shayba, *Muṣannaf* (15:85 §29768); and in the wording *wa-laka bi-mithlin* by Aḥmad; Ibn Mājah; Muslim; al-Bukhārī, *al-Adab al-mufrad*; al-Ṭabarānī; and al-Bayhaqī.

this matter, and he was now intoxicated. Then our nurturing Lord placed the children of Ādam in Paradise. However, for the children of Ādam to enter Paradise, there was a remnant of their selves that required to be cast off from them.[1] Had they not cast them off, they would have found states in Paradise that they would have been incapable of comprehending. This is why Allah made Iblīs a simple reason for the casting off of those selves.

More than that, when Iblīs entered Paradise, did he enter without knowledge of Allah, or unseen by Allah? However, **for a wisdom decreeing it, he entered and brought out Ādam and our mother Ḥawwā' to earth so that the knowledge of the children of Ādam would be completed in this life and their perfection would be completed, since our nurturing Lord says, *and We have certainly honored the children of Ādam* (Banū Isrā'īl/Isrā' 17:70), and since He made it a pillar of belief** [to believe in the foreordained decree], **the good of it and the bad of it being all from Allah**. The heart of this question reaches to this point. And this whole matter is part of the secret of *al-qadar* (the foreordained decree) without the shadow of a doubt. But its resolution is extremely difficult and to make it understood is more difficult yet, so that the knowledge of certainty and the reality of certainty would take place for the servant, and he comprehends. And when the human being realizes the wisdom for the existence of Iblīs his mind relaxes.

Iblīs has a page specific to him in the Preserved Tablet from the first of his affair, then the middle of it then the last of it. How he was at first, then where he is ending up. This is an obscure matter even for the experts in sacred Law, so how could the rest of them recognize it? This is why [it suffices to say that] Iblīs is coursing between the will of Allah and the command of Allah, whereby our nurturing Lord says, *and to each one his orientation that he turns to* (al-Baqara 2:148). Iblīs likewise has an orientation because he is subsumed under *each one*, and the upshot of his affair is in the major Judgment. After Allah judges between the servants He shall summon Iblīs for the Reckoning. That address shall restore to Iblīs his mind and he shall appear before the presence of the Almighty All-True for trial and judgment. There, Allah is the wisest of judges and nothing but justice issues from Him, and justice itself is from Him.

We have knowledge concerning the trial and judgment of Iblīs but we do not want to bring it out since it pertains to the secret of *qadar* and it is not divulged. However, we must firmly believe that our nurturing Lord is *aḥkam al-ḥākimīn* (the Wisest of judges) and that He shall rule with justice concerning Iblīs, and after that with His bounty, and Allah Most High has certainly said to Iblīs, *and verily upon you is My curse until the Day of Judgment* (Ṣād

[1] *Baqiyyatun min nufūsihim al-latī yajibu ṭarḥuhā minhum.*

38:78), and He did not say "forever." Therefore the questioner needs not anguish himself over Iblīs.

Do you have knowledge of the state of Iblīs at the time of the command to prostrate? Therefore we do not judge that his state is such and such. When Iblīs was ordered to prostrate, was he not knowledgeable? Does he need us to defend him? Furthermore, **the divine command can be disobeyed but the divine will cannot be disobeyed**. This is a rule.

There is also the secret of the foreordained decree. The proof is that Allah says, *nor have I created the jinns and human beings but so that they would worship Me* (Dhāriyāt 51:56): where is our worship? And how many of the children of Ādam do worship, although they are all commanded to worship? Yet they are rebellious and disobedient. If we said that His will is that we should disobey him we would have to say that we are forced, thereby entering into the *madhhab al-jabriyya* (doctrine of determinism)—and this is not true at all. For we do not know what is inscribed for us in the presence of Allah. If we knew what was inscribed and acted on its basis like a program it would be determinism. But by virtue of it being unseen by us and we plainly see that we have free choice, it follows that we are legally tasked—and it is with our will that we disobey.

However, does rebellious sin harm the servant—or belief?[1] **Belief is an essence, a free gift from Allah and not something acquired.**[2] **It is not possible for the servant to acquire belief** even if he has the worshipfulness of Prophets. Rather it is a bestowal from Allah. In allusion to that fact a hadith of the Prophet–upon him the blessings and peace of Allah–states, "Every newborn is born in conformity with the *fiṭra* (primordial state / disposition / nature),"[3] i.e. *islām* (submission). More than that, **since when are we a believer and a submitter?** This is the *'ilm al-ḥāl* (presently-needed knowledge)![4] And its answer is, **since the Day of *"am I not your nurturing Lord?" They said yes* (al-Aʿrāf 7:172). And was there anyone at that time that did not attend that tremendous event? Our belief was an *īmān shuhūdī* (witness-based belief),**

[1] Mawlana's position is that sin does not harm belief itself, contrary to the Mu'tazila and the Khawārij. At no point does he say that sin does not harm the believer, in conformity with the Māturīdī litotes, "we do not say that sins do not harm the believer" (*Fiqh al-akbar*), "we do not say that sins do not harm the doer as long as there is belief" (*'Aqīda Ṭaḥāwiyya*) where *īmān* and *islām* are used identically.

[2] As stated by Ibn Khafīf in his creed, i.e. an integral element as opposed to a non-essential accident. This is what Mālik b. Anas and the early Imams described "as a light cast into the heart."

[3] See Suhba I.34, second note.

[4] See Suhba I.14, second note.

and we were hearing the divine address, and we said yes, and this is a bestowal from that Day. This is why sins cannot harm belief, like a jewel that fell into impurities. Are we going to leave it there?

This is why belief is a lordly secret from Allah given to the servant, but the reality of belief has not fully appeared to us. For if this reality appeared, would we ourselves remain in the *mulk* (visible created world)? We will end up in the *malakūt* (world of invisible sovereignty).

More than that, our nurturing Lord says, *the One God shall replace their evil deeds with excellent deeds* (Furqān 25:70). "And just as My servants do not tire of committing sins, I do not tire of changing them into good deeds."[1] An example of that is that as much as you throw impurities under a tree, does it ever itself become impure? Or rather does its strength increase? Through a divine wisdom from the side of Allah, the one with high spiritual energy draws near to Allah through his obedience, while the one devoid of spiritual energy Iblīs drives into the night; but our nurturing Lord in the last third of the night changes their evil deeds into good deeds.

Question 2: "What is the meaning of *and she was certainly intent on having him, and he intended to have her. Were it not that he saw the demonstration of his nurturing Lord—* (Yūsuf 12:24)?"

Answer: Allah speaks truth. *She was certainly intent on having him, and he intended to have her.* First, he is a Messenger-Prophet, and when she was intent on having him, he intended to have her in manifestation of the fact that he was a man and not a woman, and his virility suffices women from the first to the end of the world. Secondly, this is the demonstration of his nurturing Lord. His nurturing Lord manifested it to him and informed him that "this woman is yours, but this is not the time, and you must be patient."

Question 3: "Ja'farī fiqh is the fiqh transmitted from Imam Ja'far al-Ṣādiq b. Muḥammad al-Bāqir, so he is more deserving of being followed than the four Imams. So why did a section of the Muslims put him aside and another section held fast to him? And why is it not being taught together with the [four] madhhabs as a rapprochement between Sunnis and the Shī'a?"

Answer: A question on these questions is what is the goal of these schools, what does each school claim for its follower, and to what objective exactly do they direct their follower? **Madhhab means a way that makes one reach to Allah and His Messenger**–upon him the blessings and peace of Allah. So what is the mistake that the Shīa saw in the four Schools in making the servant

[1] Per the *hadith qudsī* to that effect where the sinner, seeing this, will say to Allah, "I have more sins yet." See Suhba I.91, third note.

reach Allah and His Messenger? But if the Umma did not reach through the way of the four madhhabs we should take their madhhab? As long as these madhhabs are avenues to reach, then why the disagreement?

Question 4: "*The All-Merciful. He has taught the Qur'ān. He has created the human being. He has taught him clear speech* (Raḥmān 55:1-4). These verses impart, in their sequence, that Allah taught the Qur'ān before creating the human being, so to whom did He teach it?"

Answer: There is a question: whom was Allah addressing with his beginningless speech in pre-existence? Among the Attributes of the All-True is that he is *Mutakallim* (Speaker), and His Attribute is of a beginningless, pre-existent, everlasting nature. Was He, in pre-existence, speaking to Himself without addressee? If a person spoke without addressee it would be said of him that he was mad. This is an allusion to a secret, namely, who was being addressed by the All-True on the pre-existent Day as He was *Mutakallim*? Another question—to clarify that—is when was *lā ilāha illā-l-Lāh* written—and when *lā ilāha illā-l-Lāh* was written, next to it was written *Muḥammadun Rasūlu-l-Lāh*, and **he is the one being addressed by our nurturing Lord.**[1] Allah is saying, "I was ever a hidden treasure,"[2] and this was ever the case. And the

[1] See Suhbas I.24, I.30 and I.38.

[2] "It has come in the hadith that is *ṣaḥīḥ* (sound) through *kashf* (unveiling) but *ghayr thābit* (unestablished) per transmission from the Messenger of Allah–upon him the blessings and peace of Allah–from his nurturing Lord that He said something in the meaning of this: 'I was ever a hidden treasure and was not known. I loved to be known so I created creation and made Myself known to them, then they came to know Me.'" Ibn 'Arabī, *Futūḥāt* (3:399, chapter 198). "Its meaning is sound and inferred from the saying of Allah Most High, *nor have I created the jinns and human beings but so that they would worship Me* (al-Dhāriyāt 51:56), meaning 'that they may know Me' as Ibn 'Abbās explained it [in al-Dīnawarī, *Mujālasa* 2:93 §225 and 8:122 §3442]" per al-Qārī, *al-Asrār al-marfū'a*. It is also thus explained by Mujāhid and Ibn Jurayj in the *Tafsīrs* of al-Tha'labī, Ibn 'Abd al-Barr (*Jāmi' al-'ilm*), al-Baghawī, Abū Ḥayyān, Samīn al-Ḥalabī, Ibn Kathīr and others. "From the *maqām sirr al-sirr* (station of the secret of the secret) is 'I was a treasure hidden and I desired to be known so I created creation, whereby they know Me.' Allah is speaking of Himself. 'I was a treasure, hidden,' means no one could look at Him except by His command and His signalling permission. The Command and the Signalling Permission have not been defined yet. [Nor can they be defined] for as long as we are still in the site of this world. For it is categorically forbidden for the *dunyā* to behold al-Haqq (the All-True)! And of the totality of the Prophets: among them is he that knocked on the door of Beholding Him and did not obtain his request; and among them is he that knocked on the door of Beholding Him and obtained his secret, as happened to our liege lord Muhammad–upon him the blessings and peace of Allah. We are waiting for the emergence of the *Ṣāḥib al-zamān* (spiritual leader of end time), our liege lord Muhammad al-Mahdi–upon him peace–so that the Umma will emerge into the open. And when it emerges into the open, everything will

Messenger is saying, "I was ever a Prophet"—which conveys beginninglessness—"when Ādam was still between water and clay."[1]

Question 5: "*An afrit said, one of the jinn, 'I will bring it to you before you rise from your place, and verily I am for it indeed strong and worthy of trust.' The one with whom there was some knowledge from the Scripture said, 'I will bring it to you before your gaze returns to you!'* (al-Naml 27:39). Who is this one that has the knowledge of the Book referred to in the noble verse?"

Answer: It is one of the servants of Allah from human beings, for the rank of human beings is higher from that of the jinns, as an honor to human beings.

Question 6: "How does Islam view *ribā*, bank interest, in our society today? If we want to take a loan, there is no *bayt al-māl* (Islamic treasury)."

Answer: We are now constrained to do such a thing and are not responsible for having to give interest over our debt, but accepting [the debt] is subject to a responsibility, whereby we were constrained and have no access to a fair loan. The ruling of the sacred Law is that *al-ḍarūrāt tubīḥu al-maḥẓūrāt* (dire necessity makes impermissible things permissible). The rule is immutable. There are some people that place their money in the bank with the understanding that they are a trust, and they do not want interest for it. Still this does not free one of the responsibility. This is why we have seen that, instead of leaving the interest to the bank, it is taken and spent on the poor, and this is a sound alternative.[2]

be laid bare according to the level of each particular servant. There might be things that have never ever been seen before. It is enough, as some Shaykhs say, and especially my teacher Shaykh 'Abd Allah Fa'iz al-Daghistani–may Allah sanctify his soul–that if a single one of the beautiful-eyed houris brought out her little finger—not more than that—into this world, this world would burn up from beginning to end [due to its light]. The one who saw *what he saw* (Najm 53:11) is the Prophet–upon him the blessings and peace of Allah. Time has grown short. Nothing remains of time but a few hours—meaning, metaphorically. 'Nothing remains but seven hours' [i.e. of your lifespan: words of the angel of death to the Prophet Idris after he was raised up to heaven, see Abū al-Layth al-Samarqandī, *Baḥr al-'Ulūm*, Maryam 19:57]. And we are firmly intending that Allah Most High shall grant us the same as what He granted *Ahl al-Bayt* and the *sālikūn* (wayfarers) in this Tariqa. We pray to Allah that He shall make permanent for us this immense blessing. And from Allah comes all success. Glory and thanks to the One God, the Nurturing Lord of all the worlds." Mawlana Shaykh Nazim, Damascus Suhbas (1997-2006).

[1] See Suhba I.24, note 14.

[2] Per the fatwa of the majority of the jurists as long as one does not consider it zakat or sadaqa or a pious act or a rewardable act but rather the lesser of two evils.

Question 7: "A father died leaving orphans, so what is the wisdom when we know that Allah is the All-Just? Where is the justice?"

Answer: Allah says, "I am the *kāfil* (maintainer) of the orphan."[1] Is there a greater honor than for the nurturing Lord of the worlds to be guaranteeing and preserving that child? Is the maintenance of Allah better or the father's maintenance? So the question stems from ignorance. You may see many or most of those that were enabled to achieve success in life were orphans. So how is there not justice?

Question 8: "At the time of the stoning of Iblīs [during the Hajj], is he present at his stoning?"

Answer: As an actual form we do not see him, but as a teaching for us and a reminder that Iblīs keeps close to the servant as long as the latter still have his spirit, whoever does the stoning must say, "In spite of the devil and for the good pleasure of the All-Merciful." One should say this word in all one's acts. As for the place of stoning, that is a symbol. Iblīs exploits some of the pilgrims as he likes: whoever uses more than seven pebbles, that one is serving Iblīs.

By the sanctity of the Beloved, by the sanctity of the Fatiha.

[1] Per the verses, *do not kill your children for destitution—We provide for you and for them* (An'ām 6:151); *do not kill your children for fear of lack of food. We Ourselves provide for them and for you* (Banū Isrā'īl/Isrā' 17:31); *there is not a single animal on earth except upon the One God is due its provision* (Hūd 11:6); *how many a beast does not carry its own provision, but the One God provides it and you* ('Ankabūt 29:60); *did He not find you an orphan, then He gave refuge?* (Ḍuḥā 93:6); and per the hadith, "Whoever has left behind small ones then let them come to me. I am their *mawlā*." Narrated from Abū Hurayra by al-Dārimī, Bukhārī, Muslim and others.

49

Duty of jihad to obtain purity of heart – What is the *dunyā*? – [Allah's 24,000 daily manifestations to the heart – Your heart is the house of Allah]

I seek refuge in Allah from the accursed devil
In the Name of Allah the All-Beneficent the Most Merciful
There is no power nor strength but with Allah the High, the Magnificent
Permission, O my Master, support!
Our way is companionship, and goodness is in the congregation

The army of Islam would march from the easts to the wests with yearning and love. Thus did Sa'd b. Abī Waqqāṣ walk on top of the Tigris with his huge army. They walked on the water the way they walked on the ground. When the Persians saw that they were routed and said, "These are not human beings."[1] For that army was under the flag of the Messenger–upon him the blessings and peace of Allah–and not under one thousand flags. The Messenger–upon him the blessings and peace of Allah–said, "The faith-system is all faithful transparency."[2] All of us are in need of pure advice. The Prophets need Allah's pure advice, the Awliya and Prophets are advising the servants purely. *Naṣīḥa* is the life of the faith-system and whoever refuses it is ripe for regret and woe. Acceptance of advice is the mark of a servant's humbleness. Whoever does not accept it, then it is the mark of wretchedness. *Self-importance spurred him on to sin* (al-Baqara 2:206).

The faithful advice of our noble masters from the ocean of the sciences of the Prophet–upon him the blessings and peace of Allah–and the understanding of the discourse of the Messenger–upon him the blessings and peace of Allah–is extremely difficult at first for it needs purity of hearts. And the purity of hearts is in need of great effort until the servant is purified from this world and what it contains. For this world does not leave any purity for the servant. This is why the Prophet–upon him the blessings and peace of Allah–said, "This world is cursed, cursed is what it contains except the remembrance of Allah and what comes near it."[3]

[1] Aḥmad al-Balādhurī, *Futūḥ al-buldān* (Beirut: Maktabat al-Hilāl, 1988) p. 259 (*Fatḥ al-Madā'in*); 'Izz al-Dīn Ibn al-Athīr al-Jazarī, *Usd al-ghāba* (Zayd b. Surāqa). The Persians said, "We are not fighting against human beings; we are fighting against jinns" per al-Dhahabī, *Tārīkh al-Islām* (Year 16).

[2] See Suhba I.10.

[3] Narrated **I.** from Abū Hurayra by Ibn Mājah (*Zuhd, mathal al-dunyā*); al-Tirmidhī

What is *al-dunyā* (this world)? It is everything that turns your heart's attention away from your nurturing Lord, even if it should be one tree or a thousand trees. However, if you should have possession of the entire world but your heart is unattached to it then that does not harm you. For Allah never accepts a partner with Him in His Essence or His Attributes or His Names. Likewise He does not like to have any partner in one's love of Him. (And this is what polytheism is, not as Wahhabis define it—"invoking blessings on the Prophet after Azan is *shirk*," or "for you to rub against the window of the Prophet is *shirk*"—when they themselves are drowning in the love of this world!) This station is *and that masjids belong to the One God, so do not call, together with the One God, upon anyone else* (al-Jinn 72:18).

Likewise Allah looks at the heart of His servant in every 24 hours with 24,000 looks of manifestation. Has any of us searched his own heart to see what is in it? We are reminding you and we are not teaching you because Allah says, *and keep reminding, for verily the reminder benefits the believers* (Dhāriyāt 51:55), and He did not say, "and keep teaching." So the level of the servant will be, in the presence of his nurturing Lord, in proportion to the coming forth of the servant's heart towards his nurturing Lord. It will not be in proportion to his wealth or his appearance. This is a hidden matter between the nurturing Lord and His servant. This is why we must protect the heart, because this is more important than protecting the limbs. One is not capable of protecting

(*Zuhd, bāb,* rated *ḥasan*); Ibn Abī 'Āṣim, *Zuhd*; al-Ḥakīm al-Tirmidhī, *Nawādir*; al-Dāraquṭnī, *'Ilal* (5:89 §735, 11:45 §2117, *ṣaḥīḥ*-chained); Bayhaqī, *Shu'ab* (17: *Faḍl al-'ilm, ṭalab al-'ilm*; all with the addition "or a learned person or a learner;" (ii) Abū Sa'īd al-Khudrī by Ibn 'Abd al-Barr, *Jāmi' bayān al-'ilm* (1:133 §133) with the addition "and the rest of people are a savage mob without good in them;" (iii) Ibn Mas'ūd by Ṭabarānī, *Awsaṭ* (4:236 §4072); *Musnad al-Shāmiyyīn* (1:107 §163) in the wording "This world is cursed, cursed is what it contains, except a learned person or a learner, and the remembrance of Allah and what comes near it;" cf. al-Haythamī, *Majma' al-zawā'id* (1:122); Suyūṭī, *al-Jāmi' al-ṣaghīr* (1:420, *ḥasan*); **II.** in the wording, "except whatever is used of it for Allah Almighty" from (iv) Jābir by Ibn al-A'rābī, *Zuhd* (p. 45 §65); *Mu'jam* (2:547-548 §1069); al-Kalābādhī, *Baḥr al-fawā'id* (1:156-157); Abū Nu'aym, *Ḥilya* (3:157, 7:90); al-Ḍiyā' al-Maqdisī, *Mukhtāra* per Suyūṭī (1:420, *ṣaḥīḥ*) (v) al-Munkadir by Ibn Abī al-Dunyā, *Zuhd* (p. 26 §7); *Dhamm al-dunyā* (p. 15 §7); Bayhaqī, *Shu'ab* (71: *Zuhd*); and others; on the latter two [=iv and v] see Dāraquṭnī, *'Ilal* (14:69 §3427); (vi) 'Alī b. Abī Ṭālib by al-Shajarī, *Amālī* (2:223); (vii) Umm Hāni' by al-Dhahabī, *Mīzān* (Muḥ. b. Qāsim b. Mujammi' al-Ṭāykānī); the latter two [=vi-vii] may be forged chains; (viii) Muḥ. b. al-Munkadir in *mursal* mode by Aḥmad, *Zuhd* (p. 27 §154); Abū Dāwūd, *Marāsīl*; and **III.** as their own saying, (ix) Abū al-Dardā' by Ibn al-Mubārak, *Zuhd* (pp. 191-192 §543); al-Aṣamm, *Majmū'* (p. 121 §200); Bayhaqī, *Madkhal*; (x) Ka'b by Ibn Abī Shayba, *Muṣannaf* (19:180 §35735, 19:401 §36480); Dārimī, *Sunan* (*faḍl al-'ilm wal-'ālim*) in the wording, "This world is cursed, cursed is what it contains except a learner of goodness or its teacher."

his limbs without protecting his heart for the heart is the station of the absolute authority, and when you protect your heart and make it be with Allah, then your limbs will not trespass their limits. For there is an address coming at every moment, *and be upright as you are commanded* (al-Shūrā 42:15). Can we, after that, look upon an unrelated woman, when Allah has ordered, *tell the believers they must lower some of their gazes* (al-Nūr 24:30)?

A man came to our master the Shaykh and said, "My master, the women are naked, what is this corruption?" Our master the Shaykh said to him with severity, "How did you find out that they were naked without looking at them? Have you not heard the statement of Allah, *tell the believers they must lower some of their gazes* (al-Nūr 24:30)? You are the first one to trespass the limits set by Allah, and then you come to me to speak these words when you are sinning? Looking at the unrelated woman with an illicit look is a poisoned arrow from Iblīs by which he lays belief to ruin and when Iblīs takes control of the heart he takes control of all the limbs and puts the servant under his command. With that look, Iblīs is leading you wherever he wishes. If ʿAzrāʾīl descended at that moment to seize the soul, the return would be to Hellfire!"

One of the great Awliya recounted during the Jumuʿa sermon that Allah shall ask the servant one question on the Day of Resurrection. He will say, "O My servant, in your life I was with you, but who were you with?" When the servant answers Him, "I was with you, O my Lord," and he speaks truthfully with our nurturing Lord, then that is enough for him, he has escaped punishment and has triumphed. Therefore the human being must reflect, "Am I a slave to Allah or to someone else?" Ask your heart and you will know whether you are a slave to Allah or to someone else.

This is why "This world is cursed, cursed is what it contains, etc."[1] And this is why we are in need to purity of hearts. If we do not acquire purity by leaving the world and what it contains, darkness will descend on the hearts, and with it anxiety and sadness, but Allah is teaching us, *behold, with the remembrance of the One God are the hearts at peace!* (al-Raʿd 13:28). And when the remembrance of the All-True is in the heart, light descends with it, tranquility and mercy, and together with mercy there is gladness and peace. At that time the servant is not worried what will happen to him after a month or a year because he is under Allah's guarantee and Allah has certainly said, *behold! Verily the friends of the One God, there is no fear for them, nor shall they grieve* (Yūnus 10:62).

[1] See previous note.

So then, if a human being possessed all the wealth of the world and ruled over the world, and his heart is not a peace, that would be for him the greatest affliction. But when there is the remembrance of Allah in his heart, then his nurturing Lord has taken him under His care. Even if the whole world were engulfed in a flood of fire, his case will be like that of our liege Lord Ibrāhīm the Friend–upon him peace. He will find in the midst of the fire meadows and bliss because his reliance is upon his nurturing Lord. And **we have reached a time in which our greatest concern is this world—but whoever truly believes in the hereafter, how can his greatest concern be this world? Leave that to the people of this world and take care of your hearts that are the house of the Almighty Lord. Purify them until purity is obtained for you. At that time the manifestation will change**, whereby He says, *verily the One God does not change what is in a people until they change what is in themselves* (Ra'd 13:11).

They ask, O Shaykh, have the upheavals ended for good? But Allah is asking, *will you stop once and for all?* (al-Mā'ida 5:91). He is waiting for us to say, "we have stopped once and for all." At that time, swiftly, the manifestation will change for the best state. But He is waiting for repentance on the part of the servants.

By the sanctity of the Beloved, by the sanctity of the Fatiha.

50

[Magnifying the Holy Prophet ﷺ – The Companions repelled Iblīs from their gatherings] – The happiest of people is the one well-pleased with his Lord – Love for the righteous – 24 hours in a day – Harmony with the servants of Allah

I seek refuge in Allah from the accursed devil
In the Name of Allah the All-Beneficent the Most Merciful
There is no power nor strength but with Allah the High, the Magnificent
Permission, O my Master, support!
Our way is companionship, and goodness is in the congregation

The kings of old, at the mention of the Messenger of Allah–upon him the blessings and peace of Allah–would stand in awe and reverence. As much as we magnify the Messenger–upon him the blessings and peace of Allah–with such reverence Allah shall be pleased with us, because He Himself magnified the Prophet, exalted him, honored him, glorified him and lavished blessings on him: *verily the One God and His angels are blessing the Prophet. O you who believe! Bless him and greet him with reverent salutation* (Aḥzāb 33:56). And this is an honoring that never happened for anyone in creation, neither from the Prophets nor from the angels, except for our liege lord Muhammad–upon him the blessings and peace of Allah. Thus our gatherings are all held out of love for Allah and love for the Messenger of Allah–upon him the blessings and peace of Allah.

Mawlana Shaykh ʿAbd Allah al-Daghistani used to say that when the noble Companions attended any gathering, they had readiness to repel the assaults of Iblīs against them. For Iblīs does not leave alone any two or more that gather but he sends them of his soldiers those that would spoil the gathering. As for our time, no gathering is held except something wrong is spoken in it, to the point that the angels of mercy flee from the stench of that gathering. We have become such that we cannot smell that odor. Our type is that of the tanner who has gotten used to the smell of the hides. Mawlana al-Shaykh used to say that if Allah left the odor of the slanderer's breath spread on the face of the earth no one would be left able to eat a single morsel of food due to what they smell of his odor. This is why Allah Most High makes the angels take away this smell and put it in the Fire, which itself seeks refuge from the intensity of its stench. When the habitual slanderer of people dies the angels will bring it back to him and place it in his nose and in his grave. This is the work of Iblīs—to make gatherings be for other than the remembrance of Allah, and he does not rest night or day.

Our liege lord Shah Naqshband said, "I would observe Iblīs a lot to catch him sleeping or resting but I never saw it happen. I would always see him busy wherever people were gathering for any reason." The noble Companions had, of spiritual powers, that which enable them to repel him from their gatherings so they would not fall into his trap. Therefore we hope and ask from Allah that our gatherings will be accepted in the presence of Allah and that mercy will descend on us to purify us of sins, whereby the Prophet–upon him the blessings and peace of Allah–says, "At the mention of the righteous, mercy descends."[1] Therefore, when you gather together, mention the righteous, their deeds and their virtues, so that mercy will descend because of it. For at the mention of the unrighteous and their deeds curse and the wrath of Allah descend. So purify your gatherings from the mention of the enemies of Allah and mention the righteous and the goodness that is in them, so that Allah will dress us with something of their righteousness; and also because, in this time, there is no deliverance for us except through love of the righteous. As for love of the wretched, it will drive people to wretchedness in this life and the next. Anyone that followed or loved someone wretched, you will never find him at rest in this life or saved in the next.

Thus the love of the righteous is a salvation for all people even if we are unable to do the same as their works. The Prophet–upon him the blessings and peace of Allah–says, "**A person will be with the one he loves despite his deeds.**"[2] So with whom would you like to be on the Day of Resurrection? This

[1] Narrated in *maqṭūʿ* mode from (i) Sufyān b. ʿUyayna by Aḥmad b. Ḥanbal, *al-Zuhd* (p. 264 §1903); *al-Waraʿ*, ed. Samīr Amīn al-Zuhayrī (Riyadh: Dār al-Ṣumayʿī, 1418/1997) p. 86 §267; *Masāʾil Aḥmad riwāyat Abī Dāwūd*, ed. Ṭāriq ʿAwaḍ Allāh (Cairo: Maktabat Ibn Taymiyya, 1420/1999) p. 377 §1824; Abū Bakr Muḥ. b. Ibrāhīm b. ʿAlī Ibn al-Muqrī al-Aṣbahānī al-Khāzin, *al-Muʿjam*, ed. ʿĀdil Saʿd (Riyadh: Maktabat al-Rushd, 1419/1998) p. 75 §142; Abū Nuʿaym, *Ḥilya* (7:285); Ibn ʿAbd al-Barr, *Tamhīd* (17:429); (ii) Muḥ. b. al-Naḍr al-Ḥārithī by Abū al-Qāsim Hibat Allāh b. al-Ḥasan b. Manṣūr al-Lālikāʾī, *Karāmāt al-awliyāʾ*, ed. Aḥmad Saʿd al-Ghāmidī, 8th ed. (Riyadh: Dār Ṭayba, 1423/2003) pp. 100-101 §45; (iii) Sufyān al-Thawrī by Ibn ʿAbd al-Barr, *Jāmiʿ bayān al-ʿilm* (2:1113 §2195); (iv) Muḥammad b. Manṣūr al-Ṭūsī by al-Khaṭīb al-Baghdādī, *Tārīkh Baghdād* (Muḥ. b. Manṣūr Abū Jaʿfar al-ʿĀbid al-Ṭūsī); (v) Abū Jaʿfar Aḥmad b. Ḥamdān by Abū ʿAmr ʿUthmān b. ʿAbd al-Raḥmān Ibn al-Ṣalāḥ al-Shahrazūrī, *ʿUlūm al-ḥadīth* (Type 28); (vi) Abū ʿUthmān Saʿīd b. Ismāʿīl al-Ḥīrī (d. 298/910) by al-Dhahabī, *Tārīkh* (22:151).

[2] Narrated from (i) ʿAlī b. Abī Ṭālib by al-Ṭayālisī; al-Dārimī; (ii) Anas by Ibn al-Jaʿd; Aḥmad; (iii) Abū Dharr by Aḥmad; al-Dārimī; Abū Dāwūd; Ibn Ḥibbān; (iv) Ibn

is the foundation of the faith. Were it not for love of our nurturing Lord and love of his Messenger–upon him the blessings and peace of Allah–how would it possible for belief to settle in the heart? The illustration of that is an arid land that does not grow anything. The tree of *īmān* and *islām* takes its perpetual strength from love of Allah and His Messenger. After that, the love of the righteous is the mark of belief.

In this gathering of ours, we are speaking from the discourse of Sultan al-Awliya, for the speech of Awliya is nearer to the hearts and to the understanding of people. Mawlana would say that the happiest of people is the one that is well-pleased with his nurturing Lord wherever He put him. If He put him in the sky, or impoverished him, or enriched him, and if He raised him or put him low, if He made him sick or gave him good health—in any circumstance He puts him he will say, "You are my nurturing Lord, this is from you, and I am well-pleased with it." This person is happier and nothing matters to him.

This is important because the human being has an ego, the ego is like a child, and you will not find any limit or stability to the demands of a child. Neither does it know what it wants nor do you know what it wants. If you were to follow up each of its demands to satisfy it you would become bewildered. It might say, "Put sugar in the water," then it will ask you to take it out of it. That is the way it is with children: demands that no one can fulfill in the way the child wants. the very same attribute is found in every human being, namely the ego. If you want to follow your ego, you will not find a limit to its demands. For example, you might say, "If only Allah gave me a little bit of money like other people, if only a thousand banknotes—" and when He does give it to him, his ego asks for more, and so forth without there being any limit to its demands. You will never find it saying, "I am satisfied and pleased, O my nurturing Lord" with what it has obtained. You will never see such a person find rest or happiness. This is why Mawlana says that the happiest of people is the one that is pleased with the nurturing Lord of human beings wherever He makes him sit or in whatever state He leaves him, or whatever He gives him, he will say, "O my nurturing Lord, I am pleased." For that servant's aspiration is to be in His nurturing Lord's presence and not for his wealth to increase nor for himself to be a prisoner of this world. The prisoner of this world toils and

Mas'ūd by al-Bukhārī; Abū Ya'lā; (v) Ṣafwān b. 'Assāl by Ṭabarānī, *Awsaṭ* and *Kabīr*; (vi) Abū Hurayra by al-Mukhalliṣ, *Mukhalliṣiyyāt*; Abū Nu'aym, *Ḥilya*; (vii) Abū Mūsā al-Ash'arī by Ibn Ḥibbān; Ibn Bushkuwāl, *Ghawāmiḍ al-asmā'*; (viii-xv) Jābir b. 'Abd Allāh, Abū Qatāda, Abū Surayḥa, 'Abd Allāh b. Yazīd al-Khaṭmī, Ṣafwān b. Qudāma, 'Urwa b. Muḍarris al-Ṭā'ī, Mu'ādh b. Jabal, Abū Umāma al-Bāhilī per al-Kattānī, *Naẓm al-mutanāthir* who said it is mass-transmitted from about twenty Companions. Abū Nu'aym gathered its routes in *al-Muḥibbīn ma'a al-maḥbūbīn* per Ibn Ḥajar, *Fatḥ al-Bārī* (10:560, *'alāmat al-ḥubb fī-l-Lāh*). See also Suhba 86.

gets tired until he dies tired, and his eyes are rolling in his grave. One of them saw in a dream that a king that had died a long time before was completely decomposed, a skeleton in his grave with only his eyes still looking behind. He interpreted it as looking back to see who had taken kingship after him. This was his concern.

Therefore the most relaxed and happiest of people is the one that is satisfied with his nurturing Lord in whatever situation He puts him. When He gives him little he does not ask for more and he knows it is suffices his need. Allah Most High said, *We Ourselves have distributed between them their livelihood in the present life* (Zukhruf 43:32); and when He gives him more he gives thanks. As for the one that is displeased, his type is like the animal that walks around the waterwheel to bring out water, on whose eyes its owner has put blinders so that it does not see anything, and it thinks it has walked from one country to another by walking all day long.

What will the children of Ādam eat of all they toiled and tired themselves gathering and hoarding up? One or two plates. But can you eat the whole pot for example? No. Yet he hoards up because his ego knows no limit to its demands. This is called *nafs al-ṭifl al-madhmūma* (the child's blameworthy ego) and this is the sickness of the Umma. because of this [insatiability] they will say there is no time for prayer of servanthood. When will they find time? In the grave? In the grave there is no prayer and no fasting. So do not tire yourself. Be pleased with your nurturing Lord and your heart will be at rest. Allah has made the day 24 hours and divided them into three parts. Eight hours for the pursuit of livelihood—and He gave the opportunity for work to be in the land and at sea. Then eight hours for the work of the hereafter, because the servant is hanging on his hereafter and a human life is 70 or 80 years for example, but he is heading for the hereafter where life is eternal. There remain eight hours which Allah has appointed for the body to rest with the family or for sleep. Eight hours are enough for men after puberty. Any addition to that ruins the body just as staying up late ruins it.

Allah has certainly divided the day with just balance. So whoever observes this regimen will be at rest and will not become tired, just as sickness is not always the cause of death. A human being might live sick wishing for death — what kind of life is this? The best of matters are the middle ones. The human being must take good care of himself so that he will find, at the end of his life, the health that is appropriate for his age. It might be that a human being's health will linger before his time has come. Therefore he must preserve his state until death comes to him. Whoever tires himself will be wretched here and hereafter. This is the pure counsel of Allah for the servants. Whoever does not accept it, regret and woe will take place for him.

The ego does not want to hear any of this. But this matter will not be realized other than with strength of belief. The stronger the servant's belief is, the more he is capable of controlling the reins of his ego. An example of that is the small child: can it control a horse or drive a car. Likewise, whoever has weak belief, his ego will use him as a plaything. With the strengthening of belief the servant will become capable of control himself and drive it according to his will.

Mawlana says we say, "I believe in Allah and His angels and His Scriptures and His Messengers and the last Day and foreordained Decree, the good of it and the bad of it all being from Allah." And Allah has made it a pillar of faith for us to believe in *qadar*, the good of it and the bad of it being all from Allah Most High. This means that sovereignty belongs to Allah and the servants belong to Him likewise, and there is not one movement and not one stillness in the world except with His knowledge and His will, and nothing happens and no movement and no stillness in the world except for a certain wisdom. Belief in this fashion puts tranquility in the servant's heart. At that time he will not be fighting Allah or objecting to calamities that appear. For he will be firmly within the will of Allah and His wisdom, and all events course according to the wish and the will of our nurturing Lord.

This is why the Prophet–upon him the blessings and peace of Allah–says, *a'mālukum 'ummālukum* (your deeds are your workers).[1] For it is impossible for a servant to do righteousness and for evil to reach him, and it is impossible for him to intend goodness and for evil to reach him ever, unless there has been some deficiency from the first moment, then the defect will appear in the end. Therefore do not blame anyone for an evil you yourself have committed, and you must inspect your own states. You find your own states displayed before you. An example of that is that when some person comes to you giving you high esteem and exalting you, do you act arrogant towards him? But whoever comes to you acting arrogant, what do you do with them? And this is the truth: your deeds are your workers.

Look at the mirror. Just as you act you will behold. The deeds of people are just like a mirror. It all appears before the people. Therefore whoever keeps good company and harmony with the servants of Allah and makes his manners excellent, will contain them all and they will contain him. As for whoever does not keep good company and harmony with Allah's servants and is ill at ease with society—for the ego is savage, it does not keep good company nor harmony, and its attribute is arrogance—you will find such a person as if living in the midst of thorns. As for him that has praiseworthy manners and copes with people through good character, you will see him as if living in a garden

[1] See Suhba I.27, third to last note.

of roses and various flowers of various colors and forms. The more he looks at the servants of Allah the happier they make him. This one has put himself in Paradise while still being in the world. The other is overproud and has put himself in prison. This is why the hadith of the Messenger–upon him the blessings and peace of Allah–states, "There is no goodness in him who does not get along and with whom others do not get along."[1] Show people the best character, half of it will return to you.

Thus, when I go to Europe, over there they are all Christians but I find familiarity with them because they are the slaves of my nurturing Lord and I do not find in my heart any ill intention or enmity or envy on their part. Rather I see the wisdom of my nurturing Lord with all and I smell from each of them the smell of roses. Is this better, or for the human being to fill his breast with hatred, envy, enmity and rancor towards people, and be overproud, scowling and abhorrent to look at? The human being in this time is imprisoning himself in this world. Many are unbearable to people because of their complete lack of good character. As for the one that has good character, he is happy with the Umma of the Beloved–upon him the blessings and peace of Allah–and sees only their lights and their beauty.

Mawlana says that whoever has this attribute, its reality is that it will eventually lead him to the reality of belief. We must let our gaze be like the gaze of our nurturing Lord upon His servants, a gaze of mercy. For if the gaze of our nurturing Lord were such as the gaze of His servants to one another, all would perish! And we see how much sinning and unbelief there is, but despite that, our nurturing Lord is sending down mercy. Look at the world. Is there over it the effect of divine wrath or the effect of mercy? **If our gaze on one another were a gaze of mercy the world would be a Paradise. This is why the Messenger says, *takhallaqū bi-akhlāqi-l-Lāh* (acquire the moral traits of Allah).[2] Whoever looks with the look of mercy will be a human being otherwise he is a savage beast in the image of a human being.**

By the sanctity of the Beloved, by the sanctity of the Fatiha.

[1] Narrated from (i) Sahl b. Sa'd by Aḥmad; Rūyānī; and others; (ii) Abū Hurayra by Bazzār; Ibn 'Adī, *Kāmil*; Abū al-Shaykh, *Amthāl al-ḥadīth*; Ḥākim, *Mustadrak*; and others; (iii) Jābir by Ṭabarānī, *Awsaṭ*; al-Sulamī, *Futuwwa*; al-Naqqāsh, *Fawā'id al-'Irāqiyyīn*; and others; (iv-v) Abū Sa'īd al-Khudrī and 'Awn b. 'Abd Allāh b. 'Utba by Ṭabarānī, *Kabīr*; (vi) Ibn Mas'ūd by Tammām al-Rāzī, *Fawā'id*; and, as his own statement, Ibn Abī Shayba; Abū al-Layth al-Samarqandī, *Baḥr al-'ulūm*; Dāraquṭnī, *'Ilal*.

[2] See Suhba I.2, fifth note; Suhba I.31, third note; and Suhba I.59.

51
Do not argue even if you are in the right

I seek refuge in Allah from the accursed devil
In the Name of Allah the All-Beneficent the Most Merciful
There is no power nor strength but with Allah the High, the Magnificent
Permission, O my Master, support!
Our way is companionship, and goodness is in the congregation

Do not argue even if you are on the right. Do not argue with your wife or with your children or with anyone at all, because arguing extinguished the light of belief. Whoever you argue with, its meaning is that he will not submit to the truth. Did the Messenger–upon him the blessings and peace of Allah–argue with Abū Jahl? Did he refute him or dispute with him or wrangle with him? However, when you find someone that will accept the truth when you speak with him, then that is allowed. As for the obdurate, when he rejects your speech then say to him, *to you your faith-system and to me mine* (al-Kāfirūn 109:6). For he wants to the extinction of the light of your belief.

Do not argue even if you are on the right. For whoever you argue with will not admit it, so what is the benefit? Especially with women. Many times you will find that the reason for separations and divorce is because of argument between the two spouses. Likewise between brothers, coldness follows because of argument, and coldness between a woman and her husband is mostly because of argument. Therefore do not ever argue with her. Every issue that is found between brethren, people, neighbors, parents and children is because of arguing, and the root of separation and enmity and hatred is because of arguing. This is why Allah commanded *and do not dispute* [pl.] instead of saying, "dispute!" Rather, he said, *fight* (Barā'a/Tawba 9:29, 9:123), because with argument the two sides might be of equal weight, but fighting produces a result. This is why the Messenger–upon him the blessings and peace of Allah–did not argue with the polytheists and the Jews but he fought them and challenged them to fight, not to argue. When you are arguing with a man who is objecting, will he not injure you while you expose yourself to his assaults because he does not accept what you say? So why will you injure your belief? When you find that such is his description, withdraw quickly.

One time the Ṣiddīq was sitting with the Messenger–upon him the blessings and peace of Allah–and a man came and started to hurl abuse at the Ṣiddīq as he endured patiently. In the end, however, he answered back the man with a single word, whereupon the Messenger–upon him the blessings and peace of

Allah–rose from the gathering. The Ṣiddīq said to the Messenger–upon him the blessings and peace of Allah–"Messenger of Allah, how much did he assault me while you remained seated, and when I answered him you got up!" The Messenger–upon him the blessings and peace of Allah–said, "An angel was defending you but when you answered him"—i.e. you opened the door of argument—"the angel left and the devil came, and it is not allowed for the Prophet to sit with the devil."[1] This is a teaching to the Umma: do not defend yourself but withdraw. Allah is teaching us with His statement *and the servants of the All-Merciful who tread upon the earth lightly, and when the ignorant address them they say, "Peace"* (al-Furqān 25:63).

That is, "O My servants, be of the servants of the All-Merciful. For when you answer back those that speak ignorantly with you, you will descend to their level, but their level is ignorance." Ignorance is the mother of all dirty things, unbelief, hypocrisy and despicable acts. Ignorance is a sea in which all the vile acts live while knowledge is a sea in which all the virtues live. Allah Most High says, *so when We have recited it then follow its recitation* (al-Qiyāma 75:18). We must not recite this verse and then trample it. This would not be knowledge but ignorance. And the verse imparts that "*when We have recited it* on your tongue, O Muhammad"—and the address to the Messenger is an address to the Umma, and the command follows—"*then follow its recitation*" which contains certain rulings; it is not only for reciting.

There is no gain in arguing. Allah will send forth a seeker of the truth by any reason or by any contact, and when he is leaning to the truth, talk to him because he is fit for the way and the faith, and your nurturing Lord will make you a means for it. In order to eliminate the door of argument Allah says to the Prophet–upon him the blessings and peace of Allah–*verily you will not guide those you love, however, the One God will guide whomever He pleases* (al-Qaṣaṣ 28:56). I.e. "do not fatigue yourself, O my Beloved, trying to guide them."

Imam al-Shāfiʿī says, "I argued with a thousand learned scholars and I overcame them, and one ignoramus argued with me and overcame me." For the learned scholar has knowledge and acknowledges the truth, but the ignoramus is dominated by his ego and does not understand anything you say to follow you. Our master the Shaykh says of our liege lord Muḥyī al-Dīn Ibn ʿArabī that he had taught in the Jāmiʿ al-Ḥanābila in Damascus for forty years and at last he would say to the Awliya, "My brothers, for 40 years I have exhausted myself so that the one without mind and without thinking might

[1] Narrated from Abū Hurayra by Aḥmad (15:390 §9624); al-Bazzār (15:157 §8495); al-Quḍāʿī, *Musnad al-shihāb* (2:30 §820).

understand, but the upshot was that they trampled my shoulders and smeared my head." Our liege lord al-Shāfi'ī's speech corresponds to our liege lord Ibn 'Arabī's speech. This is why when you see from afar one whose ego is riding as its own donkey, run away from him right away. Why argue? He might bite you, or kick you, or make you abuse everyone, and that time you would leave belief.

So when you find acceptance then spare no effort, but when you find a dam do not draw near. Their hearts are covered receptacles. Their type is that of the Jews whom Allah kept them away, after which the Messenger–upon him the blessings and peace of Allah–no longer addressed them because he had no order to do so, since the Jews had said *our hearts are covered receptacles* (Baqara 2:88, Nisā' 4:155). The very same kind is found in our time in abundance. The skillful one is he that tries all upon contact until he finds among them one who is alive and ready to accept the truth. But as for the one that is like an impenetrable monolith do not draw near him.

From Allah is all success. By the sanctity of the Beloved, by the sanctity of the Fatiha.

52

Duty to consult with the Shaykh [on three matters] and to give thanks to Allah for His blessings

I seek refuge in Allah from the accursed devil
In the Name of Allah the All-Beneficent the Most Merciful
There is no power nor strength but with Allah the High, the Magnificent
Permission, O my Master, support!
Our way is companionship, and goodness is in the congregation

Consultation is an obligation for the believers so that they will not fall into a matter whose upshot will not be upright. Consultation is not for you to come to the Shaykh and say to him, for example, "I am going to Hajj, I have prepared my passport and I have purchased my ticket. What do you think?" Or "I have seen a girl and she pleased me so asked her in marriage, what do you think of it, Sayyidi?" The Shaykh's answer will be, "May Allah bless you my son." The type of such a person is like someone that came to the Shaykh with a tailored suit and asks him, "What do you think of my garment, is it adequate or not?" Since you already had it tailored and cut, and you cannot possibly make another suit out of the same cloth, then why do you ask? However, if you first came to the Shaykh with the cloth and said to him, "Sayyidi, tailor for me what is suitable for me," then that tailoring would be adequate and that is proper consultation. Not that you come to the Shaykh with a fait accompli and ask to consult with him.

There are three things a person is obligated to consult with the Shaykh about in advance: marriage, divorce and travel. Consultation is an emphasized Sunna. The murid must consult before marrying otherwise it will be a cause for the destruction of the murid. It is also an obligation for the servants to give thanks to their nurturing Lord for His blessings. It will not be true thanks until the servant acknowledges the blessing as being a blessing. An example of that is when you say, "My wife is a blessing from my nurturing Lord," it will be gratitude and acknowledgment. But whoever complains about something, then where is the gratitude? The married person must say, "O my nurturing Lord! You have honored me with a beauty queen, You have put me in a stronghold against the illicit, and You have granted me from her a pure progeny. So praise belongs to and gratitude, O my nurturing Lord!" At that time if there were 1,000 women only his wife is pleasing to him because she is his halal and the rest are haram, and the haram is poison and a fire.

The one that does not acknowledge the blessing, rarely does it stay with him. Allah brings it to an end and the result for him is affliction instead. It is like electricity. When there is a power cut you remember it is a blessing. Mawlana al-Shaykh says that **among the blessings for which we do not give what is due is that when two murids gather for companionship even the time it would take to milk two goats, Allah shall give them, of mercy and bounties, that whereby if either of them were given 2,000 years of life and spent them in worship, he would not obtain what he obtains of recompense by that suhba.**

Also part of the greatest of blessings that Allah has lavished on us is the testimony of faith. If one were to speak it, verily Allah forgives him and does not take him to account for his deeds, He protects him from the exposure of this world and the next. And whoever recognizes the immense value of the testimony of faith it is impossible that he will squander his moments but rather he will be always remembering Allah and thanking him for his blessings.

By the sanctity of the Beloved, by the sanctity of the Fatiha.

53
Matters are pledged to their own times

I seek refuge in Allah from the accursed devil
In the Name of Allah the All-Beneficent the Most Merciful
There is no power nor strength but with Allah the High, the Magnificent
Permission, O my Master, support!
Our way is companionship, and goodness is in the congregation

Everything is pledged to its own time. Whoever seeks a matter before its time shall be deprived of it. It is like citrus. If you pluck it when it is the size of a chickpea you will find it to be nothing. You must wait for its time before you can eat it. Likewise every matter has its time of ripening so that people might get its nutrition and enjoy it. Otherwise it goes to waste.

May Allah grant us understanding. By the sanctity of the Beloved, by the sanctity of the Fatiha.

54

Doubt with regard to *rizq* (provision) – [Shaykh ʿAbd al-Khāliq al-Ghujduwānī's two lessons and the murid's attainment of perfection]

I seek refuge in Allah from the accursed devil
In the Name of Allah the All-Beneficent the Most Merciful
There is no power nor strength but with Allah the High, the Magnificent
Permission, O my Master, support!
Our way is companionship, and goodness is in the congregation

I saw yellow wheat on the way. I asked, "What if we watered this wheat? Will it become green?" They answered me, "It will never become green because the time has come to harvest it so that another crop will be sowed instead." Thus has evil reached its perfection in the world and the time has come to harvest it and to harvest evil ones together with it and whoever holds fast to it, so that the world will be seeded with something in exchange, namely the choicest Umma, the noblest Umma, the best Umma. Just as the *minjal* (scythe) is not enough to harvest vast areas but rather we need large harvesters, it is the same with the harvesting of the evil ones now found between the east and the west.

Therefore do not make anyone a target for your harm—even by your intention or your thoughts—for whoever targets people, a targeting that never misses will be directed at him by the men of Allah to avenge themselves of him. The one that is in the war front, if he misses his shot, he will be struck by enemy fire; and the one that does not expect protection from the evils of his own ego will be the target of the arrow of revenge.

Allah Most High said, *they would fear a Day whose direness is universal* (Insān 76:7). These are the days and the universal direness in the skies, you cannot take refuge from it except in Allah. And Allah Almighty has caused the devil to forget two directions: above and below. This is why evil does not approach a servant that takes shelter in Allah through supplication or prostration. As for the four other sides, danger lurks from them.

Our liege lord Shaykh ʿAbd al-Khāliq al-Ghujduwānī ordered one of his murids to enter seclusion for seven years, for in his time there would be no result except with long strenuous effort, especially for Naqshbandis. The murid would enter seclusion for seven years, struggling against his ego until he would cross through all the veils and reach the objective, and he would come out of the darkness of bodies to the light of *malakūt* (invisible sovereignty). After that the Messenger–upon him the blessings and peace of Allah–came to the Shaykh with his spiritual reality and said to him, "This child of yours has achieved full readiness. Just let him understand some of the foundations of the highmost Tariqa and it is sufficiency for him."

Our liege lord Shaykh ʿAbd al-Khāliq came out with his murid to an orchard and stopped near a running river. A frog came out of it and licked the soil three times. The Shaykh said to his murid, "O my son, this frog, every 24 hours, comes out and takes three licks from the earth in fear that if it were to lick more, the earth would finish and it would die of hunger." The murid could not control his laughter and he said, "What! Will the mountains of this world finish?" Here the Shaykh made the frog speak—Shaykhs have wondrous way in the education of murids. The frog laughed at the murid's laughter and said to him, "I am right to fear that if I took more than three licks the soil would finish, and I am laughing at you because all night long you did not sleep but you have stayed up thinking about your children's provision and telling yourself, 'If I stay in seclusion for seven years, what will happen to them?' and thinking that if they sold everything that you own, it would never suffice them more than five years. O fool! The soil can very well finish but does Allah with Whom is all the provision of the servants finish?" The Shaykh said to his murid, "Do you understand O my son?" He said, "I understand, O my master."

Sultan al-Awliya Mawlana Shaykh ʿAbd Allah al-Daghistani would say that the first thing by which Iblīs leads Allah's servants astray is through doubt in provision. He puts in their hearts doubt with respect to their provision. When the servant starts doubting in his provision, he begins to doubt in the Giver of provision, in Allah. At that time his belief leaves him. If there did not remain any avenue for the servant to acquire provision for himself, at that time, if doubt enters his heart from the direction of provision, this will lay his belief to ruin. This is one of the most important teachings that the wayfarer in the path or the believer learns. For belief in this matter is one of the foundations of the edifice of submission. Water, for example, is part of provision. The servants drink it without fatigue or effort.

Then the Shaykh walked with his murid for a while and asked him to pick up a stone and strike with it an apple-tree. The murid picked up a large stone and struck one of the branches of the tree. The force of the blow caused twelve apples to fall on the ground. The Shaykh said to the murid, "O my son, look at this tree. You struck it with a stone and wounded it, and in exchange of that it has given you twelve apples. When you are more like this tree when people harm you, at that time the Umma will benefit from you." He said, "I understand, O my master." Then the Shaykh caused the murid's spiritual opening.

The latter said, "O my master, should I stay present with you now?" The Shaykh said to him, "O my son, now, even if you are in the west or in the east, there is no impediment to spiritual connection. Whatever you need will reach you. However, the body has rights and you must visit us from time to time, otherwise we will gather in spirit."

According to a person's readiness the spiritual reality of the Shaykh reached him. With these two questions that servant found sufficiency. With the two of them he reached the station of perfection. When a human being reaches the station of perfection he becomes sweet-tasting like the apple. If a servant were to try to eat an apple before its time he would spit it out. But if he waits for its ripeness it becomes sweet and beneficial.[1]

From Allah is all success. By the sanctity of the Beloved, by the sanctity of the Fatiha.

[1] This is the upshot of the previous suhba and it appear to be its completion.

55
Importance of *Khatm al-khwājagān*

I seek refuge in Allah from the accursed devil
In the Name of Allah the All-Beneficent the Most Merciful
There is no power nor strength but with Allah the High, the Magnificent
Permission, O my Master, support!
Our way is companionship, and goodness is in the congregation

There is no compulsion in the faith-system. Rectitude certainly stands clear from errancy (al-Baqara 2:256). The *Khatm* (seal) is one of the integrals of the highmost Tariqa. Without it it is impossible for the matter of Tariqa to be accomplished. The *Khatm* is once a week. Without it, it is not considered Tariqa. Our liege lord the Shaykh [ʿabd Allah al-Daghistani] has said that that if the murid leaves the daily devotions he is not considered an apostate from the Tariqa, but as for the one that leaves the Khatm al-Khwajagan, he is considered an apostate from the Tariqa. Therefore, for us, the Khatm is more important than the daily devotions, because with the Khatm the murid crosses the distances more and more than what he crosses by himself.

Allah has given the servants the choice, so whoever has a share is present, and the one that is tasked with directing the Khatm must recite it even if he is alone.

By the sanctity of the Beloved, by the sanctity of the Fatiha.

56
Foundations of asking for help towards reform

I seek refuge in Allah from the accursed devil
In the Name of Allah the All-Beneficent the Most Merciful
There is no power nor strength but with Allah the High, the Magnificent
Permission, O my Master, support!
Our way is companionship, and goodness is in the congregation

We live in the time of ruin and this time is bound for destruction. A new time shall begin that is founded on the truth. For in our time most of the foundations are built on falsehood, and "The one illicit stone in the edifice shall be the reason for its destruction."[1] A new era has dawned on us, whereby in the fifteenth century everything built on falsehood will be replaced. Thus will you find most people having no vigor for reform but we are commanded, and our job is to redress as much as we are able, even if we see destruction and ruin in every place. So be warned against corruption and taking part in destruction. For we want betterment. So if we put one stone on top of another with the intention of betterment, that will be accepted from us in the presence of our nurturing Lord.

This is why we encourage a man in the matter of reforming despite our knowledge that the matter will not be other than in the Mahdi's hand–upon him peace. Despite that we encourage a man over his intention. He says, "Help me to carry these stones" so that he will build on a basis of truth. Even if all people are involved in destruction, help him and encourage him in his intention, for reform with a single stone will be as if you had improved the whole affair from beginning to end.

When our intention is for our nurturing Lord in any help that we give our nurturing Lord will extend us a special help, but we must be extremely careful for no egotistical motive to enter into the matter. For the ego is all-treacherous and perfidious. It is imperative to beware of it. Every time it is able to stand it quickly calls people to itself and says, "Take me as a god besides Allah."

[1] A Prophetic hadith narrated from Ibn 'Umar by Ibn al-Muqrī, *Mu'jam* (p. 396 §1312, misspelled *Ibni 'ammih*); Abū Nu'aym, *Akhbār Aṣbahān* (2:123, 2:286); al-Khaṭīb, *Tārīkh Baghdād* (Aḥmad b. Muḥammad b. al-Muẓaffar); al-Quḍā'ī, *Musnad al-shihāb* (1:388 §664); al-Bayhaqī, *Shu'ab* (71: *Zuhd*); Ibn 'Asākir, *Tārīkh Dimashq* (59:296), the latter three in the wording, "Beware the illicit in building, for it is the foundation of ruin."

Despite that we must rise to reform things as much as we can. Likewise we must use wisdom so that no one feels that he is carrying too much. For if we were to ask a man to carry a chair once or twice for example, he would carry it. but if we ask him to carry it during the entire gathering he will run away. So we must ensure that tasks are like a person's winter clothing when he wears more and bears with it. But if he were to put these clothes in a suitcase and carry it he would get tired and leave it. Likewise, if you gave the ego a task in an official manner, even a to the extent of a hair, it would be as if the person is carrying a mountain and he would run away.

Therefore, whoever has an intention towards reform, let him begin with himself and work hard, whereby he will have with him a special help from Allah. For Allah Almighty says as spoken by His Prophet–upon him the blessings and peace of Allah–"Allah keeps helping the servant as long as the servant keeps helping his brother."[1] I.e. when you sacrifice yourself in the way of Allah, Allah will send you someone to join you and shoulder you. At that time he will serve you. But if you were to ask someone a service he will say to you, "What! Am I a servant?" The Messenger–upon him the blessings and peace of Allah–never tasked anyone to the point that he asked the Companions to serve him.

An example of that is if you were to uproot an olive tree from its roots to plant it it would dry up, but if you plant it while it is small it will always keep growing. This is how the Umma kept increasing from few to many, and these are the foundations. If you do not follow that style people will say this man wants us to serve him so that he will be on top of us. However, if the person forwards himself to serve as much as he is able, it will be "The master of the people is their servant."[2] And whoever comes forward with service will become the master of the people. Allah will give him value and will not let his service go to waste.

From Allah is all success. By the sanctity of the Fatiha.

[1] Narrated from Abū Hurayra by al-Ṭayālisī, *Musnad*; 'Abd al-Razzāq, *Muṣannaf*; Ibn Abī Shayba, *Muṣannaf*; Aḥmad, *Musnad*; Muslim; Ibn Mājahl Abū Dāwūd; etc.

[2] A Prophetic hadith narrated from Ibn 'Abbās, Jarīr al-Bajalī and Anas by Ibn al-Mubārak, *Jihād*; al-Sulamī, *Ādāb al-ṣuḥba*; Abū al-Qāsim al-Shahrazūrī, *Amālī*; Abū Nu'aym, *al-Arba'īn fil-mutaḥaqqiqīn min al-ṣūfiyya*; al-Khaṭīb, *Tārīkh*; and others.

57
He has put the servants wherever He wants – [Keep busy with your own faults]

I seek refuge in Allah from the accursed devil
In the Name of Allah the All-Beneficent the Most Merciful
There is no power nor strength but with Allah the High, the Magnificent
Permission, O my Master, support!
Our way is companionship, and goodness is in the congregation

One of the righteous was buried. When his murids tried to make him face towards the qibla, this wali opened his eyes, looked at him and said, "O my son, the One that directed your face has directed me. There is no need to direct me. For *verily I have turned my face to the One Who originated the heavens and the earth* (al-Anʿām 6:79). And do not fear, my son! *wherever you turn to, there is the Face of the One God* (al-Baqara 2:115)." The murid said, "O my master! Are you dead or alive so that we might take you out?" He said to him, "Finish your job and do not speak."

Allah Almighty has put the servants wherever He wants.[1] This is why the most important reminder in this time is the statement of the Messenger–upon him the blessings and peace of Allah–"Blessings to him whose own faults have kept too busy for him to look at other people's faults."[2] If people kept their looks away from one another their affairs would straighten up. But people disregard their own faults and get busy with other people's faults. At that time they will drown in rebellious sins.

Mawlana al-Shaykh used to say, "O my child, when you leave your house, do not look other than at yourself. Be busy with your own ego. And when you return home do not give your wife a chance to retell you people's news, and do not tell her what you have seen. This way you will relax. Allah has said,

[1] See Suhba I.75, second note.

[2] Narrated from (i) Anas by al-Bazzār (12:348 §6237); Ibn ʿAdī, *Kāmil* (Abān b. Abī ʿAyyāsh); Bayhaqī, *Shuʿab* (71: *Zuhd*); Khaṭīb, *Tārīkh* (ʿUmar b. Ibrāhīm b. Mūsā); and others; (ii) ʿĀʾisha by al-Dīnawarī, *Mujālasa* (4:108 §1288); (iii) Abū Hurayra by Abū Bakr Aḥmad b. Mūsā b. Mardūyah, *Juzʾ fīh mā intaqā Ibn Mardūyah ʿalā al-Ṭabarānī min ḥadīthih li-ahl al-Baṣra*, ed. Badr b. ʿAbd Allāh al-Badr (Riyadh: Aḍwāʾ al-Salaf, 1420/ 2000) p. 105-106 §43; (iv) al-Ḥusayn b. ʿAlī b. Abī Ṭālib by Abū Nuʿaym, *Ḥilya* (3:203); (v) Sufyān b. Usayd al-Ḥaḍramī by Quḍāʿī, *Musnad al-shihāb* (1:358 §613). Ibn Ḥajar rated al-Bazzār's chain from Anas fair in *Bulūgh al-marām* (*Jāmiʿ, al-rahab min masāwiʾ al-akhlāq*). Suyūṭī rated the hadith fair in *al-Jāmiʿ al-ṣaghīr* (2:71).

behold, with the remembrance of the One God are the hearts at peace! (Ra'd 13:28). Putting it into practice it blocks the devil's assaults and prevents him from laying our belief and our deeds to ruin, or ruining our relationships with others."

May Allah grant it to us. By the sanctity of the Fatiha.

58
Spending will be a reason for meeting the Mahdi

I seek refuge in Allah from the accursed devil
In the Name of Allah the All-Beneficent the Most Merciful
There is no power nor strength but with Allah the High, the Magnificent
Permission, O my Master, support!
Our way is companionship, and goodness is in the congregation

Our liege lord 'Uthmān b. 'Affān–Allah be well-pleased with him–presented to our liege lord the Messenger of Allah–upon him the blessings and peace of Allah–two ingots of gold for him to spend in the way of Allah. The Messenger made a big supplication for him and this spending is his special merit from that day and until the Day of Resurrection.[1]

As for the endtimes, when people shall spend in the way of Allah and the way of buttressing Islam, the reward for spending a single dirham will be greater than that for the spending of our liege lord 'Uthmān to the Day of Resurrection![2] And this immense merit shall end the moment the Mahdi emerges–upon him peace. In the former time, even if you spent all of the wealth of this world it would not match the reward of a single dirham in this time. And Allah has said, "O My servant, spend and I will spend on you,"[3] just as the Messenger–upon him the blessings and peace of Allah–said, "No property ever diminishes from spending alms."[4] Spending, even little, will be a reason for meeting *Ṣāḥib al-zamān*.

May Allah grant it to us. By the sanctity of the Fatiha.

[1] When 'Uthmān heard the Prophet say, "Whoever equips the army of al-'Usra"—for the campaign of Tabūk (9/630) on the border of Syro-Palestine—"he shall have Paradise," he brought the Prophet a thousand gold dinars which he poured into his lap. The Prophet picked them up with his hand and said repeatedly, "Nothing shall harm 'Uthmān after what he did today." Narrated from (i) 'Abd al-Raḥmān b. Samura by Aḥmad and Tirmidhī (*ḥasan gharīb*); (ii) 'Uthmān by Bukhārī with a different wording. It is also narrated that he equipped the army of 'Usra with seven hundred ounces of gold. Narrated from 'Abd al-Raḥmān b. 'Awf by Abū Ya'lā and Ibn 'Asākir, *Tārīkh Dimashq* (39:69). It is also narrated that he equipped them with seven hundred and fifty camels and fifty horses. Narrated from al-Ḥasan al-Baṣrī by Ibn 'Asākir (39:70).

[2] See Suhba I.44, first note and the hadith, "My Umma is like the rain..."

[3] Narrated from Abū Hurayra by al-Ḥumaydī; Aḥmad; Bukhārī; Muslim; Ibn Mājah, Abū Ya'lā; al-Ṭabarānī and others, all in the wording, "O son of Ādam, etc."

[4] Narrated from (i-iii) 'Abd al-Raḥmān b. 'Awf, Abū Hurayra and Abū Kabshat al-Anmārī from Aḥmad; al-Dārimī; Muslim; al-Tirmidhī and others.

59

[Prophets and Awliya prefer seclusion but are commanded to show themselves – Seeing Allah – The ego's arrogance] – The Israelites' repentance – [Die before you die] – Allah purifies whom He wishes – [The worst enemy – *Mawlā* not *dunyā*]

I seek refuge in Allah from the accursed devil
In the Name of Allah the All-Beneficent the Most Merciful
There is no power nor strength but with Allah the High, the Magnificent
Permission, O my Master, support!
Our way is companionship, and goodness is in the congregation

If it were up to me I would have chosen isolation and seclusion so that no one would know me. However, Allah Almighty wants for His command and His wisdom to be completed. We are slaves under His rule and under His power, complete subjects. Since He is the one that has put the servants wherever He wants[1] and we are like slaves, it is a duty to be well-pleased with our nurturing Lord–Almighty is He–whatever He does with us. The lady Maryam–upon her peace–said, *would that I had died before this, and that I were a thing forgotten, consigned to oblivion!* (Maryam 19:23). However, the will of our nurturing Lord is that she should be remembered forever.

Allah Almighty dresses His Prophets–upon them peace–and his Awliya of His exalted Attributes. If it were up to the Messenger–upon him the blessings and peace of Allah–he would have chosen to be always in seclusion, hidden. But the command of Allah came, *O immantled one! Rise and warn* (Muddaththir 74:1-2) and *so proclaim far and wide what you are commanded* (Ḥijr 15:94), i.e. show yourself to people. For **the Prophets and the Awliya are wearing the Attributes of the All-True and a Prophet is never like the rest of the people**. For he is being sent on the part of Allah Almighty. More than that, those that represent Allah in the created universe are the Messengers, and the last of the Messengers is our liege lord the Messenger of Allah–upon him the blessings and peace of Allah–the representative of the All-True, and he was dressed from the Attributes of Allah Almighty.

[1] See Suhba I.75, second note.

Were it not for the Messengers there would exist no avenue to the knowledge of the All-True. And people need to see the Attributes of the All-True personified and no only in writing. If writing were enough Allah would have sent down scrolls from the sky and He would have ordered people to go and put them into practice. He would not have sent Prophets to be looked up to. This is a wisdom, because our constitution is unsuited to be taught merely from books. But together with the Book, the All-True dresses the Prophets with His Attributes so that people will see them and so that it will become easy for them to receive [teachings] from them. The noble verse says, *there was ever for you, in the Messenger of the One God, a fine model* (Aḥzāb 33:21). How then do they dare say "the Messenger–upon him the blessings and peace of Allah–is dead and gone, he has conveyed the Message and has departed"? What is the meaning of these verses then?

For each and everyone, to the Day of Resurrection, the Messenger–upon him the blessings and peace of Allah–alone is a model. Allah mentioned that in the Qur'ān: *and verily you indeed command a sublime character* (Nūn/al-Qalam 68:4). When Allah says *sublime*, is there any yardstick by which you can measure the character of the Messenger? And when the lady 'Ā'isha–Allah be well-pleased with her–was asked about the character of the Messenger–upon him peace–she said, "His character is the Qur'ān."[1]

The Messenger–upon him the blessings and peace of Allah–was ever the representative for the character of Allah and he has instructed us to acquire the traits of character of Allah,[2] whereby **each of the traits of character of Allah is evidence for an existing attribute and the Messenger of Allah–upon him blessings and peace–was wearing, from the Attributes of Allah, something like a visible character.** People would see him appear in full sight before them while the Messenger had said, "Whoever has seen me then he has certainly seen *al-ḥaqq* (the truth)."[3] That is, he sees nothing but the All-True. And the Messenger of Allah–upon him the blessings of Allah–has said, "I have not worshipped a nurturing Lord I have not seen.[4] Rather I saw Him and I

[1] See Suhba I.31, third note.

[2] See Suhbas I.2, fifth note; I.31, third note; I.50, last note.

[3] Narrated from (i) Abū Qatāda by Aḥmad (37:291-292 §22606); Bukhārī (*Ta'bīr, man ra'ā al-Nabīy fil-manām*); Muslim (*Ru'yā, qawl al-Nabī ṣallā Allāh 'alayh wa-sallam man ra'ānī fil-manām*); (ii) Abū Sa'īd al-Khudrī by Bukhārī (ditto); (iii) Abū Hurayra by Abū Sa'īd 'Abd Allāh b. Sa'īd b. Ḥuṣayn al-Ashajj al-Kindī (d. 257/ 871), *Juz' fīhi min ḥadīth Abī Sa'īd al-Ashajj*, ed. Ismā'īl Muḥ. al-Jazā'irī (Riyadh: Dār al-Mughnī, 1422/2001) p. 284 §166; Abū Dāwūd (*Adab, fil-ru'yā*); Tirmidhī at the very end of the *Shamā'il*; (iv) 'Abd Allāh b. 'Amr by Ṭabarānī, *Kabīr* (13:634 §14558). Cf. Suhba I.61.

[4] Narrated in *maqṭū'* mode from (i) Muḥ. al-Bāqir b. 'Alī Zayn al-'Ābidīn b. al-Ḥusayn

prostrated, I saw Him and I worshipped Him, and I did not worship Him on the basis of imagination." As for the modality of the sighting then it is not taught to the servant until he enters that station.[1] At that time he will know with *'ilm al-yaqīn* (the knowledge of certainty), *'ayn al-yaqīn* (the sight of certainty) and *ḥaqq al-yaqīn* (the reality of certainty).[2] That is the station of excellence, "that you worship your nurturing Lord as if you were seeing Him, for if you are not seeing Him, then verily He sees you."[3]

There is a wisdom to "if you are not seeing Him." That is, "while you still exist you shall never see him."[4] He said to our liege lord Mūsā–upon him peace–*you shall not see Me* (al-A'rāf 7:143). "For if you are not seeing Him:" together with your existence, you cannot see Him because your ego is the greatest veil between you and your nurturing Lord. Not until the ego goes away can you know your nurturing Lord and become one of those that arrive. When our liege lord Abū Yazīd al-Bisṭāmī asked, "O my nurturing Lord! What is the way to reach You?" He said to him, "O Abū Yazīd, leave yourself behind and come. This ego of yours I do not want." For among the entirety of creatures no existence has asserted itself before the Lord of might other than the ego. It said *anā anā wa-anta ant* (I am me and You are You).[5]

by Dīnawarī, *Mujālasa* (5:395 §2257); Ibn 'Asākir, *Tārīkh* (54:282); (ii) Muḥ. b. 'Alī or his son Ja'far al-Ṣādiq by Ibn Ṭāhir al-Maqdisī, *al-Bad' wal-ṭārīkh* (1:74); Abū Sa'd Manṣūr b. al-Ḥusayn al-Rāzī al-Ābī, *Nathr al-durr fil-muḥāḍarāt*, ed. Khālid 'Abd al-Ghanī Maḥfūẓ, 4 vols. (Beirut: Dār al-Kutub al-'Ilmiyya, 1424/2004) 1:244; (ii) 'Alī b. Abī Ṭālib by Rāghib al-Aṣfahānī, *Tafsīr* (Nisā' 4:69); al-Ṭībī, *Futūḥ al-ghayb fil-kashfi 'an qinā' al-ghayb* (Nisā' 4:69); Ismā'īl Ḥaqqī, *Rūḥ al-bayān* (Mā'ida 5:6-11, Anbiyā' 21:31, Dhāriyāt 51:22-23); al-Shawkānī, *al-Bughya fī mas'alat al-ru'ya* in *al-Fatḥ al-rabbānī min fatāwā al-Imām al-Shawkānī*, ed. Muḥ. Ṣubḥī Ḥasan Ḥallāq, 12 vols. in 6 (Sanaa: Maktabat al-Jīl al-Jadīd, 2002) 2:764; Ālūsī, *Rūḥ al-bayān* (Nisā' 4:69).

[1] Per the Prophetic hadith "You shall see your nurturing Lord just as you see the moon on the night it is full" narrated from (i) Abū Hurayra by al-Tirmidhī (*ḥasan*) and (ii) Jarīr b. 'Abd Allāh al-Bajalī by al-Bukhārī and Muslim.

[2] See also Suhba I.103 for an alternate translation.

[3] See Suhba I.36, second note.

[4] Ibn 'Arabī referred to this wisdom towards the end of his very brief *Kitāb al-fanā' fil-mushāhada* (The extinction in the beholding), transl. Stephen Hirtenstein and Layla Shamash, *Journal of the Muhyiddin Ibn 'Arabi Society*, IX (1991) pp. 1-17.

[5] A Prophetic hadith about a man from the Israelites who said these words then he repented and said, "You are the Oft-Forgiving and I am the oft-sinning." Narrated from Jābir b. 'Abd Allāh by Bazzār through trustworthy narrators per al-Haythamī, *Kashf al-astār* (1:361 §755); *Majma' al-zawā'id* (2:287); Abū Ṭāhir al-Ḥasan b. Aḥmad b. Ibrāhīm b. Fīl al-Bālisī (d. 311/923), *Juz' Ibn Fīl*, ed. Mūsā Ismā'īl al-Basīṭ (Quds: Maṭba'at Mas'ūdī, 1421/2001) p. 133 §111; Ibn 'Adī, *Kāmil* (Ja'far b. Sulaymān al-Ḍuba'ī); Tammām al-Rāzī, *Fawā'id* (1:269 §659); Tha'labī (al-Baqara 2:222); Abū al-

This is why the ego is the greatest veil and must pass away, and the All-True has certainly commanded us, *and kill yourselves* (Baqara 2:54), which is recounted from the Israelites to make us understand that, out of the meanings of the Qur'ān, the least level that comes out from each letter is 24,000 meanings and wisdoms. Nor do the meanings of the first *alif* resemble those of the second *alif* for example, and so forth. Allah has retold in the Qur'ān that the reason for which the repentance of the Israelites was accepted is that they killed themselves because they had fallen into unbelief and worshipped the Calf because of their egos. They openly worshipped the Calf—and the ego is constantly looking for a calf to worship. *And they became imbued with the Calf in their hearts* (Baqara 2:93)—love of this life, and the ego worships this life, and if you do not kill it it will kill you.

This is why the jihad against the ego is the greatest jihad, for the human being's ego is his mortal enemy.[1] So when you sacrifice it and your offer it as *a tremendous sacrificial offering* (Ṣāffāt 37:107) to your nurturing Lord and you accept self-extinction, He shall give you *a pure life*,[2] an eternal life, a real life. Therefore the servants of Allah are between two choices: either that of a voluntary death, or to wait for the compulsory death, since our nurturing Lord has decreed for every soul that it must taste death (Āl 'Imrān 3:185, al-Anbiyā' 21:35, al-'Ankabūt 29:57). And **when the servant does not accept to obey the command of Allah and kill himself to reach the station of "Die before you die"[3] to triumph and be saved with a pure life, he must wait until he is shackled with the chains of divine power and the angel of death comes down to deal with that ego; but this is not a noble death.**

The noble death is to present yourself to your nurturing Lord as *a tremendous sacrificial offering.* Every time we acknowledge our weakness, as Allah Most High says, *and the human being was created weak* (al-Nisā' 4:28), Allah appoints His special care and His guidance and His mercies to be at our beck and call. That is, the more the servant feels that he or she is weak, the more Allah shall extend to them a pure help from His side. And whenever the human being sees himself as something, Allah shall leave him to himself—*Nay! Verily the human being does indeed transgress, for that he saw himself to be self-*

Qāsim al-Ḥinnā'ī, *al-Fawā'id al-Ḥinnā'iyyāt* (2:1016 §196); al-Khaṭīb, *Tārīkh* (Sa'īd b. Nuṣayr al-Baghdādī); Ibn 'Asākir, *Tārīkh* (5:149, 37:313). See also Suhbas I.89, I.95.

[1] See Suhbas I.35 and I.46, second note.

[2] *Whoever does something righteous, male or female, while a believer, then We will bring that one to life with a pure life; and We will indeed requite them their wage with the better of what they used to do* (al-Naḥl 16:97).

[3] See Suhba I.32, fourth note.

sufficient (al-'Alaq 96:6-7). When he sees himself as self-sufficient with his money or his intelligence and his worldly life and his influence, Allah entrusts him to them—and whoever is abandoned to himself has definitely perished. This is why the Messenger of Allah–upon him the blessings and peace of Allah–was constantly supplicating for himself and his Umma, "O Allah! Do not leave us to ourselves for the blink of an eye."[1]

Is there anyone that can say, "I am relying on my knowledge" or "my deeds" when every situation comes to an end? This is why **we must take the way of *sulūk* (spiritual wayfaring) on the path of *adab* (high manners), whereby the Messenger–upon him the blessings and peace of Allah–states, "My nurturing Lord has raised me and He has perfected my manners."[2] All our noble masters are holding fast to this *adab* and this hadith, and they are making it a light for them to walk by its guidance, and thus [for everyone else]. For verily the Tariqa is all high manners so that the servant will recognize his limit and his true attribute.**

Allah says, *and were it not for the bounty of the One God over you and His mercy, not one of you would become pure ever* (al-Nūr 24:21). After this who can raise his head to boast of his knowledge or his work or his strength? *But the One God purifies whomever He wishes* (al-Nūr 24:21). We are weak, and every time we acknowledge our weakness, Allah shall extend to us help from His presence. Allah has certainly said, *and the One God most surely helped you at Badr, when you were negligible* (Āl 'Imrān 3:123), not mighty but insignificant. As the Qur'ān said, *and on the day of Ḥunayn, when your large number went to your heads* (Barā'a/Tawba 9:25): when their large number went to their heads at Ḥunayn (8/630) Allah brought them low before the polytheists. At that time there were the Ten that were promised Paradise among the Companions together with the rest of the Companions, and the Messenger–upon him the blessings and peace of Allah–was present. Despite that they were routed because their large number had pleased them. The Companions themselves were routed, so how will we ourselves fare?

The worst of all enemies for all without exception is one's own soul that is between your flanks,[3] not So and so or someone else. And you will never be able to defeat your ego except with big help from Allah. This is why the Prophet–upon him the blessings and peace of Allah–would say, "O Allah! Do not leave me to myself for the blink of an eye"[4]—and where do we stand in

[1] See Suhba I.28, fifth note.

[2] See Suhba I.26, first note.

[3] See Suhba I.46, second note.

[4] See Suhba I.28, fifth note.

comparison to the Messenger of Allah? So now that he has taught us this secret, we have to take recourse to Allah for safety.

Likewise our liege lord Nūḥ, one of the Prophets of high resolve, said, *I am overcome, so take revenge!* (al-Qamar 54:10). He said–exalted is He–*and the One God is All-prevailing in His affair* (Yūsuf 12:21). We are overcome and in need of our nurturing Lord Almighty. This is why we must learn to humble themselves before Allah. The more we have travelled on any of the paths, we must increase in humbleness in the presence of Allah. Our knowledge or our devotions and our Tariqa must never be a reason for seeing ourselves as something. On the contrary we must melt away from our egos and tread the path of extinction until no trace of us remains. This is what the Prophets have come to teach us. Allah has brought out our liege lord Ādam from Paradise because of that ego and He has brought him down to the earth and said to him, "When you want to return, leave your ego behind and come; and I have foreordained death for you and your sons, and I shall subdue them with death, but blessings to him that reaches the voluntary death before the compulsory death!" So do not be a runaway slave for them [=the angels] to tie you down and bring you back to your Master.

Allah is saying, *so take flight unto the One God!* (al-Dhāriyāt 51:50)—and is there anywhere a fairer refuge and better salvation than Allah? This is why, were it not for my nurturing Lord's will, not one strand of thought would come to me so that I might speak before people, and I would leave everything so that I might be *a thing forgotten, consigned to oblivion!* (Maryam 19:23). But so that His command might be accomplished and so that He will show His wisdom, He gives my tongue speech. We hope and pray that Allah shall make this speech settle in our hearts and strengthen us against our egos, and that it will be a reason for our overwhelming power over our egos, and it will be a reason for our purification.

After that, O beloved ones of Allah and His Messenger, why are the people of religion disagreeing, on top of the worldly people in our time? Worldly people are in disagreement and mutually envious because each one of them has an objective that contravenes the other's objective. We have become the same in our time. Muslims, Tariqa people, learned scholars have all become hateful of one another. Otherwise, if their objectives became unified, they would not hate one another or envy one another or act in enmity of one another. Because our goal is Allah, Iblīs and his soldiers put disagreement between the people of Tariqa in our time besides the people of learning, because the latter are nearer to the world than the former so there is more mutual hatred among them because of love of leadership and aggrandizement and because of fame and love of exposure. But the people of Tariqa are now in the same valley for their greatest concern has become Shaykhdom, the pursuit of exposure and love of this world. This has made them enemies to one another, otherwise, if Allah were their sole objective, they would never disagree. This is what happens when the goal is no longer Allah. The goal becomes this world. Rivalry and disagreement begin. Instead of our eyes being trained on the *malakūt* (invisible sovereignty) they are now trained on the ground. But we must return to our original home country, to the *malakūt*.

More than that, do you see any wali hating another wali? How would he be a wali in the first place if he has envy or he turns to this world? Therefore, O brothers, we have to know whether our objective is *dunyā* (this world) or *Mawlā* (the protecting Friend). If you have chosen *dunyā* then you have all the insects, wild beasts and blameworthy traits in your heart. You yourself will be the center of fitna because with *dunyā* comes all evil. But if you have chosen the *Mawlā* then blessings to you!

Whoever is intending the *Mawlā*—*behold, with the remembrance of the One God are the hearts at peace!* (Raʿd 13:28), and there will not remain with you any trace of anxiety or depression because *Allāhu nāẓirī, Allāhu shāhidī, Allāhu maʿī* (Allah is my observer, Allah is my witness, Allah is with me).[1] You will forget everything other than your protecting Friend and you will be with Him. However, when you forget your protecting Friend and you choose the world, problems descend on you so that you will drown in them. You must realize that the enjoyment of this world runs out and that what is with Allah endures forever. If you feel free and bold, enter the world and drink of its anxiety and depression. But if you acknowledge your incapacity and ask for help and ease from Allah, at that time you shall relax and forget everything other than Allah.

By the sanctity of the Beloved, by the sanctity of the Fatiha.

[1] This was al-Tustarī first spiritual devotion which he would first repeat seven times then finally 11 times before sleep "without moving the tongue" as a small boy, given to him by his maternal uncle Abū ʿAbd Allāh Muḥammad b. Sawwār b. Rāshid al-Kūfī per Qushayrī, *Risāla* (Abū Muḥammad Sahl b. ʿAbd Allāh al-Tustarī). Nawawī prescribed it in *al-Adhkār* as a preventive against slipping into *ghība* (slander).

60
We must work to put out the fire of wrongdoing

I seek refuge in Allah from the accursed devil
In the Name of Allah the All-Beneficent the Most Merciful
There is no power nor strength but with Allah the High, the Magnificent
Permission, O my Master, support!
Our way is companionship, and goodness is in the congregation

"To leave one ant's weight of the prohibitions of Allah is better than the worship of the two weighty worlds."[1] If we consider that smoking is abominable—defined as what a human being hates—to the extent of an ant's weight of the prohibitions of Allah, then leaving it is better than the worship of the two weighty worlds. And who is capable of worshipping his nurturing Lord with the worship of the two weighty worlds? And we are just small individual parts of them. Nimrod kindled a furnace as big as mountains to burn our liege lord Ibrāhīm–upon him peace–and the ant—which Allah mentioned in the Qur'ān —would bring with its mouth water to put out Nimrod's fire. That is why Allah rewarded it and mentioned it in the Qur'ān and put it among the ten animals that will enter Paradise.[2] This is why it is abominable to kill an ant.

The ant would bring water in its mouth to put out Nimrod's fire—can it do that? And now, next to what is kindled in the world of the fire of wrongdoing, Nimrod's fire is like a small spark and our work is less than the work of that ant. However, if it were in the power of that ant to put out that fire it would have done so. And we know our own incapacity, and there is no possibility to

[1] Cited as a hadith in some Ḥanafī sources such as Ḥusām al-Dīn al-Sighnāqī, *al-Kāfī sharḥ al-Pazdawī*; Ḥaqqī, *Rūḥ al-bayān*; Aḥmadnagrī, *Dastūr al-'ulamā'*; Khādimī, *Barīqa maḥmūdiyya*; and Anwar Shāh Kashmīrī, *al-'Urf al-shadhīy sharḥ Sunan al-Tirmidhī*. The *thaqalayn* (two weighty ones) are the human beings and the jinns.

[2] Various hadiths cite the birds, camels, sheeps, goats, horses, bull and whales of Paradise while later scholars specified (i) the Prophet's camel mare (or his Burāq), (ii) Ṣāliḥ's camel mare, (iii) Ibrāhīm's fatted calf, (iv) Ismā'īl's ram, (v) Mūsā's cow, (vi) Yūnus' whale, (vii) Bilqīs' hoopoe, (viii) Sulaymān's ant, (ix) al-'Uzayr's donkey and (x) the dog of the sleepers of the Cave. See Abū al-'Abbās Shihāb al-Dīn Aḥmad b. Muḥammad Makkī al-Ḥusaynī al-Ḥamawī al-Ḥanafī (d. 1098/1687), *Ghamz 'uyūn al-baṣā'ir fī sharḥ al-ashbāh wal-naẓā'ir*; Shihāb al-Dīn Aḥmad b. Ghānim b. Sālim b. Muhannā al-Nafrāwī al-Mālikī (d. 1126/1714), *al-Fawākih al-dawānī 'alā risālat Ibn Abī Zayd al-Qayrawānī*; Abū al-Barakāt Aḥmad al-Dirdīr (1127-1201/1715-1786), *al-Dirdīr 'alā qiṣṣat al-mi'rāj lil-Ghayṭī* (Cairo: 'Īsā al-Bābī al-Ḥalabī, n.d.) p. 7; *Fatāwā Dār al-Iftā' al-Miṣriyya* (*Dawābb al-janna*, 'Aṭiyya Ṣaqr, May 1997).

put out the fire of wrongdoing. Nevertheless we work to put out that fire, even to the extent of an ant's work. If we had the power, all the fire of wrongdoing would be extinguished, but I am incapable, and I work just as that ant worked.

May Allah extend to us a help from His presence. By the sanctity of the Beloved, by the sanctity of the Fatiha.

61

[Two words from the Prophet – Seek your time's mercies] – Allah's hand is on the group – Reality of tasking – [Definition of muridship – Subjection of heaven and earth to the murid]

I seek refuge in Allah from the accursed devil
In the Name of Allah the All-Beneficent the Most Merciful
There is no power nor strength but with Allah the High, the Magnificent
Permission, O my Master, support!
Our way is companionship, and goodness is in the congregation

I have been informed of two words from the Holy Prophet–upon him the blessings and peace of Allah–for the sake of servanthood, and if I do not convey them I will be held to account. The Holy Prophet spoke these two words so that everyone that hears them will pay them attention and give care to them. Likewise whoever hears and does not put them into practice will be held to account in front of the Holy Prophet–upon him the blessings and peace of Allah.

First, our liege lord the Shaykh ['Abd Allah al-Daghistani] is giving the glad tidings from the Holy Prophet–upon him the blessings and peace of Allah–that we have reached a time the like of which was not reached by the Prophets or by the Awliya before, from the perspective of the immense mercy that Allah is opening to the Umma and to all of humankind. The manifestation of the mercies is immense and unprecedented. These are great glad tidings. Were it not for that vast mercy the world would be brought to ruin and no one would remain. These mercies were hidden in Allah's storehouses and nothing of them was shown to the Prophets or to the Awliya. In our time Allah opened up those storehouses to bring down mercy on the servants, since the end of the world has drawn near. It was impossible for anyone to know the extent of these mercies—neither Prophets nor Awliya—until that door was opened. At that time they would look and know. Those mercies are part of *none who is in the heavens and the earth knows the unseen except the One God* (Naml 27:65) in absolute terms. None knows until Allah brings it out into the open from His storehouses.

Mawlana says that in every moment we live in there is mercy descending, and from one moment to the next the first mercy leaves and another mercy replaces it and on and on. Whoever takes his share of those mercies has triumphed and has been saved, and whoever pays no attention to those mercies has deprived himself of them. For each mercy is proper to its time. And of the special mercies that are opened up for the Umma is, *yadu-l-Lāhi ʿalā al-jamāʿa* (The hand of Allah is *over* the group),[1] *yadu-l-Lāhi maʿa al-jamāʿa* (The hand of Allah is *with* the group).[2] And every time a gathering of dhikr is held, or a gathering of companionship and advice, those mercies descend.

The Prophet–upon him blessings and peace–says *al-dīnu al-naṣīḥa* (The faith-system is all pure counsel).[3] So whoever gathers to follow the order of the Messenger and in confirmation of his truthfulness shall obtain of that mercy in permanence. Whoever attends the gathering of *naṣīḥa* shall obtain of its mercy. If he does not attend he will not obtain that mercy that is specific to this gathering, because each gathering has a special mercy and a special manifestation. Whoever is present has obtained and gained. Whoever has not attended, even if he worshipped as much as the two weighty ones (humans and jinns) he would not obtain that mercy. Thus the believer is the product of his time.[4] Mercy descends even on two or more just as it descends on a thousand. The Messenger–upon him the blessings and peace of Allah–says, "Verily there are in your times breezes. Behold! Do expose yourselves to them."[5] Holy breezes of the eternally-besought divine "in your times," i.e. in a certain moment of your lifetime. It is never devoid of the blessings of your nurturing Lord, and the Messenger's instruction is, "Behold! Do expose yourselves to

[1] A Prophetic hadith narrated from (i) ʿUmar by Bukhārī, *Tārīkh al-kabīr*; Ṭabarānī, *Awsaṭ*; (ii) Ibn ʿUmar by Ibn Abī ʿĀṣim, *Sunna*; Dūlābī, *Kunā wal-asmāʾ*; Ṭabarānī, *Awsaṭ*; Ḥākim, *Mustadrak*; (iii) Usāma b. Sharīk by Ibn Abī ʿĀṣim, *al-Sunna*; Ibn Qāniʿ, *Muʿjam al-Ṣaḥāba*; al-Ṭabarānī, *Kabīr*; (iv) ʿArfaja b. Ḍurayḥ al-Ashjaʿī by al-Nasāʾī, *al-Mujtabā* and *al-Sunan al-kubrā*; Ibn Ḥibbān, *Ṣaḥīḥ*; (v) Ibn ʿAbbās by Abū ʿAbd Allāh Muḥ. b. Makhlad b. Ḥafṣ al-Dūrī, *Muntaqā*; Ibn Baṭṭa, *al-Ibānat al-kubrā*; al-Ḥākim, *Mustadrak*; (vi) Abū Saʿīd al-Khudrī by Ṭabarānī, *Awsaṭ* and *Musnad al-Shāmiyyīn*; (vii) al-Khabbāb b. al-Aratt by al-Ṭabarānī, *Kabīr*; and, in *mawqūf* mode, (viii) Abū ʿUbayda b. al-Jarrāḥ by al-Qāsim b. Sallām, *Amwāl*; Ibn Zanjūyah, *Amwāl*.

[2] A Prophetic hadith narrated from (i) Ibn ʿUmar by Tirmidhī, *ʿIlal*; *Sunan* (*gharīb*); Abū Nuʿaym, *Ḥilya*; (ii) Ibn ʿAbbās by al-Tirmidhī (*ḥasan*); (iii) ʿArfaja b. Ḍurayḥ al-Ashjaʿī by Ibn Ḥibbān, *Ṣaḥīḥ*; Bayhaqī, *Shuʿab* (50: *tamassuk bimā ʿalayhi al-jamāʿa*); al-Khaṭīb al-Baghdādī, *al-Faqīh wal-mutafaqqih*.

[3] See Suhba I.10.

[4] Suhrawardī, *ʿAwārif al-maʿārif* (chapter 5: definition of *taṣawwuf*).

[5] Narrated from (i) Abū Hurayra by Ibn Abī al-Dunyā, *al-Faraj baʿda al-shidda*; (ii) Ibn ʿUmar by al-Dūlābī, *al-Kunā wal-asmāʾ*; al-Khaṭīb, *Tārīkh Baghdād*; (iii) Anas by al-Ḥakīm al-Tirmidhī, *Nawādir al-uṣūl* (3:231 §963, *Aṣl* 186); Ṭabarānī, *al-Duʿāʾ* and *al-Muʿjam al-kabīr*; Abū Nuʿaym, *Ḥilya* and *Muʿjam al-Ṣaḥāba*; Bayhaqī, *Asmāʾ* and *Shuʿab*; and others; (iv) Muḥammad b. Maslama by Ṭabarānī, *Awsaṭ* and *Kabīr*; and, in *mawqūf* mode, (v) Abū al-Dardāʾ by Ibn Abī Shayba; Abū Nuʿaym, *Ḥilya*.

them." In reference to this, our Master the Shaykh says "expose yourselves" means **be sure to attend in any gathering there will be two people or more. Gather in the love of Allah and sit with them because this mercy descends on them and you will obtain it**. Mawlana al-Shaykh also says that with that mercy there are angels descending that will say, "O our nurturing Lord! Among them are people that are not qualified for that rank and that mercy, should we leave them out and give that mercy to others?" Allah shall answer them "O My angels, give it to them also, for whoever sits with those people will not be wretched. Give them of the mercy the same as what you give the rest of them and make no difference between them!"[1]

Mawlana al-Shaykh used to say that even if a *jubil munāfiq* (innate hypocrite) attended, his innate nature would be changed to belief and he would be transformed from wretchedness to bliss. When Allah gives of His mercy He boggles the mind. For Allah's giving cannot be measured by any criterion. This is why the mercy that goes away we can never bring back again even if we did the worship of the two dense species. This is why the people of the truth say, *ajallu al-karāmāt dawāmu al-tawfīq* (the most momentous of miraculous gifts is the permanence of divine enablement for success).[2] When you have agreed to a certain matter do not let worldly excuses prevent you from doing it. Rather, sacrifice the whole world in order to obtain that mercy.

For example if you have agreed to attend in a gathering of faithful advice once or twice a week then keep to that. Do not attend once and run away twice. For if that mercy were to appear to you you would travelled the world on foot so as to attend the gathering in order to obtain that mercy. And when you promise something then the angels await your coming in accordance with your promise—unless there is a legally-sanctioned excuse, which is a different matter. Otherwise, if there is no excuse, then you must observe what you promised your nurturing Lord to do, for the most momentous of miraculous gifts is the permanence of divine enablement for success—not walking on water. Iblīs can walk on water or enter a fire or fly in the air and this is worthless. Thus when you have promised a certain matter—such as praying in congregation or wearing the turban etc.—observe it faithfully and do not recant it for such counts as desertion. When you march against the enemy and then you run away, truly that is of the gravest enormities and one fears for the servant's belief because of it. This is why the Messenger–upon him the blessings and peace of Allah–instructed his Companions, "O beloved ones of Allah, when

[1] Part of a famous long Prophetic *ḥadīth qudsī* narrated from (i) Abū Hurayra by Aḥmad, al-Bukhārī, al-Tirmidhī, Ibn Abī ʿĀṣim, al-Bazzār, Ibn Ḥibbān, al-Ṭabarānī (*al-Duʿā*ʾ) and others; (ii) Ibn ʿAbbās by al-Ṭabarānī, *Ṣaghīr*; Abū Nuʿaym, *Ḥilya*.

[2] Qushayrī, *Risāla Qushayriyya* (*karāmāt al-awliyā*ʾ); Nawawī, *Bustān al-ʿārifīn* (ditto).

you promise one another a certain matter then hold fast to it,"[1] for the most momentous of miraculous gifts is the permanence of divine enablement for success.

Second, our master the Shaykh ['Abd Allah al-Daghistani] says—explaining it from the Messenger's heart–upon him blessings and peace of Allah–that Allah has said, *Allah does not task any soul except to its capacity* (Baqara 2:286). This tasking differs from one person to another. There is a secret in the tasking. Mawlana says that when a human being realizes there is goodness in a certain matter, or that it is one of the commands of Allah or of His Messenger–upon him the blessings and peace of Allah–or part of worshipfulness or part of the doing of good, then he has become tasked to implement it. Likewise with regard to prohibitions: once he finds out that a certain matter is abominable or categorically prohibited, it has become obligatory for him to leave it. But if a person does not know about a certain matter then he is not tasked.

Mawlana al-Shaykh says that **whoever puts the above rule into practice in that fashion enters the station of muridship in the Most Distinguished Naqshbandi Tariqa.** This is the way of the Prophets. Mawlana explains about the station of the murid in the Most Distinguished Tariqa that it is the manifestation of the noble verse *and He made subservient to you what is in the skies and what is on earth entirely from Him* (Jāthiya 45:13), and that **he becomes tasked with *ḥaqīqat al-taklīf* (reality of tasking), like the Companions whose tasks are other than what we have heard or seen of the matter of servanthood**. For there were, for each Companion, tasks exclusive to him—as tasking, at the station of *ghayb* (the unseen),[2] differs from tasking at the station of excellence. This is why the breath of the one at that station is dearer than the worship of the two dense species in the presence of Allah.

Therefore, **when you have realized that a certain matter is better, put it into practice right away and do not say, "there will be a time when I can do it."** If you see gold on the ground for example, will you leave it and say, "when I get back I will pick it up"? Someone else will come and take it. **This is how it always is. There are spiritual intuitions that come down. Whichever way you take you will find this world filled with the earnings of the hereafter**. And if you curb your gaze away from what is forbidden you will be given recompense as well.

[1] Per al-Baqara 2:177 and al-Naḥl 16:91, and the hadiths listing the keeping of promises as a characteristic of the Quraysh and of the believers at large; and the breaking of promises as a characteristic of the hypocrites.

[2] I.e. at the station of belief in the unseen.

At that time the created universes will be subjected to the murid: *and He made subservient to you what is in the skies and what is on earth entirely from Him* (al-Jāthiya 45:13). The universes with their immensity—because they are immense to us. But next to the magnificence of our nurturing Lord all of the universes do not even amount to less than the like of a drop in *a fathomless deep sea* (al-Nūr 24:40) without shore and without bottom. **This is His disposal for the servant to have *taṣarruf* (discretionary power) over the dwellers of the skies and the earth, such as our liege lord ʿAbd al-Qādir al-Jaylānī to whom the skies and the earth were subjected. They even have discretionary power over our liege lord ʿAzrāʾīl–upon him peace.**[1] **And this world will not be devoid of the like of our liege lord al-Jaylānī until the Day of Resurrection.** Whoever has reached that rank enters into the station of real tasking. There, you will see the modality of servanthood. *Behold! To the One God belongs the absolute faith* (al-Zumar 39:3). That is the station our liege lord ʿAlī–may Allah ennoble his countenance–when he said, "I never worshipped a nurturing Lord I could not see."[2] This station is the station of *iḥsān* (excellence), and whoever reached the station of extinction then Allah caused him to abide in His holy presence, there, all this world is subjected to him.

After that, al-Jaylānī, along with the rest of the Imams of all Tariqas, are in need of that murid the way the murid is in need of his guide. The means to arrive at the station of murid in the Most Distinguished Tariqa is that, when one knows that this matter is good, one implements it, and when one knows that that matter is evil, one stays away from it. So when you know you become tasked. And **when you know about a certain matter that it is evil, it is obligatory for you to stay away from it and to say, *lā ḥawla wa-lā quwwata illā bi-l-Lāh* (there is no power nor might but with Allah. For by yourself you cannot stay away from evil, but when you entrust yourself to Allah, your nurturing Lord will extend to you a special help from His presence and shall assist you in leaving that matter.** Just as Allah knows all secrets, He also knows a person's intention. So when you encounter something good and you are incapable of implementing it, at that time you make intention: "A person's intention is better than his deed,"[3] and "Actions are only according to intentions."[4]

[1] See the story of ʿAzrāʾīl and al-Jaylānī in Suhba I.26.

[2] See Suhba I.59, third note.

[3] A Prophetic hadith narrated from (i) Sahl b. Saʿd al-Sāʿidī by Ṭabarānī, *Kabīr*; (ii) al-Nawwās b. Samʿān al-Kilābī by Quḍāʿī, *Musnad al-Shihāb*; (iii) Anas by Bayhaqī, *Shuʿab*; (iv) Thābit al-Bunānī in *mursal* mode by Abū al-Shaykh, *Amthāl al-ḥadīth*.

[4] A famous Prophetic hadith narrated from ʿUmar b. al-Khaṭṭāb in the Six Books.

The same thing applies from the side of evil. Your ego pushes you to do it and you must do jihad against it, because your ego is bridleless and when the servant does evil he can no longer claim that he is a servant to Allah. Mawlana says that Allah is teaching all the servants—the Prophets, the believers, the depraved and the open sinner as well, since Allah says, *then He inspired it its open sin and its Godfearingness* (al-Shams 91:8). The meaning of "teaching" here is that He inspires you your right direction or your open sin but you are still free to earn—will you choose evil or will you choose goodness? And Allah must teach you that this is good for you or bad for you. This is why there is no servant but they all know goodness and evil, but the ego collaborates with Iblīs and does not collaborate with the Prophets and the Awliya over goodness. If it did collaborate with the Prophets, divine lordly support would overtake it. It is for that reason Allah teaches the servant that deeds are either good or evil.

To every human being that has recognized his deeds and his states Allah gives a light in his heart.[1] At that time he is no longer among *whoever is blind in this life, then he shall be blind in the hereafter, and more astray in his way yet* (Banū Isrā'īl/Isrā' 17:72). With the light entering the servant's heart, he will be tasked with the reality of tasking. He will be the manifestation of *and He made subservient to you what is in the skies and what is on earth* (al-Jāthiya 45:13) and that station shall take place for him.

Mawlana also says that the reason for the destruction of the previous nations of the Israelites is that they were asking their Prophets many questions and they would not put the answers into practice.[2] The absence of adducing those knowledges became the reason for their destruction. The same thing is happening in our time. People are inclined to learn or to hear, but when it comes to applying, they have no deeds. Therefore **whoever learns and acts, Allah shall save them from blindness and ignorance. He shall give them a light in their heart by which they shall know all that is between the east and the west and between the Throne and the soil, and He shall make subservient to them what is in the skies and what is on earth**. These sciences and powers are given to the seeker. As for him that walks in the way of *then they believe, then they disbelieve* (al-Nisā' 4:137), those sciences are not given to them for they have no trust. This is what the Messenger–upon him the blessings and peace of Allah–has conveyed. Mawlana says the knowledge of the first and the last is subsumed under these two matters.

By the sanctity of the Beloved, by the sanctity of the Fatiha.

[1] Cf. *Nawādir* (1:601, *Aṣl* 41) on *He shall appoint for you a discernment* (Anfāl 8:29).

[2] See Suhba I.63, first note.

62
Problems of states and nations caused by holding on to what vanishes

I seek refuge in Allah from the accursed devil
In the Name of Allah the All-Beneficent the Most Merciful
There is no power nor strength but with Allah the High, the Magnificent
Permission, O my Master, support!
Our way is companionship, and goodness is in the congregation

This world is passing away. The human being does not want to pass away from this life but passing away is foreordained for us. This is our foolishness. It is foolishness enough for us that we are asking not to pass away from this life, and that we are not turning to hold fast to Him Who never changes nor passes away ever. This world is bound to pass away and it is forewritten for us to be a fleeting shadow. And all the problems of the world —nations and states and peoples—is because of this foolishness.

From Allah is all success. By the sanctity of the Beloved, by the sanctity of the Fatiha.

63
[Mawlana Shaykh Nazim's heritage of knowledge] – With wisdom the servant draws near to Allah – Hārūt, Mārūt and magic

I seek refuge in Allah from the accursed devil
In the Name of Allah the All-Beneficent the Most Merciful
There is no power nor strength but with Allah the High, the Magnificent
Permission, O my Master, support!
Our way is companionship, and goodness is in the congregation

We have an opportunity to give every person [the chance to ask] a question on condition that he will be aiming to put into practice whatever he learns and that he will not be disputing or obdurate. For whoever has the ailment of disputation and obduracy, their kind is the same kind as Satan and Abū Jahl: there is no remedy for them. Otherwise, **for every person that asks about something that is of concern to them to benefit from it in their wayfaring in Tariqa, then we have, of sciences, from what is under the soil all the way to the Throne**.

Without benefit, then the abundance of questions was the reason for the death of past nations as the Prophet–upon him the blessings and peace of Allah–said in his hadith, that "The reason for the death of past nations was the abundance of their questions to their Prophets."[1] They learnt and they did not act. It is like a man acquiring wealth to hoard it up and not to spend it. For there is permission for the human being to acquire all the wealth in the world as long as he is spending. It is likewise with knowledge: as long as he is seeking to put into practice what he has learnt. At that time, every time he asks, the opportunity for wisdom will be opened to him.

Wisdom is a spiritual power by which one draws near to Allah, *and whoever is bestowed wisdom has been granted abundant goodness* (Baqara 2:269). For

[1] Narrated from (i) Abū Salama by Ismāʿīl b. Jaʿfar b. Abī Kathīr (d. 180/796), *Ḥadīth ʿAlī b. Ḥujr al-Saʿdī ʿan Ismāʿīl b. Jaʿfar al-Madanī*, ed. ʿUmar b. Rafūd al-Sufyānī (Riyadh: Maktabat al-Rushd, 1418/1998) p. 299 §221; (ii) Abū Hurayra by Maʿmar b. Rāshid, *Jāmiʿ*; al-Shafiʿī, *Musnad*; Ḥumaydī, *Musnad*; Ibn Rāhūyah, *Musnad*; Aḥmad, *Musnad*; Bukhārī (*al-Iʿtiṣām bil-Kitāb wal-Sunna, al-iqtidāʾ bi-Sunan Rasūli-l-Lāh*)' Muslim (*Ḥajj, farḍ al-ḥajj marratan fil-ʿumur*); Tirmidhī; Nasāʾī; and others; (iii) al-Mughīra b. Shuʿba by Ṭabarānī, *Awsaṭ*; (iv-v) Abū Umāma al-Bāhilī and ʿAlī b. Abī Ṭālib by al-Thaʿlabī (al-Māʾida 5:101); al-Wāḥidī, *Basīṭ* (ditto).

knowledge is one thing and wisdom another. Knowledge is for the servant to act freely in his world. But as for arriving at the *Malakūt* (world of invisible sovereignty) then he is in need of wisdom. And wisdom is the upshot of practice. Any person that knows and acts will acquire wisdom, and with it he may draw near to Allah.

People's whole concern nowadays is to become Dr. So and so in the science of Shari'a but when it comes to practice he will have none; only this title which has deluded him. This is a Jewish kind of affliction.[1] For these titles are not permitted. They are tolerated only for other sciences such as medicine for example. An example of that is that whoever would come to Hārūt and Mārūt insisting that he wanted to learn magic. The two angels would tell him, "Go and urinate." He would go and when he returned they would ask him, "Did you urinate?" He would say yes. Then they would ask him, "What did you see?" He would say, "Nothing." They would say to him, "You did not urinate. Go and urinate." The man would go and urinate. When he returned they would ask him, "What have you seen?" He would say, "I saw a rider on a horse coming out of me and darkness entering me." They would say to him, "That is your belief coming out of you until you learnt magic."

Therefore do not think that the Europeans are giving the doctorate degree in Shari'a before they have first laid to ruin a person's belief. They make him write dissertations that are as useless as a lifeless body with which they keep him busy for years and their goal is the destruction of Islam. They do not even know *ṭahāra* (ritual purification) and yet they claim to have knowledge.

By the sanctity of the Beloved, by the sanctity of the Fatiha.

[1] I.e. taken (i) from the rabbinate or (ii) Pharisaic. Mawlana also means the practice of receiving degrees conferred by non-Muslims. See also Suhba I.61, last note.

64
[Entrusting our testimony of faith to the Prophet – Strength in contrition] – Patient endurance in affliction is the key to deliverance

I seek refuge in Allah from the accursed devil
In the Name of Allah the All-Beneficent the Most Merciful
There is no power nor strength but with Allah the High, the Magnificent
Permission, O my Master, support!
Our way is companionship, and goodness is in the congregation

The testimony of faith is the key to the gardens of Paradise. Were it not for the bounty of Allah we would not have spoken it. How many millionaires can be found that cannot even utter it. Our liege lord Sulaymān–upon him peace–when anyone spoke in the east or the west, the wind would make their speech reach him. Does not our liege lord the Messenger of Allah–upon him the blessings and peace of Allah–have the same power? When we utter the testimony of faith and we say, *awdaʿnāhā ʿinda Rasūli-l-Lāh* (we have committed it to the presence of the Messenger of Allah), does it not reach him? Yes it does. Therefore it behooves us to ask forgiveness passionately and fervently from Allah, because we are sinning passionately and fervently and not lazily. So let our contrition also be with power and longing, not with laziness.

The Messenger–upon him the blessings and peace of Allah–asked his nurturing Lord to give him a special intercession for those that are in their twenties and up to their thirties in the Umma. Allah Most High said, *O you who believe! Obey the One God and obey the Messenger and those in authority among you* (al-Nisāʾ 4:59). If you do not like those that are in authority then go to some other country, *and the earth of the One God is vast* (Zumar 39:10). Allah has certainly said, *O My servants who have believed! Verily My earth is vast: Me, therefore—worship Me!* (ʿAnkabūt 29:56).

Long ago a man purchased a slave and took him home. Then he started eating the heart of a lettuce and he would give the outer leaves to the slave. The slave asked from his master that he sell him. His master said to him, "Stay with me, you will not find the same as me." The slave refused, so his master sold him and another one bought him. The other one took a lit candle, put it on the head of the slave, and ordered the slave to stand like a chandelier. The slave stood without a word and remained with him a long time. Whoever saw him would ask him, "Are you at peace with this station?" He would said, "For certain this is the most horrible yet, but I say nothing for fear that some other master might say to me, 'There is oil in your eyes and I want to kindle them.' So I endure." Likewise whoever is not pleased with his nurturing Lord will lose. Therefore it is an advice: endure patiently, for at the time of affliction we have nothing else but patient endurance. "Patient endurance is the key to deliverance."[1]

At times Allah Almighty manifests Himself to His servants with a manifestation of majesty and at times He does so with a manifestation of beauty. This manifestation changes in accordance with the characters of the servants. For when there is mercy in the hearts of the servants towards one another and attentiveness to the rights of the rest of people, when the elders show mercy to the juniors and the juniors show veneration of the elders, at that time the All-True manifests Himself with the manifestation of beauty and mercy descends.

However, when people are mutually envious, tyrannical, their hearts devoid of mercy, heedless of the rights of others, at that time there will be a manifestation of fierceness over the servants. He will subdue them as if they were between two millstones. This is the characteristic of this time. Therefore you must be patient. Allah says, *by the last part of the day, verily the human being is indeed in loss, except those that have believed, and have done the righteous deeds, and have enjoined one another to follow the truth, and have enjoined one another to endure steadfast!* (al-ʿAṣr 103:1-3). This is why I instruct you to endure steadfast just as our nurturing Lord has instructed us, for we have nothing else besides steadfast endurance.

It is like an animal that fell into the trap. There is no deliverance for it other than for the owner of the trap to come to take its hide for its value if it is a bear or a fox for example. As for us do we not have value? Therefore we must endure patiently until our nurturing Lord changes things. For the matter is out of our hands. Allah has said, *verily the One God does not change what is in a people until they change what is in themselves* (al-Raʿd 13:11). That is how it is. The matter is in the hand of Allah and we must be patient.

By the sanctity of the Beloved, by the sanctity of the Fatiha.

[1] Narrated as a Prophetic hadith without chain from al-Ḥusayn b. ʿAlī by al-Daylamī, *al-Firdaws* and cited as the saying of Qadi Abū ʿAlī ʿAbd al-Wahhāb b. Muḥammad al-Naysābūrī by al-Thaʿālibī, *Yatīmat al-dahr fī maḥāsin ahl al-ʿaṣr*.

65
The need for a divine pull

I seek refuge in Allah from the accursed devil
In the Name of Allah the All-Beneficent the Most Merciful
There is no power nor strength but with Allah the High, the Magnificent
Permission, O my Master, support!
Our way is companionship, and goodness is in the congregation

It is inevitable for Islam to span everything between the east and the west. It is inevitable for the faith-system of truth to prevail in every handspan of the earth, and this is a tremendous matter. Our ulema and shaykhs do not have power to bring it about. There has to come, for this affair, an extraordinary man supported from Allah who will renew the covenant of Islam. This is not some worldly matter for some leader to emerge and for people to gather behind him. Rather it requires horrific spiritual power, and from his pull he will not leave out even an ant.

Who has such a power now? What speech has effect on people? Mawlana al-Shaykh [ʿAbd Allah al-Daghistani] would say, "O my son, if the power of all Awliya were put together with the power of all Prophets in order to turn back the people that are running away from the truth it would be unable, unless Allah were to put in front of them a dam. For only the One that opened up that possibility is the One that can prevent it."

However, our job is to call out in the mosques or in every venue where we find the opportunity for that, so that we will revive the Sunna and we will speak the word of truth whether they hear or they do not hear. In this there is merit for us. We are not hoping to reform the world. We are not even capable of reforming ourselves. Thus when we say something here and you color it with your tint, it appears over there with a thousand [new] tints. More than that, this world is in need of the lordly pull that has been promised, the *Ṣāḥib al-waqt* (the spiritual leader of endtimes), our liege lord the Mahdi (the well-guided one)–upon him peace.

Our ulema that give sermons on the pulpits from the discourse of the All-True, if the mountains and the rocks heard it they would submit because they possess knowledge. However, they are missing *yaqīn* (certainty). Because of the absence of *yaqīn* in the public speakers, their addresses have no effect on people. Likewise there remains no spiritual power for the attraction of hearts, for the attraction of the pleasures of this world are stronger.

Can an ant have the strength to pull a big car? An ant might have strength to do that, but we cannot pull this world. If there is anyone to be found that claims that he has such power, let him step forward for we are certainly incapable. We are asking forgiveness of our nurturing Lord and are repenting to Him with the repentance of an impotent slave that does not possess for himself *any death, or any life, or any rising* (al-Furqān 25:3). And the Prophet–upon him the blessings and peace of Allah–has said, "When you see avarice in command, lust in the lead, preference given to this world, and everyone having a different opinion and being pleased with it; at that time, you must take care of your own self and leave the people at large!"[1] And we are in this time which the Prophet informed us about. So how can we come out to the streets?

Iblīs is actively trying to make the turbans less on the heads of the Muslims because on all the turbans there is light and mercy descending. If the Umma were only wearing the turbans without weapon the Jews would not remain a single night more, for the turban is the awe of Islam, and Allah will throw dread over the hearts of the enemies of the Muslims. If the Muslims were wearing turbans, would al-Quds remain in the hands of the Jews?

By the sanctity of the Beloved, by the sanctity of the Fatiha.

[1] Narrated from (i) Abū Tha'laba al-Khushanī by Tirmidhī, *Sunan* (*Tafsīr al-Qur'ān 'an Rasūl Allāh, wa-min sūrat al-mā'ida, ḥasan*); Abū Dāwūd, *Sunan* (*Malāḥim, al-amr wal-nahy*); Ibn Mājah, *Sunan* (*Fitan, qawlihi ta'ālā Yā ayyuhā al-ladhīna āmanū 'alaykum anfusakum*); (ii) Mu'ādh b. Jabal by Ibn Mardawayh per Suyūṭī, *Durr*.

66

[Reward of attending gatherings of faithful advice – Hankering after this world] – Contentment is an inexhaustible treasure – [Ḥabīb al-ʿAjamī's *yaqīn* vs. externalities – *A seating-place of truthfulness*] – The Day of promise and covenant – Certainty is transmitted from its possessors

I seek refuge in Allah from the accursed devil
In the Name of Allah the All-Beneficent the Most Merciful
There is no power nor strength but with Allah the High, the Magnificent
Permission, O my Master, support!
Our way is companionship, and goodness is in the congregation

"Our Tariqa is companionship, and goodness is in the congregation." This is what our liege lord Shah Naqshband pronounced 12,000 times in his life. For the Muhammadan inheritor must inevitably be a manifestation of the sciences of the Prophet–upon him blessings and peace of Allah–from the perspective that he takes from the ocean of the sciences of the noble hadiths meanings and jewels which he then gives to us. We ask for their spiritual supply and help since Allah has placed in them a secret and He has placed with them a breath of holiness from the breaths of the All-Beneficent which revives the bodies and the souls, drawing from them spiritual support, complying with their command and reviving the Sunna of the Messenger–upon him blessings and peace of Allah–who has said, "The *dīn* is *naṣīḥa*."[1] We are gathering around *naṣīḥa*. The presence of any person in the gathering of *naṣīḥa*, even if one does not take from it but 1%, nevertheless this is a gain for him because he confined himself in the way of Allah. Thus he is given the *zāhid*'s (ascetic) wage, especially in these times of ours. For *zuhd* has become a common word these days and the *zāhids* are gone or hidden.

These days are days of glory for this world. People are all directing themselves to the building up of their worldly existence, the believers and not only the unbelievers, whose share is all given to them now in this world. We see even the Muslims, whose share has been delayed to the hereafter, likewise mimicking the unbelievers in every step of their, hankering after the life of

[1] See Suhba I.10.

this world with salivating mouths. Such are our egos, demanding from us that there should be for us worldly enjoyment the way exactly as there is for them. This is why the totality of people rise to build up their worldly life and to serve it. The chief concern of the poor man is to eke out his living and the chief concern of the rich man is to add to his wealth without contenting himself with what Allah has given him. He is constantly asking for more.

Thus you will not find limits for the ego's demands. But the Messenger–upon him the blessings and peace of Allah–has said, *al-qanāʿatu kanzun lā yafnā* (Contentment is an inexhaustible treasure).[1] With anything other than contentment the servant's heart will never be at peace. One will keep toiling to add another zero to the tally of his wealth, and if you were to ask this servant for a single zero of his money he would refuse. How could he give you, for example, out of ten million dollars? That is because, the more the servant's wealth increases, the more the attribute of avarice increases in him and he holds fast to Qārūn's (Korah) attribute, although Allah has instructed, "O My servants! *Spend*" (al-Baqara 2:195, 2:267, al-Ḥadīd 57:7, al-Munāfiqūn 63:10, al-Taghābun 64:16). *And whatever expenditure you spend, then He shall replace it* (Saba' 34:39).

You will not find any remedy for avarice other than belief. For the more the servant increases in belief and certainty, the more he will increase in generosity; and the more his belief and certainty weaken, the stingier he becomes. Stinginess is what has brought the world to what they are now facing of problems. For stinginess comes from the absence of belief in the hearts, otherwise their wealthy ones would be their most generous ones. These problems were not meant to happen in the world, but whoever has all the wealth of Cress in his hand keeps asking for more to hoard, and this is what causes problems. If, however, they did their best in the way of Allah, all their problems would be solved. Allah has said, *and do what is best just as the One God has done what is best to you* (al-Qaṣaṣ 28:77), and that is when you are able to acquire the wealth of the world, and the more your wealth increases, the more you spend in return. For that does not harm you because it comes and goes in the way of Allah. But if you hoard it and you cut off all spending in the way of Allah you will have harmed yourself and all people.

[1] Narrated to that effect from (i) Jābir by al-ʿUqaylī, *Ḍuʿafāʾ*; Ibn Abī Ḥātim, *ʿIlal al-ḥadīth*; al-Ṭabarānī, *Awsaṭ*; Ibn ʿAdī, *Kāmil*; Abū al-Shaykh, *Amthāl al-ḥadīth*; Ibn Shāhīn, *al-Targhīb fī faḍāʾil al-aʿmāl*; Bayhaqī, *al-Zuhd*; Qushayrī, *Risāla*; al-Suyūṭī, *al-Jāmiʿ al-ṣaghīr* (2:94, unrated); (ii) Anas by Muḥ. b. ʿAlī b. ʿAbd Allāh al-Ṣūrī, *al-Fawāʾid al-muntaqāt wal-gharāʾib al-ḥisān ʿan al-shuyūkh al-Kūfiyyīn*; al-Quḍāʿī, *Musnad al-shihāb*; Suyūṭī, *al-Jāmiʿ al-ṣaghīr* (2:157, *ḍaʿīf*); and, in *maqṭūʿ* mode, (iii) Muḥammad b. al-Munkadir by Ibn Ḥibbān, *Rawḍat al-ʿuqalāʾ*. Cf. Sakhāwī, *Maqāṣid* (*al-qanāʿatu mālun lā yanfadu wa-kanzun lā yafnā*).

We now live in the time of common people. Their belief has become weak and we are in the greatest need to strengthen belief and especially strengthen certainty. Every person can recite, "I believe in Allah and His angels and His Books and His Messengers and in the Last Day and in foreordained destiny, the good of it and the bad of it being all from Allah Most High."[1] There are also Christians in your country that can recite these words, but will you and they then be the same? If you do not have certainty you will be on a par with them. Therefore we are only in need of certainty. The best of what a person is given after the honor of submission is certainty. For when we acquire certainty we become believers, otherwise, *say, "We submit"* (al-Ḥujurāt 49:14).

In what will certainty consist? There was, in the time of Imam Ḥasan al-Baṣrī (21-110/642-728) the Imam of the *Tābiʿīn* (Successors), a man named Ḥabīb al-ʿAjamī ("the non-Arab"),[2] one of the major people of Allah. Ḥabīb al-ʿAjamī was studying with Ḥasan al-Baṣrī because he was weak in Arabic, but Allah opened up for him the strength of belief in his heart together with the strength of certainty. One day, Imam Ḥasan al-Baṣrī came to visit Ḥabīb al-ʿAjamī where he lived. Ḥabīb brought him two loaves of bread which he disposed in front of him for him to eat. At that very time someone knocked on the door. It was a beggar asking something for the sake of Allah. Ḥabīb al-ʿAjamī took back the two loaves from in front of the Imam and gave them to the beggar. Seeing this, Imam Ḥasan al-Baṣrī said to him, "If you had a little bit of knowledge you would have given one loaf and given it to the beggar, and you would have left one loaf for the guest." Ḥabīb al-ʿAjamī did not reply anything. A few moments later someone knocked at the door again. Lo and behold, a slave was standing there, holding a large tray on which were all sorts of delicious dishes, and in the center a pouch full of gold. Ḥabīb al-ʿAjamī placed the food in front of Ḥasan al-Baṣrī and said to him, "You are an Imam

[1] These are the six branches of faith. A Prophetic hadith narrated from Ibn ʿUmar by al-Bayhaqī, *Iʿtiqād*, cf. *al-Qaḍā' wal-qadar, Shuʿab al-īmān, Manāqib al-Shāfiʿī.*

[2] Abū Muḥammad Ḥabīb b. Muḥammad al-ʿAjamī al-Baṣrī (d. 140/757) was an ascetic famous for *ṣidq al-yaqīn* (truthful certainty) and answered prayers, a student of al-Ḥasan al-Baṣrī, Ibn Sīrīn, Bakr b. ʿAbd Allāh and Abū Tamīma Ṭurayf al-Hujaymī. From him narrated the Basrans Ḥammād b. Salama, Yazīd b. Yazīd al-Khathʿamī, Ḥammād b. ʿAṭiyya, Abū ʿAwāna, Ṣāliḥ al-Murrī, Jaʿfar b. Sulaymān al-Ḍubaʿī, Kathīr b. Yasār al-Ṭufāwī, Muʿtamir b. Sulaymān, ʿUthmān b. al-Haytham and others. See al-Bukhārī, *al-Tārīkh al-kabīr* (2:326 §2635); Ḥakīm al-Tirmidhī, *Adab al-nafs*, ed. Aḥmad ʿAbd al-Raḥīm al-Sāyiḥ (Cairo: al-Dār al-Miṣriyya al-Lubnāniyya, 1413/1993) p. 30; Abū Ṭālib al-Makkī, *Qūt al-qulūb* (32: *Sharḥ maqāmāt al-yaqīn, dhikr makhāwif al-muḥibbīn*); Lālakā'ī, *Karāmāt al-awliyā'* (*mā ruwiya min karāmāt Ḥabīb al-ʿAjamī*) and others. "Ibn ʿAbd al-Barr mentioned in *Kitāb al-kunā* that 'he was trustworthy and above trustworthy, but he narrated little'" per Ibn Ḥajar, *Tahdhīb* (2:189 §347).

and this food is suitable for you, and if you had a little bit of certainty you would have known that *whatever expenditure you spend then He shall replace it* (Saba' 34:39), because my nurturing Lord is watching and He does not abandon His servant." This is the meaning of *yaqīn*.

Another day Ḥabīb al-ʿAjamī passed by the Dijla (Tigris) river and found Imam Ḥasan al-Baṣrī sitting there. He asked, "Why are you sitting?" He replied, "I am waiting for a boat to cross the river." Ḥabīb al-ʿAjamī said, "Such as you is in need of a skiff? Get up with me and let us walk on top of the water *bismi-l-Lāhi-r-Raḥmāni-r-Raḥīm*," whereupon he crossed the river from one bank to the other. Seeing this, the Imam wept. This is *yaqīn*, for in the *basmala* there is such a power, but our own conviction has not reached that level so that we might say it and walk on top of the water.

Our faith-system does not consist only in external molds but it possesses an inner reality that settles firmly in the hearts. That is what is required but in our time we have turned our *dīn* into soulless images, so you will not find anyone paying any attention to the matter of the heart. We only go by externalities and we say, "we'll continue the road to Paradise and it's enough," although the road to Paradise is open to everyone that says *lā ilāha illā-l-Lāh* (There is no god but the One God). However, beloved ones of the Prophet!–upon him the blessings and peace of Allah–**our nurturing Lord says *the God-fearing are in gardens and river water, in a seating-place of truthfulness with an All-Sovereign absolutely All-Powerful!*** (Qamar 54:54-55). **That truthful seating-place is not for everyone. It is only for the people of truthfulness and loyalty who neither substituted nor changed what they had promised Allah from the day of *"am I not your nurturing Lord?" They said yes*** (Aʿrāf 7:172).

Does anyone remember the Day of promise and covenant? No. If anyone were asked about the first thing they remember in their life they could not give the right answer. How then could they remember the Day of *am I not your Lord*? So why did the Prophets come? They came to remind us, and Allah states, *and keep reminding, for verily the reminder benefits the believers* (al-Dhāriyāt 51:55). He did not say, "and teach." The reason is that we already know, only we forgot our promise to Allah. All of us were present in the world of souls when our nurturing Lord put us in His presence and honored us by addressing us, saying, *"am I not your nurturing Lord?"* And we answered him *yes*. What is the meaning of "you are our nurturing Lord"? It means "always at all times, we will never take any lord other than You: this is our promise." Have we taken another for a lord instead of Him or not? We have taken ego, lust, world and Satan—four lords. We walk under the will of our ego and our lust and under the will of our devil and our world. This is why you will seldom find a true servant of Allah, for the majority are either a servant to their ego or a servant of lust or a servant of this world or a servant of the devil.

The human being must recognize by whose binding command he walks and for what reason he goes here and there, eats, drinks, works, leaves, thinks… When you find that you are operating by virtue of the command of Allah then give praise to Allah that you are a servant of Allah. Otherwise, do not claim to be a servant of Allah while you are operating under the volition of your ego. Therefore those that are rightly deserving to be *in a seating-place of truthfulness with an All-Sovereign absolutely All-Powerful* (Qamar 54:54-55) are the ones that did not substitute another for their nurturing Lord. Their nurturing Lord is one and one alone. That address is forever, it never stops reaching the ears of the Awliya—they hear it in every motion and stillness. O My servant, *am I not your nurturing Lord?*

In every movement and stillness Allah wants you to say, "Yes, you are my nurturing Lord" and for you to walk under His will. But lust, the world, the devil and the ego want you to believe in them, to believe that they are your nurturing lord also. Yet our nurturing Lord is saying, "Am I not your nurturing Lord? Follow Me and obey Me, I will make you lordly so that you will say to something 'Be' and it shall be."[1] Our nurturing Lord says "lordly," i.e. affiliated to Him. At that time He shall say, "O My servant, you shall have what you love because you do what I love." At that time the servant is dressed with the Attribute of servanthood in truth and will be truly a servant of Allah for he has become lordly. Those ones, their attribute is, *and He has subjected to you what is in the skies and what is on earth entirely from Him* (Jāthiya 45:13)—i.e. all human beings, jinns, the powers of the earth and the skies, the beasts of the wilderness, the whales in the sea all come under your command. For that is a servant of Allah and he is a vicegerent of Allah.

O beloved ones of Allah! This is an ocean whose bottom can never be reached. We want to walk that path, the way of servanthood. We have no claim to anything else. We do not want anything other than servanthood to our nurturing Lord alone, and we want to learn servanthood alone without ulterior motive, because the Prophets came to this end and our liege lord the Messenger of Allah–upon him the blessings and peace of Allah–and the Seal of Prophets came to teach us pure servanthood. Otherwise our servanthood is fake and our attribute remains *then they believe, then they disbelieve* (al-Nisā' 4:137). We build at times and at times we destroy. There is no firmness to be found in us.

[1] See Suhba I.34, fourth note.

This endeavor cannot be facilitated unless we learn it from its people. For when someone wants to learn a skill he takes it from its master—the confectioner from the confectioner for example, and so forth. Likewise servanthood is learned at the feet of the Prophets and, after them, from their inheritors that have inherited the certainty of Prophethood. The certainty of which we are in need is like a car without gasoline; can it run? We need certainty for the power that moves us to Allah. For it is by the power of certainty that the servant draws near to Allah, and he whose certainty falls short lags behind.

So *yaqīn* is learnt from the possessors of *yaqīn*, because a state cannot be transmitted from the lines of a book. Rather the state is transmitted from the possessors of the state when you keep close company with them. The Messenger–upon him the blessings and peace of Allah–says, "One follows the faith-system of one's close friend."[1] Whatever the latter's faith-system will be the faith-system of the former and his strength will also dictate what the other's strength will be. If you keep company with someone with weak belief you will be like him.

The beginning of *yaqīn* is with love. Every time the heart leans to the people of certainty, a door has been opened to transport their states to it. This is why it is an obligation for the believers to love Prophets and Awliya. The Prophets have gone but the Awliya never cease to be present in the Umma. Whoever seeks them, Allah will not deprive him of them and they must eventually meet up with one of them. Because of the power of his love he might even find our liege lord al-Khidr visiting him, or the Quṭb al-Ghawth, or one of the men of the unseen so that they will share their blessing with him. Therefore we ask Allah to strengthen our certainty in His Awliya because Allah states, *and do come into houses through their doors* (al-Baqara 2:189)—which is well-known and self-evident, for no one enters his house through the balcony but through the door. This why Allah is telling us to seek everything from Allah through its doors. And when you find the door, enter! Otherwise you will deprive yourself. And we ask and hope from Allah that He will gather us with His Awliya and with *Ṣāḥib al-zamān* and strengthen our belief and make us of the sincere ones.

By the sanctity of the Beloved, by the sanctity of the Fatiha.

[1] First half of a hadith that continues, "So let one watch carefully whom he takes as his close friend." Narrated from (i) Abū Hurayra by al-Ṭayālisī; Isḥāq b. Rāhūyah; Aḥmad; 'Abd b. Ḥumayd; Abū Dāwūd; Tirmidhī (*ḥasan*); and others; (ii) Sahl b. Sa'd al-Sā'idī by Ibn Abī al-Dunyā; Ibn 'Adī; Quḍā'ī; (iii) 'Ā'isha by Ibn 'Asākir, *Dhamm quranā' al-sū'*, ed. Muḥ. Muṭī' al-Ḥāfiẓ (Damascus: Dār al-Fikr, 1399/1979) p. 47; Ibn Ṣaṣrā, *Amālī* per Suyūṭī, *Jāmi' al-kabīr*; (iv) Anas per Suyūṭī (ditto); Sakhāwī, *Maqāṣid*.

67

[Tariqa principles] – Bearing with contrarieties and reverses will make you reach the reality of life

I seek refuge in Allah from the accursed devil
In the Name of Allah the All-Beneficent the Most Merciful
There is no power nor strength but with Allah the High, the Magnificent
Permission, O my Master, support!
Our way is companionship, and goodness is in the congregation

Realities cannot be reached other than in the midst of contrarieties. You will not find storehouses for free. For pearls and jewels you must dive deep until you can bring them out. It is the same in our lives. It is not important to collect volumes of books or to narrate them. What is important is to bear with contraries, because wayfaring to Allah is not an easy matter. At each breath or at each step reverses will face you. When the authorities want to open a road through mountains it places explosives to make a way, Likewise, every person has his or her own way to open by bearing with much.

Mawlana al-Shaykh [ʿAbd Allah al-Daghistani] used to say, in explanation of the hadith of the Prophet–upon him the blessings and peace of Allah–"An hour's reflection is better than the worship of seventy years,"[1] that this hadith imparts that the deeds of seventy years without reflection are worthless. For reflection gives resolve, awareness and self-respect to the human being and repels from him heedlessness and laziness. Because of reflection one gets on with one's work with vigor and self-respect.

Mawlana al-Shaykh teaches the modality of reflection thus. Reflection gives in the servant power to think of the states of this world and to prepare himself before the befalling of any contrariety, as there are related matters in the Most Distinguished Tariqa, some of which pertain to commands and prohibitions. The servant tells himself, for example, "if I were fired from my job what will I do?" Or, "if my shaykh ordered me to drink one hour before sunset whereas I am fasting, will I obey or not?" Or, "if my shaykh ordered me to marry a second woman, will I accept?" The spiritual guide might order his murid to "Get

[1] Narrated from Abū Hurayra by Abū al-Shaykh, *al-ʿAẓama* (1:299 §43, "sixty years"); Ibn al-Jawzī, *Mawḍūʿāt*. "An hour's reflection is better than standing in prayer all night" is narrated as their own statement from (i) Abū al-Dardā' by Hannād, Ibn al-Mubārak, and Aḥmad in *al-Zuhd*; Ibn Saʿd; Ibn Abī ʿĀṣim in *al-Sunna*; Abū Nuʿaym in the *Ḥilya*; and Bayhaqī in the *Shuʿab*; (ii) Ibn ʿAbbās by Abū al-Shaykh in *al-ʿAẓama*; and (iii) Ḥasan al-Baṣrī by Aḥmad, *Zuhd*; Ibn Abī Shayba; and Abū Nuʿaym.

up and go." When the murid asks, "Where to?," it detracts from followership and will count as a defect towards the guide. The murid must be like an arrow with the guide: he throws you in whatever direction he wishes, and you yourself might not like that place.

One of the shaykhs said to his murid, "Get up quickly and go!" The murid asked, "Where to, my master?" He said to him, "Sit." After a little while he said to another, "Get up and go!" The latter asked him the same question as the first. He also told him to sit. After a while he said to a third murid "Get up and go!" That murid got up and walked away without asking anything. After three steps he found himself in India. For every matter hinges on firm belief. There is no faith-system if there is no firm belief in Allah. Firm belief in Allah is that He does what He wishes and He decides what He wants in absolute terms. It is not required of you to think whether what He wants will take place or not. At that time you will fall from the rank of belief. Nor does the servant rise up to that station until he has firm belief in His Messenger–upon him the blessings and peace of Allah–that he represents the All-True and that "he is the door to Allah and my reliance." For Allah says, *and do come into houses through their doors* (al-Baqara 2:189), so you have to know what door you want to enter through. Firm conviction is what matters for the sake of that. Likewise Allah says, *and follow the path of him who has abundantly repented to Me* (Luqmān 31:15). The meaning of this is that it is obligatory to firmly believe that the Messenger–upon him the blessings and peace of Allah–has immense power by permission of Allah because he has abundantly repented to Allah.

Mawlana Shaykh ['Abd Allah al-Daghistani] explains that further by saying there was a shaykh who was with one of his students who was a scholar of external sciences. They both wanted to go to one of the towns and between them and the town there was the Tigris river. The shaykh said to his student, "if we walk alongside the river to find the bridge we will miss the prayer of maghrib and 'ishā, but the town is right ahead of us so we of we walk on the river we will reach before maghrib. Just hold on to me and say, *yā ustādhī, yā shaykhī* (O my teacher! O my shaykh!) and I shall say *yā Allāh!* But beware of saying *yā Allāh*." The shaykh walked with *bismi-l-Lāhi-r-Raḥmāni-r-Rahīm*, saying *Allāh, Allāh!* and his student was behind him, saying, *yā ustādhī, yā shaykhī*. When they reached the middle of the river the thought came to this scholar's heart, "why should I not say *yā Allāh*? Why am I saying *yā ustādh*? Isn't it more correct for me to say *yā Allāh*?" This was a fatwa from his ego. As soon as he said *yā Allāh* he sank into the water and began to drown. His shaykh caught him and said to him, "My child, say *ya ustādh* quickly!" He said *yā ustādh!* Immediately he emerged above the water and his shaykh held him.

There are two matters here. The one *who has abundantly repented* to Allah, Allah says of him, "he is with me, he walks and speaks by Me and he hears by Me."[1] When a person firmly believes in this he benefits. Therefore each person must search for someone that has abundantly repented to Allah so that he might follow him. If he makes no effort to find such a man he will be questioned about it in the divine presence. Whom did Allah address when saying *and follow the path of him who has abundantly repented to Me* (Luqmān 31:15)? Human beings or animals? And **who is that man that has abundantly repented to Allah? The earth is never devoid of them. And according to your firm belief you will benefit from him. For he is a real shaykh that has abundantly repented to Allah and who is no longer busy with creation**. Allah Most High said, *We have indeed seen the agitation of your face amid the sky, so We will verily orient you to a qibla that you are pleased with* (Baqara 2:144). **You must recognize your qibla, and for the Umma there is one qibla. Likewise there is, in the Umma, one who represents the qibla**.

When you know you must follow. An example of that is the train. When it moves and the wagons do not follow it they remain in the station. This is one of the most important teachings. Mawlana said a student who was a learned scholar came to his shaykh, our liege lord Sayyid Jamāl al-Dīn al-Ghumūqī, and asked him, "Who should I marry, my master?" The Shaykh said, "There is in the marketplace a crazy woman. Marry her." He said to him, "As you order, my master." Let everyone give thanks for their spouses. The scholar went and married her, and she was incapable of covering her own nakedness. After some time she bore him two sons. She used to forget them in the orchard and people would find them. Mawlana al-Shaykh would say of them that these two children became brilliant ulema and Allah opened for them the secret of marriage, i.e. they would both know from the Day of *am I not your nurturing Lord* who each human being should marry. Their names became famous in the regions of Daghistan since there was no one like them possessing such sciences. One time a man came to them on horseback and said, if I come down this horse my wife will be divorced thrice, and I have been on horseback for three days unable to sleep or eat. Every time I ask a shaykh he says she will be divorced if I come down, so what should I do? Hearing this the Shaykh brought a stool and said to him, get on this and then to the ground and you will have no obligation, and your three days are enough requital for what you did. If you do it again I will leave you roam for three months!

This [blessing] is from the effect of following, and Allah says, *say: "If you love the One God, then follow me, the One God will love you and forgive you*

[1] An allusion to the "hadith of Awliya." See Suhba I.70, fourth note.

your sins (Āl 'Imrān 3:31). That is, when you follow the Prophet–upon him the blessings and peace of Allah–i.e. the stations that he reaches while you are with him, but when you leave him you remain at *the lowest of the low* (al-Tīn 95:5). The Messenger–upon him the blessings and peace of Allah–is saying, *follow me*; and this is the way of salvation from the lowest depth. For example in the plane, is the passenger tasked with anything? He only sits. This is what is intended, but following is not an easy matter, for Allah is saying, *and We verily will test you with something of fear, hunger, and lack of wealth, selves, and yield* (al-Baqara 2:155). These are headings under which are subsumed the different kinds of afflictions. Is there anyone none of whose relatives dies for example? Thus will reverses come, and Mawlana is saying, test your state, i.e. there are thousands of kinds of problems and reverses for human beings. And our nurturing Lord is swearing by His might, saying, *and We verily will test you with something.*

An hour's reflection. You might say, if I lost all my money, or my car, or something, what will I do? Our liege lord Jamāl al-Dīn al-Ghumūqī had two children in the Russian empire whose rank was high. The news reached him that they had both died. Our liege lord the Shaykh called their mother and told her, "My lawful wife, if a human being gave you two jewels and placed them in trust with you then requested that they be returned, would you be deeply affected by giving them back to him?" She said, "No, I would have no right to be deeply affected or upset. Rather I would return them without any reserve." He said to her, "The two boys that were entrusted to us, their owner took them back. But receive the glad tidings that he took them back both with hearts most pure," i.e. in a state of belief, although they were with the Russian empire. And there is a secret here. We are wrong to look at things and say, "this is ours." This is the common people's way of looking, and that puts you under a burden. As for him that says, "this thing is a trust and now its owner has taken it back," he will rest. The reverse will be light for him.

The human being must know that everything in life is going to disappear but he will only be deprived of its pleasant company. Even this is hard for the human being and yet he is asked to bear with it. He said–exalted is He–*and give glad tidings to the steadfast* (Baqara 2:155). When Allah deprives you of that pleasant company while you are enduring steadfastly and patiently, He will compensate you with a pleasant company from His presence that has no end. This is why whoever reflects about reverses—"An hour's reflection is better…"[1]—that will make you fully aware that "there is One that has power over me and I belong to Him."

[1] See two notes up.

Mawlana al-Shaykh also says that **the servant cannot possibly obtain the fullness of real life without reflection about all his affairs.** With reflection it becomes easy to arrive at the truth of the real life. And **the highest directive in the Most Distinguished Tariqa is for the murid to reflect, "if, for example, this reverse befell me, would I become depressed or collapse or kill myself?** For many people kill themselves upon experiencing hardships and this is categorically prohibited. With reflection, the human being prepares himself for real life and learns patience. Allah Most High said, *and your steadfast endurance is never but by the One God* (al-Naḥl 16:127).

A learned shaykh came to Abū Yazīd al-Bisṭāmī asking to join the Most Distinguished Tariqa. Our liege lord Abū Yazīd accepted on condition that the man shaved his beard and his head, carried a bag of walnuts, stood in the square where children played, and asked from each child to slap him so that he would give him a walnut. The man refused all that so our liege lord Abū Yazid refused to give him Tariqa. That man was in fact at the height of arrogant pride and our liege lord Abū Yazīd wanted to cut off the head of his ego with that practice. However, he did not accept and he deprived himself. And that is how Tariqa is in fact the foundation of abundant repentance.

May Allah protect us and you and may He inspire us our right direction. By the sanctity of the Beloved, by the sanctity of the Fatiha.

68

[Umma's inheritance of the Mi'rāj – Everything is in the Qur'ān] – Murid's surrender to the spiritual guide – [Veil of egotism – Confirmation of belief – Spiritual illness causes remoteness from Allah]

I seek refuge in Allah from the accursed devil
In the Name of Allah the All-Beneficent the Most Merciful
There is no power nor strength but with Allah the High, the Magnificent
Permission, O my Master, support!
Our way is companionship, and goodness is in the congregation

Allah Almighty ennobles times and places. Allah has honored the night before Jumu'a and He has increased its honor this year with the Night of Mi'rāj (heavenly ascent). We hope and pray to Allah—with the blessing of our noble masters—that Allah shall dress us of the lights of this night and make us of the *ṣādiqīn* (truthful ones) and with the *ṣādiqīn*, and make us have *tawfīq* (enablement for success). For without *tawfīq* from Allah we are incapable of doing any deed, just as *ajallu al-karāmāt dawāmu al-tawfīq* (the most momentous of miraculous gifts is the permanence of divine enablement for success).[1]

We read from the words of Mawlana [Shaykh 'Abd Allah al-Daghistani], asking for blessing, that on the night of Mi'rāj, when our liege lord Jibril–upon him peace–came to invite the Messenger of Allah–upon him the blessings and peace of Allah–to the heavenly ascent to the nurturing Lord of might and magnificence, the Messenger spoke intimately with his nurturing Lord, asking Him not to deprive his Umma from this bounty, and asking for them to have a share in the Mi'rāj. For the attribute of the Messenger–upon him the blessings and peace of Allah–as Allah Most High said, is *anxious over you* (Barā'a/Tawba 9:128). Wherever he might be, he wants for his Umma to be with him and in the same station as him.

Allah Almighty ordered Jibril, "Give glad tidings to My Beloved and say to him that his Umma will have such as that Mi'rāj, and that belongs to whoever of them follows him." We are unable to follow the Messenger–upon him the blessings and peace of Allah–now, but we are able to follow his inheritors. Whoever follows the one that inherited from him, it is as if he has followed

[1] See Suhba I.61, seventh note.

the Messenger in his life. And whoever follows the Messenger or his inheritors and becomes ready, the angels of mercy come to him on one of the nights, inviting him to the Miʿrāj. But if he wants to ascend without ridding himself of his ego then this is impossible, and he will be deprived of the high stations.

Mawlana al-Shaykh is saying that Allah Most High said in the majestic Qur'ān, *and nothing moist or dry, except it is in a manifest record* (al-Anʿām 6:59). That is, this very gathering of ours is found in the Qur'ān. And how many a person comes and whatever we speak about and who benefits from them—all this is mentioned in the Qur'ān, *and nothing moist or dry, except it is in a manifest record.* Everything is found in the Qur'ān. Likewise there is in it a night Journey and a heavenly Ascent. The Pride of all existing beings–upon him the blessings and peace of Allah–knew of the moist and the dry, and thus he was giving to his inheritors of what he knew of the matters mentioned in the Qur'ān—events, disasters and all other issues—all for the sake of conveyance, for he gave them permission to speak. Likewise, the inheritor of the Messenger knows all the matters that are necessary to know in general or in detail.

Mawlana al-Shaykh is saying you have to have firm belief in the great spiritual guides in all external and inward matters of the world and the hereafter, and you will find them to be in accordance with your firm belief. And when you take a shaykh and spiritual guide hold fast to him truly. After that do not judge things but leave the judging to your guide. For he knows better about the rulings, and what might be or might not be. Otherwise, if you make yourself the judge, you will be left to yourself, and whoever is left to himself has perished. For the spiritual guide, in all matters—small or large, outward or spiritual—is more knowledgeable than you. Mawlana is saying that Allah gives understanding for these matters to whoever listens. Otherwise, he that does not listen will not understand whereas he that listens must inevitably be given understanding.

A man from the shaykhs came to visit our liege lord Shaykh Sharaf al-Dīn al-Daghistani. When he sat, our liege lord the Shaykh asked him, "Do you wish to speak so that we shall listen, or do you want to listen?" The guest said, "Rather we want to listen, for verily we are drawing from your sea." At that time our liege lord Shaykh Sharaf al-Dīn said, "Do you believe that listening is easy?" Many think that listening is easy but the contrary is true. For the one that is truly able to listen is only he that has no egotism. For egotism will never allow the servant to listen to the speech of truth, and this is the greatest veil. Do you not see that Iblīs did not listen to his nurturing Lord? And that is because of his egotism. The egotistical person cannot listen to the other. As for he that has the station of real humbleness, he hears from the young and the old. For how will you hear from a person whom you do not put ahead of yourself even if you do not see him as higher than yourself in knowledge, judgment, deed and level? At that time, when you lower yourself you, will hear from him. Otherwise then you are still claiming that you are better than him.

This is why the one that does not humble himself does not benefit from the people of truth, nor does he benefit from the lordly outpourings and the breath of the All-Beneficent that is found with the men of Allah. For there might be someone whom the possessor of a holy breath speaks to, but he does not hear from him because of his egotism, so he is deprived of the blessings of that special servant. Our liege lord al-Ghujduwānī would say ahead of the Khatm al-Khwājagān, "We want for our murid to be surrendering to us not the way the dead surrenders in the hands of the washer[1]—for this is not acceptable to us even if outwardly the dead body does not object to the washer: whichever way he turns it it follows; and yet the people of spiritual reality can hear the dead body's speech at the time it is being washed, saying 'Do not pour on me overly hot water!' or 'cold water' or 'be gentle and do not handle me in a rough manner!'"

Our master the Shaykh says that whoever wants to obtain that right guidance and the station of real life in this world and the station of "Die before you die"[2] in life, must be in the presence of the *murshid* like inanimate objects, like a dry leaf which the wind carries and flings here and there, then it casts it into the fire but not a sound comes out of it. These are the murid's highest acceptable attributes to the Naqshbandi masters. The murid must also always prepare himself for the shaykh giving him any task at any time. Let him say to himself, "If my shaykh and guide tasks me with this matter, will I be able to implement it or not?" The murid might implement it but with objection in his heart. He dares not show it but the shaykh knows and hears that objection even if the murid does not speak it. For this reason the murid will not rise in level. For the murid's actual commander and forbidder is still his own ego, and his *ṣibgha* (coloring) (al-Baqara 2:138) is still different from his shaykh's *ṣibgha*.

Mawlana al-Shaykh also says that in every moment there is a reverse, and likewise with every blessing there is a reverse, for moments and blessings are never devoid of reverses. For Allah says "I am not leaving My servant without a test."[3] Sickness, also, is two kinds, one for the body and one for the spirit. Every Muhammadan inheritor has with him the remedy to bodily or spiritual

[1] This is al-Tustarī's definition of *tawakkul* (God-reliance) in Bayhaqī, *Shuʿab* (§13).

[2] See Suhba I.32, fourth note.

[3] See al-ʿAnkabūt 29:2, al-Qiyāma 75:36.

ailments. It might be the shaykh says to whoever asks him for a remedy against cancer, "Drink the juice of a white onion." So let him drink it if only once, because what matters is firm belief and confirmation of belief. The servant, through the blessing of confirmation of belief, will obtain the station of the *ṣiddīqīn*. And Allah Almighty did not say, "woe to the confirmers of belief," but rather He said, "woe to the beliers."[1] To the extent of the confirmation of belief that is in the servant, he will rise in the levels of nearness and reach the station of the *ṣiddīqīn* which comes directly after the station of the Prophets.

There are 80,000 bad traits of character in the ego. Whoever does not concern himself to remedy them will come under the sway of the ego, lust, the devil and the world. Therefore he must struggle to rid himself of them. Our liege lord Abū Yazīd al-Bisṭāmī used to say, "All my life I never cursed Iblīs even once, for I was too afraid he might answer me saying, 'Are you not ashamed to curse me after you had been under my command for 37 years?'" This is to an extent that we may understand. Beyond, there are secrets about the harms of spiritual illnesses. Among them, that **every spiritual illness puts the servant in a state of remoteness from Allah and relegates him to his ego, just as those blameworthy traits of character take the servant far away from *ḥaẓīrat al-quds* (the sanctuary of holiness). In order to rid oneself of those stains and purify oneself of them, you must make jihad until you filter out the four elements that are in you.** Without struggling there will be no self-clearance and no cleanliness.

Mawlana al-Shaykh also says, "O my children, there is no deed of ours that does not stand in need of repentance. Nay, every deed we do we must ask forgiveness of Allah for." Therefore how can you see yourself as having kept vigil in the night of the Miʿrāj pr the nights of Ramadan with remembrance? Every deed stands in need of repentance and asking forgiveness. This repentance and contrition cut down the egotism of self-conceit, because self-conceit became the reason for the expulsion of Iblīs from the door of Allah.

May Allah protect us and you and may He inspire us our right direction. By the sanctity of the Beloved, by the sanctity of the Fatiha.

[1] See al-Ṭūr 52:11, al-Mursalāt 77:15, 19, 24, 28, 34 etc.

69

The *rūḥ* (spirit) is the vicegerent of Allah

I seek refuge in Allah from the accursed devil
In the Name of Allah the All-Beneficent the Most Merciful
There is no power nor strength but with Allah the High, the Magnificent
Permission, O my Master, support!
Our way is companionship, and goodness is in the congregation

It is possible for the *rūḥ* to be the *khalīfat Allāh* (vicegerent of Allah). The believer or the vicegerent would be, in the created universe, a *ẓarf* (container), and the created universe is *maẓrūf fīh* (contained in him). In reference to that our liege lord ʿAlī–may Allah ennoble his countenance–says, "Do you reckon yourself a small *jirm* (body) when in you is folded up the greater world?"[1] According to our noble masters, if the light of the disobedient believer were to show, it would cover up all of the skies from the intensity of its lights.[2] His being disobedient is accidental whereas the foundation is that he is a believer. Unbelief is also accidental because belief is at the foundation, just as purity is a foundation for everything and impurity is accidental. Spiritual nature is *and He blew into him of His spirit* (al-Sajda 32:9). The spirit of the human being is affiliated to Allah Almighty, transcendent, it does not accept deficiency.

From Allah is all success. By the sanctity of the Beloved, by the sanctity of the Fatiha.

[1] *Dīwān amīr al-mu'minīn al-Imām ʿAlī b. Abī Ṭālib*, ed. ʿAbd al-ʿAzīz Karam (Beirut: Mu'assasat al-Kutub al-Thaqāfiyya, 1409/1988) p. 45. Cf. Bahā' al-Dīn al-ʿĀmilī, *Kashkūl* (2:77). On microcosm see also Suhba I.28, second note; I.34, seventh note.

[2] One of them added here, "and if the light of the wali were to show, people would worship him instead of Allah."

70

Duties and benefits of reflecting about death – [*Sulṭan al-khawf* and *ʿazīmat al-sharīʿa*]

I seek refuge in Allah from the accursed devil
In the Name of Allah the All-Beneficent the Most Merciful
There is no power nor strength but with Allah the High, the Magnificent
Permission, O my Master, support!
Our way is companionship, and goodness is in the congregation

What are the benefits the servant obtains when he does a deed while fully conscious that this deed of his is the last of his deeds in this life and that he is proceeding to Allah Almighty? The matter of spiritual struggle becomes easier for him. The heart is collected in the presence of Allah Almighty. The servant will be light and vigorous in practice, from the perspective that what is required in practice is for the servant to be conscious that this deed of his is the last of his deeds which he is offering to Allah Almighty before exiting this world and proceeding to his nurturing Lord. What benefits result from this awareness?

It will be a help for the servant in the greater jihad in which he is facing himself. All the Prophets–upon them peace–came to remind the servants of Allah that ahead of them is death. Our liege lord Shaykh ʿAbd Allah al-Daghistani–may Allah always raise his ranks–says of the benefit of thinking about or remembering death that when one of us thinks about death, that thinking will be a means for the human being to live simply in this world. Thinking about death lets the servant remove himself away from the pleasures of life and the ego. Death has an authority that diminishes the desire for the pleasures of life and its appetites in the human being. Whoever considers that death is shadowing him wherever he walks—as if our liege lord ʿAzrāʾīl is awaiting the order to seize him—his appetite for food and for the rest of the desires of the ego diminishes. Love for this world diminishes in him. For "The world is the head of every sin."[1]

[1] Narrated as a Prophetic hadith from (i) al-Ḥasan al-Baṣrī in *mursal* mode by Ibn Abī al-Dunyā, *Zuhd* and *Dhamm al-dunyā*; al-Māwardī, *Aʿlām al-Nubuwwa*; al-Bayhaqī, *Shuʿab* cf. Suyūṭī, *Jāmiʿ al-ṣaghīr* (1:365, *ḍaʿīf*); and others; (ii-iii) Anas and Ḥudhayfa b. al-Yamān by Razīn per Ibn al-Athīr, *Jāmiʿ al-uṣūl*; and as a saying of (iv) Ibn Masʿūd by ʿAbd al-Razzāq, *Muṣannaf* (§5115); (v) Mālik b. Dīnār by Ibn Abī al-Dunyā, *Zuhd* and *Dhamm al-dunyā*; (vi) ʿĪsā b. Maryam by al-Ḥārith al-Muḥāsibī, *Ādāb al-nufūs*; Abū Ṭālib al-Makkī, *Qūt al-qulūb*; Abū Nuʿaym, *Ḥilya*; Mahrawānī, *Mahrawāniyyāt* 2:739-740 §71); (vii) Saʿd b. Masʿūd by Ibn ʿAsākir, *Tārīkh* (20:402). I.e. "*dunyā* is in

Since we are in great need to fight the ego in our life, to think about death, to view it as near and be aware of its nearness is a great means for us in the jihad against the ego. It is because of this that the noble verse was revealed, *verily you are dying and verily they are dying* (Zumar 39:30). Thinking about death cuts off all hope for the ego and cuts down its evil. We are struggling against ourselves to leave the love of this world because the ego is immersed in love of the world and it does not want to exit it. The great illness of the ego is love of this world. What is the remedy? To think about death. Our Imams in the Most Distinguished Naqshbandi Tariqa have said so by consensus and they have instructed those that are affiliated to the Tariqa to think about death four times a day:

1. Upon rising from sleep in the morning, with awareness of how people shall rise from death, saying, "Praise and thanks to Allah Who has given us life after He had caused us to die, and unto Him is the resurrection."

2. Between the Sunna and the obligation of the dawn prayer, whereby the Prophet–upon him the blessings and peace of Allah–would lie down on his right side and think about death.

3. After the maghrib prayer, at which time he prays over the deceased in absentia, whereby one remembers in oneself that a day shall come when people shall pray the same prayer over him. Let him prepare for that day.

4. When one puts down his head to sleep let him think about death and how he will come out of the world for death, saying, "In your Name, O Allah, do I die and live."

Whoever thinks about death, the problems of this world will seem light to him. **We have, in the jihad against the ego, only one day. For the one that is fully aware of death and its nearness to him says, "This day of mine is the last of my days in this world for tomorrow I will definitely be dead."** When you get up in the morning and you say to yourself, "O my soul! This is the last of your days in this world. Catch what you can of what remains of your time in it for you are leaving today for the hereafter. There, when you have put your ego into its proper limits, jihad will become light for you because you have shortened the distance of hope in this world. At that time you will have the most of your vigor since the more you shorten the distance, the more your strength increases for jihad. But the longer the matter is the lower the energy falls. For example the *raffāṣ* (spiral spring): when you shorten it you find that it has strength, but when you unravel it you will no longer find that strength. This is a law of physics that applies to spiritual things. To think about death pressures the ego so one has strength for jihad.

his heart, he prefers it to everything" per Aḥmad in Abū Ya'lā al-Farrā', *al-Tawakkul.*

Mawlana's explanation alludes to the saying of the Messenger–upon him blessings of Allah–"Remember the destroyer of pleasures, i.e. death."[1] So **the order to think about death four times a day is part of the orders given to those that are affiliated to the Most Distinguished Tariqa. For whoever thinks about death four times a day, this awareness of his will be an avenue for the gaze of the noble shaykhs on him.** And the gaze of the shaykhs is not like our gaze. For Allah has given them a sight from His sight,[2] and this is why they can see with Allah: "My servant does not cease to draw near to Me with voluntary deeds until I love him, etc."[3] Its meaning is that the one that keeps thinking of death four times a day is deserving and qualified for the gaze of the great shaykhs to be on him. Those that do that, it is hoped they will succeed in the jihad against the ego and be victorious in the greatest jihad. For the biggest power against the ego is fear, and the fear is death.

[1] Narrated from (i) Abū Hurayra by Ibn al-Mubārak, *Zuhd*; Ibn Abī Shayba; Aḥmad, *Musnad*; *Zuhd*; Ibn Mājah; Tirmidhī (*ḥasan*); and others; (ii) Abū Saʿīd al-Khudrī by Tirmidhī (*gharīb*); Abū al-Layth, *Tanbīh al-ghāfilīn*; (iii) Anas by Bazzār; Abū ʿArūba al-Ḥarrānī, *Juz'*; Ibn Abī Ḥātim, *'Ilal*; Ṭabarānī, *Awsaṭ*; and others; (iv) Ibn ʿUmar by Ibn al-Aʿrābī, *Muʿjam*; Ṭabarānī, *Awsaṭ*; and others; (v) Abū Salama in *mursal* mode by Ibn Abī Shayba.

[2] An allusion to the famous Prophetic hadith, "'Beware the insight of the believer, for verily he looks with the light of Allah.' Then he recited *verily there are, in that, indeed signs for the perceptive* (al-Ḥijr 15:75)." Narrated from (i) Abū Saʿīd al-Khudrī by al-Tirmidhī (*gharīb*); al-Ṭabarī; al-Ṭabarānī, *Awsaṭ*; Abū al-Shaykh, *Amthāl*; (ii-iii) Ibn ʿUmar and Thawbān by Ṭabarī; (iv) Abū Umāma by Ḥakīm al-Tirmidhī; Ṭabarānī, *Awsaṭ*; *Kabīr*; *Musnad al-Shāmiyyīn*; (v) Abū Hurayra by Abū al-Shaykh.

[3] Part of the *hadīth qudsī*, "Whoever shows enmity to a *walī* (friend) of Mine then I have certainly declared war on him. My servant does not draw near to Me with anything lovelier to Me than what I have made categorically obligatory for him. And My servant does not cease to draw near to Me with voluntary deeds until I love him. And when I love him I become his hearing with which he hears, and his sight with which he sees, and his hand with which he strikes, and his foot with which he walks. If he asks me, indeed I will certainly give him, and if he seeks refuge in Me, indeed I will certainly grant him refuge. And I do not hesitate about anything I am doing as much as I hesitate taking the life of the believer: he hates death and I hate to hurt him." Narrated from (i) Abū Hurayra by Bukhārī; Bazzār; Ibn Ḥibbān; Abū Nuʿaym, *Ḥilya*; al-Bayhaqī, *Asmā'*; *Kubrā*; *Ṣughrā*; *Zuhd*; (ii) ʿĀ'isha by Bazzār; Ibn Abī al-Dunyā, *Awliyā'*; Ḥakīm al-Tirmidhī, *Adab al-nafs*; *Nawādir*; Ṭabarānī, *Awsaṭ*; Abū Nuʿaym, *Arbaʿūn al-Ṣūfiyya*; *Ṭibb al-Nabawī*; and others; (iii) Anas by Ibn Abī al-Dunyā, *Awliyā'*; Ḥakīm al-Tirmidhī, *Nawādir*; Kalābādhī, *Baḥr*; (iv) Maymūna by Bazzār; Abū Yaʿlā; Kalābādhī, *Baḥr*; (v) Abū Umāma by Ṭabarānī, *Kabīr*; Bayhaqī, *Zuhd*; Sulamī, *Arbaʿūn fil-taṣawwuf*; (vi) ʿAlī b. Abī Ṭālib by Ismāʿīlī; (vii) Muʿādh b. Jabal by Ibn Mājah; Abū Nuʿaym, *Ḥilya*; (viii) Ḥudhayfa by Ṭabarānī, a fair chain per Ṣāliḥī, *Subul al-hudā* (10: *Jimāʿ abwāb baʿḍ āyāt waqaʿat li-aṣḥābih; wujūb iʿtiqād ithbāt karāmāt al-awliyā'*); cf. Ibn Ḥajar, *Fatḥ* (11:342); Suyūṭī, *Ḥāwī lil-fatāwī* (*al-qawl al-jalīy fī ḥadīth al-walīy*).

What is *sulṭān al-khawf* (dominant fear)? It is the one imposing its order and its rule over all. For when fear comes, all the limbs of the human being submit. The Prophets–upon them peace–came for the sake of founding dominant fear in the hearts of the servants. This is why the noble verse came at the first command *O immantled one! Rise and warn* (Muddaththir 74:1-2). The founding of the fear of death in the hearts of the servants is a warning that comprises the fear of Allah Almighty. This is why it is well-established among the sciences of the Prophet–upon him the blessings and peace of Allah–that "**The head of wisdom is fear of Allah**,"[1] for the sciences of our liege lord ʿAlī–may Allah ennoble his countenance–are part of the sciences of the Prophet.[2] And the fear of death is one of the doors of the fear of Allah.

So when the servant is qualified for the gaze of the shaykhs on him, what is the upshot of their gaze for that servant? Mawlana al-Shaykh says that that person will have journeyed on the path of the Sufis. The meaning of *ṭarīqa* is *ʿazīmat al-sharīʿa* (the high resolve of the sacred Law). For the Shariʿa is two levels: the level of dispensation and the level of high resolve. The former is for the one with weak energy and the latter is for the one with high energy. To make ablution for every single prayer, for example, is *ʿazīma*, although it is possible for you to pray all five prayers with a single ablution. Likewise prayer is allowed in every place, but attending the congregation is *ʿazīma*.

When the great shaykhs look at one of the murids, that gaze makes him reach and purifies him. With the shaykh's gaze that murid obtains mercy, cleans himself, then rises to the station of that gazer in that moment. So it is required for people of religion—any religion—to have *sulṭan al-khawf*, for thinking about death lets them to conquer their lusts and makes them live simply. Whoever has no fear cannot be of the people of religion. Whoever does not think about death, there is no fear of Allah in him at all. They are out of the way of the Prophets. The basic job of the people of religion is to lead people to live simply and remind them of death and what is after death.

By the sanctity of the Beloved, by the sanctity of the Fatiha.

[1] Narrated from (i) Zayd b. Khālid by al-Qāsim b. Mūsā b. al-Ḥasan al-Ashyab (d. 302/915), *Juzʾ al-Qāsim b. Mūsā al-Ashyab*; Abū Dharr ʿUbayd b. Aḥmad b. Muḥ. al-Harawī, *Juzʾ min fawāʾid ḥadīth Abī Dharr al-Harawī*; al-Quḍāʿī, *Musnad al-shihāb*; and others; (ii) Abū al-Dardāʾ by Abū al-Shaykh, *Amthāl al-ḥadīth*; (iii) Ibn Masʿūd by Kalābādhī, *Baḥr al-fawāʾid*; Bayhaqī, *Shuʿab*; (iv) ʿUqba b. ʿĀmir by al-Māwardī, *al-Amthāl wal-ḥikam*; Ibn ʿAsākir; (v) Khālid b. Thābit al-Rabaʿī citing the Psalms by Aḥmad, *Zuhd* per Ibn Ḥajar, *al-Maṭālib al-ʿāliya*; and as Ibn Masʿūd's own saying, Ibn Abī Shayba, *Muṣannaf*; Hannād, *Zuhd*; Abū Dāwūd, *Zuhd*; Bayhaqī, *Madkhal*; *Shuʿab*; al-Ḥakīm and Ibn Lāl per al-Suyūṭī, *al-Jāmiʿ al-ṣaghīr* (1:428, *ṣaḥīḥ*); and others.

[2] This is addressed to those that consider this saying a statement of ʿAlī. The Shīʿīs do narrate it as a saying of ʿAlī Zayn al-ʿĀbidīn b. al-Ḥusayn b. ʿAlī b. Abī Ṭālib.

71
Ḥasan Baṣrī's advice on the non-obligatory orders – [The bane of smoking]

I seek refuge in Allah from the accursed devil
In the Name of Allah the All-Beneficent the Most Merciful
There is no power nor strength but with Allah the High, the Magnificent
Permission, O my Master, support!
Our way is companionship, and goodness is in the congregation

Ḥasan al-Baṣrī–may Allah have mercy on him–was an Imam venerated and recognized by the people of external knowledge as well as the people of inward knowledge. He used to instruct two things to those that attended his gathering. The first is that a person will inevitably encounter each day something enjoined or something prohibited. So if something *ma'mūr* (enjoined) faces you—even other than categorical obligations and requirements—take it and treat it with care, even if it is something merely desirable. And if you find a chance, do not leave something desirable by saying, "this is neither *farḍ* nor *wājib*," or "this is of the Sunna, *zawā'id* (augmentations)."[1] The meaning of such statements of yours is a disparagement of the value of the Sunna—something that generates an incurable illness!

Therefore take care of the Prophetic *ādāb* (manners) because manners are a protection for the categorical obligations, the obligatory requirements and the Sunnas. When that first wall is broken, destruction befalls the Sunnas and the obligatory requirements, whereupon the latter are taken lightly. Then the categorical obligations are taken lightly until, in the end, the servant leaves them also. And when the categorical obligations are abandoned, destruction befalls belief. So do not leave manners. Even if it is something of the merely desirable, hold fast to it because it is beloved in the presence of Allah Almighty. For everything enjoined is beloved in the presence of Allah. Therefore take

[1] The *zawā'id* include all the non-obligatory acts, their *sunan* (Prophetic ways) and their *ādāb* (manners), "that whose abandonment does not entail any dislike or offense such as lengthening recitation in prayer, lengthening the bowing and the prostration and the rest of the acts of prayer, and one's acts outside of prayer including walking, dressing and eating [i.e. like the Prophet–upon him the blessings and peace of Allah], for the servant is not required to establish them and does not sin by leaving them nor does he offend [in so doing], but it is preferable to adduce them" per 'Alā' al-Dīn al-Bukhārī, *Kashf al-asrār sharḥ uṣūl al-Pazdawī* (*Aqsām al-'azīma*). See also Maryam Muḥ. Ṣāliḥ al-Ẓufayrī, *Muṣṭalaḥāt al-madhāhib al-fiqhiyya* (*al-mandūb*).

care of the things Allah loves. That is my instruction to you. Do not neglect anything even if it is something small among the things that are enjoined, for the things that are enjoined are beloved to Allah.

Second, my children, do not venture into sins and rebellious offenses by saying "these are small sins" or "this is merely disliked." [Mawlana al-Shaykh ʿAbd Allah al-Daghistani said,] **smoking is a plight, a leash that Iblīs has placed on the whole world. With this leash Iblīs is driving people to his *maḥābb* (the things he loves). Far be it that it should be of the things Allah and His Prophet love! The anger of Allah might fall on you because of the *makrūh* (disliked) and no power can lift it away**. [Ḥasan al-Baṣrī continued,] O my children, the important thing is for each of you to apply these two advices in his physical practice. Otherwise our gathering here would be *mā lā yaʿnī* (what is of no benefit), for "Part of the excellence of one's submission is to leave what is of no concern/benefit to him."[1] Give me your assurance that you will control yourselves by applying yourselves even a little in this matter.

Mawlana al-Shaykh says the good pleasure of Allah might be in a very small act that the Prophet–upon him the blessings and peace of Allah–has done. Yet the servant tires himself with valuable acts of worship, but there might be a light deed that he neglects which will be accepted in the presence of Allah, except he is doing another deed. For the human being does not know where lies Allah's greatest satisfaction. So why do you neglect the small orders? Take care of everything, because all the parts make up one thing. There should be nothing missing, as you might chance on an order at which ego, lust, the devil and the world will pounce on you so that you will leave it. Likewise you might see something forbidden, so they push you to go after it. Pay attention when some non-obligatory order happens before you. Recall my instruction. Remember Allah and say *amaddanā-l-Lāhu bi-madadikum* (may Allah extend to us help with your kind of help). If you remember Allah at the non-obligatory order, that is very precious. And when you remember your nurturing Lord at something forbidden, that remembrance of yours is more precious yet.

The real remembrance is at the orders and the prohibitions. The other kind is the remembrance of children. The original remembrance is upon practicing the non-obligatory orders. There, you remember out of true adoration of Allah. If something prohibited chances by you remember Allah. That is more precious because its merit fills the east and the west.

By the sanctity of the Beloved, by the sanctity of the Fatiha.

[1] See Suhba I.35, note 5.

72

Whoever believes in Allah, He shall guide his heart [and he will be at peace]

I seek refuge in Allah from the accursed devil
In the Name of Allah the All-Beneficent the Most Merciful
There is no power nor strength but with Allah the High, the Magnificent
Permission, O my Master, support!
Our way is companionship, and goodness is in the congregation

If Allah alone is the One that directs all, then verily His directing is without doubt to goodness. Why be anxious then? The more a person's certainty increases the more they rest easy. *And whoever believes in the One God, He shall guide his heart* (*yahdi qalbah*, Taghābun 64:11). *Yahdi* is from *hudū'* (calm).[1] When the servant believes in Allah and his belief reaches the rank of certainty, at that time tranquility takes place in the heart. The calm of belief leaves no trace of anxiety in the heart because anxiety is from weak belief. You can see people whose belief has become weak everywhere in pursuit of something they never get from morning to evening. If they could obtain it they would not disperse the next morning all over the earth. No, they wait for the next day to disperse and search again, and they return once more without having obtained their quest. If they could obtain their quest they would relax—but they do not even know their quest in the first place.

In illustration of that a man came weeping to our liege lord Jalaluddin al-Rumi, one of the major Awliya. Our liege lord Jalaluddin asked him of his problem. The man replied, "My son is seven years old and he is lost. I do not know where he is. I tried in vain to find him. My last hope is for you to find him for me." The Shaykh said, "Look, O people! Look at this man, he has lost his son and he is weeping over him because he is precious to him. Yet people have lost Allah and no one is looking for Him and trying to find Him! But which is more precious, Allah or the child?" Then he said to the man, "Ask for

[1] "Whoever believes in Allah as owning creation and command, He shall guide his heart so that it will be calm and know that Allah is worthiest of it, whereupon he shall say, 'we belong to Allah and unto Him are we returning.' And that is the interpretation of whoever read it *yahda'u qalbūh* (his heart will be at peace) [reading of Abū Bakr al-Ṣiddīq, Mālik b. Dīnar, 'Amr b. Dīnār, 'Ikrima, 'Amr b. Fā'id and others per 'Abd al-Laṭīf al-Khaṭīb, *Mu'jam al-qirā'āt* (9:491)], i.e. it will be calm, from *al-hudū'* which is stillness." Abū Manṣūr al-Māturīdī, *Ta'wīlāt al-Qur'ān*, ed. Ahmet Vanlıoğlu and Bekir Topaloğlu, 18 vols. (Istanbul: Mizan Yayınevi, 2005-2007) 15:200.

your nurturing Lord so that He will return your child to you just as He returned Yūsuf to Yaʿqūb–upon them peace."[1]

And we have lost Allah. Therefore as much as we might amass, our heart will not be at peace. Only the one that has amassed Allah has amassed everything, because all the servants' quests are with Allah. As for him that has amassed other than Allah, he has not amassed anything. If people had obtained their nurturing Lord, would you see them running right and left? Rather they would sit, and with them there is everything.

By the sanctity of the Beloved, by the sanctity of the Fatiha.

[1] See also Suhba I.11.

73
The soul of deeds is humbleness

I seek refuge in Allah from the accursed devil
In the Name of Allah the All-Beneficent the Most Merciful
There is no power nor strength but with Allah the High, the Magnificent
Permission, O my Master, support!
Our way is companionship, and goodness is in the congregation

We are all intending Allah originally, we are all coming to Allah. Whoever intends his nurturing Lord Almighty has to know what deed his nurturing Lord will accept. Our liege lord Sultan al-Awliya Shaykh ʿAbd Allah al-Daghistani–may Allah exalt his levels–says with regard to this, it is the deed that the servant does with full certainty that it is the last of his deeds and that he is coming to his nurturing Lord Almighty, cutting off all hope that he will attain that deed again after that. He is as if standing next to an executioner holding a sword who will cut off his head at the end of his prayer or his deed. **This man who is threatened with death—how will he gather up his worldly powers, his thoughts, his worldly attachments? The person that knows death is in front of him and no hope remains for him in life, how will he pray? In all humbleness.**

This is what we must do: to gather up our powers in our deeds that we offer without leaving any of our thoughts and our mind outside. For Allah does not accept any deed that is missing humbleness. When Allah manifests Himself with majesty and magnificence to His servant, that servant must gather up all his strength so that nothing distracts him other than to be under that manifestation. That is humbleness. The soul of deeds is humbleness in them. Without humbleness, deeds are like lifeless bodies. This is why no result at all comes out from multiplicity of deeds when they are devoid of humbleness. That is why the gaze of the Awliya has become focused on teaching their murids how they may obtain humbleness in their deeds. For **to the Awliya the important thing is not multitude of deeds but rather even few deeds, but with humbleness—that is what is required.**

The way to obtain humbleness in deeds is that one which Sultan al-Awliya has pointed out: that you do a deed with full certainty that you are the end of your deeds and that you are coming to Allah directly after it. The Messenger of Allah–upon him the blessings and peace of Allah–speaks the truth when he says, "Pray the prayer of someone bidding farewell."[1] That is because prayer

[1] Narrated from (i) Abū Ayyūb al-Anṣārī by Qāsim b. Sallām, *al-Khuṭab wal-mawāʿiẓ*

is the best of the acts of worship and the sum total of them. It is for this reason that the Messenger–upon him blessings and peace of Allah–pointed to it specifically. And this is not only for prayer, rather you should make the intention to do every deed brought by the Prophet–upon him the blessings and peace of Allah–as if you were bidding farewell to this world. For example, whoever wants to pray, it is required of him to wear the Messenger's turban and he must order himself to wear the turban. Whoever says, "there is time for me [=in later life] to wear the turban," at that time that deed will not have any result because he did not cut off his long hope. If he had cut off his hope from this world he would have worn the turban with full belief that that deed is his last deed.

The people of all of the religious faiths stand in need of these teachings without exception.

By the sanctity of the Beloved, by the sanctity of the Fatiha.

(pp. 196-197 §130); Aḥmad (38:484 §23498); al-Bukhārī, *al-Tārīkh al-kabīr* (6:216 §2208); Ibn Mājah (*Zuhd, ḥikma*); al-Kharā'iṭī, *I'tilāl al-qulūb*; *Makārim al-akhlāq*; *Masāwi' al-akhlāq*; and others; (ii) Ibn 'Umar by al-Ṭabarānī, *Awsaṭ*; (iii) Anas by Abū Nu'aym, *Ḥilya*; and, as their own saying, (iv) 'Awn b. 'Abd Allah by Ibn al-Mubārak, *Zuhd*; (v) 'Abd al-Malik b. 'Umayr by Ibn Abī Shayba, *Muṣannaf*; Abū Ḥātim, *Zuhd*; (vi) Mu'ādh b. Jabal by Aḥmad, *Zuhd*; (vii) 'Ubāda b. al-Ṣāmit by al-Muḥasibī, *Risālat al-mustarshidīn*; (viii) "one of the *Anṣār*" by Ibn Abī al-Dunyā, *Muḥtaḍarīn*; (ix) Sa'd b. 'Umāra al-Tha'labī by Ibn Naṣr al-Marwazī, *Ta'ẓīm qadr al-ṣalāt*; Abū Bakr al-Khallāl, *Sunna*; Ṭabarānī, *Kabīr*; Abū Nu'aym, *Ma'rifat al-Ṣaḥāba*; (x) 'Umar b. al-Khaṭṭāb by al-Dūlābī, *al-Kunā wal-asmā'*; (xi) Ibn Mas'ūd by al-Raba'ī, *Waṣāyā al-'ulamā' 'inda ḥuḍur al-mawt*; (xii) Sa'īd al-Khayr [=Sa'īd b. 'Abd al-Malik b. Marwān b. al-Ḥakam al-Umawī] by Abū Dāwūd, *Zuhd*.

74
Everything that began must have a first mover – [Those who view the universe as random chaos] – Real friendship – [The era of *Ṣāḥib al-zamān*]

I seek refuge in Allah from the accursed devil
In the Name of Allah the All-Beneficent the Most Merciful
There is no power nor strength but with Allah the High, the Magnificent
Permission, O my Master, support!
Our way is companionship, and goodness is in the congregation

He that has a beginning, must have an ending. Allah is everlasting without beginning because our existence has a beginning, so it must inevitably have one that begins is so that it might have a beginning. Without a first mover there will not be a beginning; and if we find a beginning, its must necessarily have a first mover. If we ask for a beginning for the first mover then that first mover is not a first mover but something that was begun. For everything begun has a first mover.

They say that our universe is one of many galaxies that swim or course. Do you know anything that moves without a push? For something to move, does it not need a push from behind or a pull from the front? So what is this power that lets these galaxies go forward? And where are they going to? What force is moving them? What engine is dragging them? The Arabic word *majarra* means "it is coursing," so what is dragging it? From the back or the front? For there has to be a mover for the movement of bodies. From inside it would be impossible, so from the front or from the back? And the single galaxy is formed of 200 billion stars, and in all four directions from it there are galaxies as well, all of them heading into a certain direction and moving. Where to?

There are galaxies whose light reaches us from 10 billion light-years, which means that we are observing them as they were 10 billion years ago and not at the moment that we see them through the telescope. Allah knows best where these galaxies have gone. What is important is that He said–exalted is He– *and all are in an orbit, gliding* (Yā Sīn 36:40), *and the sun runs on to its alighting-place* (Yā Sīn 36:38). So each galaxy has an alighting-place it goes to. We have said previously that whatever has a beginning must necessarily have an end, and this is the end of its alighting-place. And everything has an orbit on which it moves and which it does not go beyond, else it would collide with others.

There is no chaos in the universe and this is one of the most important points. There is a trend today that claims that there is chaos in the universe. So any universe, to them, begins in chaos and begins randomly. They deny that there is any order in the universes. However, we have established that there is One Who organizes the universes, for there necessarily must be One Who does so. It is impossible for any order to exist without an orderer. If they acknowledge there is order, Allah Almighty must be acknowledged. But the view of people now is divided in two camps: one camp acknowledges the existence of an orderer of the universe and another does not acknowledge it, although they acknowledge the existence of the order itself. In relation to the latter camp everything is random or chaotic or something else. This is the speech of someone drunk, someone devoid of logic.

So there are two parties concerning the universe: one party admit the existence of order and of the orderer in the universes, and they must necessarily admit the existence of the All-True, whereupon it is inevitable that they must acknowledge responsibility in this life and in the universe, and another party evade all responsibility and all admission of it, and they say the universe is chaos and has no end. The first party are bound by ethical restrictions and foundations and they will be the manifestation of excellent virtues. As for the second party they have no principle. We cannot tie them down to any ethical restriction because they are the very source of impieties.

We are now living in an era in which most people do not acknowledge any moral responsibility and do not want to be bound by any ethical foundations. This is why He said–exalted is He–*corruption has appeared in the land and the sea*, and Allah is warning, *so that He will cause them to taste some of what they have done.*[1] He will cause them to taste from their own handiwork so that they will taste the result of their evading all ethical foundations, whereby mercy was taken away from the Umma to the point that if one them killed half of all humankind it would not matter to him. No mercy falls into his heart at all. When the human being is left to himself he becomes like a savage predator. We cannot find in him any ethical foundations or virtues. Materialists do not think of these matters. Their school shows it.

[**Question:** how can there be real friendship?]

The meaning of friendship. In our gathering there is a group of which you are part. Have you come here of your own power? And have they come of their own power to this world? Never. Truly those that have come to be present here

[1] *Corruption has appeared in the land and the sea with what the hands of the people have earned, so that He will cause them to taste some of what they have done—perhaps they will come back* (al-Rūm 30:41).

have come out of love and through love. They have come to found friendship for the sake of Allah and not for a worldly motive. For they have no aspiration to obtain something from this world. If they had a worldly motive, there would be no care for friendship at all and no trace would be left of it. But if friendship is for Allah, it lasts and does not end.

In this time of ours people are proud to say that they live in the twentieth century, the century of civilization. Despite that, in reality, many have gone far from the reality of humanity because their social occasions have all become for this world. No one recognizes you anymore when they do not benefit from you in the worldly sense. But the Prophets–upon them peace–and the last of the Prophets, the Seal of Prophets, our liege lord Muhammad–upon him the blessings and peace of Allah–have all come in order to remove external causes between the servants and instore real love between them, to make them a single hand, a group—"the hand of Allah is with the group"[1]—the group of Allah, the group of the Prophet.

In the time of the Prophet–upon him the blessings and peace of Allah–a certain worldly matter entered between the ranks of the people of belief, at which time they became estranged from one another.[2] However, when you take away from people the worldly motive, we find them closing ranks and uniting, and forming rows before Allah with their love. They will be like a single soul because **everything that is for Allah comes with ease, and everything that is not for Allah comes with difficulty**. The difficulty that is found in this world of ours is in the problems that are without limit and without count. This is a basic cause.[3] So there will be no ease. On the contrary at every step there appears a new difficulty, and day after day the problems of the world increase and do not decrease.

Have you ever heard that problems are decreasing in the world? Since my childhood I had been hearing that the first world war would finish the problems of the world, and after but twenty years the second world war occurred, and people also thought that it would rid them of problems. On the contrary, and as you see, day after day problems increase. However, when the third world war takes place, the power of evil existing in the world that has caused the problems for humankind shall be eradicated. Very quickly we will reach the appearance of the spiritual leader of endtimes. With his sword all the problems will be resolved and nothing shall remain of them. People in his time will

[1] See Suhba I.61, first and second notes.

[2] See, e.g., Suhba I.59, battle of Ḥunayn; and the example of the battle of Uḥud.

[3] I.e. nothing is being done for the sake of Allah.

come together with divine ties and not with the ties of this world. The latter will be removed by the sword of the spiritual leader of endtimes. They were the cause of coldness, enmity, aversion and hatred between the hearts. In their place there will be love and closeness between the servants. This is the service of the spiritual leader of endtimes, and this world is in the greatest need for this event.

By the sanctity of the Beloved, by the sanctity of the Fatiha.

75
[Sin results in a repulsive savage human nature – This world is finishing] – The glad tidings of the Night journey and the Heavenly ascent

I seek refuge in Allah from the accursed devil
In the Name of Allah the All-Beneficent the Most Merciful
There is no power nor strength but with Allah the High, the Magnificent
Permission, O my Master, support!
Our way is companionship, and goodness is in the congregation

[Suhba of the Jumuʿa of *Isrā'* and *Miʿrāj* 1399/22 June 1979]

O you who believe! Obey the One God and obey the Messenger and those in authority among you (al-Nisā' 4:59). "Hear and grasp, and once you have grasped, then benefit!"[1] This is the discourse of our liege lord Shaykh ʿAbd Allah al-Daghistani. He would open his meetings with this noble verse, and this verse is to serve as a reminder always. *And keep reminding for verily the reminder benefits the believers* (al-Dhāriyāt 51:55). Every time the servant remembers, the reminder takes away heedlessness from him. What we need most to follow these days is this noble verse: *O you who believe! Obey the One God and obey the Messenger and those in authority among you.*

Be upright yourself. He said–exalted is He–*O you who believe! You are responsible for yourselves. Those who are astray cannot hurt you when you are rightly guided* (al-Mā'ida 5:105). If we ourselves have not walked on the straight path then everything will come against us. You must realize that even the ant, even the fish in the sea come against you when you are disobedient to your nurturing Lord, and you will not be qualified for the love of Allah Almighty. This is why He has placed in the hearts of the servants and the hearts of creatures aversion for you.

Disobedience of the nurturing Lord Almighty is the cause for His dressing the servant with savagery. Aversion for him is bound to fall in the heart of everyone that sees him because he is A DISOBEDIENT SLAVE. Why did Allah first command for Himself to be obeyed when He said, *Obey the One God*? Because once you have obeyed your nurturing Lord and you have become upright as He has ordered you (al-Shūrā 42:15), Allah shall dress you of

[1] See Suhba I.31, first note.

His *uns* (familiarity) and of His love and of His lights and of His majesty and of His power. Allah also commands you to obey the Messenger so that you will be dressed of the lights of the Prophet and you will be loved and brought near and accepted in his presence. And **whoever is accepted in the presence of his nurturing Lord and in the presence of His Prophet, then people will respect him and esteem him even despite themselves**. This is an important matter.

We are not walking with uprightness but according to our likes and our whim. After that we say we want all people and governors to be the way we want! There is a certain order in the world. There is a certain arrangement. *the One God has created the heavens and the earth with truth* (Ibrāhīm 14:19) *and He has disposed the balance* (al-Raḥmān 55:7). So when you walk on the path of injustice, this injustice of yours drags over you the injustice of people. But if you were to walk on the path of truth and righteousness, then all people would treat you with truth and righteousness. Hear and grasp! Do not be obdurate! Do not ram your head against the rock! Are you trying to crack the rock with your head? Your head will crack first; not the rock.

The Messenger–upon him the blessings and peace of Allah–said, "He has put the servants in whatever He wants, and to Him belongs the purpose in all that He wills."[1] You are not putting the servants in their positions—this one is a sergeant, this one is a lieutenant… There is already one that has put them in their stations and He has put you in your station. Give thanks to your nurturing Lord! This being said, O Muslims and O believers in the hereafter, where are you going? Do you know? Allah is asking and we are heedless. You must know that we are going away, we are passing away! So eat a bit less and be a bit less eager for this life, for the ravenousness of people will be the cause of the ruin of this world. We are on our way, and no one is thinking.

Now all nations—the big ones and the small ones with them—want to lay this world to ruin and leave nothing for whoever is coming after them to

[1] Part of the Sunni creed which Mawlana has mentioned before without attributing it verbatim to the Prophet (Suhbas I.57, first note; I.59, first note), spoken to that effect by Ṭabarī in explanation of Ibn 'Abbās's gloss on the verses *to Him belongs whoever is in the heavens and the earth. All are obedient unto Him. And it is He Who first produces creation then He restores it, and the latter is easier yet for Him* (Rūm 30:26-27) and confirmed by other verses such as *verily the One God is reaching His purpose* (al-Ṭalāq 65:3) and hadiths such as "O Allah, the truest word the slave may say—and each of us is Your slave—is that there is no preventer for what You give and no giver for what You prevent, and the effort of the possessor of effort avails nothing apart from You" (narrated from Ibn 'Abbās, Abū 'Ubayda, Abū Sa'īd al-Khudrī, Mu'āwiya b. Abī Sufyān, Mughīra b. Shu'ba and Ṣuhayb in the *Musnad*, *Ṣaḥīḥayn* and *Sunan*).

succeed them. They are saying, let us burn it and leave nothing. This is gluttony. This is the meaning of the verse, *corruption has appeared in the land and the sea with what the hands of the people have earned* (al-Rūm 30:41): He shall make them taste punishment with their own hands. Allah will discipline them. This world is not your and it is not mine. We are on our way, passing and not remaining, and the world is disappearing.

In every gathering you must know that from Jumuʿa to Jumuʿa we have certainly crossed a distance, and the world has become more remote, and the hereafter has drawn nearer. **We are of the children of the hereafter. Once you realize this you will relax and you will obtain loftiness in the abode of everlastingness**. Glory, praise and thanks to Allah Who has guided us to belief and submission, and Who has honored us with the Prophet of the end of times, our liege lord Muhammad–upon him peace! And this is an immense honor for us to be part of his Umma, because the honor of the Umma is proportional to the honor of its Prophet without the shadow of a doubt. And our Prophet is the best of Prophets and their leader, the best of creation and the two worlds, no Prophet comes near him in his station, people are like the earth and he is like the sky over them. None can rise above the stature of the Prophet whoever they may be, and there is no Prophet but asked to be a simple individual among the individuals that belonged to the Umma of Muhammad–upon him the blessings and peace of Allah. They asked and begged, "O our nurturing Lord! Make us of his Umma instead of our being Prophets."

Allah has dressed us with this honor and we did not have to ask for it. He has lavished blessing on us. Our Prophet is described as *anxious over you* (Tawba 9:128). That is his attribute, whereby he was not pleased to be given any merit from the presence of Allah except he would ask that his Umma would obtain the like of it as well. He was not pleased for anything to be exclusive to him but rather he wanted it to include the whole Umma. This is from the exclusive characteristics of our Prophet Muhammad–upon him the blessings and peace of Allah. Allah exalted him, honored him, magnified him and supported him with the dazzling, powerful staggering miracles. He extolled him from before time to everlastingness, and He is constantly giving him. Thus did He honor him by inviting him to His presence on the night of Heavenly ascent, and no other Prophet ever attained that Heavenly ascent other than our Prophet Muhammad–upon him the blessings and peace of Allah. The All-True–exalted is He–invited him to His presence to soothe and calm his noble heart.

That event took place for our Prophet in the world of this life before the Hijra. However, in its spiritual reality, it took place in the world of Lāhūt (Godhead) at the time the Name of Allah Almighty was written, *lā ilāha illā-l-Lāh* (there is no god but the One God), and in front of it *Muḥammadun rasūlu-l-Lāh* (Muhammad is the Messenger of the One God). From that spiritual reality a trace appeared in this world as an honor for his Umma. That honoring is permanent and constant, and it is renewed every year.

How much of honor has taken place for the Prophet and his Umma from year to year since the beginning of the matter, i.e. from the first *Miʿrāj* that took place in this world! For the same occurs every year, since last night there has taken place, of that honoring, the aggregate of all that has taken place since the very first honoring thousands of years ago,[1] nay—many times over. This honoring certainly showed from the reality of the *Miʿrāj* last night at which time the night of *Miʿrāj* joined with the night of Jumuʿa and became light upon light. On that night the Prophet–upon him the blessings and peace of Allah–was dressed with a crown from the presence of Allah Almighty which He crowned him with.

The crown of the Prophet is not a crown of kings. His crown is his turban. However, if you were to look at that turban which his nurturing Lord has dressed him with—from those lights the lights of the peerless, most magnificent Throne became more intense. And his nurturing Lord made him sit on his throne—in the Throne of Allah, where the Prophet has a special throne.[2] From the above there resulted indescribable joy last night in the Malakūt, the Jabarūt, the ʿAẓamūt, the Lāhūt—*mā shā' Allāh*. If a single drop of that joy were distributed to all people on earth they would forget food and drink and everything due to their emotion. They would be in a state until they finally meet their nurturing Lord. They would roam the deserts and the seas due to the intensity of the joy that took place in the Malakūt. He–exalted is He–said *whoever is blind in this life, then he shall be blind in the hereafter* (Banū Isrā'īl/Isrā' 17:72).

On that night which is witnessed and thanked, the people of Malakūt, the people of Allah, were crowned by their nurturing Lord with turbans of light, as if suns were rising from their heads. The Prophet–upon him blessings and peace of Allah–became the *ma'dhūn al-muṭlaq* (absolute deputy), whereby Allah gave him the glad tidings that the time had grown near for the truth to reign supreme and for falsehood to be made to perish, for the Prophet is *anxious over you* (al-Tawba 9:128). He–exalted is He–said to him, "O My Beloved! The matter is accomplished and I have turned it over to you. You are

[1] See Suhba I.24 esp. the 14th note among other proofs documented in Haddad, *The Muhammadan Light* (Chapter 5, "The progression of the Prophet's light in time").

[2] See the narrations to that effect in "The Prophet's Seating on the Throne" at https://www.livingislam.org/ir/d/pst_e.pdf

authorized absolutely and on My behalf, so receive the reins of government. Whatever you want for your Umma I have bestowed on you. Give glad tidings and do not make them run away, O my Beloved!"

The spiritual leader of endtimes, our liege lord the Mahdi–upon him peace–was represented in that august presence together with his ministers and successors. None remained, last night, of the people of spiritual reality who have preceded us, those that are present, and those whose seeds shall come, except they were in attendance in the procession in the last third of the night. They were summoned from their original stations, from the reality of the lights of the children of Ādam. It was unveiled to them so they appeared in the presence of the All-True in the same way as on the Day of *"am I not your nurturing Lord?" They said yes* (al-Aʿrāf 7:172), witnessing the lights of the All-True on our Prophet–upon him the blessings and peace of Allah–as they were standing in rows and went into prostration in the presence of the All-True with their Imam, the Imam of all, the Prophet. Allah Almighty was well-pleased with their prostration and dressed them with lights the like of which were never seen before. This sight became a magnificent sight whereby none remained among those human beings in existence except their reality was honored with those lights and all the openings and glad tidings that took place last night. If the angels were to sit with pens in their hands to write it all they would be unable to transcribe it.

What took place certainly took place! Receive the glad tidings. The good news has come that what was meant to happen over a long period of time was folded up into a shorter time so that people would not feel the hardship of the movements that would befall on the face of the earth. For Allah has dressed, from His Attribute of pure mercy, a special attribute on the *budalā'* (substitutes), *nujabā'* (highborn), *awtād* (pillars), *akhyār* (elect ones), and the angels qualified to run the affair of the world and its ultimate change. For Allah wants to change this world. He shall substitute it and change it from one era to another, and stop the era of injustice and open the era of light. He wants to close up the era of injustice and unbelief, and He wants to open the era of justice and mercy and light. This is what was decided last night. And He has given the glad tidings that all of the major events that are to take place were gathered by Allah in the Malakūt year that begins on the magnificent 15 Shaʿbān.

He has served the warning and given the glad tidings. Allah has served the warning that the haram and its people will pass away, and He has given the glad tidings that the people of the halal shall remain. Receive the glad tidings and stand firm on the truth! Deliverance is near for all humankind and not only for the believers, but rather for all that are subsumed under the address of *and We have certainly honored the children of Ādam* (Banū Isrā'īl/Isrā'

17:70). Allah has dressed them from those lights with the good news that "the end and the aftermath are in My hand and I shall not hand over the leadership of human beings to anyone. And I have entrusted them to you, O My Beloved, and I am a guardian for them." *Yā Ḥafīẓ! Yā Allāh!.*

These glad tidings have taken place by the blessing of Mawlana [Shaykh 'Abd Allah al-Daghistani]. Mawlana has graced us with this much from his station, something little. If Allah wills, you will see what which no eye has seen and hear that which no ear has heard and what has never dawned on the hearts of human beings. I am not speaking these words from books. Rather it is from the heart to the heart, and the sight of the eyes from my Master who has caused my tongue to speak.

By the sanctity of the Beloved, by the sanctity of the Fatiha.

76

[Purifying humbleness is the prayer of *miʿrāj*] – The Attribute of Allah is Power and Might [while ours is absolute incapacity – Folding of time and space at the time of the last breaths of life]

I seek refuge in Allah from the accursed devil
In the Name of Allah the All-Beneficent the Most Merciful
There is no power nor strength but with Allah the High, the Magnificent
Permission, O my Master, support!
Our way is companionship, and goodness is in the congregation

The *ṣāḥib al-zamān* (spiritual leader of endtimes=Mahdi)–upon him and upon our Prophet the best of blessings and greetings–said that when the person at prayer says *Allāhu akbar* he must come down until no trace of existence can be ascertained for him—and this is purity—until he enters into the divine presence on the spot and be at the station of the heavenly ascent of the Prophet–upon him the blessings and peace of Allah–on the night of *miʿrāj*. **Whoever raises *takbīr* (magnification) with this intention, his purification has certainly become complete, otherwise he is praying impure**. Then what are we to do? We must pray to learn and to comply with the order, like the small child who writes and erases, then writes and erases, and so forth until he becomes proficient at writing. It is obligatory for us to proceed in this manner and to go to work until the special lordly care attains us, so that we erase the trace of ego in us.

Facilitation is from Allah Most High. You must say *Allah!* with Allah and not with yourself. For whoever is with his own ego is entrusted to it. We are weak. There is no power for us nor strength. So then what is "our strength"? If we tasked some man to carry a chair off the ground he can carry it for five minutes to half an hour. The upshot is he will get tired and throw it away. This is our strength: nothing. Allah Most High said, *strength belongs to the One God entirely* (al-Baqara 2:165), *and it never strains Him to preserve them* (2:255). Likewise the attribute of the angels—the carriers of the Throne—if any single one of them were to put a single feather on earth he would make it topsy turvy, and yet these huge angels were incapable of carrying the Throne until they asked help from their nurturing Lord.[1] Allah reinforced them with the

[1] "The Throne does not carry Him, rather the Throne and its carriers are carried by

number of the angels of the seven skies and they were still unable. Then He reinforced them with the same number in addition and they were still unable to budge the Throne, until He inspired them to say, *lā ḥawla wa-lā quwwata illā bi-l-Lāhi al-ʿalīyyi al-ʿaẓīm* (there is no power nor strength but in Allah the Exalted, the Magnificent), whereupon they were able to carry the great Throne.[1] At that very moment Allah made the earth disappear from under their feet, so they grasped the Throne so that they would not fall—the Throne of the All-Beneficent. Our liege lord ʿAlī–upon him peace–said at that time it was no longer known who was carrying and who was being carried.[2] This is the strength of Allah and the attribute of the All-True: power and might.

To understand the strength of Allah we must first have belief in Allah. So the very first obligation is that we must believe in the power of the All-True, in His power over everything and this is the most elementary belief in Allah. Mawlana al-Shaykh [ʿAbd Allah al-Daghistani] told me the story of a man who was making ablution while the muezzin was raising the call to prayer. There was by him one of the possessors of a spiritual state who was also making ablution. The latter saw a sesame seed and said, "Glory to Him Whose affair is so great that He can cause the universe with all its immensity to enter inside a sesame seed without reducing its size and without increasing the size of the sesame seed!" The other man said, """This is the speech of mad people. Allah has power to do that, but He must increase the size of the sesame seed of reduce the size of the universe." As soon as he uttered this statement his foot slipped and he fell into the water gutter. He disappeared from the place of ablution and reappeared at the shore where all the water drains end up, but he was in the form of a donkey. A man ran to him, held him by the ears, hit him, rode on top of him and kept him in his possession for seven years, using him in his service. After all these years passed the donkey came one day to drink at that same shore. Its foot slipped and he reappeared at the same spot where he had made ablution seven years before, finding the same man next to him again, and the muezzin had not yet finished raising the prayer. Immediately

the subtleness of His power, subdued under His grip" per al-Ashʿarī, *al-Ibāna ʿan uṣūl al-diyāna*; "the carrier of the Throne and of its carriers is in reality Allah Himself" per al-Khaṭṭābī as cited in Bayhaqī, *al-Asmāʾ wal-Ṣifāt*; "never can the Throne carry Him, rather the Throne and the Throne-Bearers are carried up by the subtlety of His infinite might, and all are powerless in His grasp" per Ibn ʿAbd al-Salām, *al-Mulḥa fī iʿtiqād ahl al-ḥaqq* (The fair speech on the belief of the people of truth).

[1] Narrated from (i) Muʿāwiya b. Ṣāliḥ by ʿUthmān al-Dārimī, *al-Naqḍ ʿalā al-Marrīsī*; (ii) Ibn Zayd by al-Ṭabarī and Makkī (al-Ḥāqqa 69:17); (iii) Wahb b. Munabbih by Abū al-Shaykh al-Aṣbahānī, *al-ʿAẓama*; (iv) Ibn ʿAbbās by al-Thaʿlabī (Ghāfir 40:7).

[2] I.e. Allah carried both the carriers (the angels) and what they carried (the Throne) as narrated from ʿAlī al-Riḍā in the Shīʿī sources, e.g. Ṭabarsī, *Iḥtijāj*; al-Kuléní, *Kāfī*.

he said, "I repent and return to Allah! Now I know." The possessor of the spiritual state asked him, "Is He *qādir muqtadir* (Able, All-Able) or not?"

Thus, for us to believe in Allah we must believe that His Essence does not resemble our essence and His Attributes do not resemble ours. So what is the benefit is they are as described? The Attribute of Allah is absolute power while our attribute is absolute incapacity. Our Almighty nurturing Lord leaves the servant to do whatever the latter wishes. However, at his last seven breaths He does not leave him but He addresses His Beloved–upon him the blessings and peace of Allah–and says, "Now, O My Beloved, leave My slave with Me." In the last seven breaths, when the servant is in a state of agony and is unable to draw his breath, at that very time where does His nurturing Lord transport him? The Prophets themselves have no acquaintance with that—where would Iblīs be at that time?

Our nurturing Lord said on the Night of the heavenly Ascent, "O My Beloved, I have kept veiled from My servants the knowledge of how I shall treat them at the end. I have veiled this matter from everyone. Knowledge of this matter is with Me exclusively. For if they knew how I am going to treat them, I would not longer find a single one of them prostrating to Me. The human being is one and his origin is one and the same.[1] Allah Most High said, *The All-Merciful. He has taught the Qur'ān. He has created the human being* (al-Raḥmān 55:1-3).[2]

By the sanctity of the Beloved, by the sanctity of the Fatiha.

[1] See Suhba I.34; I.69.

[2] See Suhba I.48, question 4.

77
Who recited the marriage sermon for our liege lord Ādam–upon him peace?

I seek refuge in Allah from the accursed devil
In the Name of Allah the All-Beneficent the Most Merciful
There is no power nor strength but with Allah the High, the Magnificent
Permission, O my Master, support!
Our way is companionship, and goodness is in the congregation

From the sermon delivered at the marriage contract of Mehmet, the son of Mawlana al-Shaykh Nazim:

"Glory, praise and thanks to the One God Who has paired the spirits with the bodies and Who has made marriage licit and fornication illicit. Blessings, purity and peace be upon our liege lord Muhammad who has expounded to us that which is illicit and that which is permitted, and upon his Family and Companions who are indeed the people of righteousness and prosperity.

"In the Name of the One God, the All-Beneficent, the Most Merciful.

"Who recited the marriage sermon for our liege lord Ādam and our lady Ḥawwā'? **Glory to Him Who formed the child before his father!** His son recited it. The marriage sermon was recited by our liege lord Muhammad!"

By the sanctity of the Beloved, by the sanctity of the Fatiha.

78

The spirit of the Tariqa is love and followership – [Difference between love in Allah and love in the ego – The Prophet has a deputy who meets him every 24 hours and conveys from him]

I seek refuge in Allah from the accursed devil
In the Name of Allah the All-Beneficent the Most Merciful
There is no power nor strength but with Allah the High, the Magnificent
Permission, O my Master, support!
Our way is companionship, and goodness is in the congregation

Our master Shah Naqshband made this statement a pillar in the most distinguished Tariqa: "Our Tariqa is companionship," i.e. the meaning of *ṭarīqa* is *ṣuḥba*. That is why if two believers meet it is necessary to enliven that time with spiritual companionship, where the mercy that is promised for the congregation will descend. "Even if you sat a thousand years alone," Mawlana al-Shaykh ['Abd Allah al-Daghistani] used to say, "you will not find that tender care by yourself." How much will you devote yourself to worship? Yet what Allah promised to the congregation does not open up. Praise and thanks to Allah, in our gathering there is more than one, i.e. there is a congregation. The meaning of this is that whatever we speak about, we earnestly expect and hope that Allah shall grant it to us in our worldly life and in our hereafter.

Our liege lord Muhyiddin Ibn 'Arabi wrote a letter to a majestic scholar named Fakhr al-Dīn al-Rāzī, one of the major scholars, in which he said to him, "O my brother, strive for the sciences that are of necessity to you in both this world and the hereafter and do not waste your time pursuing the sciences that part with you in the hereafter."[1] Therefore it is faithful sincere advice to you: do not waste your precious life pursuing something that parts with you. For **every moment of the life of a human being is more precious than red Sulphur.**[2] What is red sulphur? It is the most precious of metals one ever heard of, and people do not see it anywhere. This is why your time is your precious lifetime and it is more precious than the red sulphur. The one that prizes his

[1] Ibn 'Arabī, *Rasā'il Ibn 'Arabī*, ed. Muḥammad 'Abd al-Karīm al-Namrī (Beirut: Dār al-Kutub al-'Ilmiyya, 1421/2001) pp. 184-187 (*risāla ilā al-imām al-Rāzī*).

[2] I.e. pure gold.

precious lifetime will not experience regret. As for the one that wastes it, he shall experience regret.

Mawlana al-Shaykh ['Abd Allah al-Daghistani] says, "Speech during companionship, even a couple of light words, is part of the sciences that are necessary in our worldly life and our hereafter." Sultan al-Awliya' said that the spirit of the Tariqa is tied fast to love and followership.[1] It is a must for every person to follow a tariqa because the tariqas let one reach Allah, and the servant must recognize that his settling-place will be with his nurturing Lord. And to follow the discipline of a tariqa is an obligation for him from whose heart his nurturing Lord has removed the veil of heedlessness.

Mawlana says that at the time of following tariqa discipline, the murid recognizes that the spirit of following is love and followership because without love there is no followership to be found and there is no spiritual wayfaring. The most important thing the servant can ask from his nurturing Lord—as Mawlana has taught—is the increase of love. O Allah, increase us in love in You! That is what really benefits the human being. So the more his love increases, the more his followership increases. After that his nearness from Allah Almighty increases. This is why Mawlana's instruction is, obtain love. Try, as much as you can, to obtain love.

What is meant by love is *al-ḥubbu fī-l-Lāh* (love in Allah). This love never leaves you—not in this world, not in the hereafter. However, to obtain this love is not an easy matter when the ego is still there because the ego does not accept for someone to love another for the sake of Allah. The ego wants all the love for itself. So love for the ego is found but love for Allah is lost. There is love among people but this is not love in Allah. Their love is for themselves. The human being loves something for the satisfaction of his ego and not for his nurturing Lord. For example, when a beautiful woman passes by all people without exception will love her. Why? Is this love in Allah? Far be it. This is love for one's own ego because if it were an old woman passing by his ego would not stir for love. Only for the young woman it stirs quickly and all people love her. Is this love in Allah? No, but rather love for the ego.

The important thing is for one to love something in Allah without giving any mind to their images or their form. He must only notice that this is my nurturing Lord's servant or that is my nurturing Lord's maidservant. When a human being loves you he will love your child also, so this love in you imparts love for everything that is affiliated with you. This is why the Messenger–upon him the blessings and peace of Allah–said, "I do not ask you anything but only

[1] See Mawlana's handwritten note to that effect at the frontispiece of this volume.

affectionate love towards kindred."[1] And this points to an important fact, i.e. "O my Umma! When your love in me is sound then I want of you to love my near relatives in *ḥasab* (position) or *nasab* (lineage). This constitutes your strength." Many say we love the Prophet–upon him the blessings and peace of Allah–but they wrong or despise his near relatives. So then this claimed love is not true. Their love is fraudulent, not purely for the sake of Allah. So **a person must know the difference between love in Allah and love in the ego**.

Our master the Shaykh ['Abd Allah al-Daghistani] would relate to me that one of the passionate lovers composed a poem in which he was saying something to the effect that "O my brethren, I do not know anything called 'love' that you are talking about. I do not believe this love of yours to be true unless I first test it so that I may confirm it as true that you are truthful lovers. When you truly love me then if I were to put you inside a meat grinder and ground you, after which you came you from the other side safe and sound by the power of Allah despite all the torment you have tasted, but your love in me has changed—then that is not true love. Rather you are a liar in that claim of love."

Thus do we recognize love. Otherwise you are merely accompanying me. For if you become upset because of a single word and you disown all the love that had lasted for years and you say, "I am upset, I do not want to see him." Where will your love be? This is a sign that he loves the other for his own ego and not for the sake of Allah. But how many people can you find that are people of this kind of love! Love in Allah is for you to respect me and honor me and prize me without anything in return. Allah loves that there should be in servants such as this love so that one's state will not change for the worse towards one's brother no matter what the other throws at him of reverses. Thus love is not an easy matter but the highest station.

How much did the Prophet–upon him the blessings and peace of Allah–bear harm from his people on the day of Uḥud? Did he imprecate against them? No. Rather he supplicated for them, "O Allah, guide my people!"[2] No hatred or enmity has settled in the chest of the Prophet–upon him the blessings and peace of Allah–for anyone. Who is the one conveying this matter? The one that conveys it is the one that is granted permission. Mawlana al-

[1] *Say, "I do not ask you over it any wage but only affectionate love towards kindred"* (Shūra 42:23).

[2] Narrated from (i-iii) Sahl b. Sa'd al-Sā'idī, Anas b. Mālik and Ibn Mas'ūd by Bukhārī and Muslim; and (iv) 'Abd Allāh b. 'Ubayd in *mursal* mode by Bayhaqī, *Shu'ab* (14: *Ḥubbu al-Nabiyyi, fī ḥadab al-Nabiyyi 'alā ummatihi wa-ra'fatihi bihim*). Cf. Abū al-Layth al-Samarqandī, *Baḥr al-'ulūm* (Āl 'Imrān 3:140); *Tanbīh al-ghāfilīn* (*kaẓm al-ghayẓ*); 'Iyāḍ, *Shifā* (I.2, *fī ḥilmihi wa-ḥtimālihi wa-'afwihi wa-ṣabrih*).

Shaykh ['Abd Allah al-Daghistani] says that the *ma'dhūn* (deputy) is able to receive what the Umma is in need of every twenty-four hours from the presence of the Messenger–upon him the blessings and peace of Allah–in the spiritual world. This deputy is able to meet with the Messenger every twenty-four hours and to receive from his presence what is needed by the *Ummat al-mutāba'a*, the *Ummat al-ijāba* and the *Ummat al-da'wa*.[1] And this is not an easy matter. This is the attribute of the *muballigh* (conveyer).

Our master the Shaykh says that conveyance from books is obligatory for all, and this is an imitation of the real deputy. Whoever reads from the books is a *muballigh*. However, he is blind, and a *muballigh* should not be blind. Allah Most High said, *say, "This is my way: I summon unto the One God with full sight, I and whoever follows me"* (Yūsuf 12:108). Allah describes the call of His Messenger as being *with full sight*, whereas the blind man cannot be a guide or a conveyer.

Who is the hypocrite? He is the one with a sick heart. Our liege lord 'Umar would ask Ḥudhayfa al-Yamānī–Allah be well-pleased with them–"I ask you by Allah and for the sake of the Messenger of Allah! Has the Messenger counted me among the hypocrites?" This is our liege lord 'Umar with all his immense status, yet he feared lest he might be of the hypocrites and he was making Ḥudhayfa al-Yamānī swear to tell him truthfully about it, because knowledge about the hypocrites, their secrets and their names was with him. **Our liege lord the Shaykh says that the hypocrite has sickness in his heart and his inward state is in ruins. The way to restore inward states is found in sticking to that *adab* (discipline)—love in Allah. For *adab* is a healing treatment for the sickness of the heart and restores the inward state back from ruin. There is no medication other than it, and compliance with *adab* is an imitation of the people of Allah.**

By the sanctity of the Beloved, by the sanctity of the Fatiha.

[1] *Ummat al-da'wa* are all those to whom the Messenger was sent with the Message. *Ummat al-ijāba* are those who have accepted the Message including the hypocrites, who have accepted it outwardly only. *Ummat al-mutāba'a* (or *al-ittibā'*) are the true believers. See Abū Zakariyyā Yaḥyā b. Abī Ṭāhir Ibrāhīm b. Aḥmad al-Salamāsī (474-550/1081-1155), *Manāzil al-A'immat al-Arba'a Abī Ḥanīfa wa-Mālik wal-Shāfi'ī wa-Aḥmad*, ed. Maḥmūd Qadaḥ (Medina: al-Jāmi'at al-Islāmiyya, 1422/2002) pp. 83-84 (*Muqaddimāt, bayān al-Umma*); Rāzī, *Tafsīr* (Ṣaff 61:10-11); 'Alā' al-Dīn al-Bukhārī, *Kashf al-asrār sharḥ uṣūl al-Pazdawī* (*ahliyyat al-ijmā'*); al-Taftāzānī, *al-Talwīḥ 'alā al-Tawḍīḥ* (*ahliyyat al-ijmā'*); Ibn al-Mulaqqin Sirāj al-Dīn 'Umar b. 'Alī b. Aḥmad, *al-Tawḍīḥ li-sharḥ al-Jāmi' al-ṣaḥīḥ*, ed. Dār al-Falāḥ, 36 vols. (Damascus: Dār al-Nawādir, 1429/2008) 19:149-150 (*Bad' al-khalq, ṣifat al-janna*, "70,000 or 700,000 shall enter Paradise...);" Ibn Ḥajar, *Fatḥ al-Bārī* (11:411, ditto).

79

Attribute of the greatest mujahid – The Prophet's renewal of the matter of Tariqa – [The possessor of *himma* obtains all the spiritual ranks before death – Pledge of dhikr from all human beings, not just Tariqa people – Mercies descend daily to the number of human beings but only rememberers get them, not violators of the solemn Covenant]

I seek refuge in Allah from the accursed devil
In the Name of Allah the All-Beneficent the Most Merciful
There is no power nor strength but with Allah the High, the Magnificent
Permission, O my Master, support!
Our way is companionship, and goodness is in the congregation

What is important is *naẓāfa* (cleanliness) and what is required is inward cleanliness. What they have is cleanliness in their garments, in their houses and in everything that shows, but what is required is cleanliness of one's inward state. The Prophet–upon him the blessings and peace of Allah–says, "Cleanliness is part of belief."[1] This is why **the servant is not counted as clean as long as there remains in him blameworthy traits.**

Mawlana al-Shaykh ['Abd Allah al-Daghistani] says that whoever rids himself of his blameworthy traits will be tasked with the reality of tasking, otherwise this will remain an imitation tasking. So the manifest externality of the sacred Law tasks the one that has reached the age of reason and puberty, but that tasking is [still] not real because it requires inward cleanliness. Until the age of puberty the legally-tasked person is counted as a child, but after the age of puberty then his ego partners with the devil and dirty works are generated from that time. This is why the servant will not be clean until his ego quits partnering with the devil.

Mawlana al-Shaykh says that even if a person were to worship to the extent of all humans and jinns, that worship is insufficient because it is missing

[1] Narrated from Ibn Mas'ūd by al-Ṭabarānī, *Awsaṭ* per al-'Irāqī, *Mughnī*; al-Khaṭīb, *Talkhīṣ al-mutashābih fīl-rasm*. Its basis is in the *Musnad* and *Sunan* as "*al-ṭuhūr* (purity) is half of belief" and "*al-wuḍū'* (ablution) is half of belief."

inward cleanliness. Thus **one may be seen worshipping his nurturing Lord from the time of puberty until above 90 years of age yet you will find that his ego is still partnering with the devil and has not cleansed itself, and you will find blameworthy traits in him**. So cleanliness is important. And if a person does not embark on spiritual wayfaring at the hand of a perfect spiritual guide, i.e. a perfect shaykh, cleanliness will not be facilitated for him. But it is the basic requirement in drawing near to Allah Almighty.

My master the Shaykh told me this suhba in al-Madīna al-Munawwara—upon its dweller the best blessing and salutation—which is where **the Messenger renewed the status of the Naqshbandi Tariqa and tied it to himself on the spot**. The wisdom of this renewal indicates that **the Messenger himself has taken charge of the protection of the most distinguished Tariqa and the protection of those affiliated with it. Our master the Shaykh would even say that whoever claims to be a *murshid* (spiritual guide) and says "my followers" will himself be a devil. Rather we are all followers of the Messenger of Allah**–upon him blessings and peace of Allah–and this makes it general, so that there will not be any splitting into factions left for it to be said, "the followers of Shaykh X, or of Shaykh Y or of Shaykh Z." So whoever observes the *adab* of the most distinguished Tariqa which the Messenger has renewed and whose *rābiṭa* has become with him will say, "the followers of our master the Messenger of Allah in the Naqshbandi Tariqa;" or "the followers of our master the Messenger of Allah in the Qadiri Tariqa;" or "the followers of our master the Messenger of Allah in the Rifaʿi Tariqa," etc. Only his followers!—whereby no *murshid* has the capacity to protect the followers by himself due to the abundance of trials and darkness and the fleeing of people away from the truth and from the right path.

Our master the Shaykh asks, **who has high spiritual energy? They are the ones that keep the *adab* of the Tariqa and they are the ones that are the wayfarers on *ʿazīmat al-sharīʿa*** (strict way of the sacred Law). **Any of them is counted as the greatest mujahid in this time of ours. A single breath of his while he is asleep is better than the worship of all humans and jinns, i.e. those of the common public that have not reached that rank**. Our master the Shaykh says that **whoever has high spiritual energy while keeping to the way of strictness in the sacred Law will obtain all the stations that Allah has allowed the servants to obtain by their striving**, and this station is below Prophethood, because Prophethood cannot be obtained by striving. **As for what is below Prophethood, then all the stations of *wilāya* (sainthood) are open. Take the way and you will obtain that rank!**[1]

[1] See also Suhba I.31 on the unacquirableness of special knowledge.

He also says that Allah opens up the opportunity for them because they have high spiritual energy and Allah will not send ʿAzrāʾīl to seize them until they will obtain all the ranks. When they become perfect and obtain their ranks Allah will send him to them. Look at the arrangement of the All-True! If a single rank remains which they have not acquired, Allah will not yet send ʿAzrāʾīl to them until they attain that station. And this is a gift from Allah to them.

Our liege lord the Shaykh says this is an important matter. People think that *dhikr* (remembrance) is only for people of Tariqa while the rest of people are not legally tasked. But it is not as they think—on the contrary. Mawlana [Shaykh ʿAbd Allah al-Daghistani] says that **since all the children of Ādam have taken the solemn covenant with their nurturing Lord on the Day of to make remembrance of Him on the Day of *"am I not your nurturing Lord?" They said yes* (al-Aʿrāf 7:172), all the seeds of human beings covenanted to the remembrance of Allah**. There is not a single servant but he made that covenant. Mawlana al-Shaykh would even say that on that Day **the hands of all the seeds of the children of Ādam were on top of one another making the pledge there. All the children of Ādam placed their hands above the hands of the Prophets and the Awliya, and above the whole of them was the hand of the Seal of Prophets–upon him the blessings and peace of Allah–then the hand of Allah Almighty**.

This is the Covenant. It certainly took place. People are heedless of this great matter. The Day of the Promise and the Covenant! There and then Allah Almighty Himself said, *verily those who pledge loyalty to you do but pledge loyalty to the One God. The hand of the One God is on top of their hands. So whoever forswears, he only forswears against himself, and whoever fulfills what he covenanted with the One God then He shall grant him an immense recompense* (al-Fatḥ 48:10). Thus did the All-True, the Almighty take the covenants of the children of Ādam on the Day of *"am I not your nurturing Lord?" They said yes.* We will certainly remember You, O our Lord!

Our master the Shaykh says, few are those who have kept their covenant which they made with their nurturing Lord on that Day. The majority have forgotten or they have made the Covenant null and void from the perspective that they forgot and they do not acknowledge it. They say, "From where did you get this? We do not remember." But they cannot remember even what day it was 15 days ago and what they ate on that day. The latter is a simple thing but it is evidence of incapacity for whoever objects to these matters and says "we do not remember." Ask him what happened exactly a year ago today and he cannot remember.

Another incapacitation is the Day of the Promise and the Covenant from where we came from one world to another world, from the world of souls we have arrived to the wombs of mothers. Do you remember your days in the womb of your mother? Impossible. Your personality which was present there? And **you were also in a state of spiritual unveiling. For the soul sees everything in the mother's womb, it glorifies Allah and it can see and witness.**[1] Mawlana al-Shaykh used to say that this witnessing on the part of the child lasts for seven or eight days then, little by little, the eyes of its heart become veiled due to the blameworthy traits of his father and mother. **We were first in the world of souls; then in the loins of fathers; then in the wombs of mothers; then we came out into the world; and you forgot what you ate only yesterday! So how can you claim that can remember everything and yet you deny this matter and what has certainly taken place?**

Mawlana al-Shaykh says that whoever violates the Covenant and does not remember it is of the unbelievers and the hypocrites, everything that was going to be given to them of the high virtue of dhikr and of that manifestation and mercy and special merits descending—because **it is to the count of all existing human beings and of the legally-tasked among them that mercy descends daily**—but every time it goes to one of them, that mercy finds the door closed for him so it returns, because it is exclusive to the rememberers. Millions of mercies return and the angels ask, "O our nurturing Lord, what should we do with these mercies?" And the answer comes, "Give them to the rememberers!" Thus the rewards of the rememberers of Allah are multiplied, especially in our time. This is why our master the Shaykh says that dhikr is not limited to the dervishes alone so that they are supposed to remember Allah while we sit and watch or they alone are legally tasked but we are not tasked, or they are Tariqa people and we are not. No! Rather, His remembrance is for everyone.

Our master the Shaykh says about the Prophets and the Awliya that they are the awakeners and the alarm-clocks of the servants, i.e. of those whose minds have gone because of [love of] this world. For this world has taken away the minds of people, and Allah is asking, *so where are you going?* (al-Takwīr 81:26). I.e. where is your mind? The job of the Prophets and Awliya is to notify the servants of their states of heedlessness, because the adornment of this world and its gilding have caused them to no longer have any mind, i.e. no sound mind. Our master the Shaykh says it is impossible for the Prophets and Awliya to do anything on their own, from the perspective that there is no capacity with them, and they are the first to acknowledge their absolute incapacity and the first to acknowledge the absolute power of the One God, the Almighty.

[1] See Suhba I.41, "every newborn is born in a state of *kashf*."

The more they confess their absolute incapacity the more the Lordly tender care reaches them.

Mawlana al-Shaykh says that the ant can carry something that is more than ten times its size. It can move it, carry it and walk on walls. When it falls it climbs up again and flees the spot from where it fell. The human being is the weakest of all. You must confess to your absolute incapacity from the bottom of your heart and not only your tongue, or else your nurturing Lord will test you—are you truthful in your confession to absolute incapacity or not? He will send you a reverse when you are unaware to test how truthful you are. Mawlana would strike a similitude for how Iblis puffs up the angry man the way the turkey struts—for Iblīs puffs and courses through the angry person's blood, inflating him. Mawlana would represent it in this way. There was a mouse that was rummaging through a Christian's pantry. It fell into a barrel of wine and began drinking and drinking until its head spun. Then it reached the edge of the barrel shouting, "Where are these cats?" This is the attribute of the angry man. What power do you have, O servant? Why do you boast? What is your strength? Confess to your incapacity and do not be like this mouse. When its head got full of wine vapors it thought itself to be a lion before the cat.

The Prophets and the Awliya are the staunchest of people in humbleness. They never raise their heads. They know their state and they know the power of the All-True. No slave raises his head except there will be empowered over him someone that will bring him low. This is why the world has become filled with those that raise their heads and this is why Allah shall bring them low. O Allah, do not leave us to ourselves! Mawlana al-Shaykh says that when a Prophet or a wali is given from the *nafas al-qudsiyya* (breath of holiness)[1] he can do everything and this world is like a ball in his hand: he holds it and throws it. But without the *nafas al-qudsiyya* they know that *they do not control for themselves any harm or benefit; and they do not control any death, or any life, or any rising* (al-Furqān 25:3). This is spiritual knowledge. Whoever reaches such certainty, all of strength protects him; and whoever does not confess to this, he is entrusted to his wealth and his work and his state, i.e. he is left to his ego. Then, everything goes to ruin.

From Allah is all success. By the sanctity of the Fatiha.

[1] See Suhba I.80, I.90.

80

Grandshaykh's service in the Dardanelles [and Palestine (1915-1917)] – The breath of holiness – Ikhwān al-Muslimīn have incurred condemnation – Prophet's knowledge of the Tablet and the Pen

I seek refuge in Allah from the accursed devil
In the Name of Allah the All-Beneficent the Most Merciful
There is no power nor strength but with Allah the High, the Magnificent
Permission, O my Master, support!
Our way is companionship, and goodness is in the congregation

The noble Qur'ān contains everything in detail and undetailed. Allah Most High says, *We have not shown neglect in anything in the Writ* (al-An'ām 6:38), and it was conveyed in the noble verse that *there is no protector today from the command of the One God, except whomever He grants mercy* (Hūd 11:43). Glory to Allah! This is a wisdom for all times.

When the Dardanelles war[1] finished–in which Mawlana al-Shaykh ['Abd Allah al-Daghistani] took part from beginning to end–they [=the Ottomans] sent him to Syria, and from Syria they were sending the army to the Hijaz. Our master the Shaykh told me, "That night until I reached morning I was in a fervent supplication, 'my nurturing Lord, do not put me in a position of power over the believers in the land of Hijaz,' as I had offered myself for the sake of fighting the unbelievers only." At dawn time a special telegram arrived from Istanbul requesting for Mawlana's troop to go to Jerusalem and for another troop to go to Hijaz. This is a miraculous gift. Mawlana added, "I was in al-Quds for a whole year. Every day I would come to the noble Rock to enter seclusion there. A black-bearded shaykh would come to me, sit on his knees and listen to me for an hour. One time I asked him, 'Where are you from, O Shaykh?' He said, 'I am the imam and the shaykh of the town of [...].'[2] Our master said to him, 'I want you to write a *ḥijāb* (amulet) for me, but leave space for an original calligraphy.' The next day the shaykh of the town brought me the *ḥijāb* and said to me, 'I have written the *ḥijāb* for you the same way that you have ordered me and I have left an empty space for the calligraphy.' After

[1] Also known as the battle of Gallipoli (1915-1916).
[2] Blank in the printed edition.

that I took part in a battle on the Nablus front against the British. At the end of the battle I felt something warm on my chest. I placed my hand there and I saw blood." Mawlana then realized that a bullet had entered four fingers above the heart and stopped there. Mawlana says, "This bullet is in my chest and I am going to my nurturing Lord carrying it."

Why did we tell this story? A servant might do everything in taking the utmost precautions to protect himself but when Allah wants, He leaves leeway for him to be hit by what has been decreed for him. *there is no protector today from the command of the One God, except whomever He grants mercy* (Hūd 11:43). Therefore do not be deluded by the preparations you make for yourselves because nothing will be of benefit to you. **To whom does the nurturing Lord grant mercy? "Those that are merciful, the All-Merciful grants them mercy."**[1] It is of the most important matters, for the servant to obtain mercy from his nurturing Lord, that there should be mercy in his heart. As for those from whose hearts mercy has been wrested out, the Lord's whip comes over them.

In the time of Mūsā all people were wishing they could have with them wealth like the wealth of Qārūn (Korah) but after the day that Allah caused the earth to swallow him they said, "Praise be to Allah that we were not in his place!"[2] Whoever rises from the level of common people in this world inevitably becomes the target of people's enmity. How many enviers must have gloated! How many an enemy exulted at this event! Yet they had been wishing they were in his place. The noble Qur'ān exposes to human beings with categorical demonstrative proofs how the aftermath will be. If the human being knew the ultimate settling-place of his fate over there, even if you were to give him all the storehouses of this world he would not accept this position [in exchange], but Allah keeps this matter covered up.

Our master the Shaykh used to narrate about our liege lord Shaykh Abū Aḥmad al-Thughūrī–may Allah sanctify his secret–who bore the station of *quṭbāniyya* (spiritual poleship) for forty years and was teacher to Shaykh Sharaf al-Dīn. There is none among the Awliya who has carried the station of

[1] Its continuation is, "Show mercy to those on earth and those in the sky shall show you mercy." A Prophetic hadith related from (i) 'Abd Allāh b. 'Amr b. al-'Āṣ by Ibn Abī Shayba; al-Ḥumaydī; Aḥmad; Abū Dāwūd; al-Tirmidhī (*ḥasan ṣaḥīḥ*); al-Ḥākim and others. It is also narrated in identical or similar terms from (ii-ix) Abū Hurayra, Jarīr, Abū Sa'īd al-Khudrī, Jābir, Ibn 'Umar, 'Imrān b. al-Ḥuṣayn, al-Ash'ath b. Qays and Ibn Mas'ūd. It is famously known as the Hadith of Mercy and is traditionally the first hadith narrated in hadith gatherings before any other. Hence it is also known as *al-musalsal bi-l-awwaliyya* (the pattern-chained with firstness).

[2] See al-Qaṣaṣ (28:76-82).

quṭbāniyya for that long because its station is extremely heavy. Forty years after burying him—in Daghistan—they transported him from his cemetery to another gravesite because they were afraid the river might take away his grave. Mawlana said that when they gathered to transport him from his grave there remained no Christian, no Jew, no Zoroastrian and none of the rest of the faith-communities in the region but they all attended there. When they raised the gravestone from over his grave a fragrant scent spread which people had never experienced the like of before, like the smell of spring in our country. The scent spread and lingered in that region for forty days and they found his body still dripping with the water of his funeral bath. When they pressed his body blood would come and flow in his veins. This is how they found him and how they transported him.

Our master the Shaykh [ʿAbd Allah al-Daghistani] said that he [=Abū Aḥmad al-Thughūrī] was the only one of the Awliya to be actually found in the grave in Russian lands. Other than him of the Awliya is taken to the land of Syro-Palestine or Mecca or al-Madīna al-Munawwara. This matter took place in the time of Mawlana. As for now, his body was transported to a grave near that of Mawlana and his *maqām* is indeed in Syro-Palestine. He is Shaykh Abū Aḥmad al-Thughūrī, he was of two wings—outward knowledge and inward knowledge.

Whenever someone's defects were mentioned in front of him he would say, "O my child, he has not gone as far as we have. He is better than us!" What humbleness is this? He is saying, "Still the bad traits of our ego are more." He would supplicate and say, "May Allah make excellent his end and our end." This was his supplication because the sole consideration for the Awliya is the last things. Their gaze is fixed on the next life—where will he settle as a result of his deeds? In bliss or in wretchedness? For the servant proceeds by *then they believe, then they disbelieve* (al-Nisā' 4:137). But if his affair settles on belief then he has triumphed and is saved. If his affair did not settle there then he has perished. So he would supplicate, "May Allah make excellent his end and our end." Likewise whenever someone came and praised someone he would hear and say, "O Allah, make him firm and make excellent his end and our end."

[In answer to a question:] The *malakūt* year (=year in terms of the world of invisible sovereignty) is from the night of mid-Shaʿbān to the night of mid-Shaʿbān of the next year. The likeness of this year is for what comes to pass of major events. In this night of mid-Shaʿban there have been determined some of the major matters and massive events for the sake of the realization of what is right and true and the destruction of falsehood.

Our master the Shaykh, Sultan al-Awliya [ʿAbd Allah al-Daghistani] says–

may Allah raise his ranks, and the speech of our master the Shaykh revives hearts and brings tranquility that repels anxiety–about the attribute of the Prophets and Awliya, that they are carrying a special trust from the presence of Allah. That trust, the Awliya use it in order to awaken the servants whose hearts have not died. The dead need Isrāfīl's trumpet for them to rise. Our liege lord Isrāfīl–upon him peace–is raising that trumpet to his mouth and if he blew in it now, not one hair of the children of Ādam would move because he would have blown at his own behest. He cannot cause even an ant to die. However, **when his nurturing Lord commands Isrāfīl to blow, He will give him a breath from the breaths of holiness, and with that breath he causes death**. Otherwise, the breath of Isrāfīl, even if all the angels of the heavens and the earths took part with him in the blowing, would not affect even an ant. However, with *nafas al-qudsiyya* (the breath of holiness)[1] that is given from the All-Merciful, when Isrāfīl blows into the trumpet—*and the trumpet was blown, then whoever was in the heavens and on the earth was thunderstruck but for whomever the One God wished* (al-Zumar 39:68).

Our master the Shaykh says that the Awliya have with them this trust and the breath of holiness. When they use it they will use it to awaken the servants and for the sake of training them on the path of the truth. There is now found whoever uses that power–the breath of holiness–but its use will not be universal. Rather, it is only to a limited extent so that people will not despair. This matter appears and affects a limited number of individuals but it does not appear over the generality of people. It is only an indication that there exists power with the Awliya. For example, the government at times digs a well and, when they find water, they close it up. When they need it, they place upon it mechanisms by which they draw up water which they use. Likewise there are certain Awliya that have that power and they have permission to use it within certain limits. However, the generality of the openings are forbidden until the order for general appearance comes.

What seethes in our countries of fitnas, Allah Almighty has warned His servants against them and against opening the door of fitna by saying, *persecution is harsher than killing* (al-Baqara 2:191). Likewise our Prophet–upon him blessings and peace of Allah–warned about fitna: "**Fitna is dormant. Allah has cursed whoever awakens it**."[2] The Prophet also notified us of the stages Islamic governance will go through after his time and until the coming

[1] See Suhba I.90.

[2] Narrated from (i) Anas by al-Rāfiʿī, *al-Tadwīn fī akhbāri Qazwīn*, cf. al-Suyūṭī, *al-Jāmiʿ al-ṣaghīr* (2:135, *ḍaʿīf*); and as *al-fitnatu rātiʿa* (fitna is grazing), (ii) Ibn ʿUmar by Nuʿaym b. Ḥammād, *Fitan*; (iii) Abū al-Dardāʾ by Abū Nuʿaym, *Ḥilya*.

of the Hour saying, "**There shall be after me caliphs, and after the caliphs emirs, and after the emirs kings, and after the kings tyrants. After that there shall come out a man from the people of my House that will fill the earth with justice and right just as it had been filled with injustice and transgression.**"[1] The latter indicates that when you have reached the age of the tyrants, bear with it steadfastly and nothing more, because Allah has promised—and His promise is true—*the One God has promised those of you who believe and do righteous deeds that He shall indeed grant them succession in the land just as He granted those who were before them succession; and that He shall indeed empower for them their faith-system with which He is well-pleased for them; and that He shall indeed give them in exchange, after their fear, safety, as they worship Me without associating anything with Me* (al-Nūr 24:55). Even if the entirety of the people are unbelievers it does not matter to you. He Himself is granting you succession. So if you move, you will have stirred up a fitna, which is *harsher than killing*, and Allah has cursed whoever stirs it up.

Our nurturing Lord has given us glad tidings but we are denying His blessing and showing ingratitude by not listening to that good news. We have become *fāsiq* (depraved). Therefore we have no permission to move against those in power ever until Allah Himself replaces those people. The meaning of this is that Allah is supporting those in power. When He wants to replace them He will not support them. There is a wisdom there. And you want to stand against them? You cannot without there being fitna.

More than that, Allah has made it clear by the tongue of His Messenger–upon him the blessings and peace of Allah–*ittaqū mawāqiʿ al-tuham*, "Guard yourselves against the contexts that prompt condemnations."[2] I.e. do not put yourself in the station of condemnation. Those Ikhwān al-Muslimīn fell into the station of condemnation and this is a huge mistake. Because of their falling there they have attracted blame no matter what they did. It is like the example

[1] See Suhba I.44, second note. Cf. Suhba I.5, second note.

[2] Also translatable as "Steer clear of suspicious situations" and "Steer clear of spots that give rise to accusations." Something to that effect was related in *mawqūf* mode from (i) ʿUmar b. al-Khaṭṭāb by Zubayr b. Bakkār, *al-Muwaffaqiyyāt*, ed. Sāmī Makkī al-ʿĀnī (Beirut: ʿĀlam al-Kutub, 1416/1996) p. 32 §46; Abū Dāwūd, *al-Zuhd*; Ibn Abī al-Dunyā, *al-Ṣamt*; Ibn ʿAdī, *Kāmil* (Yaʿqūb b. Isḥāq al-Anṣārī); Khaṭīb, *Tārīkh Baghdād*; Ibn ʿAsākir, *Tārīkh Dimashq* (44:359); al-Rāfiʿī, *al-Tadwīn*; and (ii) an unnamed Companion through Ibn al-Musayyib by Abū al-Shaykh, *al-Tawbīkh wal-tanbīh*; al-Bayhaqī, *Shuʿab* (57: *Ḥusn al-khuluq, faṣl fī tark al-ghaḍab*). Cf. Zabīdī, *Itḥāf* (7:283). One time Mawlana Shaykh Nazim avoided taking a bottle of water even inside the car that picked him up at night after *tarawīḥ* in London—although parched—lest it give rise to ill thinking on the part of onlookers, and he quoted this report.

of a man who entered a winery with an empty bottle and came out with a full bottle. If he were to say "I bought vinegar," who will listen to him or believe him? The meaning of this is, do not pass through a place on which there is condemnation—and the Messenger–upon him the blessings and peace of Allah–left nothing [blameworthy] except he warned against it. Whoever does not give ear to that, let him never blame anyone but himself.[1]

From Allah is all success. By the sanctity of the Beloved, by the sanctity of the Fatiha.

[In answer to a question:][2] Is not knowledge one of the Attributes of the All-True? So does Allah have any need of the Pen and the Tablet? Does He have any need for the knowledge of the Pen or the knowledge of the Tablet? Does Allah look at the Tablet in order for His knowledge to increase? Is the knowledge of the Tablet for the benefit of One God? What are we saying—that the Pen and the Tablet are part of the Attribute of the One God? *That is the extent of their knowledge!* (al-Najm 53:30).

The knowledge of Allah is without beginning. The one that stands in need for that particular knowledge is the Prophet–upon him the blessings and peace of Allah. Even if we said that "part of your knowledge, O Muhammad, is the knowledge of the Tablet and the Pen," we would not be adding anything to him because **he–upon him the blessings and peace of Allah–is the manifestation of the knowledge of the first and the last.**[3] And he is the one concerning whom the nurturing Lord of the worlds has said *and never have We sent you but as a mercy for the worlds* (al-Anbiyā' 21:107). Are not this life and the next part of *the worlds*? So what can you do if gives from this knowledge to some people?

[1] This is the wording of the report from 'Umar b. al-Khaṭṭāb cited in the above note.

[2] About verse 154 in al-Būṣīrī's *Burda* addressing the Prophet with the words, *fa-inna min jūdika al-dunyā wa-ḍarratahā / wa-min 'ulūmika 'ilma al-lawḥi wal-qalami* (for verily part of your munificence are this world and the next, and part of your sciences is the knowledge of the Tablet and the Pen). For the commentaries of the reliable scholars on this passage see Haddad, *Albani and His Friends*, 2nd ed. (pp. 184-190).

[3] I.e. the Qur'ān. See also the first part of the hadith of the Highest Assembly (=the angels): "I felt drowsy in my prayer until I dozed off. Lo and behold, I found myself in front of my nurturing Lord in the best form. He said: 'O Muḥammad!' I replied: 'At Your service, O my nurturing Lord!' He said: 'Over what do the Highest Assembly compete?' I said, 'I do not know, O my nurturing Lord.' This went on three times. Then I saw Him put His palm between my shoulders and I felt the coolness of His fingers in my innermost, whereupon everything in heaven and on earth became manifest to me and I knew." Narrated from Mu'ādh b. Jabal by Dāraquṭnī, *al-Ru'ya* (p. 340 §254) and its basis is in al-Tirmidhī, (*Tafsīr, min Sūrat Ṣād, ḥasan ṣaḥīḥ*).

Allah has prevented them from understanding because of their narrow-mindedness. If there exists some person that is neither male nor female, how can you make them understand something about men? Can you make them understand? Their understanding is limited. Is there any contradiction to the categorical proof-texts in this verse, "and part of your sciences is the knowledge of the Tablet and the Pen"? Whoever objects does so because of their obduracy and arrogance in themselves just as took place among the pontiffs of the Quraysh against the Prophethood of the Messenger, and their statement, why did you receive revelation but we did not? Those ones will never succeed.

By the sanctity of the Beloved, by the sanctity of the Fatiha.

81
The world is under control

I seek refuge in Allah from the accursed devil
In the Name of Allah the All-Beneficent the Most Merciful
There is no power nor strength but with Allah the High, the Magnificent
Permission, O my Master, support!
Our way is companionship, and goodness is in the congregation

Ibrahim Ad-ham loved hunting. One day as he was running after a gazelle a caller called out to him from the whip that was tied to his saddle, "O Ibrahim! Is this what you were created for or what you were commanded?" This was a lordly call. He left the gazelle and returned, although hunting and fishing on land and water are licit. However, the activity of the hunter and the fisher is not something praised and blessed. Our liege lord ʿĪsā b. Maryam imprecated them when he said "There is no blessing in a hunter/fisher." When Allah prohibited fishing on the Sabbath for the Jews, they dug ponds so that the fish would come into them.[1] *Their fish would come to them on their Sabbath-day, appearing on the surface of the water* (Aʿrāf 7:163), so they would dig and open up ponds so that the fish would go down into them on the Sabbath-day. They would claim that they are not hunting but on the next day they would come and catch the fish. It became trickery, so Allah became angry with them and turned them into apes and swine.[2] They lived on for a few days in that form, after which they died.

Allah is not restricted by anything. He does what He wishes and He decides what He wants. When He wants something *He says for it, "Be!"—and it is* (Yā Sīn 36:82). This world in which we live is controlled by the order of *the Sunna* (custom, way) *of the One God* (al-Aḥzāb 33:38, 33:62). Allah has appointed for it customs, i.e. laws, i.e. causes and effects for everything. This is why causes appear from which effects result. Without a man and a woman getting together, by the power of Allah, it is possible for the woman to give birth to a child—this is the power of Allah. But the custom of Allah is for the two of them to get together for the woman to become pregnant. So then Allah is not restricted by this matter because when He wants something *He says for it, "Be!"—and it is.*

[1] See the Quranic commentaries on al-Baqara 2:65 and al-Aʿrāf 7:163.

[2] See the Quranic commentaries on al-Māʾida 5:60, 5:115.

Birds do not have reasons. Everyone's reason moves them. Do bees work with their own minds? No, but their craft boggles the minds. They are in need of three things—reason, knowledge, craft. Yet whoever claimed that bees possess reason? If it possessed reason it would not come to bite the human being only then to die. So they have no reason. If you knew that you would die immediately after mating with a woman would you still mate with her? So then there must be one that is arranging and moving everything, and He is the One that is controlling them and moving them, and were it not for Him they could not produce a single drop of honey. "Each is facilitated for that for which it was created."[1] There is a kind of bee called *zalqaṭ*[2] (yellow wasp) that does not produce honey and there is also the *dabbūr* (bumblebee) that eats the bees. There is the *iḥyā' al-mutaṣarrif* (reviving by the one with discretionary power) who has discretionary power over creatures and whose task is the reviving of this matter. At the foundation the reviving is from Allah but there appears causes for it.

From Allah is all success. By the sanctity of the Fatiha.

[1] Part of the Prophetic hadith on foreordained destiny, "There is not a single soul among you but its residence is already known in Paradise and Hell." They said, "Messenger of Allah—then what are we working for?" He said, "Work! For each is facilitated for that which he was created for." Narrated from (i-xiii) Abū Bakr al-Ṣiddīq, 'Umar b. al-Khaṭṭāb, 'Alī b. Abī Ṭālib, Jābir, Surāqa b. Mālik b. Ju'shum, Sa'd b. Abī Waqqāṣ, 'Imrān b. Ḥuṣayn, Dhū al-Liḥya Shurayḥ b. 'Āmir al-Kilābī, Abū al-Dardā', Ibn Mas'ūd, Abū Ḥumayd al-Sā'idī, Abū Asīd Ḥudhayfa b. Asīd, Anas and Abū Hurayra in the Six Books, the *Musnad* and elsewhere.

[2] Or *zurquṭa*.

82

Some virtues of the blessings on the Prophet – Praying at the times of greatest merit – [Tariqa high resolve forbids speaking of people's defects – Keep steadfast endurance and do not get angry]

I seek refuge in Allah from the accursed devil
In the Name of Allah the All-Beneficent the Most Merciful
There is no power nor strength but with Allah the High, the Magnificent
Permission, O my Master, support!
Our way is companionship, and goodness is in the congregation

My nurturing Lord! Expand for me my breast, make easy for me my case, and undo a knot in my tongue so that they will understand my statement (Ṭa Ha 20:25-28). Allah Almighty supports His friends with the breath of holiness.

Our master Sultan al-Awliya [Shaykh ʿAbd Allah al-Daghistani] says that when Allah ordered the people of belief to invoke blessings and greetings of purity and peace on our Prophet–upon him blessings and peace of Allah–they asked Him, "How should we invoke blessings on you and greet you, O Messenger of Allah?" The Messenger taught them, "Say, O Allah, bless Muhammad and the Family of Muhammad and greet them."[1] This is a teaching of the Messenger and there are many different ways of invoking noble blessings using which there is no impediment, but according to our honorable masters the Prophet's teaching is best. *Allāhumma ṣalli ʿalā Muḥammadin wa-ʿalā āli Muḥammadin wa-sallim.*

Our master the Shaykh says that *ṣalawāt* are magnification of the Prophet. Allah has commanded the believers to magnify and venerate our liege lord Muhammad–upon him the blessings and peace of Allah–and Mawlana says that **it is to the extent of our magnification of our liege lord Muhammad that we earn the good pleasure of Allah Almighty. This is an important report. This is why the doctrine of the people of truth is the magnification of the Messenger–upon him the blessings and peace of Allah.**

As much as we magnify the Messenger of Allah we shall be earning more from Allah. This is why the one that invokes blessings on the Prophet–upon him the blessings and peace of Allah–every day to a certain amount –even if

[1] See *The Musnad of Ahl al-Bayt*, second hadith for full wording and documentation.

he invokes blessings on the Prophet a thousand times—Allah has promised that he will not see straitened circumstances whether in this life or in the next, his body will be prohibited for the Fire and he will not be burnt whether by the fire of this life or by the fire of the hereafter, and he will be protected against strifes. Our master the Shaykh used to say **the greatest mujahid has that [devotion], one thousand invocations of blessings on the Prophet daily. Even the breath with which he breathes in his sleep is better and more excellent than the worship of the common public one and all.**

Our master the Shaykh says that the people of high resolve on Monday, Thursday and Friday—three days, or the nights that precede them—hold fast to one thousand *ṣalawāt* and when they want to add to one thousand in the nights as opposed to the days, Allah creates from each invocation an angel from His power that has 70,000 wings, each wing carrying 70,000 heads, each head possessing 70,000 tongues, and this angel plunges in the sea of the Prophet–upon him the blessings and peace of Allah–then comes out and shakes the water off its feathers. From each of these drops Allah creates angels that keep invoking blessings on the Prophet until the Day of Resurrection. The reward will be given and inscribed into the records of that servant. That is the immense virtue that is promised for now.

Mawlana also instructed that the five prayers must be prayed in the meritorious time because offering prayers in the meritorious time is an obligation for the people of high resolve. Mawlana explained the meritorious time by saying, "'The Hajj is 'Arafa'[1] and on the day of 'Arafa a person must be on the mountain of 'Arafāt." He said that on that day Allah opens up a manifestation on the people that are present on the day of 'Arafāt. Whoever is present, they have obtained that gaze and with that manifestation they become a Hājj, i.e. one's Hajj is now complete. He said the rest of the rituals are like the engraving.[2] The foundation is to stand in 'Arafāt and to be present if only for a portion of that time so that that manifestation will reach him even for a brief moment—he will be a Hājj. As for the rest of the pilgrimage rituals such as circumambulation, running [between Ṣafā and Marwa], casting the stones, sacrificing and donning the sacred garb, they are all engraving on top of that manifestation that lasts two hours.[3]

[1] A Prophetic hadith narrated from 'Abd al-Raḥmān b. Ya'mur Dīlī by Aḥmad (31:63-64 §18773-774); Abū Dāwūd (*Manāsik, man lam yudrik 'Arafa*); Tirmidhī (*Ḥajj, mā jā'a fīman adraka al-imām bi-jam'*; *Tafsīr*, al-Baqara 2:203, *ḥasan ṣaḥīḥ*); al-Nasā'ī (*Manāsik al-Ḥajj, farḍ al-wuqūf bi-'Arafa*); Ibn Mājah (*Manāsik, man atā 'Arafata qabl al-fajr laylata jam'*); al-Dārimī (*Manāsik, bi-mā yatimm al-Ḥajj*); and others.

[2] I.e. the metaphorical throne has been firmly set, the rest is like the engraving on it.

[3] Per the Prophetic hadith, "Whoever prays this prayer of ours and has come to 'Arafa

This is the excellence of the particular time because there is a divine gaze on it. This gaze gives immense value to that time. Mawlana says that because of that divine gaze, the servants get cleaned of any blameworthy traits of character that are in them and they become pure. With that manifestation the angels descend with that mercy in that time. Just as this matter takes place in ʿArafāt, likewise in the five prayers there is the most excellent time. The gaze of the All-True is there and because of it the angels descend with that mercy. Mawlana says that **the most excellent time is from the call to prayer until half an hour or one hour later. In the early time there will be the manifestation of the good pleasure of Allah. In the middle time there is the mercy of Allah and in the late time the forgiveness of Allah**. If the time between *ẓuhr* and *ʿaṣr* is three hours the manifestation in the first hour is the good pleasure of Allah, in the second the mercy of Allah and in the third the forgiveness of Allah. The divine gaze falls in the beginning of the time, in the first half hour or the first hour.

Just as the divine gaze that falls on ʿArafāt burns away crimes that were incurred by the children of Ādam, likewise the gaze that falls on the five prayers burn away the crimes and the blameworthy traits of character that are in the worshipper. Nothing of that is left. It is all burnt away and cleaned up so that it does not move to the hereafter. As for the rest of the time, the gaze is not there but mercy remains. Allah Most High has said, *verily the prayer forbids indecency and wrongdoing; and indeed the remembrance of the One God is greater* (ʿAnkabūt 29:45). These prayers now serve to forbid indecency and wrongdoing. As for the eternal bliss of the servant, it is in the first of the time because he earns the gaze of Allah. This is why it is a duty for the people of resolve to observe that and to do their prayer in the preferred time. After that, the people of resolve must observe and give value to the Sunnas just as they give value to the categorical obligations.

Mawlana asks, what is the duty of the people of high resolve towards people? Whoever holds fast to the strictness of the sacred Law, how must his interaction or his state be with all the servants of Allah? For our nurturing Lord has said, *and We have certainly honored the children of Ādam* (Banū Isrāʾīl/Isrāʾ 17:70). **He did not distinguish between human beings because they are all sorts and all kinds that are without limit and without count. Rather He gathered them and He included them all in the honor from His presence. This is important. The outlook of the one that holds fast to the strictness of the Law must be the same as the gaze of the All-True–glorified is He. In**

before that during part of the night or part of the day, his Hajj is complete and he has finished his *tafath* (unkemptness)." Narrated from ʿUrwa b. Muḍarris by al-Ṭaḥāwī, *Aḥkām al-Qurʾān*; *Sharḥ mushkil al-āthār*; *Sharḥ maʿānī al-āthār*.

the presence of our nurturing Lord there is no distinction, and the people of *ʿazīma* must know with certainty that all human beings—whether depraved or open sinners or unbelievers—are subsumed under the address *We have certainly honored* and this honoring is comprising all! He did not specify one section of them but made the honoring inclusive of all. This firm conviction is necessary, and when they recognize that they are all subsumed under that address, the people of firm resolve must refrain from speaking out about people's blemishes.

This is the correct manner for the people of high resolve in the most distinguished Tariqa no matter what the blemishes of the others are. Let it be. You are inherently not allowed to look at the blemishes of anyone, let alone speak about them. That is forbidden! It is a duty to guard the tongue and the gaze. Mawlana is saying that all human beings are honored, but you might hear from one of them a word or there might come to you some gesture that is rough on their part in whatever form, which your ego dislikes. Mawlana says that if there comes to you from any person by hand or verbally that which disturbs you, your nurturing Lord addresses you on the spot, saying, "O My servant! listen to what I say! *but whoever pardons and conciliates, his wage rests upon the One God* (al-Shūrā 42:40). This is My instruction O My servant. I pardon him, and with the blessing of your pardon there will be reconciliation between you. It will be a process of reconciliation between people. Take your recompense from Me." This requires endurance so that one will take one's recompense from Allah Almighty. Instead we say, "O Allah, we want to wage war against him and exact our right, we do not want anything from You." Thus does the servant respond. "I want to follow the devil and I am not following You" whereas Allah is saying, *whoever pardons and conciliates.*

Heed your nurturing Lord and earn His good pleasure. Do not heed the devil and destroy yourself. At that time you will become the example of divine anger because the Prophet–upon him the blessings and peace of Allah–says, "Fitna is asleep. Allah has cursed whoever awakens it,"[1] and *ṣabr* (endurance) is the key to Paradise[2]—its door does not open except with endurance. Mawlana says, if one of the children of Ādam heard Iblīs saying to him, "Eat from this, my filth," would he eat it? Iblīs is tasking that servant, he is activating him,

[1] See Suhba I.80, fifth note.

[2] Per the Prophetic hadiths I. "Endurance and preparing for a reward are among the things that free the necks from Hellfire, and they bring their doer into Paradise without reckoning," narrated from al-Ḥakam b. ʿUmayr by al-Ṭabarānī, *al-Muʿjam al-kabīr*; II. "The *fuqarāʾ al-ṣubur* (all-enduring poor)—they are the ones sitting with Allah on the Day of Resurrection," narrated from (i) Ibn ʿUmar by Abū al-Ḥasan al-Azdī, *Min ḥadīth Mālik b. Anas* §69); and (ii) ʿUmar by al-Qushayrī, *Risāla* (*al-Faqr*).

he is making him angry, and he is saying to him, "Eat." When he eats he becomes like the mouse that fell into the wine jar, became drunk and started shouting, "Where are the cats?" This is how he becomes when he gets angry, meaning Iblīs is feeding the servant his filth. But when you endure you will be demolishing him.

You must know that the human being is not infallible and that when he gets angry his mind disappears and no trace of mind or belief remains with him. Endure patiently. The first moment is difficult then it becomes easy, but we break down from the first test. This is why, if we endure patiently from the first of the test we will overcome our ego, and Allah supports His servant and catches him. Mawlana says that enduring servant will be like a magnet for the care and support of Allah, and his endurance will be a cause for the guidance of that servant.

By the sanctity of the Beloved, by the sanctity of the Fatiha.

83
The excellence of the *basmala* – The Praiseworthy Station – The nib of the Pen

I seek refuge in Allah from the accursed devil
In the Name of Allah the All-Beneficent the Most Merciful
There is no power nor strength but with Allah the High, the Magnificent
Permission, O my Master, support!
Our way is companionship, and goodness is in the congregation

Writing exists from the time of our liege lord Idrīs.[1] He was the first one to write with his hand, in Aramaic. When Allah created the light of our liege lord Muhammad–upon him the blessings and peace of Allah–He created from his light the most exalted Pen, then He created the preserved Tablet. He ordered the Pen to write what is and what shall be.[2] The Pen is created by Allah. The first thing the Pen wrote is *bismi-l-Lāhi-r-raḥmāni-r-raḥīm*. Its writing took 700 of our years and whoever says *bismi-l-Lāhi-r-raḥmāni-r-raḥīm* a single time to express magnification, Allah has promised him to give him the reward of 700 years. Our age will not reach 700 years but Allah in His bounty has given to the Umma of the Beloved, because of a single naming, the reward of 700 years. Allah is the bestower of immense bounty. When He gives, nothing diminishes from His storehouses. He awaits whoever will ask him so that He will give him.

The holder of the Pen is carrying it. Who is "the Pen"? He is one of the creatures of Allah in charge of whom is a Muhammadan inheritor. The holder of the Pen is the purity of origin of the Messenger of Allah. The Muhammadan inheritor is in charge of it on *yawm al-maḥshar* (the Day of the Regathering). When Allah judges between the servants as He has promised us: *so whoever does even a small ant's weight in goodness shall see it and whoever does even a small ant's weight in evil shall see it* (Zalzala 99:7-8). And He shall pass final judgment and separate the servants—these go to Paradise, and these go to

[1] Narrated as part of a long hadith from (i) Abū Dharr by al-Ṭaḥāwī, *Mushkil* (14:385 §5695); Ibn Ḥibbān, *Ṣaḥīḥ* (2:76-77 §361) and others; (ii) Ibn Isḥāq by Ibn Hishām, *Sīra* (1:3). See also Abū ʿArūba al-Ḥusayn b. Muḥammad al-Ḥarrānī, *al-Awā'il*, ed. Mashʿal al-Muṭayrī (Beirut: Dār Ibn Ḥazm, 1424/2003) p. 51 §19; Abū Hilāl al-ʿAskarī, *al-Awā'il*, ed. Muḥ. al-Sayyid al-Wakīl (Ṭanṭā: Dār al-Bashīr, 1408/1987) p. 423; al-Thaʿlabī; al-Jurjānī, *Darj*; and others.

[2] A Prophetic hadith narrated from ʿUbāda b. al-Ṣāmit by Ṭayālisī and Ibn al-Jaʿd in their *Musnads*; al-Tirmidhī (*gharīb*); Ibn Abī ʿĀṣim, *al-Sunna*; al-Firyābī, *al-Qadar*; al-Ṭabarī (al-Qalam 68:1); Ibn Qāniʿ, *Muʿjam al-Ṣaḥāba*; al-Ājurrī, *al-Sharīʿa*.

Hellfire.[1] After that, *He decrees what He will* (al-Mā'ida 5:1) and *He does what He wants* (Āl 'Imrān 3:40, al-Ḥajj 22:18).[2]

He shall call the Messenger–upon him the blessings and peace of Allah–and He shall make him sit in the seat of judgment. That is the praiseworthy Station. He shall say to him, " I have passed judgment exactly as I have promised, after which I am absolutely free." Allah is free with His will, His acts, His handiwork, His creation. Everything is justice from Him. He shall order the Prophet–upon him blessings and peace–to sit in the station of judgment. He shall give him the most exalted Pen and say to him, "I have passed judgment between the servants and I am now handing over the judgment to you. So you may send whomever you wish to Paradise and whomever to Hellfire."[3] At the same time Allah shall manifest Himself with the mercy of ninety-nine Names from the beautiful Names of Allah. After that He shall manifest Himself with the mercy of the greatest Name of Allah. It shall join them so that, under that manifestation, a thing will be seen as something else. All the servants will be dressed with the manifestations of mercy and it shall purify them. At that time where will the Messenger find any attribute or any trace of anyone so that he should send him to Hellfire? And the Pen shall write the command of the Prophet. Our liege lord Sharaf al-Din [al-Daghistani] said that the nib of the Pen is Mawlana Shaykh 'Abd Allah–may Allah sanctify his secret. And this is from the vast mercy of Allah.

May Allah grant us and you the best end.

[1] A Prophetic hadith narrated from (i) 'Abd al-Raḥmān b. Qatāda al-Sulamī by al-Ṭabarī; Ibn Qāni', *Mu'jam al-Ṣaḥāba*; (ii) Hishām b. Ḥakīm by al-Firyābī, *al-Qadar*; al-Ājurrī, *al-Sharī'a*; al-Ṭabarānī, *Musnad al-Shāmiyyīn*; Ibn Mandah, *al-Radd 'alā al-Jahmiyya*; al-Bayhaqī, *al-Asmā' wal-ṣifāt*; (iii) Ibn 'Abbās by al-Ājurrī, *al-Sharī'a*; (iv) Abū Hurayra in *mawqūf* mode by al-Bayhaqī, *al-Qaḍā' wal-qadar*; al-Ḥasan in *maqṭū'* mode by al-Firyābī (ditto).

[2] See Suhbas I.24; I.34; II.4.

[3] See to this effect the Prophetic hadith:
إِنَّ رَبِّي اسْتَشَارَنِي فِي أُمَّتِي مَاذَا أَفْعَلُ بِهِمْ، فَقُلْتُ: مَا شِئْتَ أَيْ رَبِّ، هُمْ خَلْقُكَ وَعِبَادُكَ، فَاسْتَشَارَنِي الثَّانِيَةَ، فَقُلْتُ لَهُ كَذَلِكَ، فَقَالَ: لَا أُحْزِنُكَ فِي أُمَّتِكَ يَا مُحَمَّدُ
"Verily my nurturing Lord has consulted me with regard to my Umma: 'What should I do with them?' So I said, 'Whatever You wish, yes, my nurturing Lord! They are Your creatures and Your servants.' Then He asked my advice a second time so I said to Him likewise. Then He said, 'I shall not make you sad with regard to your Umma, O Muhammad!'" Narrated from (i) Ḥudhayfa b. al-Yamān by Aḥmad (38:361 §23336), a fair report with a fair chain per Ibn Kathīr, *Bidāya* (*dhikr mā warada fīl-ḥawḍ al-Nabawī al-Muḥammadī*) and al-Haythamī, *Majma' al-zawā'id* (10:71); Abū Bakr al-Shāfi'ī, *Ghaylāniyyāt* (p. 682 §927); and (ii) 'Awf b. Mālik al-Ashja'ī by Ibn Khuzayma, *al-Tawḥīd* (*dhikr takhyīr Allah Nabiyyahu*).

84

"Fitna is dormant, Allah curses whoever awakens it" – *Whoever pardons and conciliates, his wage rests upon the One God* – Rank of readiness in Tariqa – Pharaoh's judgment against himself – [Can women be soldiers?] – *Fiṭra* in slaughtering

I seek refuge in Allah from the accursed devil
In the Name of Allah the All-Beneficent the Most Merciful
There is no power nor strength but with Allah the High, the Magnificent
Permission, O my Master, support!
Our way is companionship, and goodness is in the congregation

Any human being that follows the devil is inevitably eating of its filth.[1] So "Fitna is dormant, Allah has cursed whoever awakens it."[2] There is no power nor strength but with Allah the High, the Magnificent! The Prophet – upon him the blessings and peace of Allah–said, "Endurance is the key to Paradise."[3] *And persecution is harsher than killing* (Baqara 2:191). Iblīs's job is to make fitna happen. A thousand fitnas are found every day. With your wife, your children, your siblings, your neighbors. He says: "This is a ʿAlawī." "This is a Shīʿī." "This is a Communist." "This is a Satanist." There are a thousand fitnas.

Mawlana [Shaykh ʿAbd Allah al-Daghistani] and our honorable Shaykhs teach us how the All-True looks upon His servants and we must look upon them just as the All-True looks upon them. And this shall save us from falling into fitnas. He–exalted is He–said, *and We have certainly honored the children of Ādam* (Banū Isrā'īl/Isrā' 17:70). He said *the children of Ādam* and He did not say Arab, Turk, Sunni, Shiʿi or anything else. Has not their nurturing Lord dressed them with the attribute of humanness? So then He has honored them. He–exalted is He–is saying, "they are My servants, I have honored them," i.e. "I have given them value. All of them, in My presence, have immense value." The servant must look at them the way his nurturing Lord looks at them: "this

[1] See Mawlana's remark further down, "We use coarse language so that one will feel repulsion. When you feel repulsion, you will rise from the station of *the inciteful ego* (Yūsuf 12:53) to the station of *the indictive soul* (al-Qiyāma 75:2)."

[2] See Suhba I.80, fifth note.

[3] See Suhba I.82, sixth note.

is the servant of my Lord," "that is the servant of my Lord." All human beings—their forelocks are in whose hand? In the hand of Allah, so that Iblīs cannot interfere, i.e. He did not leave their forelocks to Iblīs. Mawlana [Shaykh ʿAbd Allah] has explained this noble verse for 40 years: *and We have certainly honored the children of Ādam* (Banū Isrā'īl/Isrā' 17:70). He was saying, "if I sat from the beginning of this world to its end explaining this verse or clarifying the meanings contained in the ocean of *We have honored*, I would not be able to."

Despite that, we have said that Iblīs is walking among us. How did he enter the space of Paradise and cause fitna to befall our mother Ḥawwā' and our father Ādam in the first place? Is he going to leave their children in peace? We are living as a collective but we believe that we are living as individuals. This is why, when a human being mixes with other human beings, he wants to be the only one to rule in every aspect. He does not like to listen to anyone or to do anyone else's will. He wants to be independent and alone in his opinion, and he wants for everything to run according to his will. But even in your own house it is impossible to achieve this. Your wife does not do your bidding, nor do your children, nor do your father and mother, nor do your siblings, and nor do your neighbors. No one in command and no one under orders does what you want. There is always confrontation, contradiction and disagreement.

Our master the Shaykh says that from the moment you wake up and until you sleep you may see that which displeases you to see or to hear because people are not under the control of your will. Each one of them wants to proceed as he himself likes. Hence his moves are not acceptable to you. You run away from him. He is the opposite of lovely to you. He shows harshness which he himself does not see. On the contrary it is natural to him and he reckons himself innocent of any wrongdoing. As long as people's harshness has no end then the divine instruction to us is, *but whoever pardons and conciliates, then his wage rests upon the One God* (Shūrā 42:40). We have to hold fast to this instruction. *Whoever pardons* despite people's harshness *and conciliates, then his wage rests upon the One God.* Allah Most High is saying, *and We have appointed some of you as a trial for others—will you patiently endure? And your nurturing Lord is ever All-Seeing* (al-Furqān 25:20). Our harshness towards one another—this is a test from Allah for us.

Our master the Shaykh says that whoever has reached the level of readiness in the most distinguished Tariqa may see Iblīs. Likewise, he may also see from the start Iblīs's underlings among human beings. He recognizes them unmistakably. He may look at a man and very quickly his heart recognizes that he is of the camp of Iblīs and his troops. One might recognize at the first sight that a person is one of Iblīs's soldiers. Another, as soon as he hears someone's name, he will know from the start that he is one of them. **The heart will not make mistakes.**[1] Many times one hears someone's name and at the mere mention of his name the heart banishes him. At the peak of readiness one may see Iblīs walking with that person and likewise his *qarīn* (peer). **We use coarse language so that one will feel repulsion. When you feel repulsion, you will rise from the station of *the inciteful ego* (Yūsuf 12:53) to the station of *the indictive soul* (al-Qiyāma 75:2).** You are the slave of Allah and your master knows what He dressed you with and where you are removing your garment from yourself.

Mawlana recounted that one of the Companions sent his brother—also a Companion—to ask for a woman in marriage. When he went to make the proposal the family said to him, "we will not give our daughter to your brother but we will marry her to you if you accept." They married off their daughter to that man. The latter remained out of sight for a week and was nowhere to be found. At last his brother found him and asked him where he had been. He said, "I got married." He asked, "What happened regarding the proposal?" He said, "They married her off to me and out of shame before you, I did not show myself to you." He said to him, "O my brother, are you ashamed? I am the one that should be ashamed. I put my gaze on your share. It is you who must forgive me and do not ask me to forgive you!" The other one quickly repented and asked forgiveness of Allah, saying, "I am the one that did wrong by asking for your share. Forgive me, O my brother."

This is a divine order. When one of the rulings of Allah appears and our ego desires something different we must repent. "We repent and we return to Allah." We have committed wrong, O our nurturing Lord! How many matters, when we want them but the opposite appears, we become upset. But when the command of Allah and His will appear, we must quickly keep our heart still and be at peace. This is the meaning of *behold, with the remembrance of the One God are the hearts at peace!* (Ra'd 13:28). **When you remember Allah has willed it—in this way the heart quickly is at peace. But for someone to reach that rank is very difficult. For the ego is inciteful of evil. When you have expelled your egotism from between yourself and your nurturing Lord, at that time you will have obtained that station.**

In the hereafter our scrolls will be unrolled and the human being will look at his scrolls right away. For each human being seventy scrolls are recorded against him in his world.[2] In the hereafter his scrolls are unrolled, and the

[1] As meant in the instruction "always follow the first inspiration" (Shaykh Hisham).

[2] Narrated from ʿAbd Allāh b. ʿAmr b. al-ʿĀṣ by I. al-Khaṭīb al-Baghdādī, *al-Amālī bi-*

matter of the hereafter is not like the matter of this world—you open the book and you read the first page from the first line to the last, then you turn the page and so forth, no. Over there, there is immediate totality. The vision of the human being will be total and all-inclusive. He will appear, look and read all his life in a single gaze that encompasses all his life. At that time it will be said to him, what is your judgment concerning that man? He himself will judge himself so that there can be no injustice, just as Firʿawn passed judgment against himself. Two angels came to him in the form of human beings and asked him, "Our king sent us to you to ask you about a slave that ran away from him after he had immersed him in his bounty. What is his requital?" He replied, "To drown in the sea!" When they decided to leave, to leave no doubt to Firʿawn, they said, "We want a document signed and sealed by you because our king might not accept from us a mere verbal report. So give us a paper sealed with the ruling." They took the paper and they showed it to him at the time he was drowning, saying to him, "This is your judgment against yourself."[1]

Therefore, on the Day of Resurrection, there will be no leeway for the servant to object and say, "this judgment does not suit me, this is injustice." And after each has passed judgment on himself, Allah is not obligated to agree with his verdict. He is free to forgive or to punish. *Then He shall forgive whomever He wishes and He shall punish whomever He wishes* (Baqara 2:284). No one can force Him. Mawlana says, "Take your nurturing Lord's good pleasure and forgive others, because severity does not generate other than regrets, and whoever was granted gentleness has been provided the goodness of this world and the next." It is general advice for us to use gentleness no matter the cost, even if it is high. Allah said, *there is no protector today from the command of the One God, except whomever He grants mercy* (Hūd 11:43). The hard-hearted will be killed. As for the possessors of heart filled with mercy, they are sources of mercy for the servants. They abide.

In our time hearts have become like stone, even those of women let alone men. The hearts of women have turned to stone, they have gone far from the sources of mercy, and you see the strangest things in their treatment of their husbands and their children. Can women be soldiers? They cannot—unless the attribute of mercy has disappeared from the woman's heart. "As you judge, so will you be judged."[2]

jāmiʿ Dimashq, ed. pp. 92-93 §33 (seventy-seven scrolls); II. Aḥmad; al-Tirmidhī; Ibn Ḥibbān; al-Ḥākim; al-Baghawī, *Sharḥ al-Sunna*; and others (ninety-nine scrolls).

[1] İsmail Hakkı Bursevî, *Tafsīr rūḥ al-bayān* (al-Ṣāffāt 37:24-26).

[2] *Kamā tadīnū tudānū*. Part of a longer hadith narrated (i) in *mursal* mode from Abū Qilāba (d. 104/722), from the Prophet–upon him blessings and peace–by ʿAbd al-

The Prophet–upon him the blessings and peace of Allah–says, "Those that are merciful, the All-Merciful grants them mercy."[1] His Name is the All-Merciful but this cycle shall become complete this year at the appearance of the completion of the noble verse [in which] the noble angels [queried] Allah by saying, *"Will You place in it those who will spread corruption in it and shed blood,*[2] from the perspective of complete corruption giving rise to general bloodshed whereas mercy is present. If a human being wanted to slaughter [even] a bird, the innate disposition of the possessor of a pure heart will refuse to do so, and were it not that Allah has ordered slaughtering he would not slaughter. This is why Allah ordered for us to say, at the time of slaughtering, *bismi-l-Lāh* (in the Name of the One God). Glory to the one Who made slaughtering licit with *bismi-l-Lāh, Allāhu akbar!* This makes it lighter on the pure soul and makes the slaughtering valid. otherwise the pure nature does not want to slaughter. That is from the soundness of the conscience and the purity of belief. For the Prophet himself did slaughter, and there is none among creatures who is more compassionate and merciful than out Prophet–upon him the blessings and peace of Allah–and also slaughtering is obedience to the divine command.

So then you must choose. Is it necessary to listen to Iblīs and take his assent? Or rather is it necessary to listen to your nurturing Lord and obtain His good pleasure? When something of the harshness of people appears to you, you are ordered to pardon and conciliate. "Pardon your brother and conciliate and take your reward from Me!" Iblīs says, "Beat him! Kill him so that you will vent your anger! How can you sit still in the face of his harshness?" When we

Razzāq, *Muṣannaf* and through him, Bayhaqī, *al-Zuhd al-Kabīr* and *al-Asmā' wal-Ṣifāt*, ed. ʿAbd Allāh al-Ḥāshidī, 2 vols. (Jeddah: Maktabat Sawādī, 1413/1993) 1:197 §132=ed. Muḥ. Zāhid al-Kawtharī (Beirut: Dār Iḥyā' al-Turāth al-ʿArabī, n.d., repr. of the 1358/1939 Cairo edition) p. 79; (ii) with a continuous *musnad* but very weak chain from Ibn ʿUmar by Ibn ʿAdī, *al-Kāmil fīl-Ḍuʿafā'* (7:348); and (iii) as a saying of Abū al-Dardā' and Mālik b. Dīnār quoting the Torah, by Aḥmad, *Zuhd*. Its meaning is confirmed by several narrations in *Ṣaḥīḥ al-Bukhārī*: *lā tūkī fa-yūkā ʿalayki; lā tuḥṣī fa-yuḥṣiya ʿalayki; lā tūʿī fa-yūʿiya Allāh ʿalayki* all in *Kitāb al-Zakāt, al-taḥrīḍ ʿalā al-ṣadaqa* and the next chapter, also *Kitāb al-Hiba, hibat al-mar'a li-ghayr zawjihā*. It is a leitmotiv of Judeo-Christian Scripture (cf. Jg 1:7, Ps 137:8, Ob 1:15, Mk 4:24, Lk 6:38) and an Arabic proverb cf. ʿAskarī (310-ca. 400/922-1010), *Jamharat al-Amthāl* (§1460), Abū al-Faḍl al-Maydānī (d. 518/1124), *Majmaʿ al-Amthāl* (*kamā*), and al-Zamakhsharī, *al-Mustaqṣā min Amthāl al-ʿArab* (*k-m-y*). Mawlana is hereby referring to the Day of Judgment. "*Yawm al-Dīn* is 'the Day of Retribution;' whence 'As you judge, so will you be judged'" (Bayḍāwī, al-Fātiḥa 1:4).

[1] See Suhba I.80, third note.

[2] The completion of the statement is, *"while we extol with Your praise and we keep holy for You?" He said, "Verily I know what you do not know"* (al-Baqara 2:30).

listen to Iblīs the result will be to fall into affliction. At that time you will be either killer or killed, and affliction happens. Allah Most High said, *but whoever pardons and conciliates, then his wage rests upon the One God* (Shūrā 42:40), and Mawlana explains the Messenger's hadith, "Endurance is the key to Paradise"[1] to mean that by enduring you will enter Paradise, and you will also be in Paradise in this world as a result of your endurance. And whoever does not endure, pain will still smite him. You do not want to endure because this is too heavy for you, but likewise even if you do not endure. For affliction descends and then in spite of yourself you must endure all the same. This is why we supplicate, *Allāhumma iḥfaẓnā min sāʿat al-ghafla*. "O Allah, guard us against the moment of heedlessness." In one instant you follow Iblīs and after that you will be in pain all your life. An eyeblink brings you the regret of a lifetime.

May Allah protect us and you by the sanctity of the Beloved, by the sanctity of the Fatiha.

[1] See Suhba I.82, sixth note.

85

One's safety is in keeping custody of the tongue – [Allah curses whoever awakens fitna]

I seek refuge in Allah from the accursed devil
In the Name of Allah the All-Beneficent the Most Merciful
There is no power nor strength but with Allah the High, the Magnificent
Permission, O my Master, support!
Our way is companionship, and goodness is in the congregation

The human being is not infallible. It means the human being errs and sins. A man might come to you acting harshly towards you. You must endure patiently all people. Not all people are Prophets or saints. They might be ignorant. When one of them acts with ignorance you must have endurance and forbearance. For the ones that are ignorant are following the devil to the point they will become ignorant, and if they were following their nurturing Lord they would not be ignorant. When one behaves ignorantly towards you, you must not act ignorantly with them also. Allah Most High says, *and the servants of the All-Merciful who tread upon the earth lightly, and when the ignorant address them they say, "Peace"* (al-Furqān 25:63). In order for you to be safe and sound from the evil of people and be safe from the evil of your own ego and from the evil of the devil, and so that you will be of the honored ones, do not stoop to the level of ignorance. You will have safety in the two abodes.

Our master the Shaykh [ʿAbd Allah al-Daghistani] said that the follower of the *ʿazīmat al-sharīʿa* (the high resolve of the sacred Law) must take good care of certain matters so that he will rise up to the stations of nearness in the presence of Allah Almighty. What we are referring to is the most high stations. There are also the intermediate stations and the lower stations. Our master the Shaykh recounted that in the time of the Prophet–upon him the blessings and peace of Allah–on a certain night at a late hour, Jibril came down with an important matter from the presence of Allah to His Messenger. In light of the gravity of the matter the Messenger of Allah sent word for Bilāl to call out to the people so that they would gather in the noble Mosque. The time was late. The Companions became alarmed and were asking themselves, are we under attack by the enemy? When they gathered, the Messenger of Allah conveyed to them the command of his nurturing Lord, namely, "O Muhammad! convey the news that whoever brings up the report of something that has already passed and has been dead and buried—even if it took places two hours before—and fitna flares up because of it, then that will be a reason for incurring the curse of Allah and of His Messenger. It will be the awakening of fitna. Fitna is dormant, Allah has cursed whoever awakens it![1] This is the matter that Jibril has brought and which he has ordered to be announced on the spot, before the morning, so that no one should bring up the report of something that is already buried and gone."

On that night our liege lord Abū Bakr al-Ṣiddīq placed the stone in his mouth.[2] He could not speak unless he removed that stone and he would not remove it other than to eat, sleep or pray. The rest of the time he would put it in so that he would not speak or mention something. Allah then informed His Messenger about it and told him to tell Abū Bakr to remove the stone from his mouth because his tongue had become a *lisān ṣidq* (tongue of truthfulness), and nothing would come out of it but truthfulness. As for us, how many a stone must we put into our mouths so that we might guard our tongues? And once word comes to us that our tongue has become a *lisān ṣidq*—at that time we may speak whatever we wish.

The Aws and the Khazraj were two tribes that were always at odds and fighting one another in Medina before the Hijra. Islam came and put out the fitna between them. One day they were sitting and discussing how on a certain day such and such happened, and you did this, and you were following misguidance, and they were disputing, no, we were following the truth and you were following falsehood, etc. They began to disagree and they ended up drawing swords against one another, each of the two sides claiming to be right.[3]

[1] See Suhba I.80, fifth note.

[2] He is said to have done so for years per Qushayrī, *Risāla* (chapter on silence). This is also related about the oft-smiling gentle-mannered Syrian shaykh Abū Yaḥyā ʿAbd Allāh b. Abī Zakariyyā al-Khuzāʿī al-Rabbānī (d. 117/735) by Abū Nuʿaym in *Ḥilyat al-awliyā'* (5:152) who did this for years to learn silence.

[3] Bayḍāwī said about the verse, *O you who believe, if you obey a party of those who received the Scripture, they will turn you back, after your having believed, into unbelievers* (Āl ʿImrān 3:100): "It was revealed in reference to a group of the Aws and the Khazraj that were sitting together and conversing when the Jew Sha's b. Qays passed by and was vexed by their rapport and sociability, so he ordered a young man of the Jews to sit with them, remind them of the day of [the battle of] Buʿāth and declaim to them some of the poetry to that effect. The Aws had won that battle. The young man did so, after which the group contended among themselves with mutual boasts, anger flared up and they shouted, 'to arms! to arms!' Large numbers rallied to each side. At that point the Messenger of Allah–upon him the blessings and peace of Allah–went over to them and said, 'Do you all invoke Jāhiliyya while I am here in your midst, and after Allah has honored you with Islam, severed from you the matter of Jāhiliyya, and brought your hearts into harmony?' They realized that it was a satanic provocation and

This is the fitna that happened between the Aws and the Khazraj until Allah ordered that nothing [bad] that happened in the past—even two hours before—should be brought up again, and whoever did that incurs the curse of Allah and of His Messenger. This is an important matter especially in this time of ours, when people are falling into deadly crises because of their tongues. It is all the more important because the Messenger–upon him the blessings and peace of Allah–instructed that a person's safety is in the guarding of his own tongue.[1] The less you speak, the safer you will be, and the more you speak, the more you will be held to account in this world and the next. Too many fall into disasters because of their tongues, but the Messenger–upon him the blessings and peace of Allah–instructed, "Whoever believes in Allah and the last Day then let him speak goodness or be silent."[2]

From Allah is all success. By the sanctity of the Fatiha.

a plot from their enemies. They threw down their weapons, embraced one another and walked away with the Messenger." Narrated from (i) Ibn Isḥāq by Ibn Hishām, *Sīra* (1:556); (ii) Zayd b. Aslam by al-Ṭabarī; Thaʿlabī; Baghawī and others. See also al-Wāḥidī, *Asbāb al-nuzūl*; al-Suyūṭī, *al-Durr al-manthūr*; Ibn Ḥajar, *al-ʿUjāb fī bayān al-asbāb*, ed. ʿAbd al-Ḥakīm Muḥammad al-Anīs, 2 vols. (Dammām: Dār Ibn al-Jawzī, 1418/1997) 2:720-722 §216.

[1] See the next note and the many hadiths to that effect collected by Ibn Abī al-Dunyā in his book *al-Ṣamt*.

[2] Narrated from (i) Abū Shurayḥ al-ʿAdawī al-Khuzāʿī by Mālik; Aḥmad; al-Dārimī; al-Bukhārī; Muslim; Ibn Mājah; al-Tirmidhī; (ii) ʿAbd Allāh b. ʿAmr b. al-ʿĀṣ by Aḥmad; (iii) Abū Hurayra by Aḥmad; al-Bukhārī; Muslim; Ibn Mājah; Abū Dāwūd; Tirmidhī; (iv) Abū Umāma by al-Ṭabarānī, *Kabīr*; al-Bayhaqī, *Zuhd*; (v) an unnamed Muzanī Companion by Aḥmad; (vi) ʿĀ'isha by Aḥmad.

86

[The wali is nothing without the divine gift] – Who is the sincere one? – [The Umma's three types: Prophet-like, interceded for, honored]

I seek refuge in Allah from the accursed devil
In the Name of Allah the All-Beneficent the Most Merciful
There is no power nor strength but with Allah the High, the Magnificent
Permission, O my Master, support!
Our way is companionship, and goodness is in the congregation

They say "the Shaykh knows everything." Allah knows everything! And, in reality, Allah Almighty is giving the wali from *nafas al-qudsiyya* (the breath of holiness) and, with the latter, he will know everything. Then He withdraws it from him and He leaves him on his own: at that point he will be like inanimate objects! Why does Allah act like this? In order to teach them **that they are nothing. They have no power. They are nothing without the breath of holiness. You are nothing, you do not know and you do not work. This is a proclamation.**

Iblīs perished due to his self-admiration. The most harmful thing for the servants and the worshippers, that which causes them to descend and fall deeper than the level of the uneducated masses or the level of the enviers, is their self-admiration while they know their actual state. This is why Allah does not leave this power with the Awliya. Daily He withdraws it from them so that they know that it is a gift from Allah—when this runs out you realize its value and how precious it is—as a proclamation to them that they have nothing without the breath of holiness which is of the breaths of the All-Beneficent. And this is the secret of *wilāya* (protective divine friendship).[1] So do not say that "the Shaykh knows." For he knows when Allah gives him the breath of holiness. At that time do not object to the words of the shaykhs, because they have come out of the level of the common masses and have become with Allah Almighty. Their speech is the speech of Allah, their knowledge is from the knowledge of the All-True, their power is from the power of the All-True, their hearing is from the hearing of the All-True. Everything is with the All-True. They are now with Allah, in His company.[2]

[1] *And there was never, for him, any faction to help him besides the One God, and he could not defend himself at all. Therein does protective friendship belong to the One True God. It is far better as a reward and far better as an outcome!* (al-Kahf 18:43-44).

[2] Per the *ḥadīth qudsī* of the Awliya in al-Bukhārī. See Suhba I.70, fourth note.

Our master the Shaykh [ʿAbd Allah al-Daghistani] said as a teaching for us that *adab* (high manners) dictate that there is danger in speaking [ill] about someone in his absence. It is subsumed under the Prophet's warning that you should not be speaking about something that happened [even] two hours before because curses will come down and the murid must strictly avoid the contexts of cursing since it is the opposite of mercy. If a fire comes down, what will happen? It will burn him. Likewise, when curses descend on the works of the servant they burn them. Therefore you must avoid all the contexts because of which curses descend on the works of the servants.

Mawlana al-Shaykh says that the Pride of all beings has given a personal guarantee to whoever observes these proprieties.[1] He–upon him the blessings and peace of Allah–is saying that he is his teacher and they shall have no fear whether in this world or the next, and I defend them, and these ones will not leave any of the highest ranks except they will obtain them, and these ones are those whose single breath while they sleep is worthier than the worship of all of the common masses. Mawlana al-Shaykh says that this *adab* of which we described a small part in the beginning, shall make the people of high resolve entitled to take from the storehouses of the All-True because they are trustworthy and there is no treachery with them. When no more treachery remains, the opportunity is given to them to have complete discretion over the storehouses of the All-True. These are the sincere ones.

Who is the sincere one? Mawlana said it is he who finds no heaviness in what the Messenger has brought. With everything that he ever brought they find high energy to put it into practice and it does not bear heavily on them. Likewise to leave something that is forbidden is easy for them because of their sincerity. These are the sincere ones, and the one who is sincere at the command of Allah and at His prohibition finds no fatigue or heaviness in complying with its obligation or its prohibition. From that you can tell he is sincere. These are the sincere ones and these are the believers, and the submitters are the ones Allah mentioned in the Qurʾān.

Mawlana asks, when will we ourselves be Muslims? When we continue after these ones whose names Allah mentions in the Qur'ān such as our liege lord Ibrāhīm or our liege lord Mūsā–upon them peace–and we do as they did. Allah spoke of them to the effect that these Muslims are the first group from

[1] Per the Prophetic hadith "Whoever guarantees for me what is between his jawbones and what is between his legs, I guarantee Paradise for him" / "Whoever controls this and this"—pointing to his tongue and groin—"I guarantee for him Paradise," narrated from (i) al-Zubayr by Maʿmar b. Rāshid and al-Bayhaqī, *Shuʿab*; (ii-iii) Jābir b. ʿAbd Allāh and Sahl b. Saʿd by Abū Yaʿlā; (iv) Abū Hurayra by Ibn ʿAdī and al-Taymī, *al-Targhīb wal-tarhīb*; (v) Ibn Masʿūd by Abū Nuʿaym, *Ḥilya*.

the Umma of our liege lord Muhammad-upon him blessings and peace of Allah. They are the people of high resolve. There is a second group from the Umma of the Beloved that regularly pray the five prayers and keep to the pre-prayer practice of reciting three witnessings of faith and asking forgiveness seventy times. These ones, the Prophet will be an intercessor for them, for they are subsumed under the hadith, "My intercession is for those of my Umma who are guilty of enormous sins."[1] These ones, their progress is *then they believe, then they disbelieve* (Nisā' 4:137). The Messenger of Allah–upon him the blessings and peace of Allah–will intercede for them and they will become of the people of Tariqa. They are under the mercy of Allah and sins are not counted against them.[2] There is a third group of the Umma of our liege lord Muhammad–upon him the blessings and peace of Allah–who are described by the noble verse *and We have certainly honored the children of Ādam* (Banū Isrā'īl/Isrā' 17:70). They are under a divine honoring.

Our liege lord the Shaykh says that whoever is part of those who are addressed here, do not look at their defects, even if it may be a fornicator or a depraved one or an open sinner. Do not weigh the deeds of people and rule over them, saying this is a depraved sinner, an open sinner, an unbeliever. This is not up to you. He is in the hand of Allah. He weighs the works of the servants. He judges their depravity and their open sins, and they are His servants from the perspective that He has honored them. It is not up to you to follow up on the defects of people. Even the Prophet–upon him the blessings and peace of Allah–was not given jurisdiction over the Balance of deeds because it is Allah Almighty Who weighs out their deeds and passes judgment on them.

This [second][3] group are given the choice to mention *Allāh* daily 1,500 times and invoke one hundred blessings on the Prophet, *Allāhumma ṣalli ʿalā Muḥammadin wa-ʿalā āli Muḥammadin wa-sallim.* Whoever keeps to this spiritual practice will not leave this life before first entering under the gaze that is obtained by the first group of the people of high resolve in Shariʿa and in Tariqa. They are given the choice and the verse *Allah does not task any soul except to its capacity* (Baqara 2:286) encompasses them.

The third group of the Umma of the Prophet, even if they do not pray and they do not fast, and they commit all of the forbidden acts, they too enter under the hadith of the Prophet–upon him the blessings and peace of Allah–

[1] Narrated from Jābir, Anas, Ibn ʿUmar, Ibn ʿAbbās and Umm Salama through mostly sound chains in the *Musnads* and *Sunan* etc.. See more on this type in Suhba I.95.

[2] As clarified at the very end of Sura I.96.

[3] The transcription has "third."

"The human being is with whomever he loves despite his deeds."[1] These ones have entered into mercy because of love. Thus did the Messenger–upon him the blessings and peace of Allah–say that everything is linked to love and conviction. The more you have with you love and conviction for the host of the righteous the more you will benefit. Otherwise you will not be able to obtain the high levels through this prayer of yours or this this practice of yours or through this fasting of yours. If this servant that neither prays nor fasts does not harm any of the Muslims and does not object to the Muslims in their prayer and their fasting but he loves them for their righteous deeds —this attribute of the third group will be a cause for accompanying the righteous and the believers on the Day of Resurrection.[2]

Our proof to that effect is the dog of the Companions of the Cave: it loved and accompanied the Companions of the Cave. No matter how much they chased it away and beat it, its love for them remained despite that, although the dog is originally impure. Yet Allah will purify it and cause it to enter Paradise with them.[3] Mawlana asks, did that dog pray and fast? But because of its love for its companions it entered with them. Allah purified it and put it with them in Paradise. This is sufficient evidence and it is definitive. **Whoever has love towards the righteous and towards the believers, no matter what he does, will be with them in Paradise**. Mawlana says that any human being that says "I believe in Allah" and "I am a believer in Allah," will his nurturing Lord leave him? By the mere virtue of saying "I am a believer in Allah," "I am a believer in the oneness of Allah," "I believe in Allah" and he has nothing else other than that. Will his nurturing Lord leave him? No, He will not leave him. Does it become the magnificence of the nurturing Lord and His munificence to leave a servant that believes in Him?

Mawlana says that Allah has cursed the unbelief of the unbelievers and He did not curse their bodies. He cursed their works. If He had cursed their bodies, none of them would have purified himself by saying *lā ilāha illā-l-Lāh Muḥammadun Rasūlu-l-Lāh*. It would have been necessary for his body to be changed as well. Note well that if the divine curse had fallen on the bodies of the unbelievers they could not have purified themselves by saying the witnessing of faith. So then the divine curse is falling on the discourse of unbelief, and when he utters the witnessing of faith he becomes pure.

[1] See Suhba 50, second note.

[2] In a more recent suhba available online Mawlana Shaykh Nazim specified about the abovementioned hadith that the definite article *al-* in *al-mar'u* (the human being) denotes both *istighrāq* (totality) and *jins* (genus).

[3] See Suhba I.60, second note.

I.86

Now we have reached the station of the discourse on the five stations of the heart and Mawlana will explain these stations.

From Allah is all success. By the sanctity of the Fatiha.

87
Attributes of the five stations of the heart – How the servants will see their deeds on the Day of Resurrection – [The greatest Name of Allah in the human being]

I seek refuge in Allah from the accursed devil
In the Name of Allah the All-Beneficent the Most Merciful
There is no power nor strength but with Allah the High, the Magnificent
Permission, O my Master, support!
Our way is companionship, and goodness is in the congregation

Sultan al-Awliya Mawlana al-Shaykh ʿAbd Allah al-Daghistani–may Allah sanctify his secret–said that Allah has given the human being five stations in his heart. These are the attributes of these five stations.

The first station is *maqām al-qalb* (the Station of the Heart). It is given to whoever has *firāsa* (insight). The insight of the believers is a reality which Allah gives to the believer as a light in his heart. The Prophet–upon him the blessings and peace of Allah–says, "Beware the insight of the believer for he sees with the light of Allah."[1] This light unveils the first of the stations of the heart. **This station is in the believer and in the rest of people. For the people of insight, whatever will happen or whatever settles in the human heart gets unveiled**. Allah Almighty has given them that light and that power.

Even with Iblīs this light can be found—for he looks into the first of the

[1] Narrated from (i) Abū Umāma al-Bāhilī by al-Ṭabarānī, *Kabīr* (8:121 §7497); *Awsaṭ* (3:311-312 §3254); and *Musnad al-Shāmiyyīn* (3:183-184 §2042) with a fair chain per Haythamī, *Majmaʿ al-zawāʾid* (10:268); Ibn ʿAbd al-Barr, *Jāmiʿ bayān al-ʿilm* (1:677 §1197); al-Ḥakīm al-Tirmidhī, *Nawādir* (3:591 §1153, 3:637 §1174, *ṣaḥīḥ*); Ibn ʿAdī, *Kāmil*; Abū Nuʿaym, *Ḥilya* and *Arbaʿīn al-ṣūfiyya*; al-Khaṭīb, *Tārīkh*; Bayhaqī, *Zuhd*. Both Suyūṭī in the *Laʾāli'* and Shawkānī in the *Fawāʾid* declared it fair; (ii) Abū Saʿīd al-Khudrī by Tirmidhī (*gharīb*); Bukhārī, al-*Tārīkh al-kabīr*; Ṭabarī (Ḥijr 15:75 *verily there are, in that, indeed signs for the discerners*); Ṭabarānī, *Awsaṭ* (8:23 §7843); Abū Nuʿaym, *Ḥilya* and others; (iii-v) Thawbān, Ibn ʿUmar and Abū Hurayra by Ṭabarī, Abū al-Shaykh, Abū Nuʿaym, Ibn Abī Ḥātim and others. It is further confirmed by the Prophetic report "Allah has servants who know [what lies hidden] by *tawassum* (reading the signs)" from (vi) Anas b. Mālik by al-Bazzār, *Musnad*; al-Ṭabarī; Quḍāʿī, *Musnad al-shihāb*; Abū Nuʿaym, *Ṭibb*; Ibn al-Sunnī, *Ṭibb*; all with fair chains per Ibn Ḥajar, *Mukhtaṣar zawāʾid al-Bazzār*, al-Haythamī (10:268) and al-Sakhāwī, *Maqāṣid*.

stations of the heart and he knows what runs into the servant's heart.[1] It is well-known that the seat of the human being's intention is the heart. Whenever you intend goodness Iblīs looks and hurries to corrupt for you that intention and change it. This [station] is subjected to him. Iblīs knows what courses through the heart. What power is this? But the first of the stations of the heart is also made compliant to the real believers, and they have discretion over it. The true believer knows what is coursing through your heart and he knows its wisdom, whereas Iblīs cannot know the wisdom.

The second is the station of *al-sirr* (the secret). It is more hidden than the station of the heart. Allah has brought into being or subjected this station for the imams of the Tariqas, not only the Naqshbandis. It is not possible for the power of the ego, whim, the devil or the world to enter or even approach the station of the secret. It is forbidden [to them]. This [station] has been and continues to be unveiled to you also, because it is only opened for the imams of all the Tariqas. You have to reach that rank in their stations so that you will be given of their lights so that it will be unveiled to you. But you have been and continue to be heedless and unaware of the knowledge of the station of the secret in your heart, what secrets it contains and what our nurturing Lord has deposited therein of storehouses. However, Allah Almighty has certainly entrusted over it the imams of all the Tariqas and they are the ones responsible from the aspect of preservation and from the aspect of spiritual opening for the servant.

So these ones guard that station. When the servant reaches a level where he can control it, they open and give to him from the station of the secret. But **if he is not qualified, they keep it for him so that no harm or defect will affect the servant. Yet they have to give and open that station to the servant before his exit from this world, and they must perfect him until he dies. At the time of death they must open that station for him** as they are accountable on the Day of Resurrection before the All-True for the station of the secret for the servants. Our master the Shaykh says, look how much Allah has given of jurisdiction and ability and power to his Awliya the noble shaykhs! They are *qudamā' al-wasāṭa* (the forerunners of mediation) and He made them forerunners for the disobedient ones.

[1] Per the hadith, "Verily the devil runs wherever the human being's blood runs" narrated from (i) Anas by Aḥmad; Bukhārī, *Adab mufrad*; Muslim; Abū Dāwūd; (ii) Jābir by Aḥmad; Dārimī; Tirmidhī; Ṭaḥāwī, *Mushkil*; and others; (iii) Ṣafiyya bint Ḥuyay by 'Abd al-Razzāq; Ibn Rāhūyah; Aḥmad; Bukhārī; Muslim; Ibn Mājah; Abū Dāwūd; (iv) Abū Hurayra by Ibn al-Muqri', *Mu'jam*; in *mawqūf* mode: (v) Ibn Mas'ūd by Abū Yūsuf, *Āthār*; Abū Nu'aym, *Ḥilya*; (vi) Ibn 'Umar by Dūlābī, *Kunā*; Ṭabarānī, *Kabīr*; Ibn al-Muqri', *Mu'jam*; in *maqṭū'* mode: (vii) Ibn al-Musayyib by Ibn Abī Shayba.

I.87

Then Mawlana explained **the station of the secret of the secret, the third of the stations of the heart**. Allah has made it exclusive to the imams of the Naqshbandi masters and He has entrusted to them the station of the secret of the secret in the heart. That is also even more hidden, and the strength of the imams of the rest of the Tariqas is insufficient for them to look at that station but only our Naqshbandi masters can, those that have full knowledge of the station of the secret of the secret in the heart—and their number is 7007 imams of the Naqshbandi masters—and they alone are the ones in charge of preserving and guarding the station of the secret of the secret with the generality of people also, and not only with the believers.

Their duty is to perfect that servant until he receives his trust from the station of the secret of the secret. **When the servant has not reached perfection in his life they have to perfect him without fail at the end of the time until they give him the key to his storehouses because he is their owner.** *And We have certainly honored the children of Ādam* (Banū Isrā'īl/Isrā' 17:70). According to this honoring He has given storehouses at each of the stations of the heart. However, for you to obtain the station of *rushd* (mature rectitude) and until your *rushd* becomes firm they are the ones guarding those trusts on your behalf because they cannot benefit anyone but you. You are their owner and none of the rest of the people has any share of them with you. All have these storehouses, and our Naqshbandi masters have to perfect the Umma, and all human beings must prepare themselves to receive the key to the storehouses.

As for the fourth of the stations of the heart it is *akhfā* (more hidden). Our nurturing Lord is saying to the Beloved, "O Muhammad, I have certainly given you the station of *al-akhfā* (the more hidden) in the hearts of My servants. I have given it to you and it is exclusive to you." Whatever exists of the storehouses which Allah has stored into the station of more hidden are known only to the Messenger of Allah-upon him the blessings and peace of Allah. No one else can see them and he is the only one governing this station. **All the hearts of human beings are subsumed under this matter. Unbelief appears only at the first station—the heart—and it receives no regard because it is forbidden for that unbelief to move to the station of the secret, the station of the secret of the secret, the station of more hidden and the station of hiddenness.**

Mawlana asks, what is the wisdom of our nurturing Lord in that Iblīs can enter the first of the stations of the heart? Yet what happens there gets no regard and the servant is not harmed by it. At times people ask, will we be responsible for these passing thoughts? Mawlana says you are not responsible at all until you speak them out or act upon them. Mawlana says, leave Iblīs work and fatigue himself at the first station trying to corrupt it, since it receives no regard. This is good news! Mawlana said that Shaykh Muḥyī al-Dīn Ibn ʿArabī was explaining and giving a commentary on the noble verse, *so whoever does even a small ant's weight in goodness shall see it and whoever does...* (Zalzala 99:7-8). He was saying that whoever does this much goodness will see, and also whoever does this much evil will see, however, he was saying that Allah will change their bad deeds into good deeds, then He shall show them to them in the form of the most excellent and righteous deeds and not as bad deeds. *The One God shall replace their evil deeds with excellent deeds* (Furqān 25:70).[1] This is how he would explain [it].[2]

So **it is unbecoming of Allah's grandeur for Him to become occupied with the human being's bad deeds. Rather He will substitute them, clean them away and not let them show. This is why some angels are found glorifying with the words, "O You Who have brought out the beautiful and covered up the ugly!"**[3] What do you think then about the Day of the Regathering when Allah has let down His cover over the servants? What can be unveiled anymore of the blemishes of the heart? The angels are raising the glorification, "O You Who have brought out the beautiful and covered up the ugly!" **He brings out the bad deeds as good deeds. This is our nurturing Lord and this is the understanding of the Awliya; and the All-True says, "I am exactly as My servant thinks of Me."**[4] If only we think of our nurturing Lord in this way we will find Him exactly like this. **And this opens up an immense reach for us—just as you think of your nurturing Lord, thus will you find Him to be.**

"My expectation of my nurturing Lord is that He shall substitute my bad deeds with excellent deeds." And thus shall you find Him to be. We hear many of the people *that have exceeded all bounds to their own detriment* (al-Zumar 39:53) say *verily Allah is Most Forgiving, Most Merciful* (Baqara 2:173 etc.). If they are truthful, the All-True will not manifest Himself on the Day of Resurrection other than as *Most Forgiving, Most Merciful.* He shall inspire the disobedient sinners on the Day of the Regathering [to say], "O our nurturing

[1] See Suhba I.31, 11th paragraph.

[2] See Ibn ʿArabī, *Futūḥāt* chapters 47, 70 (*waṣl fī faṣl mā akala ṣāḥibu al-tamri wal-zarʿ min tamrihi wa-zarʿih*), 74, 200, 207, 345, 369 (*waṣl* 21), 403.

[3] Narrated from (i) Ubay b. Kaʿb by al-ʿUqaylī, *al-Ḍuʿafāʾ* (Zahdam b. al-Ḥārith); al-Khaṭīb, *al-Muttafaq wal-muftaraq* (2:1004); Ibn Qudāma, *Faḍl yawm al-tarwiya wa-ʿArafa*; (ii) ʿAbd Allāh b. ʿAmr b. al-ʿĀṣ by al-Ḥākim, *Mustadrak* (1:729 §1998); al-Bayhaqī, *al-Daʿawāt al-kabīr* (1:329 §238); al-Rāfiʿī, *al-Tadwīn*; (iii) Ibn ʿAbbās by al-Bayhaqī, *al-Asmāʾ wal-ṣifāt* (1:145-147 §90).

[4] See Suhba I.8, second note.

Lord, we did not expect You to be thus!" and on the spot the manifestation will be according to the expectation they had of Him in their life in the world. "My expectation of You is that I am hoping for Your mercy, Your gift, Your forgiveness, Your generosity! I never thought—not even once—that You are severe in punishment! I exceeded all bounds against my own soul but I was seeking refuge in the hem of Your mercy! O my nurturing Lord, I knew with certainty that Your mercy is vaster than my sins and that it is impossible for my sins to overcome Your mercy—never!"

If the servants proceeded in this fashion, matters would fix themselves in every sphere of life and people would be able to relax. However, *they continue to disagree* (Hūd 11:118), and the spiritual leader of endtimes shall come at a time of great dissent among the people as a just arbiter. Allah shall substitute the bad deeds of the servants into excellent deeds, and with His gently kindness and His generosity He shall make them appear in this beautiful way. "*Mā shā' Allāh!* All that shows of you is everything beautiful, O My servants!" Mawlana says that outside the eight gardens of Paradise there are seven hells that are like outside toilets, and all the impurities that issued from human beings will be thrown there.

Mawlana says, [these are] four stations in the heart of the servant over which the Messenger of Allah–upon him the blessings and peace of Allah–was made to rule. The carrier of the shaykhs in their stations and the carrier of the believers, also, is the Messenger of Allah. They are all under his guardianship. And Allah Almighty is saying, "O Muhammad! **The fifth of the stations of the heart for My servant [is the station of *al-khafā'* (hiddenness)]**. This I do not give to anyone, it is with Me. The heart of My servant is My throne—'The heart of the believer is the throne of Allah.'[1] This is Mine." **He said–exalted is He–*the All-Merciful over the Throne has established Himself*** (Ṭa Ha 20:5).[2] May He be glorified! Look—the fifth of the

[1] Cited thus chainless by 'Alī al-Qārī at the end of the commentary on *qadar* in the hadith of *islām, īmān, iḥsān* in *Mirqāt al-mafātīḥ sharḥ Mishkāt al-maṣābīḥ* (1309/1892 ed. 1:52) and İsmail Hakkı in *Ruḥ al-bayān* (A'rāf 7:1). 'Abd al-'Azīz al-Ghumārī in *al-Tahānī min al-ta'qīb 'alā Mawḍū'āt al-Ṣaghānī* (Cairo: Dār al-Anṣār, 1982) p. 54 said it is narrated in the wording, "Allah has vessels from among the people of the earth and the vessels of your nurturing Lord are the hearts of His righteous servants." See the latter hadith's documentation in *Qari's Encyclopedia of Forgeries* (entries "Neither My heaven nor My earth can contain Me but the soft, humble heart of my believing servant can contain Me" and "The heart is the house of the Lord").

[2] See the words of Ibn 'Aṭā' [=Abū al-'Abbās Aḥmad b. Muḥammad b. Sahl b. 'Aṭā' al-Adamī al-Baghdādī d. 309/921] connecting this verse with the meaning of the statement that the heart of the believer is the throne of Allah as quoted by Ruzbehan Baqli (d. 606/1210), *Tafsīr 'arā'is al-bayān fī ḥaqā'iq al-Qur'ān* (1:476, Ṭa Ha 20:5).

stations belongs to Allah. Mawlana says that although the Messenger is under the safeguarding of Allah and He is an infallible Prophet, yet no one knows of the station of hiddenness in the hearts of human beings anything but their nurturing Lord–Almighty is He–regardless whether one is a Prophet or a wali or a believer or an unbeliever. They have no jurisdiction over that station at all. And if the servants of Allah knew how Allah was going to treat them in the next life they would live in any way their egos wished.

Our nurturing Lord is saying "this is in My hand and none knows other than Me what is found therein of the storehouses of *and We have certainly honored the children of Ādam* (Banū Isrā'īl/Isrā' 17:70)." **The secret of belief is stored therein. From where and in what way can Iblīs come near? Allah shall open up the secret of that matter for His servant. But when the servant is able and readies himself, a ray of those lights is opened for him.** If his readiness is not complete He will leave him until his last breaths, when only seven breaths remain of the life of the servant. At that time Allah orders the Prophet–upon him the blessings and peace of Allah–"Leave My servant with me." What takes place between Allah and the servant and how He prepares him and makes him ready Allah knows best. Then He opens for him from that station also.

Mawlana says that Allah knows who has reached the station of "Die before you die."[1] Allah knows who is going to be a manifestation of that station and patiently endure with striving and hardships in his wayfaring until he causes his ego to die before the compulsory death. That one knows of those secrets and an opening is given to him to the extent of what he learnt in this world. For if a complete opening were to happen to him, this world would not be able to bear for that servant to walk on it. It has not strength.[2] Mawlana says that if Allah opened up from that station even something like a pinhole to the extent of an atom of light over this world and the next, both would be as if they had never existed. They would burn up from the intensity of those lights. This is what is hidden with our nurturing Lord Almighty.

Mawlana says that **in every single one of the hearts of human beings, in the five stations, there is a manifestation of the greatest Name of Allah**. This is why Mawlana used to say that "the greatest Name of Allah is the children of Ādam—it is the human being under this manifestation!"[3] There is so much

[1] See Suhba I.32, fourth note.

[2] See Suhba I.69, second note.

[3] I.e. the greatest Name is manifested in the fifth station of a human being's heart. I had first heard the statement Mawlana reported from Mawlana Shaykh 'Abd Allah that "the greatest Name of Allah is the human being" from Shaykh Muṣṭafā 'Alaylī in Beirut in the 2000s and it is a stumbling-block of momentous consequence unless it is

power in the heart! And the Day of the Regathering, when the judgment is finished according to *whoever does even a small ant's weight in goodness shall see it and whoever does even a small ant's weight in evil shall see it* (Zalzala 99:7-8), at that time Allah shall open up, together with the manifestations of the ninety-nine beautiful Names of Allah, the manifestation of the greatest Name of Allah until all people are seen wearing that manifestation. At that time there shall appear in the human being the greatest Name of Allah, and it will be seen [as if] he himself is the greatest Name of Allah. This is on top of the fact, already now, that all creatures are living by the mercy of the name of Allah *al-Raḥmān* (the All-Beneficent).

In the presence of Allah all human beings are on a par in consideration of the five stations [of the heart], and the greatest Name of Allah that rises in the station of hiddenness. They are, in the presence of their nurturing Lord, manifestations of the greatest Name of Allah, all of them without exception—and there is no regard given to the first of the five stations. Mawlana says there is no difference between any two human beings in the presence of their nurturing Lord because Allah is not susceptible of deficiency and no deficiency can affect our nurturing Lord as a consequence of the unbelief of people or their rebellious sins or their depravity. Nor does any increase result for Him out of their worship. This is why the look of the All-True to the servants is on a par in consideration of the stations of the secret, the secret of the secret, the more hidden and hiddenness. No regard is given to the first station, the station of the heart—because Iblīs acts there—but more importantly the greatest Name of Allah manifests itself in the station of hiddenness, whereby that is where the Throne of Allah is set up. *The All-Merciful over the Throne has established Himself* (Ṭa Ha 20:5).

We shall stop here. This matter will be explained, and the fact that all the servants in the presence of our nurturing Lord are equally under His mercy.

From Allah is all success. By the sanctity of the Beloved, by the sanctity of the Fatiha.

pondered and qualified in light of what Mawlana Shaykh Nazim explained elsewhere in this collection and in such as his Suhba of *The Joy of Cyprus in the Association of Rajab* (Damascus: Dār al-Aḥbāb, 1422/2002) pp. 7-8 ("Oneness of Being," The Divine Names and Attributes, Oneness); p. 19 (Revering the Divine Secret in Man). See also al-Kharrāz's quotation to that effect under Ruzbehan Baqli's commentary on the Verse of Light (al-Nūr 24:35) in *'Arā'is al-bayān*. "We are a group whose works are unlawful to peruse, since the Sufis, one and all, use terms in technical senses by which they intend other than what is customarily meant by their usage among scholars, and those who interpret them according to their usual significance commit unbelief" per Ibn 'Arabī as cited in the supplements to *Reliance of the Traveller* (p. 1080).

88
Questions and answers on creed and Quranic commentary

I seek refuge in Allah from the accursed devil
In the Name of Allah the All-Beneficent the Most Merciful
There is no power nor strength but with Allah the High, the Magnificent
Permission, O my Master, support!
Our way is companionship, and goodness is in the congregation

Question: is *taqwā* (guarding oneself from divine displeasure) first or belief in absolute terms? Answer: without belief *taqwā* is inconceivable. Yet with the presence of *taqwā* belief begins. With the appearance of *taqwā* in the servant belief appears. Belief is a foundation but what pulls a person to belief is his inclination to *taqwā*. *O you who believe! Guard yourself from the One God and be with the truthful ones* (al-Tawba 9:119). Belief together with *taqwā* followed by keeping company with the truthful ones. The greatest foundation in Islam according to the people of spiritual reality is the welfare of the world with belief and with *taqwā* and the companionship of the truthful ones, without whom the welfare of the world is inconceivable.

Belief does not become perfect by itself, only with *taqwā*. *Taqwā* reforms the individual while keeping company with the truthful ones reforms society. The welfare of the individual is in *taqwā* while the welfare of society is for them to meet with the truthful ones. The reason for the ruin of the world is because we have marched against the noble verse, *so let those that act in defiance of His/his*[1] *command beware lest a trial smite them, or lest there smite them a painful punishment!* (al-Nūr 24:63). They did not beware. This is why they fell in and they were afflicted "with a fitna that shall make the wise bewildered,"[2] "fitnas that are like chunks of dark night."[3]

Can any human being solve the problems of a handspan of the lands of Cyprus or Palestine? Those that act proud and boast of their minds have no

[1] Allah's or the Prophet's–upon him the blessings and peace of Allah (Bayḍāwī).

[2] Part of a Prophetic hadith narrated from (i) Abū Mūsā al-Ash'arī by al-Ṭabarānī, *Awsaṭ* (2:65 §1263); (ii) Abū al-Dardā' by al-Khaṭīb, *al-Faqīh wal-mutafaqqih* (2:342); Ibn 'Asākir, *Dhamm man lā ya'malu bi-'ilmih*. It is also transmitted as the fragment of a divine threat to the doctors of the Israelites narrated from (iii) Muḥammad b. Ka'b al-Quraẓī from Sa'd al-Maqburī by Sa'īd b. Manṣūr, *Sunan*; and (iv) Wahb b. Munabbih by Ibn Abī al-Dunyā, *al-'Uqūbāt*.

[3] See Suhba I.24, third note.

mind. Allah Most High says, *and if you quarrel about something then refer it back to the One God and His Messenger* (al-Nisā' 4:59). But they do not refer it except to their minds, and the more they refer it to their minds, the lower they sink, since their minds are their god and it is letting them perish.

Question: He said–exalted is He–*By the night-star when it plunges* (al-Najm 53:1). What is the real meaning of this star and who is it?

Answer: you have certainly asked one who is well apprised! Allah Most High said, *so ask of it one who is well apprised* (al-Furqān 25:59). Allah knows best and His Messenger knows best whom of His servants He chose by that question about *the piercing star* which is mentioned in the noble verses *by the sky and the night star! And what has told you what the night star is? The piercing star* (al-Ṭāriq 86:1-3). It is the Messenger of Allah–upon him the blessings and peace of Allah.[1]

When the Messenger of Allah asked Jibril, "How old are you?" He said to him, "O my master, O Messenger of Allah! Here there is a star that rises from the Throne once every 70,000 years, and I have witnessed it 70,000 times. As for how many times it has risen before that, I do not know." The Prophet–upon him the blessings and peace of Allah–asked him, "Have you found out who that star was, O Jibril?" He said, "I do not know who he is." The Prophet said, "That star is your Prophet, O Jibril.[2] I was a Prophet when Ādam was still between water and clay."[3] Allah knows best how long before that he first appeared. This is an expression of the Muhammadan reality, a mere glimpse, and not the emergence of the Muhammadan reality. For if it actually appeared would Jibril and the worlds remain? Nothing would remain.

Question: [In the Sura of] *woe to every oft-reviler, inveterate backstabber* (Humaza 104:1), what is *the Fire of the One God, ablaze* (104:6)?

Answer: it is the fire of woe and regrets. May Allah protect us and you.

By the sanctity of the Beloved, by the sanctity of the Fatiha.

[1] As stated by Ja'far al-Ṣādiq and al-Sulamī per Qadi 'Iyāḍ, *al-Shifā* (I.1.5) and Ibn Diḥya. This was cited by al-Sakhāwī, *al-Qawl al-badī' filṣalāt 'alā al-Ḥabīb al-Shafī'* (al-Thāqib, al-Najm); al-Suyūṭī, *al-Riyāḍ al-anīqa fī sharḥ asmā' khayr al-khalīqa* (al-Najm al-thāqib) and *al-nahjat al-sawiyya fil-asmā' al-nabawiyya* (ditto); 'Abd al-Bāsiṭ al-Bulqīnī, *al-Wafā bi-sharḥ al-iṣṭifā min asmā' al-Muṣṭafā* (al-Najm). Sahl al-Tustarī in his *Tafsīr* said *al-Najm al-thāqib* refers to the Prophet's noble heart.

[2] Cited to here by Nūr al-Dīn al-Ḥalabī (d. 1044/1634) in *Insān al-'uyūn fī sīrat al-Amīn al-Ma'mūn*, known as *al-Sīrat al-ḥalabiyya* (at the end of the very first chapter on the noble Prophetic genealogy) who says he saw it in a book entitled *al-Tashrīfāt fil-khaṣā'iṣ wal-mu'jizāt* as narrated from Abū Hurayra.

[3] See Suhba I.24, note 14 on the latter hadith.

89

"Tie down knowledge with writing" – [Purpose of knowledge – Faith in Awliya increases you in faith in Allah and His Prophet – Real love of the Shaykh – Coming to the houses through their doors]

I seek refuge in Allah from the accursed devil
In the Name of Allah the All-Beneficent the Most Merciful
There is no power nor strength but with Allah the High, the Magnificent
Permission, O my Master, support!
Our way is companionship, and goodness is in the congregation

The Messenger of Allah–upon him the blessings and peace of Allah–said, "Tie down knowledge with writing."[1] Why knowledge? Because knowledge is a restraint in itself. When you restrain yourself then that knowledge is a beneficial knowledge. Otherwise, then your ego is tying you down with that manacle for knowledge has become incriminating evidence against you! So either you must put your ego in shackles or your ego shall put you in shackles. Either you will be your ego's prisoner or your ego will be your prisoner. Either you will be your ego's donkey or your ego will be your donkey. Anger makes the servant his ego's donkey. **When you are unable to tie down your ego with [your] knowledge, that knowledge has become a conclusive proof against you on the Day of Resurrection.**[2]

[1] Narrated I. from (i) Anas by Luwayn al-Miṣṣīṣī, *Juz' Luwayn*; al-Ḥakīm al-Tirmidhī, *Nawādir al-uṣūl*; Abū al-Shaykh, *Ṭabaqāt al-muḥaddithīn bi-Aṣbahān*; al-Dāraquṭnī, *'Ilal*; Ibn Shādhān, *al-Fawā'id al-muntaqāt*; Ibn Ṭāhir al-Mukhalliṣ, *Mukhalliṣiyyāt*; Ḥākim, *Mustadrak*; Bayhaqī, *Madkhal* and others; (ii) Ibn 'Abbās by Ibn 'Adī, *Kāmil*; (iii) 'Abd Allāh b. 'Amr by Ibn 'Asākir, *Tārīkh*; Ibn al-Jawzī, *'Ilal*; and II. as their own statement from Anas by Muḥ. b. 'Abd Allāh al-Baṣrī al-Anṣārī (d. 215/830) [a descendant of Anas], *Ḥadīth Muḥammad b. 'Abd Allāh al-Baṣrī*; Ibn Sa'd, *Ṭabaqāt*; Zuhayr b. Ḥarb, *al-'Ilm*; Ibn Abī Khaythama, *al-Tārīkh al-kabīr*; Ṭabarānī, *Kabīr*; Abū Nu'aym, *Tārīkh Aṣbahān*; Ibn 'Abbās by Ibn Sa'd, *Ṭabaqāt*; Zuhayr b. Ḥarb, *al-'Ilm*; (iv) 'Umar b. al-Khaṭṭāb by Ibn Abī Shayba, *Muṣannaf*; Dārimī, *Sunan*; Ḥākim, *Mustadrak*; Bayhaqī, *Madkhal*; (v) Ibn 'Umar by Dārimī; and (vi) 'Umar b. 'Abd al-'Azīz by Balādhurī, *Ansāb al-ashrāf*. See also Khaṭīb al-Baghdādī's compilation of the reports to that effect entitled *Taqyīd al-'ilm* (The tying down of knowledge) where he narrates it as a Prophetic hadith from 'Abd Allāh b. 'Amr, Anas, and, as their own statement, 'Umar b. al-Khaṭṭāb, (vii) 'Alī b. Abī Ṭālib, Ibn 'Abbās and Anas.

[2] "What fends from you the conclusive proof of ignorance is knowledge, and what fends from you the conclusive proof of knowledge is practice;" "Verily Allah shall

Our liege lord Muḥyī al-Dīn Ibn 'Arabī wrote to Fakhr al-Dīn al-Rāzī—he was an arch-erudite scholar: "O leading scholar of the Muslims! Take from knowledge and work on acquiring whatever knowledge will accompany you and benefit you in this world and after death and in the hereafter."[1] For there are many types of knowledge that a servant acquires for the sake of this life and from which he will benefit only right here, but he will not benefit from them in the hereafter. As for the types of knowledge that the people of spiritual reality know and which Muḥyī al-Dīn means, then they will be an engraving on the servant's heart whereby he increases in belief in Allah and in love and nearness to Allah Almighty. This is the point of knowledge. If it is not increasing you in belief and love and nearness to Allah, such knowledge is considered hot air.

Our master Shaykh 'Abd Allah al-Daghistani was concerned, through everything he said, only for the servant's strong faith in his nurturing Lord Almighty and in His Prophet–upon him the blessings and peace of Allah–to increase. That takes place by way of the Muhammadan inheritor. Your love, your strong faith in the Muhammadan inheritor increase you in your strong faith and love and certainty and belief in the Messenger of Allah and Allah Almighty. Without foundation there can be no edifice. This is a rule of life.

Allah Most High said, *and follow the path of him who has abundantly repented to Me* (Luqmān 31:15). You cannot follow anyone until you first believe that he has abundantly repented to Allah. At that time there will be love for him so that you can follow him. After that the result of that station is for your strong faith in the Messenger of Allah to increase, and for your love in the Messenger of Allah to increase, and for your strong faith in Allah and your love in Allah to increase.

pardon the illiterate on the Day of Resurrection in a way He shall not pardon the ulema." Respectively narrated from 'Alī b. Abī Ṭālib and Anas b. Mālik by al-Khaṭīb al-Baghdādī, *Iqtiḍā' al-'ilm al-'amal* (Knowledge's exigency of practice). He narrates in the same work the following sayings: "This world is ignorance and wasteland except knowledge, and knowledge is damning evidence except its being put into practice" (Sahl al-Tustari); "The greater your knowledge the more certain the conclusive proof against you" (Sarīy al-Saqaṭī); "Knowledge is beautiful for whoever puts it into practice, but for whoever does not, how harmful!" (Bishr al-Ḥāfī); "Everyone that does not examine through knowledge what Allah holds against him, then knowledge is a conclusive proof against him and a curse" (Ibn Sam'ūn); "Knowledge that does not benefit you harms you" (Ibn 'Uyayna)—"he means that if it does not benefit him by being put into practice it harms him by being a conclusive proof against him" (Abū Ma'mar). See also Ibn 'Asākir's class in the Great Mosque of Damascus entitled *Dhamm man lā ya'mal bi-'ilmih* (Blame of who does not practice what he knows).

[1] See Suhba I.78, first note.

What is important is for you to make your ego accept to have firm conviction in one person. For the ego that had the audacity, when its nurturing Lord asked it, "Who am I and who are you?" to reply, "I am who I am and you are who you are,"[1] to raise its head before the All-True and say such a thing, how will you ask it to humble itself for a person such as itself, someone of its own human species? You yourself might say *sayyidī* (my master) to a man such as yourself without truthfulness, only for some self-interest. Otherwise the ego would not accept for you to say *sayyidī* to anyone unless there is some selfish advantage. Mawlana says we do not want this. So before there is a possibility for the servant to love Allah and His Messenger–upon him the blessings and peace of Allah–and for his faith in Allah and His Messenger to increase, his way passes by the obligation to first accept a shaykh.

Mawlana used to say that acquiring love in the shaykh and following the shaykh is also not an easy matter. Mawlana al-Shaykh was addressing famous shaykhs—and among them Ibrāhīm al-Ghalāyīnī—saying, "O Shaykh Ibrāhīm, do not be deceived by the love of the followers because they are kissing your hands! Do not be deceived, for you will not find among those that kiss your hands and show you love for you any real love. For if you were to hurt one of them with pin he would draw a dagger against you without fail if only with a word. He would reject any love of the shaykh, his heart would become cold, and he would change from love to enmity and hatred. And there are some of the knowledgeable ones that for a mere word would take offense and part ways with you. This is why Allah is saying, I will not leave My servant without test. There must be a trial by which I test them—will they be fit or unfit for servanthood?"

Look at the Companions of the Cave, how much they beat that dog and harmed it, and yet it never left them but kept walking with them. He said to them, "even if you kill me I am with you. I will not part ways with you, O friends of Allah!" And you, when you recognize the shaykh to be a wali, how can you part ways with him? At the time of testing how do you take offense from him and turn away from him? The following verse gathers up all the tricks of the ego. Allah Most High say, *and of people is he who worships the One God from afar, so if some good happens to him he feels at peace with it, but if a trial befalls him he recedes to his former way* (Ḥajj 22:11).

It is the most difficult thing for a servant to lower himself to another servant like himself because his ego did not lower itself to the Lord of the worlds but

[1] See Suhba I.59, ninth note.

it raised its head and said, "I am me and you are you."[1] And in order to acquire the stations of nearness to Allah and to the Messenger of Allah, there is only one way, which is for you to follow a Muhammadan inheritor. Otherwise you cannot build up your strong faith in the Messenger of Allah–upon him the blessings and peace of Allah–and increase your love in him and in Allah. Allah Most High says *and follow the path of him who has abundantly repented to Me* (Luqmān 31:15). **This is why no one can reach without abundant repentance to *him who has abundantly repented* to Allah.** Otherwise his knowledge will be hot air and his works will be hot air. For with the presence of pride and self-importance he will never lower himself to say, "you are my nurturing Lord." This is the meaning of *and do come into houses through their doors* (al-Baqara 2:189). How will you enter otherwise? From the windows? They will not welcome you.

Whoever comes in contravention of manners and principles they will never welcome him. This is important information. As a teaching for us He is saying, you must look at all creatures as being all equal before the majestic presence of the All-True. There is no sectarianism, no nationalism. Over there, there is no "I" and "you." You have to know that in the majestic presence of the All-True all human beings are a single kind whose attribute is well-honored: *and We have certainly honored the children of Ādam* (Banū Isrā'īl/Isrā' 17:70). This is why, with the Prophets, there is no beholding other than the beholding of the All-True. Were it not the case then why did the Messenger–upon him the blessings and peace of Allah–say, "No Arab has any superiority over any non-Arab except with Godfearingness. All of you come from Ādam, and Ādam comes from dust."[2]

It is up to Him–exalted is He–to let the servants be in whatever condition He wants and, more than that, to dress His servants from the station of Prophethood, from the station of divine friendship, and from the stations of belief or of submission. That is from His bounty. Or He may dress His servants with unbelief, hypocrisy, depravity and open sin, and this is from His justice. There can be no objection to His decision. You must only keep good manners with everyone. When you see someone who was given ranks from Allah that is from His bounty, and when He dresses you with something you must

[1] See previous note.

[2] The first half is narrated from (i) Abū Sa'īd al-Khudrī by 'Abd Allāh b. al-Mubārak, *Musnad*; Aḥmad, *Musnad* (38:474 §23489); Abū al-Shaykh, *al-Tawbīkh*; (ii) Jābir by Abū Nu'aym, *Ḥilya* (3:100); al-Bayhaqī, *Shu'ab*. The second half is narrated from (iii) Ibn 'Umar by Tirmidhī (*Tafsīr*, al-Ḥujurāt 49:13, *gharīb*); also from (iv) Abū Hurayra by Aḥmad (14:349 §8735); Abū Dāwūd (*Adab, al-tafākhur bil-aḥsāb*); (*Tafsīr*, Ḥujurāt 49:13, *ḥasan ṣaḥīḥ*) (vi) Ḥudhayfa by al-Bazzār.

recognize that it is from His bounty. Or, when you that the one whose states or deeds displease you, you must recognize that if he himself were not carrying that matter, you would have been carrying it. This is good manners with all. There is no difference between the servants.

Every human being has a role in this world that will emerge from him, and every human being was given a heart by Allah, and the heart has five stations.[1] The first of them is subjected such that Iblīs may come in and out. That is why, since Iblīs interferes, it receives no regard. As for the rest of the stations he cannot interfere. The hearts of the servants are in the hand of the All-Merciful and the believer's heart is the throne of Allah. *The All-Merciful over the Throne has established Himself* (Ṭa Ha 20:5).[2] These stations are *qalb* (heart), *sirr* (secret), *sirr al-sirr* (secret of the secret), *akhfā* (more hidden) and *khafā'* (hiddenness). They are present in everyone.

The first of the above stations appears in the deeds of the servant but the latter four of these stations are hidden. Nothing appears of them but their work is proceeding also. The first [of the latter four stations] is administered among the rest of the Tariqas except the Naqshbandis. The station of the secret of the secret is entrusted among the Naqshbandi masters. As for the station of "more hidden" then it is in the hand of the Messenger–upon him the blessings and peace of Allah–and the station of hiddenness is in the hand of Allah. He is *All-Effecter of what He wants* (Burūj 85:16). In this fashion, Mawlana says, human beings are all equal in the presence of Allah. So then there is no regard given to the first station.

From Allah is all success. By the sanctity of the Fatiha.

[1] See Suhbas I. 25 and I.87.

[2] See Suhba I.87, seventh and eight notes.

90

No harm ensues for Allah from the unbelief of the servants – [The breath of holiness – Prophethood and sainthood are bestowed, not acquired – The pursuit of spiritual knowledge – Divine mercy far exceeds the mercy of Prophets and Awliya]

I seek refuge in Allah from the accursed devil
In the Name of Allah the All-Beneficent the Most Merciful
There is no power nor strength but with Allah the High, the Magnificent
Permission, O my Master, support!
Our way is companionship, and goodness is in the congregation

The servants are all equal in the presence of their Almighty nurturing Lord. All of them are under the divine address of *and We have certainly honored the children of Ādam* (Banū Isrā'īl/Isrā' 17:70). There is no difference between them because our nurturing Lord is not affected by the acts of the servants and no diminishment ensues for Him from their unbelief or because they say, "Allah exists" or "He does not exist" or their attribution of a partner to Him, or of a son. Just because the servant says something baseless there does not ensue any harm or diminishment for our nurturing Lord, just as there ensues no benefit for Him from the worship of the worshippers, as much as they say *lā ilāha illā-l-Lāh*, *Allāhu akbar*, and magnify and worship. There results no increase for the magnificence of Allah.

The evidence that the matter is as mentioned above is what our master the Shaykh related to me. The story of Ibrāhīm the intimate friend of the All-Merciful–upon him and upon our Prophet the blessings and peace of Allah–indicates that Allah Himself is the one that views the servants as equal and treats them equally, or esteems them to be all equal in His presence even if they disbelieve, even if they transgress, and there never ceases to remain value for them in the presence of their nurturing Lord. Our master Shaykh ʿAbd Allah recounted that in the time of our liege lord Ibrāhīm–upon him peace–there was a group of people that had reached extremes in unbelief and rebellious sins. They rejected his message and they never accepted to enter into the faith of the truth. Worse, they went against him and they harmed him until our liege lord Ibrāhīm imprecated them with the supplication that Allah gave to His Prophets, with *nafas al-qudsiyya* (the breath of holiness). When they call upon Him with that breath their call does not go unanswered. It is answered.

Our master the Shaykh says that this account instructs us that Allah never left it to any person to interfere in the affairs of the servants no matter what the status of the latter is. Mawlana says that servants become Prophets because of the existence of the breath of holiness with them. Likewise they will become Awliya because of the existence of the breath of holiness with them. Likewise one will become the intimate friend of Allah for the same reason. Allah bestows the breath of holiness on anyone He wishes until they become an intimate friend. Mawlana says this is a signal for us that **no one can become something by himself. Allah alone is the One that makes some Prophets, Awliya, an intimate friend. It is impossible for anyone to do what he himself wants but it is Allah that makes him do it.**

Just as Allah makes His servant a wali or a Prophet with the breath of holiness, likewise He gives life to the servants and, when He wishes, He causes their death with the breath of holiness. Likewise, when Allah gives our liege lord Isrāfīl the breath of holiness he will blow the blast of the thunderstroke whereupon all will die and none shall remain alone among creatures. When Allah wants to bring the servants back to life He will likewise give Isrāfīl the breath of holiness and the latter will blow the next blast which will bring back life.[1] One trumpet-blast that causes death, one trumpet-blast that causes life. This is the breath of holiness. That is the most important thing with every Prophet and wali, and that breath of holiness is permanently found with them. As for our liege lord Isrāfīl, then he is given that breath of holiness at the time of the blast only, then it is taken back from him.

Mawlana says, *al-dīnu al-naṣīḥa* (The faith-system is all pure counsel).[2] This gathering of ours is a gathering held to the intention of following the speech of the Prophet–upon him the blessings and peace of Allah–who has said that *dīn* is *naṣīḥa*. We are gathered together to hear pure advice. This is why Mawlana is saying that there is a holy gaze that is trained on you on the part of the All-True and on the part of the Messenger–upon him the blessings

[1] There are three blasts in all, the first being the *nafkhat al-faza*ʿ (alarm-blast), the second the thunderstroke that puts all to death and the third the revival that regathers all. The first trumpet-blast is referred to at the opening of Ḥajj 22:1-2. The second trumpet-blast is mentioned in Yā Sīn 36:49; al-Ṭūr 52:45; al-Ḥāqqa 69:13; and less explicitly in other verses as well, putting all to death. The third trumpet-blast is mentioned in Yā Sīn 36:53; al-Ṣāffāt 37:19; Qāf 50:42; al-Nāziʿāt 79:13; and other verses, reviving all for the *maḥshar* (regathering) to the *mawqif* (waiting-station). The latter two blasts are successively referred to in al-Nāziʿāt 79:6-7.

[2] See Suhba I.10.

and peace of Allah. For no servant comes out aspiring to receive knowledge and *naṣīḥa* so as to increase in belief and certainty and love in Allah and in His Messenger, but the angels lower their wings[1] so that people may walk on them, and that is magnification for whoever seeks knowledge and pursues *naṣīḥa*. What is *naṣīḥa* for? So that the servant will increase in belief, certainty, love and nearness to Allah. That is why the angels bring down their wings, in good pleasure at what that group are is doing. Therefore there is a blessed gaze from Allah and His Messenger–upon him the blessings and peace of Allah. And when we say "the gaze of the All-True and the Messenger," the gaze of the Awliya will be on us, and this sitting of ours shall push back darkness from seventy bad gatherings and lift away affliction from them. Thus did Mawlana al-Shaykh give us glad tidings.

Then he said that Ibrāhīm, the intimate friend of the All-Merciful who had been given of the breath of holiness, imprecated against the group until Allah caused them to perish. That night our liege lord Ibrāhīm saw in dream [the message,] "slaughter your son Ismā'īl." (Mawlana says that if Allah informs and teaches His servant, the servant will know. Otherwise he will be like inanimate objects, not knowing anything.) So in compliance with the command of Allah, Ibrāhīm came to his son and placed the knife and pressed it hard on his neck, but at the time of the act his liver caught fire and smoke came out of his nose. His heart burnt up out of mercy for his child as Allah was looking upon them. Allah made it so that smoke would come up and his heart would burn up. (This is very strong evidence. If you were to say that "smoke came out of him" it would be unbelief, but for the people of spiritual reality it is Allah Most High that made the smoke come out of his heart, because for the people of spiritual reality there is no movement and no stillness other than by the permission and the command and the will of Allah Most High. This is the doctrine of the people of spiritual reality.) Our nurturing Lord said, addressing our liege lord Ibrāhīm–upon him peace, "O Ibrāhīm, do you think I do not have mercy towards My servants—those ones whom you asked to be destroyed—to the extent of your mercy towards this son of yours? Did I create them just like that, without mercy? If you had estimated that My mercy towards My servants was at least to the extent of your mercy towards your son, you would not have made this supplication for Me to destroy them when I am the one that created them and honored them. Had I ever done that without any mercy towards them, and love? I have with Me mercy and love for My servants—no matter how much they disobey or

[1] For heavenly ease and safety as well as immense honor. A Prophetic hadith narrated from (i) Ṣafwān b. 'Assāl al-Murādī by Aḥmad; al-Nasā'ī; al-Bayhaqī and others; (ii) Abū al-Dardā' by Aḥmad; al-Dārimī; Ibn Mājah; Abū Dāwūd and others.

disbelieve—that is not less than your mercy towards your child and your love for him."

No one knows how much our nurturing Lord's love is. None can assess it—neither a Prophet nor a wali. Look and see whether our nurturing Lord has counted this unbelief or that rebellious sin against them, or that speech! Rather He covered it up for them. Allah does not count but a Prophet counts this unbelief and sin, and, likewise, a wali counts it against people. Yet it is Allah alone Who is the concerned party. If He wishes to pardon He pardons, He grants mercy, He forgives. For the servant is His servant; and if He pardons who can say to Him "why did You pardon?" He [=the questioner] himself is in the utmost need of His pardon. Even the Prophets and the Awliya are in need of His pardon–exalted is He. Allah Almighty is of exalted magnificence. Glorified and Holy is He! He does not sink to look at our sins. Rather He flings them into the sea of the All-Merciful and He substitutes them with excellent deeds.[1] I have heard that in some countries water is scarce so they recycle wastewater that runs in big buildings and in certain stores. It is purified of contamination and eliminable impurities then water remains that can be reused to irrigate the soil. If the servant is able to recycle wastewater, then how much more is our nurturing Lord able to substitute our bad deeds with excellent deeds! Does He not have more power?

After that Allah rebuked our liege lord Ibrāhīm–upon him peace–and He said to him, "By My glory and might, O Ibrāhim! This time in respect of you I did not reject your request with regard to the people and I have caused them to perish. But if you were to do this again, I would remove you from the assembly of the Prophets."[2] This is severity from Allah Most High. Hence all Prophets and Awliya are afraid to imprecate their people no matter how much they have reached in corruption, *so that the One God would bring to pass a matter that was to be accomplished* (al-Anfāl 8:42, 8:44). He is most knowing of His servants. This is what Allah has done [even] with a people that had *exceeded all bounds to their own detriment* (Zumar 39:53) and reached the farthermost limit in unbelief and rank disobedience.

[1] al-Furqān 25:70.

[2] When Allah took up Ibrāhīm to show him *the preternal dominion of the heavens and the earth* (An'ām 6:75), Ibrāhīm saw a servant committing fornication so he imprecated him and he died. Then he saw another fornicating so he imprecated him and he died. Then he saw another and he wanted to imprecate but Allah said, "Slow down, Ibrāhīm! For your prayer is answered, but I have three ways of treating My servants: either he will repent and I will relent towards him, or I will bring out of him a pure progeny, or he might linger doing what he does—but I am behind him, i.e. I have power over him. Bring down My servant so that My servants will not perish!" Cited from 'Aṭā' and Salmān by Abū al-Layth, *Baḥr al-'ulūm* (An'ām 6:75).

Mawlana said that if it were up to us, what would we have done? We would have cursed them. Allah alone is the Creator, and with Him there is vast mercy. When our liege lord Mūsā imprecated Qārūn and Allah caused the earth to swallow the latter, Qārūn was beseeching Mūsā and asking for his forgiveness. He called for his mercy seventy times but our liege lord Mūsā–upon him peace–did not turn towards him. In the end our nurturing Lord said to him, "O Mūsā! He besought you seventy times so that you might grant him mercy but you did not turn to him. By My glory and might! If he had called me once I would have delivered him and I would have pardoned him.[1] You did not grant him mercy because you did not create him. However, I created him." This is immense glad tidings!

Then Allah said to our liege lord Ibrāhīm, "O Ibrāhīm, I have not given you of the oceans of My mercy other than a drop from the tip of a needle. Yet with this mercy your liver has burnt up out of mercy for your child. Is My mercy for My slaves less than your mercy for your child? I am not in need of mercy. It is all for My slaves, whom I have honored and whom I have made My vicegerents. Why do you interfere between Me and them?"

May Allah grant us understanding. By the sanctity of the Beloved, by the sanctity of the Fatiha.

[1] Narrated from Ibn ʿAbbās by ʿAbd al-Razzāq, Ṭabarī, Ibn Abī Ḥātim and al-Zajjāj in their *Tafsīrs* (Qaṣaṣ 28:82); Ibn Abī Shayba, *Muṣannaf* (16:535 §32504); and Ibn ʿAsākir, *Tārīkh Dimashq* (61:95-96).

91

[Rebelling against authority] – Who sows the wind reaps the whirlwind – Reason has limited power – Solving the world crisis

I seek refuge in Allah from the accursed devil
In the Name of Allah the All-Beneficent the Most Merciful
There is no power nor strength but with Allah the High, the Magnificent
Permission, O my Master, support!
Our way is companionship, and goodness is in the congregation

[Various answers of Mawlana al-Shaykh Nazim to some questions.] The murid is in the hand of the shaykh in order for the murid to journey to Allah. The murid's shaykh is more knowledgeable of it than he is and this fact is clear. This is why the shaykh opens up leeway for him to move him. For the murid, from the aspect of "for that which he was created for,"[1] he must complete his role in this world—and you will see the murid falling into error and his shaykh cleaning him up—and although *to each one his orientation that he turns to*, nevertheless, *so race to the good things* (Baqara 2:148).

Our nurturing Lord is not bound by the sacred Law. No legal rulings bind Him. He is *All-Effecter of whatever He wishes* (Hūd 11:107, Burūj 85:16). what is binding on the servant is *so race to the good things*, i.e. do not tread the way of evil. Whenever the human being is forced to do something he is excused (Baqara 2:173, Naḥl 16:106). Mistakes are excused (Baqara 2:286, Aḥzāb 33:5). Forgetfulness is excused (Baqara 2:286). When a person writhes in pain at the thought of his evildoing, that will be an avenue for the substitution of bad deeds to good ones.

Mawlana al-Shaykh [ʿAbd Allah al-Daghistani] said that our liege lord Muḥyī al-Dīn Ibn ʿArabī said[2] in the explanation of *and whoever does even a small ant's weight in evil shall see it* (Zalzala 99:8) that yes, our nurturing Lord shall make him see even a small ant's weight of evil, but in a form substituted to excellent deeds,[3] and this is appropriate to the generosity of our nurturing

[1] Part of the Prophetic hadith on foreordained destiny. See Suhba I.81, third note.

[2] See Ibn ʿArabī, *Futūḥāt* (chapter 234).

[3] To the point the forgiven sinner will want more of his past sins to be counted and will say, "I also have other sins I do not see here." A Prophetic hadith narrated from Abū Dharr by Wakīʿ, *Zuhd*; Aḥmad (35:313 §21393); Muslim; Tirmidhī, *Sunan* and

Lord. Even a small child will understand, but he will not know the meaning of the parents' love. That understanding is too far from him.

The battle between good and evil is a dam that does not stop work but it reduces speed, as also do the unacceptable deeds that require repentance from the servant and for which he must ask forgiveness. The meaning of this is the condemnation of the work of his own soul. This condemnation gives him strength and orients him towards the race to good things (Baqara 2:148). For there is not one servant with a pure heart except he will condemn ugly matters, and his condemnation gives him strength to propel himself towards Allah Almighty. This is why the servant is between good and evil, and this battle endures.

Question: Why does Allah not respond to the supplicant's cry for help?

Answer: How many a sick person in the hospital cries out for the physician to remove the splint from his hand or his foot? Does the physician hear? He will not do other than what he considers to be in the interest of the patient. As for us, and so that the people of Islam will not run away, Allah has ordered us, *O you who believe! Obey Allah* (Nisā' 4:59, Anfāl 8:20, Muḥammad 47:33) *and endure steadfastly* (al-Anfāl 8:46) until Allah changes it.

It is difficult to change the state of things. To rebel against the authority is not an easy matter, because that population in that level will be in agreement with the government even in its inward thoughts. And when they brought themselves low, they were humiliated. "Your deeds are your workers."[1] It is like the Turks. They were glorious in the time of the kings. After the glory of Islam they abolished the sultanate then they abolished the caliphate then they objected to religion, and people went along with them. Allah had given them might with the sultans but they were forever insisting, "we want other than them, we want freedom." By "freedom" is meant not being bound by any stricture from the side of religion. This is the freedom which populations mean. Turks want freedom so that they will not be bound by any religious laws and rules, and this is the result.

"Whoever sows the wind reaps the whirlwind" i.e. something worse. Now, in Turkey, in the universities, young men are eating one another. These ones are the post-caliphate generation, i.e. this generation emerged from their hand. They planted this in their heart and this was never the matter of the

Shamā'il (on the Prophet's smile); Ibn Abī al-Dunyā, *Hawātif* and *Qaṣr al-amal*; al-Bazzār; and others. The Prophet smiled so widely his molars showed, so this report was included in Aḥmad Ghumārī's *Shawāriq al-anwār al-munīfa bi-ẓuhūr al-nawājidh al-sharīfa* and 'Aṭā' Allāh b. Fayḍ al-Sindī's *al-Arba'ūn fil-tabassum wal-ḍaḥik.*

[1] See Suhba I.27, third note and Suhba I.28, seventh note.

sultans. This is why a rule has come in conformity with their deeds and their intentions, and patient endurance is necessary. *Verily the One God does not change what is in a people until they change what is in themselves* (Ra'd 13:11). Allah says, *corruption has appeared in the land and the sea with what the hands of the people have earned* (al-Rūm 30:41), and it is not from the outside. It is not from the sky nor from under the earth but rather *with what the hands of the people have earned.* Because of our acts, *so that He will cause them to taste some of what they have done* (al-Rūm 30:41).

If Allah were to take people to account over all their deeds the final Hour would come. They tried all the roads and they found them all impracticable. But the road of the faith-system is practicable. However they act overproud. They return to all the other roads and they find them still impracticable. *And if you quarrel about something then refer it back to the One God and His Messenger* (al-Nisā' 4:59). Until they refer the matter back to Allah and His Messenger they will have no solution ever. So let them eat one another. It is of the honoring of the servants that the All-True has given them freedom of choice. The human being sees himself and sees his self-respect. The completion of your self-respect is in your return to Allah and His Messenger. If you do not accept, then taste your violence against one another (An'ām 6:65).

Allah does not act out of emotion. Men are prone to emotion. We are in the midst of immense mercy but the servant is unaware. If something smites him, Allah shall compensate him. Mawlana used to say that even a mosquito-bite would repel punishment from the next life to fifty thousand levels. The one that understands understands; and the one that does not understand will understand when it comes to pass. It is inevitable that the human being will be exposed to harm. Whatever smites people they will be given its compensation. If Allah judged on the basis of sentiment everything would fall apart. Nuclear war in the presence of Allah is one of the avenues of moving to the interlife. There are a thousand different ways to moving there, and means without limit and without count. That is why every single servant must inevitably move there in whatever fashion it happens. He will meet his demise in one of a thousand different ways. All that is asked is the opening of the door for the soul to exit the prison of the body.

What happens at the moment of death? Whoever has not tasted does not know. The *rūḥ* (spirit) alone is the one that comprehends in life and after death. *Then We lifted from you your blindfold, so your sight today is iron-sharp* (Qāf 50:22). Today we are wearing a blindfold. Set free the spirit that is shackled by the body. Your body has put it in shackles. Set it free from its shackles. Free it from the prison of the five senses. When it is set free it will return whence it came. *And they have not reckoned the One God by His true reckoning* (al-An'ām 6:91, al-Zumar 39:67). He is the Greatest of the greatest Who takes over everything while we are the smallest of the smallest, so how can we reckon Allah? For example the fish in the wide ocean, if you could ask it to define this wide ocean that has no beginning and no end—can it? So what can the one with limited mind and limited strength understand? He cannot possible encompass knowledge of Allah. We are the ones encompassed, not the ones encompassing. How can that fish inside the vast ocean out-ocean the ocean? But when that fish cannot comprehend, will it deny the existence of the ocean just because it fails to understand? Will the fish say I do not understand this? Will a dot be tasked to embrace the vast ocean?

After arrival understanding will increase, but he will not comprehend. If he comprehended his heart would explode. Allah Most High said, *and We have more* (Qāf 50:35). If He did not have anything additional so as to give more to His servant, how could He be a nurturing Lord?

Question: how can the crisis of the world be solved?

Answer: it can be solved by abolishing interest all over the world, shutting down all industry for forty days with no production for goods to diminish and until the available products are sold, and making all manufactures work only by day or only by night.

The majority of the world's problems are the over-expansion of industries and manufactures. The solution would be, instead of gathering up industries in one large land, to place divisions of them in many areas and to make each area specific to a single kind of production. The reduction of the size of the production plant will reduce the pressure put on the large ones. It will follow that the rural populations will not be a burden for the urban ones.

Fourth, no sale nor purchase other than by cash, no credit and no installments. Fifth, doing away with paper money and using gold and silver instead so that people will see gold and silver in their hands. Sixth, Let meat be slaughtered once a week and let no animal be slaughtered before one year of age while the adult animal must not be slaughtered before three years of age. Seventh, all the factories that produce nonessential luxuries must be closed and turned into food and drink production for the benefit of the servants. Eighth, unnecessary travel is forbidden on one day of the week to save petrol. The rest of the week let cars be allowed to circulate according to odd and even plate numbers. We want to slow down the speed of the traffic of the world in this fashion.

By the sanctity of the Beloved, by the sanctity of the Fatiha.

92

Slander causes diminishment in the faith of the slandered – Allah is the wisest of judges – Awliya are sources of the holiest outpouring

I seek refuge in Allah from the accursed devil
In the Name of Allah the All-Beneficent the Most Merciful
There is no power nor strength but with Allah the High, the Magnificent
Permission, O my Master, support!
Our way is companionship, and goodness is in the congregation

In the post-dawn suhba in the mosque of al-Mahdī in Damascus,[1] every Quranic verse or noble Prophetic hadith without fail contains the sciences of the first and the last. Mawlana [Shaykh 'Abd Allah al-Daghistani] says that **the Friends of Allah each have competence and authority to receive 24,000 thousands of the meanings of each verse or hadith**. More than that, **if a human being acted in observance of the exigency of a single Quranic verse, it would be enough for him until the Day of Resurrection**. That is, he will not finish putting its commands into practice until he moves on to the second verse and so forth. From this noble verse it is possible to receive the knowledge of spiritual openings. Mawlana said, **if a human being acted in observance of the noble verse and applied as it truly should be applied, he himself would become a sign from the signs of Allah**.

Mawlana said, we want to explain one verse of the noble Qur'ān whereby our nurturing Lord says, ***would anyone of you like to eat the flesh of his brother, dead***—*then you would abominate it!* Its completion is, *and beware the One God. Verily the One God is Oft-Relenting, Most Merciful* (al-Ḥujurāt 49:12). Our Almighty nurturing Lord with this noble verse pointed out the most evil trait of character in human beings. He alluded to slander because this sickness has spread to all people, and if all creatures do not clean themselves of it they can never obtain the stations of nearness to Allah Almighty.

Mawlana says in explanation of this verse that **even the wolf does not eat the flesh of its own kind**. So the meaning of one that eats the flesh of his brother is that he is a greater evil than the wolf. If there were for slanderers a lowlier and more despicable description than this, Allah would have used it to describe them. But because there exists no attribute lowlier, he indicated it: *to*

[1] I.e. the mosque of Mawlana Shaykh 'Abd Allah al-Daghistani on Mount Qasyūn.

eat the flesh of his brother, dead. As many blameworthy traits as were mentioned in the Qur'ān, the very worst of them fell on the slanderers of people. Whoever slanders people is the most evil of people in character because it is the most evil attribute of humankind.

In confirmation of this our master the Shaykh related a story that happened in the time of the Messenger –upon him the blessings and peace of Allah. Two of the Companions came to the Prophet and said, "Messenger of Allah, we are feeling strong stomach cramps. Please medicate us with your medication. We want a treatment." The Messenger said to them, "You have eaten raw meat and that is the cause of your stomach ailment." They said, "Messenger of Allah, we did not eat any meat." He repeated what he had said. They swore, "By Allah, Messenger of Allah! We have not tasted a morsel of meat for a fortnight." The Messenger became angry and said, "You did eat raw meat. Make yourselves vomit." Whereupon chunks of raw meat—carrion—came out of their mouths and the cramps stopped. The Companions were puzzled by this and they asked him, "What is this, Messenger of Allah?" I.e. what is the wisdom and from where did this come when we have not eaten any meat? He said to them, "On your way here you passed by the house of So and so and you began to slander him, did you not? This is slander and this is the result."

Mawlana said that slander will also be a cause for the diminishment of the *dīn* (faith) of the one being slandered. Why? Because as a result of your slander, darkness descends on that person and there remains no vigor for worship and divine service. You yourself will be the cause of that effect. For our nurturing Lord brought creatures into being only for worship. He said–exalted is He–*and I did not create the jinns and human beings but so that they would worship Me* (al-Dhāriyāt 51:56). **By slandering that servant you have harmed him and you will be the reason for changing that for which he was created, i.e. servanthood, as if you had killed the *dīn* of that person by reason of your slandering him.** This is why the most evil of people are the slanderers.

Mawlana is saying that the killing of the *dīn* of a person is worse than killing a thousand human beings. The pride of creations–upon him the blessings and peace of Allah–said, O servants of Allah, did not your nurturing Lord Almighty say in His glorious Book, *is not the One God indeed the Wisest of judges?* (al-Tīn 95:8). Yes He did, He alone is the Wisest of judges, so that you will not yourselves dare to judge anyone by saying he is an evildoer or a depraved person or an open sinner. You must know that the Wisest of judges is the nurturing Lord of the worlds. So why did you yourself venture to judge, and you pre-empted the judgment of the nurturing Lord of the worlds, and you pre-empted for that person to redress himself after this day? This is hidden polytheism[1] on your part! As much as the servant might be an inveterate sinner, he is not infallible. There might issue from a servant a thousand mistakes but when he errs that error is not forever held against that servant as long as the door of repentance is open. It might be his heart will be inspired to repent. What do you know?

Thus did the Messenger–upon him the blessings and peace of Allah–advise the Companions. O my Companions, do you not recognize that Allah is the wisest of judges? Why do you yourselves judge that servant? Even I do not judge over the servants for this jurisdiction is not with me. Therefore slander is forbidden and the slanderer is someone that claims partnership with Allah, as if he is a partner in judgment! But Allah has no partner.

Mawlana said that the Quranic verses of Allah are oceans, endless oceans that would never end even if they were explained from pre-existence to everlastingness. For each Quranic verse represents the knowledges of the All-True and likewise the hadiths of the Prophet–upon him the blessings and peace of Allah–are like the signs of Allah Almighty. The Awliya swim in those oceans to the extent of their ability in knowledge and in accordance with *and above every possessor of knowledge there is one with vaster knowledge* (Yūsuf 12:76). In this fashion each wali plunges into those oceans and takes of the pearls and jewels to the extent of his ability. Every Prophet and every wali enters and takes of them to the extent of his capacity.

It is impossible for the showing of incapacity to come to an end. Every Prophet and every wali confesses incapacity on their part. **When the servant recognizes and admits his absolute incapacity and says, "I have no capacity, I am powerless," at that time Allah strengthens the servant with a holy strength, and He subjects to them the ability to enter into those oceans and grasp what they want. At that time the servant never tires and is never sated from receiving the pearls of meanings and the pearls of spiritual realities because he has become supported by Allah and is not left to his own strength. Rather, the holiest outpouring is coursing in him from the presence of Allah.** Until the servant reaches that station, his status will be like that of a battery-operated machine that stops when the batteries are empty. But the one that has become connected with his nurturing Lord is receiving a *sabīl* (waterway) from the heart to the heart and he represents a *fayḍ aqdas* (holiest outpouring).

The Friends of Allah are always present in this world whether openly or in a hidden way. In our time all the Awliya that are supported with external miraculous gifts have disappeared. Otherwise, if a single miraculous gift ap-

[1] See Suhba 96, third note.

peared, the whole world would be filled with their renown. So the Friends of Allah exist but they do not appear in the open. If they showed their miraculous gifts the activities of the evildoers would break down. Whoever wanted to crawl to evildoing with a single step, the earth would be ordered to subdue him, and if all the nations came together to free a man from the earth they could not. The wali would say to the earth's ear, "Grab the feet of every evildoer." And the earth hears. The miraculous gift of the Awliya would be in that. Why does the wali not carry it out? For evil has to reach its peak because it is of the signs of the Hour, after which follows the emergence of the Mahdi. An allegory of that is that when the lady of the house puts the food on the fire she keeps watching it and only when it is cooked will she put out the fire. This is an important matter which the Messenger of Allah speaks about.[1]

The Friends of Allah exist in every period of history. They are the wellsprings of the holiest outpouring. It flows from them to the servants and the seekers. If there is anyone into whose heart the holiest outpouring does not flow, he is a dead person moving about. His heart has died, whereas the life of the heart is with the holiest outpouring from the presence of Allah. This outpouring searches for pure, intact, clean hearts so that it would pour into them. When the servant acknowledges absolute incapacity that outpouring runs into him. But when he contents himself with his own ego, at that time this door is closed. Why does Mawlana speak of these things? Because they are among the high manners that are indispensable for us in every time of history, especially in the time of transition from one period to another. Whatever harms our morales and high spirits the Awliya shall forcefully remove it so that no harm will smite one at the time of the coming events.

Our liege lord ʿAlī said–may Allah ennoble his countenance–"Whoever guards himself from Allah lives blessed and journey in the lands of Allah secure"[2] until he passes on. And we are in the days or in the time of transition from period to period, hence the Awliya do not want for the same disease to move from this period to the next. Whoever is pure and clean and unscathed will remain until the time of the Mahdi. As for the one with blameworthy traits and the slanderer he cannot move from period to period. He must clean himself of his own will so that he can reach that time.

By the sanctity of the Beloved, by the sanctity of the Fatiha.

[1] See Suhba I.44, second note.

[2] Narrated to here as a Prophetic hadith from (i) Samura by Abū Nuʿaym, *Tārīkh Aṣbahān* (2:217 "in the lands of his enemy"); (ii) ʿAlī b. Abī Ṭālib by Abū Nuʿaym, *Ḥilya* (2:175 "in His lands").

93

Divine help through the servant's acknowledgment of his incapacity – The least level of the people of Paradise – [*The nurturing Lord of the worlds*]

I seek refuge in Allah from the accursed devil
In the Name of Allah the All-Beneficent the Most Merciful
There is no power nor strength but with Allah the High, the Magnificent
Permission, O my Master, support!
Our way is companionship, and goodness is in the congregation

All the ranks that are dressed upon the servant are given to him to the extent of his acknowledgment of his own incapacity. The more they recognize Allah the more the magnificence and grandeur of the All-True shows, and the more the magnificence and grandeur of the All-True shows, the smaller they become in their own eyes. The more Allah shows with His power—at that time what does the human being see? What remains of his own power and his own claims? Human beings show off power through the things that were subjugated for him. If he wants even to pick up a stone from the earth and throw it he needs power. And it is Allah that has subjugated for him the power that exists on earth. Yet people show off with power, although without that subjugation it is undoubted that the human being has the least capacity of all. And the more he confesses to his incapacity, the more he will keep receiving extensive help from Allah.

When does that lordly extension of help become cut off? When he begins to forget that power that comes from Allah and when he sees himself and his state as the be-all and end-all, Quickly this power that supports him is cut off and he remains in darkness and incapacity, otherwise, as long as he continues to acknowledge complete incapacity then help keeps coming without interruption. This is why the Messenger of Allah–upon him the blessings and peace of Allah–would keep supplicating, "O Allah! Do not leave me to myself for the blink of an eye."[1]

Mawlana says that as long as the servant acknowledges his incapacity, Allah shall open for him an opportunity to glorify in the ocean of power and in the ocean of knowledge. Whatever Allah has given them—and it is abundant—nevertheless, when their gaze falls on what Allah has with Him, they see it

[1] See Suhba I.28, fifth note.

[=what they have] as nothing yet. In allusion to this He said–exalted is He–*and you have not been given of knowledge but a little* (Banū Isrā'īl/Isrā' 17:85). It is permanently little because whatever you have been given is limited and fit to increase, whereas what is with Allah has no beginning for it to have an end. and it is not subsumed by any delimitation or enumeration. *What is with you runs out and what is with the One God abides* (al-Naḥl 16:96), i.e. it abides from pre-existence to everlastingness, it has no beginning and no end. The Prophets and the Awliya know this, just as it is impossible for them to comprehend what is with Allah. For if they had the possibility of knowing everything that is with Allah, those ones would be partners in the knowledge of Allah and this is impossible. There is no possibility for the servants to partner with Allah since He is without partner, and He is the All-Giver. He pours out over His servants from pre-eternity to everlastingness. The servant asks, is there more? and Allah says *and We have more* (Qāf 50:35).

This is the matter that makes hearts relax and be at peace. For the servant thinks about what would happen with us if the giving ran out. Do not fear. There is no possibility for what is with Allah to run out. May Allah grant us and you to enter Paradise. May Allah grant us to enter the abode of generosity—His generosity.

There are open invitations over there, in the gardens of Paradise. The turn comes for the one with the lowest of all the ranks of Paradise to invite all of the people of Paradise to his place.[1] When we want to invite people we think, how many will come? You must know, is it within your means? What do you think about whoever wants to invite the people of Paradise? It is an invitation they have never seen in their own gardens of Paradise. It is special to him, so that the happiness of the invitees and the happiness of the inviter would be complete. He will offer them what has not come up with them of the different kinds of blessings, food and drink, and he will dress them with tunics, then he will crown each and everyone—with *be! and it shall be* (al-Baqara 2:117, Āl 'Imrān 3:47, 3:59 etc.)—with crowns in the form of turbans. The men of Paradise do not sport beards or moustaches except our liege lord Ādam. He is the father of humankind so he is bearded.[2] All others have, instead of beard

[1] Narrated from Abū Hurayra by Aḥmad (16:544-545 §10932); al-Tha'labī (Zukhruf 43:71); Abū Nu'aym, *Ṣifat al-janna*. See Muḥ. Ibn Qayyim al-Jawziyya, *Ḥādī al-arwāḥ ilā bilād al-afrāḥ*, chapters 40 (The lowest-ranked of the people of Paradise); 59 (The intervisitations of the people of Paradise); 60 (The souks of Paradise).

[2] Al-Sakhāwī said in *al-Maqāṣid al-ḥasana*, "I have seen it handwritten by one of the scholars that this was said about Ādam, but I do not know anything firm about that." A Prophetic hadith states, "All the men of Paradise are beardless except Mūsā b. 'Imrān. His beard reaches to his navel." Narrated from (i) Ibn Mas'ūd by Ṭabarānī per Ibn

and moustaches, a green light, and their crowns are turbans. After the crowning, there also appears with the host, in his gardens of Paradise, that which no eye has seen, no ear has heard of and which has never dawned on the heart of any human being. And he shall give everyone gifts appropriate to all their stations—and he himself is in the lowest of the ranks of Paradise.

The Prophet–upon him the blessings and peace of Allah–says that after all return to their gardens of Paradise they will find with them all that they have seen and which has pleased them, even the palaces or anything else that pleased them, they will find they will find it in their possession, yet it will not diminish anything in the least from their host's storehouses of blessings and gardens. It will only be in honor of those people who were given of the storehouses of Paradise by Allah that which no eye has seen and no ear has heard of. If the storehouses of the lowest-ranked of the people of Paradise are such, then what do you think about the storehouses of the nurturing Lord of the worlds?

We think that the phrase "Lord of the worlds" is easy. What greatness and magnificence does such a phrase denote? *Praise belongs to the One God, the nurturing Lord of the worlds* (Fātiḥa 1:2). It is because of this that He described Himself as *the nurturing Lord of the worlds, the All-Beneficent, the Most Merciful, the Owner of the Day of Reckoning* (Fātiḥa 1:2-4), the All-Revered, the All-Magnified, the One Whose worlds cannot be counted to begin to indicate the magnificence of the All-True, the Majestic and Exalted.

May Allah grant it to us and you by the sanctity of the Beloved, by the sanctity of the Fatiha.

Ḥajar in Sakhāwī's *Maqāṣid*; (ii) Jābir by ʿUqaylī, Ibn ʿAdī, Abū Nuʿaym and Khaṭīb. Qurṭubī (*Tadhkira*) said the same is said of his brother Hārūn.

94

Individual rights and public rights – Rights of Allah and rights of servants

I seek refuge in Allah from the accursed devil
In the Name of Allah the All-Beneficent the Most Merciful
There is no power nor strength but with Allah the High, the Magnificent
Permission, O my Master, support!
Our way is companionship, and goodness is in the congregation

Crimes in penal law is in two categories: individual right and public right. In the presence of Allah, however, sins are not categorized in this fashion but as the right of servants and the right of Allah. The right of Allah is according to two possible wills: either He wants to pardon everything or He wants to punish. He has absolute freedom. However, He will question about the rights of the servants so that the ones that were deprived of their rights will either relent or they will demand retaliation on the Day of Regathering. That is so that no injustice remains unrequited at that time.

Our master the Shaykh [ʿAbd Allah al-Daghistani] said about Nūḥ's flood that there was an old woman who used to bring milk to our liege lord Nūḥ–upon him peace–and she would request of him not to forget her when the flood takes place and to tell her beforehand so that she would embark with him. The flood took place and ended, and our liege lord Nūḥ disembarked. During that time Allah confined that old woman in her house because she had no milk to sell. After a while she took the milk again to our liege lord Nūḥ and she asked him about that flood. Has it happened or not yet? He answered her, "Glory to Allah! You are alive? Where were you? The flood took place and people drowned!" She said to him, "O Prophet of Allah! I did not see it. I was in my house and I was unaware of it. But one day my cow went to graze and came back all muddied so I was wondering about that." This is from Allah's protection of her.

When Allah wants to put His servants in His safeguard, you must not fear. Although our acts attract problems to us, nevertheless as long as you keep the best opinion, you do not think that your nurturing Lord will let you down, you say, "I have reached evening and morning by the grace of Allah," do not think that He will let you reach morning and evening without safety and without blessing. Just take care of your opinion. For it has been transmitted in the [Divine] Hadith, "I am exactly as My servant thinks of Me."[1]

We have reached morning and we have reached evening by His grace and bounty. Praise belongs to Allah. By the sanctity of the Fatiha.

[1] See Suhba I.8, second note.

95
[God-given knowledge is partial and there is no partnership for anyone with Allah in knowledge] – The station of judgeship is for the Messenger – [Prostration is indispensable in worship] – Actions are according to conclusions

I seek refuge in Allah from the accursed devil
In the Name of Allah the All-Beneficent the Most Merciful
There is no power nor strength but with Allah the High, the Magnificent
Permission, O my Master, support!
Our way is companionship, and goodness is in the congregation

Allah Almighty opens up for Prophets and Awliya the door of spiritual knowledge and He lets them swim in the oceans of spiritual knowledges and realities. Still the servant is servant and the Lord is Lord. Allah Almighty gives of the sciences and the spiritual knowledges, but these God-given knowledges are countable and limited no matter how abundant they are. They cannot be considered more than something little: *and you have not been given of knowledge but a little* (Banū Isrā'īl/Isrā' 17:85). If they knew just as the All-True knows, it would necessarily ensue that they are partners with Allah in His knowledge, whereas He is free of partners. Whatever is given to the servant is only a part. As for the whole, it remains with Allah Almighty.

Mawlana [Shaykh 'Abd Allah al-Daghistani] says that when our Prophet–upon him the blessings and peace of Allah–said, "I am a helpless servant," Allah made him the *qāsim* (distributor) to all the Prophets, the Awliya, the believers and the totality of creatures. For the station of distributorship is with the Prophet and he is the one that distributes to one and all on behalf of the All-True. Al-Qāsim is the Messenger of Allah–upon him the blessings and peace of Allah–the like of whom no one has humbled himself in the presence of Allah Almighty. His statement "I am a helpless servant"[1] shows the perfection of humbleness.

[1] E.g. in the hadiths "I eat the way a the servant eats and I sit the way the servant sits for I am only a servant"; "Do not aggrandize me the way 'Īsā b. Maryam was aggrandized for I am only a servant, so say, 'His servant and Messenger'"; "I am only a servant, I do not know other than what Allah has taught me;" "I am only a servant under orders, whatever I am ordered I do."

Mawlana says Prophets have the station of Prophethood while Awliya have the stations of sainthood and believers have the ranks of belief. Whatever was reserved especially for them of knowledges and spiritual openings is distributed to them from the ocean of the knowledges of the Prophet–upon him the blessings and peace of Allah. For Allah pours into the ocean of the Prophet and from the latter he distributes and divides to the Awliya and the others. This is the attribute of the Messenger of Allah–upon him the blessings and peace of Allah. This is why he is the manifestation of the knowledges of the first and the last.[1] He knows the ancients and he knows those of the latter days. He is the Pride of existent beings. Despite all that he is not a judge in front of the divine presence of the Almighty All-True. However, towards creatures, then he is our judge and ruler. Mawlana says that if the Messenger were a judge in the presence of Allah he would not have waited for Jibril to descend to him but he would have ruled without waiting.

Mawlana says that **Allah shall give the Prophet the station of judgeship together with the reality of Prophethood on the Day of the Regathering, and He shall dress him with the station of judgeship after Allah has judged all the servants** by virtue of the verse *so whoever does even a small ant's weight in goodness shall see it and whoever does even a small ant's weight in evil shall see it* (Zalzala 99:7-8). **After He rules between the servants and passes judgment He will call the Prophet–upon him the blessings and peace of Allah–and He will send him to the *Praiseworthy Station*** (Banū Isrā'īl/Isrā' 17:79) **and make him *the Wisest of judges* over the people of the Regathering.**[2] Every person must recognize that the Prophet reached this station because of humbling himself.

"Who humbles himself for Allah, Allah elevates him."[3] No one has humbled himself the way the Messenger of Allah humbled himself. This is why all the

[1] See Suhba I.80, 11th note and the last words of Suhba I.61.

[2] This is the gist of the many reports to the effect that Allah will make the Prophet sit on the Throne. See Suhba I.75, fourth note.

[3] A Prophetic hadith narrated from (i) Abū Hurayra by Ismā'īl b. Ja'far, *Ḥadīth 'Alī b. Ḥujr al-Sa'dī 'an Ismā'īl b. Ja'far al-Madanī* (p. 339 §271); Aḥmad (12:139 §7206, 14:552 §9008); Dārimī (*Zakāt, faḍl al-ṣadaqa*); Muslim (*al-Birr wal-ṣila, istiḥbāb al-'afwi wal-tawāḍu'*); Tirmidhī (*al-Birr wal-ṣila, al-tawāḍu', ḥasan ṣaḥīḥ*); (ii) Abū Sa'īd al-Khudrī by Aḥmad (18:250 §11723); Ibn Mājah (*Zuhd, al-barā'a min al-kibr*); Abū Ya'lā; and as their own saying (iii-iv) Salmān and Ibn Mas'ūd by Wakī, *Zuhd*; Aḥmad, *Zuhd*; Ibn Abī al-Dunyā, *al-Tawāḍu' wal-khumūl*; (v) 'Umar b. al-Khaṭṭāb by Ibn 'Uyayna, *Ḥadīth Sufyān b. 'Uyayna riwāyata al-Marwazī*; Ibn Abī Shayba, *Muṣannaf*; Ibn Shabba, *Tārīkh al-Madīna*; Abū Dāwūd, *Zuhd*; (vi) Bukayr b. al-Ashajj by Bukhārī, *al-Tārīkh al-kabīr*; (vii) Ibn al-Sammāk by al-Zubayr b. Bakkār, *al-Muwaffaqiyyāt*; (viii) Ka'b al-Aḥbār by Ibn Abī al-Dunyā, *al-Shukr*. Mujāhid said that when Allah sent

stations of nearness are opened to him. The Prophets came for the realization of this goal, because the human being is tyrannical and overproud, he must not submit to anyone. And because the ego had the audacity to say, "I am me and you are you"[1] instead of submitting and saying, "You are my nurturing Lord and I am Your servant." This is its attribute. The ego was originally made overproud. This is why the Prophets came to realize this goal. When the servant humbles himself the way is facilitated for him to obtain all the ranks, and the divine enablement towards success will be inseparable from him in all his affairs. As for the overproud and tyrannical he is detested by people and in the presence of the Lord of the worlds.

This is what Mawlana is indicating when he says that the more the servant humbles himself the worthier he is in the presence of Allah and His Messenger. This is why the best of the acts of piety to draw near to Allah is for the servant to prostrate to Him. Prostration represents perfect outward humbleness in the servant, and without it no act of drawing near will be acceptable to Allah, because all such acts do not weigh the like of a single prostration. Without it, it is as if one were to read the Qur'ān without the Fatiha. Is there any Sura that can fill in for the Fatiha in the Qur'ān? On the other hand the Opening of the Book can fill in for the whole Qur'ān. This is why its recitation according to Imam al-Shāfiʿī and Imam al-Aʿẓam[2] is a categorical obligation and a requirement. Without its recitation neither worship nor prayer can be accomplished. In the same way it is possible for the servant to do all kinds of pious acts, but if he does not prostrate, all his work remains incomplete and unfinished. The servant will not be recorded as a servant until he places his forehead on the ground in prostration to his exalted and majestic nurturing Lord. For this is the sign of the perfection of humbleness being outwardly expressed in the servant.

You will often see that most people find pious deeds easy to do except prostration. Most of them object so that they will not have to prostrate. This is because of the ego. That is why the Prophets came to break their egos until they prostrate. For they easily prostrate to idols but it is difficult for them to prostrate to the nurturing Lord of the worlds. Among the outward aspects of humbleness is for a person to humble himself to the young and the old and to not get angry against anyone. This needs training because humbleness is the

the flood all the mountains raised their heads except al-Jūdī. It humbled itself for Allah so Allah raised it over all of them and made the ark alight on it per ʿAbd al-Razzāq, *Tafsīr* (al-Qamar 54:9-15).

[1] See Suhba I.59, ninth note.

[2] "The Greatest Imam," as Imam Abū Ḥanīfa is called by the Ḥanafīs.

highest of the ranks of servanthood and the most difficult of them to obtain. For every time you want to humble yourself your ego rebels against you and says, "This is my attribute! How dare you humble me! I want gloriousness not lowliness!" Your ego would accept everything except quitting egotism. It will say, "I worship, I pray, I fast—with my egotism," because your ego will address you and say, "I have prayed! I do not owe anyone anything!" It loves to say favor is from me and not from anyone else.

You must know that prayer and fasting and Hajj are something immense for you, and your ego desires to use them to increase its own arrogance. That is why *woe then to the worshippers that are unmindful of their prayer* (Mā'ūn 107:4-5): they are unmindful of their nurturing Lord and they cater to their egos instead of serving Him. They magnify themselves and they increase in pride and arrogance. Is this servanthood? The ego's pride keeps showing and works to increase. This is the pursuit of the ego, and the people of ego want by any possible means to extract arrogance from wealth, from reputation, from knowledge of this world or even from the aspect of religion also. He will go on Hajj a lot of times so that it will be said he went on Hajj a lot of times. All the while the ego does not acknowledge anything —no nurturing Lord, no Awliya and no Prophets. It only says me and me alone.

Mawlana says—moving on from the explanation of the Prophet's humbleness to the explanation of the state of Iblīs who is the paragon of pride—that just as the Messenger–upon him the blessings and peace of Allah–possesses utmost humbleness, Iblīs is at the opposite extreme in possessing utmost haughtiness. He is someone that worshipped his nurturing Lord 2,000 years, showing Him sincerity, and he was of those brought near. Then he brought into servanthood an instant that contradicts servanthood and he followed after the pride of his ego. He turned from the presence of Allah to his own ego, whereby he brought in, in one instant, his own will together with the will of Allah, i.e. he manifested his will in front of Allah.

Mawlana asks, when is the servant truly humble and when will he be harboring pride? Iblīs for 2,000 years did not show any will. He was following the will of Allah and he was the servant of his nurturing Lord. Then, in an instant, he showed his own will together with the will of our nurturing Lord, and he followed his own will, and he became the servant of himself. By so doing he left behind the station of humbleness and he manifested the station of arrogant pride. At that time he fell the way that a plane that runs out of fuel in mid-air falls before reaching its destination. It breaks into pieces and does not arrive. This is why the Awliya ask refuge from Allah from the moment of heedlessness, because it causes one to perish even if he had been worshipping 2,000 years only to follow his own ego in the end. He will have come out of the worship of Allah and he will have become a worshipper of himself. It is no longer fit for him to be in the presence of the All-True. Allah says, "I am the All-Sublime![1] There is no partner for Me[2] in My sublimity."[3]

This is why the Prophet–upon him the blessings and peace of Allah–says, "Actions are only according to conclusions."[4] So **whoever prays is fulfilling the categorical obligation. However, to reach the stations of servanthood, one must come out of the station of ego. Iblīs worshipped his nurturing Lord but was not given the divine enablement of success in coming out of the station of ego. His worship did not bring him out. Therefore you must recognize what station you yourself are in. Are you in the station of servanthood or the station of ego? You will not be able to know without a *murshid* (spiritual guide).**

This is why every person needs a spiritual guide to medicate them. Otherwise they will enter the sphere of the doers of ugly things *and they reckon they excel in handiwork!* (Kahf 18:104). But they are far from that because they are at the station of ego. **They are the *aṣḥāb al-kabā'ir* (doers of enormities) whom the Prophet**–upon him the blessings and peace of Allah –**has promised his intercession** when he said, "My intercession is for those of my Umma who are guilty of enormous sins."[5] Through the blessing of his intercession our work will become accepted and our bad deeds will be substituted with excellent deeds. Otherwise how will our prayer ever be complete and accepted?

From Allah is all success. By the sanctity of the Fatiha.

[1] A Prophetic *hadīth qudsī* narrated from Ibn 'Umar by Aḥmad, *Musnad*; al-Nasā'ī, *al-Sunan al-kubrā*; and others.

[2] A Prophetic *hadīth qudsī* narrated from Abū Hurayra and Abū Sa'īd al-Khudrī by 'Abd b. Ḥumayd, *Musnad*; Ibn Mājah; al-Tirmidhī (*ḥasan*); and others.

[3] "Sublimity is My cloak alone." A Prophetic *hadīth qudsī* narrated from Abū Hurayra by al-Ṭayālisī; al-Ḥumaydī; Ibn Abī Shayba; Ibn Rāhūyah; Aḥmad; and in the *Sunan*.

[4] Narrated from (i) Sahl b. Sa'd al-Sā'idī by Ibn al-Ja'd, *Musnad*; Aḥmad; al-Bukhārī; and others; (ii) Mu'āwiya b. Abī Sufyān by Abū Ya'lā; Ibn Ḥibbān; (iii) 'Ā'isha by Ibn Ḥibbān; al-Bayhaqī, *al-I'tiqād*; Ibn 'Asākir, *Tārīkh*; (iv) 'Alī b. Abī Ṭālib by Ṭabarānī, *Awsaṭ*; (v) Muḥ. b. Ka'b al-Quraẓī by Abū al-Layth, *Tanbīh al-ghāfilīn*; Ibn Baṭṭa, *Ibāna*; (vi) Ibn 'Abbās by al-Lālakā'ī, *I'tiqād*; Ibn Bishrān, *Amālī*.

[5] See Suhba I.86, fourth note.

96

Meaning of fear of Allah – Real servanthood is to follow the divine will free of *shirk khafīy* – Abū Bakr and ʿAlī's high station – [Secret of the Qur'ān]

I seek refuge in Allah from the accursed devil
In the Name of Allah the All-Beneficent the Most Merciful
There is no power nor strength but with Allah the High, the Magnificent
Permission, O my Master, support!
Our way is companionship, and goodness is in the congregation

When Iblīs openly displayed his will—i.e. his ego's will in the face of the will of his nurturing Lord—he was expelled from servanthood and his deeds became *scattered motes* (Furqān 25:23). Mawlana [Shaykh ʿAbd Allah al-Daghistani] says that the servant must always think so that he will be wide awake. "What do you think is the deed that would be the reason for all my good deeds to be demolished?" For there are certain words, certain acts because of which all of the good work one has done until that time will be demolished. It is like Iblīs's motion that ended up as the cause for the destruction of his righteous deeds. Therefore it is a duty for the believer to be paying attention lest Iblīs will cause him to fall into doing something that will become a cause for the destruction of all his good deeds. This is the meaning of "the fear of Allah."[1]

Mawlana says that our work will become *scattered motes*, but this does not mean that the servant will not be given anything in exchange for these works. Rather Allah never mislays any recompense even a small ant's weight, but **the meaning of its becoming *scattered motes* is there will no longer remain any driving force in that work to propel it towards the stations of nearness to Allah, i.e. that work will no longer serve to make the servant arrive to real life, eternal life and the reality of belief in his lifetime because its power has been lost**. An example would be when a person buys milk and wants to make yoghurt and cheese with it, but if any dirt is found in the container the milk will turn bad. Because of that it is not good for anything, but in spite of that it is not thrown away. Instead it is consumed. Likewise, any deed in which is found the *wakham* (taint) of the ego is turned for the worse by it, it is corrupted by it. As a result it will not bring him high.

[1] See Suhba I.70, fifth note.

The human being's great affliction is his sitting alone with his ego. His keeping good company with his ego is what deprives him of keeping good company with Allah. it deprives him from sitting with Allah and it distracts him from Allah. The ego is forever keeping the servant busy according to its will. It is the head of fitna and problems and upheavals. It never leaves us to sit alone with Allah. Everyone of you wants to sit with us in private but he does not think of sitting in private with his nurturing Lord because the ego comes, and the devil comes, and this world and whim all come to keep you busy away from your nurturing Lord.

Mawlana says that, in the face of his nurturing Lord's will and the will of His Prophet–upon him the blessings and peace of Allah–the servant's displaying of his own will is *shirk khafīy* (hidden polytheism).[1] It means "O nurturing Lord, You want this but I do not like this. Rather I want something else." But the foundation in the reality of servanthood is for the servant to follow the will of Allah and His Messenger. Every time you go back to your own will it means that you have gone back from doing the will of Allah. This is the *shirk khafīy* about which the Messenger of Allah has warned when he said, "Hidden polytheism in my Umma is stealthier than the creeping of the ant."[2] Is the creeping of the ant audible? It comes to you stealthily while you are not paying any attention to it. When you display something contravening the will of Allah and His Messenger, you have certainly committed hidden polytheism. Outwardly you do not know, but all of your work has gone unregarded because of it. Mawlana says that he that pays no attention to these minute matters in the faith-system, his work will have turned bad and become corrupt without his notice.

Then Mawlana moves on to speak about Ādam after explaining Iblīs's situation. He said that Allah made eight gardens of Paradise licit to him with all of their contents except that tree which He forbade to him. Allah Most High said, *but do not approach this Tree* (al-Baqara 2:35), until our mother Ḥawwā' prevailed on him and swayed the will of our liege lord Ādam–upon him peace–and they decided to eat from it. So what was the result? Whoever displays will in contravention of Allah will never succeed. Allah expelled him

[1] See Suhba 96, third note.

[2] Narrated from (i) Abū Mūsā al-Ash'arī by Ibn Abī Shayba; Aḥmad; al-Bukhārī, *al-Tārīkh al-kabīr*; (ii) Ma'qil b. Yasār by al-Bukhārī, *al-Adab al-mufrad*; Abū Ya'lā; (iii) Abū Bakr al-Ṣiddīq by Aḥmad b. 'Alī al-Marwazī, *Musnad Abī Bakr al-Ṣiddīq*; Abū Ya'lā, *Musnad*; (iv) Ḥudhayfa by Abū Ya'lā; (v) Ibn 'Abbās by al-Ḥakīm al-Tirmidhī, *Nawādir*; Ibn Abī Ḥātim (Baqara 2:22); (vi) 'Ā'isha by Ḥakīm al-Tirmidhī, *Nawādir*; 'Uqaylī, *Ḍu'afā'*; Abū Nu'aym, *Ḥilya*; in *mursal* mode, (vii) Mujāhid by Hannād b. Sarīy, *Zuhd*; (viii) Ibn Jurayj by al-Ḥakīm al-Tirmidhī, *Nawādir*; and as his own saying, (ix) Ibn Mas'ūd by Wakī', *Zuhd*; Ibn Ḥibbān, *Thiqāt*.

from Paradise. He even removed from him the garments of Paradise so that he came down to earth naked. The time was night. When the dawn rose and light came up our liege lord Ādam made two prostrations to Allah—so the two cycles of the dawn prayer are from our father Ādam. This is the reason he was brought out of Paradise. Therefore be in compliance and do not be in contravention. The one who is in compliance always wins.

Mawlana asked, did any *shirk khafīy* (hidden polytheism) show from some of the Companions? He replied yes.[1] For this reason only two among the noble Companions have certainly reached their trust in the presence of Allah on Day of *am I not your nurturing Lord* (al-Aʿrāf 7:172). The first of the two is Abū Bakr al-Ṣiddīq, who was the manifestation of "Die before you die,"[2] for he possessed no will with the Messenger of Allah and no personal opinion. Rather he arrived with him to the highest degrees of trusting confirmation and his attribute with him was like that of a dead man: he would follow the Prophet–upon him the blessings and peace of Allah–in everything the way a person's shadow follows him. This is why anything Allah was pouring into the breast of the Prophet, the Prophet would then pour it into the breast of Abū Bakr.[3] For there was complete acceptance with him for everything that the Prophet brought.

With the Awliya also, it is opened to them to the extent of what they find in their hearts of acceptance or its absence. Secrets are not an easy matter. Whenever the murid walks with his own will—i.e. with his mind—it will be impossible for him to come out of the station of mind to the station of secret until he accepts them [=secrets] and until he digests some of the secrets. This is why there will be no spiritual opening for him. For as long as the murid remains with his ego, no secret will be revealed to him—not until he is with his shaykh. At that time his shaykh will look at him and see—is he like him? When he finds there is acceptance with his murid, he will gift him from the secrets to the heart. Our liege lord ʿAlī says–may Allah ennoble his countenance–"If I were to speak from my secret you would kill me before I rise."[4] O noble Companions of the Messenger of Allah, when will you yourself

[1] The Prophet–upon him the blessings and peace of Allah–said, "Shall I not tell you of that which is, in my view, more fearful for you than the arch-liar false Messiah? Hidden polytheism." Narrated from Abū Saʿīd al-Khudrī by Aḥmad and Ibn Mājah.

[2] See Suhba I.32, fourth note.

[3] See Suhba I.21, third note.

[4] Narrated as the saying of (i) Ḥudhayfa by Maʿmar b. Rāshid, *Jāmiʿ* (11:52 §19889); Nuʿaym b. Ḥammād, *Fitan*; (ii) Abū Hurayra by al-Bukhārī, *al-Tārīkh al-kabīr* (4:183 §2416, Sakan b. Ismāʿīl); Abū Zurʿa al-Dimashqī, *al-Fawāʾid al-Muʿallala*; its basis is in Bukhārī's *Ṣaḥīḥ*; (iii) al-Aswad b. Khalaf b. ʿAbd Yaghūth by Bukhārī, *al-Tārīkh al-kabīr*

be a holder of a secret? Not until you are your master's shadow. When you find in yourself acceptance, at that time Allah shall gift you of those secrets to your satiety. Here is our liege lord Abū Bakr al-Ṣiddīq into whose breast Allah poured what He had poured into the breast of the Messenger of Allah–upon him the blessings and peace of Allah.[1]

As for the second one it is our liege lord 'Alī–may Allah ennoble his countenance. He did not have any hidden *shirk* because he also did not display any will of his own in the face of the Prophet's will. "I am the city of knowledge and 'Alī is its gate."[2] I.e. whatever the Messenger of Allah had been given was also given to 'Alī. For the Messenger of Allah–upon him the blessings and peace of Allah–had requested our liege lord 'Alī to behold him for a while. At that time he beheld and witnessed the reality of the Messenger of Allah–upon him the blessings and peace of Allah–as he really was, and from that witnessing he obtained of the sciences of spiritual openings.[3]

Mawlana asks, what was the reason for which the Messenger gifted him that look and that witnessing? Mawlana says that our liege lord 'Alī, likewise, was following him like his shadow. That is why such a station took place for him among the Companions. Mawlana said that our liege lord 'Alī is without the shadow of a doubt the victorious lion of Allah, but despite that he did not use that prodigious force that was with him without the will of the Prophet–upon him the blessings and peace of Allah. He never imprecated anyone, and this is a difficult thing because any person that is shown to possess a certain power will inevitably be driven by his ego to harm another human being, even with his own children!

The upshot of the talk is, *ṭifl al-nafs al-madhmūma* (the childish blame-worthy ego) develops with a person from infancy and it is difficult to leave it. Our liege lord 'Alī, despite having this power, never hurt anybody and never used force except under the will of the Prophet–upon him the blessings and peace of Allah. Thus there were two Companions only who obtained the trusts from the secret of the Qur'ān among the Companions. As for the rest, they left this load with the Messenger of Allah and went, so the Messenger remained under the Companions' load.

(1:29 §35, 1:444 §1423); al-Bayhaqī, *Dalā'il* (2:61); (iv) Khalaf b. 'Abd Yaghūth by Ibn Abī 'Āṣim, *al-Āḥād wal-mathānī* (al-Aswad b. Khalaf).

[1] See two notes up.

[2] A Prophetic hadith narrated from 'Alī and Ibn 'Abbās by al-Tirmidhī and others. See its full documentation in Haddad, *The rightly-guided Caliphs* (pp. 251-252).

[3] For more details on this witnessing see Mawlana Shaykh Hisham Kabbani's Rajab 1413 (December 1992) suhba entitled "Advice of the broken-hearted – You are in perpetual ascension."

Now that the time for the emergence of the secret of the Qur'ān into view has come and as a service to all the Companions at the beginning of the matter, those trusts and spiritual openings have been opened and given to all the Companions, and they have become guardians of the secret of the Qur'ān. This service was accomplished at the hand of Mawlana Sultan al-Awliya. This is why Mawlana said that our liege lord 'Alī, when an opening was granted to him from the secret of the Qur'ān, addressed our liege lord 'Umar saying, "O 'Umar, if I were to divulge one of the secrets that have been given to me you would not have left me but you would have killed me.[1] And these secrets are in our hearts and they shall not emerge into view until you are like us in regard to acceptance."

There are trusts with our nurturing Lord Almighty. For them to be given, our nurturing Lord looks upon His servant. When He finds that there is acceptance with him, it is given. For the ego refuses the secret and says, "I do not accept." So stay with your mind. Once you accept We are there with the giving. This is why it is a duty for the human being to break the ego and shatter it to pieces. When you break it you will succeed in acquiring all the secrets, otherwise the servant will be left with his ego.

This is a suhba. Mawlana is saying that he has no expectation that we will hold fast to it and put it into practice because this is the business of the men of Allah. However, we ourselves hear and recognize where we stand now. We are claiming that we have reached to the Throne of Allah—this is imagination. We are still in *the lowest of the low* (al-Tīn 95:5) and have not yet climbed up to the surface of the earth! May Allah extend to us a special help from Him so that we shall be in His presence.

By the sanctity of the Beloved, by the sanctity of the Fatiha.

[1] See four notes up.

97
[Kaʿb al-Aḥbar – ʿUmar and ʿUthmān's stations – Prophets and Awliya]

I seek refuge in Allah from the accursed devil
In the Name of Allah the All-Beneficent the Most Merciful
There is no power nor strength but with Allah the High, the Magnificent
Permission, O my Master, support!
Our way is companionship, and goodness is in the congregation

Kaʿb al-Aḥbār[1] was of the Jewish scholars. He had knowledge of the Gospel, the Torah, the Psalms and the noble Qurʾān. He submitted in the time of our liege lord ʿUmar although he was already there in the time of the Prophet and in the time of Abū Bakr, but he did not submit until the time of our liege lord ʿUmar. The latter even asked him, "Kaʿb, you were there in the time of the Best of creation and you did not show your belief, then you were there in the time of the best of people and you did not show your belief. so why have you only shown it now?" He replied, "Commander of the believers, what you say is true. I was watching all the signs mentioned in our scriptures that would take place about the Prophet of the end times. Every time I saw a sign just as it was mentioned in the Scripture it would increase me in certainty that he is indeed that Prophet. All of the signs were complete in his lifetime and our books also mentioned two signs that would take place after his time: he would have two ministers that would also be his successors. I waited for these two signs to emerge and I saw the first minister become the first successor and the second minister the second successor. So there remained nothing to prevent me from proclaiming my belief and my submission." Allah made him a conclusive proof over all the scholars of the people of Scripture—"this is one of yours." He watched all the signs until he found them conforming exactly. Mawlana says Kaʿb's knowledge was abundant, whereby he possessed knowledge from the station of Jibril and everything under it, but not of what is over it, for they are spirit-related knowledges.

[1] Abū Isḥāq Kaʿb al-Aḥbār b. Mātiʿ al-Ḥimyarī (68bh-34/556-655) was an erudite rabbi from Yemen who converted to Islam after the death of the Prophet–upon him blessings and peace–and came to Medina in ʿUmar's caliphate then moved to Syro-Palestine and died in Homs. He is trustworthy in hadith and is of the *Tābiʿīn* from whom junior Companions and many Successors related reports such as Muʿāwiya, Abū Hurayra, Ibn ʿAbbās, ʿAbd Allāh b. ʿAmr and Saʿīd b. al-Musayyib. His narrations are in the Four *Sunan*. He died aged over 100 in the caliphate of ʿUthmān.

We had said that two of the Companions had reached the reality of the secret of the Qur'ān, namely our liege lord Abū Bakr and our liege lord 'Alī–Allah be well-pleased with them. As for the rest of the Companions, they left that trust to be carried by the Messenger of Allah–upon him the blessings and peace of Allah. Our liege lord 'Uthmān–Allah be well-pleased with him –is of the rightly-guided Caliphs. Due to the intensity of his modesty the devil was too timid to approach him. He is the one that gathered the Qur'ān, he was the most generous man among the noble Companions and he was the son-in-law of the Prophet–upon him blessings and peace of Allah–[twice,] Dhūl-Nūrayn, "he of the two lights." All of these ranks and this servanthood were with him. Yet, our master the Shaykh says that he did not wholly come out from his own will the way our liege lord Abū Bakr did and our liege lord 'Alī did. For he would do certain things as part of his own will. That is why he did not reach the spirit-related knowledges. And part of the reasons for his becoming a shahid and his killing is that he used his own will together with the will of the Prophet–upon him the blessings and peace of Allah.

Our liege lord 'Umar used to say, "In my time of ignorance there are three things I never did which Islam prohibited strenuously. I found that leaving them were markers of a sound mind. The first is that I never lied in my time of ignorance. For when lying manifests itself in a servant his worth falls to the extent of his lying—and is there any measurement for lying? Thus did I recognize that this is unacceptable." Islam declares terrible war on mendacity. If the servant steers clear of it he would reach the greatest happiness. Lying is like a false lantern that stays lit until *'ishā'* then it goes out. It is not the unbelievers that should be ashamed but the Muslims when they lie. Our liege lord 'Umar says, "when lying manifests itself in a servant his worth falls to the dust and he becomes dirt, even though the attribute of lying came from the Jews.[1] Also, belief does not endure together with lying, so how can it endure with the rest of ugly deeds and sins? Our liege lord 'Umar said, "I never lied in my life. I never drank alcoholic drinks.[2] It is enough stupidity for a man to

[1] See Āl 'Imrān 3:75-78.

[2] Many Arabs forbade themselves from drinking intoxicants in the time of Ignorance, among them Abū Bakr al-Ṣiddīq, 'Uthmān b. 'Affān, 'Uthmān b. Maẓ'ūn, al-'Abbās b. Mirdās al-Sulamī, Qays b. 'Āṣim al-Minqarī, Qiss b. Sā'ida al-Ayādī, 'Ubayd b. al-Abraṣ, 'Abd Allāh b. Jad'ān, Maqīs b. Ṣubāba, Bashīr al-Thaqafī, al-Aslūm al-Yāmī, Ḥarb b. Umayya, Hishām b. al-Mughīra, his brother al-Walīd b. al-Mughīra, Umayya b. Khalaf, Qays b. 'Āṣim and countless others. See Jawād 'Alī, *al-Mufaṣṣal fī tārīkh al-'arab qabla al-islām*, 2nd ed., 10 vols. (Baghdad: Jāmi'at Baghdād, 1413/1993) 4:670-672, 49: *al-Ḥayāt al-yawmiyya, khumūr*). 'Umar swore he "drank hard" in pre-Islamic times as narrated by al-Bayhaqī, *al-Sunan al-kubrā* (10:214) but he stopped when the verse of prohibition (Mā'ida 5:90-91) was revealed as narrated by Ṭabarī and others.

strive to disable his mind. And I never looked at people's women for I never liked for anyone to look at my women."

The one that belies the Friends of Allah, the Prophet–upon him the blessings and peace of Allah–belies him. If there were any Prophethood now, the Awliya would be Prophets. However, it was sealed with the Seal of Prophets; and the immense worth of the Prophet in the presence of his nurturing Lord is through his *wilāya* (Friendship), as *wilāya* is more ancient than *nubuwwa* (Prophethood). The foundation is *wilāya* and without it there would not be any Prophethood. An illustration of that is the existence of deputies upon whom ministership is conferred. So the foundation is for every Prophet to be a *walī* upon whom Prophethood is conferred—and whoever belies the wali belies the Prophet. So Prophethood is external while Friendship is internal, so whoever belies the Prophet commits unbelief while whoever belies the wali does not commit unbelief, because his status is hidden no matter how much the wali becomes famous as possessing his *wilāya*, because it is an internal matter.[1]

Our liege lord ʿUmar added, "I did not drink alcohol because I did not count it as self-respect for a man to use something that invalidates his reason," for such is foolishness and reason is the pride of human beings, and when one's mind is gone he becomes animal-like, so how could anyone accept for that honor to be removed from him and to descend to the rank of animals? "And likewise I would keep safe the honor of others so that no one would violate mine." Yet, despite all that, our liege lord ʿUmar–Allah be well-pleased with him–would at times show *nuqṣāniyya* (defectiveness). For he would show his manliness, draw out his sword and request from the Messenger the permission to cut off a man's head; i.e. he would not wait for the Messenger himself to order him to do that. First wait for the command that comes on the part of the Messenger, then comply, because the Shariʿa consists in putting into practice whatever the Prophet has brought of orders, and to wait for what comes next.

So the attribute of our liege lord ʿUmar was in this fashion and he did not obtain the spirit-related types of knowledge, whereas our liege lord ʿAlī was his minister and would explain to him whatever was obscure to him. Mawlana

[1] See al-Ḥakīm al-Tirmidhī, *Sīrat al-awliyā'* in *Thalāthat muṣannafāt lil-Ḥakīm al-Tirmidhī*, ed. Bernd Radtke (Beirut: [German Institute for Oriental Studies], 1992) pp. 51-52 §74, translated as *The Life of the the Friends of God* in Bernd Radtke and John O'Kane, *The Concept of Sainthood in Early Islamic Mysticism* (Richmond: Curzon Press, 1996) p. 119 §74; Ibn ʿArabī's words in *Risāla fil-wilāya* and *Fuṣūṣ al-ḥikam* per Chodkiewicz, *Sceau* (pp. 70-71) and Addas, *Ibn ʿArabī* (pp. 101-102); *al-ʿAbādila*, ed. ʿAbd al-Qādir Aḥmad ʿAṭā (Cairo: Maktabat al-Qāhira, 1389/1969) p. 82.

says that the sciences of realities were not opened up for our liege lord 'Umar. Had they been opened up for him our chain of transmission would have been *Nabī* → *Ṣiddīq* → *'Umar*; but these knowledges were not in his possession. This is why the chain has *Nabī* → *Ṣiddīq* → *Salmān*. The reality proceeded with Salmān al-Fārisī and not with 'Umar, just as in his lifetime, our liege lord 'Umar did not see the reality of our liege lord the Messenger of Allah the way that our liege lord 'Alī had seen it.[1] The latter had seen the image of the reality of the Messenger of Allah only once, and because of that single sight, it was opened for him of the real knowledges and he became a door for the sciences.

When our liege lord Uways al-Qaranī asked 'Umar, "Did you see the Messenger of Allah O 'Umar?" He simply replied, "I was always with him."[2] He said, "What did you see of him? Describe him for me." So he described him as he had seen him—an external description for the noble Prophetic traits. Our liege lord Uways al-Qaranī said, "This is also how Abu Jahl and all the eminencies of the Quraysh saw him, exactly in that form, and you have not added anything to their description. With the light of your belief you have remained at the same level as them in sight."

That sight is not realized and is not facilitated until the servant comes out from the station of the ego or the station of *the lowest of the low* (al-Tīn 95:5), and the door for this is open.

From Allah is all success. By the sanctity of the Beloved, by the sanctity of the Fatiha.

[1] See Suhba I. 96, ninth note.

[2] On the narrations from Usayr b. Jābir al-Kūfī of Uways al-Qaranī's meeting with 'Umar b. al-Khaṭṭāb and 'Umar's request to Uways to ask forgiveness for him per the Prophet's instruction see Ibn al-Mubārak, *Musnad* (pp. 18-19 §34); *al-Zuhd wal-raqā'iq* (2:59-61); Ibn Sa'd, *al-Ṭabaqāt al-kubrā* (long entry on Uways al-Qaranī); Ibn Abī Shayba, *Muṣannaf* (*dhikr Uways al-Qaranī*); Aḥmad, *Zuhd* (*Uways al-Qaranī*); *Musnad* (1:372-373 §266); Muslim (*Faḍā'il al-Ṣaḥāba, min faḍā'il Uways al-Qaranī*); Ibn Abī Khaythama, *al-Tārīkh al-Kabīr* (3:202-221 §4506-4544); and others.

98

Have faith in the shaykh's knowledge of this world and of the *dīn* (faith-system) equally – Miraculous gifts of Shaykh ʿAbd al-Khāliq al-Ghujduwānī – [All human beings have goodness in them]

I seek refuge in Allah from the accursed devil
In the Name of Allah the All-Beneficent the Most Merciful
There is no power nor strength but with Allah the High, the Magnificent
Permission, O my Master, support!
Our way is companionship, and goodness is in the congregation

I am speaking to you from the tongue of *Ṣāḥib al-zamān ʿalayhissalām* (the spiritual leader of endtimes). He is not authorized as of yet to address you directly, so I address you on his behalf. You will see, at the time that he emerges, that he will speak in this manner and in this style. So whoever attends this circle of ours will obtain the same as the one that sits with *Ṣāḥib al-zamān* will obtain. Whatever virtues and merits are found in his sitting are present in this one as well. Our gathering is but a segment of his sitting. This is glad tidings.

Mawlana [Shaykh ʿAbd Allah al-Daghistani] says that if you were to look for this knowledge in the books from the beginning of this world until the end of this world, it would be extremely difficult for you to obtain the like of these sciences. For they are not derived from book-reading but rather they are a manifestation of *and whom We had taught, from Our side, a certain knowledge* (al-Kahf 18:65). I.e. Mawlana's knowledge is not from book-reading but from the teaching of the All-True to him. Mawlana says that the reason for the spiritual opening of the sciences to the servant is the acknowledgment of absolute incapacity and the relinquishing of everything he knows. His attribute will be like the attribute of the Prophet–upon him the blessings and peace of Allah–in the divine presence—"my nurturing Lord knows and I do not know"—and like the attribute of the Companions in the presence of the Prophet—"Allah and His Messenger know best, we do not know," until all the Companions became oceans of knowledge.

This is a true acknowledgment of incapacity: Allah and His Messenger know best and we do not know. When you want to obtain something of the teaching of the All-True you must, in the sitting of the people of spiritual truth, firmly believe that "they know best and we do not know." For they will not put anything into the jug that is full, but if they find it empty they will fill it. And in accordance with emptiness—i.e. to the extent of his earnest pursuit—the true student is recognized. **The successors in their wake also say, "Our shaykh knows best and we do not know." The very least rank of a murid is for the latter to observe high manners towards his shaykh and to hold firm belief in his with regard to the affairs of this world and of the faith-system.** This is the lowest rank of the murid's magnification of his shaykh or of his firm belief in him. Do not say, "what does the shaykh know of the affairs of this world?" For he knows of the matter of this world and of the faith-system equally.

What do you think if we were to try and teach the shaykh the principles? Now the shaykh has become lower than you and you have become above him! Principles are poured over from above. When you look down on the shaykh you have deprived yourself of the spiritual intuitions. For when the murid makes himself higher through his own mind and his own opinion, inevitably he will be deprived of the shaykh's blessing. Besides this matter, Allah has made goodness and blessing with everyone. With every human being there is found goodness and blessing. So when someone looks down on any other person no matter who they are, he deprives himself of the blessing of that person and of his goodness. This is why whoever humbles himself with everyone will obtain of the blessing and the goodness of that person, whose secret he is not cognizant of.

Mawlana [Shaykh ʿAbd Allah] said there was a wretched man from whom people never felt safe, not with regard to their possessions, not with regard to their lives and not with regard to their reputations for 37 years. At last the man died. People exulted. It was like a festival day for them. When they all gathered to bury him his bier could not be moved and they could not carry him forward from his place. They kept trying but to no avail. It was as if he was stuck to the ground. They said, "What is this ordeal? Alive and dead he is such a weight on us?" The news reached our liege lord ʿAbd al-Khāliq al-Ghujduwānī–Allah sanctify his secret–who came and tried to lift the bier but again it would not move. He asked the villagers, "Who here knows of any good deed that this man did?" They replied, "We never saw anything but affliction from him. Praise to Allah, he is dead so that we can rest easy!" Then he asked his wife and children. They said he had another wife. They sent for her and when she came the shaykh asked her the same question. She said, "Praise be to Allah that he died, for I never saw any good coming from him ever!" But he kept asking her with such severity that he reminded her of something in her heart. She felt fear and she said, "He came to me one day and said, 'Woman, today something happened with me and I am still wondering how such a thing occurred. I was in my usual occupation'—he was a highway robber—'and I saw a man carrying a box. I greeted him, although I never greet anyone nor do I return anyone's greeting, then I walked with him and I asked him about the box. He said it was honey and that he was going to visit Shaykh 'Abd al-Khāliq al-Ghujduwānī because he attended the *khatm* at his place, and after the *khatm* the Shaykh treats everyone to honey. So I carried the box for him and walked with him a certain distance. I gave it back to him at the parting of the roads and I greeted him, and I regret not taking the box from him, and I am wondering what happened to me.'"

When Shaykh 'Abd al-Khāliq al-Ghujduwānī heard this he exclaimed, "Glory to Allah! O my nurturing Lord, this is Your servant, he served me, and You have promised us that whoever rises to serve us will not be shamed, not in this world and not in the next." At that time they saw the bier moving and rising, and they started walking behind it as it was above their heads and they could not touch it. Thus, with even a small service, there is a promise from Allah that He will not put to shame whoever serves the Awliya and whoever loves them. This man did not know any love but he now have this service to his credit according to this foundation. Our liege lord 'Abd al-Khāliq al-Ghujduwānī was well-pleased with this service and on the spot it became an answered prayer from Allah. All the people walked behind him. They said, "This is the miraculous gift of al-Ghujduwānī."

When they lowered him into the grave, green leaves came down from the sky over their heads. On them were written the names of those that were present, announcing to them the promise of Paradise! Whoever got that green leaf on his head would turn to bliss. At that time that man's tongue spoke in clear speech, saying, "O my master al-Ghujduwānī, these people all were harmed by me in my life and this is their witness, but because of a small service done to you I have obtained a generous gift, and with this generous gift I asked my nurturing Lord to grant bliss to all that had been harmed by me. My nurturing Lord inspired me to make this request and then He granted it!"

What Allah does is something wondrous. It is not known how He will grant mercy to His servant and how He will lavish generosity on him. Why did we retell this story today? So that everyone should know that Allah has put goodness in him, and blessing, even if he is such as that man. Because of a small service—something we would consider insignificant—those people obtained bliss, so how much goodness was in this man, although he was wretched? Allah's affairs can never be known, and how He disposes goodness with His servants! Even if it is the most wretched of people he will make him a cause for goodness and blessing to ensue, and if it is not immediate they will obtain it later.

Therefore one must be humble with everyone. Even if the other is arrogant and tyrannical, let it not bother you. Give him the higher place and let him trample you down, you will obtain [goodness] from him because the Lord of might has placed in His servants a point of goodness and blessing so that it would be earned from him. But what is the benefit if you look down on the shaykhs, whereas the shaykhs are filled with goodness and blessing? You are only depriving yourself of their goodness, not only the awliya and the shaykhs but even ordinary people. It must be without fail that Allah has placed in him goodness even to the extent of a dot, and it might be that this dot will cause you to join absolute goodness and you will be in bliss.

From Allah is all success. By the sanctity of the Beloved, by the sanctity of the Fatiha.

99

[Be patient and do not pass judgment on others] – A murid's following of his shaykh's order – Reality of "Whoever depends on Allah it is enough for him" – [Why does a person not reach unveiling?]

I seek refuge in Allah from the accursed devil
In the Name of Allah the All-Beneficent the Most Merciful
There is no power nor strength but with Allah the High, the Magnificent
Permission, O my Master, support!
Our way is companionship, and goodness is in the congregation

Our liege lord 'Umar, despite his immense rank, *kāna yataqaddamu 'alā* (was at times forward with) the Messenger of Allah in his opinion and his will. He would speak out his opinion when something displeased him. He would say, "Messenger of Allah, let me strike the neck of this hypocrite!"[1] But the Pride of all beings would reply to him, "O 'Umar, how do you pass judgment that this is a hypocrite when I do not recognize the hypocrite until my nurturing Lord informs me of him?" Thus, and yet we pass judgment on people with every sort of judgment which are never ours to pass in the first place. Every situation passes and the human being's heart was named *qalb* (turnover) because of the intensity of its shifts. You will seldom find someone whose heart stays firm on a single state in permanence. There are shifts and turns, and "the nurturing Lord turns them over in any way He wishes."[2]

When you yourself pass judgment over a human being it might be that after a brief moment or after a day that judgment disappears. No trace remains of what you used to claim there was in him. This is why, when you look at people,

[1] Spoken about I. 'Abd Allāh b. Ubay b. Salūl the chief of the Medinan hypocrites as narrated from (i) Jābir by Aḥmad; Bukhārī; Muslim; Tirmidhī; II. Dhū al-Khuwayṣira Ḥurqūṣ b. Zuhayr the head of the Khawārij: (ii) Abū Sa'īd al-Khudrī by Ibn Wahb, *Muwaṭṭa'*; Muslim; Nasā'ī, *Kubrā*; and others; also Jābir by Aḥmad, al-Dārimī, in the *Ṣaḥīḥayn*, Ibn Mājah; III. Ḥāṭib b. Abī Balta'a the Badrī Companion who had spied for the Quraysh: (iii) 'Alī by Wāqidī, *Maghāzī* (2:797-798); 'Abd al-Razzāq, *Tafsīr* (al-Mumtaḥana 60:1); Ibn Hishām (2:398); al-Bukhārī; Muslim; Abū Dāwūd; Tirmidhī; and others; IV. a Jew who had insulted the Prophet: (iv) Anas by Ṭayālisī; V. Ḥakam b. Kaysān the captive pagan chief: (v) Miqdād b. 'Amr by al-Wāqidī, *Maghāzī* (1:15); Ibn Sa'd, *Ṭabaqāt*; VI. Ibn Sayyād the pseudo-Prophet: (vi) Ibn Mas'ūd by Aḥmad.

[2] Part of a Prophetic hadith documented in Suhba 100, penultimate note.

their characters and their acts, you must have patient endurance. You must not pass judgment over one that he is a hypocrite or a transgressor or an obdurate person, because he might change. This is important.

The Pride of all beings—when he acknowledged complete incapacity in the presence of Allah, his nurturing Lord made him a *ḥākim* (judge) over all human beings: *qāsim* (distributor) and, at the same time, *ḥākim* over them. Mawlana says that when the servant relinquishes will—the partial and the complete—and follows the will of Allah and His Messenger–upon him the blessings and peace of Allah–his nurturing Lord delimits a certain limit for him, because it is the most difficult thing for the ego when a human being relinquishes his will to follow the will of another. So this is in need of jihad. However, you might find a person walking behind another only out of fear of him, or in the hope he will obtain certain worldly benefits from him. Without these two motivations he will not follow him. I.e. from one's own free acceptance and without the pursuit of any worldly gain it is very difficult for someone to follow another. Therefore it needs jihad because it is hard on his ego. And this is *ināba* (delegation): for you to come and delegate another and say, "I have left my own will and subsumed it to your will. Whatever way you command me I will proceed."

Following this matter is difficult. I would say to Mawlana, *'murnī sayyidī* (command me, my master!) and he would reply, "Nazim Efendi, I cannot find anyone that can carry a command." This is why, in everything, Mawlana would give a choice to the murids. He would say, *mukhayyar yā waladī* (it's your choice my son). And whenever the shaykh gives a choice to his murids, it means the human ego will find leeway to act freely. One will say to himself, "Leaving the command is by my own choice, and I shall choose whatever I like," because there might come, of commands, that which your ego will not like. What will you do when this is the command? You have to obey when you have covenanted the Shaykh over a certain matter, and that is difficult.

Al-Ghujduwānī said to his murid in the gathering, "Get up, my son, go to the house and cut off the head of your father who is sleeping next to your mother." He got up and left the gathering in a hurry. After a while he returned holding a sack in his hand. The Shaykh ordered him to open it. He did, and behold, it was the head of a priest who had entered by ruse into his mother's presence. This Shaykh possessed *kashf* (spiritual unveiling) and he had ordered the son to cut of the head of "his father" knowing full well there was a impostor there, but he nevertheless said, "cut off your father's head." If he had said "there is an impostor there," it would have been natural to carry out the order.

The person's situation will be as had happened on our liege lord Mūsā's part with our liege lord al-Khiḍr. Our liege lord al-Khiḍr scuttled the boat, killed the child and raised up the wall, and our liege lord Mūsā objected. Its meaning is, how would our liege lord Mūsā acted if our liege lord al-Khiḍr had ordered him to scuttle the boat? Would he have complied? Our liege lord Mūsā would not have borne to comply with this order. This is why the affair of the people of spiritual truth is not an easy matter.

Mawlana used to say, "Nazim Efendi, do not say, *'murnī* (order me) because no one is able to comply with the order." All of you say, *amrak sayyidī* (at your command my master) if it suits your egos but when it comes against your ego's desire you will say no. This is a matter we fail to recognize, and we fail to recognize the shaykh also. That is why the easiest way is for the shaykh to say to you "as you choose." He gives you the choice. This is a teaching. From choice, a person will progressively go up until he complies with the exigency of the order. For bearing with the order is a very high rank. This is why, when the human being leaves his will, at that time he becomes fit to carry the order and it becomes easy for him to proceed under the shaykh's will. Otherwise it is very difficult.

Our liege lord 'Abd al-Qādir al-Jaylānī's shaykh said to him, "O my son, you must marry. Look for a suitable girl and marry her." Our liege lord al-Jaylānī proposed to one of the most beautiful girls and she belonged to a rich family. On the night before Jumu'a, the night of the wedding, everything was made ready and the bride was adorned and awaited. Then the shaykh sent one of his murids to the groom the command that he must divorce the girl and donate to her the house with all its furnishings, whereupon he said, *'alā al-ra'si wal-'ayn* (just as you wish) and as ordered by my shaykh! He divorced her and he gifted her the house and its contents. So then the murid—the groom—carried out the order on the spot. This is an order.

The shaykh is an educator. He knows the foundations of the way to deliver you from the grip of your ego when he gives you any order. (When it conforms with your wish you follow it, but whatever displeases you, you leave. At that time you will be like that murid, like the Jews who would believe in some of the verses and disbelieve in some (al-Baqara 2:85). Whatever suited their egos they would accept and whatever did no suit them they rejected.) Whoever endures patiently in this fashion with his ego's will, Allah Almighty will appoint for every person patient endurance with spiritual struggle when it reaches that limit. At that time He will send *rīḥ al-ṣabā* (the easterly wind) which, to the people of spiritual truth, is like the Prophet's Burāq because it brings one to his destination. The *rīḥ al-ṣabā* comes, envelops and protects him against that harshness, and gives him authorization to enter the sea of spiritual realities. He gives him from the attribute of divine power until he can swim in the seas of spiritual realities in the presence of Allah. At that time the servant recognizes something of the awesome power of Allah Almighty and he recognizes something of the reality of the fairness of the All-True. At that time he recognizes the meaning of *man tawakkala ʿalā-l-Lāhi kafāh* (whoever trusts in the One God, He suffices him).[1] This is truth.

Mawlana asks, when must you surrender and trust? Whoever passes on everything over to Allah, such a person is called a *fāsiq* (depraved one) by the people of spiritual truth. Mawlana says that the servant may run and strive within the limits of his capacity, but after that he surrenders and trusts in Allah. Otherwise, whoever turns over everything to Allah and does not do what is within his capacity, he will be a *fāsiq*. For it belongs to the servant to labor and plant, but it does not belong to him to cause the plant to grow or the sky to rain. This is not in the servant's hand. **You must surrender and trust in what is neither within your capacity nor in your hand. However, when you have the ability to do something but instead you turn over the matter, you will be a depraved one**. And "whoever trusts in the One God, He suffices him" without doubt, but on condition that you do not neglect that which you have capacity to do.

Mawlana al-Shaykh used to say that when the range of striving ends, Allah opens for him the door of the knowledges and will be his teacher. But as for him who still has range to work yet leaves it incomplete while saying, "I trust in Allah," he will be deprived of arrival to these realities. Awliya are watching. They know your capacity and your limits when you fall short. They hold the trusts and will not give them to you. When the servant does not fall short and keeps striving, he too has a limit; but matters do not proceed according to our effort. For **as much as you put effort into it, your work will not make you reach the ranks to Allah. Still you must strive and you must not leave out anything that you have the capacity for**. When you leave it out, then "whoever trusts in the One God, He suffices him" will not be realized. The servant will be left alone and the door will remain closed in his face.

[1] Part of a Prophetic hadith narrated from (i) ʿAmr b. al-ʿĀṣ by Ibn Mājah (*Zuhd, al-tawakkul wal-yaqīn*) whose complete wording is, "Verily there is in every valley a branch of the heart of the human being, so he whose heart follows all the branches, Allah does not care in what valley He will cause him to die, and whoever trusts in the One God He suffices him without need of branching off;" also narrated as the saying of (ii) ʿUmar by Balādhurī, *Ansāb al-ashrāf*; (iii) Masrūq by Aḥmad, *Zuhd*; Bayhaqī, *al-Qaḍāʾ wal-qadar*. It is the same meaning as the verse *and whoever trusts in the One God, then He is his sufficiency* (Ṭalāq 65:3). Cf. Ibn Abī Jamra's commentary on the hadith of the Companions whose commander ordered them to enter into a fire in Ibn Ḥajar, *Fatḥ al-Bārī* (8:60, *sariyyat ʿAbd Allāh b. Ḥudhāfat al-Sahmī*).

Why is a person not reaching spiritual openings and unveilings? Because he does not first offer what is in his capacity and he does not practice what is in his purview. He waits for everything to come to him for free. It is not going to happen. *But the ones that strove in Us, We will indeed show them Our ways* (al-'Ankabūt 29:69). And what is your striving? It is to the extent of your capacity. *The One God does not task any soul except to its capacity* (al-Baqara 2:286). It might someone's capacity is two cycles of prayer only while another's is a hundred cycles. It is in accordance to the Shaykh's rule: he gives you and tasks you then you are falling short. Whoever wants to obtain those stations, then the merit of effort is to the extent of ability. *So beware the One God to your utmost* (al-Taghābun 64:16).

Mawlana used to say, "This suhba is from the tongue of *Ṣāḥib al-zamān* (the spiritual leader of endtimes). The latter is not authorized to mingle with people and to address them, so I speak on his behalf, and this gathering of mine is only a segment of his gathering."

From Allah is all success. By the sanctity of the Beloved, by the sanctity of the Fatiha.

100

The hearts of kings are in the Hand of the All-Merciful – Was al-Ḥajjāj an evildoer or a just man?

I seek refuge in Allah from the accursed devil
In the Name of Allah the All-Beneficent the Most Merciful
There is no power nor strength but with Allah the High, the Magnificent
Permission, O my Master, support!
Our way is companionship, and goodness is in the congregation

O you who believe! Obey the One God and obey the Messenger and those in authority among you (al-Nisā' 4:59). And this is an important order for the protection of the servants in this world and the hereafter. This is why Mawlana repeats, in every gathering, that "O my brothers, hear and grasp, and once you have grasped, then benefit![1] Hear the boundaries and do not transgress."

I was in Aleppo at the same time as these days last year, at which time we visited the brothers. There was a famous shaykh there who saw, as he was giving the sermon, a person of influence. So he was giving the sermon with vehemence as Iblīs was inflating him. Most of the preachers fall into the trap of Iblīs especially while giving the sermon. They reckon they possess a spiritual power or an external power because of the presence of those thousands of worshippers. Iblīs suggests to him that this power can back him up. But this is baseless whether from the spiritual side or from the side of those congregations filling the mosques. And this is from the zeal of youth, he thinks that in his sermon he will fix the world or change conditions.

This is why Iblīs makes it very beloved to preachers to attack the regimes that are found in various countries, for they do not know the secret, which is that it is Allah alone that is ruling or that appoints the rulers over the servants, with His will, as something suitable for them, and all of them are oblivious to that secret. It is irrefutable that their outlook is far from the will of Allah and they reckon that those rulers came on their own, by themselves. They think that Allah was asleep and that when He woke up, He saw the rulers sitting there, and He has no power to remove them. Does our nurturing Lord sleep? *Neither fatigue nor sleep ever affect Him* (Baqara 2:255). May He be glorified! His will–exalted is He–is for these rulers to be exactly where they are, for each

[1] See Suhba I.31, first note.

time has its men. Allah appoints for this time its men, then another time comes, and so forth, and nothing endures but Allah.

I told that shaykh a story a story I had heard from my teacher and master Shaykh ʿAbd Allah that had taken place at the time of al-Ḥajjāj,[1] the tyrant that was famous for his cruelty, for filling the prisons with prisoners and for killing until heads piled up like hills. This was his habit. One day al-Ḥajjāj wanted to ask a certain question. He ordered for ten of the nobles and the scholars to be brought so that he might ask them. When they came he asked them, "Am I just or unjust in my rule?" They said, "Our liege lord, you are the soul of justice. Far be it that you should be unjust." He said to the executioner, "Cut off their heads." The next day he summoned others and asked them the same question. They said, "You have not trodden the path of justice." He said, "So I am unjust? Cut off their heads." And he summoned others. Thus was he cutting off the heads of the ulema.

One day there was a group on their way to see al-Ḥajjāj. One of the wise fools saw them and asked them, where are you going? They replied, "Do you not know we are on our way to the slaughterhouse?" He said, "Where is the slaughterhouse?" They said, "Where al-Ḥajjāj is." He went with them and walked ahead of them in the presence of al-Ḥajjāj. He said to him, "Ḥajjāj!" without any title. These are my group and I am put in charge of them and I am their spokesman, so do not bother to ask them anything. Ask me and I will answer you." Those behind him stood trembling. Al-Ḥajjāj said, "Am I just or am I a tyrant in my rule?" He replied, "Far be it that you should be either! Rather you have been put in power over us according to our deeds." Al-Ḥajjāj said, "Release!" Then he addressed the people. "Servants of Allah! I am neither a tyrant nor am I just. But because of your deeds, my nurturing Lord has empowered me over you. Do not attribute to me any injustice or any justice!"

Thus would Mawlana always say, "My children, you must keep high manners with Allah and with the holder of power." And the Messenger–upon

[1] al-Ḥajjāj b. Yūsuf b. al-Ḥakam al-Thaqafī (42-95/662-714) was an Umayyad general and strongman under ʿAbd al-Malik b. Marwān b. al-Ḥakam and his son al-Walīd. He was "an oppressive tyrant, a hater of the Prophetic family, devious, bloodthirsty, yet he possessed courage and audacity, cunning, superlative intelligence, purity of speech, eloquence and magnification of the Qur'ān. He besieged Ibn al-Zubayr in the Kaʿba and lobbed boulders at it with mangonels at the time, after which he humiliated the dwellers of the two Inviolable Sanctuaries and ruled over Iraq and the east for twenty years. He would delay prayers from their times until Allah eradicated him. We hate him for the sake of Allah, which is of the staunchest ropes of faith. Yet he has good deeds buried deep in the sea of his sins. His case is resigned to Allah." Shams al-Dīn al-Dhahabī, *Siyar aʿlām al-nubalā'* (Risāla ed. 4:343).

him the blessings and peace of Allah–has instructed that our interaction with the holder of power should be marked with gentleness and respect.[1] Mawlana says, "Do not despise a holder of power because it is Allah that has dressed him with this station. Do not despise him no matter what his attribute is; but respect him, because Allah has dressed him with this respect. You must keep manners with rulers. Even if a policeman comes, our nurturing Lord has dressed him with this attribute. If you have erred with him he will humiliate you because he is a holder of power and not you."

I said to that preacher, "There is no need of this *khuṭba*. It is as if you are slandering the one you are speaking about, and people have become like drug-dependent addicts with the talk of reviling rulers. When they hear that they become happy. But Allah is commanding, *O you who believe! Obey the One God and obey the Messenger and those in authority among you* (al-Nisā' 4:59). The meaning of that is that if any party or any individual among them contravenes the command of Allah, there shall smite them harm because it is forbidden to despise the holder of power. It has come in the divine Hadith, 'I am the king of kings, the hearts of kings are in My hand! If you obey Me I make them a mercy over you, and if you disobey Me I make them a vengeful punishment against you. So do not busy yourself with the revilement of kings but repent to Me!'[2] This is our method, and this is the correct manner demanded by the Speech of Allah and of His Messenger as a *ḥadīth qudsī*. The noble Quranic verse is enough, while the hadith explains it in a clearer fashion. Allah gives dominion, and are you yourself trying to wrest it from Him?" This is an *iltifāt* (apostrophic redirection) from *ghayb* (absence) to *shuhūd* (witnessing).[3]

This is what we have learnt from the manners and practice of Mawlana

[1] Per the *ḥadīth qudsī* below. Also, "When the noble of a people comes to you, treat him in a noble manner," narrated from (i) Ibn 'Umar by Ibn Mājah and Bazzār; (ii) Ibn 'Abbās by Ibn Shabba, *Tārīkh al-Madīna*; (iii) Jarīr al-Bajalī by Ibn Abī al-Dunyā, *Makārim al-akhlāq*; (iv) Abū Hurayra by Bazzār; (v) Anas by al-Kharā'iṭī, *Makārim al-akhlāq*; (vi) al-Sha'bī in *mursal* mode by Ibn Abī Shayba and Abū Dāwūd, *Marāsīl*.

[2] Narrated as a Prophetic *ḥadīth qudsī* from (i) Abū Dardā' by Ibn Ḥibbān, *Majrūḥīn*; al-Dāraquṭnī, *'Ilal*; al-Ṭabarānī, *Awsaṭ* (9:9 §8962); Abū Nu'aym, *Ḥilya* (2:388). It is also narrated as a quotation from the Prophet Dāwūd or one of the sapiental books from (ii) Mālik b. Mighwal by Ibn Abī Shayba, *Muṣannaf*; (iii) Mālik b. Dīnār by Ibn Abī al-Dunyā, *al-'Uqūbāt*; *al-Tawba*; Abū Nu'aym, *Ḥilya*.

[3] Mawlana Shaykh Nazim is pointing out that the verse of al-Nisā' 4:59 uses the third person in reference to Allah, the Prophet and those in authority, whereby the third person in grammar refers to the absent and the unseen. In contrast, the *ḥadīth qudsī* shifts to the second person which implies direct address and mutual witnessing. On this famous and frequent Quranic rhetorical figure see al-Bayḍāwī on al-Fātiḥa 1:1-5.

[Shaykh ʿAbd Allah Daghistani]. For he had himself experienced, in Turkey, the harshest of seditions after the demise of the Ottoman Caliphate and the substitution of the Islamic regime to a secular regime. He faced all the fitnas in that time. Praise belongs to Allah, none of the murids were harmed. How many were hanged, killed, their houses were laid to ruin! But–praise belongs to Allah–by His favor none of the murids of Mawlana Shaykh ʿAbd Allah Daghistani were harmed and none of the murids of Mawlana Shaykh Sharafuddin either. All men were forced to wear a *burnayṭa* (European-style hat)[1] except Mawlana with his turban, and all people were forbidden to assemble and conduct the dhikr but Mawlana would do dhikr and supplicate. This is the meaning of the discourse of our liege lord ʿAlī–Allah ennoble his countenance–"Whoever guards himself of Allah lives blessed and journeys in the lands of Allah secure."[2] Whoever puts that verse into practice is one who guards himself, and Allah will not empower over him any human or beast because each one's forelock is in the hand of Allah (Hūd 11:56).

This is our way. The Messenger–upon him blessings and peace of Allah–has certainly described the features of this particular time caused by the works of people and their going completely astray. And Allah is expounding to us, "O My servants, do not revile the kings but repent to Me and I will change their hearts," for "the hearts" of kings "are between the two fingers of Allah, He turns them over any way He wishes."[3] You (sing.) are incapable of changing the rulers but the way of repentance is the most secure way. Allah will make the man himself a believer that serves Islam and He will overturn him, *and that is in no wise arduous for the One God* (Ibrāhīm 14:20). Repent (pl.) to Allah!

Our liege lord Ādam is teaching us manners: when He brought him down to earth he said, "I have wronged myself, this wrong is my own wrong against myself, and You never wronged me, O my Lord!" At Ādam's landing place in Ceylon, he stood up on one leg for 300 years weeping[4]—his tears turned into

[1] Per the (unrepealable) Turkish "Hat Law" of November 1925 followed by the 1934 "Law Relating to Prohibited Garments."

[2] See Suhba I.92, last note.

[3] A Prophetic hadith narrated from (i) Umm Salama by ʿAbd b. Ḥumayd; (ii) ʿAbd Allāh b. ʿAmr b. al-ʿĀṣ by Aḥmad and Muslim; (iii) Anas by Aḥmad; al-Tirmidhī (*ḥasan ṣaḥīḥ*) and Ibn Mājah; (iv) ʿUbāda b. al-Ṣāmit by Ibn ʿAdī; (v-vii) Nuwwās b. Simʿān, ʿĀʾisha, Abū Dharr per Tirmidhī: see Ḥasan Wāʾilī, *Nuzhat al-Albāb fī Qawl al-Tirmidhī, "wa-fīl-bāb,"* 6 vols. (Riyadh: Dār Ibn al-Jawzī, 1426/2005) 5:2980-2984.

[4] On the mountain of Sarandīb (the Arabic name for present-day Sri Lanka). Narrated from Ḥasan al-Baṣrī and Wahb b. Munabbih by Ibn Abī al-Dunyā, *al-Riqqa wal-Bukāʾ* and *al-ʿUqūbāt*. It is adduced in the *Tafsīrs* (Baqara 2:36) of Abū al-Layth, al-Baghawī,

diamonds—until Allah manifested Himself to him: *then Ādam welcomed from his nurturing Lord certain words* (al-Baqara 2:37). With broken hearts say, "O our nurturing Lord, we have wronged ourselves!" Every quest has its door and its states. *And do come into houses through their doors* (al-Baqara 2:189). Everything is there in our sacred Law.

From Allah is all success. By the sanctity of the Beloved, by the sanctity of the Fatiha.

Ibn al-Jawzī, al-Qurṭubī, Abū Ḥayyān, al-Naysābūrī, al-Thaʿālibī and others.

101

Who is the companion of *Ṣāḥib al-zamān*? – Miraculous gifts of the Muhammadan inheritor – [Attending a suhba means getting the high levels mentioned therein]

I seek refuge in Allah from the accursed devil
In the Name of Allah the All-Beneficent the Most Merciful
There is no power nor strength but with Allah the High, the Magnificent
Permission, O my Master, support!
Our way is companionship, and goodness is in the congregation

Among the Companions, only our liege lord Abū Bakr and our liege lord ʿAlī are the one that received their trusts from the Messenger–upon him the blessings and peace of Allah. As for the rest, their trusts remained with him. Mawlana [Shaykh ʿAbd Allah Daghistani] had explained for all the Companions a reason for their lagging behind their obtainment of that trust, namely because there was still a self-based will in them in the presence of the will of Allah and His Messenger. This is the matter that held them back.

One morning I went to see Mawlana Shaykh ʿAbd Allah. He said, "Nazim Efendi, after I made that suhba about the Companions in the presence of *Ṣaḥib al-zamān* (the spiritual leader of endtimes) and the Caliphs, all the noble Companions were as happy as one could be, because I spoke about the aspect of the shortcoming found in them, and it is obligatory for us, whenever we mention anyone's imperfection, to complete him. That completion took place and the required cleanliness for the obtainment of the trusts while they are in the interlife. *Ṣāḥib al-zamān* opened up for them what had been opened up for the two Companions Abū Bakr and ʿAlī–Allah be well-pleased with them–in their lives and he gave them their trusts. They reached perfection from Mawlana's side, and this is the job of the *ṣāḥib*.

Then he explained, who is the *ṣāḥib* (companion) of *Ṣāḥib al-zamān*? For there is indeed a *ṣāḥib* for him. He is Mawlana al-Shaykh ʿAbd Allah al-Daghistani, while *Ṣāḥib al-zamān* is our liege lord the Mahdi. Mawlana Shaykh ʿAbd Allah says, "Give thanks to your nurturing Lord that he Has made you attend the gathering of the man who is the deliverer for all the followers of the noble Shaykhs and the noble Awliya who are captives at the hands of the enemies—*nafs, dunyā, hawā, shayṭān*—whereby there are many followers whom Iblīs has captured. Give thanks to Allah for making you attend the gathering of the man who has such a mandate, to set free the followers one and all from the hand of Iblis. Allah has dressed him with this power so that he is capable of delivering all the captives among the followers of the Awliya." I asked, "O my master, does this mandate comprise the past Ummas of the Prophets?" He said yes, that servant was certainly given authority for the sake of the past Ummas one and all, to save the nations of the Prophets from the hand of Iblīs and those that remained outside the sphere of the Prophets and lagged behind or ran away. He can also gather up all that have strayed far from the nations of the Prophets that did not respond to their Prophets and strayed far from them. How much of a miraculous gift has Allah given to that wali!

Mawlana says of the meaning of "The Prophets are alive in their graves,"[1] is that every Prophet is alive in his grave: if we dig up their graves we will find them exactly as on the day that they were buried there. This means that Allah Almighty has brought into being, in exchange for each Prophet, one of the Awliya to do his work in every age as a protection for the nation of that Prophet. For example, if you are an inheritor for our liege lord Mūsā–upon him peace–your service will be a revival, as if our liege lord Mūsā were alive and serving his Umma. That wali also serves to deliver the captives of the Umma. Whatever is found of defect in the nation of Mūsā, that wali must complete them and protect them.

In every age there is one of the Awliya rising to do the service of that Prophet for the protection of his Umma. This is the meaning of a Prophet being alive. Mawlana said, "after I pass on this job will pass to someone after me so that he will run this matter." **Mawlana said that "when we speak about the shortcomings of any servant due to his flaws or his falling short, on the spot he gets cleaned up of that shortcoming and he is perfected."** For if we speak without carrying out actual service such speech will be slander and fault-finding, which is categorically forbidden. Why? Because we do not speak about the shameful flaws of people to satisfy our egos or in envy or out of enmity against certain people. However, Awliya are like the physician, he lays bare his patient to see his illness and gives him the remedy. Likewise the

[1] "The Prophets are alive in their graves, praying." A Prophetic hadith narrated from Anas by Abū Ya'lā and Bayhaqī in *Ḥayāt al-anbiyā'*. Ibn Ḥajar rated its chain sound in *Fatḥ al-Bārī* as did Suyūṭī in *Anbā' al-adhkiyā' bi-ḥayāt al-Anbiyā'*, adding: "The life of the Prophet–upon him blessings and peace of Allah–in his grave and that of the rest of the Prophets is known to us as *'ilman qaṭ'iyyan* (categorical knowledge)." Imam Aḥmad "frequently said that the Prophets are alive in their graves praying and that the grave-dweller recognizes his visitors the day of Jumu'a" per Abū Bakr al-Khallāl, *al-'Aqīda lil-Imām Aḥmad bi-Riwāyat al-Khallāl*. See Sayyid Muḥammad b. 'Alawī al-Mālikī, *The Life of the Prophets in Their Graves*.

Awliya do not speak of that flaw for slander and to delight in what is haram but rather, when they speak of any flaw, they do not leave it in the servant, so that Allah will not ask the latter of his shortcomings. For his purity has become perfect from the time of puberty until that age: the wali has purified him with a holy gaze and the breath of holiness. He only mentioned his shortcoming or his flaw in order to replace it with perfection or to deliver him from shameful flaws. It is only for these two reasons that they speak.

This type of spiritual guidance is exclusive to Mawlana's person [=Shaykh ʿAbd Allah Daghistani]. This type of *irshād* was not given to the early generations and will not be given to the later ones, and the *taṣarruf* (discretionary power) of Mawlana al-Shaykh covers what lies between the east and the west. In this time of ours he is the Muhammadan inheritor, and he has the authority to appear in 700,000 places at the same time through a spiritual power. In the time of our liege lord Abū Yazīd the Muhammadan inheritor would appear in 24,000 places. In our time, the Muhammadan inheritor—the absolute mujtahid—can appear in 700,000 places. It is with this power that Mawlana has operated. And now, also, in as many forms as Mawlana wishes to appear he may, even though he is in the interlife. A thousand forms he appears in, he walks in the souks, he sits in the gatherings, and he will be present between east and west. That is, his service is permanent, and this is a miraculous gift for the cleansing of the Umma of Muhammad–upon him the blessings and peace of Allah–and its perfecting, and it has always been a running service.

This type of spiritual guidance is exclusive to us. Mawlana said that, more than that, Allah has promised us that whatever spiritual station we have explained and detailed to the brothers in our gathering, even if the deeds of those in attendance are not enough, they will reach that station merely by sitting in attendance and hearing and accepting that suhba. That is enough to make them reach those stations. **Mawlana said, "I have been ordered that for whoever sits in my gathering, hears and accepts, I must make him reach that station." We have no right to show something to those who are in attendance and then to disappoint them. Rather we show it to him in order to give it to him, not in order to deprive him. This is why, whatever station we speak of in the suhba, that station is taking place for those that are present**. This matter that the spiritual guide is ordered with, is to make those that are present reach those stations. Therefore we are not progressing through our knowledge. On the Day of Resurrection we shall see lofty stations because of the suhba of the Prophets and the Awliya. Through their high spiritual energies, as many of the spiritual stations they explain to us, we will inevitably reach.

From Allah is all success. By the sanctity of the Beloved, by the sanctity of the Fatiha.

102

[*Adab* with Allah and His apportionment] – A person's worth is the worth of his manners – He has put the servant where He wanted – [Do not question the position of others and their doings]

I seek refuge in Allah from the accursed devil
In the Name of Allah the All-Beneficent the Most Merciful
There is no power nor strength but with Allah the High, the Magnificent
Permission, O my Master, support!
Our way is companionship, and goodness is in the congregation

A person's worth is estimated according to his *adab* (manners), and not his *dhahab* (gold). The latter estimation is that of the ignorant. With the people of spiritual reality he is estimated according to character. Mawlana asked, what is the highest *adab*, and what is the spirit of the Shariʿa, and what is the spirit of the Tariqa? The highest *adab* is for the servant to give up "why is this happening?" and "no!" when the apportionments of the All-True are taking their course, for each of these reactions signifies objection. So this is the highest *adab*. This what how the attribute of the servant must be. However, for him to truly achieve that, then that is extremely difficult and not an easy matter, for objection will come to the servant from a thousand different directions when the apportioned decrees of the All-True take their course. This means that the servant must make sure his will is with the will of Allah *in weal and woe* (Āl ʿImrān 3:134). In weal, every person is in agreement, but at the manifestation of woe—at that time, for one to agree with the will of Allah, then this is high manners.

Every person under orders says to the one giving him orders in the work of this world, "at your command, just as you wish." Even if he does not like the order he will say, "as you command, my master," no matter how much you dislike the order, especially in the military. But insofar as he is under orders the person must execute it whether he likes it or not. He must not say "why?" or "no!" Is it not fitting that the servant should do exactly the same with his nurturing Lord? Is it not even more appropriate for him to say to his nurturing Lord, "My Lord, we accept"? This is why there is a supplication that says, *raḍḍinā bi-qaḍā'ik* (make us well-pleased with Your decree).[1]

[1] Narrated as a *duʿā* from Fatḥ b. Saʿīd al-Mawṣilī by Ibn Abī al-Dunyā, *al-Riḍā ʿani-l-*

This matter is difficult but it is *adab*. For even if you object to the order it is not going to change. So it is best that you reconcile yourself with Allah. It is better than to go to war, which is all hardship. If you contravene your nurturing Lord, the burden will be heavier on you but when you reconcile with Him, He lifts it away from you. Outwardly you are under the burden but in reality He is carrying it for you. This is what the people of spiritual reality are seeking. "We do not ask you to repel the decree but *lutf* (subtle kindness) in it." With pincers you pull out teeth, but how much will one suffer if he does this. If, however, he goes to the dentist, he might administer a local pain-killer and do he same task but with gentleness. The result is the same.

This is how things are. When the servant gives up objection and resigns himself and says, "O my Lord, here is your weak servant, grant me kindness in keeping with Your generosity! O my Lord, I am a helpless servant. Your subtle kindness in the Decree, and not its rejection." At that time, outwardly, it be begins as the servant is made to bear with it, but in reality Allah is carrying on his behalf. This is important. A person might see a thousand sights as he walks the earth. So if you see some man with some woman, do not look at them—"what are they doing?"—and do not object to them. Every human being is busy or made to be at his station, or every person is settled on some matter. He has put the servant wherever He wants to.[1]

For example the army sets up checkpoints, stops traffic and checks them. When your turn comes you must follow orders without adding or subtracting anything. It is the same with the people with whom you live. Each one of them is put in a certain station. We on our part think that maybe so and so is in an incorrect station: this has now become a rejection of the apportionment of the All-True Who has set him up there. Why did He set him up there? Every human being is standing at a certain station, and it is impossible for the stations of human beings to be as you yourself like them, is it? If you yourself were tasked with setting up all creatures, would you be able to achieve that? If you were to set them up, you might see so and so is unsuited to be in such and such a place and you will say, what if we changed this one instead of that one, etc. We cannot set up creatures according to what is suitable for them. Their nurturing Lord knows best about His servants and has set them up in what is suitable for them. However, when we go back to our egos, our egos refuse and say, "These appointments are unsuitable."

How should we appoint? Should we place a group in a forward place, and place someone forward in the place of a group? Allah knows best about His

Lāh bi-qaḍā'ih and Abū Nuʿaym, *Ḥilya*, both in the wording *arḍinā bi-qaḍā'ik*.

[1] See Suhbas I.28, 57, 59, 75.

servants, and we do not know the wisdom. Everything exists for a wisdom, and according to its wisdom, its nurturing Lord put it in a certain place. This is an important matter. The servant must see everything as put in its place until its nurturing Lord changes its place from there and puts it somewhere else. Everything is ordered, as there is no mistake in the arrangement of the All-True. Far from it! You must know and say to yourself that "my knowledge falls short and I am short-sighted and I do not know whether this matter is well-suited or not." As for your nurturing Lord He knows. So even if, outwardly, you see something wrong, nevertheless, in the presence of the people of spiritual reality, that is the soul of rightness. This is why they see the affairs of the servants and they do not say "why this?" or "this is unsuitable." Because it is Allah Who is the apportioner and every movement and stillness that the possessor of *adab* sees, he does not ask "why did it happen?" Rather the affair proceeds according to His arrangement–exalted is He–and this requires training. Let one instruct himself and tell his ego, "You are wrong. Your nurturing Lord knows best the affair of His servants. Whether one's movements are from corruption or from righteousness, He knows best. It is possible for you to see something as evil but its upshot will be goodness. It is also possible that it points to something good but it turns out to be a misperception, and it reverts itself to become something evil."

Do not believe your ego but believe your nurturing Lord. Believe that your nurturing Lord has set up His servants in certain jobs, and that all have jobs they are doing, either in goodness or in evil. When you see that you have been employed in goodness, give thanks to your nurturing Lord. And when you see that certain people have been employed in evil, also give praise to your nurturing Lord, whereby they are the ones that took on the burden of that evil from you, and had they not taken it on, you would be the one taking it on. At that time be fair to that servant because he is carrying, or he is the display of evil. Show mercy and be fair to him, say, "May Allah help him in what he is bearing." This is not an easy matter. For example what soldiers carry: it is not as they wish. What is their secret between themselves and their nurturing Lord? We do not know, but Allah knows—*and for that did He create them* (Hūd 11:119).

In short, you must keep *adab* with everyone. When you yourself show little *adab* with people, they will show little *adab* with you; but when you make excellent your *adab* with them, you will not find other than *adab*. This is a foundational rule that never changes. When you stand in front of the mirror, if you laugh then your image will laugh, and the reverse is also true.

May Allah grant us and you excellent *adab*. By the sanctity of the Beloved, by the sanctity of the Fatiha.

103

[Spiritual intuitions are from divine *fayḍ* in the Shaykh's heart] – Bearing with reverses is [the one sign of belief and] the means to spiritual sciences and openings – [The servants' sins cannot overcome the mercy of their Lord] – Deeds of human beings between the spirit and the body

I seek refuge in Allah from the accursed devil
In the Name of Allah the All-Beneficent the Most Merciful
There is no power nor strength but with Allah the High, the Magnificent
Permission, O my Master, support!
Our way is companionship, and goodness is in the congregation

O Allah, grant us to stand firm in that which You have placed us in! Mawlana [Shaykh ʿAbd Allah Daghistani] says that every human being is meant to concern himself with his own situation and his own station without turning right or left. Mawlana says that for a person to be busy with his own mission is from the strength of belief, whereas abandoning one's own mission and busying oneself with what is of no concern or benefit to him is from weakness of belief or absence of belief. For example, we are sitting here and our job is to listen. When there are problems happening outside, if you happen to turn to them, Mawlana says this is from the weakness of belief or the absence of belief. For our job is right here and not out there. It is part of the murid's *adab* to be busy with his mission and not to be busy with what is of no concern or benefit to him. This is why "Part of the excellence of one's submission is to leave what is of no concern/benefit to him."[1]

Mawlana said the murid must concern himself with the guarding of his heart towards his spiritual guide, and there must not occur in the murid's heart any bad thought towards his spiritual guide. For Iblīs might throw thoughts into the murid's heart so that he will separate from his shaykh. Someone comes up asking, "how is this shaykh speaking such things, how is his state such and such, how is his status such and such." He will bring you fleeting thoughts until he spoils what is between you and the shaykh. Mawlana says that for a bad thought to come to the heart of the murid against his shaykh is more harmful than disbelieving in the Prophets. Why? Because were it not for

[1] See Suhba I.35, note 5.

that evidence—i.e. were it not for your shaykh—you would know nothing of the reality of the Prophets, and you would never achieve real belief in the Prophets. **For the servant to say, *āmantu bi-l-Lāhi wa-malā'ikatihi wa-kutubihi wa-rusulihi* (I believe in Allah, His angels, His Books, His Messengers) is an easy thing, but to achieve real belief in the Messengers is not ascertained except by your following your shaykh the way the Umma follows its Prophet, which teaches you how the reality of following must be, or the reality of believing in your Prophet, which takes place through the shaykh.** And just as it is impermissible to allow any fleeting thought in your mind against your Prophet, likewise it is impermissible to allow any fleeting thought in your mind against your shaykh, for were it not for the *imdād* (lending of spiritual help) from the shaykh, we would never get to know our Prophet. Therefore it is more harmful than unbelief in the Prophets for the murid to allow any fleeting thought against his shaykh in his heart. Likewise **the shaykh is permanently watching the hearts of the murids and what is revolving in them. Is the heart present? Is it in agreement? In disagreement? Or heedless? In whatever description the murid's heard is in, the shaykh looks at the hearts of the murids. If he finds the heart in agreement and present, he will pour over it from the outpourings of the All-True.** But if he finds that heart heedless, closed up, nothing of the spiritual intuitions will enter it. This is why it is obligatory for him to be in agreement and present with the shaykh permanently.

Mawlana asked, when does the servant achieve realization of true belief?[1] This is important. We are ordered to make our belief true and real so that we can rise and progress from imitative belief to real belief. This is required and we are legally tasked to achieve this realization. Mawlana asked when does real belief take place? One sign for real belief is that as many reverses descend on a human being without any objection on his part, or he did not object to any of them and he endured patiently and bore with it: at that time it will be real belief. Think about how many things happen in a single day, things you do not like. You might be upset with them, you might curse or quarrel or get angry or fight, or they make you commit disbelief. We seek refuge in Allah! There are so many different kinds of reverses and troubles that your ego dislikes. And this is constantly coming down. When one misses you another one will smite you. This is why, when reverses come up, you must control your nerves, neither collapsing nor resisting. The meaning of this is that you have power for endurance that comprises these reverses. For if there is not originally any power, this structure cannot be loaded onto it.

[1] See Suhba I.4 on the signs of real belief vs. imitative belief.

This is why **the servant is exposed all life long to every aspect of its pains, its worries, its problems and agitations, and to everything which the ego dislikes and is averse to. Despite all that, it is unable to run away from it. If one misses the other will reach. Count, each day, how many reverses you either hear or see. Likewise interaction with people, you will find in it what you dislike. What is the position of the true believer in that context? It is that he must put up with and bear with everything without objecting to anything! The true believer is like a high mountain. No matter how many storms there are, nothing moves it from its foundation**.

This is why Mawlana said, it is obligatory for the true believer to bear with everything. Do not say I cannot bear. Your nurturing Lord is looking at your request. When you ask of Him strength to carry, He will give it to you here and hereafter. According to your requests, you will find Him giving you. O our nurturing Lord! Strengthen our belief and strengthens our certainty! So the more our certainty strengthens and increases, the more our belief increases. Our master the Shaykh said that all the sciences and the openings are opened for the servant because of his bearing with reverses. The proverb says, "When you do not dig for a well you will not find a source." Likewise, bearing with reverses is a means for knowledges and openings in the station of true belief, whereby Mawlana says, *ʿilm al-yaqīn* (certainty of knowledge), *ʿayn al-yaqīn* (certainty of sight), *ḥaqq al-yaqīn* (certainty of reality):[1] these are the levels of knowledge, while the key to those knowledges is to bear with reverses. Mawlana says that at the time a person faces a reverse his state changes, and such a change negates belief because it reduces it. Reverses are the things the ego hates and dislikes.

In the unbeliever, coloring and change take place from state to state at the occurrence of reverses whereas the believer stands firm because he is tied, connected. His tie and connection makes him firm. As for the unbeliever he has no tie or connection, so he turns with the wind. Mawlana said that the Prophet–upon him the blessings and peace of Allah–likened the believer to the *sarw* (cypress) and said, "O Abu Bakr, the believer is like the cypress. It keeps its state in summer and winter, it is an evergreen and its state is firm. It does not shed its leaves. As for the hypocrite he is like the *kūsā* (squash) because this tree fills the world when it sees space, it keeps growing as if there was nothing else besides it, but when storms begin you find no trace of it at all."[2] Such is the hypocrite when reverses occur, nowhere to be found. But you will find him active in whatever he likes.

[1] See also Suhba I.59 for an alternate translation.

[2] I. "The likeness of the believer is as an evergreen whose leaves neither fall nor does

Mawlana said the mercy of Allah is vast and the sins of the servants will never overcome the mercy of their nurturing Lord. If all the sewers of the world poured into this ocean, will they overcome the ocean? Never, rather the ocean will purify them. And oceans are but a drop in the oceans of the All-True. This is why the sins of the servants will never overcome the oceans of mercy. **Our master the Shaykh said that as much as you commit sins, the result will be that the mercy of Allah is going to overtake them. "My mercy has primacy over My wrath."**[1] This is why the doors of Paradise are open for the servants. If one has missed entering through one, he will enter through the second door, or the third, and so forth. Eight Paradises whose doors are open for the servant. Mawlana says that for all human beings there is bliss in store, even if what has appeared in the world of this life is their unbelief, their atheism, their rebellious sins.

What counts is the ultimate end. The Prophet–upon him the blessings and peace of Allah–said, "Actions are only according to conclusions."[2] How it will be concluded for the servant is what is important. When he concluded with an acceptable deed, he did it, or he spoke about it, or if he was unable and it only fell into his heart without any open mention of this acceptable deed—because of it Allah will appoint for him a path to Paradise. **This is why the ultimate end of every human being is a hidden matter. This is between him and his nurturing Lord, and this is not known. Allah knows best the secret. This is why Mawlana says, even if his unbelief is apparent, yet in the ultimate end, how will it be sealed for him?**

If Allah asked them, "What were you doing in your world?" they will be inspired to answer, "Whatever You wanted us to do we were doing, we did not swerve. If You made us conform we acted in conformity. If You wanted us to act in contravention we did so. Only according to Your will have we ever been, O nurturing Lord of the worlds!" The servants will be inspired to say this answer. "You have left us to do whatever we wanted—*do what you will* (Fuṣṣilat 41:40)—so we have done what we will and now we have come." Allah will not take to account any of these because they are not qualified to be taken to account. Mawlana says that at that time the bodies of human beings are

their color change, it is the date palm." Narrated from Ibn ʿUmar by al-Bukhārī. II. "The likeness of the believer is as the stalk that grows, the winds blow on it and wrestle it down at times, and at other times straighten it up, while the likeness of the hypocrite is as the oak tree that stands firm on its trunk, nothing moving it until it is uprooted once and for all." Narrated from Abū Hurayra, Jābir and Kaʿb b. Mālik in various wordings by Aḥmad, Dārimī, Bukhārī, Muslim, al-Tirmidhī and others.

[1] See Suhba I.34, 10th note.

[2] See Suhba I.95, penultimate note.

inanimate earth while their spirits are from light in the presence of their nurturing Lord. *Say, "The spirit is of the command of my nurturing Lord"* (Banū Isrā'īl/Isrā' 17:85). Nothing comes from inanimate objects. The deceased will sleep forty years, does any deed emerge from him? Never.

Our nurturing Lord says, *say, "The spirit is of the command of my nurturing Lord."* Its meaning is that the spirit is a ray from the light of the Essence of the All-True and it does not suffer any diminishment. This light is pure and no impurity can be conceived to touch it. Nothing can be imagined to darken it. Can light bear any impurity? Never. Darkness cannot overcome light. Thus it is impossible for any darkness to appear from the servant's spirit. Bodies are inanimate objects, nothing comes from them. More than that, the deeds of human beings are not ascribed to their bodies or to their spirits. One does not say, this is the work of the body, or this is the work of the spirit. So the bodies are inanimate objects and the spirit is from Allah. Both sides justify his stand before the Lord of Might. Mawlana says that at that time there will appear from them as with the stone and the metal. When you strike one with the other sparks come out. Where were they before? Inside the metal or inside the stone?

Mawlana says that **the acts of human beings appear between the spirit and the body by the power of Allah. At that time the power of Allah will be given to the deeds of human beings one and all. At that time the meaning of "the good of it and the bad of it is from Allah"[1] shall come. Why did Allah say that the latter was a categorical obligation for us? So that we would believe that good and evil are from Allah. And you must recognize that acts are not ascribed to the body or to the spirit**. Therefore whatever issues from them is by the power of Allah. He held sway over it at that time. This is why, on the Day of Resurrection, our deeds will appear as forms coming to the Day of the Regathering. Our deeds will be created and given form at the Station, and judgment will be passed over them. When Allah passes judgment on the Day of Resurrection on these forms of the ugly deeds they will appear in the form of that particular servant and they will be thrown into Hellfire. While they are burning, the spirit of that servant will be as if imprisoned until Allah passes judgment over him. I.e. in proportion with the extent of darkness present in the person, his reality will appear at that time, and this punishment will be in this form and this fashion. When this punishment ends, the spirit will return to its station, and this is resigned to the knowledge of Allah Most High.

By the sanctity of the Beloved, by the sanctity of the Fatiha.

[1] See Suhba I.66, third note.

104
[*Dastūr* and *madad* signify breaking of the ego] – Story of Ahmad al-Badawi with the *Quṭb* – Tariqa is for piercing through the veils – Be with the truthful – [The lights of Naqshbandis prevail]

I seek refuge in Allah from the accursed devil
In the Name of Allah the All-Beneficent the Most Merciful
There is no power nor strength but with Allah the High, the Magnificent
Permission, O my Master, support!
Our way is companionship, and goodness is in the congregation

The sign of belief is the expansion of the chest. When you say *madad* (support!), the ego gets broken. This Shaykh X, despite his lofty status, says, "O my master, the ego says to the human being what the devil said to Firʿawn when he was intent on repenting, 'Do not repent, because people hold the belief that you are their god, so how will you repent?'" Likewise the *mutamashyikhūn* (self-made shaykhs) are told by the devil, "People are coming to you so display to people that you are everything. Nay, put yourself above everyone," just as Firʿawn said *"I am your supreme nurturing lord!"* (Nāziʿāt 79:23), "and never accept to say, *dastūr yā sayyidī, madad* (permission, O my Master, support!).[1] The significance of *dastūr* is the breaking of the ego.

The lordly Imam 'Abd al-Wahhāb al-Saʿrānī (898-973/1493-1565) used to say, "I never sat for sincere advice except I first asked permission by saying, *madad yā sayyidī*. I would ask permission from *ṣāḥib al-waqt* (the authority of the time), from the caliph of the Messenger of Allah, from the caliph of Allah." When the speaker asks permission and says, *dastūr yā sayyidī*, a special *madad* comes to him. As for the one that sits tyrant-like he is locked out and left to his ego, ruining his state and ruining himself.

[1] *Dastūr*, pl. *dasātīr*, from Pers. *dastūr* (custom, privilege, perk, cf. *OED*, art. *dustoor*), has six meanings per the authors of *al-Muʿjam al-jāmiʿ fīl-muṣṭalaḥāt al-ʿuthmāniyya dhāt al-uṣūl al-ʿarabiyya wal-fārisiyya wal-turkiyya wal-ayyūbiyya wal-mamlūkiyya* (Encyclopedic dictionary of Ottoman terms with Arabic, Persian, Turkish, Ayyubid and Mamluk origins), ed. Ḥassān Ḥallāq and ʿAbbās Ṣabbāgh (Beirut: Dār al-Nahḍat al-ʿArabiyya, 1430/2009) p. 92 including the one given above. Other senses are "vizier," "regional government office," "law, principle, or scholarly principle," "Zoroastrian high priest," and "an exclamation from someone startled by a frightful event."

Our liege lord Ahmad al-Badawi–Allah sanctify his secret–reached to the station of *kalīmu-l-Lāh* (conversing with Allah), i.e. one who is addressed by Allah with His speech directly, from behind the veil. That is the station of our liege lord Mūsā–upon him peace–and part of the address of the All-True to the servants. One day the *Quṭb* (spiritual pole) of the time saw him and said to him, "O Ahmad, come! I have your key." He replied to him, "I have no need of your keys. I will not take the key other than from the All-Opener. I will obtain it from Him–the Almighty–and I do not want a key from you." Why do we mention this story? The servant is with his ego and the ego refuses that he should do without its own striving and apart from its rank. Our liege lord Ahmad Badawi replied to the *Quṭb*, "I do not want it from you, but from Him."

A person's ego will never let him yield. But the custom of Allah imposes upon you that you must follow after the people of Allah and surrender yourself to them, and you must declare in the presence of the All-True that your have surrendered yourself as a sacrificial ram. At that time something of the gift of the All-True shall reach the servant and the servant shall be with Allah. Otherwise it is not with mere speech that creatures can say "I am with Allah." They are lying. Rather they are with their egos. If they were really with Allah things would change to their advantage. How is our state with our egos? The ego is ruling us. Your ego refuses for anyone to interfere in its affairs.

Also, the servant will never be with Allah until he is first with the people of Allah. *O you who believe! Guard yourself from the One God and be with the truthful ones* (Tawba 9:119). Those who have not exchanged their covenant with Allah for something else until it became correct to attribute truthfulness to them and their nurturing Lord called them truthful ones. This is a recommendation from the presence of Allah: one that is truthful with Allah and His Messenger–upon him the blessings and peace of Allah–and there is no treachery with them. Who is the truthful one? They are the people of Allah,[1] *Men who have been true to what they covenanted with the One God* (Aḥzāb 33:23). The elucidation [of *the truthful ones*] is their covenant with Allah. How can they be with Allah and yet they leave the truthful ones? We accuse our nurturing Lord of abandoning us, but have you yourself walked with the truthful ones then your nurturing Lord neglected you? And your nurturing Lord said be *with* the truthful ones and He did not say *of*, because we are not qualified for that. But for us to be in their company—it is possible. People have the effrontery to say, "Allah has ignored us although we are with Him." This is a lie. We are not with Allah, for if we were with Him, this tender care would walk with us.

[1] See Ruzbehan Baqli, *Tafsīr ʿarāʾis al-bayān fī ḥaqāʾiq al-Qurʾān* (Tawba 9:119).

When a lamp goes out, what does it indicate? That the power was cut from the main power station. This indicates that tender care is not with us because we are separated from Allah, we prostrate to the idols, we lie and we claim that we are with Allah, and Allah never accepts lies. The human ego does not accept to yield easily. Imam Ahmad al-Badawi longed to see our nurturing Lord. That station was that of our liege lord Mūsā when he said, *let me see, that I may look at You*. Allah Most High said, *you shall not see Me* (al-A'rāf 7:143). Its meaning is that as long as you yourself are still existing you shall not see Me. With your claim to existence you shall not see Me; and everyone that claims existence shall not see Him.

Our liege lord Ahmad al-Badawi said, "O my nurturing Lord, let me see that I may look at you." He said, "You shall not see Me. The keys to this door were given to So and so." His nurturing Lord sent him to that *Quṭb* so that he would erase his egotism. He said to him, "You shall not be given the key, and even if you spent two thousand years the door shall not be opened and you shall not enter. I have given the key to my servant So and so, take it from him and come." For he was coming with his ego.

Our liege lord Mūsā, with his lofty status in the presence of Allah—of Prophet-Messenger and of those of strong resolve—said, *let me see, that I may look at You*. He said *you shall not see Me* (A'rāf 7:143), these are the serails of absolute Oneness, the serails of kings, there is no admittance for two, it does not accommodate "Me and you." Once no trace of you remains then come. The ocean of pure monotheism does not accept any duality—let alone three! Four! He said, "I have given the key to that wali, and that wali shall pulverize your egotism, then you may come." *Lan tarānī* (you shall not see Me), this is an emphasized future negation, *abadan* (ever). As long as there remain in you your egos and with your existence there is no possibility, until you yourself sacrifice your ego with death. "Die before you die."[1]

Our liege lord Ahmad al-Badawi returned in search of that *Quṭb*, but first he had given precedence to his ego, and only second did he begin to look for him. The search proved difficult until he despaired. At that time the wali unveiled himself so that our liege lord Ahmad could see him and he said to him, "You came, O Ahmad? You came, O my master? You have surrendered?" "I have surrendered." He turned to him with a single spiritual turn, removed everything from his chest, brought him down from that station and put on the ground. He was in al-Thurayyā (the Pleiades) and he put him in *al-tharā* (the soil). He left nothing of him, his state, his knowledge, his deeds. He left nothing for him that he could rely on. He left him for six months not knowing

[1] See Suhba I.32, fourth note.

how to pray. Before that, he was not praying other than for his ego, not for his nurturing Lord. He had made his ego a god and an imam, he would prostrate to his ego and remember his ego, "there is no god but my ego." This is an example of someone who is at the station of ego without any *murshid* (spiritual guide) educating him. For the ego strives to be a god over a person.

Why does Mawlana [Shaykh 'Abd Allah Daghistani] say, "We are the people of enormous sins, the Messenger–upon him the blessings and peace of Allah–shall intercede for us"? Because at *maqām al-nafs* (the station of ego) any deed you do is counted as one of the enormities.[1] For you are working to satisfy your ego or, at the very least, for an ego-driven motive even with the pursuit of the hereafter: your ego will not submit until you placate it with all kinds and all sorts of ranks through palaces and wide-eyed houris. At that time you will agree to worship in the hope of living in gardens of Paradise and in bliss. This is the exultation of the ego and this is the station of whoever worships his nurturing Lord at the station of the ego, and he is of the people of enormous sins.[2] The veils were not torn up for him so that he could worship his nurturing Lord in the field of pure monotheism with true worship. (There is no harm in being with our *nafs* when we are sick).

What is the way to pierce through these veils and rise? There are five billion people in the world. How many of them are presidents of nations? 200 presidents? And people are all hoping to become president. Is this possible? But as for the one asking to become a wali, his way is open. You must come out of the field of your ego and become free of its dictate. At that time you will become a wali. To leave the surface of the earth until you escape gravity — how difficult that is! But beyond gravity is there any difficulty? All you need to do is cross over the threshold of gravity. All the paths and sacred laws were brought into existent so that it would be possible for you to cross this, and when you cross it you will become a servant to Allah.

Everything has its principles. *And do come into houses through their doors*

[1] Because of the hidden *shirk* that it implies. See Suhba 96.

[2] This paragraph illustrates the position related from 'Alī Zayn al-'Ābidīn by Abū Nu'aym, *Ḥilya* (3:134); Ibn 'Asākir, *Tārīkh* (41:409-410); Ibn al-Jawzī, *Ṣifat al-ṣafwa* ('Alī b. al-Ḥusayn b. 'Alī b. Abī Ṭālib *'alayhim al-salām*); Yāfi'ī, *Mir'āt al-jinān* (year 94); Ibn Kathīr, *Bidāya* (year 94, 'Alī b. al-Ḥusayn) in his famous statement, "Some people worship out of fear and this is the worship of slaves. Some worship out of desire and this is the worship of merchants. Some worship Him in gratitude and this is the worship of the free." The author of *Nuzhat al-majālis* attributes it to Ma'rūf al-Karkhī while al-Qārī in his commentary on Tirmidhī's *Shamā'il* attributes it to 'Alī b. Abī Ṭālib. Others famous forms of a similar view came from Rābi'a al-'Adawiyya and Abū Manṣūr al-Ḥallāj.

(al-Baqara 2:189). *But the ones that strove in Us, We will indeed show them Our ways* ('Ankabūt 29:69). The logic that inspires us this[1] is a divine outpouring and it does not stray from the logic of the verse. The precondition is jihad against the ego, and when you are enabled to have success in waging jihad, your nurturing Lord has promised you: *and He has subjected to you what is in the skies and what is on earth entirely from Him* (Jāthiya 45:13). But what is important is to cross this distance. Moreover, our nurturing Lord says, *Allah does not task any soul except to its capacity* (Baqara 2:286). There is no assertion of impossibility. Perhaps with the Prophet's hadith–upon him the blessings and peace of Allah–for example, "The loveliest of deeds to Allah are the most permanent ones, even if they are few." I.e. what is asked is not abundance of deeds but regularity of the servant in worship.

The indication there is for the servant to keep boundaries. This is what matters, and not the performance of deeds, which is easy since Allah did not task us to be *of* the truthful ones—which would be an assertion of impossibility. Rather, *be with the truthful ones* (al-Tawba 9:119). If He had said, be of the truthful ones, who would have been able? Very rare few. But He gave leeway and made it light. For example, if no one could board a plane except pilots, then who could board? This is a tasking beyond capacity, it spells impossibility. But it is enough for the murids to be together with the truthful one, like a single locomotive pulling a hundred train compartments. Only chain the cars together and to the locomotive and everything will go, because the power is in the first one. Wherever it goes they will go with it. **Your own jihad is to be in the company of the truthful ones. This is what is missing from those human people**.

There is also a clarification needed for Mawlana's discourse so that no point should remain misunderstood, because our goal is difficult. **When you have missed a train there is a second one, and up to 124,000 ones. And the greatest sign is love. When the chain of love is found then do not fear!** Wherever this group will be arriving is also the same station where you will arrive and sit.

(Our liege lord Abū Yazīd al-Bisṭāmī the Sultan of the Knowers used to say, "For 37 years I had been doing jihad against my ego. In the end I examined myself and I still saw a belt on my midsection,"[2] i.e. I am still with my unbelief. Therefore do not praise yourself and say, "I have submitted." Do not trust in yourself lest a test might come and throw you into the depth of the fire. After

[1] I.e. this connection between Mawlana's discourse and the Quranic verses he cites.

[2] Narrated by al-Nawawī in *Bustān al-'ārifīn*.

all the struggle and effort Abū Yazīd himself is saying, "I found the belt still strapped on myself."[1])

This is why you see the love of the people of Scripture for our liege lord ʿĪsā is beyond description. Do you reckon this love will be left unchecked? Yet we, the Umma of the Beloved, do not have love for our Prophet the like of their love for theirs. From the intensity of their love for him they have made him a god in their view. Despite that, Allah will not leave them and He will not leave the Christians; nor the pseudo-shaykhs—since "Whoever imitates a people then he is one of them."[2] But for someone to be at the spiritual station is one thing, and for one to see it on TV is something else. They take pleasure in sights, but those that have entered the station are something else.

That *Quṭb* had left Shaykh Ahmad Badawi for six months without showing himself to him. All that time Ahmad al-Badawi was looking for him while struggling with himself intensely. His station was at the Pleiades and now it was in the soil, but he endured steadfastly because Allah had told him, go to that one. After six months that *Quṭb* appeared to him. Our liege lord Ahmad asked him, "Where were you?" He replied, "I have not left you. I was right there with you, but you did not see me." Then that *Quṭb* directed himself with *ḥaqīqat al-tawajjuh* (the reality of focusing the heart)[3] to our liege lord Ahmad al-Badawi and poured down into his heart, just as the Messenger of Allah–upon him the blessings and peace of Allah–had poured down into the heart of Abū Bakr al-Ṣiddīq. He made him be at the same station that he was before, but not through Ahmad's own work, rather out of the bounty of his nurturing Lord at the hand of the *Quṭb*.

At that point there is no egotism. It is no longer *mamhūr bi-muhr al-nafs* (imprinted with the imprint of the ego). *This is from the bounty of my nurturing Lord* (al-Naml 27:40). This is a farthermost limit and it is not an easy thing. At that time he got the key to open. For he had become without self. Lights came down on him and he was dressed with them. The light of *walah* (bewilderment) was coming out of his eyes, from the two Attributes of the majesty and the beauty of the All-True. That light, were it to hit any human

[1] I.e. the distinctive sign of non-Muslims.

[2] Narrated from (i) Ibn ʿUmar by Ibn Abī Shayba; Aḥmad; ʿAbd b. Ḥumayd; Abū Dāwūd; and others; (ii) Abū Hurayra by Abū Umayya al-Ṭarasūsī, *Musnad*; Bazzār; and others; (iii) Ḥudhayfa by Bazzār; Ṭabarānī, *Awsaṭ*; (iv) ʿUmar by Ibn Ḥadhlam, *Juzʾ min ḥadīth al-Awzāʿī li-bni Ḥadhlam*.

[3] Also translatable as the power of alignment of the shaykh's heart with the murid's and of the murid's heart towards his spiritual goal. See Mawlana al-Shaykh Nazim's suhba "The Final Limit" in *Mercy Oceans' Lovestreams* (pp. 101-110).

being, it would kill him like a thunderbolt. This is why he would wear a face-veil after that station had become unveiled to him. One of the eminent seniors among our Naqshbandi masters retold this account in his gathering, then he turned his address to one of the murids and said to him, “O my child, what would your state have been if you had faced Ahmad al-Badawi with that light?” That one—who had reached the station of murid in the Naqshbandi Tariqa—replied, “O my master, I do not know, but if had been in front of my master Ahmad al-Badawi my *walah* would have burned him despite his *walah*.”

This is why **our beginning is the end of all the other Tariqas**. The lights of the Naqshbandis are stronger by far because their station begins above the station of Jibril, whereas the rest begin from below the station of Jibril. It is like the Prophets. They know the immense level of the Prophet–upon him and them the blessings and peace of Allah–and this is why every Prophet requested to be part of the Umma of the Beloved instead of being a Prophet.

By the sanctity of the Beloved, by the sanctity of the Fatiha.

105

Fiṭra matters more than Islam, belief [and deeds] – Did the Messenger rely on his work? – [*Fiṭra* takes you to your station] – Story of our liege lord ʿAlī with the Jewish doctors of the Law

I seek refuge in Allah from the accursed devil
In the Name of Allah the All-Beneficent the Most Merciful
There is no power nor strength but with Allah the High, the Magnificent
Permission, O my Master, support!
Our way is companionship, and goodness is in the congregation

Mawlana Sultan al-Awliya ʿAbd Allah Fa'iz al-Daghistani–may Allah sanctify his secret–said that the Messenger of Allah–upon him the blessings and peace of Allah–did not obtain any level through his work. This points to a spiritual reality, namely that people do not reach the levels with their deeds but from the bounty of Allah Most High. It is not by *kasb* (earning) but by *wahb* (bestowal) from Allah Almighty. The evidence that it is the case is the statement of the Prophet–upon him the blessings and peace of Allah–"Do not leave us to ourselves for the blink of an eye."[1] This is sufficient evidence that the Messenger did not reach any level through his work.

Mawlana says that the Messenger–upon him the blessings and peace of Allah–from the start never accepted any rank either in exchange for his work. This is an important matter. Because of that, Shah Naqshband used to say that for the servant to possess a pure *fiṭra* (primordial state / disposition / nature) is better than *īmān* and *islām*. For there to be with the servant a strong qualification or *fiṭra* is better than his *islām* and his *īmān*, because *īmān* and *islām* appear in the servant and, together with it, there will be a lot of deficiency. However, the *fiṭra* that Allah originally created people with is a leaven and a pristine jewel in the servant. That is the important thing with Allah. The Prophet said, *al-nāsu maʿādin* (human beings are minerals),[2] i.e.

[1] See Suhba I.28, fifth note.

[2] Its continuation is, "the best of them in pagan times are the best of them in Islam once they become learned and understand. You will find that some of the best people are those who hate this great matter the most until they become involved in it." Narrated from (i) Abū Hurayra by Ṭayālisī; al-Shāfiʿī; Ḥumaydī; Ibn Rāhūyah; Aḥmad; al-Bukhārī; Muslim; and others; (ii) Jābir by Aḥmad; Ibn ʿAbd al-Barr, *Jāmiʿ bayān al-ʿilm*; (iii) Abād b. Saʿīd b. al-ʿĀṣ by Ibn Khayyāṭ, *Ṭabaqāt*; (iv) Umm Salama by Ibn Abī al-

they are not all the same mineral. Every human being has a special jewel and this jewel is under the upbringing of one of the beautiful Names of Allah. This is why ***fiṭra* is what matters and not the external works from *īmān* and *islām*. For in our *īmān* there is boundless and countless deficiency! And Allah does not treat us in consideration of our deeds but rather in consideration of the original *fiṭra*. This is why Shah Naqshband says, "What is important for us is *fiṭra*," i.e. the original jewel existing in the human being. This *fiṭra* is more important than all the acts of worship**.

Mawlana [Shaykh 'Abd Allah Daghistani] says, in confirmation of Shah Naqshband's statement, that one night after the *'ishā* prayer, the Prophet–upon him blessings and peace of Allah–addressed the Companions (and such address is general to the Umma also, for he is a Prophet to all). He said to them, "O my noble Companions, pray when you like and when you do not like, do not pray. Whatever of the two [you choose] is one and the same." He spoke to this sense. "Because the pen has written, and the records are dry, and this will not change. Thus, my Companions, you will not obtain any rank with your deeds, but only with His bounty and His generosity and His mercy–exalted is He! For He has already written and arranged everything on His own part."[1]

Mawlana is saying, pay attention! **Even if you strove with the strength of the Prophet–upon him the blessings and peace of Allah–you will not obtain the least of the level than the one Allah has given you**. This points to our weakness, and our helplessness points to His generosity. Think: if you had the strength of the Prophet–upon him the blessings and peace of Allah–and you are worshipping with that power and without any contravention, still you will never obtain the least level of what Allah has given you! What is the status of deeds then? Have we prayed or not? Have we acted or not? If we acted with the power of the Prophet of the end of times, whose two cycles of prayer outweigh all the deeds of the two weighty worlds of the human beings and the jinns, and the angels—for they do not reach their extent—still, even though we have worshipped with that power, we would not obtain the least level of

Dunyā, *al-Ḥilm*; al-Ḥākim; (v) Ibn 'Abbās by Ibn Sakhtūyah al-Muzakkī, *al-Muzakkiyāt*; Ibn 'Adī, *Kāmil*; Abū al-Shaykh, *Amthāl al-ḥadīth*; Bayhaqī, *Shu'ab* (74: *al-jūd wal-sakhā'*); (vi) Sahl b. Sa'd al-Sā'idī by al-Māwardī, *al-Amthāl wal-Ḥikam*.

[1] See Suhba I.81, penultimate note as well as the Prophetic hadith, "None of you will enter Paradise with his deeds," narrated from (i) Abū Hurayra by Aḥmad; Bukhārī; Bazzār and others; (ii) Jābir by Aḥmad; Muslim and others; (iii) 'Ā'isha by Bukhārī; Muslim and others; (iv) Asad b. Kurz by Bukhārī, *al-Tārīkh al-kabīr*; al-Ṭabarānī, *Kabīr*; *Musnad al-Shāmiyyīn*; Abū Nu'aym, *Ma'rifat al-Ṣaḥāba*; al-Ḍiyā' al-Maqdisī, *al-Mukhtāra*; (v) Sharīk b. Ṭāriq by Ibn Qāni', *Mu'jam al-Ṣaḥāba*; Ṭabarānī, *Kabīr*.

that which Allah has conferred on us out of His bounty.

Consider the example of your works. If you want to build an edifice from the earth to the sky, is it possible at all? If you brought together everything for its construction, still, it would not suffice to reach there. It means you are falling short. However, Allah, with His generosity, shall give you and shall make you reach your high rank. What happened with our deeds then? They remained here. Our work starts from the ground and you are building on it righteous deeds to progress higher, and when you are busy in this manner, a lordly elevator descends from the presence of Allah, you are invited to sit and it takes you there. This is important. Why have creatures fallen into destructive matters? Because of their reliance on acts. Iblīs, due to reliance on his works, came down and fell. This is why **our master the Shaykh's concern was always, in his spiritual directives and his counsels, that no human being should rely on his acts**.

The Companions said to the Messenger–upon him the blessings and peace of Allah: "Messenger of Allah, then why should we endure hardships in the nights, and why should we get up and wash in the cold days to pray? Why should we not leave deeds?" He said, "If you want to leave them leave them. If you want not to pray then do not pray." They said, "Then we are free." They went out and decided not to come to prayer that night. When the time for azan came and our liege lord Bilal went up for the reminder, all the Companions that heard it got up and came to the mosque. After the prayer the Messenger–upon him the blessings and peace of Allah–asked them, "How did you come after you had resolved not to come? How did you leave your houses, your women, your beds? Why did you come?" They said, "Messenger of Allah, by Allah! When we heard Bilal's azan our beds became like beds of thorns and our houses like prisons. We wanted to set ourselves free from them and we came here and reached to Paradise." The Messenger of Allah–upon him the blessings and peace of Allah–said, "O my Companions! The secret for which you were created is activating you and it is not in your hands, and every human being has this secret—that for which one was created. That is what is activating him."

That is meaning of Shah Naqshband's statement, "What is important for us is the human being's original *fiṭra*." ***Fiṭra* is found in the station of *khafā* (hiddenness).**[1] ***Fiṭra* is what activates you and orients you and takes you to your station, and to the rank that is with Him—not what you have founded of ranks. What you have done is bound for ruin and what He has given you is the original**. He said–exalted is He–*and We turned to what they had done*

[1] See Suhbas I.25 and I.87.

of works then We made it scattered motes (al-Furqān 25:23). Mawlana says, "If the Messenger–upon him the blessings and peace of Allah–himself did not rely on his deeds which he did with his strength and his will, what is left of our deeds? And how can we ourselves claim that we pray, or attend the congregation with the people of dhikr or Tariqa? How is it possible that we can claim this?"

Mawlana represented our works as what our liege lord ʿAlī–Allah be well-pleased with him–said about women, "O women! There is no doing without you and there is no goodness in you."[1] Just as our liege lord ʿAlī said of women, likewise his discourse applies to our deeds: there is no goodness in our deeds but they are indispensable. Our deeds are like women. You must firmly believe that our works are inappropriate, as there is no benefit from our deeds and there is no doing without them. This is why we must work whether there is goodness in them or not. Mawlana says that when the believing woman shows her face to people, Allah Almighty calls to His angels, "Come, all of you, My angels, and stoke the furnace for her!" The more her act repeats itself, the more the furnace increases in intensity until it is blacker than tar, and the bodies of the people of Hellfire burn until the tooth of each of them is like a mountain. What is the wisdom? The permanence of their punishment. Mawlana asks what is the greatest affliction for the people of the Fire? That there is no death there. They wish it but they cannot find it. We ask Allah's kindness! Their edges burn with a green fire and Allah return their frame so that they burn again.[2] Thus there is no death there.

Mawlana says that twenty-five of *al-falāsifat al-qissīsīn al-dahriyyīn* (eternalist priest philosophers) attended the gathering of our liege lord ʿAlī. They did not believe in Allah, or His Messenger, or Resurrection, or Paradise or Hell. They were *ibāḥiyyūn* (libertine freethinkers) who did not bind themselves with any restriction. They had come to debate our liege lord ʿAlī–may Allah ennoble his countenance–about the matters of belief. They addressed our liege lord ʿAlī by saying, "You are fools because you bind yourselves with baseless matters. You fear the Day of Resurrection and you put yourselves in narrow confines and hardships. As for ourselves we live happy and we do what pleases us. This is why you are fools and we are wise."

Our liege lord ʿAlī said to them, "Yes, we want to follow you because you are wise, but I have a question. If you answer it, you must be following the truth and we are following falsehood." They said, "Ask!" Our liege lord ʿAlī said,

[1] Cited in the Shīʿī sources: Ṭabarsī, *Majmaʿ al-bayān* (Āl ʿImrān 3:14); al-Murtaḍā Ḥusayn al-Mūsawī, *Nahj al-balāgha*; Kāfī al-Dīn ʿAlī b. Muḥammad al-Laythī, *ʿUyūn al-ḥikam*; Bahāʾ al-Dīn Muḥammad b. Ḥusayn al-Ḥārithī al-ʿĀmilī, *al-Kashkūl*.
[2] See al-Nisāʾ 4:56.

"Will there come a day when we are exactly equal you and us? When the agonies of death come to us, will any trace of this happiness and pleasure remain?" They said, "All pleasure ends." Our liege lord ʿAlī said, "We ourselves are far from the pleasure of life and we do not abandon ourselves to live as we please, so when we enter the agonies of death this hardship shall end and at that time we shall be equal. If the matter is as you claim—no Reckoning, no record of deeds, no Fire and no Paradise, the result will be that you have won nothing and we have lost nothing. However, if there is a hereafter, a Reckoning, a Judgment, a Paradise and a Hellfire, we will be saved and will have won. What about you?" Our liege lord ʿAlī struck the head of the priests with his finger as he said, "Think about this matter!" He had cornered them with his argument. They wanted to escape and run away but there was no way out from our liege lord ʿAlī's discourse. Their leader reflected then he said, "O ʿAlī! You have spoken true. Your way is safe and we are immensely mistaken. We beg you to teach us belief right away. We bear witness that there is no god but the One God and that Muhammad is the Messenger of the One God. This is indeed the truth and we will not accept to be fools." They entered Islam and they became honored with *īmān* through the gentle wisdom of our liege lord ʿAlī.

Mawlana said our liege lord ʿAlī is not like our liege lord ʿUmar. If it were ʿUmar he would have killed them. True knowledge gives its owner gentle wisdom and our liege lord ʿAlī possessed the secret that the Messenger–upon him the blessings and peace of Allah–had given him. Because he had this secret, he now possessed steadfast endurance. Mawlana said the Messenger–upon him the blessings and peace of Allah–would send our liege lord ʿAlī at times on journeys no one knew about. It was a secret between the two of them. On one occasion a *mārid* (giant) as tall as a minaret came and took him to fight a certain people. During the battle he felt slightly disturbed by them so he let out a yell by which he caused all the souls of the shahids and their swords to appear. They appeared to give him assistance. Then he completed the fighting and gained victory over the enemy. At that time of the emergence of the Mahdi our liege lord ʿAlī will come and there will be with him 12,000 men of his descendants and in his form. Their swords will be like fire and they will have [the sword] Dhū al-Fiqār with them.

Our liege lord the Shaykh said to me that another time the Messenger of Allah–upon him the blessings and peace of Allah–ordered our liege lord ʿAlī–Allah sanctify his countenance–to pe present at Mount Uḥud and told him, "Someone will come to you, do what he orders." There came to him the Prophet Rāzīn–upon him peace–the legatee of our liege lord ʿĪsā and one of the Israelite Prophets.[1] He came there and took him to the far west where are found Wādī al-Salām, Wādī al-Sibāʿ, Wādī al-Zaytūn, Ziʾr al-ʿAlā and Jabal Aws—five stations where the sun sets. He took him there and he stayed three months. He married one of their daughters and had a progeny there. Mawlana al-Shaykh said that from our liege lord ʿAlī there are 12,000 riders with his form, his strength and his knowledge. That progeny is found in this number. If one passes on another replaces him, to the age of the spiritual leader of endtimes, when our liege lord the Mahdi shall raise the *takbīr*. In Syro-Palestine, upon hearing his *takbīr*, 12,000 will appear before him as will our liege lord ʿAlī with his physical power together with these powers, in addition to the angels and the jinns. These are special brigades for *Ṣāḥib al-zamān*. They will be present for the cleaning of the world from the stain of unbelief. O Allah! Reunite us with them.

[Question: Why did Allah not make the servants devoid of free choice?]

Allah left us free to choose and He did not confine us, so that we would not see ourselves are restricted and so that every person might run free with his freedom. For if it were apparent in us that we had no free will, how would our state be? We would leave everything and not do any of our deeds. However, this is the secret of the nurturing Lord. He facilitated it for us so that He would protect us from destructive ways. An example for this is that you take your children to the beach and you let them swim and play, but you are watching them. You do not go far from them, because children do not know where danger lies. As for you, you are watching them and, if you perceive any danger around them you interfere.

May Allah protect us and you. By the sanctity of the Beloved, by the sanctity of the Fatiha.

[1] "Between ʿĪsā and Muḥammad–upon them blessings and peace–there were 600 or 569 years and four Prophets: three of them Israelites and one of them an Arab, Khālid b. Sinān al-ʿAbsī" (Bayḍāwī, al-Māʾida 5:19). The names of the three Israelites are discussed in the commentaries under Yā Sīn 36:13-14. See also Ibn Ḥajar, *Fatḥ al-Bārī* (*Aḥādīth al-anbiyāʾ*, 6:467 [Yā Sīn 36:13] and 6:489 [Maryam 19:16]).

106

Be a searcher for the truth – The submission of our liege lord 'Umar – Deeds have no inherent result in the divine presence – Meaning of "The best of deeds are the most arduous"

I seek refuge in Allah from the accursed devil
In the Name of Allah the All-Beneficent the Most Merciful
There is no power nor strength but with Allah the High, the Magnificent
Permission, O my Master, support!
Our way is companionship, and goodness is in the congregation

How were the noble Companions once, and what did they become? Mawlana [Shaykh 'Abd Allah Daghistani] says that our liege lord 'Umar would not sit at a table until there were before him a hundred different types of food. One day he heard that "his sister was now believing in Muhammad" -upon him the blessings and peace of Allah. His anger was intense and it flared as a fire. He went to cut off her head. When he arrived he hit her and was intent on killing her. She said to him, "O 'Umar! No matter what you do, even if you kill me, I will never recant the faith of Muhammad–upon him the blessings and peace of Allah. Do what you see fit." At that time he fell silent and thought about how this sister of his never used to talk back to him no matter what he did to her, and now she was answering back. There must be a wisdom there. He said to her, "What does Muhammad recite to you? Recite it to me." She recited, *By the night-star when it plunges! Your companion has not erred. Nor does he speak of his own whim. It is nothing but revelation revealed. The one of mighty powers has taught him* (al-Najm 53:5).[1] Our liege lord 'Umar was deeply moved by the mellifluence of the speech. He had not heard any of it before. A spiritual state took over 'Umar and he left her.

He headed for the Messenger of Allah–upon him the blessings and peace of Allah–intending not to return until he had verified his case. When the Companions saw 'Umar heading over in this fashion—he was carried his sword in a reverse fashion that meant kill or be killed—their hearts were shaken and alarmed, except our liege lord 'Alī drew his sword, stood at the

[1] Or the beginning of the Sura of Ṭa Ha (20) as narrated in Ibn Isḥāq, Ibn Hishām, Ibn Ḥibbān and Ibn Kathīr's *Sīras*; Aḥmad, *Faḍā'il al-Ṣaḥāba*; Ibn 'Asākir, *Tārīkh*; etc. all as narrated from his sister Fāṭima bint al-Khaṭṭāb b. Nufayl al-Qurashiyya.

door and said, "If that is 'Umar then here is 'Alī." He readied himself for him but the Pride of creatures called him, "O 'Alī! Sheathe your sword, for Jibril has just given me the glad tidings that 'Umar was coming in search of the truth. Do not fear, for whoever comes searching for the truth then no fear should be felt from him. Let him come in." So our liege lord 'Alī let go of his sword.

Mawlana said, see how Allah opens all doors before the seeker of truth. This is excellent news. The Companions were worshipping with the Messenger of Allah–upon him the blessings and peace of Allah–in the mosque of Khayf. When our liege lord 'Umar submitted he said, "Are we not following the truth, Messenger of Allah? Why hide and why fear?" The possessor of the truth wields great authority. Allah made our liege lord 'Umar for this service and this was his job. With him the number of the Companions became forty and with him Islam emerged into the open. Thus he is the manifestation of the Islamic faith. He said, "We want to show ourselves, Messenger of Allah!" He climbed a high spot and raised the *takbīr* announcing his submission. When Abū Jahl heard him he sent the children after him with instructions to pelt him with stones. This is why when he was saying *ḥayya 'alā al-ṣalāt* (come to prayer) he would turn right, and when he was saying *ḥayya 'alā al-falāḥ* (come to success) he would turn left, to see who was throwing the stone among the children so that he would teach their fathers a lesson. This is how our liege lord 'Umar submitted, and through him Allah showed Islam into full view.

The seeker of the truth must necessarily reach the truth. All you need to do is be a seeker of the truth. Even if you are in the farthermost end of the earth and among a people of ignorance living in a time of darkest ignorance! Just as our liege lord 'Umar lived in the Jahiliyya (Time of ignorance) and yet sought after the truth and reached it, likewise it is possible for a person to live in any country—England, America, Russia—and, if he is a seeker of the truth, he must necessarily reach it. Allah shall make him reach it. This is why you will see in western countries the number of those that declare their submission and openly announce it constantly increasing. Why? Although their upbringing was amidst the darkness of unbelief, yet by mere virtue of their reflection about the truth, Allah Almighty made them reach. This is a secret. Among the Muslims also are those that want to reach the truth and they have truthfulness in this matter. Allah will inevitably make them reach to the heart of the truth.

Mawlana told the story of our liege lord 'Alī with the priests—we retold it in the previous suhba—and he said that the Messenger of Allah–upon him the blessings and peace of Allah–had not obtained any rank through his works. I.e. he obtained the ranks as a gift from Allah Almighty. **Whoever considers**

that they obtained ranks as a result of their own deeds, you will find with them full of passion and eagerness for work because they imagine that the obtainment of ranks is through their deeds. They do not know that even for the Messenger of Allah–upon him the blessings and peace of Allah–his work is not enough to reach those ranks on the part of Allah. Whoever realizes about that reality that he will not obtain any rank even if he has the power of all the Prophets, and has ascertained this knowledge and this station, work will become for him as if dragging a mountain—and at that time, *aḥsanu al-a'māli ashaqquhā* (The best of deeds are the most arduous).[1] At that time one will be counted of the enduring ones because he truly knows there is no result from this work of his. Yet **you must work and at the same time you must recognize that this work cannot make you reach the least rank in the presence of Allah—until your nurturing Lord bestows on you that rank from His presence. And the ranks are given to the children of Ādam from the Day of *"am I not your nurturing Lord?"*** (al-A'rāf 7:172), i.e. from the day that Allah honored the servants—*and We have certainly honored the children of Ādam* (Banū Isrā'īl/Isrā' 17:70). So then is it you that have worshipped Him until He honored you? Or rather is it Him that has dressed you with His bounty?

May Allah keep us and you! By the sanctity of the Beloved, by the sanctity of the Fatiha.

[1] Famously attributed—without chain—to Ibn 'Abbās by the lexicographers, e.g. al-Farāhidī, *al-'Ayn*; al-Qāsim b. Sallām, *Gharīb al-ḥadīth*; Ibn Qutayba, ditto; al-Ḥarbī, ditto; al-Azharī, *Tahdhīb al-lugha*; Jawharī, *Ṣiḥāḥ*; Abū 'Ubayd al-Harawī, *Gharībayn*; Ibn al-Jawzī, *Gharīb al-ḥadīth* etc. It is a rule inferred from the Prophetic hadith "The reward [for your Hajj] is proportional to your fatigue," narrated from 'Ā'isha by al-Bukhārī and Muslim as stated by al-Qārī in *al-Asrār al-marfū'a*.

Bibliography

'Abd al-Razzāq al-Ṣan'ānī. *Muṣannaf.* With Ma'mar b. Rāshid, *Jāmi'*. Ed. Ḥabīb al-Raḥmān al-A'ẓamī. 2nd ed. 11 vols. Gujerat, India: al-Majlis al-'Ilmī, 1304/ 1983.

Abū Dāwūd Sulaymān b. al-Ash'ath al-Sijistānī. *Sunan.* Ed. Muḥ. 'Awwāma. 2nd ed. 5 vols. Jeddah: Dār al-Qibla lil-Thaqāfat al-Islāmiyya; Beirut: Mu'assasat al-Rayyān, 1425/2004.

Abū Nu'aym al-Aṣbahānī, Aḥmad b. 'Abd Allāh b. Isḥāq. [*al-Muntakhab min*] *Dalā'il al-Nubuwwa.* Ed. Muḥ. Rawwās Qal'ajī and 'Abd al-Barr 'Abbās. 2 vols. in 1. 2nd ed. Beirut: Dār al-Nafā'is, 1419/1999.

_______. *Ḥilyat al-Awliyā' wa-Ṭabaqāt al-Aṣfiyā'.* 10 vols. Cairo: Maktabat al-Khānjī & Maktabat al-Sa'āda, 1932-1938. Rept. Beirut: Dār al-Kitāb al-'Arabī, 1967-1968.

_______. *Ma'rifat al-Ṣaḥāba.* Ed. 'Ādil b. Yūsuf al-'Azzāzī. 7 vols. Riyadh: Dār al-Waṭan lil-Nashr, 1419/1998.

Abū al-Shaykh al-Aṣbahānī al-Anṣārī, Abū Muḥammad 'Abd Allāh b. Muḥ. b. Ja'far b. Ḥayyān. *al-'Aẓama.* Ed. Riḍā' Allāh Mubārakfūrī. 5 vols. Riyadh: Dār al-'Āṣima, 1418/1998.

_______. *Ṭabaqāt al-Muḥaddithīn bi-Aṣbahān.* Ed. 'Abd al-Ghafūr al-Balūshī. 4 vols. Beirut: Mu'assasat al-Risāla, 1412/1992.

Abū Ya'lā al-Mawṣilī al-Tamīmī, Aḥmad b. 'Alī b. al-Muthannā. *Musnad.* Ed. Ḥusayn Salīm Asad, 14 vols. Damascus: Dār al-Ma'mūn lil-Turāth, 1407-1987.

Aḥmad b. Muḥammad b. Ḥanbal b. Hilāl b. Asad al-Shaybānī, Abū 'Abd Allāh. *Faḍā'il al-Ṣaḥāba.* Ed. Waṣiyyullāh Muḥ. 'Abbās. 2 vols. Beirut, Mu'assasat al-Risāla, 1403/ 1983.

_______. *al-Musnad.* Ed. Shu'ayb al-Arnā'ūṭ et al. 50 vols. Beirut: Mu'assasat al-Risāla, 1999-2001.

_______. *al-Zuhd.* Ed. Muḥ. 'Abd al-Salām Shāhīn. Beirut: Dār al-Kutub al-'Ilmiyya, 1420/1999.

al-Ājurrī. *al-Sharī'a.* Ed. 'Abd Allāh al-Dumayjī. 6 vols. Riyadh: Dār al-Waṭan, 1418/ 1997.

al-Ālūsī, Abū al-Faḍl Shihāb al-Dīn Maḥmūd b. 'Abdallāh. *Rūḥ al-Ma'ānī fī Tafsīr al-Qur'ān al-'Aẓīm wal-Sab' al-Mathānī.* 30 vols. in 15. Cairo: Idārat al-Ṭibā'at al-Munīriyya, 1345/1926. Rept. Beirut: Dār Iḥyā' al-Turāth al-'Arabī, [1970?].

al-Aṣamm al-Naysābūrī, Abū al-'Abbās Muḥammad b. Ya'qūb b. Yūsuf. *Majmū' fīhi Muṣannafāt Abī al-'Abbās al-Aṣamm wa-Ismā'īl al-Ṣaffār.* Ed. Nabīl Sa'd al-Dīn Jarrār. Beirut: Dār al-Bashā'ir al-Islāmiyya, 1425/2004.

al-'Askarī, Abū Hilāl al-Ḥasan b. 'Abd Allāh b. Sahl b. Sa'īd. *al-Awā'il.* Ed. Muḥ. al-Sayyid al-Wakīl. Ṭanṭā: Dār al-Bashīr, 1408/1987.

al-Baghawī, Abū Muḥammad al-Ḥusayn b. Mas'ūd al-Farrā'. *Tafsīr al-Baghawī al-Musammā Ma'ālim al-Tanzīl.* Ed. 'Abd al-Razzāq al-Mahdī. 5 vols. Beirut: Dār Iḥyā' al-Turāth al-'Arabī, 1420/2000.

al-Bayḍāwī, Nāṣir al-Dīn Abū Sa'īd 'Abd Allah b. 'Umar. *Anwār al-Tanzīl wa-Asrār al-Ta'wīl.* Ed. Heinrich Leberecht Fleischer. 2 vols. Leipzig: Vogel, 1846-1848.

_______. *Muntahā al-Munā fī Sharḥ al-Asmā' al-Ḥusnā*. Ed. Nizār Ḥammādī. Sharjah: al-Markaz al-ʿArabī lil-Kitāb, [2001?].

_______. *Tafsīr al-Qāḍī al-Bayḍāwī al-Musammā Anwār al-Tanzīl wa-Asrār al-Ta'wīl wa-maʿahu Ḥāshiyat al-ʿAllāmat al-Suyūṭī al-Musammāt Nawāhid al-Abkār wa-Shawārid al-Afkār*. Ed. Māhir Adīb Ḥabbūsh [et al.]. 12 vols. Istanbul: Maktabat al-Irshād and Dār al-Lubāb, 1443/2022.

al-Baghawī, Abū Muḥammad al-Ḥusayn b. Masʿūd al-Farrā'. *Sharḥ al-Sunna*. Ed. Shuʿayb Arnā'ūṭ. 2nd ed. 15 vols. Beirut: al-Maktab al-Islāmī, 1403/1983.

al-Bayḍāwī, Nāṣir al-Dīn Abū Saʿīd Abū al-Khayr ʿAbd Allah b. ʿUmar b. Muḥammad b. ʿAlī. *Tafsīr al-Qāḍī al-Bayḍāwī al-Musammā Anwār al-Tanzīl wa-Asrār al-Ta'wīl wa-maʿahu Ḥāshiyat al-ʿAllāmat al-Suyūṭī al-Musammāt Nawāhid al-Abkār wa-Shawārid al-Afkār*. Ed. Māhir Adīb Ḥabbūsh [et al.]. 12 vols. Istanbul: Maktabat al-Irshād and Dār al-Lubāb, 1443/2022.

al-Bayhaqī, Abū Bakr Aḥmad b. al-Ḥusayn. *al-Asmā' wal-Ṣifāt*. Ed. ʿAbd Allāh al-Ḥāshidī. 2 vols. Jeddah: Maktabat al-Sawādī, 1413/1993.

_______. *al-Daʿawāt al-Kabīr*. Ed. Badr ʿAbd Allāh al-Badr. 2 vols. Kuwait: Gharās lil-Nashr wal-Tawzīʿ, 2009.

_______. *Dalā'il al-Nubuwwa wa-Maʿrifat Aḥwāl Ṣāḥib al-Sharīʿa*. Ed. ʿAbd al-Muʿṭī Qalʿajī. 7 vols. Beirut: Dār al-Kutub al-ʿIlmiyya and Dār al-Rayyān lil-Turāth, 1408/1988.

_______. [*Shuʿab al-Īmān*]. *al-Jāmiʿ li-Shuʿab al-Īmān*. Ed. ʿAbd al-ʿAlī ʿAbd al-Ḥamīd Ḥāmid. 14 vols. Riyadh: Maktabat al-Rushd, 1423/2003.

_______. *al-Sunan al-Kubrā*. With Ibn al-Turkmānī's *al-Jawhar al-Naqī*. 10 vols. Hyderabad Deccan: Maṭbaʿat Majlis Dā'irat al-Maʿārif al-ʿUthmāniyya, 1355/1937.

al-Bazzār, Abū Bakr Aḥmad b. ʿAmr b. ʿAbd al-Khāliq. [*Musnad.*] *al-Baḥr al-Zakhkhār al-Maʿrūf bi-Musnad al-Bazzār*. Ed. Maḥfūẓ al-Raḥmān Zayn Allāh et al. 18 vols. Beirut: Mu'assasat ʿUlūm al-Qur'ān; Medina: Maktabat al-ʿUlūm wal-Ḥikam, 1409-1430/1988-2009.

al-Bukhārī, Muḥ. b. Ismāʿīl b. Ibrāhīm al-Juʿfī. *al-Jāmiʿ al-Ṣaḥīḥ wa-huwa al-Jāmiʿ al-Musnad al-Ṣaḥīḥ al-Mukhtaṣar min Umūri Rasūl Allāh Ṣallā Allāhu ʿalayhi wa-Sallam wa-Sunanih wa-Ayyāmih*. 2nd ed. 8 vols. in 3. Ed. Muḥ. Zuhrī al-Ghamrāwī et al. Būlāq: al-Maṭbaʿat al-Kubrā al-Amīriyya, 1314/1896. Rept. Cairo: al-Maṭbaʿat al-Maymūniyya [Muṣṭafā Bābī al-Ḥalabī], 1323/1905.

_______. *al-Tārīkh al-Kabīr*. Ed. Sayyid Hāshim al-Nadwī et al. 9 vols. Hyderabad Deccan: Dā'irat al-Maʿārif al-ʿUthmāniyya, 1360/1941.

Chodkiewicz, Michel. *Le Sceau des saints*. Paris: Gallimard, 1986.

al-Dārimī, Abū Muḥammad ʿAbd Allāh b. ʿAbd al-Raḥmān b. al-Faḍl. *Sunan al-Dārimī*. Ed. Muṣṭafā Dīb al-Bughā. 2 vols. Damascus: Dār al-Qalam, 1412/1991.

al-Daylamī al-Hamadhānī, al-Kiyā Abū Shujāʿ Shīrūyah b. Shahradār b. Shīrūyah b. Fannākhusrū. *al-Firdaws bi-Ma'thūr al-Khiṭāb*. Ed. al-Saʿīd b. Basyūnī Zaghlūl. 6 vols. Beirut: Dār al-Kutub al-ʿIlmiyya, 1406/1986.

_______. *Firdaws al-Akhbār bi-Ma'thūr al-Khiṭāb al-Mukharraj ʿalā Kitāb al-Shihāb*. With *Musnad al-Firdaws* by Abū Manṣūr Shahradār b. Shīrūyah b. Shahradār b. Shīrūyah b. Fannākhusrū al-Daylamī and *Tasdīd al-Qaws* by Ibn Ḥajar al-ʿAsqalānī.

Ed. Fawwāz Zamarlī, Muḥ. al-Muʿtaṣim Billāh al-Baghdādī. 5 vols. Beirut: Dār al-Kitāb al-ʿArabī, 1407/1987.

al-Dhahabī, Muḥammad b. Aḥmad b. ʿUthmān al-Turkmānī. *Mīzān al-Iʿtidāl fī Naqd al-Rijāl, wa-yalīhi Dhayl Mīzān al-Iʿtidāl lil-Imām Abī al-Faḍl ʿAbd al-Raḥīm b. al-Ḥusayn al-ʿIrāqī*. Ed. ʿAlī Muḥ. Muʿawwaḍ et al. 8 vols. Beirut: Dār al-Kutub al-ʿIlmiyya, 1416/1995.

_______. *Tārīkh al-Islām wa-Wafayāt al-Mashāhīr wal-Aʿlām*. Ed. ʿUmar ʿAbd al-Salām Tadmurī. 2nd ed. 52 vols. Beirut: Dār al-Kitāb al-ʿArabī, 1409/ 1989.

al-Dīnawarī, Abū Bakr Aḥm. b. Marwān. *al-Mujālasa wa-Jawāhir al-ʿIlm*. Ed. Mashhūr Salmān. 10 vols. Bahrain: Jamʿiyyat al-Tarbiya al-Islāmiyya; Beirut: Dār Ibn Ḥazm, 1419/1999.

al-Ghazālī, Zayn al-Dīn Abū Ḥāmid Muḥammad b. Muḥ. b. Muḥ. *Iḥyāʾ ʿUlūm al-Dīn*. Ed. al-Lajnat al-ʿIlmiyya bi-Dār al-Minhāj. 10 vols. Jeddah: Dār al-Minhāj lil-Nashr wal-Tawzīʿ, 1432/2011.

al-Ghumārī, Aḥmad b. Muḥammad b. al-Ṣiddīq. *al-Mudāwī li-ʿIlal al-Jāmiʿ al-Ṣaghīr wa-Sharḥay al-Munāwī*. 6 vols. Cairo: Dār al-Kutbī and al-Maktabat al-Makkiyya, 1996.

al-Ḥākim al-Naysābūrī, Abū ʿAbd Allāh Muḥ. b. ʿAbd Allāh b. al-Bayyiʿ. *al-Mustadrak ʿalā al-Ṣaḥīḥayn*. With Dhahabī's *Talkhīṣ al-Mustadrak*. Ed. Muṣṭafā ʿAbd al-Qādir ʿAṭā. 2nd ed. 5 vols. Beirut: Dār al-Kutub al-ʿIlmiyya, 1422/2002.

al-Ḥakīm al-Tirmidhī. *Khatm al-awliyāʾ*. Ed. ʿUthmān Yaḥyā. Beirut: Maʿhad al-Ādāb al-Sharqiyya, 1964.

_______. *Nawādir al-Uṣūl fī Maʿrifat Akhbār al-Rasūl*. Ed. Nūr al-Dīn Shukrī al-Būrdurī. 5 vols. Jeddah: Dār al-Minhāj, 1436/2015.

Ḥaqqī al-Burūsawī, Ismāʿīl b. Muṣṭafā b. Čawush (İsmail Hakkı Bursevî). *Tafsīr Rūḥ al-Bayān*. Ed. Ḥāfiẓ Muḥ. Khayrī and Aḥmad Rifʿat. 10 vols. Istanbul: al-Maṭbaʿat al-ʿUthmāniyya, 1330-1346/1912-1928.

al-Haythamī, Nūr al-Dīn ʿAlī b. Abī Bakr. *Majmaʿ al-Zawāʾid wa-Manbaʿ al-Fawāʾid*. 10 vols. Beirut: Dār al-Fikr, 1412/1992.

al-Ḥumaydī al-Qurashī al-Asadī, Abū Bakr ʿAbd Allāh b. al-Zubayr. *Musnad*. Ed. Ḥasan Salīm Asad. 2 vols. Damascus: Dār al-Saqqā, 1996.

Ibn ʿAbd al-Barr al-Namarī, Abū ʿUmar Yūsuf b. ʿAbd Allāh b. Muḥammad. *Bahjat al-Majālis wa-Uns al-Mujālis*. Ed. Muḥ. Mursī al-Khawlī. 2 vols. Cairo: al-Dār al-Miṣriyya lil-Taʾlīf, 1387-1390/1967-1970. Rept. Beirut: Dār al-Kutub al-ʿIlmiyya, 1401/1981.

_______. *Jāmiʿ Bayān al-ʿIlm wa-Faḍlih*. Ed. Abū al-Ashbāl al-Zuhayrī. 2 vols. Dammam: Dār Ibn al-Jawzī, 1414/1994.

_______. *al-Tamhīd li-mā fil-Muwaṭṭaʾ min al-Maʿānī wal-Asānīd*. Ed. Mūṣṭafā b. Aḥmad al-ʿAlawī et al. 26 vols. Rabat: al-Maṭbaʿat al-Malakiyya, 1387-1412/1967-1992.

Ibn Abī ʿĀṣim al-Shaybānī, Abū Bakr b. Aḥmad b. ʿAmr b. al-Ḍaḥḥāk. *al-Sunna*. Ed. Bāsim Jawābira. 2 vols. Riyadh: Dār al-Ṣumayʿī, 1419/1998.

Ibn Abī Ḥātim al-Rāzī al-Ḥanẓalī, Abū Muḥammad ʿAbd al-Raḥmān b. Muḥammad b. Idrīs b. al-Mundhir al-Tamīmī. *Tafsīr al-Qurʾān al-ʿAẓīm Musnadan ʿan Rasūl*

Allāh ṣallā Allāhu ʿalayhi wa-sallam wal-Ṣaḥābati wal-Tābiʿīn. Ed. Asʿad Muḥ. al-Ṭayyib. 14 vols. Mecca and Riyadh: Maktabat Nizār Muṣṭafā al-Bāz, 1417/1997.

Ibn Abī Shayba al-ʿAbsī al-Kūfī, Abū Bakr ʿAbd Allāh b. Muḥammad. *al-Muṣannaf*. Ed. Muḥ. ʿAwwāma. 26 vols. Beirut: Dār Qurṭuba, 1428/2006.

Ibn Abī Shayba al-ʿAbsī al-Kūfī, Abū Jaʿfar Muḥammad b. ʿUthmān. *al-ʿArsh*. Ed. Muḥammad b. Khalīfa al-Tamīmī. Riyadh: Maktabat al-Rushd and Sharikat al-Riyāḍ, 1418/1998.

Ibn ʿAdī al-Jurjānī, Abū Aḥmad ʿAbd Allāh b. ʿAdī b. Muḥammad b. Mubārak. *al-Kāmil fī Ḍuʿafāʾ al-Rijāl*. Ed. ʿĀdil Aḥmad ʿAbd al-Mawjūd et al. 9 vols. Beirut: Dār al-Kutub al-ʿIlmiyya, 1418/1997.

Ibn ʿArabī, al-Ḥātimī al-Ṭāʾī, Muḥyī al-Dīn Abū ʿAbd Allāh Muḥammad b. ʿAlī. *L'Arbre du Monde*. Transl. of *Shajarat al-kawn* by Maurice Gloton. Paris: Les Deux Océans, 1990.

_______. *al-Futūḥāt al-Makkiyya*. Ed. Muḥammad al-Zuhrī al-Ghamrāwī. 4 vols. Būlāq: al-Maṭbaʿat al-Maymaniyya, 1329/1911.

_______. *al-Futūḥāt al-Makkiyya*. Ed. Osman Yahya. Cairo: al-Hayʾat al-Miṣriyya al-ʿĀmma lil-Kitāb, 1408/1988.

_______. *La Profession de Foi*. Transl. of *Tadhkirat al-khawāṣṣ wa-ʿaqīdat ahl al-ikhtiṣāṣ* by Roger Deladrière. Paris: Sindbad, 1985.

Ibn ʿAsākir, Thiqat al-Dīn Abū al-Qāsim ʿAlī b. al-Ḥasan b. Hibat Allāh al-Dimashqī. *Muʿjam al-Shuyūkh*. Ed. Wafāʾ Taqī al-Dīn. 3 vols. Beirut: Dār al-Bashāʾir al-Islāmiyya, 1421/2000.

_______. *Tārīkh Madīnat Dimashq*. Ed. Muḥibb al-Dīn al-ʿAmrawī. 80 vols. Beirut: Dār al-Fikr, 1421/2001.

Ibn Abī Khaythama Zuhayr b. Ḥarb, Abū Bakr Aḥmad. *al-Tārīkh al-Kabīr al-Maʿrūf bi-Tārīkh Ibn Abī Khaythama*. Ed. Ṣalāḥ b. Fatḥī Halal. 4 vols. Cairo: al-Fārūq al-Ḥadītha, 1424-1427/2004-2006.

Ibn Ḥajar al-ʿAsqalānī, Shihāb al-Dīn Abū al-Faḍl Aḥmad b. ʿAlī. *Fatḥ al-Bārī bi-Sharḥ Ṣaḥīḥ al-Bukhārī*. Ed. Muḥammad Fuʾād ʿAbd al-Bāqī and Muḥibb al-Dīn al-Khaṭīb. 13 vols. Beirut, Dār al-Maʿrifa, 1379/1959.

_______. *al-Iṣāba fī Tamyīz al-Ṣaḥāba*. Ed. 8 vols. in 4. Cairo: al-Maṭbaʿat al-Sharafiyya, 1327/1909. Rept. in 5 vols. with indices Beirut: Dār al-Kutub al-ʿIlmiyya, n.d.

_______. *Natāʾij al-Afkār fī Takhrīj Aḥādīth al-Adhkār*. Ed. Ḥamdī al-Salafī. 2nd ed. 5 vols. Damascus and Beirut: Dār Ibn Kathīr, 1429/2008.

Ibn Ḥibbān al-Bustī, Abū Ḥātim Muḥammad b. Ḥibbān b. Aḥmad. *Ṣaḥīḥ Ibn Ḥibbān bi-Tartīb Ibn Balbān*. Ed. Shuʿayb Arnāʾūṭ. 2nd ed. 18 vols. Beirut: Muʾassasat al-Risāla, 1414/1993.

Ibn Hishām al-Maʿāfirī, Abū Muḥ. ʿAbd al-Malik. *al-Sīrat al-Nabawiyya*. Ed. Muṣṭafā al-Saqqā et al. 2nd ed. 4 vols. in 2. Beirut: Dār al-Wifāq, 1375/1955.

_______. *al-Tījān fī Mulūk Ḥimyar*. Ed. Sayyid Zayn al-ʿĀbidīn al-Mūsawī. Hyderabad Deccan: Dāʾirat al-Maʿārif al-ʿUthmāniyya, 1347/1928.

Ibn al-Jaʿd b. ʿUbayd al-Jawharī, ʿAlī. *Musnad Ibn al-Jaʿd*. Ed. ʿĀmir Aḥmad Ḥaydar. Beirut: Muʾassasat Nādir, 1410/1990.

Ibn al-Jawzī al-Qurashī al-Baghdādī, Abū al-Faraj ʿAbd al-Raḥmān b. ʿAlī b. Muḥ. *al-Mawḍūʿāt*. Ed. ʿAbd al-Raḥmān ʿUthmān. 3 vols. Medina: al-Maktabat al-Salafiyya, 1386-1388/1966-1968.

_______. *al-Mawḍūʿāt min al-Aḥādīth al-Marfūʿāt*. Ed. Nūr al-Dīn b. Shukrī Būyājīlār. 4 vols. Riyadh: Aḍwā' al-Salaf, 1418/1997.

Ibn Kathīr al-Qurashī al-Baṣrī al-Dimashqī, Abū al-Fidā' Ismāʿīl b. ʿUmar. *al-Bidāya wal-Nihāya*. Ed. ʿAbd Allāh al-Turkī. 21 vols. Cairo: Dār Hajar, 1417/1997.

_______. *Tafsīr al-Qur'ān al-ʿAẓīm*. Ed. Muṣṭafā al-Sayyid Muḥammad et al. 15 vols. Jīza: Mu'assasat Qurṭuba, 1421/2000.

Ibn Mājah Yazīd al-Qazwīnī, Abū ʿAbd Allāh Muḥammad. *Sunan*. Ed. Bashshār ʿAwwād Maʿrūf. 6 vols. Beirut: Dār al-Jīl, 1418/1998.

Ibn al-Mubārak b. Wāḍiḥ al-Marwazī al-Ḥanẓalī, Abū ʿAbd al-Raḥmān ʿAbd Allāh. *al-Musnad*. Ed. Ṣubḥī al-Badrī al-Sāmarrā'ī. Riyadh: Maktabat al-Maʿārif, 1407/1987.

_______. *al-Zuhd wal-raqā'iq*. With Nuʿaym b. Ḥammād's additions in his narration of the same. Ed. Ḥabīb al-Raḥmān al-Aʿẓamī. 2 vols. in 1. Malegaon, India: Majlis Iḥyā' al-Maʿārif, 1386/1966. Rept. Beirut: Dār al-Kutub al-ʿIlmiyya, n.d.

Ibn Saʿd b. Manīʿ al-Zuhrī al-Hāshimī–*waliyyuhum*–al-Baṣrī al-Baghdādī, Abū ʿAbd Allāh Muḥammad. *al-Ṭabaqāt al-Kubrā*. Ed. Iḥsān ʿAbbās. 9 vols. Beirut: Dār Ṣādir, 1957-1968.

al-Kattānī, Abū ʿAbd Allāh Muḥ. b. Jaʿfar b. Idrīs. *Naẓm al-Mutanāthir min al-Ḥadīth al-Mutawātir*. Ed. Sharaf Ḥijāzī. Cairo: Dār al-Kutub al-Salafiyya, 1328/ 1910; rept. Beirut: Dār al-Kutub al-ʿIlmiyya, 1980.

_______. *Miʿrāj al-Nabī*. 4th ed. (Damascus: Dār al-Qur'ān, 1392/1072.

al-Kharkūshī al-Naysābūrī, Abū Saʿd ʿAbd al-Malik b. Abī ʿUthmān Muḥammad b. Ibrāhīm. [*Sharaf al-Muṣṭafā*.] *Manāḥil al-Shifā wa-Manāhil al-Ṣafā bi-Taḥqīq Kitāb Sharaf al-Muṣṭafā*. Ed. Abū ʿĀṣim Nabīl b. Hāshim al-Ghamrī Āl Bā ʿAlawī. 5 vols. Beirut: Dār al-Bashā'ir al-Islāmiyya, 1424/2003.

al-Khaṭīb al-Baghdādī, Abū Bakr Aḥmad b. ʿAlī b. Thābit. *al-Faqīh wal-Mutafaqqih*. Ed. ʿĀdil al-ʿAzāzī. 2 vols. Dammām: Dār Ibn al-Jawzī, 1997.

_______. *Iqtiḍā' al-ʿIlm al-ʿAmal*. Ed. Muḥ. Nāṣir al-Albānī. 5th ed. Beirut: al-Maktab al-Islāmī, 1404/1984.

_______. *al-Jāmiʿ li-akhlāq al-rāwī wa-ādāb al-sāmiʿ*. Ed. Muḥammad ʿAjāj al-Khaṭīb. 2 vols. Beirut: Mu'assasat al-Risāla, 1412/1991.

_______. [*Tārīkh Baghdād*.] *Tārīkh Madīnat al-Salām wa-Akhbār Muḥaddithīhā wa-Dhikr Quṭṭānihā al-ʿUlamā'*. Ed. Bashshār ʿAwwād Maʿrūf. 17 vols. Beirut: Dār al-Gharb al-Islāmī, 1422/2001.

al-Māwardī, Abū al-Ḥasan ʿAlī b. Muḥammad b. Ḥabīb. *Adab al-dunyā wal-dīn*. Ed. al-Lajnat al-ʿIlmiyya bi-Dār al-Minhāj. Jeddah: Dār al-Minhāj, 1343/2013.

al-Mizzī, Abū al-Ḥajjāj Yūsuf b. ʿAbd al-Raḥmān b. Yūsuf. *Tahdhīb al-Kamāl fī Asmā' al-Rijāl*. Ed. Bashshār Maʿrūf. 35 vols. Beirut: Mu'assasat al-Risāla, 1402-1413/1982-1992.

Muslim b. al-Ḥajjāj b. Muslim al-Qushayrī al-Naysābūrī. [*Ṣaḥīḥ*.] *al-Jāmiʿ al-Ṣaḥīḥ*. 8 vols. [Istanbul]: al-Maṭbaʿat al-ʿĀmira, 1334/1916.

al-Nasāʾī, Abū ʿAbd al-Raḥmān Aḥmad b. Shuʿayb b. ʿAlī. *Sunan al-Nasāʾī bi-Sharḥ al-Ḥāfiẓ Jalāl al-Dīn al-Suyūṭī wa-Ḥāshiyat al-Imām al-Sindī*. 8 vols. [Cairo]: al-Maṭbaʿat al-Miṣriyya, 1348/1930. Rept. 8 vols. in 4. Beirut: Dār Iḥyāʾ al-Turāth al-ʿArabī, n.d.

______. *al-Sunan al-Kubrā*. Ed. Ḥasan ʿAbd al-Munʿim Shalabī et al. 12 vols. Beirut: Muʾassasat al-Risāla, 1421/2001.

al-Nawawī, Muḥyī al-Dīn Abū Zakariyyā Yaḥyā b. Sharaf b. Marīy al-Dimashqī. *al-Adhkār*. Ed. Bashīr Muḥammad ʿUyūn. Damascus: Dār al-Bayān; Taif: Maktabat al-Muʾayyad, 1408/1988.

______. *Tahdhīb al-asmāʾ wal-lughāt*. 3 vols. Cairo: Idārat al-Ṭibāʿat al-Munīriyya, [1927?]. Rept. Beirut: Dār al-Kutub al-ʿIlmiyya, 1977.

al-Qālī, Abū ʿAlī Ismāʿīl b. al-Qāsim b. ʿAydhūn. *al-Amālī*. Ed. Muḥ. ʿAbd al-Jawād al-Aṣmaʿī. 2nd ed. 4 vols. Cairo: Dār al-Kutub al-Miṣriyya, 1344/1926.

al-Qārī, Mullā ʿAlī b. Sulṭān Muḥammad al-Harawī. *al-Asrār al-Marfūʿa fil-Akhbār al-Mawḍūʿa*. Ed. Muḥ. Luṭfī al-Ṣabbāgh. 2nd ed. Beirut: al-Maktab al-Islāmī, 1406/1986.

Qawwām al-Sunna Abū al-Qāsim Ismāʿīl b. Muḥ. b. al-Faḍl b. ʿAlī al-Qurashī al-Ṭulayḥī al-Taymī al-Aṣbahānī. *al-Targhīb wal-Tarhīb*. Ed. Ayman Ṣāliḥ Shaʿbān. 3 vols. Cairo: Dār al-Ḥadīth, 1414/1993.

al-Quḍāʿī, Abū ʿAbd Allāh Muḥammad b. Salāma b. Jaʿfar. *Musnad al-Shihāb*. Ed. Ḥamdī al-Salafī. 2 vols. Beirut: Muʾassasat al-Risāla, 1405/1985. 2nd ed. 1407/ 1986.

al-Qurṭubī, Abū ʿAbd Allāh Muḥ. b. Aḥm. b. Abī Bakr. [*Tafsīr*.] *al-Jāmiʿ li-Aḥkām al-Qurʾān wal-Mubayyin li-mā Taḍammanahu min al-Sunna wa-Āy al-Furqān*. Ed. ʿAbd Allāh b. ʿAbd al-Muḥsin al-Turkī and Muḥ. Riḍwān ʿAraqsūsī. 24 vols. Beirut: Muʾassasat al-Risāla, 1427/2006.

al-Qushayrī al-Naysābūrī al-Shāfiʿī, Zayn al-Islām Abū al-Qāsim ʿAbd al-Karīm b. Hawāzin b. ʿAbd al-Mālik. *Laṭāʾif al-Ishārāt: Tafsīr Ṣūfī Kāmil lil-Qurʾān*. Ed. Ibr. Bayyūnī. 6 vols. Cairo: al-Hayʾat al-Miṣriyyat al-ʿĀmma, 1390/1971. Rept. 2000 in 3 vols.

______. *al-Miʿrāj*. Ed. ʿAlī Ḥusayn ʿAbd al-Qādir. Cairo: Dār al-Kutub al-Ḥadītha, 1964.

al-Rūyānī, Abū Bakr Muḥammad b. Hārūn. *Musnad*. Ed. Ayman ʿAlī Abū Yamānī. 2 vols. Cairo: Muʾassasat Qurṭuba, 1416/1996.

al-Sakhāwī, Abū al-Khayr Shams al-Dīn Muḥ. b. ʿAbd al-Raḥmān b. Muḥ. *al-Maqāṣid al-Ḥasana fī Bayān Kathīr min al-Aḥādīth al-Mushtahara ʿalā al-Alsina*. Ed. ʿAbd Allāh Muḥ. al-Ṣiddīq. Cairo: Maktabat al-Khānjī, 1955. Rept. Beirut: Dār al-Kutub al-ʿIlmiyya, 1399/1979.

Sakūnī, Abū ʿAlī ʿUmar b. Muḥammad b. Ḥamd b. Khalīl. *Arbaʿūna masʾala fī uṣūl al-dīn*. Ed. Yūsuf Aḥnānā. Beirut: Dār al-Gharb al-Islāmī, 1993.

al-Shajarī, Yaḥyā b. al-Ḥusayn. [*al-Amālī al-ḥadīthiyya*.] *al-Amālī wa-hiya al-shahīra bil-amālī al-khamīsiyya*. 2 vols. Cairo: Maṭbaʿat al-Fajjāla, 1376/1957. Rept. 3rd ed. Beirut: ʿĀlam al-Kutub, 1403/1983.

al-Silafī al-Aṣbahānī, Abū Ṭāhir Aḥm. b. Muḥ. b. Aḥm. *Muʿjam al-safar*. Ed. ʿAbd Allāh ʿUmar al-Bārūdī. Mecca: al-Maktabat al-Tijāriyya, 1382/1963. Rept. Beirut: Dār al-Fikr, 1414/1993.

al-Suyūṭī, Jalāl al-Dīn Abū al-Faḍl ʿAbd al-Raḥmān b. Kamāl al-Dīn Abī Bakr. *al-Durr al-manthūr*

______. *al-Jāmiʿ al-Ṣaghīr fī Aḥādīth al-Bashīr al-Nadhīr*. Ed. Ibrāhīm ʿAbd al-Ghaffār al-Dusūqī. 2 vols. Bulaq: Dār al-Ṭibāʿat al-ʿĀmira,1286/1869.

______. *Muʿtarak al-Aqrān fī Iʿjāz al-Qurʾān*. Ed. Aḥmad Shams al-Dīn. 3 vols. Beirut: Dār al-Kutub al-ʿIlmiyya, 1408/1988.

al-Ṭabarānī, Abū al-Qāsim Sulaymān b. Aḥmad b. Ayyūb al-Lakhmī al-Shāmī. *al-Duʿāʾ*. Ed. Muḥ. Saʿīd al-Bukhārī. 3 vols. Beirut: Dār al-Bashāʾir al-Islāmiyya, 1407/1987.

______. *al-Muʿjam al-Awsaṭ*. Ed. Ṭāriq b. ʿAwaḍ Allāh b. Muḥammad and ʿAbd al-Muḥsin al-Ḥusaynī. 10 vols. Cairo: Dār al-Ḥaramayn, 1415/1995.

______. *al-Muʿjam al-Kabīr*. Ed. Ḥamdī ʿAbd al-Majīd al-Salafī. 2nd ed. 25 vols. Baghdad: Wizārat al-Awqāf, 1984-1990. Rept. Cairo: Maktabat Ibn Taymiyya, n.d.

______. *Musnad al-Shāmiyyīn*. Ed. Ḥamdī ʿAbd al-Majīd al-Salafī. 4 vols. Beirut: Muʾassasat al-Risāla, 1405/1984.

al-Ṭabarī, Abū Jaʿfar Muḥammad b. Jarīr. *Tafsīr al-Ṭabarī: Jāmiʿ al-Bayān ʿan Taʾwīl Āy al-Qurʾān*. Ed. ʿAbd Allāh b. ʿAbd al-Muḥsin al-Turkī et al. 26 vols. Cairo: Dār Hajar, 1422/2001.

al-Ṭaḥāwī, Abū Jaʿfar Aḥmad b. Muḥ. b. Salāma al-Azdī. *al-ʿAqīdat al-Ṭaḥāwiyya*. Ed. Muḥammad b. Ṣāliḥ al-Shawādifī. Riyadh: Madār al-Waṭan, 1427/2006.

______. *Sharḥ Maʿānī al-Āthār*. Ed. Muḥ. Zahrī al-Najjār et al. 5 vols. Beirut: ʿĀlam al-Kutub, 1414/1994.

______. *Sharḥ Mushkil al-Āthār*. Ed. Shuʿayb al-Arnāʾūṭ. Beirut: Muʾassasat al-Risāla, 1415/1994.

al-Thaʿlabī al-Naysābūrī, Abū Isḥāq Aḥmad b. Muḥammad b. Ibrāhīm. *al-Kashf wal-Bayān ʿan Tafsīr al-Qurʾān*. Ed. Ṣalāḥ Bāʿ Uthmān et al. 33 vols. Jeddah: Dār al-Tafsīr, 1436/2015.

al-Tirmidhī, Abū ʿĪsā Muḥ. b. ʿĪsā b. Sawra. [*Sunan*.] *al-Jāmiʿ al-Ṣaḥīḥ*. Ed. Aḥm. Shākir et al. 5 vols. 2nd ed. Cairo: Muṣṭafā Bābī al-Ḥalabī, 1398/1978.

al-Wāḥidī al-Naysābūrī, Abū al-Ḥasan ʿAlī b. Aḥmad. *al-Tafsīr al-Basīṭ*. Ed. Muḥ. Ṣāliḥ al-Fawzān et al. 25 vols. Riyadh: Jāmiʿat Muḥ. b. Saʿūd, 1430/2009.

Yaʿqūb b. Sufyān al-Fasawī, Abū Yūsuf. *al-Maʿrifa wal-Tārīkh*. Ed. Akram Ḍiyāʾ al-ʿUmarī. 4 vols. Medina: Maktabat al-Dār, 1410/1990.

al-Zabīdī, Muḥammad b. Muḥammad Murtaḍā al-Ḥusaynī. *Itḥāf al-Sādat al-Muttaqīn bi-Sharḥ Asrār Iḥyāʾ ʿUlūm al-Dīn*. With the text of al-Ghazālī's *Iḥyāʾ ʿUlūm al-Dīn* in the margins, ʿAbd al-Qādir b. ʿAbd Allāh al-ʿAydarūs Bā ʿAlawī's *Taʿrīf al-Aḥyāʾ bi-Faḍāʾil al-Iḥyāʾ*, and al-Ghazālī's *al-Imlā ʿan Ishkālāt al-Iḥyā*. 10 vols. Cairo: al-Maṭbaʿat al-Maymaniyya, 1311/1893.

Index of Quranic Verses

Fātiḥa
1:2, 132
1:2-4, 407
1:4, 170

Baqara
2:11, 59
2:22, 418
2:31, 188
2:34, 132
2:35, 418
2:37, 441
2:54, 158, 266
2:73, 89
2:85, 433
2:88, 245
2:93, 266
2:115, 259
2:117, 406
2:138, 301
2:144, 295
2:148, 109, 227, 397, 398
2:155, 296
2:165, 325
2:173, 378, 397
2:177, 276
2:189, 292, 294, 388, 441, 461
2:191, 344, 359
2:195, 288
2:206, 217, 233
2:255, 150, 202, 437
2:256, 191, 255
2:267, 288
2:269, 281
2:284, 362
2:286, 207, 276, 371, 397, 435, 461

Āl ʿImrān
3:26, 146
3:28, 30, 137
3:31, 296
3:40, 358
3:47, 406
3:59, 406
3:123, 267
3:134, 447
3:169, 63, 184
3:185, 266
3:191, 109, 225

Nisāʾ
4:1-4, 118
4:28, 199, 266
4:34, 46
4:59, 283, 319, 384, 398, 399
4:76, 152
4:137, 28, 89, 183, 278, 291, 343, 371
4:148, 196
4:155, 245

Māʾida
5:1, 358
5:9, 135
5:91, 236
5:105, 319

Anʿām
6:38, 341
6:59, 300
6:65, 399
6:73, 199
6:79, 259
6:91, 108, 119, 400

Aʿrāf
7:143, 265, 459
7:156, 172
7:163, 349
7:172, 108, 121-123, 167, 228, 290, 323, 337, 419, 473
7:180, 152
7:204, 131

Anfāl
8:20, 398
8:42, 394
8:44, 394
8:46, 398

Barāʾa/Tawba
9:25, 267
9:29, 243
9:33, 162
9:51, 23
9:94, 199
9:105, 199
9:119, 383, 458, 461
9:123, 243
9:128, 52, 299, 321, 323

Yūnus
10:24, 163
10:25, 45, 217
10:31, 74
10:55, 213
10:62, 235

Hūd
11:6, 232
11:43, 341-342, 362
11:56, 440
11:107, 74, 172, 397
11:118, 379
11:119, 449

Yūsuf
12:21, 268
12:24, 219, 229
12:53, 41, 133, 359, 361
12:76, 29, 150, 403
12:108, 334

Raʿd
13:9, 199
13:11, 29, 129, 236, 284, 399
13:28, 235, 260, 269, 361
13:33, 97

Ibrāhīm
14:19, 320
14:20, 440

Ḥijr
15:18, 195
15:26, 118

15:44, 89
15:75,307,375
15:78-79, 129
15:87, 151
15:94, 263

Naḥl
16:8, 57, 118, 172
16:91, 276
16:96, 406
16:97, 266
16:106, 397
16:127, 297

Banū Isrā'īl/ Isrā'
17:1, 115, 117
17:21, 45
17:31, 232
17:44, 55
17:70, 27, 95, 108,121,134-135,142,169, 227,324,353, 359-360,371, 377,380,388, 391, 473
17:72,278,322
17:78, 64
17:79, 412
17:85, 145, 406, 411, 455

Kahf
18:21, 213
18:43-44, 369
18:65, 28, 41, 150, 427
18:104, 415
18:107, 121

Maryam
19:1, 141, 188
19:17, 134
19:23,263,268
19:57, 231

Ṭa Ha
20:5, 379, 381, 389
20:14, 143
20:18, 104
20:25-28, 351
20:114, 193

Anbiyā'
21:30, 56
21:35, 266
21:91, 145
21:107, 186, 346

Ḥajj
22:11,180,387
22:18, 358
22:26, 46
22:47, 49
22:74, 146

Mu'minūn
23:1-11, 85
23:92, 199

Nūr
24:19, 196
24:21, 267
24:30, 235
24:35,185,381
24:40, 277
24:55, 49, 136, 213, 345
24:63, 383

Furqān
25:3, 286, 339
25:20, 360
25:23, 193, 417, 468
25:59, 384
25:63,244,365
25:70, 153, 229, 378, 394

Shu'arā'
26:88-89, 67, 76
26:89, 128
26:189, 129

Naml
27:6, 142, 145, 186-187
27:39, 231
27:40,173,462
27:65,127,273
27:88, 146

Qaṣaṣ
28:13, 213
28:35, 40
28:56, 244
28:77, 288

'Ankabūt
29:45, 65, 67, 353
29:56, 283
29:57, 266
29:60, 232
29:69, 67, 435, 461

Rūm
30:26-27, 320
30:41, 59, 316, 321, 399

Luqmān
31:15,41, 124, 294-295, 386, 388

Sajda
32:6, 199
32:9, 145, 303

Aḥzāb
33:5, 397
33:21,188,264
33:23, 458
33:38, 349
33:56, 237
33:62, 349
33:72, 89

Saba'
34:39,288,290

Yā Sīn
36:36, 57
36:38, 315
36:40, 315
36:82, 349

Ṣāffāt
37:24-26, 362
37:96, 74
37:107, 266

Ṣād
38:12-14, 129
38:26, 89
38:39, 173
38:75, 170
38:78, 228

Zumar
39:10, 283
39:3, 180, 216, 277
39:30, 306
39:53,378,394

39:67, 108, 119, 400
39:68, 344

Fuṣṣilat
41:40, 454
41:53, 144

Shūrā
42:15, 202, 235, 319
42:23, 333
42:30, 135
42:40, 354, 360, 364

Zukhruf
43:32, 240

Jāthiya
45:13, 110, 132, 276-278, 291, 461
45:23, 89, 219

Aḥqāf
46:24, 129

Muḥammad
47:18, 200
47:33, 398

Fatḥ
48:1, 128
48:10, 337
48:28, 162

Ḥujurāt
49:8, 179, 217
49:12, 401
49:14, 289

Qāf
50:21, 168
50:22, 399
50:35, 154, 217, 400, 406

Dhāriyāt
51:21, 132
51:50, 139, 268
51:55, 97, 234, 290, 319
51:56, 215, 228, 230, 402

Najm
53:1, 384
53:5, 471
53:11, 231
53:18, 146
53:30, 346

Qamar
54:1, 128, 162
54:10, 268
54:54-55, 155, 290, 291

Raḥmān
55:1-4, 230, 327
55:7, 320
55:29, 170

Wāqiʿa
56:61, 57

Ḥadīd
57:3, 119
57:7, 288
57:13, 115

Ḥashr
59:9, 100

Ṣaff
61:9, 162
61:10-11, 334
61:13, 136, 213

Jumuʿa
62:5, 206

Munāfiqūn
63:10, 288

Taghābun
64:11, 311
64:16, 288, 435

Ṭalāq
65:3, 320, 434

Taḥrīm
66:12, 145

Mulk
67:22, 40

Nūn/Qalam
68:4, 151, 264

Ḥāqqa
69:18, 45

Jinn
72:18, 234
72:26, 199

Muddaththir
74:1-2, 263, 308
74:31, 171
74:50-51, 217

Qiyāma
75:2, 359, 361
75:14, 216
75:18, 244

Insān
76:7, 137, 251

Mursalāt
77:30, 89

Nāziʿāt
79:23, 457

Takwīr
81:5, 196
81:10, 196
81:26, 338

Inshiqāq
84:19, 172, 201

Burūj
85:16, 389, 397

Ṭāriq
86:1-3, 384

Fajr
89:14, 176

Shams
91:8, 278

Ḍuḥā
93:5, 152
93:6, 232

Sharḥ
94:4, 117, 142

Tīn
95:4, 134
95:5, 28, 77, 296, 421, 426
95:8, 402

ʿAlaq
96:6-7, 267

Qadr
97:3, 209

Bayyina
98:5, 216

Zalzala
99:7-8, 357, 378, 381, 412
99:8, 397

ʿAṣr
103:1-3, 286

Humaza
104:1, 386

Māʿūn
107:4-5, 416

Kāfirūn
109:6, 245

Ikhlāṣ
112:1,147,149

Index of Reports

Abū Bakr is in Paradise, ʿUmar is in Paradise, 153
Abū Bakr was the first of the believers, 106
Actions are only according to conclusions, 415, 454
Actions are only according to intentions, 277
Ādam and everyone after him are under my flag, 117
Ādam stood up on one leg for 300 years weeping, 440
All of you come from Ādam, and Ādam comes from dust, 388
All the men of Paradise are beardless except Mūsā, 406
Allah alone is al-Mudabbir (the Knower and Disposer), 141
Allah has servants who know what lies hidden, 375
Allah has vessels from among the people of the earth, 379
Allah is my observer, Allah is my witness, Allah is with me, 269
Allah keeps helping the servant as long as..., 258
Allah ordered the Pen to write what is and what shall be, 357
Allah shall cause the renewer of the faith to appear in one night, 162
Allah shall pardon the illiterate on the Day of Resurrection, 386
Allah will make the Prophet sit on the Throne, 412
all-enduring poor—they are the ones sitting with Allah, The, 354
angels lower their wings for knowledge seekers, The, 71, 393
angels of the seven skies were unable to budge the Throne, The, 326
Anger flared up and they shouted, 'to arms! to arms!', 366
As you are, so shall your governors be, 129-130
As you judge, so will you be judged, 362-363
Ask and you shall be given, 152
At the mention of the righteous, mercy descends, 47, 238
Awaiting deliverance is worship, 49, 130, 213
Be a victim of oppression and do not be an oppressor, 93
Be like the better one of the two sons of Ādam, 93
believer is as an evergreen, The, 453
believer is like the cypress, The, 453
believer's prayer is his *miʿrāj*, The, 116
best of deeds are the most arduous, The, 473
best of them in pagan times are the best in Islam, The, 465
Better than the Kaʿba, better than the Throne..., 155
Between me [Jibril] and the Throne are seventy veils of light, 66

Beware the insight of the believer, 307, 375
Blessings to him whose own faults have kept busy, 74, 259
Cleanliness is part of belief, 335
Contentment is an inexhaustible treasure, 287-288
death of past nations was the abundance of their questions, The, 281
Did you cut open his heart?, 80
Die before you die, 157-158, 263, 266, 301, 380, 419, 459
dīn is all *naṣīḥa*, The, 73-74, 131, 233, 274, 287, 392-393
dīn began as a stranger, The, 213
dīn is all transaction, The, 160
Do not be angry, 90, 218
Do not busy yourself with the revilement of kings but repent, 439
Do not greet the Jews of my Umma with salam, 210
Do not imitate Jews and polytheists, 209
Do not initiate salam to the Jews and the Christians, 210
Each is born with belief, 167
Each is facilitated for that for which it was created, 350, 397
Earth shall never be devoid of Awliya, 113
Earth will never lack forty men similar to the Friend of the Merciful, 113
Ego is the most relentless enemy of a human being, 66, 176
Endurance and preparing for a reward…, 354
Endurance is the key to Paradise, 354
Even if there remains only one day for the Umma…, 162
Every epoch has a king whom Allah sends…, 130
Every hundred years there shall come someone…, 48
Every newborn is born with the *fiṭra*, 167, 228
Every serious matter that is not begun with..., 68
faith-system is all pure counsel, the: see "*Dīn* is all…"
first creation is the Messenger of Allah, The, 186
First I warn you against your own ego, 221
Fitna is dormant. Allah has cursed whoever awakens it, 344, 359, 366
fitna shall make the wise bewildered, A, 383
Fitnas that are like chunks of dark night…, 114, 383
For 37 years I had been doing jihad against my ego, 461
For each human being seventy scrolls are recorded, 361
fornicator does not fornicate while he is a believer, The, 223
From them strife issues and to them it returns, 210
From you and back to you, O Muhammad, 187

Gehenna's open doors will flap in the winds, 170
Guard yourselves against the contexts that prompt condemnations, 345
Had Jibril moved past his station he would have been burnt, 65
Hajj is 'Arafa, The, 352
hand of Allah is *over* the group, The, 274
hand of Allah is *with* the group, The, 41, 274, 317
He has put the servants in whatever He wants, 320
He says to a thing, "Be" and it will be, 169
He whose two days are identical is defrauded, 73
head of wisdom is fear of Allah, The, 308
hear and grasp, and once you have grasped, benefit, 149, 319, 437
heart of the believer is the throne of Allah, The, 379
Hearts are between the two fingers of Allah, 431, 440
Help me against your own *nafs*, 222
Hidden polytheism in my Umma is stealthier…, 419-420
hour's reflection is better than the worship of seventy years, An, 293
human being is the copy of the Motherbook, The, 170
Human beings are minerals…, 465
I also have other sins I do not see here, 229, 397
I am exactly as My servant thinks of Me, 69, 379, 410
I am me and You are You, 265, 387, 413
I am the All-Sublime, 415
I am the city of knowledge and 'Alī is its gate, 420
I am the maintainer of the orphan, 234
I am the Mover and the All-Doer of what I want, 72
I am the servant of Allah in the Motherbook, 117
I ask Your love, the love of those who love You, 76
I believe in Allah and His angels and His Books…, 289
I guarantee Paradise…, 370
I have expanded your breast for you and relieved you, 117
I have forgiven her all her sins because of the mercy she showed, 53
I have given you an Umma from the end of times, 153
I have not worshipped a nurturing Lord I have not seen, 264
I never lied in my life. I never drank, 424
I shall not make you sad with regard to your Umma, 358
I was a Prophet when Ādam was between water and clay, 117, 142, 231, 384
I was already the Seal of Prophets when Ādam was still…, 117
I was ever a hidden treasure…, 230

I was given *jawāmiʿ al-kalim*, 200
I was only sent to complete high manners, 160
I was ordered to fight people until they say…, 181
Iblīs knows what runs into the servant's heart, 376
Ibrāhīm imprecated a group that had reached extremes in unbelief, 393
Ibrāhīm saw a servant committing fornication so he imprecated him, 394
If a man with full certainty were to recite…, 85
If I were to speak from my secret you would kill me, 419
If Mūsā were alive he would have no alternative…, 187
If my Umma has followed uprightness then they have one day…, 49
If the faith of Abū Bakr was weighed…, 143
Iḥsān (excellence) is for you to worship Him as if you see Him, 180
In the morning every joint of yours must pay a *ṣadaqa*, 55
Injustice does not last, and if it lasts, it destroys, 101
Intervisitations of the people of Paradise, 406
Is it not a human soul?, 96
It is heavily attended by the angels, 64
It is not allowed for the Prophet to sit with the devil, 244
Jibril said, *kāf*. The Prophet said, "I know", 189
Knowledge can only be through learning…, 219
Knowledge is two types: one is by the heart…, 205
Knowledge that does not benefit you harms you, 386
Lā ilāha illā-l-Lāh is My fortress, and whoever enters…, 139
least level of someone who enters Paradise…, The, 154
Leaving one ant's weight of the prohibitions is better…, 271
Make us well-pleased with Your decree!, 447
man hidden in the light of the Throne hadith, The, 155
Many a transmitter of knowledge does not himself understand…, 30
master of the people is their servant, The, 258
men of Paradise do not sport beards except Ādam, The, 406
Messenger of Allah, let me strike the neck of this hypocrite!, 431
molar of the people of hell is as big as Mount Uḥud, The, 217
Muslim is he from [the harm of] whose tongue…, The, 101
My Companions are as the stars…, 161
My God, You are my goal and Your good pleasure…, 155
My intercession is for those guilty of enormous sins, 371, 415
My mercy has primacy over My wrath, 172, 454
My nurturing Lord has consulted me with regard to my Umma, 358

My nurturing Lord has raised me and perfected my manners, 124, 222, 267
My servant does not cease to draw near to Me…, 307
Never dismiss any *ma'rūf* (goodness) as insignificant, 53
No Arab has any superiority over any non-Arab except…, 388
No human being fills a worse vessel than a belly, 91
No property ever diminishes from spending alms, 261
None has been harmed as much as I have been harmed, 102
None of you will enter Paradise with his deeds, 462-466
O Allah, do not leave me to my ego for the blink of an eye, 133
O Allah, guide my people!, 333
O Allah, You are my nurturing Lord, there is no god but You, 137
O Muḥammad! Describe for us your Lord, 147
O Mūsā! He [Qārūn] besought you seventy times, 395
O My servant, spend and I will spend on you, 261
O women! There is no doing without you and no goodness in you, 468
O You Who have brought out the beautiful and covered up the ugly, 378
One follows the faith-system of one's close friend, 292
One illicit stone in the edifice shall be the reason for its destruction, 257
One of them will be given the reward of fifty of you, 211
One third for food, one third for drink and one third for air, 91
Out of them dissension came forth and back to them shall it return, 210
Over what do the Highest Assembly compete?, 346
Part of the excellence of one's submission is to leave…, 177, 225, 310, 451
Patient endurance is the key to deliverance, 284
pebbles glorified Allah in the Prophet's hand, The 57
pen has written and the records are dry, The, 466
People are either an oppressor or a victim of oppression, 93
person will be with the one he loves despite his deeds, A, 238
person's intention is better than his deed, A, 277
The piercing star is the Messenger of Allah, 384
Pray the prayer of someone bidding farewell, 313
Prophet is *al-Ḥāshir* (the Gatherer), The, 200
Prophet made a big supplication for 'Uthmān b. 'Affān, The, 261
Prophet manifests the knowledge of the first and the last, The, 346
Prophet would stand up for a funeral bier, even for an unbeliever, The 96
Prophets are alive in their graves, praying, The 444
Remember the destroyer of pleasures, i.e. death, 307
Reward is proportional to fatigue, 473

Show mercy to those on earth, 342
Sidrat al-muntahā is where the angels' knowledge ends, 66
Someone famous might have no value for Allah whereas..., 198
stomach is a container…, The 91
Sublimity is My cloak alone, 415
Substitutes in this Community are thirty like Ibrāhīm, The, 113
That star is your Prophet, O Jibril, 388
There are 360 joints in a human being…, 60
There are open invitations in the gardens of Paradise, 406
There is in every valley a branch of the heart of the human being…, 434
There is no blessing for me in a morning wherein I have not gained…, 73
There is no goodness in him who does not get along, 242
There is no partner for Me in My sublimity, 415
There is no preventer for what You give…, 320
There is not a single soul among you but its residence…, 350
There shall be after me caliphs, and after the caliphs emirs, 211, 345
There shall be Prophethood among you for as long as Allah wishes, 55
There shall be strifes in which the one lying down is better, 59
There shall come up to you from all over the world students, 175
There will be a tyrannical kingship for as long as Allah wishes, 55
There will be a massive slaughter, 136-137
There will be caliphate after the pattern of Prophethood, 55
There will never cease to be a group from my Umma…, 46
These go to Paradise, and these go to Hellfire, 358
This is your son Aḥmad; he is the First and the Last, 186
This world is cursed, cursed is what it contains except dhikr, 233
Those that are merciful, the All-Merciful grants them mercy, 342, 363
Through them (the *Abdāl*) people receive rain and are given help, 113
Tie down knowledge with writing, 385
Truly there is a servant to whom Allah gave the choice…, 105
Turbans are the crowns of the Arabs, 209
Two prostrations of inadvertence compensate every addition…, 65
Verily there are in your times (spiritual) breezes…, 274
Wall up these doors except the door of Abū Bakr, 105
We have returned from the minor jihad to the greater jihad, 176
What does Muhammad recite to you? Recite it to me, 471
What fends from you the conclusive proof of ignorance…, 385
Whatever Allah has poured into my chest I have certainly poured…, 105

When Allah Almighty created Ādam He showed him..., 186
When one knows oneself..., 144
When the noble of a people comes to you..., 439
When the servant supplicates for his brother..., 226
When you see avarice in command, lust in the lead..., 286
Whenever you see the dying person's gaze raised..., 116
Who humbles himself for Allah, Allah elevates him, 412
Whoever believes let him speak goodness or be silent, 367
Whoever deceives us then he is not of us, 216
Whoever endures succeeds, 61
Whoever guarantees for me what is between his jawbones..., 370
Whoever guards himself from Allah lives blessed, 404
Whoever has left behind small ones, I am their guardian, 234
Whoever has seen me then he has certainly seen the truth, 264
Whoever imitates a people then he is one of them, 462
Whoever knows himself knows his nurturing Lord, 144-145
Whoever practices what he knows, Allah shall teach him, 191
Whoever prays this prayer of ours and has come to ʿArafa..., 353
Whoever pursues knowledge and dies..., 69
Whoever shows enmity to a *walī* of Mine..., 307
Whoever sits with those people will not be wretched, 275
Whoever strives to come nearer to Me one hand-span..., 68
Whoever targets us is not part of us, 177
Whoever trusts in the One God, He suffices him, 434
world is a carcass and its seekers are dogs, The, 221
world is the head of every sin, The, 305
Worship Allah as if you see Him, 180
Writing exists from the time of our liege lord Idrīs, 357
Written in light on the leg of the Throne..., 117
You are as if you had never been in this world, 58
You are only standing up for your brothers the angels, 96
You shall indeed be hand-picked, 158
You shall see your nurturing Lord, 265
Your deeds are your workers, 130, 135, 241, 398
Your worst enemy is your own ego that is between your flanks, 221-222

General Index

12,000 descendants of our liege lord 'Alī, 470
12,000 heavenly ascents, 29, 105-108, 113-116, 119
12,000 pronouncements of Shah Naqshband, 287
124,000 Ādams, 113, 117-118, 170-172
124,000 Awliya, 114, 461
124,000 Prophets, 114, 118
24,000 looks of manifestation, 234
24,000 meanings, 141, 266
'Abd al-Khāliq al-Ghujduwānī, 155, 251, 301, 427, 428-429, 432
'Abd Allah al-Daghistani, 8, 23-30, 47, 52, 56, 63-64, 67, 71, 74-75, 79, 95, 99, 101, 103, 105, 108, 111, 114-115, 122-125, 137, 149-151, 154, 165, 170, 176, 179, 183, 191, 197, 202, 215, 217, 231, 237, 252, 273, 276, 285, 293-294, 299, 305, 310, 313, 319, 324, 326, 331-337, 341, 343, 351, 358-359, 365, 370, 375, 380, 386, 391, 397, 401, 409, 411, 417, 427-428, 438, 440, 443, 445, 451, 460, 466, 471
'Abd al-Qadir al-Jaylani, 65, 125-126, 153, 157, 169, 170, 277, 433
Abū Aḥmad al-Thughūrī, 342-343
Abū Bakr al-Ṣiddīq, 37, 65, 71-72, 105-107, 115-116, 130, 143, 149, 151, 243, 311, 350, 366, 418-420, 424, 426, 443, 453, 462
Abū Ḥanīfa, 80, 93, 413
Abū Jahl, 77, 243, 281, 472
Abū Yazīd al-Bisṭāmī, 44, 111, 123, 159, 197-198, 265, 297, 302, 445, 461
adab, pl. *ādāb*, 8, 35, 90, 97, 124, 128, 199, 218, 267, 309, 334, 336, 370, 447-451
age of progress, 133, 137
Ahmad al-Badawi, 457-463
Ahmad al-Rifa'i, 172
akhlāq, 151-160, 259, 314, 439; see also high manners
akhyār, 161, 323
'ālam al-iṭlāq, 145
'Alī b. Abī Ṭālib, 203, 277, 303, 308, 420-426, 440, 443, 465-472
an ant, 42, 271-272, 285, 286, 344
angel of death, 96, 231, 266; see also Azrā'īl
angels, 23, 25, 29, 42, 56, 64-66, 69, 81, 96, 99, 108, 118, 123, 125, 133, 155, 199, 202, 218, 226, 237, 241, 268, 275, 282, 289, 300, 323-326, 338, 344, 346, 352-353, 362-363, 378, 393, 452, 466, 468, 470
anger, angry, 27, 42, 68, 89-91, 215-219, 222, 310, 339, 349, 351, 354-355, 363, 366, 402, 413, 452, 471
appetite, appetitive, 27, 89-90, 192, 223, 305
Arabs, 158, 209, 424
asking forgiveness, 8, 36, 218, 283, 286, 302, 371 398, 426; see also repentance
atoms, 119, 126, 147, 152, 165
Aws and the Khazraj, 366-367
awtād, 323
'aẓamūt, 35, 153, 322
'Azāzīl, 226
'azīmat al-sharī'a, 35, 305, 308, 336, 365
'Azīz Maḥmūd Hudā'ī, 197, 202
'Azrā'īl, 123, 126, 235, 277, 305, 337
Badr, 267
Barzakh, 55
barzakhī, 58
basmala, 8, 35, 290, 357
Bayt al-ma'mūr, 63, 64, 65
beautiful Names, 47, 57, 113, 119, 149, 152, 169, 358, 381, 466
belief in the unseen, 71, 276
blameworthy traits, 30, 68, 108, 181, 183, 184, 269, 302, 335-338, 353, 401, 404
breath of holiness, 36, 287, 339, 341, 344, 351, 369, 391-393, 445
budalā', 323

certainty, 31, 35-37, 42, 48, 63, 79, 85, 145, 160, 171, 197, 227, 265, 285, 288-289, 292, 311, 313, 339, 354, 379, 386, 393, 423, 453; see also *yaqīn*
character of the Messenger, 264, see also *akhlāq*; high manners
cleanliness, 302, 335-336, 443
cleanness of the heart, 45; see also purification
Companions of the Cave, 387
custom of Allah, 349, 458
Cyprus, 21, 24, 32, 111, 381, 383
Dardanelles war, 341
Day of the Regathering, 37, 127, 155, 159, 172, 198, 203, 357, 378, 381, 392, 409, 412, 455
depravity (*fisq*), depraved (*fāsiq*), 345, 371, 381, 388, 434
dervishes, 338
the devil, 8, 37, 41, 44, 51-52, 91, 122, 128, 152, 232, 244, 251, 260, 291, 302, 310, 335-336, 354, 359, 365, 376, 418, 424, 457; see also Satan
Dhūl-Fiqār, 203
discipline, 35, 37, 128, 195, 202, 321, 332, 334
disobedience, 91, 225, 319, 394
divine enablement for goodness, see *tawfīq*
dunyā defined, 234
ego, *passim*; control of ego, 132, 180; ego, whim, the devil and the world, 62, 91, 159, 443; your ego, 91, 133, 216-218, 222, 239-240, 265-268, 278, 291, 306, 354, 385-387, 414, 432-433, 443, 449-452, 459-460
egotism, 42, 79, 81, 100, 176, 215, 217, 218, 219, 299, 300, 301, 302, 361, 414, 459, 462
eight days of *kashf* for newborns, 202, 338
eight hours for livelihood, eight for the hereafter, eight for sleep, 240
eight Paradises, 155, 379, 418, 454
electrons, 147
emotions, 27, 89, 159
endurance, enduring harm, 27, 52, 61, 102, 283-284, 297, 351, 354-355, 364-365, 399, 432-433, 452, 469
envy, envious, 42, 97, 242, 268, 269, 284, 445
fake servanthood, 291
fake worship, 216
Fakhr al-Dīn al-Rāzī, 118-119, 331, 386
faqih, 150
Fir'awn, 129, 362, 457
fitna, 35, 59, 161, 269, 344-345, 359-360, 365-367, 383, 418
fiṭra, 35, 167, 228, 465, 467; see also newborns
five stations of the heart, 25, 121, 373, 375-381, 389, 470
food, 76, 91, 100, 101, 142, 154, 191, 232, 237, 289, 305, 322, 400, 404, 406, 471
foolishness, 150, 279, 425
fornication, 91, 223, 329, 394
foundations of obligatory belief, 185
frequent repetition, 183
friendship, 37, 115, 315, 316, 369, 388
galaxies, 315
gaze of the Awliya, 126, 313, 393
Ghazālī, 44-46, 51-52, 80, 111, 132, 160
Ghujduwānī, see 'Abd al-Khāliq al-Ghujduwānī
good character, 242
greatest mujahid, 335-336, 352
Ḥabīb al-'Ajamī, 287-290
ḥaqīqa, 33, 35, 79-80, 171
ḥaqīqat al-jadhba, 35, 127
ḥaqīqat al-naẓar, 127
ḥaqīqat al-tawajjuh, 35, 462
harmful souls, 196
Harun al-Rashid, 157
Hārūt and Mārūt, 282
Ḥasan al-Baṣrī, 51, 58, 73, 130, 135, 176, 261, 289-293, 305, 310, 440
ḥaẓīrat al-quds, 302
heart, *passim*; hearts, 17, 19, 25, 28, 43, 46-48, 77, 102-103, 107-108, 114-116, 130-131, 137, 141, 160, 168, 170, 197, 233-236, 239, 245, 252, 260, 266, 268-269, 284-290, 296, 308, 318-319, 324, 342, 344, 361-362, 366, 377-380, 389, 404, 406, 419, 421, 437-441, 452, 471; see also five stations of the heart

heavenly Ascent, see *Mi'rāj*
heedlessness, 293, 319, 332, 338, 364, 414
high manners, 8, 124, 142, 151, 160, 191, 198, 222, 225, 267, 370, 404, 428, 439, 447
high spiritual energy (*himma*), 36, 37, 83, 85, 86, 229, 336, 337
Hijaz, 341
Ḥimṣ, 423
honored, honoring 29, 53, 61, 95, 101, 108, 117, 119, 121, 132-135, 141-142, 150, 169, 171, 185, 227, 237, 247, 290, 299, 321-324, 353-354, 359, 365-366, 369, 371, 377, 380, 388, 391, 393, 395, 399, 469, 473
Ḥudhayfa al-Yamānī, 334
human perfection, 27, 90, 99
human station, 29, 179
humbleness, 26, 233, 268, 301, 313, 325, 339, 343, 411-414
Ḥunayn, 267, 317
huwiyya, 119, 199
hypocrisy, hypocrites 41, 196, 244, 275-276, 334, 338, 388, 431-432, 453-454, 490
Iblīs, 66, 79, 81, 95, 108, 126, 130, 151, 152, 192, 215, 217, 225, 226, 227, 228, 229, 232, 235, 237, 238, 252, 268, 275, 278, 286, 300, 302, 310, 327, 339, 354, 359, 360, 363, 369, 375, 377, 380, 381, 389, 414, 415, 417, 418, 437, 444, 451, 467
Ibn 'Arabī, Muḥyī al-Dīn, 19, 58, 114, 118, 128, 144, 170, 180, 187, 200, 206, 230, 244, 265, 331, 378, 381, 386, 397, 425, 478
Ibrāhīm–upon him peace, 271, 370, 391-395
Ibrahim Ad-ham, 349
iḥsān, 24, 36, 180, 277, 379
iḥyā' al-mutaṣarrif, 350
'ilm al-ḥāl, 86, 228
īmān shuhūdī, 229
imitative belief, 55, 452
incapacitation, 337
incapacity, 21, 121-122, 162, 269, 271, 325, 327, 337-339, 403, 404-405, 427, 432
inheritors, see Muhammadan inheritors
intermediacy / intermediary, 37, 105, 142, 185-189, 226
invisible sovereignty, 12, 36, 64, 79-80, 85, 103, 110-112, 145, 153, 159, 169, 188, 229, 252, 269, 282, 343; see also *malakūt*
inward knowledge, 79
irshād, 26, 33, 128, 445
'Īsā–upon him peace, 25, 48, 93, 104, 144, 163, 191, 271, 305, 349, 411, 462, 469-470
Isrāfīl, 344, 392
Istanbul, 111, 202, 203, 311, 341
istighfār, 218
jabarūt, 36, 153, 161, 322
Ja'far al-Ṣādiq, 80, 229, 265, 384
Jalaluddin Rumi, 19, 75, 311
Jamāl al-Dīn al-Ghumūqī, 165, 295, 296
jihad, 36, 66-69, 102, 158, 175-176, 212, 221-222, 233, 266, 278, 302, 305-307, 432, 461; greatest jihad, 66, 176, 222, 266, 307
job, 293; of the believers, 257, 285; of the murid, 259; of the people of religion, 308; of the Prophets and Awliya, 338; of Iblīs, 359; of *Ṣāḥib al-zamān*, 443; of Grandshaykh 'Abd Allah's successor, 444; of the listener, 451; of 'Umar b. al-Khaṭṭāb, 472
Ka'b al-Aḥbār, 66, 423
karāma, pl. *karāmāt*, 36, 127, 201, 203, 275, 289, 299, 307; see also miraculous gift
kashf, 21, 36, 58, 128, 167, 172, 197-198, 201-202, 230, 257, 338, 432, 483, 535
Khālid b. al-Walīd, 203
Khatm al-Khwajagan, 255, 301
Khiḍr–upon him peace, 292
knowledge, 19, 23-25, 28-32, 36, 42, 55-57, 63-66, 69-73, 79-80, 83-86, 105-106, 109-115, 130, 133, 137, 144-145, 149-150, 153, 161, 165, 169-176, 183, 191-193, 199-206, 215, 218-222, 227-228, 231, 241, 244, 257, 264-268, 278, 281-282, 285, 289, 301,

309, 327, 334, 336, 339, 341, 343, 346-347, 350, 369, 376-377, 385-393, 400-405, 411, 414, 420, 423, 425, 427, 444-445, 449, 453, 455, 460, 469-470, 473
lā ilāha illā-l-Lāh Muḥammadun Rasūlu-l-Lāh, 117, 185-186, 206, 372
ladunnī, 36, 150
lāhūt, 36, 153, 187, 322
legally tasked, 53, 67, 132, 135, 183, 216, 218, 228, 337, 338, 452
light in the heart, 278
losing money, 205
lust, lustful, 27, 89-91, 222, 286, 290-291, 302, 310
macrocosm / microcosm of human beings, 132, 170, 303
magic, 281-282
magnification of the Prophet, 29, 104, 108, 153, 185, 237, 351
Mahdi–upon him peace, 19, 25-26, 36, 47-50, 104, 130, 153, 157, 163, 173, 203, 231, 257, 261, 285, 323, 325, 404, 443, 469-470; see also *Ṣāḥib al-zamān*
majāl al-iṭlāq, 36, 169
malakūt, 27, 36, 64, 80, 85, 103, 110, 114- 115, 145, 152- 153, 159-161, 169, 181, 185, 188-189, 229, 252, 269, 282, 322-323, 343; *malakūt*-affiliated men, 189; see also invisible sovereignty
maqām al-nafs, see station of ego
mark of servanthood, 139
Maryam–upon her peace, 263
medication, 191, 334, 402
microcosm, see macrocosm
milḥān, 101
miraculous gift(s), 24, 36, 125, 169, 201, 341, 403, 429, 444-445, see also *karāma*
Mi'rāj, 65, 105-107,115-116, 150-153, 171, 187, 299-302, 319, 322, 327; see also 12,000 heavenly ascents
Muhammadan heart, 106, 116, 126, 150, 198
Muhammadan inheritors, 46, 52, 71, 113-114, 176, 201-202, 215, 292, 300
Muhammadan light, 201
Muhammadan Reality, 171, 187-188
Muhammadan sciences, 206
mujāhada, 67, 68, 69
mu'jiza, pl. *mu'jizāt*, 36, 103-104, 201, 384
mukallaf, 27, 131, 135
murid(s), 24, 26, 27, 32, 52, 67, 107, 123-126, 155, 158, 181, 218, 219, 247-252, 255, 259, 273, 276-277, 294, 297, 301, 308, 313, 332, 370, 397, 419, 428, 431, 432-433, 440, 451-452, 461-463
Mūsā–upon him peace, 43, 53, 63, 93, 96-97, 104, 114, 124, 161, 163, 187, 195, 200, 216, 239, 259, 265, 271, 308, 342, 370, 383, 395, 406, 418, 433, 444, 458-459
Nablus, 342
nafas al-qudsiyya, 36, 339, 344, 369, 391
Names for Allah, 119, 152
Naqshbandi Tariqa, 105, 116, 276, 306, 336, 463; Naqshbandis, 251, 376, 389, 457, 463
nāsūtiyya, 37, 186
newborns are born in a state of *kashf*, 202; see also *fiṭra*
Nimrod, 271
nujabā', 323
obduracy, obdurate, 42, 75, 77, 102, 215, 243, 281, 320, 347, 432
oppression, oppressors, 93
other Tariqas, 463
outward knowledge, 79
Palestine, 341, 343, 383
perfect *murshid*, 41-44
perfect purity, 67
Pharaoh, see Fir'awn
pleasure, 26, 28, 51-52, 76-77, 89, 91, 125, 155, 159, 172, 181, 212, 232, 310, 351, 353-354, 362-363, 393, 462, 469
Preserved Tablet, 227, 341, 346-347, 357
pride, proud, 42-43, 99, 212, 222, 226, 242, 297, 317, 383, 388, 399, 402, 413-414, 425
pure life, 266

pure monotheism, 144, 146, 155, 176, 181, 459, 460
purification, 28, 37, 46-48, 67, 101-102, 268, 282, 325
Qadiri Tariqa, 336
Qārūn, 288, 342, 395
Quds, 265, 286, 341
Quṭb, 24, 32, 37, 109-110, 197-198, 292, 457-459, 462; *quṭb al-aqṭāb*, 128; *quṭb al-bilād*, 128; *quṭb al-ghawth*, 128; *quṭb al-irshād*, 128; *quṭb al-mutaṣarrif*, 128
quwwa ḥuḍūriyya, 183
rabbānī, 169, 265
Rāzīn, 469
real belief / reality of belief, 28, 55-58, 183, 229, 242, 417, 452
real remembrance, 310
rebellious sins, 198, 259, 381, 391, 454
reflection, 206, 293, 296, 297, 472
reformism, 216, 257-258, 285
repentance, 27, 89, 91, 236, 263, 266, 286, 297, 302, 388, 398, 403, 440; see also asking forgiveness
revolution, revolutionaries, 31, 130
Rifa'i Tariqa, 336
righteousness, 238, 241, 320, 329, 449
rūḥāniyya, 58; see also spiritual reality
ṣabr, 61, 354
Sa'd b. Abī Waqqāṣ, 233
ṣāfī, 168
Ṣāḥib al-zamān, 36-37, 104, 128, 223, 285, 317, 323, 325, 379, 427, 435, 443, 470
Sa'īd b. al-Musayyab, 423
ṣalāt al-wusṭā, 64
Satan, 33, 281, 290; see also the devil
Saṭīḥ the soothsayer, 195
servanthood, 37, 150, 157, 181, 192, 218, 226, 240, 273, 276-277, 291-292, 387, 402, 414-418, 424
al-Shāfi'ī, 65, 80, 133, 180, 244, 289, 358, 413, 465
Shah Naqshband, 123, 127, 165, 197, 238, 287, 331, 465-467
Shamshūn, 209
Sharaf al-Din al-Daghistani, 47, 96, 300, 342, 440
Shari'a, 8, 31, 33, 96, 106, 127, 153, 179, 207, 282, 308, 371, 425, 447
ṣibgha, 301
Ṣiddīq, see Abū Bakr al-Ṣiddīq
Ṣiddīqiyya, 116
slander, slanderers, 237, 269, 401-404, 439, 444
smoking, 271, 309-310
spending in the way of Allah, 62, 261, 281, 288-290
the spirit, 30, 37, 123, 145, 176, 302, 332, 399, 424-425, 447, 451, 455
spirit of the human being, 303
spiritual guide, 27, 36, 41, 80, 104, 293, 299-300, 336, 415, 445, 451, 460
spiritual leader of endtimes, see *Ṣāḥib al-zamān*
spiritual life, 123, 184
spiritual powers, 103-104, 108-111, 145, 238
spiritual presence, 37, 52, 58, 126, 179, 201
spiritual reality, 27, 35, 79-81, 90, 95, 99, 102, 106, 119, 121, 123, 133, 137, 146, 159, 169, 179-180, 191, 201, 217, 252-253, 301, 322-323, 383, 386, 393, 447-449, 465; see also *rūḥāniyya*
spiritual unveiling, see *kashf*
spirituality, 72
staggering miracle, see *mu'jiza*
station of more hidden (*akhfā*), 377
station of ego, 36, 90, 121, 181, 415, 460
station of the heart, 375
station of hiddenness (*khafā'*), 25, 377-381, 389
station of incapacity, 121, 122
station of Jibril, 185, 187, 423, 463
station of the secret, 230, 376-377, 389
station of the secret of the secret, 230, 377, 389
stations of nearness, 99, 100, 172, 365, 388, 401, 413, 417
Sultan 'Abd al-Ḥamīd, 212
Sultan Ahmad, 202, 203
sultān al-dhikr, 165
sulṭan al-khawf, 37, 308
Syria, 41, 44, 341; Syro-Palestine, 26, 207, 212, 261, 343, 423, 470

the Tablet, see Preserved Tablet
Tabūk, 261
tamkīn, 37, 102
taqwā, 37, 47, 383
Tariqa people, 268, 335, 338
tawfīq, 275, 299, 413, 415
thinking about death, 306-308
Tigris, 233, 290, 294
Tripoli, 5, 23, 24, 41, 44, 221
truthfulness, 47, 63, 155, 206, 274, 287, 290, 291, 366, 387, 458, 472
turban, 203, 207, 209, 275, 286, 314, 322, 406, 440
Turkey, 210, 212, 398, 440
tyrants, 59, 100, 203, 211-212, 345
ʿubūdiyya, see servanthood
Uḥud, 217, 317, 333, 469
ulema, 42, 69, 111, 157, 162, 170, 201, 212, 285, 295, 386, 438
ʿUmar b. al-Khaṭṭāb, 53, 107, 115-117, 209, 222, 277, 314, 334, 345-346, 350, 385, 412, 421-426, 431, 469-472
Ummat al-daʿwa, 334
Ummat al-ijāba, 334
Ummat al-mutābaʿa, 334
unbelief, 29, 81, 95, 100, 103, 108, 125-129, 163, 168, 177, 242, 244, 266, 323, 372, 377, 381, 388-394, 425, 452, 454, 462, 470, 472
unknowable, 147
uns, 320
ʿUthmān b. ʿAffān, 423
Uways al-Qaranī, 426
veils, 66, 124, 201, 217, 251, 457, 460
vicegerents, 95, 132, 176, 395
voluntary death, 158, 266-268
voluntary deeds, 51, 307
waḥdāniyya, 144
Wahhabis, 210, 234
wasīla, see intermediacy
wayfaring, 37, 47, 145, 216, 267, 281, 293, 332, 336, 380
worshipfulness, 37, 121, 216, 225, 228, 276
Ya'jūj and Ma'jūj, 163
yaqaẓa, 183
yaqīn, 35-37, 79, 85, 160, 221, 265, 285-292, 434, 453; see also certainty
yawm al-ʿarḍ, 45
zāhid, 38, 287
zinā, 91
zuhd, 74, 221, 287

www.ingramcontent.com/pod-product-compliance
Lightning Source LLC
Chambersburg PA
CBHW030508080526
44586CB00011B/115
9781938058820